More praise for
Women Who Run With the Wolves

"Millennia of humans have gathered around fires to hear words that transferred hard-won wisdom and allowed dreams of unlimited possibilities. In a modern world that limits wisdom to 'facts,' and women's access even to those, Dr. Estés has restored the fire—for us all."

> —GLORIA STEINEM
> Author of *Revolution from Within*

"Rare is the scholar who also has the *don* of story-teller poet, as Estés demonstrates with such unrelenting eloquence. This is a contemporary codice—extraordinarily precious not only for its immense wisdom but for its wealth and mastery of language. Clarissa Pinkola Estés is a formidable writer."

> —ANA CASTILLO
> Author of *My Father Was a Toltec*

"This is a terrific book! Dr. Pinkola Estés has hit the dark rich center. I thank her!"

> —NATALIE GOLDBERG
> Author of *Wild Mind* and *Long Quiet Highway*

"This book articulated things I had felt . . . but were not named or spoken with such clarity and wisdom until now."

> —WILMA MANKILLER
> Former Chief of The Cherokee Nation
> Author of *Mankiller*

Please turn the page for more reviews . . .

"Clarissa Pinkola Estés has brought forth, through the wisdom, struggle, and riches of her life, a groundbreaking text in *Women Who Run With the Wolves*. As a Jungian analyst, a poet, and *cantadora*, she has cracked open the dominant culture and exposed its myths and, in the process, given us new ones. With each story, if we dare to face our wild nature, we begin an excavation of the soul. Dr. Estés' courage to unmask the truth allows us to realize our own. She demands, through the depth of this brave and holy work, that women confront what we fear the most, our own power. I believe this is a book we grow into and through."

—Terry Tempest Williams
Author of *Refuge*

"My copy of *Women Who Run With the Wolves* came to me as a gift from one who not only knew me well, but loved me well. 'You need this,' she told me. When finally—far away from home and terribly worn down—I pulled the book out and dipped into it, I realized she was right. Estés gives story as sustenance ... vital to the survival of the soul. What Clarissa Pinkola Estés has done is more than give us stories and parables by which we construct our stronger selves. She has given us a vision of life as a shared enterprise, the female heart not just embattled, but vibrant and open to hope. It is a book I, too, give to those I love."

—Dorothy Allison
Author of *Bastard Out of Carolina*

"This is the work of a born poet—oracular, salvific, and luminous with the natural prayer of the soul. . . . I am in awe of its sheer fluency, moving between the languages of spirituality, myth, and medicine with such clarity and courage. No one has written this before, no one has dared to break so many boundaries of thought."

—CAROLYN FORCHÉ
Author of *The Country Between Us*

"With lyrical power and grace, Clarissa Pinkola Estés brings forth the ancient wisdom of our ancestors and applies contemporary insight that makes these stories *jump* with meaning for our spiritually hungry souls. She invites women and men alike into the realm of the Spirit of truth, a Spirit that heals, awakens, challenges, connects, and laughs. This book will be honored in generations to come as one of the truly profound spiritual testimonies of our time."

—MATTHEW FOX
Author of *Original Blessing*

"A fascinating collection of transformative stories with feminist-oriented interpretations, both enlightening and empowering for every woman in search of her own inner spirit."

—Barbara G. Walker
Author of *The Woman's Encyclopedia of Myths and Secrets*

"Through myth, fairy tale, and an extended 'soul conversation,' Estés calls back into life the wild neglected places of the feminine psyche. This is an inspiring and compassionate book."

—JULES CASHFORD
Jungian Analyst, London
Coauthor of *The Myth of the Goddess*

Please turn the page for more reviews . . .

"A hearty, spicy stew to feed all women who are feeling burned-out, stifled, sluggish, or just plain old tired. If those descriptions hit home, take a bowl of Estés stew to cure what she calls *hambre del alma*, starvation of the soul, and read on. . . . *Women Who Run With the Wolves* is a feminine manifesto for all women regardless of age, race, creed, or religion, to return to their . . . roots. Look in the mirror . . . Estés argues that our similarities outweigh our differences. . . . She is *cantadora*, *curandera*, midwife, mentor."

—*Hispanic* Magazine

"Full of wonderful, passionate, poetic, psychologically potent words and images that will inspire, instruct, and empower women to be true to their own nature, and thus in touch with sources of creativity, humor, and strength."

—JEAN SHINODA BOLEN, M.D.
Author of *Goddesses in Everywoman*
and *Ring of Power*

"As I was reading this, the Gypsy tapped me lightly on the left shoulder, sleepwalked me across the room, and pulled out a scratchy orthophonic recording of Ma Rainey singing *Trust No Man*, Bessie Smith with *It's Right Here for You* and *St. Louis Blues*, and Ida Cox belting out *Wild Women Don't Have the Blues*. 'Talk about archetypes,' she told me as she laid the record on the turntable, 'Estés has been there and back.'"

—CLARIBEL ALEGRIA
Author of *Family Album:*
Guerrilla Poems of El Salvador

WOMEN WHO RUN WITH THE WOLVES

Myths and Stories
of the Wild Woman Archetype

Clarissa Pinkola Estés, Ph.D.

BALLANTINE BOOKS • NEW YORK

A Ballantine Book
Published by The Random House Publishing Group
Copyright © 1992, 1995 by Clarissa Pinkola Estés, Ph.D.

Published in the United States by Ballantine Books, an imprint of The Random House Publishing Group, a division of Random House, Inc., New York, and simultaneously in Canada by Random House of Canada Limited, Toronto.

Grateful acknowledgment is made to the following for permission to reprint previously published material:

Houghton Mifflin Company: Excerpt from "The Red Shoes" poem in *The Book of Folly* by Anne Sexton. Copyright © 1972 by Anne Sexton. Reprinted by permission of Houghton Mifflin Co. All rights reserved.

Simon & Schuster and Methuen London: Excerpt from *for colored girls who have considered suicide/when the rainbow is enuf* by Ntozake Shange. Copyright © 1975, 1976, 1977 by Ntozake Shange. Reprinted by permission of Simon & Schuster and Methuen London.

W. W. Norton & Company, Inc., and Adrienne Rich: Excerpt from "Diving into the Wreck" reprinted from *The Fact of a Doorframe, Poems Selected and New, 1950–1984,* by Adrienne Rich. Copyright © 1975, 1978 by W. W. Norton & Company, Inc. Copyright ©1981 by Adrienne Rich. Reprinted by permission of the author and the publisher, W. W. Norton & Company, Inc.

www.ballantinebooks.com

ISBN 978-0-345-40987-4

Printed in the United States of America

First Hardcover Edition: June 1992
First Trade Paperback Edition: September 1995
First Mass Market Paperback Edition: January 1997

OPM   49   48   47   46

A kedves szüleimnek
Mária és Joszef,
Mary and Joseph,
Szeretlek benneteket.

y
Para todos los que yo amo
que continúan desaparecidos.

CONTENTS

THE BOUNTY OF WILD WOMAN

⚡ FOREWORD

We are all filled with a longing for the wild. There are few culturally sanctioned antidotes for this yearning. We were taught to feel shame for such a desire. We grew our hair long and used it to hide our feelings. But the shadow of Wild Woman still lurks behind us during our days and in our nights. No matter where we are, the shadow that trots behind us is definitely four-footed.

CLARISSA PINKOLA ESTÉS, PH.D.
Cheyenne, Wyoming

WOMEN
WHO RUN
WITH THE WOLVES

Singing Over
the Bones

Wildlife and the Wild Woman are both endangered species.

Over time, we have seen the feminine instinctive nature looted, driven back, and overbuilt. For long periods it has been mismanaged like the wildlife and the wildlands. For several thousand years, as soon and as often as we turn our backs, it is relegated to the poorest land in the psyche. The spiritual lands of Wild Woman have, throughout history, been plundered or burnt, dens bulldozed, and natural cycles forced into unnatural rhythms to please others.

It's not by accident that the pristine wilderness of our planet disappears as the understanding of our own inner wild natures fades. It is not so difficult to comprehend why old forests and old women are viewed as not very important resources. It is not such a mystery. It is not so coincidental that wolves and coyotes, bears and wildish women have similar reputations. They all share related instinctual archetypes, and as such, both are erroneously reputed to be ingracious, wholly and innately dangerous, and ravenous.

My life and work as a Jungian psychoanalyst, poet, and *cantadora*, keeper of the old stories, have taught me that women's flagging vitality can be restored by extensive "psychic-archeological" digs into the ruins of the female underworld. By these methods we are able to recover the ways of the natural instinctive psyche, and through its personification in the Wild Woman archetype we are able to discern the ways and means of woman's deepest nature.

The modern woman is a blur of activity. She is pressured to be all things to all people. The old knowing is long overdue.

The title of this book, *Women Who Run With the Wolves: Myths and Stories of the Wild Woman Archetype*, came from my study of wildlife biology, wolves in particular. The studies of the wolves *Canis lupus* and *Canis rufus* are like the history of women, regarding both their spiritedness and their travails.

Healthy wolves and healthy women share certain psychic characteristics: keen sensing, playful spirit, and a heightened capacity for devotion. Wolves and women are relational by nature, inquiring, possessed of great endurance and strength. They are deeply intuitive, intensely concerned with their young, their mates, and their pack. They are experienced in adapting to constantly changing circumstances; they are fiercely stalwart and very brave.

Yet both have been hounded, harassed, and falsely imputed to be devouring and devious, overly aggressive, of less value than those who are their detractors. They have been the targets of those who would clean up the wilds as well as the wildish environs of the psyche, extincting the instinctual, and leaving no trace of it behind. The predation of wolves and women by those who misunderstand them is strikingly similar.

So that is where the concept of the Wild Woman archetype first crystallized for me, in the study of wolves. I've studied other creatures as well, such as bear, elephant, and the soul-birds—butterflies. The characteristics of each species give abundant metaphoric hints into what is knowable about the feminine instinctual psyche.

The wild nature passed through my spirit twice, once by my birth to a passionate Mexican-Spanish bloodline, and later, through adoption by a family of fiery Hungarians. I was raised up near the Michigan state line, surrounded by woodlands, orchards, and farmland and near the Great Lakes. There, thunder and lightning were my main nutrition. Cornfields creaked and spoke aloud at night. Far up in the north, wolves came to the clearings in moonlight, prancing and praying. We could all drink from the same streams without fear.

Although I did not call her by that name then, my love for Wild Woman began when I was a little child. I was an aesthete rather than an athlete, and my only wish was to be an ecstatic wanderer.

Rather than chairs and tables, I preferred the ground, trees, and caves, for in those places I felt I could lean against the cheek of God.

The river *always* called to be visited after dark, the fields *needed* to be walked in so they could make their rustle-talk. Fires *needed* to be built in the forest at night, and stories *needed* to be told outside the hearing of grown-ups.

I was lucky to be brought up in Nature. There, lightning strikes taught me about sudden death and the evanescence of life. Mice litters showed that death was softened by new life. When I unearthed "Indian beads," fossils from the loam, I understood that humans have been here a long, long time. I learned about the sacred art of self-decoration with monarch butterflies perched atop my head, lightning bugs as my night jewelry, and emerald-green frogs as bracelets.

A wolf mother killed one of her mortally injured pups; this taught a hard compassion and the necessity of allowing death to come to the dying. The fuzzy caterpillars which fell from their branches and crawled back up again taught single-mindedness. Their tickle-walking on my arm taught how skin can come alive. Climbing to the tops of trees taught what sex would someday feel like.

My own post–World War II generation grew up in a time when women were infantilized and treated as property. They were kept as fallow gardens . . . but thankfully there was always wild seed which arrived on the wind. Though what they wrote was unauthorized, women blazed away anyway. Though what they painted went unrecognized, it fed the soul anyway. Women had to beg for the instruments and the spaces needed for their arts, and if none were forthcoming, they made space in trees, caves, woods, and closets.

Dancing was barely tolerated, if at all, so they danced in the forest where no one could see them, or in the basement, or on the way out to empty the trash. Self-decoration caused suspicion. Joyful body or dress increased the danger of being harmed or sexually assaulted. The very clothes on one's shoulders could not be called one's own.

It was a time when parents who abused their children were

simply called "strict," when the spiritual lacerations of profoundly exploited women were referred to as "nervous breakdowns," when girls and women who were tightly girdled, tightly reined, and tightly muzzled were called "nice," and those other females who managed to slip the collar for a moment or two of life were branded "bad."

So like many women before and after me, I lived my life as a disguised *criatura*, creature. Like my kith and kin before me, I swagger-staggered in high heels, and I wore a dress and hat to church. But my fabulous tail often fell below my hemline, and my ears twitched until my hat pitched, at the very least, down over both my eyes, and sometimes clear across the room.

I've not forgotten the song of those dark years, *hambre del alma*, the song of the starved soul. But neither have I forgotten the joyous *canto hondo*, the deep song, the words of which come back to us when we do the work of soulful reclamation.

Like a trail through a forest which becomes more and more faint and finally seems to diminish to a nothing, traditional psychological theory too soon runs out for the creative, the gifted, the deep woman. Traditional psychology is often spare or entirely silent about deeper issues important to women: the archetypal, the intuitive, the sexual and cyclical, the ages of women, a woman's way, a woman's knowing, her creative fire. This is what has driven my work on the Wild Woman archetype for over two decades.

A woman's issues of soul cannot be treated by carving her into a more acceptable form as defined by an unconscious culture, nor can she be bent into a more intellectually acceptable shape by those who claim to be the sole bearers of consciousness. No, that is what has already caused millions of women who began as strong and natural powers to become outsiders in their own cultures. Instead, the goal must be the retrieval and succor of women's beauteous and natural psychic forms.

Fairy tales, myths, and stories provide understandings which sharpen our sight so that we can pick out and pick up the path left by the wildish nature. The instruction found in story reassures us that the path has not run out, but still leads women deeper, and more deeply still, into their own knowing. The tracks we all are following are those of the wild and innate instinctual Self.

I call her Wild Woman, for those very words, *wild* and *woman*, create *llamar o tocar a la puerta*, the fairy-tale knock at the door of the deep female psyche. *Llamar o tocar a la puerta* means literally to play upon the instrument of the name in order to open a door. It means using words that summon up the opening of a passageway. No matter by which culture a woman is influenced, she understands the words *wild* and *woman*, intuitively.

When women hear those words, an old, old memory is stirred and brought back to life. The memory is of our absolute, undeniable, and irrevocable kinship with the wild feminine, a relationship which may have become ghosty from neglect, buried by over-domestication, outlawed by the surrounding culture, or no longer understood anymore. We may have forgotten her names, we may not answer when she calls ours, but in our bones we know her, we yearn toward her; we know she belongs to us and we to her.

It is into this fundamental, elemental, and essential relationship that we were born and that in our essence we are also derived from. The Wild Woman archetype sheaths the alpha matrilineal being. There are times when we experience her, even if only fleetingly, and it makes us mad with wanting to continue. For some women, this vitalizing "taste of the wild" comes during pregnancy, during nursing their young, during the miracle of change in oneself as one raises a child, during attending to a love relationship as one would attend to a beloved garden.

A sense of her also comes through the vision; through sights of great beauty. I have felt her when I see what we call in the woodlands a Jesus-God sunset. I have felt her move in me from seeing the fishermen come up from the lake at dusk with lanterns lit, and also from seeing my newborn baby's toes all lined up like a row of sweet corn. We see her where we see her, which is everywhere.

She comes to us through sound as well; through music which vibrates the sternum, excites the heart; it comes through the drum, the whistle, the call, and the cry. It comes through the written and the spoken word; sometimes a word, a sentence or a poem or a story, is so resonant, so right, it causes us to remember, at least for an instant, what substance we are really made from, and where is our true home.

These transient "tastes of the wild" come during the mystique of inspiration—ah, there it is; oh, now it has gone. The longing for her comes when one happens across someone who has secured this wildish relationship. The longing comes when one realizes one has given scant time to the mystic cookfire or to the dream-time, too little time to one's own creative life, one's life work, or one's true loves.

Yet it is these fleeting tastes which come both through beauty as well as loss, that cause us to become so bereft, so agitated, so longing that we eventually must pursue the wildish nature. Then we leap into the forest or into the desert or into the snow and run hard, our eyes scanning the ground, our hearing sharply tuned, searching under, searching over, searching for a clue, a remnant, a sign that she still lives, that we have not lost our chance. And when we pick up her trail, it is typical of women to ride hard to catch up, to clear off the desk, clear off the relationship, clear out one's mind, turn to a new page, insist on a break, break the rules, stop the world, for we are not going on without her any longer.

Once women have lost her and then found her again, they will contend to keep her for good. Once they have regained her, they will fight and fight hard to keep her, for with her their creative lives blossom; their relationships gain meaning and depth and health; their cycles of sexuality, creativity, work, and play are re-established; they are no longer marks for the predations of others; they are entitled equally under the laws of nature to grow and to thrive. Now their end-of-the-day fatigue comes from satisfying work and endeavors, not from being shut up in too small a mind-set, job, or relationship. They know instinctively when things must die and when things must live; they know how to walk away, they know how to stay.

When women reassert their relationship with the wildish na-ture, they are gifted with a permanent and internal watcher, a knower, a visionary, an oracle, an inspiratrice, an intuitive, a maker, a creator, an inventor, and a listener who guide, suggest, and urge vibrant life in the inner and outer worlds. When women are close to this nature, the fact of that relationship glows through them. This wild teacher, wild mother, wild mentor supports their inner and outer lives, no matter what.

So, the word *wild* here is not used in its modern pejorative sense, meaning out of control, but in its original sense, which means to live a natural life, one in which the *criatura*, creature, has innate integrity and healthy boundaries. These words, *wild* and *woman*, cause women to remember who they are and what they are about. They create a metaphor to describe the force which funds all females. They personify a force that women cannot live without.

The Wild Woman archetype can be expressed in other terms which are equally apt. You can call this powerful psychological nature the instinctive nature, but Wild Woman is the force which lies behind that. You can call it the natural psyche, but the archetype of the Wild Woman stands behind that as well. You can call it the innate, the basic nature of women. You can call it the indigenous, the intrinsic nature of women. In poetry it might be called the "Other," or the "seven oceans of the universe," or "the far woods," or "The Friend."[1] In various psychologies and from various perspectives it would perhaps be called the id, the Self, the medial nature. In biology it would be called the typical or fundamental nature.

But because it is tacit, prescient, and visceral, among *cantadoras* it is called the wise or knowing nature. It is sometimes called the "woman who lives at the end of time," or the "woman who lives at the edge of the world." And this *criatura* is always a creator-hag, or a death Goddess, or a maiden in descent, or any number of other personifications. She is both friend and mother to all those who have lost their way, all those who need a learning, all those who have a riddle to solve, all those out in the forest or the desert wandering and searching.

In actuality, in the psychoid unconscious—an ineffable layer of psyche from which this phenomenon emanates—Wild Woman has no name, for she is so vast. But, since this force engenders every important facet of womanliness, here on earth she is named many names, not only in order to peer into the myriad aspects of her nature but also to hold on to her. Because in the beginning of retrieving our relationship with her she can turn to smoke in an instant, by naming her we create for her a territory of thought and feeling within us. Then she will come, and if valued, she will stay.

So, in Spanish I call her *Río Abajo Río*, the river beneath the river; *La Mujer Grande*, the Great Woman; *Luz del abismo*, the light from the abyss; *La Loba*, the wolf woman; or *La Huesera*, the bone woman.

She is called in Hungarian, *Ö, Erdöben*, She of the Woods, and *Rozsomák*, The Wolverine. In Navajo, she is *Na'ashjé'ii Asdzáá*, The Spider Woman, who weaves the fate of humans and animals and plants and rocks. In Guatemala, among many other names, she is *Humana del Niebla*, The Mist Being, the woman who has lived forever. In Japanese, she is *Amaterasu Omikami*, The Numina, who brings all light, all consciousness. In Tibet she is called *Dakini*, the dancing force which produces clear-seeing within women. And it goes on. She goes on.

The comprehension of this Wild Woman nature is not a religion but a practice. It is a psychology in its truest sense: *psukhē/psych*, soul; *ology* or *logos*, a knowing of the soul. Without her, women are without ears to hear her soultalk or to register the chiming of their own inner rhythms. Without her, women's inner eyes are closed by some shadowy hand, and large parts of their days are spent in a semi-paralyzing ennui or else wishful thinking. Without her, women lose the sureness of their soulfooting. Without her, they forget why they're here, they hold on when they would best hold out. Without her they take too much or too little or nothing at all. Without her they are silent when they are in fact on fire. She is their regulator, she is their soulful heart, the same as the human heart that regulates the physical body.

When we lose touch with the instinctive psyche, we live in a semi-destroyed state and images and powers that are natural to the feminine are not allowed full development. When a woman is cut away from her basic source, she is sanitized, and her instincts and natural life cycles are lost, subsumed by the culture, or by the intellect or the ego—one's own or those belonging to others.

Wild Woman is the health of all women. Without her, women's psychology makes no sense. This wilderwoman is the prototypical woman . . . no matter what culture, no matter what era, no matter what politic, she does not change. Her cycles change, her symbolic representations change, but in essence, *she* does not change. She is what she is and she is whole.

She canalizes through women. If they are suppressed, she struggles upward. If women are free, she is free. Fortunately, no matter how many times she is pushed down, she bounds up again. No matter how many times she is forbidden, quelled, cut back, diluted, tortured, touted as unsafe, dangerous, mad, and other derogations, she emanates upward in women, so that even the most quiet, even the most restrained woman keeps a secret place for her. Even the most repressed woman has a secret life, with secret thoughts and secret feelings which are lush and wild, that is, natural. Even the most captured woman guards the place of the wildish self, for she knows intuitively that someday there will be a loophole, an aperture, a chance, and she will hightail it to escape.

I believe that all women and men are born gifted. However, and truly, there has been little to describe the psychological lives and ways of gifted women, talented women, creative women. There is, on the other hand, much writ about the weakness and foibles of humans in general and women in particular. But in the case of the Wild Woman archetype, in order to fathom her, apprehend her, utilize her offerings, we must be more interested in the thoughts, feelings, and endeavors which strengthen women, and adequately count the interior *and* cultural factors which weaken women.

In general, when we understand the wildish nature as a being in its own right, one which animates and informs a woman's deepest life, then we can begin to develop in ways never thought possible. A psychology which fails to address this innate spiritual being at the center of feminine psychology fails women, and fails their daughters and their daughters' daughters far into all future matrilineal lines.

So, in order to apply a good medicine to the hurt parts of the wildish psyche, in order to aright relationship to the archetype of the Wild Woman, one has to name the disarrays of the psyche accurately. While in my clinical profession we do have a good diagnostic statistical manual and a goodly amount of differential diagnoses, as well as psychoanalytic parameters which define psychopathy through the organization (or lack of it) in the objective psyche and the ego-Self axis,[2] there are yet other defining behaviors and feelings which, from a woman's frame of reference, powerfully describe what is the matter.

What are some of the feeling-toned symptoms of a disrupted relationship with the wildish force in the psyche? To chronically feel, think, or act in any of the following ways is to have partially severed or lost entirely the relationship with the deep instinctual psyche. Using women's language exclusively, these are: feeling extraordinarily dry, fatigued, frail, depressed, confused, gagged, muzzled, unaroused. Feeling frightened, halt or weak, without inspiration, without animation, without soulfulness, without meaning, shame-bearing, chronically fuming, volatile, stuck, uncreative, compressed, crazed.

Feeling powerless, chronically doubtful, shaky, blocked, unable to follow through, giving one's creative life over to others, life-sapping choices in mates, work, or friendships, suffering to live outside one's own cycles, overprotective of self, inert, uncertain, faltering, inability to pace oneself or set limits.

Not insistent on one's own tempo, to be self-conscious, to be away from one's God or Gods, to be separated from one's revivification, drawn far into domesticity, intellectualism, work, or inertia because that is the safest place for one who has lost her instincts.

To fear to venture by oneself or to reveal oneself, fear to seek mentor, mother, father, fear to set out one's imperfect work before it is an opus, fear to set out on a journey, fear of caring for another or others, fear one will run on, run out, run down, cringing before authority, loss of energy before creative projects, wincing, humiliation, angst, numbness, anxiety.

Afraid to bite back when there is nothing else left to do, afraid to try the new, fear to stand up to, afraid to speak up, speak against, sick stomach, butterflies, sour stomach, cut in the middle, strangled, becoming conciliatory or nice too easily, revenge.

Afraid to stop, afraid to act, repeatedly counting to three and not beginning, superiority complex, ambivalence, and yet otherwise fully capable, fully functioning. These severances are a disease not of an era or a century, but become an epidemic anywhere and anytime women are captured, anytime the wildish nature has become entrapped.

A healthy woman is much like a wolf: robust, chock-full, strong life force, life-giving, territorially aware, inventive, loyal, roving. Yet, separation from the wildish nature causes a woman's personality to become meager, thin, ghosty, spectral. We are not meant to be puny with frail hair and inability to leap up, inability to chase, to birth, to create a life. When women's lives are in stasis, or filled with ennui, it is always time for the wildish woman to emerge; it is time for the creating function of the psyche to flood the delta.

How does Wild Woman affect women? With her as ally, as leader, model, teacher, we see, not through two eyes, but through the eyes of intuition which is many-eyed. When we assert intuition, we are therefore like the starry night: we gaze at the world through a thousand eyes.

The wild nature carries the bundles for healing; she carries everything a woman needs to be and know. She carries the medicine for all things. She carries stories and dreams and words and songs and signs and symbols. She is both vehicle and destination.

To adjoin the instinctual nature does not mean to come undone, change everything from left to right, from black to white, to move the east to west, to act crazy or out of control. It does not mean to lose one's primary socializations, or to become less human. It means quite the opposite. The wild nature has a vast integrity to it.

It means to establish territory, to find one's pack, to be in one's body with certainty and pride regardless of the body's gifts and limitations, to speak and act in one's behalf, to be aware, alert, to draw on the innate feminine powers of intuition and sensing, to come into one's cycles, to find what one belongs to, to rise with dignity, to retain as much consciousness as possible.

The archetype of the Wild Woman and all that stands behind her is patroness to all painters, writers, sculptors, dancers, thinkers, prayermakers, seekers, finders—for they are all busy with the work of invention, and that is the instinctive nature's main occupation. As in all art, she resides in the guts, not in the head. She can track and run and summon and repel. She can sense, camouflage, and love deeply. She is intuitive, typical, and normative. She is utterly essential to women's mental and soul health.

So what compromises the Wild Woman? From the viewpoint

of archetypal psychology as well as in ancient traditions, she is the female soul. Yet she is more; she is the source of the feminine. She is all that is of instinct, of the worlds both seen and hidden—she is the basis. We each receive from her a glowing cell which contains all the instincts and knowings needed for our lives.

". . . She is the Life/Death/Life force, she is the incubator. She is intuition, she is far-seer, she is deep listener, she is loyal heart. She encourages humans to remain multi-lingual; fluent in the languages of dreams, passion, and poetry. She whispers from night dreams, she leaves behind on the terrain of a woman's soul a coarse hair and muddy footprints. These fill women with longing to find her, free her, and love her.

"She is ideas, feelings, urges, and memory. She has been lost and half forgotten for a long, long time. She is the source, the light, the night, the dark, and daybreak. She is the smell of good mud and the back leg of the fox. The birds which tell us secrets belong to her. She is the voice that says, 'This way, this way.'

"She is the one who thunders after injustice. She is the one who turns like a great wheel. She is the maker of cycles. She is the one we leave home to look for. She is the one we come home to. She is the mucky root of all women. She is the things that keep us going when we think we're done for. She is the incubator of raw little ideas and deals. She is the mind which thinks us, we are the thoughts that she thinks.

"Where is she present? Where can you feel her, where can you find her? She walks the deserts, woods, oceans, cities, in the barrios, and in castles. She lives among queens, among *campesinas*, in the boardroom, in the factory, in the prison, in the mountain of solitude. She lives in the ghetto, at the university, and in the streets. She leaves footprints for us to try for size. She leaves footprints wherever there is one woman who is fertile soil.

"Where does she live? At the bottom of the well, in the headwaters, in the ether before time. She lives in the tear and in the ocean. She lives in the cambia of trees, which pings as it grows. She is from the future and from the beginning of time. She lives in the past and is summoned by us. She is in the present and keeps a chair at our table, stands behind us in line, and drives ahead of us on the road. She is in the future and walks backward in time to find us now.

"She lives in the green poking through snow, she lives in the rustling stalks of dying autumn corn, she lives where the dead come to be kissed and the living send their prayers. She lives in the place where language is made. She lives on poetry and percussion and singing. She lives on quarter notes and grace notes, and in a cantata, in a sestina, and in the blues. She is the moment just before inspiration bursts upon us. She lives in a faraway place that breaks through to our world.

"People may ask for evidence, for proof of her existence. They are essentially asking for proof of the psyche. Since we are the psyche, we are also the evidence. Each and every one of us is the evidence of not only Wild Woman's existence, but of her condition in the collective. We are the proof of this ineffable female numen. Our existence parallels hers.

"Our experiences of her within and without are the proofs. Our thousands and millions of encounters with her intra-psychically through our night dreams and our day thoughts, through our yearnings and inspirations, these are the verifications. The fact that we are bereft in her absence, that we long and yearn when we are separated from her; these are the manifestations that she has passed this way. . ."[3]

My doctorate is in ethno-clinical psychology, which is the study of both clinical psychology and ethnology, the latter emphasizing the study of the psychology of groups, and tribes in particular. My post-doctoral diploma is in analytical psychology, which is what certifies me as a Jungian psychoanalyst. My life experience as *cantadora/mesemondó*, poet, and artist informs my work with analysands equally.

Sometimes I am asked to tell what I do in my consulting room to help women return to their wildish natures. I place substantial emphasis on clinical and developmental psychology, and I use the simplest and most accessible ingredient for healing—stories. We follow the patient's dream material, which contains many plots and stories. The analysand's physical sensations and body memories are also stories which can be read and rendered into consciousness.

Additionally, I teach a form of powerful interactive trancing that is proximate to Jung's active imagination—and this also produces stories which further elucidate the client's psychic journey. We elicit the wildish Self through specific questions, and through examining tales, legends, and mythos. Most times we are able, over time, to find the guiding myth or fairy tale that contains all the instruction a woman needs for her current psychic development. These stories comprise a woman's soul drama. It is like a play with stage instructions, characterization, and props.

The "craft of making" is an important part of the work I do. I seek to empower my clients by teaching them the age-old crafts of the hands . . . among them the symbolic arts of talisman making, *las ofrendas* and *retablos*—these being anything from simple ribbon sticks to elaborate sculpture. Art is important for it commemorates the seasons of the soul, or a special or tragic event in the soul's journey. Art is not just for oneself, not just a marker of one's own understanding. It is also a map for those who follow after us.

As you might imagine, work with each person is customized in the extreme, for it is true that people are made one to a kind. But these factors remain constant in my work with people, and these are the fundament for all humans' work before them today, my own work as well as yours. The craft of questions, the craft of stories, the craft of the hands—all these are the making of something, and that something is soul. Anytime we feed soul, it guarantees increase.

I hope you will see that these are tangible ways to soften old scar tissue, balm old wounds, and envision anew, thereby restoring the old skills that make the soul visible in down-to-earth ways.

The tales I bring here to elucidate the instinctual nature of women are in some cases, original stories, and in other cases, are distinct literary renderings that I have written based on those peculiar ones given into my keeping by my *tias y tios, abuelitas y abuelos, omahs and opahs*, the old ones of my families—those whose oral traditions have been unbroken for as far back as we can remember. A few are written documents of my own firsthand encounters, some from long time passing, and all from the heart. They are presented in all faithful detail and archetypal integrity. It is with the permission and blessing of three living generations of familial healer-tellers who understand the subtleties and requirements of story as healing phenomena that I carry these forward.[4]

Additionally, here are some of the questions I pose to my analysands and others to whom I offer counsel in order for them to remember themselves. I also detail for you some of the craft—the experiential and artful play that assists women in retaining the numen of their work in conscious memory. All these help to bring about convergence with the precious wildish Self.

Stories are medicine. I have been taken with stories since I heard my first. They have such power; they do not require that we do, be, act anything—we need only listen. The remedies for repair or reclamation of any lost psychic drive are contained in stories. Stories engender the excitement, sadness, questions, longings, and understandings that spontaneously bring the archetype, in this case Wild Woman, back to the surface.

Stories are embedded with instructions which guide us about the complexities of life. Stories enable us to understand the need for and the ways to raise a submerged archetype. The stories on the following pages are the ones, out of hundreds that I've worked with and pored over for decades, and that I believe most clearly express the bounty of the Wild Woman archetype.

Sometimes various cultural overlays disarray the bones of stories. For instance, in the case of the brothers Grimm (among other fairy-tale collectors of the past few centuries), there is strong suspicion that the informants (storytellers) of that time sometimes "purified" their stories for the religious brothers' sakes. Over the course of time, old pagan symbols were overlaid with Christian ones, so that an old healer in a tale became an evil witch, a spirit became an angel, an initiation veil or caul became a handkerchief, or a child named Beautiful (the customary name for a child born during Solstice festival) was renamed *Schmerzenreich*, Sorrowful. Sexual elements were omitted. Helping creatures and animals were often changed into demons and boogeys.

This is how many women's teaching tales about sex, love, money, marriage, birthing, death, and transformation were lost. It is how fairy tales and myths that explicate ancient women's mysteries have been covered over too. Most old collections of fairy tales and mythos existent today have been scoured clean of the scatological, the sexual, the perverse (as in warnings against), the pre-Christian, the feminine, the Goddesses, the initiatory, the medicines for various psychological malaises, and the directions for spiritual raptures.

But they are not lost forever. I was given as a child many of what I know to be unvarnished and uncorrupted themes of the stories of eld, many of which I bring to this work. But even story fragments, as they exist today, can foreshadow the shape of the entire story. I've poked about in what I playfully call fairy-tale forensics and paleomythology, even though, as its heart, reconstruction is a long, intricate, and contemplative endeavor. When such would be effective, I use various forms of exegesis, comparing leitmotifs, taking anthropological and historical inferences into account, and forms both new and old. This method, in part, reconstructs from ancient archetypal patternings learned through my years of training in analytical and archetypal psychology, which preserve and study all the motifs and plots in fairy tales, legends, and mythos in order to apprehend the instinctual lives of humans. I gain an assist from templates that lie in the imaginal worlds, the collective images of the unconscious, and those drawn up through dreams and non-ordinary states of consciousness. A final polish might be gained by comparing the story matrices with archeological evidence from the ancient cultures themselves, such as ritual pottery, masks, and figurines. Simply put, in fairy-tale locution, I spend much time raking the ashes with my nose.

I have been studying archetypal patterns for some twenty-five years, and myths, fairy tales, and folklore from my familial cultures for twice as long. I have learnt a vast body of knowledge about the bones of stories, and know when and where the bones are missing in a story. Through the centuries, various conquests of nations by other nations, and both peaceful and forced religious conversions, have covered over or altered the original core of the old stories.

But there is good news. For all the structural tumble-down in existing versions of tales, there is a strong pattern that still shines forth. From the form and shape of the pieces and parts, it can be determined with good accuracy what has been lost from the story and those missing pieces can be redrawn accurately—often revealing amazing understructures which begin to heal women's sadness that so much of the old mysteries has been destroyed. It is not quite so. They have not been destroyed. All one might need, all that we might ever need, is still whispering from the bones of story.

Collecting the essence of stories is a constant paleontologic endeavor. The more story bones, the more likely the integral structure can be found. The more whole the stories, the more subtle twists and turns of the psyche are presented to us and the better opportunity we have to apprehend and evoke our soulwork. When we work the soul, she, the Wild Woman, creates more of herself.

As a child, I was lucky to be surrounded by people from many of the old European countries and Mexico. Many members of my family, my neighbors, and friends had recently arrived from Hungary, Germany, Romania, Bulgaria, Yugoslavia, Poland, Czechoslovakia, Serbo-Croatia, Russia, Lithuania, and Bohemia as well as Jalisco, Michoacán, Juárez, and many of the *aldeas fronterizas* villages at the Mexico/Texas/Arizona borders. They, and many others—Native Americans, people from Appalachia, Asian immigrants, and many African-American families from the South—came to farm, to pick, to work in the ash pits and steel mills, the breweries, and in domestic jobs. Most were not educated in the academic sense, yet they were intensely wise. They were the bearers of a valuable and almost pure oral tradition.

Many of my family and neighboring people who surrounded me had survived forced labor camps, displaced person camps, deportation camps, and concentration camps where the storytellers among them had lived a nightmare version of Scheherazade. Many had had their family lands taken, had lived in immigration jails, had been repatriated against their wills. From these rustic storytellers I first learned the tales people tell when life may turn to death and death may turn to life at any moment. Because their transmissions to me were so filled with suffering and with hope, when I later grew old enough to read fairy stories printed in books, the latter seemed curiously starched and ironed flat in comparison.

As a young adult I migrated west toward the Continental Divide. I lived amidst loving Jewish, Irish, Greek, Italian, Afro-American, and Alsatian strangers who became kindred spirits and friends. I've been blessed to know some of the rare and old Latino communities from the southwestern U.S.A., such as Trampas, and Truchas, New Mexico. I was fortunate to spend time with Native American friends and relatives, from the Inuit in the North, through the Pueblo and Plains peoples in the West, to the Nahuas, Lacandones, Tehuanas, Huicholes, Seris, Maya-Quichés, Maya-Caqchiqueles, Mésquitos, Cunas, Nasca/Quechuas, and Jivaros in Central and South America.

I've traded stories with sister and brother healers at kitchen tables and under grape arbors, in henhouses and dairy barns, and while patting tortillas, tracking wildlife, and sewing the millionth cross-stitch. I've been lucky to share the last bowl of chili, to sing with gospel women so as to raise the dead, and to sleep under stars in houses without roofs. I've sat down to the fire or dinner, or both, in Little Italy, Polish Town, the Hill Country, Los Barrios, and other ethnic communities throughout the urban Midwest and Far West, and most recently traded stories about *sparats*, bad ghosts, with man-*griot* friends in the Bahamas.

I have been double-lucky that wherever I've gone the children, the matrons, the men in their prime, and the old coots and crones—the soul-artists—have crept out of the woods, jungles, meadows, and sandhills to regale me with caws and kavels. And I too, to them.

There are many ways to approach stories. The professional folk-lorist, the Jungian, Freudian, or other sort of analyst, the ethnologist, anthropologist, theologian, archeologist, each has a different method, both in collecting tales and the use to which they are put. Intellectually the way I developed my work with stories was through my training in analytical and archetypal psychology. For more than half a decade during my psychoanalytic education I studied amplification of leitmotifs, archetypal symbology, world mythology, ancient and popular iconology, ethnology, world religions, and interpretation.

Viscerally, however, I come to stories as a *cantadora*, keeper of the old stories. I come from a long line of tellers: *mesemondók*, old Hungarian women who might as easily tell while sitting on wooden chairs with their plastic pocketbooks on their laps, their knees apart, their skirts touching the ground, or while wringing the neck of a chicken . . . and *cuentistas*, old Latina women who stand, robust of breast, hips wide, and cry out the story *ranchera* style. Both clans storytell in the plain voice of women who have lived blood and babies, bread and bones. For us, story is a medicine which strengthens and arights the individual and the community.

Those who have taken on the responsibilities of this craft, and are committed to the numen behind the craft, are direct descendants of an immense and ancient community of holy people, troubadours, bards, griots, cantadoras, cantors, traveling poets, bums, hags, and crazy people.

I once dreamt I was telling stories and felt someone patting my foot in encouragement. I looked down and saw that I was standing on the shoulders of an old woman who was steadying my ankles and smiling up at me.

I said to her, "No, no, come stand on *my* shoulders for you are old and I am young."

"No, no," she insisted, "this is the way it is supposed to be."

I saw that she stood on the shoulders of a woman far older than she, who stood on the shoulders of a woman even older, who stood on the shoulders of a woman in robes, who stood on the shoulders of another soul, who stood on the shoulders . . .

I believed the old dream-woman about the way it was supposed to be. The nurture for telling stories comes from the might and endowments of my people who have gone before me. In my experience, the telling moment of the story draws its power from a towering column of humanity joined one to the other across time and space, elaborately dressed in the rags and robes or nakedness of their time, and filled to the bursting with life still being lived. If there is a single source of story and the numen of story, this long chain of humans is it.

Story is far older than the art and science of psychology, and will always be the elder in the equation no matter how much time passes. One of the oldest ways of telling, which intrigues me greatly, is the passionate trance state, wherein the teller "senses" the audience—be it an audience of one or of many—and then enters a state in the "world between worlds," where a story is "attracted" to the trance-teller and told through her.

The trance-teller calls on *El duende*,[5] the wind that blows soul into the faces of listeners. A trance-teller learns to be psychically double-jointed through the meditative practice of story, that is, training oneself to undo certain psychic gates and ego apertures in order to let the voice speak, the voice that is older than the stones. When this is done, the story may take any trail, be turned upside down, be filled with porridge and dumped out for a poor person's feast, be filled with gold for the taking, or chase the listener into the next world. The teller never knows how it will all come out, and that is at least half of the moist magic of story.

This is a book of tellings about the ways of the Wild Woman archetype. To try to diagram her, to draw boxes around her psychic life, would be contrary to her spirit. To know her is an ongoing process, a lifelong process, and that is why this work is an ongoing work, a lifelong work.

So here are some stories to apply to yourself as soul vitamins, some observations, some map fragments, some little pieces of pine pitch for fastening feathers to trees to show the way, and some flattened underbrush to guide the way back to *el mundo subterráneo*, the underground world, our psychic home.

Stories set the inner life into motion, and this is particularly important where the inner life is frightened, wedged, or cornered. Story greases the hoists and pulleys, it causes adrenaline to surge, shows us the way out, down, or up, and for our trouble, cuts for us fine wide doors in previously blank walls, openings that lead to the dreamland, that lead to love and learning, that lead us back to our own real lives as knowing wildish women.

Stories like "Bluebeard" bring us news of just what to do about the women's wound that will not cease its bleeding. Stories like "Skeleton Woman" demonstrate the mystical power of relationship and how deadened feeling can return to life and deep loving once again. The gifts of Old Mother Death are to be found in the character of Baba Yaga, the old Wild Hag. The little doll who shows the way when all seems lost raises one of the lost womanly and instinctual arts to the surface again in "Vasalisa the Wise."[6] Stories like "*La Loba*," a bone woman in the desert, teach about the transformative function of the psyche. "The Handless Maiden" recovers the lost stages of the old initiation rites from ancient times, and as such offers a timeless and lifelong guidance for all the years of a woman's life.

It is our brush with the wild nature that drives us not to limit our conversations to humans, not to limit our most splendid movements to dance floors, nor our ears only to music made by human-made instruments, nor our eyes to "taught" beauty, nor our bodies to approved sensations, nor our minds to those things we all agree upon already. All these stories present the knife of insight, the flame of the passionate life, the breath to speak what one knows, the courage to stand what one sees without looking away, the fragrance of the wild soul.

This is a book of women's stories, held out as markers along the path. They are for you to read and contemplate in order to assist you toward your own natural-won freedom, your caring for self, animals, earth, children, sisters, lovers, and men. I'll tell you right now, the doors to the world of the wild Self are few but precious. If you have a deep scar, that is a door, if you have an old, old story, that is a door. If you love the sky and the water so much you almost cannot bear it, that is a door. If you yearn for a deeper life, a full life, a sane life, that is a door.

The material in this book was chosen to embolden you. The work is offered as a fortification for those on their way, including those who toil in difficult inner landscapes, as well as those who toil in and for the world. We must strive to allow our souls to grow in their natural ways and to their natural depths. The wildish nature does not require a woman to be a certain color, a certain education, a certain lifestyle or economic class . . . in fact, it cannot thrive in an atmosphere of enforced political correctness, or by being bent into old burnt-out paradigms. It thrives on fresh sight and self-integrity. It thrives on its own nature.

So, whether you are an introvert or extrovert, a woman-loving woman, a man-loving woman, or a God-loving woman, or all of the above: Whether you are possessed of a simple heart or the ambitions of an Amazon, whether you are trying to make it to the top or just make it through tomorrow, whether you be spicy or somber, regal or roughshod—the Wild Woman belongs to you. She belongs to all women.

To find her, it is necessary for women to return to their instinctive lives, their deepest knowing.[7] So, let us push on now, and remember ourselves back to the wild soul. Let us sing her flesh back onto our bones. Shed any false coats we have been given. Don the true coat of powerful instinct and knowing. Infiltrate the psychic lands that once belonged to us. Unfurl the bandages, ready the medicine. Let us return now, wild women howling, laughing, singing up The One who loves us so.

For us the issue is simple. Without us, Wild Woman dies. Without Wild Woman, we die. *Para Vida*, for true life, both must live.

CHAPTER I

The Howl:
Resurrection of the
Wild Woman

La Loba, The Wolf Woman

I must reveal to you that I am not one of the Divine who march into the desert and return gravid with wisdom. I've traveled many cookfires and spread angel bait round every sleeping place. But more often than the getting of wisdom, I've gotten indelicate episodes of *Giardiasis*, *E. coli*,[1] and amebic dysentery. Ai! Such is the fate of a middle-class mystic with delicate intestines.

Whatever wisdom or notion I espied on my travels to odd places and unusual people, I learned to shelter, for sometimes old father Academe, like Kronos, still has an inclination to eat the children before they can become either curative or astonishing. Over-intellectualization can obscure the patterns of the instinctual nature of women.

So, to further our kinship relationship with the instinctual nature, it assists greatly if we understand stories as though we are inside them, rather than as though we are outside of us. We enter into a story through the door of inner hearing. The spoken story touches the auditory nerve, which runs across the floor of the skull into the brainstem just below the pons. There, auditory impulses are relayed upward to consciousness or else, it is said, to the soul . . . depending on the attitude with which one listens.

Ancient dissectionists spoke of the auditory nerve being divided into three or more pathways deep in the brain. They surmised that the ear was meant, therefore, to hear at three different

23

levels. One pathway was said to hear the mundane conversations of the world. A second pathway apprehended learning and art. And the third pathway existed so the soul itself might hear guidance and gain knowledge while here on earth.

Listen then with soul-hearing now, for that is the mission of story.

Bone by bone, hair by hair, Wild Woman comes back. Through night dreams, through events half understood and half remembered, Wild Woman comes back. She comes back through story.

I began my own migration across the United States in the 1960s, looking for a settling place that was dense with trees, fragrant with water, and populated by the creatures I loved: bear, fox, snake, eagle, wolf. The wolves were being systematically exterminated from the upper Great Lakes region; no matter where I went, the wolves were being hounded in one way or another. Although many spoke of them as menaces, I always felt safer when there were wolves in the woods. Out West and in the North in those times, you could camp and hear the mountains and forest sing, sing, sing at night.

But, even there, the age of scope rifles, Jeep-mounted klieg lights, and arsenic "treats" caused an age of silence to creep over the land. Soon, the Rockies were almost empty of wolves too. That is how I came to the great desert which lies half in Mexico, half in the United States. And the further south I traveled, the more stories I heard about wolves.

You see, it is told that there is a place in the desert where the spirit of women and the spirit of wolves meet across time. I felt I was onto something when in the Texas borderlands I heard a story called "*Loba* Girl" about a woman who was a wolf who was a woman. Next I found the ancient Aztec story of orphaned twins being breast-fed by a she-wolf till the children were old enough to stand on their own.[2]

And finally, from the old Spanish land-grant farmers and Pueblo people of the Southwest, I heard one-line reports about the bone people, the old ones who bring the dead back to life; they were said to restore both humans and animals. Then, on one of my own ethnographic expeditions, I met a bone woman and have never been quite the same since. Allow me to present a firsthand account and introduction.

~~~~~~~~~~~~~~~~~~~~~~~~~~~~~~~~~~~

La Loba

THERE IS AN OLD WOMAN who lives in a hidden place that everyone knows in their souls but few have ever seen. As in the fairy tales of Eastern Europe, she seems to wait for lost or wandering people and seekers to come to her place.

She is circumspect, often hairy, always fat, and especially wishes to evade most company. She is both a crower and a cackler, generally having more animal sounds than human ones.

I might say she lives among the rotten granite slopes in Tarahumara Indian territory. Or that she is buried outside Phoenix near a well. Perhaps she will be seen traveling south to Monte Albán[3] in a burnt-out car with the back window shot out. Or maybe she will be spotted standing by the highway near El Paso, or riding shotgun with truckers to Morelia, Mexico, or walking to market above Oaxaca with strangely formed boughs of firewood on her back. She calls herself by many names: *La Huesera*, Bone Woman; *La Trapera*, The Gatherer; and *La Loba*, Wolf Woman.

The sole work of *La Loba* is the collecting of bones. She collects and preserves especially that which is in danger of being lost to the world. Her cave is filled with the bones of all manner of desert creatures: the deer, the rattlesnake, the crow. But her specialty is wolves.

She creeps and crawls and sifts through the *montañas*, mountains, and *arroyos*, dry riverbeds, looking for wolf bones, and when she has assembled an entire skeleton, when the last bone is in place and the beautiful white sculpture of the creature is laid out before her, she sits by the fire and thinks about what song she will sing.

And when she is sure, she stands over the *criatura*, raises her arms over it, and sings out. That is when the rib bones and leg bones of the wolf begin to flesh out and the creature becomes furred. *La Loba* sings some more, and more of the creature comes into being; its tail curls upward, shaggy and strong.

And *La Loba* sings more and the wolf creature begins to breathe.

And still *La Loba* sings so deeply that the floor of the desert shakes, and as she sings, the wolf opens its eyes, leaps up, and runs away down the canyon.

Somewhere in its running, whether by the speed of its running, or by splashing its way into a river, or by way of a ray of sunlight or moonlight hitting it right in the side, the wolf is suddenly transformed into a laughing woman who runs free toward the horizon.

So remember, if you wander the desert, and it is near sundown, and you are perhaps a little bit lost, and certainly tired, that you are lucky, for *La Loba* may take a liking to you and show you something—something of the soul.

~~~~~~

We all begin as a bundle of bones lost somewhere in a desert, a dismantled skeleton that lies under the sand. It is our work to recover the parts. It is a painstaking process best done when the shadows are just right, for it takes much looking. *La Loba* indicates what we are to look for—the indestructible life force, the bones.

The work of *La Loba* can be thought of as representing *un cuento milagro*, a miracle story. It shows us what can go right for the soul. It is a resurrection story about the underworld connection to Wild Woman. It promises that if we will sing the song, we can call up the psychic remains of the wild soul and sing her into a vital shape again.

La Loba sings over the bones she has gathered. To sing means to use the soul-voice. It means to say on the breath the truth of one's power and one's need, to breathe soul over the thing that is ailing or in need of restoration. This is done by descending into the deepest mood of great love and feeling, till one's desire for relationship with the wildish Self overflows, then to speak one's soul from that frame of mind. That is singing over the bones. We cannot make the mistake of attempting to elicit this great feeling of love from a lover, for this womens' labor of finding and singing the creation hymn is a solitary work, a work carried out in the desert of the psyche.

Let us consider *La Loba* herself. In the symbolic lexicon of the psyche, the symbol of the Old Woman is one of the most widespread archetypal personifications in the world. Others are the Great Mother and Father, the Divine Child, the Trickster, the Sorceress(er), the Maiden and Youth, the Heroine-Warrior, and the Fool(ess). Yet, a figure like *La Loba* can be considered vastly different in essence and effect, for she is symbolic of the feeder root to an entire instinctual system.

In the Southwest the archetype of the old woman can also be apprehended as old *La Que Sabe*, The One Who Knows. I first came to understand *La Que Sabe* when I lived in the Sangre de Cristo mountains in New Mexico, under the heart of Lobo Peak. An old witch from Ranchos told me that *La Que Sabe* knew everything about women, that *La Que Sabe* had created women from a wrinkle on the sole of her divine foot: This is why women are knowing creatures; they are made, in essence, of the skin of the sole, which feels everything. This idea that the skin of the foot is sentient had the ring of a truth, for an acculturated Kiché tribeswoman once told me that she'd worn her first pair of shoes when she was twenty years old and was still not used to walking *con los ojos vendados*, with blindfolds on her feet.

The wild essence that inhabits nature has been called by many names and crisscrosses all nations down through the centuries. These are some of the old names for her: *The Mother of Days* is the Mother-Creator-God of all beings and doings, including the sky and earth; *Mother Nyx* has dominion over all things from the mud and dark; *Durga* controls the skies and winds and the thoughts of humans from which all reality spreads; *Coatlicue* gives birth to the infant universe which is rascally and hard to control, but like a wolf mother, she bites her child's ear to contain it; *Hekate*, the old seer who "knows her people" and has about her the smell of humus and the breath of God. And there are many, many more. These are the images of what and who lives under the hill, far off in the desert, out in the deep.

By whatever name, the force personified by *La Loba* records the personal past and the ancient past for she has survived generation after generation, and is old beyond time. She is an archivist of feminine intention. She preserves female tradition. Her whiskers sense the future; she has the far-seeing milky eye of the old crone; she lives backward and forward in time simultaneously, correcting for one side by dancing with the other.

The old one, The One Who Knows, is within us. She thrives in the deepest soul-psyche of women, the ancient and vital wild Self. Her home is that place in time where the spirit of women and the spirit of wolf meet—the place where mind and instincts mingle, where a woman's deep life funds her mundane life. It is the point where the I and the Thou kiss, the place where, in all spirit, women run with the wolves.

This old woman stands between the worlds of rationality and mythos. She is the knucklebone on which these two worlds turn. This land between the worlds is that inexplicable place we all recognize once we experience it, but its nuances slip away and shape-change if one tries to pin them down, except when we use poetry, music, dance, or story.

There is speculation that the immune system of the body is rooted in this mysterious psychic land, and also the mystical, as well as all archetypal images and urges including our God-hunger, our yearning for the mysteries, and all the sacred instincts as well as those which are mundane. Some would say the records of humankind, the root of light, the coil of dark are also here. It is not a void, but rather the place of the Mist Beings where things are and also are not yet, where shadows have substance and substance is sheer.

One thing about this land is certain, it is old . . . older than the oceans. It has no age; it is ageless. The Wild Woman archetype funds this layer, emanating from the instinctual psyche. Although she can take on many guises in our dreams and creative experiences, she is not from the layer of the mother, the maiden, the medial woman, and she is not the inner child. She is not the queen, the amazon, the lover, the seer. She is just what she is. Call her *La Que Sabe*, The One Who Knows, call her Wild Woman, call her *La Loba*, call her by her high names or by her low names, call her by her newer names or her ancient ones, she remains just what she is.

Wild Woman as an archetype is an inimitable and ineffable force which carries a bounty of ideas, images, and particularities for humankind. Archetype exists everywhere and yet is not seeable in the usual sense. What can be seen of it in the dark cannot necessarily be seen in daylight.

We find lingering evidence of archetype in the images and symbols found in stories, literature, poetry, painting, and religion. It would appear that its glow, its voice, and its fragrance are meant to cause us to be raised up from contemplating the shit on our tails to occasionally traveling in the company of the stars.

At *La Loba*'s place, the physical body is, as poet Tony Moffeit writes, "a luminous animal,"[4] and the body's immune system seems, via anecdotal reports, to be strengthened or weakened by conscious thought. At *La Loba*'s place, the spirits manifest as personages and *La voz mitológica*, The Mythological Voice of the deep psyche, speaks as poet and oracle. Things of psychic value, once dead, can be revived. Also, the basic material of all stories existent in the world ever, began with someone's experience here in this inexplicable psychic land, and someone's attempt to relate what occurred to them here.

There are various names for this locus betwixt the worlds. Jung called it variously the collective unconscious, the objective psyche, and the psychoid unconscious—referring to a more ineffable layer of the former. He thought of the latter as a place where the biological and psychological worlds share headwaters, where biology and psychology might mingle with and influence one another. Throughout human memory this place—call it Nod, call it the home of the Mist Beings, the crack between the worlds—is the place where visitations, miracles, imaginations, inspirations, and healings of all natures occur.

Though this site transmits great psychic wealth, it must be approached with preparation, for one may be tempted to joyously drown in the rapture of one's time there. Consensual reality may seem less exciting by comparison. In this sense, these deeper layers of psyche can become a rapture-trap from which people return unsteady, with wobbly ideas and airy presentments.

That is not how it is meant to be. How one is meant to return is wholly washed or dipped in a revivifying and informing water, something which impresses upon our flesh the odor of the sacred.

Each woman has potential access to *Río Abajo Río*, this river beneath the river. She arrives there through deep meditation, dance, writing, painting, prayermaking, singing, drumming, active imagination, or any activity which requires an intense altered consciousness. A woman arrives in this world-between-worlds through yearning and by seeking something she can see just out of the corner of her eye. She arrives there by deeply creative acts, through intentional solitude, and by practice of any of the arts. And even with these well-crafted practices, much of what occurs in this ineffable world remains forever mysterious to us, for it breaks physical laws and rational laws as we know them.

The care with which this psychic state must be entered is recorded in a small but powerful story of four rabbis who yearned to see the most sacred Wheel of Ezekiel.

The Four Rabbinim

ONE NIGHT four rabbinim were visited by an angel who awakened them and carried them to the Seventh Vault of the Seventh Heaven. There they beheld the sacred Wheel of Ezekiel.

Somewhere in the descent from *Pardes*, Paradise, to Earth, one Rabbi, having seen such splendor, lost his mind and wandered frothing and foaming until the end of his days. The second Rabbi was extremely cynical: "Oh I just dreamed Ezekiel's Wheel, that was all. Nothing *really* happened." The third Rabbi carried on and on about what he had seen, for he was totally obsessed. He lectured and would not stop with how it was all constructed and what it all meant . . . and in this way he went astray and betrayed his faith. The fourth Rabbi, who was a poet, took a paper in hand and a reed and sat near the window writing song after song praising the evening dove, his daughter in her cradle, and all the stars in the sky. And he lived his life better than before.[5]

Who saw what in the Seventh Vault of the Seventh Heaven, we do not know. But we do know that contact with the world wherein the Essences reside causes us to know something beyond the usual hearing of humans, and fills us with a feeling of expansion and grandeur as well. When we touch the authentic fundament of The One Who Knows, it causes us to react and act from our deepest integral nature.

The story recommends that the optimal attitude for experiencing the deep unconscious is one of neither too much fascination nor too little, one of not too much awe but neither too much cynicism, bravery yes, but not recklessness.

Jung cautions in his magnificent essay "The Transcendent Function"[6] that some persons, in their pursuit of the Self, will overaestheticize the God or Self experience, some will undervalue it, some will overvalue it, and some who are not ready for it will be injured by it. But still others will find their way to what Jung called "the moral obligation" to live out and to express what one has learned in the descent or ascent to the wild Self.

This moral obligation he speaks of means to live what we perceive, be it found in the psychic Elysian fields, the isles of the dead, the bone deserts of the psyche, the face of the mountain, the rock of the sea, the lush underworld—anyplace where *La Que Sabe* breathes upon us, changing us. Our work is to show we have been breathed upon—to show it, give it out, sing it out, to live out in the topside world what we have received through our sudden knowings, from body, from dreams and journeys of all sorts.

La Loba parallels world myths in which the dead are brought back to life. In Egyptian mythos, Isis accomplishes this service for her dead brother Osiris, who is dismembered by his evil brother, Set, every night. Isis works from dusk to dawn each night to piece her brother back together again before morning, else the sun will not rise. The Christ raised Lazarus, who had been dead so long he "stinketh." Demeter calls forth her pale daughter Persephone from the Land of the Dead once a year. And *La Loba* sings over the bones.

This is our meditation practice as women, calling back the dead and dismembered aspects of ourselves, calling back the dead and dismembered aspects of life itself. The one who re-creates from that which has died is always a double-sided archetype. The Creation Mother is always also the Death Mother and vice versa. Because of this dual nature, or double-tasking, the great work before us is to learn to understand what around and about us and what within us must live, and what must die. Our work is to apprehend the timing of both; to allow what must die to die, and what must live to live.

For women, "*El río abajo río*, the river-beneath-the-river world," the Bone Woman home place, contains direct knowing about seedlings, root stock, the seed corn of the world. In Mexico, women are said to carry *la luz de la vida*, the light of life. This light is located, not in a woman's heart, not behind her eyes, but *en los ovarios*, in her ovaries, where all the seed stock is laid down before she is even born. (For men, exploring the deeper ideas of fertility and the nature of seed, the cross-gender image is the furry bag, *los cojones*, the scrotum.)

This is the knowing to be gained in being close to Wild Woman. When *La Loba* sings, she sings from the knowing of *los ovarios*, a knowing from deep within the body, deep within the mind, deep within the soul. The symbols of seed and bone are very similar. If one has the root stock, the basis, the original part, if one has the seed corn, any havoc can be repaired, devastations can be resewn, fields can be rested, hard seed can be soaked to soften it, to help it break open and thrive.

To have the seed means to have the key to life. To be with the cycles of the seed means to dance with life, dance with death, dance into life again. This embodies the Life and Death Mother in her most ancient and principled form. Because she turns in these constant cycles, I call her the Life/Death/Life Mother.

If something is lost, it is she to whom one must appeal, speak with, and listen to. Her psychic advice is sometimes harsh or difficult to put into practice, but always transformative and restorative. So when something is lost, we must go to the old woman who always lives in the out-of-the-way-pelvis. She lives out there, half in and half out of the creative fire. This is a perfect place for women to live, right next to the fertile *huevos*, their eggs, their female seeds. There the tiniest ideas and the largest ones are waiting for our minds and actions to make them manifest.

Imagine the old woman as the quintessential two-million-year-old woman.[7] She is the original Wild Woman who lives beneath and yet on the topside of the earth. She lives in and through us and we are surrounded by her. The deserts, the woodlands, and the earth under our houses are two million years old, and then some.

I'm always taken by how deeply women like to dig in the earth. They plant bulbs for the spring. They poke blackened fingers into mucky soil, transplanting sharp-smelling tomato plants. I think they are digging down to the two-million-year-old woman. They are looking for her toes and her paws. They want her for a present to themselves, for with her they feel of a piece and at peace.

Without her, they feel restless. Many women I've worked with over the years began their first session with some variation of: "Well, I don't feel bad, but I don't feel good either." I think that condition is not a great mystery. We know it comes from not enough muck. The cure? *La Loba*. Find the two-million-year-old woman. She is caretaker of the dead and dying of woman-things. She is the road between the living and the dead. She sings the creation hymns over the bones.

The old woman, Wild Woman, is *La voz mitológica*. She is the mythical voice who knows the past and our ancient history and keeps it recorded for us in stories. Sometimes we dream her as a disembodied but beautiful voice.

As the hag-maiden, she shows us what it means to be, not withered, but wizened. Babies are born wizened with instinct. They know in their bones what is right and what to do about it. It is innate. If a woman holds on to this gift of being old while she is young and young while she is old, she will always know what comes next. If she has lost it, she can yet reclaim it with some purposeful psychic work.

La Loba, the old one in the desert, is a collector of bones. In archetypal symbology, bones represent the indestructible force. They do not lend themselves to easy reduction. They are by their structure hard to burn, nearly impossible to pulverize. In myth and story, they represent the indestructible soul-spirit. We know the soul-spirit can be injured, even maimed, but it is very nearly impossible to kill.

You can dent the soul and bend it. You can hurt it and scar it. You can leave the marks of illness upon it, and the scorch marks of fear. But it does not die, for it is protected by *La Loba* in the underworld. She is both the finder and the incubator of the bones.

Bones are heavy enough to hurt with, sharp enough to cut through flesh, and when old and if strung, tinkle like glass. The bones of the living are alive and creatural in themselves; they constantly renew themselves. A living bone has a curiously soft "skin" to it. It appears to have certain powers to regenerate itself. Even as a dry bone, it becomes home for small living creatures.

The wolf bones in this story represent the indestructible aspect of the wild Self, the instinctual nature, the *criatura* dedicated to freedom and the unspoiled, that which will never accept the rigors and requirements of a dead or overly civilizing culture.

The metaphors in this story typify the entire process for bringing a woman to her full instinctual wildish senses. Within us is the old one who collects bones. Within us there are the soul-bones of this wild Self. Within us is the potential to be fleshed out again as the creature we once were. Within us are the bones to change ourselves and our world. Within us is the breath and our truths and our longings—together they are the song, the creation hymn we have been yearning to sing.

This does not mean we should walk about with our hair hanging in our eyes or with black-ringed claws for fingernails. Yes, we remain human, but also within the human woman is the animal instinctual Self. This is not some romantic cartoon character. It has real teeth, a true snarl, huge generosity, unequaled hearing, sharp claws, generous and furry breasts.

This Self must have freedom to move, to speak, to be angry, and to create. This Self is durable, resilient, and possesses high intuition. It is a Self which is knowledgeable in the spiritual dealings of death and birth.

Today the old one inside you is collecting bones. What is she re-making? She is the soul Self, the builder of the soul-home. *Ella lo hace a mano*, she makes and re-makes the soul by hand. What is she making for you?

Even in the best of worlds the soul needs refurbishing from time to time. Just like the adobes here in the Southwest, a little peels, a little falls down, a little washes away. There is always an old round woman with bedroom-slipper feet who is patting mud slurry on the adobe walls. She mixes straw and water and earth, and pats it back on the walls, making them fine again. Without her, the house will lose its shape. Without her, it will wash down into a lump after a hard rain.

She is the keeper of the soul. Without her, we lose our shape. Without an open supply line to her, humans are said to be soulless or damned souls. She gives shape to the soul-house and makes more house by hand. She is the one in the old apron. She is the one whose dress is longer in the front than in the back. She is the one who patta-pat-pats. She is the soul-maker, the wolf-raiser, the keeper of things wild.

So, I say to you with affection, imagistically—be you a Black wolf, a Northern Gray, a Southern Red, or an Arctic White—you are the quintessential instinctual *criatura*. Although some might really prefer you behave yourself and not climb all over the furniture in joy or all over people in welcome, do it anyway. Some will draw back from you in fear or disgust. Your lover, however, will cherish this new aspect of you—if he or she be the right lover for you.

Some people will not like it if you take a sniff at everything to see what it is. And for heaven's sakes, no lying on your back with your feet up in the air. Bad girl. Bad wolf. Bad dog. Right? Wrong. Go ahead. Enjoy yourself.

People do meditation to find psychic alignment. That's why people do psychotherapy and analysis. That's why people analyze their dreams and make art. That is why some contemplate tarot cards, cast I Ching, dance, drum, make theater, pry out the poem, and fire up their prayers. That's why we do all the things we do. It is the work of gathering all the bones together. Then we must sit at the fire and think about which song we will use to sing over the bones, which creation hymn, which re-creation hymn. And the truths we tell will make the song.

These are some good questions to ask till one decides on the song, one's true song: What has happened to my soul-voice?

What are the buried bones of my life? In what condition is my relationship to the instinctual Self? When was the last time I ran free? How do I make life come alive again? Where has *La Loba* gone to?

The old woman sings over the bones, and as she sings, the bones flesh out. We too "become" as we pour soul over the bones we have found. As we pour our yearning and our heartbreaks over the bones of what we used to be when we were young, of what we used to know in the centuries past, and over the quickening we sense in the future, we stand on all fours, four-square. As we pour soul, we are revivified. We are no longer a thin solution, a dissolving frail thing. No, we are in the "becoming" stage of transformation.

Like the dry bones, we so often start out in a desert. We feel disenfranchised, alienated, not connected to even a cactus clump. The ancients called the desert the place of divine revelation. But for women, there is much more to it than that.

A desert is a place where life is very condensed. The roots of living things hold on to that last tear of water and the flower hoards its moisture by only appearing in early morning and late afternoon. Life in the desert is small but brilliant and most of what occurs goes on underground. This is like the lives of many women.

The desert is not lush like a forest or a jungle. It is very intense and mysterious in its life forms. Many of us have lived desert lives: very small on the surface, and enormous under the ground. *La Loba* shows us the precious things that can come from that sort of psychic distribution.

A woman's psyche may have found its way to the desert out of resonance, or because of past cruelties or because she was not allowed a larger life above ground. So often a woman feels then that she lives in an empty place where there is maybe just one cactus with one brilliant red flower on it, and then in every direction, 500 miles of nothing. But for the woman who will go 501 miles, there is something more. A small brave house. An old one. She has been waiting for you.

Some women don't want to be in the psychic desert. They hate the frailty, the spareness of it. They keep trying to crank a rusty jalopy and bump their way down the road to a fantasized shining city of the psyche. But they are disappointed, for the lush and the wild is not there. It is in the spirit world, that world between worlds, *Río Abajo Río*, that river beneath the river.

Don't be a fool. Go back and stand under that one red flower and walk straight ahead for that last hard mile. Go up and knock on the old weathered door. Climb up to the cave. Crawl through the window of a dream. Sift the desert and see what you find. It is the only work we *have* to do.

You wish psychoanalytic advice?

Go gather bones.

CHAPTER 2

Stalking the Intruder:
The Beginning
Initiation

Bluebeard

In a single human being there are many other beings, all with their own values, motives, and devices. Some psychological technologies suggest we arrest these beings, count them, name them, force them into harness till they shuffle along like vanquished slaves. But to do this would halt the dance of wildish lights in a woman's eyes; it would halt her heat lightning and arrest all throwing of sparks. Rather than corrupt her natural beauty, our work is to build for all these beings a wildish countryside wherein the artists among them can make, the lovers love, the healers heal.

But what shall we do with those inner beings who are quite mad and those who carry out destruction without thought? Even these must be given a place, though one in which they can be contained. One entity in particular, the most deceitful and most powerful fugitive in the psyche, requires our immediate consciousness and containment—and that one is the natural predator.

While the cause of much human suffering can be traced to negligent fostering, there is also within the psyche naturally an innate *contra naturam* aspect, an "against nature" force. The *contra naturam* aspect opposes the positive: it is against development, against harmony, and against the wild. It is a derisive and murderous antagonist that is born into us, and even with the best parental nurture the intruder's sole assignment is to attempt to turn all crossroads into closed roads.

38

This predatory potentate[1] shows up time after time in women's dreams. It erupts in the midst of their most soulful and meaningful plans. It severs the woman from her intuitive nature. When its cutting work is done, it leaves the woman deadened in feeling, feeling frail to advance her life; her ideas and dreams lay at her feet drained of animation.

Bluebeard is a story of such a matter. In North America, the best known Bluebeard versions are the French and the German.[2] But I prefer my literary version in which the French and the Slavic are mingled, like the one given to me by my Aunt Kathé (pronounced "Katie"), who lived in Csíbrak near Dombovar in Hungary. Among our cadre of farmwomen tellers, the Bluebeard tale is begun with an anecdote about someone who knew someone who knew someone who had seen the grisly proof of Bluebeard's demise. And so we begin.

THERE IS A HANK OF BEARD which is kept at the convent of the white nuns in the far mountains. How it came to the convent no one knows. Some say it was the nuns who buried what was left of his body, for no one else would touch it. Why the nuns would keep such a relic is unknown, but it is true. My friend's friend has seen it with her own eyes. She says the beard is blue, indigo-colored to be exact. It is as blue as the dark ice in the lake, as blue as the shadow of a hole at night. This beard was once worn by one who they say was a failed magician, a giant man with an eye for women, a man known by the name of Bluebeard.

'Twas said he courted three sisters at the same time. But they were frightened of his beard with its odd blue cast, and so they hid when he called. In an effort to convince them of his geniality he invited them on an outing in the forest. He arrived leading horses arrayed in bells and crimson ribbons. He set the sisters and their mother upon the horses and off they cantered into the forest. There they had a most wonderful day riding, and their dogs ran beside and ahead. Later they stopped beneath a giant tree and Bluebeard regaled them with stories and fed them dainty treats.

The sisters began to think, "Well, perhaps this man Bluebeard is not so bad after all."

They returned home all a-chatter about how interesting the day had been, and did they not have a good time? Yet, the two older sisters' suspicions and fears returned and they vowed not to see Bluebeard again. But the youngest sister thought if a man could be that charming, then perhaps he was not so bad. The more she talked to herself, the less awful he seemed, and also the less blue his beard.

So when Bluebeard asked for her hand in marriage, she accepted. She had given his proposal great thought and felt she was to marry a very elegant man. Marry they did, and after, rode off to his castle in the woods.

One day he came to her and said, "I must go away for a time. Invite your family here if you like. You may ride in the woods, charge the cooks to set a feast, you may do anything you like, anything your heart desires. In fact, here is my ring of keys. You may open any and every door to the storerooms, the money rooms, any door in the castle; but this little tiny key, the one with the scroll-work on top, do not use."

His bride replied, "Yes, I will do as you ask. It all sounds very fine. So, go, my dear husband, and do not have a worry and come back soon." And so off he rode and she stayed.

Her sisters came to visit and they were, as all souls are, very curious about what the Master had said was to be done while he was away. The young wife gaily told them.

"He said we may do anything we desire and enter any room we wish, except one. But I don't know which one it is. I just have a key and I don't know which door it fits."

The sisters decided to make a game of finding which key fit which door. The castle was three stories high, with a hundred doors in each wing, and as there were many keys on the ring, they crept from door to door having an immensely good time throwing open each door. Behind one door were the kitchen stores, behind another the money stores. All manner of holdings were behind the doors and everything seemed more wonderful all the time. At last, having seen all these marvels, they came finally to the cellar and, at the end of the corridor, a blank wall.

They puzzled over the last key, the one with the little scrollwork on top. "Maybe this key doesn't fit anything at all." As they said this, they heard an odd sound—"errrrrrrrrrrr." They peeked around the corner, and—lo and behold!—there was a small door just closing. When they tried to open it again, it was firmly locked. One cried, "Sister, sister, bring your key. Surely this is the door for that mysterious little key."

Without a thought one of the sisters put the key in the door and turned it. The lock scolded, the door swung open, but it was so dark inside they could not see.

"Sister, sister, bring a candle." So a candle was lit and held into the room and all three women screamed at once, for in the room was a mire of blood and the blackened bones of corpses were flung about and skulls were stacked in corners like pyramids of apples.

They slammed the door shut, shook the key out of the lock, and leaned against one another gasping, breasts heaving. My God! My God!

The wife looked down at the key and saw it was stained with blood. Horrified, she used the skirt of her gown to wipe it clean, but the blood prevailed. "Oh, no!" she cried. Each sister took the tiny key in her hands and tried to make it as it once was, but the blood remained.

The wife hid the tiny key in her pocket and ran to the cook's kitchen. When she arrived, her white dress was stained red from pocket to hem, for the key was slowly weeping drops of dark red blood. She ordered the cook, "Quick, give me some horsehair." She scoured the key, but it would not stop bleeding. Drop after drop of pure red blood issued from the tiny key.

She took the key outdoors, and from the oven she pressed ashes onto it, and scrubbed some more. She held it to the heat to sear it. She laid cobweb over it to staunch the flow, but nothing could make the weeping blood subside.

"Oh, what am I to do?" she cried. "I know, I'll put the little key away. I'll put it in the wardrobe. I'll close the door. This is a bad dream. All will be aright." And this she did do.

Her husband came home the very next morning and he strode

into the castle calling for his wife. "Well? How was it while I was away?"

"It was very fine, sir."

"And how are my storerooms?" he rumbled.

"Very fine, sir."

"How are my money rooms?" he growled.

"The money rooms are very fine also, sir."

"So everything is good, wife?"

"Yes, everything is good."

"Well," he whispered, "then you'd best return my keys."

Within a glance he saw a key was missing. "Where is the smallest key?"

"I . . . I lost it. Yes, I lost it. I was out riding and the key ring fell down and I must have lost a key."

"What have you done with it, woman?"

"I . . . I . . . don't remember."

"Don't lie to me! Tell me what you did with that key!"

He put his hand to her face as if to caress her cheek, but instead seized her hair. "You infidel!" he snarled, and threw her to the floor. "You've been into the room, haven't you?"

He threw open her wardrobe and the little key on the top shelf had bled blood red down all the beautiful silks of her gowns hanging there.

"Now it's your turn, my lady," he screamed, and dragged her down the hall and into the cellar till they were before the terrible door. Bluebeard merely looked at the door with his fiery eyes and the door opened for him. There lay the skeletons of all his previous wives.

"And now!!!" he roared, but she caught hold of the door frame and would not let go. She pleaded for her life, "Please! Please, allow me to compose myself and prepare for my death. Give me but a quarter hour before you take my life so I can make my peace with God."

"All right," he snarled, "you have but a quarter of an hour, but be ready."

The wife raced up the stairs to her chamber and posted her sisters on the castle ramparts. She knelt to pray, but instead called out to her sisters.

"Sisters, sisters! Do you see our brothers coming?"

"We see nothing, nothing on the open plains."

Every few moments she cried up to the ramparts, "Sisters, sisters! Do you see our brothers coming?"

"We see a whirlwind, perhaps a dust devil in the distance."

Meanwhile Bluebeard roared for his wife to come to the cellar so he could behead her.

Again she called out, "Sisters, sisters! Do you see our brothers coming?"

Bluebeard shouted for his wife again and began to clomp up the stone steps.

Her sisters cried out, "Yes! We see them! Our brothers are here and they have just entered the castle."

Bluebeard strode down the hall toward his wife's chamber. "I am coming to get you," he bellowed. His footfalls were dense; the rocks in the hallway came loose, the sand from the mortar poured onto the floor.

As Bluebeard lumbered into her chamber with his hands outstretched to seize her, her brothers on horseback galloped down the castle hallway and charged into her room as well. There they routed Bluebeard out onto the parapet. There and then, with swords, they advanced upon him, striking and slashing, cutting and whipping, beating Bluebeard down to the ground, killing him at last and leaving for the buzzards his blood and gristle.

~~~~~~~~~~~~~~~~~~~~~~~~~~~~~~~~~~~~~~~

The Natural Predator of the Psyche

Developing a relationship with the wildish nature is an essential part of women's individuation. In order to accomplish this, a woman must go into the dark, but at the same time she must not be irreparably trapped, captured, or killed on her way there or back.

The Bluebeard story is about that captor, the dark man who inhabits all women's psyches, the innate predator. He is a specific and incontrovertible force which must be memorized and restrained. To restrain the natural predator[3] of the psyche it is necessary for women to remain in possession of all their instinctual powers. Some of these are insight, intuition, endurance, tenacious loving, keen sensing, far vision, acute hearing, singing over the dead, intuitive healing, and tending to their own creative fires.

In psychological interpretation we call on all aspects of the fairy tale to represent the drama within a single woman's psyche. Bluebeard represents a deeply reclusive complex which lurks at the edge of all women's lives, watching, waiting for an opportunity to oppose her. Although it may symbolize itself similarly or differently in men's psyches, it is the ancient and contemporary foe of both genders.

It is difficult to completely comprehend the Bluebeardian force, for it is innate, meaning indigenous to all humans from birth forward, and in that sense is without conscious origin. Yet I believe we have a hint of how its nature developed in the preconscious of humans, for in the story, Bluebeard is called "a failed magician." In this occupation he is related to figures in other fairy tales which also portray the malignant predator of the psyche as a rather normative-looking but immeasurably destructive mage.

Using this description as an archetypal shard, we compare it to what we know of failed sorcery or failed spiritual power in mythohistory. The Greek Ikaros flew too close to the sun and his waxen wings melted, catapulting him to earth. The Zuni myth "The Boy and the Eagle" tells of a boy who would have become a member of the eagle kingdom but for thinking he could break the rules of Death. As he soared through the sky his borrowed eagle coat was torn from him and he fell to his doom. In Christian myth, Lucifer claimed equality with Yahweh and was driven down to the underworld. In folklore there are any number of sorcerers' apprentices who foolishly dared to venture beyond their actual skill levels by attempting to contravene Nature. They were punished by injury and cataclysm.

As we examine these leitmotifs, we see the predators in them desire superiority and power over others. They carry a kind of psychological inflation wherein the entity wishes to be loftier than, as big as, and equal to The Ineffable, which traditionally distributes and controls the mysterious forces of Nature, including the systems of Life and Death and the rules of human nature, and so forth.

In myth and story we find that the consequence for an entity attempting to break, bend, or alter the operating mode of The Ineffable is to be chastened, either by having to endure diminished ability in the world of mystery and magic—such as apprentices who are no longer allowed to practice—or lonely exile from the land of the Gods, or a similar loss of grace and power through bumbling, crippling, or death.

If we can understand the Bluebeard as being the internal representative of the entire myth of such an outcast, we then may also be able to comprehend the deep and inexplicable loneliness which sometimes washes over him (us) because he experiences a continuous exile from redemption.

The problem posed in the Bluebeard tale is that rather than empowering the light of the young feminine forces of the psyche, he is instead filled with hatred and desires to kill the lights of the psyche. It is not hard to imagine that in such a malignant formation there is trapped one who once wished for surpassing light and fell from Grace because of it. We can understand why thereafter the exiled one maintains a heartless pursuit of the light of others. We can imagine that it hopes that if it could gather enough soul(s) to itself, it could make a blaze of light that would finally rescind its darkness and repair its loneliness.

In this sense we have at the beginning of the tale a formidable being in its unredeemed aspect. Yet this fact is one of the central truths the youngest sister in the tale must acknowledge, that all women must acknowledge—that both within and without, there is a force which will act in opposition to the instincts of the natural Self, and that that malignant force *is what it is*. Though we might have mercy upon it, our first actions must be to recognize it, to protect ourselves from its devastations, and ultimately to deprive it of its murderous energy.

All creatures must learn that there exist predators. Without this knowing, a woman will be unable to negotiate safely within her own forest without being devoured. To understand the predator is to become a mature animal who is not vulnerable out of naïveté, inexperience, or foolishness.

Like a shrewd tracker, Bluebeard senses the youngest daughter is interested in him, that is, willing to be prey. He asks for her in marriage and in a moment of youthful exuberance, which is often a combination of folly, pleasure, happiness, and sexual intrigue, she says yes. What woman does not recognize this scenario?

Naive Women as Prey

The youngest sister, the most undeveloped one, plays out the very human story of the naive woman. She will be captured temporarily by her own interior stalker. Yet, she will out in the end, wiser, stronger, and recognizing the wily predator of her own psyche on sight.

The psychological story underlying the tale also applies to the older woman who has not yet completely learned to recognize the innate predator. Perhaps she has begun the process over and over again but, lacking guidance and support, has not yet finished with it.

This is why teaching stories are so nourishing; they provide initiatory maps so even work which has hit a snag can be completed. The Bluebeard story is valuable to all women, regardless of whether they are very young and just learning about the predator, or whether they have been hounded and harassed by it for decades and are at last readying for a final and decisive battle with it.

The youngest sister represents a creative potential within the psyche. A something that is going toward exuberant and fissioning life. But there is a detour as she agrees to become the prize of a vicious man because her instincts to notice and do otherwise are not intact.

Psychologically, young girls and young boys are as though asleep about the fact that they themselves are prey. Although sometimes it seems life would be much easier and much less painful if all humans were born totally awake, they are not. We are all born *anlagen*, like the potential at the center of a cell: in biology the *anlage* is the part of a cell characterized as "that which will become." Within the anlage is the primal substance which in time will develop, causing us to become a complete someone.

So our lives as women are ones of quickening the anlage. The Bluebeard tale speaks to the awakening and education of this psychic center, this glowing cell. In service of this education, the youngest sister agrees to marry a force which she believes to be very elegant. The fairy-tale marriage represents a new status being sought, a new layer of the psyche about to be unfurled.

However, the young wife has fooled herself. Initially she felt fearful of Bluebeard. She was wary. However, a little pleasure out in the woods causes her to overrule her intuition. Almost all women have had this experience at least once. As a result she persuades herself that Bluebeard is not dangerous, but only idiosyncratic and eccentric. Oh, how silly. Why am I so put off by that little old blue beard? Her wildish nature, however, has already sniffed out the situation and knows the blue-bearded man is lethal, but the naive psyche disallows this inner knowing.

This error of judgment is almost routine in a woman so young that her alarm systems are not yet developed. She is like an orphan wolf pup who rolls and plays in the clearing, heedless of the ninety-pound bobcat approaching from the shadows. In the case of the older woman who is so cut away from the wild that she can barely hear the inner warnings, she too proceeds, smiling naively.

You might well wonder if all this could be avoided. As in the animal world, a young girl learns to see the predator via her mother's and father's teachings. Without parents' loving guidance she will certainly be prey early on. In hindsight, almost all of us have, at least once, experienced a compelling idea or semi-dazzling person crawling in through our psychic windows at night and catching us off guard. Even though they're wearing a ski mask, have a knife between their teeth, and a sack of money slung over their shoulder, we believe them when they tell us they're in the banking business.

However, even with wise mothering and fathering, the young female may, especially beginning about age twelve, be seduced away from her own truth by peer groups, cultural forces, or psychic pressures, and so begins a rather reckless risk-taking in order to find out for herself. When I work with older teenage girls who are convinced that the world is good if they only work it right, it always makes me feel like an old gray-haired dog. I want to put my paws over my eyes and groan, for I see what they do not see, and I know, especially if they're willful and feisty, that they're going to insist on becoming involved with the predator at least once before they are shocked awake.

At the beginning of our lives our feminine viewpoint is very naive, meaning that emotional understanding of the covert is very faint. But this is where we all begin as females. We are naive and we talk ourselves into some very confusing situations. To be uninitiated in the ways of these matters means that we are in a time of our life when we are vulnerable to seeing only the overt.

Among wolves, when the bitch leaves her pups to go hunting, the young ones try to follow her out of the den and down the path. She snarls at them, lunges at them, and scares the bejeezus out of them till they run slipping and sliding back to the den. Their mother knows her pups do not yet know how to weigh and assess other creatures. They do not know who is a predator and who is not. But in time she will teach them, both harshly and well.

Like wolf pups, women need a similar initiation, one which teaches that the inner and outer worlds are not always happy-go-lucky places. Many women do not even have the basic teaching about predators that a wolf mother gives her pups, such as: if it's threatening and bigger than you, flee; if it's weaker, see what you want to do; if it's sick, leave it alone; if it has quills, poison, fangs, or razor claws, back up and go in the other direction; if it smells nice but is wrapped around metal jaws, walk on by.

The youngest sister in the story is not only naive about her own mental processes, and totally ignorant about the murdering aspect of her own psyche, but is also able to be lured by pleasures of the ego. And why not? We all want everything to be wonderful. Every woman wants to sit upon a horse dressed in bells and go riding off through the boundless green and sensual forest. All humans want to attain early Paradise here on earth. The problem is that ego desires to feel wonderful but a yen for the paradisical, when combined with naïveté, makes us not fulfilled, but food for the predator.

This acquiescence to marrying the monster is actually decided when girls are very young, usually before five years of age. They are taught to not see, and instead to "make pretty" all manner of grotesqueries whether they are lovely or not. This training is why the youngest sister can say, "Hmmm, his beard isn't really *that* blue." This early training to "be nice" causes women to override their intuitions. In that sense, they are actually purposefully taught to submit to the predator. Imagine a wolf mother teaching her young to "be nice" in the face of an angry ferret or a wily diamondback rattler.

In the tale, even the mother colludes. She goes on the picnic, "goes along for the ride." She doesn't say a word of caution to any of her daughters. One might say the biological mother or the internal mother is asleep or naive herself, as is often the case in very young girls, or in unmothered women.

Interestingly, in the tale, the older sisters demonstrate some consciousness when they say they do not like Bluebeard even though he has just entertained and regaled them in a very romantic and paradisical manner. There is a sense in the story that some aspects of the psyche, represented by the older sisters, are a little more developed in insight, that they have "knowing" which warns against romanticizing the predator. The initiated woman pays attention to the older sisters' voices in the psyche; they warn her away from danger. The uninitiated woman does not pay attention; she is as yet too identified with naïveté.

Say, for instance, a naive woman keeps making poor choices in a mate. Somewhere in her mind she knows this pattern is fruitless, that she should stop and follow a different value. She often even knows how to proceed. But there is something compelling, a sort of Bluebeardian mesmerization, about continuing the destructive pattern. In most cases, the woman feels if she just holds on to the old pattern a little longer, why surely the paradisical feeling she seeks will appear in the next heartbeat.

At another extreme, a woman involved in a chemical addiction most definitely has at the back of her mind a set of older sisters who are saying, "No! No way! This is bad for the mind and bad for the body. We refuse to continue." But the desire to find Paradise draws the woman into the marriage to Bluebeard, the drug dealer of psychic highs.

Whatever dilemma a woman finds herself in, the voices of the older sisters in her psyche continue to urge her to consciousness and to be wise in her choices. They represent those voices in the back of the mind that whisper the truths that a woman may wish to avoid for they end her fantasy of Paradise Found.

So the fateful marriage occurs, the mingling of the sweetly naive and the dastardly unlit. When Bluebeard leaves on his journey, the young woman does not realize that even though she is exhorted to do anything she wishes—except that one thing—she is living less, rather than living more. Many women have literally lived the Bluebeard tale. They marry while they are yet naive about predators, and they choose someone who is destructive to their lives. They are determined to "cure" that person with love. They are in some way "playing house." One could say they have spent much time saying, "His beard isn't really so blue."

Eventually a woman thus captured will see her hopes for a decent life for herself and her children diminish more and more. It is to be hoped that she will finally open the door to the room where all the destruction of her life lies. While it may be the woman's actual mate who denigrates and dismantles her life, the innate predator within her own psyche concurs. As long as a woman is forced into believing she is powerless and/or is trained to not consciously register what she knows to be true, the feminine impulses and gifts of her psyche continue to be killed off.

When the youthful spirit marries the predator, she is captured or restrained during a time in her life that was meant to be an unfoldment. Instead of living freely, she begins to live falsely. The deceitful promise of the predator is that the woman will become a queen in some way, when in fact her murder is being planned. There is a way out of all of this, but one must have a key.

The Key to Knowing: The Importance of Snuffling

Ah, now this tiny key; it provides entry to the secret all women know and yet do not know. The key represents permission to know the deepest, darkest secrets of the psyche, in this case the something that mindlessly degrades and destroys a woman's potential.

Bluebeard continues his destructive plan by instructing his wife to compromise herself psychically; "Do whatever you like," he says. He prompts the woman to feel a false sense of freedom. He implies she is free to nourish herself and to revel in bucolic landscapes, at least within the confines of his territory. But in reality, she is not free, for she is constrained from registering the sinister knowledge about the predator, even though deep in the psyche she already truly comprehends the issue.

The naive woman tacitly agrees to remain "not knowing." Women who are gullible or those with injured instincts still, like flowers, turn in the direction of whatever sun is offered. The naive or injured woman is then too easily lured with promises of ease, of lilting enjoyment, of various pleasures, be they promises of elevated status in the eyes of her family, her peers, or promises of increased security, eternal love, high adventure, or hot sex.

Bluebeard forbids the young woman to use the one key that would bring her to consciousness. To forbid a woman to use the key to conscious self knowledge strips away her intuitive nature, her natural instinct for curiosity that leads her to discover "what lies underneath" and beyond the obvious. Without this knowing, the woman is without proper protection. If she attempts to obey Bluebeard's command not to use the key, she chooses death for her spirit. By choosing to open the door to the ghastly secret room, she chooses life.

In the tale her sisters come to visit and "they were, as all souls are, very curious." The wife gaily tells them, "We can do anything, except for one thing." The sisters decide to make a game out of finding which door the little key fits. They again have the proper impulse toward consciousness.

Some psychological thinkers, including Freud and Bettelheim, have interpreted episodes such as those found in the Bluebeard tale as psychological punishments for women's sexual curiosity.[4] Early in the formulation of classical psychology women's curiosity was given quite a negative connotation, whereas men with the same attribute were called investigative. Women were called nosy, whereas men were called inquiring. In reality, the trivialization of women's curiosity so that it seems like nothing more than irksome snooping denies women's insight, hunches, intuitions. It denies all her senses. It attempts to attack her most fundamental powers: differentiation and determination.

So, considering that women who have not yet opened the

forbidden door tend to be the same women who walk right into the Bluebeard's arms, it is fortuitous that the older sisters have the proper wildish instincts for curiosity intact. These are the shadow-women of the individual woman's psyche, the tics and nudges in the back of a woman's mind that re-mind her, put her back in her right mind about what is important. Finding the little door is important, disobeying the predator's order is important, and finding out what is so special about this one room is essential.

For centuries, doors have been made both of stone and wood. In certain cultures, the spirit of the stone or wood was thought to be retained in the door, and it too was called upon to act as guardian of the room. Long ago there were more doors to tombs than to homes, and the very image of *door* meant something of spiritual value was within, or that there was something within which must be kept contained.

The door in the tale is portrayed as a psychic barrier, as a kind of sentry that is placed in front of the secret. This guard reminds us again of the predator's reputation as a mage—a psychic force that twists and tangles us up as though by magic, keeping us from knowing what we know. Women strengthen this barrier or door when they discourage themselves or one another from thinking or diving too deeply, for "you may get more than you bargained for." In order to breach this barrier, a proper counter-magic must be employed. And the fitting magic is found in the symbol of the key.

Asking the proper question is the central action of transformation—in fairy tales, in analysis, and in individuation. The key question causes germination of consciousness. The properly shaped question always emanates from an essential curiosity about what stands behind. Questions are the keys that cause the secret doors of the psyche to swing open.

Though the sisters know not whether treasure or travesty lies beyond the door, they summon their goodly instincts to ask *the* precise psychological question, "*Where* do you think that door is, and *what* might lie beyond it?"

It is at this point that the naive nature begins to mature, to question, "What is behind the visible? What is it which causes that shadow to loom upon the wall?" The youthful naive nature begins to understand that if there is a secret something, if there is a shadow something, if there is a forbidden something, it needs to be looked into. Those who would develop consciousness pursue all that stands behind the readily observable: the unseen chirping, the murked window, the lamenting door, the lip of light beneath a sill. They pursue these mysteries until the substance of the matter is laid open to them.

As we shall see, the ability to stand what one sees enables a woman to return to her deep nature, there to be sustained in all thoughts, feelings, and actions.

The Animal Groom

So though the young woman attempts to follow the orders of the predator, and agrees to be ignorant about the secret in the cellar, she can only comply for so long. Finally she puts the key, the question, to the door and finds the shocking carnage in some part of her deep life. And that key, that tiny symbol of her life, suddenly will not cease its bleeding, will not cease to give the cry that something is wrong. A woman may try to hide from the devastations of her life, but the bleeding, the loss of life's energy, will continue until she recognizes the predator for what it is and contains it.

When women open the doors of their own lives and survey the carnage there in those out-of-the-way places, they most often find they have been allowing summary assassinations of their most crucial dreams, goals, and hopes. They find lifeless thoughts and feelings and desires; ones which were once graceful and promising but now are drained of blood. Whether these hopes and dreams be about desire for relationship, desire for an accomplishment, a success, or a work of art, when such a gruesome discovery is made in one's psyche, we can be sure the natural predator, also often symbolized in dreams as the animal groom, has been at work methodically destroying a woman's most cherished desires, concerns, and aspirations.

In fairy tales, the animal groom character is a common motif that can be understood to represent a malevolent thing disguised as a benevolent thing. This or some proximate characterization is always present when a woman carries naive presentiments about something or someone. When a woman is attempting to avoid the facts of her own devastations, her night dreams are likely to shout warnings to her, warnings and exhortations to wake up! or get help! or flee! or go for the kill!

Over the years, I've seen many women's dreams with this animal groom feature or this things-are-not-as-nice-as-they-seem aura. One woman dreamt of a beautiful and charming man, but when she looked down, there was a loop of cruel barbed wire beginning to uncoil from his sleeve. Another woman dreamt that she was helping an old person cross the street and the old person suddenly smiled diabolically and "melted" on her arm, burning her deeply. Yet another woman dreamt of eating with an unknown friend whose fork flew across the table, mortally wounding the dreamer.

This not seeing, not understanding, not perceiving that our internal desires are not concomitant with our external actions; this is the spoor left behind by the animal groom. The presence of this factor in the psyche accounts for why women who say they wish to have a relationship instead do all they can to sabotage a loving one. This is how women who set goals to be here, there, or wherever by such and such time never even begin the first leg of the journey, or abandon it at the first hardship. This is how all the procrastinations which give rise to self-hatred, all the shame-feelings which are pushed down and away to fester, all the new beginnings which are sorely needed, and all the long overdue endings are not met. Wherever the predator lurks and works, everything is derailed, demolished, and decapitated.

The animal groom is a widespread symbol in fairy tales, the general story going something like this: A strange man courts a young woman who agrees to be his bride, but before the wedding day she takes a walk in the woods, becomes lost, and as darkness falls, climbs into a tree to be safe from predators. As she waits out the night, along comes her betrothed with a spade over his shoulder. Something about her groom-to-be gives him away as being not truly human. Sometimes it is his strangely formed foot, hand, arm, or hair that is decidedly outré and gives him away.

He begins to dig a grave beneath the very tree she sits in, all the while singing and muttering about how he will murder his latest bride-to-be and bury her in this grave. The terrified girl conceals herself all night long, and in the morning when the groom-to-be is gone, she runs home, reports him to her brothers and father, and the men waylay the animal groom and kill him.

This is a powerful archetypal process in women's psyches. The woman is adequately perceptive, and though she too at first agrees to marry that natural predator of the psyche, and although she too goes through a period of being lost in the psyche, she wills out at the end, for she is able to see into the truth of it all, and she is able to hold it in consciousness and take action to resolve the matter.

Ah, so then comes the next step, even more difficult yet, and that is to be able to stand what one sees, all one's self-destruction and deadness.

Blood Scent

In the tale, the sisters slam shut the door to the killing chamber. The young wife stares at the blood on the key. A whimper rises within her. "I must scrub this blood off or he will know!"

Now the naive self has knowledge about a killing force loose within the psyche. And the blood on the key is women's blood. If it were only blood from having one's frivolous fantasies sacrificed, there would be but a nick of blood on the key. But it is so much more serious, for the blood represents a decimation of the deepest and most soulful aspects of one's creative life.

In this state a woman loses her energy to create, whether it be solutions to mundane matters in her life, such as school, family, friendships, or her concerns with compelling issues in the larger world, or with issues of spirit—her personal development, her art. This is not a mere procrastination, for it continues over weeks and months of time. She seems flattened out, filled with ideas perhaps, but deeply anemic and more and more unable to act upon them.

The blood in this story is not menstrual blood, but arterial blood from the soul. It not only stains the key, it runs down the entire persona. The dress she wears as well as all the gowns in her wardrobe are stained by it. In archetypal psychology, clothing can personify the outer presence. The *persona* is a mask a person shows to the world. It hides much. With proper psyche padding and disguises, both men and women can present a near-perfect persona, a near-perfect facade.

When the weeping key—the crying question—stains our personas, we cannot any longer hide our travails. We can say what we like, present the most smiling facade, but once we have seen the shocking truth of the killing room, we can no longer pretend it does not exist. And seeing the truth causes us to bleed energy even more. It is painful; it is artery cutting. We must try to immediately correct this terrible state.

So, in this fairy tale, the key also acts as container; it contains the blood which is the memory of what one has seen and now knows. For women, the key always symbolizes entrée to a mystery or into knowledge. In other fairy tales, the symbolic key is often represented by words such as "Open Sesame," which Ali Baba shouts to a ragged mountain, causing the entire mountain to rumble and crack open so he can pass through. In a more picaresque manner, at Disney Studios, the fairy godmother in Cinderella chortles "Bibbity-bobbity-boo!" and pumpkins turn into carriages and mice into coachmen.

In the Eleusinian mysteries, the key was hidden on the tongue, meaning the crux of the thing, the clue, the trace, could be found in a special set of words, or key questions. And the words women need most in situations similar to the one described in Bluebeard are: What stands behind? What is not as it appears? What do I know deep in my *ovarios* that I wish I did not know? What of me has been killed, or lays dying?

Any and all of these are keys. And if a woman has been leading a half-dead life, the answers to these four questions are very likely to come up with blood on them. The killing aspect of the psyche, part of whose job it is to see that no consciousness occurs, will continue to assert itself from time to time and twist off or poison any new growth. It is its nature. It is its job.

So, in a positive sense, it is only the insistent blood on this key which causes the psyche to hold on to what it has seen. You see, there is a natural censoring of all negative and painful events that occur in our lives. The censoring ego most certainly wishes to forget it ever saw the room, ever saw the cadavers. This is why Bluebeard's wife attempts to scour the key with horsehair. She tries everything she knows, all the remedies for lacerations and deep wounds from women's folk medicine: cobwebs, ash, and fire—all associated with the weaving of life and death by the Fates. But not only does she fail to cauterize the key, neither can she end this process by pretending it is not occurring. She cannot stop the tiny key from weeping blood. Paradoxically, as her old life is dying and even the best remedies will not hide that fact, she is awake to her blood loss and therefore just beginning to live.

The formerly naive woman must face what has occurred. Bluebeard's killing of all his "curious" wives is the killing of the creative feminine, the potential that develops all manner of new and interesting life. The predator is particularly aggressive in ambushing woman's wildish nature. At the very least, it seeks to scorn, and at the most to sever a woman's connection to her own insights, inspirations, follow through, and more.

Another woman I worked with, an intelligent and gifted woman, told me of her grandmother, who lived in the Midwest. Her grandmother's idea of a really good time was to board the train to Chicago and wear a big hat, and walk down Michigan Avenue looking in all the shop windows and being an elegant lady. By hook or by crook or by fate, she married a farmer. They moved out into the midst of the wheatlands, and she began to rot away in that elegant little farmhouse that was just the right size, with all the right children, and all the right husband. She had no more time for that "frivolous" life she'd once led. Too much "kids." Too much "women's work."

One day, years later, after washing the kitchen and living room floors by hand, she slipped into her very best silk blouse, buttoned her long skirt, and pinned on her big hat. She pressed her husband's shotgun to the roof of her mouth and pulled the trigger. Every woman alive knows why she washed the floors first.

A starved soul can become so filled with pain, a woman can no longer bear it. Because women have a soul-need to express themselves in their own soulful ways, they must develop and blossom in ways that are sensible to them and without molestation from others. In this sense, the key with blood could be said to also represent a woman's female bloodlines, those who have gone before her. Who among us does not know at least one female loved-one who lost her instincts to make good choices for herself, and was forced therefore to live a marginal life or worse? Perhaps you yourself are that woman.

One of the least discussed issues of individuation is that as one shines light into the dark of the psyche as strongly as one can, the shadows, where the light is not, grow even darker. So when we illuminate some part of the psyche, there is a resultant deeper dark to contend with. This dark cannot be let alone. The key, the questions, cannot be hidden or forgotten. They must be asked. They must be answered.

The deepest work is usually the darkest. A brave woman, a wisening woman, will develop the poorest psychic land, for if she builds only on the best land of her psyche, she will have for a view the least of what she is. So do not be afraid to investigate the worst. It only guarantees increase of soul power through fresh insights and opportunities for re-visioning one's life and self anew.

It is in this psychic kind of land development that Wild Woman shines. She is not afraid of the darkest dark, in fact she can see in the dark. She is not afraid of offal, refuse, decay, stink, blood, cold bones, dying girls, or murderous husbands. She can see it, she can take it, she can help. And this is what the youngest sister of the Bluebeard tale is learning.

The skeletons in the chamber represent, in the most positive light, the indestructible force of the feminine. Archetypally, bones represent that which can never be destroyed. Stories of bones are essentially about something in the psyche that is difficult to destroy. The only thing that we possess that is difficult to destroy is our soul.

When we talk about the feminine essence, we're really talking about the feminine soul. When we talk about the bodies scattered in the cellar, we're saying something has happened to the soul-force and yet, even though its outer vitality has been taken away, even though life has essentially been wrung out of it, it has not been destroyed utterly. It can come back to life.

It comes back to life through the young woman and her sisters, who ultimately are able to break the old patterns of ignorance, by being able to behold a horror and not look away. They are able to see, and to stand what they see.

Here we are again at *La Loba*'s place, at the archetypal bone woman's cave. Here we have the remnants of what once was the full woman. However, unlike the cyclical life and death aspects of the Wild Woman archetype who takes the life that is ready to die, incubates it, and hurls it back into the world again, Bluebeard only kills and dismantles a woman until she is nothing but bones. He leaves her no beauty, no love, no self, and therefore no ability to act in her own behalf. To remedy this, we as woman must look to the killing thing that has gained hold of us, see the result of its grisly work, register it all consciously, and retain it in consciousness, and then act in *our*, not its, behalf.

The cellar, dungeon, and cave symbols are all related to one another. They are ancient initiatory environs; places to or through which a woman descends to the murdered one(s), breaks taboos to find the truth, and through wit and/or travail triumphs by banishing, transforming, or exterminating the assassin of the psyche. The Bluebeard tale lays out the work for us with clear instructions: track the bodies, follow instincts, see what you see, call up psychic muscle, dismantle the destructive energy.

If a woman does not look into these issues of her own deadness and murder, she remains obedient to the dictates of the predator. Once she opens the room in the psyche that shows how dead, how slaughtered she is, she sees how various parts of her feminine nature and her instinctual psyche have been killed off and died a lowly death behind a facade of wealth. Now that she sees this, now that she registers how captured she is and how much psychic life is at stake, now she can assert herself in an even more powerful manner.

Backtracking and Looping

Backtracking and looping are terms that describe an animal diving underground to escape, and then popping up behind the predator's back. This is the psychic maneuver which Bluebeard's wife effects in order to reestablish her sovereignty over her own life once again.

Bluebeard, upon discovering what he deems to be his wife's deceit, seizes her by her hair and drags her down the stairs. "Now it is your turn!" he roars. The killing element of the unconscious rises up and threatens to destroy the conscious woman.

Analysis, dream interpretation, self-knowing, exploration, all are undertaken because they are ways of backtracking and looping. They are ways of diving down and coming up behind the issue and seeing it from a different perspective. Without the ability to see, truly see, what is learned about ego-self and the numinous Self slips away.

In Bluebeard, the psyche now tries to avoid being killed. No longer naive, it has become cunning; it pleads for time to compose itself—in other words, time to strengthen itself for the final battle. In outer reality, we find women planning their escapes too, whether from an old destructive mode, a lover, or a job. She stalls for time, she bides her time, she plans her strategy and calls up her power internally, before she makes an external change. Sometimes it is just this kind of immense threat from the predator that causes a woman to change from being an adaptive dear to having the hooded eye of the watchful.

Ironically, both aspects of the psyche, the predator and the young potential, reach their boiling point. When a woman understands that she has been prey, both in the outer and inner worlds, she can hardly bear it. It strikes at the root of who she is at center, and she plans, as she must, to kill the predatory force.

Meanwhile her predatory complex is enraged that she has pried open the forbidden door, and is busily making its rounds, attempting to cut off all avenues of her escape. This destructive force becomes murderous, and says the woman has violated the holy of holies and now must die.

When opposing aspects of a woman's psyche both reach their flash points, a woman may feel incredibly tired, for her libido is being drawn away in two opposite directions. But even if a woman is fatigued unto death with her miserable struggles, no matter what they might be, even though she be starved of soul, she must yet plan her escape; a woman must force herself forward anyway. At this critical time it is like being in subzero weather for a day and a night. In order to survive, we must not give in to the fatigue. To go to sleep now is certain death.

This is the more profound initiation, a woman's initiation into her proper instinctive senses wherein the predator is identified and banished. This is the moment in which the captured woman moves from victim status into shrewd-minded, wily-eyed, sharp-eared status instead. This is the time that almost superhuman effort manages to drive the so-tired psyche to its final work. The key questions continue to help, for the key continues to bleed its wise blood even as the predator forbids consciousness. His maniacal message is, "For consciousness—you die." Her response is to trick him into thinking she is his willing victim while she plans his demise.

Among animals there is said to be a mysterious psychic dance between predator and prey. It is said, if the prey gives a certain kind of servile eye contact, and a certain kind of shiver that causes a faint rippling of the skin over its muscles, that the prey acknowledges its weakness to the predator and agrees to become the predator's victim.

There are times to shiver and run, and there are times to not. At this critical time, a woman must not shiver, and must not grovel. Bluebeard's young wife's plea for time to gather herself together is not the signal of submission to the predator. It is her shrewd way of gathering her energy up into muscle. Like certain creatures of the forest, she is poised to make an all-out strike against the predator. She dives into the ground to escape the predator, then unexpectedly surfaces behind him.

Giving the Cry

When Bluebeard bellows for his wife and she stalls for dear time, she is trying to rouse energy to overwhelm the captor, whether that specifically or in combination be a destructive religion, husband, family, culture, or a woman's negative complexes.

Bluebeard's wife pleads for her life, but craftily. "Please," she whispers, "allow me to prepare for my death."

"Yes," he snarls, "but be ready."

The young woman summons her psychic brothers. What do these represent in a woman's psyche? They are the more muscled, more naturally aggressive propellants of the psyche. They represent the force within a woman which can act when it is time to kill off malignant impulses. Although this attribute is here portrayed by the male gender, it can be portrayed by either gender—and by other things which are genderless, such as the mountain which snaps shut on the intruder, the sun which descends for an instant to burn the marauder to a crisp.

The wife races up the stairs to her chamber and posts her sisters on the ramparts. She cries up to her sisters, "Do you see our brothers coming yet?" And her sisters call down that they see nothing yet. As Bluebeard roars for his wife to come to the cellar so he can behead her, again she cries, "Do you see our brothers coming?" And her sisters call down that perhaps they see a little dust devil or a whirlwind off in the distance.

Here we have the entire scenario of a woman's surge of intra-psychic power. Her sisters—the wiser ones—take center stage in this last initiatory step; they become her eyes. The woman's cry travels over a long intra-psychic distance to where her brothers live, to where those aspects of psyche that are trained to fight, to fight to the death if necessary, live. But initially, the defending aspects of psyche are not immediately as close by to conscious-ness as they ought to be. Many women's alacrity and fighting natures are not as close to consciousness as is efficient.

A woman must practice calling up or conjuring her contentious nature, her whirlwind, dust-devil-like attributes. The symbol of the whirling wind represents a central force of determination which, when focused rather than scattered, gives tremendous energy to a woman. With this more fierce attitude at the ready, she will not lose consciousness or be interred along with the rest. She will solve, for once and for all, the interior woman-killing, her loss of libido, the loss of her passion for life. While the key questions provide the opening and loosening required for her liberation, without the eyes of the sisters, without the muscle of the sword-wielding brothers, she cannot fully succeed.

Bluebeard shouts for his wife and begins to clomp up the stone steps. His wife cries to her sisters, "And now, do you see them now?" And her sisters cry down, "Yes! We see them now, they are almost here." Her brothers gallop down the hall. They charge into her room and drive Bluebeard out onto the parapet. There, with swords, they kill him and leave what is left of him for the carrion eaters.

When women re-surface from their naïveté, they draw with them and to themselves something unexplored. In this case the now wiser woman draws an internal masculine energy to her aid. In Jungian psychology, this element has been named *animus*; a partly mortal, partly instinctual, partly cultural element of a woman's psyche that shows up in fairy tales and in dream symbols as her son, husband, stranger, and/or lover—possibly threatening depending on her psychic circumstances of the moment. This psychic figure is particularly valuable because it is invested with qualities which are traditionally bred out of women, aggression being one of the more common.

When this opposite-gender nature is healthy, as symbolized by the brothers in "Bluebeard," it loves the woman it inhabits. It is the intra-psychic energy which helps her to accomplish anything she asks. He is the one who has psychic muscle where she may have differing gifts. He will aid and assist her in her bid for consciousness. For many women, this contra-sexual aspect bridges between the worlds of internal thought and feeling—the outer world.

The stronger and more integrally vast the animus (think of the animus as a bridge) the more able, easily, and with style the woman manifests her ideas and her creative work in the outer world in a concrete way. A woman with a poorly developed animus has lots of ideas and thoughts but is unable to manifest them in the outer world. She always stops short of the organization or implementation of her wonderful images.

The brothers represent the blessing of strength and action. With them, in the end, several things occur: one is that the vast and disabling ability of the predator is neutralized in a woman's psyche. And second, the blueberry-eyed maiden is replaced by one with eyes awake, and third, a warrior to each side of her if she but calls for them.

The Sin-eaters

Bluebeard is through and through a "cutting" story about severing and reunion. In the final stage of the story, Bluebeard's body is

left for the flesh-eaters—the cormorants, raptors, and buzzards—
to carry away. Here we have a very strange and mystical ending.
In ancient times there were souls called sin-eaters. These were
personified by spirits, birds, or animals, sometimes humans, who
somewhat like the scapegoat, took on the sins, that is, the psychic
waste of the community, so people could be cleansed and re-
deemed from the detritus of difficult life or life not well lived.

We have seen how the wild nature is exemplified by the finder
of the dead, the one who sings over the bones of the dead, bringing
them back to life again. This Life/Death/Life nature is a central
attribute of the instinctual nature of women. Likewise, in Norse
mythology, the sin-eaters are carrion eaters who devour the dead,
incubate them in their bellies, and carry them to Hel, who is not
a place but a person. Hel is the Goddess of life and death. She
shows the dead how to live backward. They become younger
and younger until they are ready to be reborn and re-released back
into life.

This eating of sins and sinners, and the subsequent incubation
of them, and their release back into life once more, constitutes an
individuation process for the most base aspects of the psyche. In
this sense it is right and proper that energy is drawn out of the
predatory elements of the psyche, killing them so to speak, draining their powers. Then they may be returned to the compassionate
Life/Death/Life Mother, to be transformed and re-issued, hope-
fully in a less contentious state.

Many scholars who have studied this tale think Bluebeard represents a force which is not redeemable.[5] But I sense additional
ground for this aspect of the psyche—not a transformation from
mass murderer into Mr. Chips, but more like a person who must
be in an asylum, but a decent place with trees and sky and proper
nourishment, and perhaps music to soothe, but not banished to a
back ward in the psyche to be tortured and reviled.

On the other hand, I do not want to portray that there is no such
thing as manifest and irredeemable evil, for that also exists.
Throughout time there is the mystical sense that any individuation
work done by humans also changes the darkness in the collective
unconscious of all humans, that being the place where the predator
resides. Jung once said that God became more conscious[6] as

humans became more conscious. He postulated that humans cause the dark side of God to become struck with light when they rout their personal demons out into the light of day.

I do not claim to know how it all works, but following archetypal pattern, it would look and work something like this: Instead of reviling the predator of the psyche, or running away from it, we dismember it. We accomplish this by not allowing ourselves divisive thoughts about our soul-life and our worth in particular. We capture invidious thoughts before they become large enough to do any harm, and we dismantle them.

We dismantle the predator by countering its diatribes with our own nurturant truths. Predator: "You never finish anything you start." Yourself: "I finish many things." We dismantle the assaults of the natural predator by taking to heart and working with what is truthful in what the predator says and then discarding the rest.

We dismantle the predator by maintaining our intuitions and instincts and by resisting the predator's seductions. If we were to list all our losses up to this point in our lives, remembering times when we were disappointed, when we were powerless against torment, when we had a fantasy filled with frosting and frou-frou, we would understand that those are vulnerable sites in our psyches. It is to those desirous and underprivileged parts that the predator appeals in order to hide the fact that its sole intention is to drag you to the cellar and leech your energy as a blood transfusion for himself.

In the finale of the Bluebeard story his bones and gristle are left for the buzzards. This gives us a strong insight into transformation of the predator. That is the last task for a woman in this Bluebeardian journey: to allow the Life/Death/Life nature to pick the predator apart and carry it off to be incubated, transformed, and released back into life.

When we refuse to entertain the predator, its strength is extracted and it is unable to act without us. We, in essence, drive it down into the layer of the psyche where all creation is as yet unformed, and let it bubble in that etheric soup till we can find a form, a better form for it to fill. When the predator's psychic *energum* is rendered, it is formable to some other purpose. We are creators then; the raw substance reduced down becomes then the stuff of our own creation.

Women find that as they vanquish the predator, taking from it what is useful and leaving the rest, they are filled with intensity, vitality, and drive. They have rendered from the predator what has been stolen from them, vigor and substance. To render the predator's energy and turn it to something useful can be understood in these ways: The predator's rage can be rendered into a soul-fire for accomplishing a great task in the world. The predator's craftiness can be used to inspect and understand things from a distance. The predator's killing nature can be used to kill off that which must properly die in a woman's life, or what she must die to in her outer life, these being different things at different times. Usually, she knows exactly what they are.

To render the parts of Bluebeard is like taking the medicinal parts of the deadly nightshade, or the healing elements of the poisonous belladonna plant, and using these materials carefully and for healing and helping. What ash of the predator is left then will indeed rise up again, but in much smaller form, much more recognizably, and with much less power to deceive and destroy— for you have rendered many of its powers which it plied destructively, and you have turned these powers toward the useful and the relevant.

Bluebeard is one of several teaching tales that I believe are important for women who are young, not necessarily in years, but in some part of their minds. It is a tale of psychic naïveté, but also of powerfully breaching the injunction against "looking." It is a tale about finally cutting down and rendering the natural predator of the psyche.

It is my belief that story is meant to set the inner life back into motion again. The Bluebeard story is a medicine which is particularly important to apply where the inner life of a woman has become frightened, or wedged or cornered. Story solutions lessen fear, elicit doses of adrenaline at just the right times, and most importantly for the captured naive self, cut doors into walls which were previously blank.

Perhaps most elementally, the Bluebeard story raises to consciousness the psychic key, the ability to ask any and all questions about oneself, about one's family, one's endeavors, and about life all around. Then, like the wildish being who sniffs things out, snuffles into and under and around to discover what a thing is, a woman is free to find true answers to her deepest and darkest questions. She is free to wrest the powers from the thing which has assailed her and to turn those powers which were once used against her to her own well-suited and excellent uses. That, is a wildish woman.

The Dark Man in Women's Dreams

The natural predator of the psyche is not only found in fairy tales but also in dreams. There is a universal initiatory dream among women, one so common that it is remarkable if a woman has reached age twenty-five without having had such a dream. The dream usually causes women to jolt awake, striving and anxious.

This is the pattern of the dream: The dreamer is alone, often in her own home. There are one or more prowler-types outside in the dark. Frightened, she dials[7] the emergency phone number for help. Suddenly, she realizes, the prowler is inside the house with her . . . close to her . . . perhaps she can feel his breath . . . perhaps he is even touching her . . . and she cannot ring the emergency number. The dreamer awakens instantly, breathing gutturally, heart like a crazy drum.

There is a strong physical aspect to having a dream of the dark man. The dream is often accompanied by sweats, struggles, hoarse breathing, heart pounding, and sometimes cries and moans of fear from the dreamer. We could say the dream-maker has dispensed with subtle messages to the dreamer and now sends images which shake the neurological and autonomic nervous system of the dreamer, thereby communicating the urgency of the matter.

The antagonist(s) of this "dark man" dream are usually, in women's own words, "terrorists, rapists, thugs, concentration camp Nazis, marauders, murderers, criminals, creeps, bad men, thieves." There are several levels to the interpretation of such a dream, depending on the life circumstances and interior dramas surrounding the dreamer.

For instance, often such a dream is a reliable indicator that a woman's consciousness, as in the case of a very young woman, is just beginning to gain awareness of the innate psychic predator. In other instances, the dream is a harbinger; the woman dreamer has just discovered, or is about to discover and begin liberating, a forgotten and captive function of her psyche. Under yet other circumstances the dream is about an increasingly intolerable situation in the culture outside the dreamer's personal life, one in which she is being called to either fight or flee.

First let us understand the subjective ideas in this motif as applied to the personal and interior life of the dreamer. The dark man dream tells a woman what predicament she is facing. The dream tells about a cruel attitude toward herself as personified by the thug in the dream. Like Bluebeard's wife, if the woman can consciously gain hold of the "key" question about this matter and answer it honestly, she can be set free. Then the muggers, lurkers, and predators of the psyche will exert much less pressure on her. They will fall away to a distant layer of the unconscious. There she can deal with them conscientiously instead of in crisis.

The dark man in women's dreams appears when an initiation— a psychic change from one level of knowing and behavior to another more mature or more energetic level of knowledge and action—is imminent. This dream occurs to the as-yet-to-be-initiated, as well as to those who are veterans of several rites of passage, for there is always more initiation. No matter how old a woman becomes, no matter how many years pass, she has yet more ages, stages, and more "first times" awaiting her. That is what initiation is all about: it creates an archway which one prepares to pass through to a new manner of knowing and being.

Dreams are *portales*, entrances, preparations, and practices for the next step in consciousness, the "next day" in the individuation process. So, a woman might have a dream of the predator when her psychic circumstances are too quiescent or complacent. We could say that this occurs in order to raise a storm in the psyche so that some energetic work can be done. But also a dream like this affirms that the woman's life needs to change, that the woman dreamer has gotten caught in some hiatus or ennui as regards a difficult choice, that she is reluctant to take the next step, go the next distance, that she is shying away from wresting her own power away from the predator, that she is not used to being/acting/ striving at full bore, in all-out capacity.

Additionally, dark man dreams are also wake-up calls. They say: Pay attention! Something has gone radically amiss in the outer world, in personal life, or in the outer collective culture. Classical psychological theory tends to, by absolute omission, split the human psyche away from relationship to the land on which humans live, away from knowledge of the cultural etiologies of malaise and unrest, and also to sever psyche from the politics and policies which shape the inner and outer lives of humans—as though that outer world were not just as surreal, not just as symbol-laden, not just as impacting and imposing upon one's soul-life as the inner din. The land, the culture, and the politics in which one lives contribute every bit as much to the individual's psychic landscape and are as valuable to consider in these lights as one's subjective milieu.

When the outer world has intruded on the basic soul-life of one individual or of many, dark man dreams come in legions. It has been fascinating to me to have gathered dreams from women afflicted by something gone wrong in the outer culture, such as those living near the poisonous smelter at York City,[8] Idaho, to dreams dreamt by some extremely conscious women actively involved in social action and environment protection, such as *las guerrillas compañeras*, warrior sisters in the Quebrada outback of Central America,[9] women in the *Cofradios des Santuarios*[10] in the United States, and civil rights proponents in Latino County.[11] They all dream many dark man dreams.

Generally, it would appear that to the naive or noncognizant dreamers, these are meant as wake-up calls: "*Hola!* Pay attention, you're in danger." And to those women who are quite conscious and involved in social action, the dark man dream seems to be almost a tonic which reminds the woman what she is up against, which encourages her in turn to stay strong, stay vigilant, and continue the work at hand.

So, when women dream of the natural predator, it is not always or solely a message about the interior life. Sometimes it is a message about the threatening aspects of the culture one lives in, whether it be a small but brutal culture at the office, one within their own family, the lands of their neighborhood, or as wide as their own religious or national culture. As you can see, each group and culture appears to also have its own natural psychic predator, and we see from history that there are eras in cultures during which the predator is identified with and allowed absolute sovereignty until the people who believe otherwise become a tide.

While much psychology emphasizes the familial causes of angst in humans, the cultural component carries as much weight, for culture is the family of the family. If the family of the family has various sicknesses, then all families within that culture will have to struggle with the same malaises. In my heritage, there is a saying *cultura cura*, culture cures. If the culture is a healer, the families learn how to heal; they will struggle less, be more reparative, far less wounding, far more graceful and loving. In a culture where the predator rules, all new life needing to be born, all old life needing to be gone, is unable to move and the soul-lives of its citizenry are paralyzed with both fear and spiritual famine.

Why this intruder which, in women's dreams, most often takes the shape of an intrusive male, seeks to attack the instinctual psyche and its wildish knowing powers in particular, no one can say for certain. We say it is the nature of the thing. Yet we find this destructive process exacerbated when the culture surrounding a woman touts, nourishes, and protects destructive attitudes toward the deep instinctual and soulful nature. Thusly, these destructive cultural values—to which the predator avidly agrees—grow stronger within the collective psyche of all its members. When a society exhorts its people to be distrustful of and to shun the deep instinctual life, then an autopredatory element in each individual psyche is strengthened and accelerated.

Yet even in an oppressive culture, in whichever women the Wild Woman still lives and thrives or even glimmers, there will be "key" questions asked, not only the ones we find useful for insight into ourselves but also ones about our culture. "What stands behind these proscriptions I see in the outer world? What goodness or usefulness of the individual, of the culture, of the earth, of human nature has been killed, or lies dying here?" As these issues are examined, the woman is enabled to act according to her own abilities, according to her own talents. To take the world into one's arms and to act toward it in a soul-filled and soul-strengthening manner is a powerful act of wildish spirit.

It is for this reason that the wildish nature in women must be preserved—and even, in some instances, guarded with extreme vigilance—so that it is not suddenly abducted and garroted. It is important to feed this instinctive nature, to shelter it, to give it increase, for even in the most restrictive conditions of culture, family, or psyche, there is far less paralysis in women who have remained connected to the deep and wild instinctual nature. Though there be injury if a woman is captured and/or tricked into remaining naive and compliant, there is still left adequate energy to overcome the captor, to evade it, to outrun it, and eventually to sunder and render it for their own constructive use.

There is one other specific instance in which women are highly likely to experience dark man dreams and that is when one's internal creative fire is smoking and banking all by itself, when there is little fuel left in the corner, or when the white ashes grow deeper every day yet the cookpot remains empty. These syndromes can occur even when we are veterans at our art, as well as when we first seriously begin to apply our gifts outwardly. They occur when there is a predatory intrusion into the psyche, and as a result we find every reason to do anything and everything except sit there, or stand there, or travel there in order to execute whatever it is that we hold dear.

In these cases, the dark man dream, even though accompanied by heart-jumping fear, is not an ominous dream. It is a very positive one about a proper and timely need to awaken to a destructive movement within one's own psyche, to that which is stealing one's fire, intruding on one's vim, robbing one of the place, the space, the time, the territory to create.

Often the creative life is slowed or stopped because something in the psyche has a very low opinion of us, and we are down there groveling at its feet instead of bopping it over the head and running for freedom. In many cases what is required to aright the situation is that we take ourselves, our ideas, our art, far more seriously than we have before. Due to wide breaks in matrilineal (and patrilineal) succor over many generations, this business of valuing one's creative life—that is, valuing the utterly original, beauteous, and artful ideas and works which issue from the wildish soul—has become a perennial issue for women.

In my consulting room I have watched as certain poets toss their pages of work onto the sofa as though their poetry were refuse rather than treasure. I have seen artists bring their paintings to session, banging them against the door frame on their way in. I have seen the green gleam in women's eyes as they try to disguise their anger that others seem able to create and that they themselves, for some reason, cannot.

I have heard all the excuses that any woman might knit up: I'm not talented. I'm not important. I'm not educated. I have no ideas. I don't know how. I don't know what. I don't know when. And the most scurrilous of all: I don't have time. I always want to shake them upside down until they repent and promise to never tell falsehoods again. But I don't have to shake them up, for the dark man in dreams will do that, and if not he, then another dream actor will.

The dark man dream is a scary dream, and scary dreams are most often very good for creativity; they show the artist what will happen to them if they allow themselves to be fried up into talented derelicts. This dark man dream is often enough to scare a woman back into creating again. At the very least, she can create work which elucidates the dark man in her own dreams.

The threat of the dark man serves as a warning to all of us—if you don't pay attention to the treasures, they will be stolen from you. In this manner, when a woman has one or a series of these dreams, it infers that a huge gate is opening to the initiatory grounds where her revaluing of her gifts can occur. There, whatever has been incrementally destroying her or robbing her can be recognized, apprehended, and dealt with.

When a woman works to espy the predator of her own psyche, and if she will acknowledge its presence and do necessary battle with it, the predator will move to a much more isolated and unobtrusive point in the psyche. But if the predator is ignored, it becomes increasingly and deeply hateful and jealous, with a desire to silence the woman forever.

At a very mundane level, it is important for a woman having dark man and Bluebeardian sorts of dreams to cleanse her life of as much negativity as she can. Sometimes it is necessary to limit or thin out certain relationships, for if a woman is outwardly surrounded by persons who are antagonistic to or careless about her deep life, her interior predator is fed by this and develops extra muscle within her psyche, and more aggression toward her.

Women are often highly ambivalent about aggression toward the intruder, for they think it is a "damned if I do, damned if I don't" situation. If she doesn't break away, the dark man becomes her keeper and she his slave. If she does break away, he pursues her relentlessly, as though he owns her. Women fear that he will hunt them down in order to bring them back into submission, and this fear is reflected in the contents of their dreams.

And so it is common for women to kill off their entirely original, creative, soulful, and wildish natures in response to threats from the predator. That is why the women lie as skeletons and cadavers in Bluebeard's cellar. They learnt of the trap, but too late. Consciousness is the way out of the box, the way out of the torture. It is the path away from the dark man. And women are entitled to fight tooth and nail to have it and keep it.

In the Bluebeard story we see how a woman who falls under the spell of the predator rouses herself and escapes him, wiser for the next time. The story is about the transformation of four shadowy introjects which are in particular contention for women: have no integrity of vision, have no deep insight, have no original voice, have no decisive action. In order to banish the predator, we must unlock or pry ourselves and other matters open to see what is inside. We must use our abilities to stand what we see. We must speak our truth in a clear voice. And we must be able to use our wits to do what needs be about what we see.

When a woman's instinctual nature is strong, she intuitively recognizes the innate predator by scent, sight, and hearing . . . anticipates its presence, hears it approaching, and takes steps to turn it away. In the instinct-injured woman, the predator is upon her before she registers its presence, for her listening, her knowing, and her apprehension are impaired—mainly by introjects which exhort her to be nice, to behave, and especially to be blind to being misused.

Psychically, it is difficult at first glance to tell the difference between the uninitiated, who are as yet young and therefore naive, and women who are injured in instinct. Neither knows much about the dark predator, and both are therefore still credulous. But fortunately for us, when the predatory element of a woman's psyche is on the move, it leaves behind unmistakable tracks in her dreams. These tracks eventually lead to its discovery, capture, and containment.

The cure for both the naive woman and the instinct-injured woman is the same: Practice listening to your intuition, your inner voice; ask questions; be curious; see what you see; hear what you hear; and then act upon what you know to be true. These intuitive powers were given to your soul at birth. They have been covered over, perhaps by years and years of ashes and excrement. This is not the end of the world, for these can be washed away. With some chipping and scraping and practice, your perceptive powers can be brought back to their pristine state again.

By retrieving these powers from the shadows of our psyches, we shall not be simple victims of internal or external circumstances. No matter how culture, personality, psyche, or other might demand women be dressed and behaved, no matter how others may wish to keep all females in a gaggle with ten dozing *dueñas*, chaperones, nearby, no matter what pressures attempt to compress a woman's soulful life, they cannot change the fact that a woman is what she is, and that this is dictated by the wild unconscious, and that it is very, very good.

It is crucial for us to remember that when we have dark man dreams there is always an opposing, that is, a balancing power, poised and waiting to help us. When we initiate wildish energy in order to balance the predator, guess who immediately shows up? Wild Woman comes diving over whatever fences, walls, or obstructions the predator has erected. She is not an icon, to be hung on the wall like a *retablo*, religious painting. She is a living being who comes to us anywhere, under any conditions. She and the predator have known each other a long, long time. She tracks him through dreams, through stories, through tales, and through women's entire lives. Wherever he is, she is, for she is the one who balances his predations.

Wild Woman teaches women when not to act "nice" about protecting their soulful lives. The wildish nature knows that being "sweet" in these instances only makes the predator smile. When the soulful life is being threatened, it is not only acceptable to draw the line and mean it, it is required. When a woman does this, her life cannot be interfered with for long, for she knows immediately what is wrong and can push the predator back where it belongs. She is no longer naive. She is no longer a mark or a target. And this is the medicine that causes the key—the little one with the scrollwork on top—to finally, cease its bleeding.

CHAPTER 3

Nosing Out the Facts: The Retrieval of Intuition as Initiation

The Doll in Her Pocket: Vasalisa the Wise

Intuition is the treasure of a woman's psyche. It is like a divining instrument and like a crystal through which one can see with uncanny interior vision. It is like a wise old woman who is with you always, who tells you *exactly what the matter is, tells you exactly whether you need to go left or right*. It is a form of The One Who Knows, old *La Que Sabe*, the Wild Woman.

In the traditions I was raised in, dedicated storytellers were always off under some psychic hill, up to their knees in story dust, brushing away centuries of dirt, digging under overlays of culture and conquests, numbering every frieze and fresco of story they could find. Sometimes a story has been reduced to powder, sometimes portions and details are missing or rubbed out, often the form is intact but the coloring is destroyed. But even so, every dig holds hope for finding an entire body of story intact and unbroken. The following tale is just such an incredible treasure.

To my mind, the old Russian tale "Vasalisa"[1] is a woman's initiation story with few essential bones astray. It is about the realization that most things are not as they seem. As women we call upon our intuition and instincts in order to sniff things out. We use all our senses to wring the truth from things, to extract nourishment from our own ideas, to see what there is to see, to know what there is to know, to be the keepers of our own creative fires, and to have intimate knowing about the Life/Death/Life cycles of all nature—this is an initiated woman.

Stories with Vasalisa as a central character are told in Russia, Romania, Yugoslavia, Poland, and throughout all the Baltic countries. In some instances, the tale is commonly called "Wassilissa the Wise." I find evidence of its archetypal roots dating back at least to the old horse-Goddess cults which predate classical Greek culture. This tale carries ages-old psychic mapping about induction into the underworld of the wild female God. It is about infusing human women with Wild Woman's primary instinctual power, intuition.

The pattern for my literary version of the Vasalisa tale spun here was given to me by my aunt Kathé. It begins with one of the oldest storytelling devices, "Once there was, and once there was not . . ."[2] This paradoxical phrase is meant to alert the soul of the listener that this story takes place in the world between worlds where nothing is as it first seems. So let us begin.

Vasalisa

ONCE THERE WAS, and once there was not, a young mother who lay on her deathbed, her face pale as the white wax roses in the sacristy of the church nearby. Her young daughter and her husband sat at the end of her old wooden bed and prayed that God would guide her safely into the next world.

The dying mother called to Vasalisa, and the little child in red boots and white apron knelt at her mother's side.

"Here is a doll for you, my love," the mother whispered, and from the hairy coverlet she pulled a tiny doll which like Vasalisa herself was dressed in red boots, white apron, black skirt, and vest embroidered all over with colored thread.

"Here are my last words, Beloved," said the mother. "Should you lose your way or be in need of help, ask this doll what to do. You will be assisted. Keep the doll with you always. Do not tell anyone about her. Feed her when she is hungry. This is my mother's promise to you, my blessing on you, dear daughter."

And with that, the mother's breath fell into the depths of her body where it gathered up her soul and rushed out from between her lips, and the mother was dead.

The child and her father mourned for a very long time. But, like the field cruelly plowed under by war, the father's life rose green from the furrows again, and he married a widow with two daughters. Although the new stepmother and her daughters spoke in polite tones and always smiled like ladies, there was something of the rodent behind their smiles which Vasalisa's father did not perceive.

Sure enough, when the three women were alone with Vasalisa, they tormented her, forced her to wait on them, sent her to chop wood so her lovely skin would become blemished. They hated her because she had a sweetness about her that was otherworldly. She was also very beautiful. Her breasts were bounding while theirs dwindled from meanness. She was helpful and uncomplaining while the stepmother and stepsisters were, among themselves, like rats in the offal pile at night.

One day the stepmother and stepsisters simply could not stand Vasalisa any longer. "Let . . . us . . . conspire to make the fire go out, and then let us send Vasalisa into the forest to Baba Yaga, the witch, to beg fire for our hearth. And when she reaches Baba Yaga, well, old Baba Yaga will kill her and eat her." Oh, they all clapped and squeaked like things that live in the dark.

So that evening, when Vasalisa came home from gathering wood, the entire house was dark. She was very concerned and inquired of her stepmother, "What has happened; what will we have to cook with? What will we do to light the darkness?"

The stepmother admonished, "You stupid child. Obviously we have no fire. And I can't go out into the woods because I am old. My daughters can't go because they are afraid. So you are the only one who can go out into the forest to find Baba Yaga and get a coal to start our fire again."

Vasalisa replied innocently, "Well all right, yes, I'll do that," and so she set out. The woods became darker and darker, and sticks cracked under her feet, frightening her. She reached down in the long deep pocket of her apron and there was the doll her dying mother had given her. And Vasalisa patted the doll in her pocket and said, "Just touching this doll, yes, I feel better."

And at every fork in the road, Vasalisa reached into her pocket and consulted the doll. "Well, should I go to the left or should I go to the right?" The doll indicated "Yes," or "No," or "This way," or "That way." And Vasalisa fed the doll some of her bread as she walked and followed what she felt was emanating from the doll.

Suddenly a man in white on a white horse galloped by and it became daylight. Farther on, a man in red sauntered by on a red horse, and the sun rose. Vasalisa walked and walked and just as she came to the hovel of Baba Yaga, a rider dressed in black came trotting on a black horse, and rode right into Baba Yaga's hut. Swiftly it became night. The fence made of skulls and bones surrounding the hut began to blaze with an inner fire so the clearing there in the forest glowed with an eerie light.

Now the Baba Yaga was a very fearsome creature. She traveled, not in a chariot, not in a coach, but in a cauldron shaped like a mortar which flew along all by itself. She rowed this vehicle with an oar shaped like a pestle, and all the while she swept out the tracks of where she'd been with a broom made from the hair of a person long dead.

And the cauldron flew through the sky with Baba Yaga's own greasy hair flying behind. Her long chin curved up and her long nose curved down, and they met in the middle. She had a tiny white goatee and warts on her skin from her trade in toads. Her brown-stained fingernails were thick and ridged like roofs, and so curled over she could not make a fist.

Even more strange was the Baba Yaga's house. It sat atop huge, scaly yellow chicken legs, and walked about all by itself and sometimes twirled around and around like an ecstatic dancer. The bolts on the doors and shutters were made of human fingers and toes and the lock on the front door was a snout with many pointed teeth.

Vasalisa consulted her doll and asked, "Is this the house we seek?" and the doll, in its own way, answered, "Yes, this is what you seek." And before she could take another step, Baba Yaga in her cauldron descended on Vasalisa and shouted down at her, "What do *you* want?"

And the girl trembled. "Grandmother, I come for fire. My house is cold . . . my people will die . . . I need fire."

Baba Yaga snapped, "Oh yesssss, I know you, and your people. Well, you useless child . . . you let the fire go out. That's an ill-advised thing to do. And besides, what makes you think I should give you the flame?"

Vasalisa consulted her doll and quickly replied, "Because I ask."

Baba Yaga purred, "You're lucky. That is the right answer."

And Vasalisa felt very lucky she had given the right answer.

Baba Yaga threatened, "I cannot possibly give you fire, until you've done work for me. If you perform these tasks for me, you shall have the fire. If not . . ." And here Vasalisa saw Baba Yaga's eyes turn suddenly to red cinders. "If not, my child, you shall die."

So Baba Yaga rumbled into the hovel and laid down upon her bed and ordered Vasalisa to bring her what was cooking in the oven. In the oven was enough food for ten people and the Yaga ate it all, leaving just a tiny crust and a thimble of soup for Vasalisa.

"Wash my clothes, sweep the yard and clean my house, prepare my food, and separate the mildewed corn from the good corn and see that everything is in order. I will be back to inspect your work later. If it is not done, *you* will be my feast." And with that Baba Yaga flew off in her cauldron with her nose as the windsock and her hair as the sail. And it became night again.

Vasalisa turned to her doll as soon as the Yaga had gone. "What shall I do? Can I complete these tasks in time?" The doll assured her she could, and to eat a little and go to sleep. Vasalisa fed the doll a little too, then she slept.

In the morning, the doll had done all the work and all that remained was the meal to be cooked. In the evening the Yaga returned and found nothing undone. Pleased, in a way, but not pleased because she could find no fault, Baba Yaga sneered, "You are a very lucky girl." She then called on her faithful servants to grind the corn and three pairs of hands appeared in midair and began to rasp and crush the corn. The chaff flew in the house like a golden snow. Finally it was done and Baba Yaga sat down to eat. She ate for hours and ordered Vasalisa on the morrow to again clean the house, sweep the yard, and launder her clothes.

The Yaga pointed to a great mound of dirt in the yard. "In that pile of dirt are many poppy seeds, millions of poppy seeds. And I want, in the morning, to have one pile of poppy seeds and one pile of dirt, all separated out from each other. Do you understand?"

Vasalisa almost fainted. "Oh my, how am I going to do that?" She reached into her pocket and the doll whispered, "Don't worry, I will take care of it." That night Baba Yaga snored off to sleep and Vasalisa tried . . . to pick . . . the . . . poppy seeds . . . out . . . of . . . the . . . dirt. After a time, the doll said to her, "Sleep now. All will be well."

Again the doll accomplished these tasks, and when the old woman returned home, all was done. Baba Yaga spoke sarcastically through her nose. "Welllll! Lucky for you that you were able to do these things." She called for her faithful servants to press the oil from the poppy seeds, and again three pairs of hands appeared, and did so.

While the Yaga was smearing her lips with grease from her stew, Vasalisa stood nearby. "What are you staring at?" barked Baba Yaga.

"May I ask you some questions, Grandmother?" asked Vasalisa.

"Ask," ordered the Yaga, "but remember, too much knowledge can make a person old too soon."

Vasalisa asked about the white man on a white horse.

"Aha," said the Yaga fondly, "that first is my Day."

"And the red man on the red horse?"

"Ah, that is my Rising Sun."

"And the black man on the black horse?"

"Ah yes, that is the third and he is my Night."

"I see," said Vasalisa.

"Come, come child. Wouldn't you like to ask more questions?" wheedled the Yaga.

Vasalisa was about to ask about the pairs of hands that appeared and disappeared, but the doll began to jump up and down in her pocket, so instead Vasalisa said, "No, Grandmother. As you yourself say, to know too much can make one old too soon."

"Ah," said the Yaga, cocking her head like a bird, "you are

wiser than your years, my girl. And how did you come to be this way?"

"By the blessing of my mother," smiled Vasalisa.

"Blessing?!" screeched Baba Yaga. "Blessing?! We need no blessings around this house. You'd best be on your way, daughter." She pushed Vasalisa out into the night.

"I'll tell you what, child. Here!" Baba Yaga took a skull with fiery eyes from her fence and put it on a stick. "Here! Take this skull on a stick home with you. There! There's your fire. Don't say another word. Just be on your way."

Vasalisa began to thank the Yaga, but the little doll in her pocket began to jump up and down, and Vasalisa realized she must just take the fire and go. She ran for home through the dark forest, following the turns and twists in the road as the doll told her which way to go. Vasalisa came through the forest carrying the skull, with fire blazing from its ear, eye, nose, and mouth holes. Suddenly, she became frightened of its weight and its eerie light and thought to throw it away. But the skull spoke to her and urged her to calm herself and to continue toward the home of her stepmother and stepsisters. And this she did.

As Vasalisa came nearer and nearer to her house, her stepmother and stepsisters looked out the window and saw a strange glow dancing through the woods. Closer and closer it came. They could not imagine what it could be. They had decided that Vasalisa's long absence meant she was dead by now and her bones dragged away by animals and good riddance.

Vasalisa advanced closer and closer to home. And as the stepmother and the stepsisters saw it was her, they ran to her, saying they had been without fire since she'd left, and no matter how hard they had tried to start one, it always went out.

Vasalisa entered the house feeling triumphant, for she had survived her dangerous journey and brought fire back to her home. But the skull on the stick watched the stepsisters' and the stepmother's every move and burnt into them, and by morning it had burnt the wicked trio to cinders.

And there we have it, an abrupt ending to kick people out of the fairy tale and back into reality again. There are many endings of this sort in fairy tales. They are the equivalent of saying Boo! to bring listeners back to mundane reality.

Vasalisa is a story of handing down the blessing on women's power of intuition from mother to daughter, from one generation to the next. This great power, intuition, is composed of lightning-fast inner seeing, inner hearing, inner sensing, and inner knowing.

Over generations, these intuitive powers became as buried streams within women, buried by disuse and unfounded charges of disrepute. However, Jung once remarked that nothing was ever lost in the psyche. I think we can be confident that things lost in the psyche are all still there. So too, this well of women's instinctual intuition has never been lost, and whatever is covered over can be brought back out again.

To grasp the import of such a tale, we understand that all its components represent characterizations of a single woman's psyche. So all aspects of the story belong to and elucidate an individual psyche undergoing an initiatory process. Initiation is enacted by completing certain tasks. In this tale there are nine tasks for the psyche to complete. They focus on learning something of the ways of the Old Wild Mother.

Through completion of these tasks, a woman's intuition—that knowing being who walks wherever women walk, looking at all things in their lives and commenting on the truth of it all with swift accuracy—is re-set into woman's psyche. The goal is a loving and trusting relationship with this being whom we have come to call "the knowing woman," the essence of the Wild Woman archetype.

In the rite of the old wild female Goddess, Baba Yaga, these are the tasks of initiation:

The First Task—Allowing the Too-Good Mother to Die

In the opening of the tale, the mother is dying and bequeaths to her daughter an important legacy.

The psychic tasks of this stage in a woman's life are these: *Accepting that the ever-watchful, hovering, protective psychic*

mother is not adequate as a central guide for one's future instinc-
tual life (the too-good mother dies). Taking on the task of being on
one's own, developing one's own consciousness about danger,
intrigue, politic. Becoming alert by oneself, for oneself. Letting die
what must die. As the too-good mother dies, the new woman
is born.

In the tale, the initiatory process begins when the dear and good
mother dies. She is not there to touch Vasalisa's hair anymore. In
all our lives as daughters, there is a time when the good mother of
the psyche—the one which served us appropriately and well in
earlier times—turns into a too-good mother, one which by virtue
of her overly safeguarding values—begins to prevent us from
responding to new challenges and thereby to deeper development.

In the natural process of our maturing, the too-good mother
must become thinner and thinner, must dwindle away until we are
left to care for ourselves in a new way. While we always retain a
core of her warmth, this natural psychic transition leaves us on our
own in a world that is not motherly to us. But wait. This too-good
mother is not all she at first seems. Under the blanket, she has a
tiny doll to give her daughter.

Ah, there is something of the Wild Mother underneath this
figure. But the too-good mother cannot completely live this out,
for she is the milk-teeth mother, the blessed one every baby needs
in order to gain a toehold in the psychic world of love. So even
though this too-good mother cannot live and influence beyond a
certain point in a girl's life, she does right by her offspring here.
She blesses Vasalisa with the doll, and this, as we see, is a great
blessing indeed.

This dramatic psychological dwindling of the over-arching
mother occurs as a girl moves from the fur-lined nest of pre-
adolescence to the jolting jungle of adolescence. For some girls,
however, the process of developing a new, more shrewd, inner
mother—the mother called intuition—was only half completed
then, and women so inducted have wandered for years wishing for
and wanting the complete initiatory experience, and patching
themselves up as best they could.

The arresting of a woman's initiation process occurs for various
reasons, such as when there has been too much psychological

hardship early in one's life—especially when there has been no consistent "good-enough" mother in the early years.[3] The initiation may also be stalled or uncompleted because there is not enough tension in the psyche—the too-good mother has the stamina of a formidable weed and lives on, waving her leaves and overprotecting her daughter even though the script says, "Exit stage left *now*." In this situation, women often feel too timid to proceed into the woods and resist it all they can.

For these, as well as other adult women for whom the rigors of life itself chip and distance them from their deeply intuitive lives, and whose plaint is often, "I am so tired of taking care of myself," there is a good and wise remedy. A re-affirming of, a re-tracing or re-initiation will re-set the deep intuition, regardless of a woman's age. And it is the deep intuition that knows what is good for us, knows what we need next, and knows it with lightning speed . . . if we will just take down its dictation.

Vasalisa's initiation begins with learning to let die what must die. This means to let die the values and attitudes within the psyche which no longer sustain her. Especially to be examined are those long-held tenets which make life too safe, which overprotect, which make women walk with a scurry instead of a stride.

The time during which the childhood "positive mother" dwindles—and her attitudes die away as well—is always a time of great learning. Although there is a period in all our lives during which we rightfully remain close to the protective psychic mother (for instance, when we are actual children, or during recovery from an illness or psychological or spiritual trauma, or when our lives are in danger and being quiet will keep us safe), and even though we retain large stores of her succor for life, there also comes a time to change mothers, so to speak.[4]

If we stay overly long with the protective mother within our own psyches, we find ourselves impeding all challenges to ourselves and therefore blocking further development. While I do not in any way advise that a woman ought to throw herself into torturous or abusive situations, I do mean she must set for herself a something in life that she is willing to reach for and therefore take risks for. It is through this process that she sharpens her intuitive powers.

Among wolves, when a wolf mother nurses her pups, she and they spend much time lazing about. Everyone slumps over everyone else in a great puppy-pile; the outer world and the world of challenges are far away. However, when the wolf mother finally trains the pups to hunt and forage, she shows them her teeth more often than not, she snaps and demands they keep up, she shoves them down if they don't do what she requires.

And so it is in order to pursue further development that we exchange the hovering internal mother which was so apt for us when we were young for another kind of mother, one who lives even deeper in the psychic wilderlands, one who is both escort and teacher. She is a loving mother, but also fierce and demanding.

Most of us will not let the too-good mother die just because it is time. Although this too-good mother may not allow our most vivid energies to surface, it is so nice to be with her, so comfortable, why leave? Often we hear voices within our minds which encourage us to hold back, to stay safe.

These voices say things like, "Oh, don't say *that*," or "You can't do *that*," or "Well you're certainly not one of my children [friends, peers] if you do that," or "It's dangerous out there," or "Who knows what will become of you if you insist on leaving this warm nest," or "You're just going to humiliate yourself you know," or even more insidious still, "Pretend you are taking risks, but secretly stay here with me."

These are all voices of the frightened and rather exasperated too-good mother within the psyche. She cannot help herself; she is what she is. Yet if we merge with the too-good mother for too long, our lives and our gifts for expression fall into the shadows, and we become scant instead of strong.

And worse, what occurs when one compresses a vivid energy and allows it no life? Like the magic porridge pot in the wrong hands, it grows, and grows, and *grrrrows* until it explodes! spilling all of its goodness onto the ground. So, we must be able to see that for the intuitive psyche to be invigorated, the nice hovering protector must recede. Or perhaps more accurately, we eventually find ourselves pushed out of that nice cozy tête-à-tête, not because we planned it that way, not because we were completely ready—no one is ever completely ready—but because there is something waiting for us at the edge of the woods, and it is our fate to meet it.

Guillaume Apollinaire wrote: "We took them to the edge and bade them fly. They held on. 'Fly!' we said. They held on. We pushed them over the edge. And they flew."

It is typical for women to be afraid to let the too-comfortable and too-safe life die. Sometimes a woman has reveled in the protection of the too-good mother, and so desires to continue ad infinitum. She must be willing to feel anxious sometimes, otherwise she might as well have stayed in the nest.

Sometimes a woman is afraid to be without security or without certainty, for even a short time. She has more excuses than dogs have hairs. She must just simply dive in and stand not knowing what will happen next. It is the only thing which will retrieve her intuitive nature. Sometimes a woman is so bound up in being the too-good mother to other adults that they have latched onto her *tetas*, teats, and are not about to let her leave them. In this case a woman has to kick them off with her hind leg and go on anyway.

And since the dreaming psyche compensates for, among other things, that which the ego will not or cannot acknowledge, a woman's dreams during such a struggle will be filled, compensatorily, with chases, dead ends, cars that will not start, incomplete pregnancies, and other symbols which image life not going forward. In her guts a woman knows there is a deadliness in being the too-sweet self for too long.

So loosening our hold on the glowing archetype of the ever-sweet and too-good mother of the psyche is the first step. We are off the teat and learning to hunt. There is a wild mother waiting to teach us. But in the meantime the second task is to hold on to the doll while we learn its uses.

The Second Task—Exposing the Crude Shadow

In this part of the tale, the "bad-rotten" stepfamily[5] marches into Vasalisa's world and begins to make her life miserable. The tasks of this time are: *Learning even more mindfully to let go of the overly positive mother. Finding that being good, being sweet, being nice will not cause life to sing. (Vasalisa becomes a slave, but it does not help.) Experiencing directly one's own shadow nature, particularly the exclusionary, jealous, and exploitative aspects of self (the stepmother and stepsisters). Acknowledging these unequivocally. Making the best relationship one can with the worst parts of oneself. Letting the pressure build between who one is taught to be and who one really is. Ultimately working toward letting the old self die and the new intuitive self be born.*

The stepmother and stepsisters represent the undeveloped but provocatively cruel elements of the psyche. They are shadow elements, meaning aspects of oneself which are considered by the ego to be undesirable or not useful and are therefore relegated to the dark. On one hand, shadow material can be quite positive, for often a woman's gifts are pushed into the dark, hidden there and waiting to be discovered. On the other hand, negative shadow material—that which busily kills off or detains all new life—can also be turned to one's use, as we shall see. When it erupts, and we finally identify its aspects and sources, we are made all the stronger and wiser.

In this stage of initiation, a woman is harassed by the petty demands of her psyche which exhort her to comply with whatever anyone wishes. Compliance causes a shocking realization that must be registered by all women. That is, to be ourselves causes us to be exiled by many others, and yet to comply with what others want causes us to be exiled from ourselves. It is a tormenting tension and it must be borne, but the choice is clear.

Vasalisa is disenfranchised, for she inherits and is inherited by a family that cannot understand or appreciate her. As far as they're concerned, she is unnecessary. They hate and revile her. They treat her as The Stranger, the untrustworthy one. In fairy tales, the role of the stranger or the outcast is usually played by the one who is most deeply connected to the knowing nature.

The stepmother and stepsisters can be understood as creatures set into a woman's psyche by the culture to which a woman belongs. The stepfamily in the psyche is different from the "soul family," for it is of the superego, that aspect of psyche which is structured according to each particular society's expectations—healthy or not—for women. These cultural—that is, superego—overlays and injunctions, are not experienced by women as emanating from the soul-Self psyche, but are felt as if they come from "out there," from some other source which is not innate. The cultural/superego overlays can be very positive or they can be very detrimental.

Vasalisa's stepfamily is an intra-psychic ganglia which pinches off the nerve to life's vitality. They enter as a chorus of unredeemed hags who taunt, "You can't do it. You're not good enough. You're not bold enough. You're stupid, insipid, vacant. You don't have time. You're only good for simple things. You're only allowed to do this much and no more. Give up while you're ahead." As Vasalisa is not yet fully conscious of her powers, she allows this evil crimp in her lifeline. In order for her to regain her life, something different, something life-giving must occur.

The same is true for us. We can see in the story that Vasalisa's intuition into what is happening around her is quite flimsy, and that the father of the psyche doesn't notice the hostile environment either; he is also too-good and has no intuitive development himself. It is interesting to note that daughters who have naive fathers often take far longer to awaken.

We too are pinched off when the stepfamily within us and/or surrounding us tells us we are not much to begin with and insists we focus on our shortcomings, rather than perceiving the cruelty whirling around us—be it emanating from within our psyches or from without in the culture. However, to see into or through something requires intuition and also the strength to stand upon what one sees. Like Vasalisa we may try to be nice when we ought to be knowing. We may have been taught to set aside acute insight in order to get along. However, the reward for simply being nice[6] in oppressive circumstances is to be mistreated all the more. Although a woman feels that if she is herself she will alienate others, it is just this psychic tension that is needed in order to make soul and to create change.

So the stepmother and stepsisters scheme to send Vasalisa away. They secretly plot, "Go into the forest, Vasalisa, go to Baba Yaga, and if you survive, ha ha—which you won't—then we might accept you." This is a very critical idea because many women are stuck halfway through this initiation process—sort of hanging half in and half out of the hoop. Although there is a natural predator in the psyche, one who says, "Die!" and "Bah!" and "Why don't you give up?" on a rather automatic basis, the culture in which a woman lives, and the family in which she was raised, can painfully exacerbate that natural but moderate nay-saying aspect in the psyche.

For instance, women who are raised in families that are not accepting of their gifts often set off on tremendously big quests— over and over, and they do not know why. They feel they must have three Ph.D.s or that they have to hang upside down from Mount Everest, or that they must execute all manner of dangerous, time-consuming, and money-eating endeavors to try to prove to their families that they have worth. "Now will you accept me? No? Okay (sigh), watch this." The stepfamily ganglia of course belongs to us by whichever means we received it, and it is our work to deal with it in an empowered manner. However, we can see that for the deep work to continue, trying to prove one's worth to the chorus of jealous hags is pointless, and as we shall see, in fact impedes the initiation.

Vasalisa does the everyday chores without complaint. To submit without complaint is heroic-seeming, but in fact causes more and more pressure and conflict between the two oppositional natures, one too-good and the other too-demanding. Like the conflict between being overadaptive and being oneself, this pressure builds to a good end. A woman who is torn between these two is in a good way, but she must take the next steps.

In the story, the stepwomen so squeeze the burgeoning psyche that through their machinations the fire goes out. At this point a woman begins to lose her psychic bearings. She may feel cold, alone, and willing to do anything to bring back the light again. This is just the jolt the too-nice woman needs in order to continue her induction into her own power. One might say that Vasalisa has to meet the Great Wild Hag because she needs a good scare. We have to leave the chorus of detractors and plunge into the woods. There is no way to both stay and go.

Vasalisa, like us, needs some guiding light that will differentiate for her what is good for her and what is not. She cannot develop by standing around being everyone's bootjack. Women who try to make their deeper feelings invisible are deadening themselves. The fire goes out. It is a painful form of suspended animation.

Conversely, and perhaps somewhat perversely, when the fire is put out, it helps to snap Vasalisa out of her submission. It causes her to die to an old way of life and to step with shivers into a new life, one which is based on an older, wiser kind of inner knowing.

The Third Task—Navigating in the Dark

In this part of the tale, the dead mother's legacy—the doll— guides Vasalisa through the dark to the house of Baba Yaga. These are the psychic tasks of this time: *Consenting to venture into the locus of deep initiation (entering the forest), and beginning to experience the new and dangerous-feeling numen of being in one's intuitive power. Learning to develop sensitivity as regards direction to the mysterious unconscious and relying solely on one's inner senses. Learning the way back home to the Wild Mother (heeding the doll's directions). Learning to feed intuition (feeding the doll). Letting the frail know-nothing maiden die even more. Shifting power to the doll, i.e., intuition.*

Vasalisa's doll is from the provisions of the Old Wild Mother. Dolls are one of the symbolic treasures of the instinctual nature. In Vasalisa's case, the doll represents *la vidacita*, the little instinctual life force that is both fierce and enduring. No matter what mess we are in, it lives out a life hidden within us.

For centuries humans have felt that dolls emanate both a holiness and *mana*[7]—an awesome and compelling presence which acts upon persons, changing them spiritually. For instance, among rustic healers, the mandrake root is praised for its resemblance to the human body, with arms and legs of root, and a gnarl for a head. It is said to be charged with great spiritual power. Dolls are believed to be infused with life by their makers. Some are used in rites, ritual, hoodoo, love spells, and general mischief. When I lived among the Cuna in the isles off Panama, their small wooden figures were used as markers of authority to remind one of one's own power.

Museums throughout the world are filled to overflowing with idols and figurines made of clay, wood, and metals. The figurines from Paleolithic and Neolithic times are dolls. Art galleries are filled with dolls. In modern art, Segal's life-size gauze-wrapped mummies are dolls. Ethnic dolls fill railway gift shops and the gas stations on major interstates. Among royalty, dolls have been given as gifts since ancient times as tokens of goodwill. In rustic churches throughout the world there are saint-dolls. The saint-dolls are not only bathed on a regular basis and dressed in handmade clothing, but also "taken for walks" so that they might see the conditions of the fields and of the people, and therefore intercede with heaven in the humans' behalf.

The doll is the symbolic *homunculi*, little life.[8] It is the symbol of what lies buried in humans that is numinous. It is a small and glowing facsimile of the original Self. Superficially, it is just a doll. But inversely, it represents a little piece of soul that carries all the knowledge of the larger soul-Self. In the doll is the voice, in diminutive, of old *La Que Sabe*, The One Who Knows.

The doll is related to the symbols of leprechaun, elf, pixie, fairy, and dwarf. In fairy tales these represent a deep throb of wisdom within the culture of the psyche. They are those creatures which go on with the canny and interior work, who are tireless. The psyche works even when we sleep, most especially when we sleep, even when we are not fully conscious of what we are enacting.

In this way the doll represents the inner spirit of us as women; the voice of inner reason, inner knowing, and inner consciousness. The doll is like the little bird in fairy tales who appears and whispers in the heroine's ear, the one who reveals the hidden enemy and what to do about it all. This is the wisdom of the *homunculus*, the small being within. It is our helper which is not seeable, per se, but which is always accessible.

There is no greater blessing a mother can give her daughter than a reliable sense of the veracity of her own intuition. Intuition is handed from parent to child in the simplest ways: "You have good judgment. What do you think lies hidden behind all this?" Rather than defining intuition as some unreasoned faulty quirk, it is defined as truly the soul-voice speaking. Intuition senses the directions to go in for most benefit. It is self-preserving, has a grasp of underlying motive and intention, and it chooses what will cause the least amount of fragmenting in the psyche.

The process is similar in the fairy tale. Vasalisa's mother has set an enormous boon on her daughter by binding the doll and Vasalisa to one another. Being bound to one's intuition promotes a confident reliance on it, no matter what. It changes a woman's guiding attitude from "what will be, will be" to "let me see all there is to see."

What does this wildish intuition do for women? Like the wolf, intuition has claws that pry things open and pin things down, it has eyes that can see through the shields of persona, it has ears that hear beyond the range of mundane human hearing. With these formidable psychic tools a woman takes on a shrewd and even precognitive animal[9] consciousness, one that deepens her femininity and sharpens her ability to move confidently in the outer world.

So now Vasalisa is on her way to gain an ember to rekindle the fire. She is in the dark, in the wilds, and can do nothing *but* listen to the inner voice coming from the doll. She is learning to rely on that relationship, and she is learning yet one more thing—she learns to feed the doll.

What does one feed intuition so that it is consistently nourished and responsive to our requests to scan our environs? One feeds it life—one feeds it life by listening to it. What good is a voice without an ear to receive it? What good is a woman in the wilds of megatropolis or daily life unless she can hear and depend upon the voice of *La Que Sabe*, The One Who Knows?

I've heard women say it, if not a hundred times, then a thousand times: "I knew I should have listened to my intuition. I sensed that I should/should not have done such and such, but I didn't listen." We feed the deep intuitive self by listening to it and acting upon its advice. It is a personage in its own right, a magical dollish-sized being which inhabits the psychic land of the interior woman. In this way it is like the muscles in the body. If a muscle is not used, eventually it withers. Intuition is exactly like that: without food, without employment, it atrophies.

The feeding of the doll is an essential cycle of the Wild Woman archetype—she who is the keeper of hidden treasures. Vasalisa feeds the doll in two ways, first with a bit of bread—a bit of life for this new psychic venture, and secondly by finding her way to the Old Wild Mother, the Baba Yaga. By listening to the doll—at every turn and every fork in the road—the doll indicates which way is "home."

The relationship between the doll and Vasalisa symbolizes a form of empathic magic between a woman and her intuition. This is the thing that must be handed down from woman to woman, this blessed binding, testing, and feeding of intuition. We, like Vasalisa, strengthen our bond with our intuitive nature by listening inwardly at every turn in the road. "Should I go this way, or this way? Should I stay or go? Should I resist or be flexible? Should I run away or toward? Is this person, event, venture true or false?"

The breaking of the bond between a woman and her wildish intuition is often misunderstood as the intuition itself being broken. This is not the fact. It is not intuition which is broken, but rather the matrilineal blessing on intuition, the handing down of intuitive reliance between a woman and all females of her lines who have gone before her—it is that long river of women that has been dammed.[10] A woman's grasp of her intuitive wisdom may be weak as a result, *but* with exercise it will come back and become fully manifested.[11]

The dolls serve as talismans. Talismans are reminders of what is felt but not seen, what is so, but is not immediately obvious. The talismanic numen of the image of the doll reminds us, tells us, sees ahead for us. This intuitive function belongs to all women. It is a massive and fundamental receptivity. Not receptivity as once touted in classical psychology, that is, as a passive vessel. But receptivity as in possessing immediate access to a profound wisdom that reaches down into women's very bones.[12]

The Fourth Task—Facing the Wild Hag

In this part of the tale, Vasalisa meets the Wild Hag face-to-face. The tasks of this meeting are these: *Being able to stand the face of the fearsome Wild Goddess without wavering; that is, facing the imago of the fierce mother (meeting up with the Baba Yaga). Familiarizing oneself with the arcane, the odd, the "otherness" of the wild (residing at Baba Yaga's house for a while). Bringing some of her values into our lives, thereby becoming ourselves a little odd in a goodly way (eating her food). Learning to face great power—in others, and subsequently one's own power. Letting the frail and too-sweet child die back even further.*

Baba Yaga lives in a house squatting on chicken legs. It whirls and spins when it has a mind to. In dreams, the symbol of house comments on the organization of the psychic space a person inhabits, both consciously and unconsciously. Ironically, if this story were a compensatory dream, the eccentric house would infer that the subject, in this case Vasalisa, is too unremarkable, too middle-of-the-road, and needs to twirl and whirl in order to find out what it's like to dance like a crazy chicken once in a while.

Now we can see that the Yaga's house is of the instinctual world and that Vasalisa needs more of this element in her personality. This chicken-legged house walks about, twirls even, in some hippity-hop dance. This house is alive, bursting with enthusiasm, with joyous life. These attributes are the main fundaments of the archetypal psyche of Wild Woman; a joyous and wild life force, where houses dance, where inanimates such as mortars fly like birds, where the old woman can make magic, where nothing is what it seems, but for the most part, is far better than it seemed to begin with.

Vasalisa began with what we might call a flattened-out mundane personality. It is just this "hyper-normalcy" that creeps up on us till we have a routine life, and a lifeless life without our really meaning to. This encourages the neglect of intuition[13] which in turn produces lack of light in the psyche. We must do something then, we must set out into the woods, go find the scary woman, or else one day as we are nodding down the street a manhole cover will snap open and *whoosh* we will be snatched by some unconscious thing that will throw us about like a rag—joyously or otherwise, mostly otherwise, but for good outcome.[14]

The giving of the intuitive doll by the original sweet mother is incomplete without the task-giving and testing done by the Old Wild One. Baba Yaga is the marrow of the instinctive and integrated psyche. We know this from her knowledge of all that has gone before. "Oh yes," she says when Vasalisa arrives, "I know of

you and your people." Further, as in her other incarnations as the
Mother of Days and *Mother Nyx* (Mother Night,[15] a Life/Death/
Life Goddess), old Baba Yaga is the keeper of the sky and earth
beings: Day, Rising Sun, and Night. She calls them "my Day, my
Night."

Baba Yaga is fearsome, for she represents the power of annihilation and the power of the life force at the same time. To gaze into
her face is to see *vagina dentata,* eyes of blood, the perfect newborn child and the wings of angels all at once.

And Vasalisa stands there and accepts this wild Mother divinity, wisdom, warts, and all. One of the most remarkable facets
of the Yaga portrayed in this tale is that though she threatens, she
is just. She does not hurt Vasalisa as long as Vasalisa affords her
respect. Respect in the face of great power is a crucial lesson. A
woman must be able to stand in the face of power, because ultimately some part of that power will become hers. Vasalisa faces
Baba Yaga *not* obsequiously, not boastfully or filled with brag-
gadocio, neither running away nor hiding. She presents herself
honestly and just as herself.

Many women are in recovery from their "Nice-Nice" complexes, wherein, no matter how they felt, no matter who assailed
them, they responded so sweetly as to be practically fattening.
Though they might have smiled kindly during the day, at night
they gnashed their teeth like brutes—the Yaga in their psyches
was fighting for expression.

This too-nice over-adaptation in women often occurs when they
are desperately afeared of being disenfranchised or found "unnecessary." Two of the most poignant dreams I've ever heard concerned a young woman who definitely needed to be less tame. The
first dream was that she inherited a photo album—a special one
with pictures of the "Wild Mother." How happy she was, until the
next week when she dreamt she opened a similar album and there
was a horrid old woman looking out at her. The hag was
possessed of mossy teeth and had black betel juice running down
her chin.

Her dream is typical of women who are recovering from being
too sweet. The first dream demonstrates one side of the wild
nature—the benign and bountiful, and all that is well with her

world. But when the mossy Wild Woman is presented to her, well, ah, uh, er . . . could we put this off for a while? The answer is no.

The unconscious in its brilliant way is offering this dreamer an idea about a new way of living that is not just the two-toothed frontal smile of the too-nice woman. To face this wild and creative power in ourselves is to gain access to the myriad faces of the subterrene feminine. These belong to us innately, and we may choose to inhabit whichever ones serve us best at whichever time.

In this initiation drama, Baba Yaga is instinctive nature in the guise of the witch. Like the word *wild*, the word *witch* has come to be understood as a pejorative, but long ago it was an appellation given to both old and young women healers, the word *witch* deriving from the word *wit*, meaning wise. This was before cultures carrying the one-God-only religious image began to overwhelm the older pantheistic cultures which understood the Deity through multiple religious images of the universe and all its phenomena. But regardless, the ogress, the witch, the wild nature, and whatever other *criaturas* and integral aspects the culture finds awful in the psyches of women are the very blessed things which women often need most to retrieve and bring to the surface.

A good deal of literature on the subject of women's power states that men are afraid of women's power. I always want to exclaim, "Mother of God! So many women themselves are afraid of women's power." For the old feminine attributes and forces are vast, and they *are* formidable. It is understandable that the first time they come face-to-face with the Old Wild Powers, both men and women take one anxious look and make tracks; all you see of them is flying paw-pads and frightened tails.

If men are going to ever learn to stand it, then without a doubt women have to learn to stand it. If men are ever going to understand women, women are going to have to teach the configurations of the wild feminine to them. To this end, the dream-making function of the psyche carries the Yaga and all her cohorts right into women's bedrooms at night through the dreamtime. If we are lucky, the Yaga will leave her big broad footprints in the carpet at our bedsides. She will come to peer at those who do not know her. If we are late to our initiations, she wonders why we do not come to visit her, and comes to visit us in night dreams instead.

One woman I worked with dreamed of women in long ragged nightgowns happily eating things you would never find on a restaurant menu. Another woman dreamed of an old woman in the shape of an old clawfoot bathtub that rattled its pipes and threatened to burst them unless the dreamer knocked out a wall so the tub could "see." A third woman dreamt that she was one of three blind old women, except she kept losing her driver's license and had to keep leaving her group in order to search for it—in a sense it could be said that she had difficulty remaining identified with the three Fates—the powers which guide life and death in the psyche. But in time, she too learned to stand it, learned to stay close to what she once feared—her own wildish nature.

All these creatures in dreams remind the woman dreamer of her elemental self: the Yaga Self, the enigmatic and intense power of the Life/Death/Life Mother. Yes, we are saying that to be Yaga-ish is good, and that we must be able to stand it. To be strong does not mean to sprout muscles and flex. It means meeting one's own numinosity without fleeing, actively living with the wild nature in one's own way. It means to be able to learn, to be able to stand what we know. It means to stand and live.

The Fifth Task—Serving the Non-Rational

In this part of the tale, Vasalisa has asked Baba Yaga for fire, and the Yaga agrees—but only if Vasalisa will do some household chores for her in exchange. The psychic tasks of this time of learning are these: *Staying with the Hag; acclimating to the great wildish powers of the feminine psyche. Coming to recognize her (your) power and the powers of inner purifications; unsoiling, sorting, nourishing, building energy and ideas (washing the Yaga's clothes, cooking for her, cleaning her house, and sorting out the elements).*

Not so long ago, women were deeply involved in the rhythms of life and death. They inhaled the pungent odor of iron from the fresh blood of childbirth. They washed the cooling bodies of the dead as well. The psyches of modern women, especially those from industrial and technological cultures, are often deprived of these close-up and hands-on blessed and basic experiences. But there is a way for the novice to fully participate in the sensitive aspects of the life and death cycles.

Baba Yaga, the Wild Mother, is the teacher whom we can consult in these matters. She instructs the ordering of the house of the soul. She imbues an alternate order to the ego, one where magic can happen, joy can be done, appetite is intact, things are accomplished with gusto. Baba Yaga is the model for being true to the Self. She teaches both death and renewal.

In the tale, she teaches Vasalisa how to care for the psychic house of the wild feminine. Laundering the Baba Yaga's clothes is a fabulous symbol. In the old countries, and still today, in order to launder one's clothes one descends to the river, and there makes the ritualistic ablutions that people have made since the beginning of time in order to renew the cloth. This is a very fine symbol for a cleansing and purification of the entire bearing of the psyche.

In mythology, the woven cloth is the work of the Life/Death/Life mothers. For instance, in the East there are the Three Fates: *Clotho*, *Lachesis*, and *Atropos*. In the West there is *Na'ashjé'ii Asdzáá*, the Spider Woman, who gave the gift of weaving to the Diné (Navajo). These Life/Death/Life mothers teach women sensitivity to what must die and what shall live, to what shall be carded out, to what shall be woven in. In the tale, Baba Yaga charges Vasalisa do the laundry to bring this weaving, these patterns known to the Life/Death/Life Goddess, out into the open, to consciousness; handling them, washing them, renewing them.

To wash something is a timeless purification ritual. It not only means to purify, it also means—like baptism from the Latin *baptiza*—to drench, to permeate with a spiritual numen and mystery. In the tale the washing is the first task. It means to make taut again that which has become slackened from the wearing. The clothes are like us, worn and worn until our ideas and values are slackened by the passing of time. The renewal, the revivifying, takes place in the water, in the re-discovering of what we really hold to be true, what we really hold sacred.

In archetypal symbolism, clothing represents *persona*, the first view the public gains of us. Persona is a kind of camouflage which lets others know only what we wish them to know about us, and nothing more. But there is an older meaning to *persona*, one found in all the MezoAmerican rites, one well known to *cantadoras y cuentistas y curanderas*, healers. The persona is not simply a mask to hide behind, but rather a presence which eclipses the mundane personality. In this sense, persona or mask is a signal of rank, virtue, character, and authority. It is the outward significator, the outward display of mastery.[16]

I like very much this initiatory task which requires a woman to cleanse the personae, the clothing of authority of the great Yaga of the forest. By washing the Yaga's clothes, the initiate herself will see how the seams of persona are sewn, what patterns the gowns take. Soon she herself will have some measure of these personae to place in her closet amidst others she has fashioned throughout her life.[17]

It is easy to imagine that the Yaga's marks of power and authority—her clothes—are made as she herself is fashioned psychologically: strong, enduring. To wash her laundry is a metaphor through which we learn to witness, examine, and take on this combination of qualities. We learn how to sort, mend, and renew the instinctive psyche through a *purificatio*, the washing of the fibers of being.

Vasalisa's next task is to sweep the hut and the yard. In Eastern European fairy tales, brooms are often made of sticks from trees and bushes, and sometimes the roots of wiry plants. Vasalisa's work is to sweep this object made of plant matter over the floors and the yard to keep the place clear of debris. A wise woman keeps her psychic environ uncluttered. She accomplishes such by keeping a clear head, keeping a clear place for her work, working at completing her ideas and projects.[18]

For many women, this task requires that they clear a time each day for contemplation, for a space to live in that is clearly their own with paper, pens, paints, tools, conversations, time, freedoms that are for this work only. For many, psychoanalysis, contemplation, mediation, the taking of solitude, and other experiences of descent and transformation provide this special time and place for the work. Each woman has her own preferences, her own way.

If this work can take place in Baba Yaga's hut, so much the better. Even near the hut is better than far away. In any event, one's wild life has to be kept ordered on a regular basis. It is not good enough to go to it for one day, or a few, once a year.

But because it is Baba Yaga's hut that Vasalisa sweeps, because it is Baba Yaga's yard, we are also speaking of keeping unusual ideas clear and ordered. These ideas include those which are uncommon, mystical, soulful, and uncanny.[19]

To sweep the premises means not only to begin to value the nonsuperficial life but to care for its orderliness. Sometimes women become confused about soulful work, and neglect its architecture till it is taken back by the forest. Gradually the structures of the psyche are overgrown until they finally are but a hidden archeologic ruin in the psyche's unconscious. A cyclical and critical sweeping will prevent this from occurring. When women have cleared space, the wild nature will better thrive.

To cook for Baba Yaga, we ask literally, how does one feed the Baba Yaga of the psyche, what does one feed so wild a Goddess? Firstly, to cook for the Yaga, one lays a fire—a woman must be willing to burn hot, burn with passion, burn with words, with ideas, with desire for whatever it is that she truly loves. It is actually this passion which causes the cooking, and a woman's original ideas of substance are what is cooked. To cook for the Yaga, one must arrange that one's creative life has a consistent fire under it.

Most of us would do better if we became more adept at watching the fire under our work, if we watched more closely the cooking process for nourishing the wild Self. Too often we turn away from the pot, from the oven. We forget to watch, forget to add fuel, forget to stir. We mistakenly think the fire and the cooking are like one of those feisty houseplants that can go without water for eight months before the poor thing keels over. It is not so. The fire bears, *requires* watching, for it is easy to let the flame go out. The Yaga must be fed. There's hell to pay if she goes hungry.

So, it is the cooking up of new and completely original things, of new directions, of commitments to one's art and work that continuously nourishes the wild soul. These same things nourish the Old Wild Mother and give her sustenance in our psyches. Without the fire, our great ideas, our original thoughts, our yearnings and longings remain uncooked, and everyone is unfulfilled. On the other hand, anything we do which has fire will please her and nourish us all.

In the development of women, all these motions of "home-keeping," the cooking, the washing, the sweeping, quantify something beyond the ordinary. All these metaphors offer ways to think about, to measure, feed, nourish, straighten, cleanse, order the soul-life.

In all these things Vasalisa is initiated, and her intuition helps her accomplish the tasks. The intuitive nature carries the ability to measure things at a glance, to weigh in an instant, to clear off the debris around an idea, and to name the essence of the thing, to fire it with vitality, to cook raw ideas, to make food for the psyche. Vasalisa, through the doll of intuition, is learning to sort, understand, keep in order, and clear and clean the psychic premises.

Additionally, she learns that the Wild Mother requires much nourishment in order to do her work. Baba Yaga cannot be put on a lettuce leaf and black coffee diet. If one wishes to be close to her, one has to realize that she has appetite for certain things. If one is to have a relationship with the ancient feminine, one must cook up much.

Through these chores, Baba Yaga teaches, and Vasalisa learns not to cringe away from the big, the mighty, the cyclical, the unforeseen, the unexpected, the vast and grand scale which is the size of Nature, the odd, the strange, and the unusual.

Women's cycles according to Vasalisa's tasks are these: To cleanse one's thinking, renewing one's values, on a regular basis. To clear one's psyche of trivia, sweep one's self, clean up one's thinking and feeling states on a regular basis. To build an enduring fire beneath the creative life, and cook up ideas on a systematic basis, means especially to cook, and with originality, a lot of unprecedented life in order to feed the relationship between oneself and the wildish nature.

Vasalisa, via her time with the Yaga, will eventually integrate some of the manner and style of the Yaga. And we too; it is our job, in our own limited human way, to pattern ourselves after her. And this we learn to do, yet we are awed at the same time, for in Baba Yaga–land there are things that fly in the night and are arisen again at daybreak, all summoned and bidden by the wild instinctual nature. There are the bones of the dead which still speak, and there are winds and fates and suns, moon, and sky which all live in her great trunk. But she keeps order. Day follows night, season follows season. She is not haphazard. She is both Rhyme and Reason.

In the story, the Yaga finds Vasalisa has completed all the tasks set before her and the Yaga is pleased, but also a little disappointed that she cannot rail against the girl. And so, just to make sure Vasalisa doesn't take anything for granted, Baba Yaga lets her know: "Though you managed to do my work once doesn't mean you can do it again. So here, here's another day of tasks. Let's see how you do, dearie . . . or else."

Vasalisa again, via the aegis of intuitive guidance, accomplishes the work, and the Yaga gives her the grumpy and begrudging stamp of approval . . . the kind that always comes from old women who have lived a long time and who have seen much, and somewhat wish they hadn't, and are rather proud they have.

The Sixth Task—Separating This from That

In this part of the tale, Baba Yaga requires two very demanding tasks of Vasalisa. A woman's psychic tasks are these: *Learning fine discrimination, separating one thing from the other with finest discernment, learning to make fine distinctions in judgment (sorting the mildewed corn from the good corn, and sorting the poppy seeds from a pile of dirt). Observing the power of the unconscious and how it works even when the ego is not aware (the pairs of hands which appear in the air). More learning about life (corn) and death (poppy seeds).*

Vasalisa is asked to separate four substances, mildewed corn from whole corn, and poppy seed from dirt. The intuitive doll completes the sorting of one from the other. Sometimes this sorting process occurs at such a deep level it is barely conscious to us, until one day . . .

The sorting spoken of in the tale is the kind which occurs when we face a dilemma or question, but not much is forthcoming to help us solve it. But leave it alone and come back to it later and there may be a good answer waiting for us where there was nothing before. Or "go to sleep, see what you dream,"[20] perhaps the two-million-year-old woman will come visit you from the night land. Perhaps she will be bearing the solution, or will show you that the answer is under your bed, or in your pocket, in a book, or behind your ear. It is an observable phenomenon that a question asked before bedtime, with practice, often elicits an answer upon awakening. There is something in the psyche, something of the intuitive doll, something under, over, or in the collective unconscious which sorts the materials while we sleep and dream.[21] And reliance on this attribute is also part of the wild nature.

Symbolically, the mildewed corn carries a dual meaning. As a liquor, mildewed corn may be used both as an inebriative and as a medication. There is a fungal condition called corn-smut—a rather fuzzy black fungus which is found in mildewed corn—this being reputed to be hallucinogenic.

It is hypothesized by various scholars that hallucinogens from wheat, barley, poppies, or maize were used in the old Eleusinian Goddess rites in Greece. Additionally, the sorting of the corn that the Yaga bids Vasalisa do is also related to the gathering of medicines by *curanderas*, the old woman-healers one can still observe at this work throughout North, Central, and South America today. We see the woman-healer's ancient remedies and treatments also in the poppy seed, which is a soporific and barbiturate, as well as in the dirt, which has been used since ancient times and is still used today in poultices and as packs, in baths, and even for ingestion under certain circumstances.[22]

This is one of the loveliest phrasings in the story. The fresh corn, mildewed corn, poppy seed, and dirt are all remnants of an ancient healing apothecary. These substances are used as balms, salves, infusions, and poultices to hold other medicines on the body. As metaphors, they are also medicines for the mind; some nourish, others put to rest, some cause languor, others, stimulation. They are facets of the Life/Death/Life cycles. Baba Yaga is not only asking Vasalisa to separate this from that, to determine the difference between things of like kind—such as real love from false love, or nourishing life from spoiled life—but she is also asking her to distinguish one medicine from another.

Like dreams, which can be understood on the objective level but still retain a subjective reality, these elements of food/medicines also have symbolic guidance for us. Like Vasalisa, we have to sort out our psychic healing agents, to sort and sort and sort to understand that food for the psyche is also medicine for the psyche, and to wring the truth, the essence, out of these elements for our own nourishment.

All these elements and tasks are teaching Vasalisa about the Life/Death/Life nature, the give-and-take of caring for the wild nature. Sometimes, in order to bring a woman closer to this nature, I ask her to keep a garden. Let this be a psychic one or one with mud, dirt, green, and all the things that surround and help and assail. Let it represent the wild psyche. The garden is a concrete connection to life and death. You could even say there is a religion of garden, for it teaches profound psychological and spiritual lessons. Whatever can happen to a garden can happen to soul and psyche—too much water, too little water, infestations, heat, storm, flood, invasion, miracles, dying back, coming back, boon, healing, blossoming, bounty, beauty.

During the life of the garden, women keep a diary, recording the signs of life-giving and life-taking. Each entry cooks up a psychic soup. In the garden we practice letting thoughts, ideas, preferences, desires, even loves, both live and die. We plant, we pull, we bury. We dry seed, sow it, moisten it, support it, harvest.

The garden is a meditation practice, that of seeing when it is time for something to die. In the garden one can see the time coming for both fruition and for dying back. In the garden one is moving with rather than against the inhalations and the exhalations of greater wild Nature.

Through this meditation, we acknowledge that the Life/Death/Life cycle is a natural one. Both life-giving and death-dealing natures are waiting to be befriended, forever loved. In this process, we become like the cyclical wild. We have the ability to infuse energy and strengthen life, and to stand out of the way of what dies.

The Seventh Task—Asking the Mysteries

After the successful completion of her tasks, Vasalisa asks the Yaga some good questions. The tasks of this time are these: *Questioning and trying to learn more about the Life/Death/Life nature and how it functions (Vasalisa asks about the horsemen). Learning the truth about being able to understand all the elements of the wild nature ("to know too much can make one old too soon").*[23]

We all begin with the question "What am I, really? What is my work here?" The Yaga teaches us that we are Life/Death/Life, that this is our cycle, this is our special insight into the deep feminine. When I was a child one of my aunts told me our family's legend of "The Watery Women." She said that at the edge of every lake there lived a young woman with old hands. Her first job was to put *tüz*—what I can only describe to you as souls or "soul-fire"—into dozens of beautiful porcelain ducks. Her second job was to wind the wooden keys in the ducks' backs. When the winding-keys ran out, and the ducks fell over, their bodies shattered, she was to flap her apron at the souls as they were released and shoo them up into the sky. Her fourth job was to put *tüz* into more beautiful porcelain ducks, wind their keys, and release them to their lives. . . .

The *tüz* story is one of the clearest about exactly what it is the Life/Death/Life Mother does with her time. Psychically, Mother Nyx, Baba Yaga, the Watery Women, *La Que Sabe*, and Wild Woman represent different pictures, different ages, moods, and aspects of the Wild Mother God. The infusion of *tüz* into our own ideas, our own lives, the lives of those we touch, that is our work. The shooing of the soul to its home, that is our work. The releasing of a shower of sparks to fill the day, and creating a light so we can find our way through the night, that is our work.

Vasalisa asks about the men on horseback she has seen while finding her way to Baba Yaga's hut; the white man on the white horse, the red man on the red horse, the black man on the black horse. The Yaga, like Demeter, is an old horse-mother Goddess, associated with the power of the mare, and fecundity as well. Baba Yaga's hut is a stable for the many colored horses and their riders.

These pairs pull the sun up and across the sky by day, and pull the cover of darkness over the sky at night. But there is more.

The black, red, and white horsemen symbolize the ancient colors connoting birth, life, and death. These colors also represent old ideas of descent, death, and rebirth—the black for dissolving of one's old values, the red for the sacrifice of one's preciously held illusions, and the white as the new light, the new knowing that comes from having experienced the first two.

The old words used in medieval times are *nigredo*, black; *rubedo*, red; *albedo*, white. These describe an alchemy[24] which follows the circuit of the Wild Woman, the work of the Life/Death/Life Mother. Without the symbols of daybreak, rising light, and mysterious dark, she would not be who she is. Without the rising of hope in our hearts, without the steady light—no matter if a candle or a sun—to tell us this from that in our lives, without a night from which all things can be soothed, from which all things can be born, we too would not benefit from our wildish natures.

The colors in the tale are extremely precious, for each has its death nature and its life nature. Black is the color of mud, the fertile, the basic stuff into which ideas are sown. Yet black is the color also of death, the blackening of the light. And black has even a third aspect. It is also the color associated with that world between the worlds which *La Loba* stands upon—for black is the color of descent. Black is a promise that you will soon know something you did not know before.

Red is the color of sacrifice, of rage, of murder, of being tormented and killed. Yet red is also the color of vibrant life, dynamic emotion, arousal, *eros*, and desire. It is a color that is considered strong medicine for psychic malaise, a color which rouses appetite. There is throughout the world a figure known as the red mother.[25] She is not as well known as the black mother or black madonna, but she is the watcher of "things coming through." She is especially propitiated by those who are about to give birth, for whosoever leaves this world or comes into this world has to pass through her red river. Red is a promise that a rising up or a borning is soon to come.

White is the color of the new, the pure, the pristine. It is also the color of soul free of the body, of spirit unencumbered by the physical. It is the color of the essential nourishment, mother's milk. Conversely, it is the color of the dead, of things which have lost their rosiness, their flush of vitality. When there is white, everything is, for the moment, *tabula rasa*, unwritten upon. White is a promise that there is nourishment enough for things to begin anew, that the emptiness or the void would be filled.

Besides the horsemen, both Vasalisa and her doll are dressed in red, white, and black as well. Vasalisa and her doll are the alchemical *anlagen*. Together they cause Vasalisa to be a little Life/Death/Life Mother in-the-becoming. There are two epiphanies or life-givings in the story. Vasalisa's life is revivified by the doll and by her meeting with Baba Yaga, and thereby through all the tasks she masters. There are also two deaths in the story: that of the original too-good mother and also that of the stepfamily. Yet we see easily that the deaths are proper, and that they ultimately cause the young psyche a much fuller life.

So this letting live, letting die, is very important. It is the basic and natural rhythm which women are meant to understand . . . and live. Grasping this rhythm lessens fear, for we anticipate the future, and the ground swells and the emptyings out it will hold. The doll and the Yaga are the wild mothers of all women; they provide the penetrating intuitive gifts from the personal level as well as the divine. This is the extreme paradox and teaching of the instinctual nature. It is a sort of Wolf Buddhism. What is one, is both. What is two, makes three. What lives shall die. What dies shall live.

This is what Baba Yaga means when she says, "to know too much can make one old too soon." There is a certain amount we all should know at each age and each stage of our lives. In the tale, to know the meaning of the hands that appear and wring out the oil from the corn and the poppy seed, both life-giving and death-dealing medicines in and of themselves, is to ask to know too much. Vasalisa asks about the horses, but not about the hands.

When I was a young adult, I asked my friend Bulgana Robnovich, an elderly teller from the Caucasus who lived in a tiny Russian farm community in Minnesota, about the Baba Yaga. How did she see this part of the tale where Vasalisa "just knows" to stop asking questions? She looked at me with the lashless eyes of an old dog and said, "Dere are simply tings vich cannot be known." She smiled bewitchingly, crossed her thick ankles, and that was that.

To try to understand the mystery of the appearing and disappearing servants who come in the form of disembodied hands is akin to trying to absolutely comprehend the core of the numinosum. By warning Vasalisa away from the question, the doll and the Yaga caution Vasalisa about calling upon too much of the numinosity of the underworld all at once, and this is right and proper, for though we visit there, we do not want to become enraptured and thereby trapped there.

It is another set of cycles the Yaga alludes to here, cycles of a woman's life. As a woman lives them, she will understand more and more of these interior feminine rhythms, among them the rhythms of creativity, of birthing psychic babies and perhaps also human ones, the rhythms of solitude, of play, of rest, of sexuality, and of the hunt. One need not push it, the understanding will come. Some things must be accepted as being out of our reach, even though they act upon us, and we are enriched by them. There is a saying in my family: "Some things are God's business."

So, by the end of these tasks, "the legacy of the wild mothers" is deepened and intuitive powers emanate from both the human and soulful sides of the psyche. Now we have the doll as teacher on one side, and the Baba Yaga on the other.

The Eighth Task—Standing on All Fours

Baba Yaga is repelled by Vasalisa's blessing from her deceased mother, and gives Vasalisa light—a fiery skull on a stick—and tells her to go. The tasks of this part of the tale are these: *Taking on immense power to see and affect others (receiving the skull). Looking at one's life situations in this new light (finding the way back to the old stepfamily).*

Is Baba Yaga repelled because Vasalisa has received her mother's blessing, or rather is she just repelled by blessedness in general? Actually, not quite either. Considering the later monotheistic overlays to this story, it would also appear that here the story has been shifted to make the Yaga seem afeared of Vasalisa's having been blessed, thereby demonizing this Old Wild Mother (from perhaps as far back in time as the Neolithic era) with an eye to elevating the newer Christian religion and discouraging the older one.

The original word in the story might have been changed to *blessing* to encourage conversion, but I think the essence of original and archetypal meaning is still present. The issue of the mother's blessing can be interpreted this way: The Yaga is not repelled by the fact of the blessing, but is rather put off by the fact that the blessing is from the too-good mother; the nice, the sweet, the darling of the psyche. If the Yaga is true to form, she would not care to be too close to, nor for too long near, the too conforming, the too demure side of the feminine nature.

Although the Yaga could blow life's breath into a mouse-child with infinite tenderness, she could be said to know well enough to stay in her own land. Her land is the underworld of the psyche. The too-good mother's land is that of the topside world. Although sweetness can fit into the wild, the wild cannot long fit into sweetness.

When women integrate this aspect of the Yaga, they change from accepting without question every tinker, every barb, every dadoo, every everything that comes their way. To gain a little distance from the sweet blessing of the too-good mother, a woman gradually learns to not just look, but to squint and to peer, and then, more and more, to suffer no fools.

Having now, through serving the Yaga, created a capacity within herself which she did not have before, Vasalisa receives a portion of the wild Hag's power. Some women are afraid this deep knowing via instinct and intuition will cause them to be reckless or thoughtless, but this is an unfounded fear.

Quite the contrary; lack of intuition, lack of sensitivity to cycles, or not following one's knowing, causes choices which turn out poorly, even disastrously. More often this Yagaian kind of knowledge moves women by small increments, and most often gives direction by conveying clear pictures of "what lies beneath or behind" the motives, ideas, actions, and words of others.

If the instinctive psyche warns "Beware!" then the woman must pay heed. If the deep intuition says "Do this, do that, go this way, stop here, go forward," the woman must make corrections to her plan as needed. Intuition is not to be consulted once and then forgotten. It is not disposable. It is to be consulted at all steps along the way, whether the woman's work be clashing with a demon in the interior, or completing a task in the outer world. It does not matter whether a woman's concerns and aspirations are personal or global. Before all else, every action begins with strengthening the spirit.

Now let us consider the skull with fiery light. It is a symbol associated with what some old-style archeologists called "ancestral worship."[26] In later archeo-religious versions of the story, the skulls on sticks are said to be those of humans whom the Yaga has killed and eaten. But in the older religious rites which practiced ancestral kinship, bones were recognized as the agents for calling the spirits, the skulls being the most salient part.[27]

In ancestral kinship, it is believed that the special and timeless knowledge of the old ones of the community lives on in their very bones after death. The skull is thought to be the dome which houses a powerful remnant of the departed soul . . . one which, if asked, can call the entire spirit of the dead person back for a time in order to be consulted. It is easy to imagine that the soul-Self lives right in the bony cathedral of the forehead, with the eyes as windows, mouth as door, and ears as the winds.

So when the Yaga gives Vasalisa a lighted skull, she is giving her an old-woman icon, an "ancestral knower," to carry with her for life. She is initiating her into a matrilineal legacy of knowing, one which, in the caves and canyons of the psyche, remains whole and thriving.

So, off goes Vasalisa into the dark forest with the fiery skull. She wandered about to find the Yaga, now she returns to home more sure, more certain, hips aimed straight ahead. This is the ascent from the initiation of deep intuition. Intuition has been set into Vasalisa like a center jewel in a crown. When a woman has come this far, she has managed to leave the protection of her own inner too-good mother, learned to expect and deal with adversity in the outer world in a powerful rather than complicit manner. She has become aware of her own shadowy and inhibitory stepmother and stepsisters and the destruction they mean to do to her.

She has negotiated through the dark while listening to her inner voice, and has been able to stand the face of the Hag, which is a side of her own nature, but also the powerful wild nature. Thus she is enabled to understand awesome and conscious power, her own and that of others. No more "But I'm afraid of him/her/it."

She has served the Hag Goddess of the psyche, fed the relationship, purified the personae, kept clear thinking. She has gotten to know this wild feminine force and its habits. She has learned to differentiate, to separate thought from feelings. She has learned to recognize the great wild power in her own psyche.

She has learned about Life/Death/Life, and women's gift about it all. With these newly acquired Yaga skills, she need not lack in confidence or potency anymore. Having been given the legacy of the mothers—intuition from the human side of her nature, and a wild knowing from the *La Que Sabe* side of the psyche—she is well enabled. She goes forward in life, feet placed surely, one after the other, womanly. She has coalesced all her power and sees the world now and her life through this new light. Let us see what happens when a woman behaves thusly.

The Ninth Task—Recasting the Shadow

Vasalisa journeys toward home with the fiery skull on the stick. She almost throws it away but the skull reassures her. Once back home, the skull watches the stepsisters and stepmother, and burns them to ashes. Vasalisa lives well and for a long time afterward.[28]

These are the psychic tasks of this time: *Using one's acute vision (fiery eyes) to recognize and react to the negative shadow of one's own psyche and/or negative aspects of persons and events in the outer world. Recasting the negative shadows in one's psyche with hag-fire (the wicked stepfamily which formerly tortured Vasalisa is turned to cinders).*

Vasalisa has the fiery skull held before her as she walks through the forest, and her doll indicates the way back. "Go this way, now this way." Vasalisa, who used to be a blueberry-eyed sweet-muffin, is now a woman walking with her power preceeding her.

A fiery light emanates from the eyes, ears and nose, and mouth of the skull. It is another representation of all the psychic processes which have to do with discrimination. It is also related to ancestor kinship and therefore to remembering. If the Yaga had given Vasalisa a knee-bone on a stick, that would require a different symbolic rendering. If she had given her a wrist-bone, a neck-bone, or any other bone—other than, perhaps, the female pelvis—it would not mean the same thing.[29]

So the skull is another representation of intuition—it does not hurt the Yaga or Vasalisa—it has a discrimination of its own. Vasalisa now carries the blaze of knowing; she has those fierce senses. She can hear, see, smell, and taste things out, and she has her Self. She has the doll, she has Yaga sensibilities, now she has the fiery skull as well.

Momentarily Vasalisa becomes afraid of the power she carries, and she thinks to throw the fiery skull away. With this formidable power at her behest, it is no wonder the ego thinks perhaps it would be better, easier, safer, to discard this burning light, for it is so much, and through it Vasalisa has become so much. But a supernatural voice from the skull instructs her to stay calm and to proceed. And this she is able to do.

Each woman who retrieves her intuition and Yaga-like powers reaches a point where she is tempted to throw them away, for what is the use of seeing and knowing all these things? This skull-light is not forgiving. In its light, the old are elderly; the beautiful, lush; the silly, foolish; the drunk are drunken; the unfaithful are infidels; things which are incredible are noted as miracles. Skull-light sees what it sees; it is an eternal light, and right out front, shining ahead of a woman, like a presence which goes a little bit before her and reports back to her what it has found ahead. It is her perpetual reconnaissance.

Yet, when one sees and senses thusly, then one has to work to do something about what one sees. To possess good intuition, goodly power, causes work. It causes work firstly in the watching and comprehending of negative forces and imbalances both inward and outward. Secondly, it causes striving in the gathering up of will in order to do something about what one sees, be it for good, or balance, or to allow something to live or die.

It is true, I will not lie to you; it is easier to throw away the light and go back to sleep. It is true, it is hard to hold the skull-light out before us sometimes. For with it, we clearly see all sides of ourselves and others, both the disfigured and the divine and all conditions in between.

Yet, with this light the miracles of deep beauty in the world and in humans come to consciousness. With this penetrating light one can see past the bad action to the good heart, one can espy the sweet spirit crushed beneath hatred, one can understand much instead of being perplexed only. This light can differentiate layers of personality, intention, and motives in others. It can determine consciousness and unconsciousness in self and others. It is the wand of knowing. It is the mirror in which all things are sensed and seen. It is the deep wild nature.

Yet, there are times when its reports are painful and almost too much to bear: for also the fiery skull points out where there are betrayals brewing, where there is faintness of courage in those who speak otherwise. It points out envy lying like cold grease behind a warm smile; it points out the looks which are mere masks for dislike. As regards oneself, its light is equally bright: it shines on our treasures and on our foibles.

It is these knowings which are the most difficult to face. It is at this point that we always want to throw away all this damnable shrewd knowing of ours. It is here that we feel, if we will not ignore it, a strong force from the Self saying, "Do not throw me away. Keep me. You'll see."

As Vasalisa weaves through the forest, she no doubt is thinking too about the stepfamily which had maliciously sent her off to die, and though she herself is sweet of heart, the skull is not sweet; its work is to be sight-full. So when she wishes to toss it away, we know that she is thinking of the pain it causes to know some things and certain things about self, about others, about the nature of the world.

She arrives home and the stepmother and stepsisters tell her they had no fire, no energy while she was away, that no matter what they did, they could not make light. And this is the exact truth in any woman's psyche when she is in her wildish power. During that time, the things which have oppressed her have no libido, it is all taken up in the good journey. Without libido, the nastier aspects of the psyche, those which exploit the creative life of a woman or encourage her to squander her life with minutiae, these become like gloves with no hands in them.

The fiery skull begins to peer at the stepsisters and stepmother, watching and watching them intently. Can a negative aspect of psyche be reduced to cinder by being watched and watched? Yes, indeed it can. Holding it in consistent consciousness can cause the thing to dehydrate. In one version of the tale, the errant family members are burnt to a crisp, in another version, to three small black cinders.

The three small black cinders hold a very old and interesting idea. The little black *dit*, or dot, is often thought of as the beginning of life. In the Old Testament when that God made First Man and First Woman, he fashioned them from earth, dirt, mud, depending on which translation one reads. Just how much earth? No one says. But among other creation stories, the beginning of the world and of its inhabitants is often made from the dit, from one grain, one single tiny dark dot of something.[30]

In this manner, the three small cinders are in the province of the Life/Death/Life Mother. They are reduced down almost to nothing in the psyche. They are deprived of libido. Now something new can occur. In most cases when we consciously deprive a psychic thing of juice, it shrivels, and its energy is released or reconfigured.

There is another side to this draining of the destructive stepfamily. One cannot keep the consciousness one has earned by meeting the Hag Goddess and carrying the fiery light, and so forth, if one lives with cruel people outwardly or inwardly. If you are surrounded by people who cross their eyes and look with disgust up at the ceiling when you are in the room, when you speak, when you act and react, then you are with the people who douse passions—yours and probably their own as well. These are not the people who care about you, your work, your life.

A woman must choose her friends and lovers wisely, for both can become like a bad stepmother and rotten stepsisters. In the case of our lovers, we often invest them with the power of a great Mage—a great magician. This is easy to do, for if we become truly intimate, it is like unlocking a lead crystal *atelier*, a magic one, or so it feels to us. A lover can engender and/or destroy even our most durable connections to our own cycles and ideas. The destructive lover must be avoided. A better sort of lover is one finely wrought of strong psychic muscle and tender flesh. For Wild Woman it also helps if the lover is just a little bit "psychic" too, a person who can "see into" her heart.

When the wildish woman has an idea, the friend or lover will never say "Well, I don't know . . . sounds really dumb [grandiose, undoable, expensive, etc.] to me." A right friend will never say that. They might say instead . . . "I don't know if I understand. Tell me how you see it. Tell me how it will work."

Having a lover/friend who regards you as a living growing *criatura*, being, just as much as the tree from the ground, or a ficus in the house, or a rose garden out in the side yard . . . having a lover and friends who look at you as a true living breathing entity, one that is human but made of very fine and moist and magical things as well . . . a lover and friends who support the *criatura* in you . . . these are the people you are looking for. They will be the friends of your soul for life. Mindful choosing of friends and lovers, not to mention teachers, is critical to remaining conscious, remaining intuitive, remaining in charge of the fiery light that sees and knows.

The way to maintain one's connection to the wild is to ask yourself what it is that *you* want. This is the sorting of the seed from the dirt. One of the most important discriminations we can make in this matter is the difference between things that beckon to us and things that call from our souls.

This is how it works: Imagine a smorgasbord laid out with whipped cream and salmon and bagels and roast beef, and fruit salad, and green enchiladas and rice and curry and yogurt and many, many things for table after table after table. Imagine that you survey it all and that you see certain things that appeal to you. You remark to yourself, "Oh! I would really like to have one of those, and one of that, and some of this other thing."

Some women and men make all their life decisions in this way. There is around and about us a constant beckoning world, one which insinuates itself into our lives, arousing and creating appetite where there was little or none before. In this sort of choice, we choose a thing because it just happened to be beneath our noses at that moment in time. It is not necessarily what we want, but it is interesting, and the longer we gaze at it, the more compelling it becomes.

When we are connected to the instinctual self, to the *soul* of the feminine which is natural and wild, then instead of looking over whatever happens to be on display, we say to ourselves, "What am I hungry for?" Without looking at anything outwardly, we venture inward, and ask, "What do I long for? What do I wish for now?" Alternate phrases are "What do I crave? What do I desire? For what do I yearn?" And the answer usually arrives rapidly: "Oh, I think I want . . . you know what would be really good, is some this or that . . . ah yes, that's what I really want."

Is that on the smorgasbord? Maybe yes and maybe no. In most cases, probably not. We will have to quest for it a little bit—sometimes for a considerable time. But in the end we shall find it, and be glad we took soundings about our deeper longings.

This discrimination which Vasalisa learns as she separates poppy seeds from dirt and mildewed corn from fresh corn, is one of the most difficult things to learn, for it takes spirit, will, and soulfulness and it often means holding out for what one wants. Nowhere can this be seen more clearly than in the choice of mates and lovers. A lover cannot be chosen *à la smorgasbord*. A lover has to be chosen from soul-craving. To choose just because something mouth-watering stands before you will never satisfy the hunger of the soul-Self. And that is what intuition is for; it is a direct messenger of the soul.

To amplify further, if you are presented with an opportunity to buy a bicycle, or an opportunity to travel to Egypt and see the Pyramids, you have to set the opportunity aside for the moment, enter into yourself, and ask, "What am I hungry for? What do I long for? Maybe I'm hungry for a motorcycle instead of a bicycle. Maybe I'm hungry for a trip to see my grandmother, who's coming up in years." The decisions do not have to be so large. Sometimes the matter to be weighed is taking a walk versus making a poem. Momentous or mundane, the idea is to have consulted the instinctual self through one or several aspects available to you; these symbolized by the doll, the old Baba Yaga, and the fiery skull.

Another way to strengthen connection to intuition is to refuse to allow anyone to repress your vivid energies . . . that means your opinions, your thoughts, your ideas, your values, your morals, your ideals. There is very little right/wrong or good/bad in this world. There is, however, useful and not useful. There are also things that are sometimes destructive, as well as things which are engendering. There are actions that are properly integrated and intentioned and those that are not. But as you well know, a garden has to be turned in the fall in order to prepare it for the spring. It cannot bloom all the time. But let your own innate cycles dictate the upsurges and the downward cycles of your life, not other forces or persons outside yourself, nor negative complexes from within.

There are certain constant entropies and creatings which are a part of our inner cycles. It is our task to synchronize with them. Like the chambers of a heart which fill and empty and fill again, we "learn to learn" the rhythm of this Life/Death/Life cycle instead of becoming martyred by it. Liken it to jump rope. The rhythm already exists; you sway back and forth until you are copying the rhythm. Then, you jump in. That's how it is done. It is no more fancy than that.

Further, intuition provides options. When you are connected to the instinctual self, you always have at least four choices . . . the two opposites and then the middle ground, and "taken under further contemplation." If you're not vested in the intuitive, you may think you only have one choice, and that it seems an undesirable one. And perhaps you feel that you ought to suffer about it. And submit. And force yourself to do it. No, there's a better way. Listen to the inner hearing, the inner seeing, the inner being. Follow it. It knows what to do next.

One of the most remarkable things about using intuition and the instinctive nature is that it causes a surefooted spontaneity to erupt. Spontaneity doesn't mean being unwise. It is not a "pounce-and-blurt" attribute. Good boundaries are still important. Scheherazade, for instance, had pretty good boundaries. She used her cleverness to please while at the same time positioning herself to be valued. Being real doesn't mean being reckless, it means allowing *La voz mitológica*, The Mythological Voice, to speak. One does this by shutting off the ego for a while and letting that which wishes to speak, speak.

. In the consensual reality, we all have access to little wild mothers in the flesh. These are women who, as soon as you see them, something in you leaps, and something in you thinks, "MaMa." You take one look and think, "I am her progeny, I am her child, she is my mother, my grandmother." In the case of *un hombre con pechos*—figuratively, a man with breasts—you might think, "Oh grandfather" or "Oh my brother, my friend." You just know that this man is nurturing. (Paradoxically they are strongly masculine and strongly feminine at the same time. They are like fairy godmother, like mentor, like the mother you never had, or did not have long enough; that is an *un hombre con pechos*.)[31]

All these human beings could be called little wild mothers. Usually everyone has at least one. If we are lucky, throughout a lifetime we will have several. You are usually grown or at least in your late adolescence by the time you meet them. They are vastly different from the too-good mother. The little wild mothers guide you, burst with pride over your accomplishments. They are critical of blockages and mistaken notions in and around your creative, sensual, spiritual, and intellectual life.

Their purpose is to help you, to care about your art, and to reattach you to the wildish instincts, and to elicit your original best. They guide the restoration of the intuitive life. And they are thrilled when you make contact with the doll, proud when you find the Baba Yaga, and rejoicing when they see you coming back with the fiery skull held out before you.

We have seen that to remain a dummling and too-sweet is dangerous. But perhaps you still are not convinced; perhaps you're thinking, "Oh lordy, who wants to be like Vasalisa?" And I'm telling you, you do. You want to be like her, accomplish what she has accomplished, and follow the trail she has left behind, for it is the way of retaining and developing your soul. The Wild Woman is the one who dares, who creates, and who destroys. She is the primitive and inventing soul that makes all creative acts and arts possible. She creates a forest around us and we begin to deal with life from that fresh and original perspective.

So, here at the end of the re-setting of initiation into the feminine psyche, we have a young woman with formidable experiences who has learnt to follow her knowing. She has endured through all the tasks to a full initiation. The crown is hers. Perhaps recognizing intuition is the easier of the tasks, but holding it in consciousness and letting live what can live, and letting die what must die, is by far the more strenuous, yet so satisfying aim.

Baba Yaga is the same as Mother Nyx, the mother of the world, another Life/Death/Life Goddess. The Life/Death/Life Goddess is always also a creator Goddess. She makes, fashions, breathes life into, she is there to receive the soul when the breath has run out. Following her footprints, we endeavor to learn to let be born what must be born, whether all the right people are there or not. Nature does not ask permission. Blossom and birth whenever you feel like it. As adults we need little permission but rather more engendering, much more encouraging of the wild cycles, much more original vision.

To let things die is the theme at the end of the tale. Vasalisa has learned well. Does she collapse into a fit of high-pitched shrieking as the skull burns into the malicious ones? No. What must die, dies.

How does one make such a decision? One knows. *La Que Sabe* knows. Ask within for her advice. She is the Mother of the Ages. Nothing surprises her. She has seen it all. For most women, to let die is not against their natures, it is only against their training. This can be reversed. We all know in *los ovarios* when it is time for life, when it is time for death. We might try to fool ourselves for various reasons, but we know.

By the light of the fiery skull, we know.

✒ CHAPTER 4

The Mate: Union
With the Other

Hymn for the Wild Man: Manawee

If women want men to know them, really know them, they have to teach them some of the deep knowing. Some women say they are tired, that they already have done too much in this area. I humbly suggest they have been trying to teach a man who does not care to learn. Most men want to know, want to learn. When men show that willingness, then is the time to reveal things; not just because, but because another soul has asked. You will see. So, here are some of the things which will make it much easier for a man to understand, for him to meet a woman halfway; here is a language, our language.

In mythos, as in life, there is no doubt that the Wild Man seeks his own down-under-the-earth bride. In tales among the Celts, there are famous pairs of Wild Gods who love one another so. They often live under a lake where they are the protectors of the underlife and the underworld. From Babylonian mythos, the cedar-thighed Inanna calls to her lover, The Bull Plow, "Come cover me with your wildness." In modern times, even now in the upper Midwest, the Mother and Father of God are still said to roll about in their spring bed, making thunder.

Similarly, there is no one a wildish woman loves better than a mate who can be her equal. Yet, over and over perhaps since the beginning of infinity, those who would be her mate are not quite

121

sure they comprehend her true nature. What does a woman truly desire? This is an ancient question, a soulful riddle about the wildish and mysterious nature which all women possess. While the hag in Chaucer's "The Wife of Bath" croaked out that the answer to this question was that women wished to have sovereignty over their own lives, and this is indeed an irrevocable fact, there is yet another and equally powerful truth which answers this question as well.

Here is a story that replies to the age-old question about women's true nature. Those who endeavor in the ways and means shown in the story shall be lover and mate to the wildish woman forever. Long ago Miss V. B. Washington gifted me with a little African-American story that I have amplified into a literary story here I call Manawee.

~~~~~~~~~~~~~~~~~~~~~

Manawee

THERE WAS A MAN who came to court two sisters who were twins. But their father said, "You may not have them in marriage until or unless you can guess their names." Manawee guessed and guessed, but he could not guess the names of the sisters. The young women's father shook his head and sent Manawee away time after time.

One day Manawee took his little dog with him on a guessing visit, and the dog saw that one sister was prettier than the other and the other sister was sweeter than the other. Though neither sister possessed all virtues, the little dog liked them very much, for they gave him treats and smiled into his eyes.

Manawee failed to guess the names of the young women again that day and trudged home. But the little dog ran back to the hut of the young women. There he poked his ear under one of the side walls and heard the women giggling about how handsome and manly Manawee was. The sisters, as they spoke, called each other by name and the little dog heard, and ran as fast as he could back to his master to tell him.

But on the way, a lion had left a big bone with meat on it near the path, and the tiny dog smelled it immediately, and without another thought he veered off into the brush dragging the bone. There, he happily licked and snapped at the bone till all the flavor was gone. Oh! the tiny dog suddenly remembered the forgotten task, but unfortunately, he had also forgotten the names of the young women as well.

So back he ran to the twin sisters' hut a second time, and this time it was night, and the young women were oiling each other's arms and legs and readying themselves as though for a celebration. Again the little dog heard them call each other by name. He hopped up in the air in a fit of delight, and was racing back down the path to the hut of Manawee when from the brush came the smell of fresh nutmeg.

Now there was nothing the little dog loved more than nutmeg. So he took a quick turn off the path and sped to where a lovely kumquat pie sat cooling on a log. Well, soon the pie was all gone, and the little dog had lovely nutmeg breath. As he trotted home with a very full belly, he tried to think of the young women's names, but again, he had forgotten them.

So finally the little dog raced back to the sisters' hut again, and this time the sisters were readying themselves to be wed. "Oh no!" thought the little dog, "there is hardly time left." And when the sisters called each other by name, the little dog put the names into his mind and sped away, absolutely and resolutely determined that nothing would stop him from delivering the precious two names to Manawee right away.

The little dog spied some small fresh kill on the trail, but ignored it and vaulted over it. The little dog, for a moment, thought he smelled a curl of nutmeg on the air, but he ignored it and instead ran and ran toward home and his master. But the little dog did not plan for a dark stranger to leap out of the bush and grab him by the neck and shake him so hard his tail almost fell off.

For that is what happened, and all the while the stranger shouted, "Tell me those names! What are the names of the young women so I may win them."

The little dog thought he himself would faint from the tight fist about his neck, but he fought bravely. He growled, he scratched, he kicked, and finally bit the giant stranger between the fingers, and the little dog's teeth stung like wasps. The stranger bellowed like a water buffalo, but the little dog would not let go. The stranger ran off into the bush with the little dog dangling from his hand.

"Let go, let go, let go of me, little dog, and I will let go of you," pleaded the stranger. And the little dog snarled between its teeth, "Do not come back or you won't see morning ever again." And so the stranger escaped into the bush, moaning and holding his hand as he ran. And the little dog proceeded to half hobble and half run down the path to Manawee.

Even though his pelt was bloody and his jaws ached, the names of the young women were clear in his mind, and he limped up to Manawee beaming. Manawee gently washed the little dog's wounds, and the little dog told him the whole story and the two names of the young women as well. Manawee raced back to the village of the young women with the little dog on his shoulders riding high, the dog's ears flying like two horse tails.

When Manawee reached the father with the names of his daughters, the twin sisters received Manawee completely dressed to journey with him; they had been waiting for him all along. That is how Manawee won two of the most beautiful maidens of the riverland. And all four, the sisters, Manawee, and the little dog, lived in peace together for a long time to come.

Krik Krak Krout, now this story's out.
Krik Krak Krun, now this story's done.[1]

~~~~~~~~~~~~~~~~~~~~~~~~~~~~~~~~~~~

The Dual Nature of Women

With folk stories, as with dreams, we can understand their contents subjectively, all the symbols portraying aspects of a single person's psyche, but we can also understand tales objectively, as they relate to conditions and relations in the outer world. Here let us talk about the Manawee tale more in terms of relationship between a woman and her mate, keeping in mind that many times "as it is without, it is also within."

This story unravels an old, old secret about women, and it is this: to win the wildish woman's heart, a mate would understand her natural duality through and through. Although we could understand the two women in the tale ethnologically as brides-to-be in a polygamous culture, from an archetypal perspective, this story speaks about the mystery of two powerful feminine forces within a single woman.

The Manawee story contains all the essential facts for being close to the wildish woman. Manawee, through his faithful dog, guesses the two names, the two natures of the feminine. He cannot win unless he solves the mystery. And he must use his own instinctual self—as symbolized by the dog—to accomplish it.

Anyone close to a woman is in fact in the presence of two women; an outer being and an interior *criatura*, one who lives in the topside world, one who lives in the world not so easily seeable. The outer being lives by the light of day and is easily observed. She is often pragmatic, acculturated, and very human. The *criatura*, however, often travels to the surface from far away, often appearing and then as quickly disappearing, yet always leaving behind a feeling: something surprising, original, and knowing.

Understanding this dual nature in women sometimes causes men, and even women themselves, to close their eyes and hail heaven for help. The paradox of women's twin nature is that when one side is more cool in feeling tone, the other side is more hot. When one side is more lingering and rich relationally, the other may be somewhat glacial. Often one side is more happy and elastic, while the other has a longing for "I know not what." One may be sunny, while the other is bittersweet and wistful. These "two-women-who-are-one" are separate but conjoined elements which combine in the psyche in thousands of ways.

The Power of Two

While each side of a woman's nature represents a separate entity with different functions and discriminate knowledge, they must, like the brain with its *corpus callosum*, have a knowing or a translation of one another and therefore function as a whole. If a woman hides one side or favors one side too much, she lives a very lopsided life which does not give her access to her entire power. This is not good. It is necessary to develop both sides.

There is much to be learned about the strength of Two when we examine the symbol of twins. Throughout the world since ancient times, twins have been thought to be endowed with supernatural powers. In some cultures, there is an entire discipline devoted to the balancing of the nature of twins, for they are thought to be two entities which share one soul. Even after their deaths, twins are fed, spoken to, given gifts, and sacrifices.

In various African and Carib communities the symbol of twin sisters is said to possess *juju*—the mystical energy of the soul. Therefore it is required that twins be impeccably taken care of lest a bad fate befall the entire community. One precaution from the hoodoo religion of Haiti requires that twins always be fed exactly the same measured portions in order to summarily allay all jealousy between them, but more so, to prevent the wasting away of one of them, for if one dies, so shall the other, and the special soulfulness they bring to the community will be lost.

Likewise, a woman has tremendous powers when the dual aspects of psyche are consciously recognized and beheld as a unit; held together rather than held apart. The power of Two is very strong and neither side of the duality should be neglected. They need be fed equally, for together they bring an uncanny power to the individual.

I once heard a story from an old African-American man in the mid-South. He came out of an alley as I was sitting amidst the graffiti of an inner-city "park." Some people would call him crazy, for he spoke to anyone and no one. He shuffled along with one finger held out as though to test the wind's direction. *Cuentistas* recognize such persons as having been touched by the gods. In our tradition, we'd call such a man *El bulto*, The Bundle, for souls such as he carry a certain kind of ware and show it to any who will look, anyone who has the eyes to see it and the sense to shelter it.

This particular kindly *El bulto* gave me this story. It is about a certain kind of ancestral transmission. He called the story "One Stick, Two Stick." "This is the way of the old African kings," he whispered.

In the story, an old man is dying, and calls his people to his side. He gives a short, sturdy stick to each of his many offspring, wives, and relatives. "Break the stick," he instructs them. With some effort, they all snap their sticks in half.

"This is how it is when a soul is alone and without anyone. They can be easily broken."

The old man next gives each of his kin another stick, and says, "This is how I would like you to live after I pass. Put your sticks together in bundles of twos and threes. Now, break these bundles in half."

No one can break the sticks when there are two or more in a bundle. The old man smiles. "We are strong when we stand with another soul. When we are with others, we cannot be broken."

Likewise, when both sides of the dual nature are held close together in consciousness, they have tremendous power, and cannot be broken. This is the nature of the psychic duality, of twinning, the two aspects of woman's personality. By itself the more civilized self is fine . . . but somehow lonely. By itself, the wildish self is also fine, but wistful for relationship with the other. The loss of women's psychological, emotional, and spiritual powers comes from separating these two natures from one another and pretending one or the other no longer exists.

This tale can be viewed as being about masculine duality as well as female duality. The Manawee man has his own dual nature: a human nature, and an instinctive nature as symbolized by the dog. His human nature, while sweet and loving, is not enough to win the courtship. It is his dog, a symbol of his instinctual nature, that has the ability to creep near the women and with his keen listening hear their names. It is the dog that learns to overcome superficial seductions and retain the most important knowings. It is Manawee's dog that has sharp hearing and tenacity, that has the instincts to burrow under walls and to find, to chase, and to retrieve valuable ideas.

As in other fairy tales, masculine forces can carry Bluebeardlike or murderous Mr. Fox sorts of energy and thereby attempt to demolish the dual nature of women. That sort of suitor cannot tolerate duality and is looking for perfection, for *the one* truth, *the one* immovable, unchangeable *feminina substancia*, feminine substance, embodied in *the one* perfect woman. Ai! If you meet this kind of person, run the other way as fast as you can. It is better to have a Manawee-type lover both within and without: He is a much better suitor, for he is intensely devoted to the idea of the Two. And the power of the Two is in acting as one integral entity.

So Manawee wishes to touch this most ubiquitous but mysterious combination of soul-life in woman, and he has a sovereignty all of his own. Since he is himself a wildish, natural man, he resonates to and has a taste for the wildish woman.

Among that cumulative tribe of masculine figures in a woman's psyche whom Jungians call *animus*, there is also a Manawee-like attitude, which finds and claims a woman's duality, finding it valuable, courtable, and desirable, instead of devilish, ugly, and to be disdained.[2] Manawee, whether as an internal or external figure, represents a fresh but faith-filled lover whose central desire is to name and understand the mysterious and numinous double in women's nature.

The Power of Name

Naming a force, creature, person, or thing has several connotations. In cultures where names are chosen carefully for their magical or auspicious meanings, to know a person's true name means to know the life path and the soul attributes of that person. And the reason the true name is often kept secret is to protect the owner of the name so that he or she might grow into the power of the name, to shelter it so that no one will either denigrate it or distract from it, and so that one's spiritual authority can develop to its full proportions.

In fairy tales and folktales there are several additional aspects to the name, and these are at work in the tale of Manawee. Although there are some tales wherein the protagonist searches for the name of a malevolent force in order to have power over it, more so the questing after the name is in order to be able to summon that force or person, to call that person close to oneself, and to have relationship with that person.

The latter is the case in the Manawee story. He travels back and forth, back and forth, in sincere efforts to draw the power of "the Two" close to him. He is interested in naming them, *not* in order to seize their power but instead to gain self-power *equal* to theirs.

To know the names means to gain and retain consciousness about the dual nature. Wish as one may, and even with the use of one's might, one cannot have a relationship of depth without knowing the names.

The guessing of the names of the dual nature, of the two sisters, is as difficult a task initially for women as it is for men. But there need not be extensive angst about it. If we are interested to find the names, then we are already on the right path.

And what are the exact names of these two symbolic sisters in a woman's psyche? The names of the dualities of course vary from person to person, but they tend to be opposites of some sort. Like much of the natural world, they at first may seem so vast as to be without pattern or repetition. But close observation of the dual nature, asking after it and hearing its answers will soon reveal a pattern to it all, a pattern that is vast, it is true, but that has a stability like waves ebbing and flowing; its high and low tides are predictable, its deeper currents are mappable.

In the matter of guessing the names, to say a person's name is to make a wish or a blessing over them each time their name is called. We name these dual temperaments in ourselves in order to marry—ego to spirit. This naming and marrying is called, in human words, self-love. When it occurs between two individual persons, it is called loving another.

Manawee guesses and guesses, but cannot guess the names of the twins with his mundane nature alone. The dog, as representative of the intuitive, acts in Manawee's service. Women often crave a mate who has this kind of endurance and the wit to continue trying to understand her deep nature. When she finds a mate of that substance, she will give lifelong loyalty and love.

In the tale, the twins' father acts as the guardian of the mystical pair. He is symbolic of an actual intra-psychic feature which insures the integrity of things "staying together" and not being split apart. It is he who tests the worthiness, the "rightness," of the suitor. It is good for women to have such a watcher.

In this sense it could be said that a healthy psyche tests new elements which apply to it for inclusion; that the psyche has an integrity about it, a screening process. A healthy psyche containing a fatherly watchman does not just admit any old thought, attitude, or person, only those which are sentient or striving to become so.

The father of the two sisters says, "Wait. Until you convince me you are interested in really knowing about the true essence—the true names—you may not have my daughters." The father is saying, You can't have understanding of women's mysteries just for the asking. You must do the work first. You must endure in pursuing this matter. You must divine yourself ever closer to the real truth of this female soul puzzle, this endeavor which is both descent and riddle.

The Tenacious Dog Nature

The little dog in the story shows exactly how psychic tenacity works. Dogs are the magicians of the universe. By their presence alone, they transform grumpy people into grinning people, sad people into less sad people; they engender relationship. As in the ancient Babylonian epic "Gilgamesh," wherein Inkadu, the hairy animal/man, counterbalances Gilgamesh, the too-rational king, the dog is one entire side of man's dualistic nature. He is the woods nature, the one who can track, who knows by sensing what is what.

The dog likes the sisters because they feed him and smile at him. The mystical feminine readily understands and accepts the instinctual nature of the dog. Dogs represent, among other things, he (or she) who loves from the heart easily and long, who forgives effortlessly, who can run long, and fight, if necessary, to the death. The dog nature[3] gives concrete clues to how a mate will win the heart of the dual sisters . . . and the wildish woman—the main clue being, "keep returning."

. Manawee fails to guess the names again and trudges home. But the little dog runs back to the hut of the young women and listens till he hears their names. In the world of archetypes, the dog nature is both psychopomp—messenger between the topside world and the dark-lit world—and chthonic—that of the darker or farther back regions of the psyche, that which has been called the under-world for eons. It is this sensibility that a mate reaches into in order to understand duality.

The dog is similar to the wolf, only a little more civilized, although as we see in the rest of the story, not by much. This little dog as psychopomp represents the instinctive psyche. It hears and sees differently than a human. It travels to levels the ego would never think of by itself. It hears words and instructions that the ego cannot hear. And it follows what it hears.

Once, at a science museum in San Francisco, I entered a chamber filled with microphones and speakers that simulated a dog's hearing. When a palm tree waved in the wind, it sounded like Armageddon; when footsteps approached from far off, it was like a million sacks of cornflakes being crunched right in my ear. The world of the dog is filled with constant cataclysmic sound . . . sound that we, as humans, do not register at all. But the little dog does.

The canid hears outside the range of "human" hearing. This mediumistic—as in medial—aspect of the instinctual psyche intuitively hears the deep work, the deep music, the deep mysteries of the feminine psyche. It is this nature that is able to know the wild nature in women.

Creeping Seductive Appetite

It is not by accident that men and women struggle to find deeper sides of their natures and yet become distracted for any number of reasons, mostly pleasures of various sorts. Some become addicted to those pleasures and stay forever entangled there and never continue with their work.

The little dog is also at first distracted by its appetites. Appetites are often charming little *forajidos*, robbers, dedicated to the theft of time and libido. Yours. Jung remarked that some control must be placed on human appetite. Otherwise, as you can see, one will stop for every bonehock in the road, every pie on a log.

Mates who seek to name the dualities may, like the dog, lose their resolve as they are tempted off the path. This may especially occur if they are feral or starved creatures themselves. Too, they may lose their memory of what they were about. They may be tempted/attacked by something from their own unconscious which wishes to force itself upon women for exploitative gain or wishes to entice women for its own pleasure, or in an effort to banish a hunter's emptiness.

On the way back to his master, the dog is distracted by a luscious bone, and in the process, forgets the young women's names. This episode embodies a very common occurrence in deep psychic work: the distractions of appetite interfere with the primary process. Not a month goes by that I do not hear an analysand saying, "Well, I became distracted from my deep work because I became hot sexually and it took seven days to quench the blaze" or ". . . because I decided this week was just the right time to give all my five hundred houseplants a haircut" or ". . . because I began seven new creative ventures, had a great time at it, and then decided that none of them truly showed real promise and dropped them all."

So you see, the bone on the road is waiting for all of us. It has the luscious stink a dog can hardly refuse. At worst it is likely a favorite addiction, one which already has cost us and cost us. But even if we have failed time and again, we must try again, till we can pass it by and get on with the primary work.

The momentum of deep work is similar to sexual arousal in that it begins from ground zero, accelerates in plateaus, becomes sustained and intense. If the plateaus are interrupted harshly (imagine a loud and unexpected noise), one must begin all over again. There is a similar arousal tension in working with the archetypal layer of the psyche. If the tension is interrupted, one has to start nearly from scratch. So, there are many bones on the road, juicy, nice, interesting, savagely exciting bones. But somehow they cause us to be carried off into an amnesia, to not only forget where we are in the work but to forget what the work was to begin with.

The Koran wisely advises that we will be called upon to account for all the permitted pleasures in life we did not enjoy while on earth. However, too much or even a little bit of a good thing at the wrong time can cause a gross loss of consciousness. Then, instead of a sudden rush of wisdom, we walk about like an absentminded professor muttering, "Now where was I?" It takes weeks, sometimes months, to recover from these distractions of ours.

In the story, the dog runs back to the sisters' hut, again hears their names, and races off once more. This canid has the right instinct to try again and again. But, oh-oh, there's a kumquat pie which distracts him, and he forgets the names again. Another aspect of appetite has assaulted the creature and again drawn him from his task, and although his gut is satisfied, the soul's work is not.

We begin to understand that this process of remaining conscious, and particularly of not giving in to distracting appetites while trying to elicit psychic connection, is a long process, and one that is difficult to hold to. We see the wily little dog trying his damnedest. Yet it is a long way from the deep archetypal unconscious back to the conscious mind. It is a long way down to the names, and a long way back to the surface again. Holding knowledge in consciousness is hard when there are snares along the path.

The kumquat pie and the bone represent distracting seductions that are in their own ways delicious . . . in other words, there are elements of everyone's psyches that are devious, trickerish, and scrumptious. These elements are anti-consciousness; they thrive by keeping things dark and exciting. Sometimes it is hard to remind ourselves that we are holding out for the excitement of the light.

In this story, the dog is the light-bringer; he is trying to bring up conscious connection to the mystical twin nature. "Something" rhythmically attempts to prevent this, something that is unseen but most assuredly is the positioner of bones and the fixer of pies. No doubt this is the dark stranger, another version of the natural predator of the psyche that opposes consciousness. Because of this naturally occurring opposer in the psyche of all persons, even the most healthy psyche is susceptible to losing its place. Remembering the real task, and reminding ourselves over and over in practically mantra fashion, will bring us back to consciousness.

Achieving Fierceness

The little dog learns the names of the women one more time and races back to his master. He ignores the feast on the road and the enticing smells from the bush. Here we see the consciousness of the psyche rising. The instinctive psyche has learned to curb itself, prioritize, and focus. It refuses to be diverted. It is now intent.

But from nowhere a dark thing suddenly jumps out at the little dog. The stranger shakes the dog and shouts, "Tell me those names! What are the names of the young women so I may win them?!" The stranger does not care for duality or the finer points of the psyche. To him the feminine is a possession to be won and nothing more.

The stranger can be personified by an actual person in the outer world or by a negative complex within. It does not matter which, for the devastating effect is the same. This time the dog engages in unrestrained battle. Whether male or female, this occurs in outer life when an incident, a slip of words, an odd thing of some sort, jumps out and tries to make us forget who we are. There is always something in the psyche that tries to rob us of the names. There are many name robbers in the outer world also.

In the story, the little dog fights for its life. Sometimes the only way we learn to hold on to our deeper knowing is because a stranger jumps out. Then we are forced to fight for what we find dear—fight to be serious about what we are about, fight to develop past our superficial spiritual motives, which Robert Bly calls "the desire to feel groovy,"[4] fight to hold on to the deeper knowledge, fight to finish what we have begun.

The little dog fights to keep the names and thusly conquers the repetitive slide into unconsciousness. Once the battle is fought, amazingly the dog has not lost the names, for that is what they were fighting over, knowledge about the wild feminine. Whoever possesses it has a power equal to that of the woman herself. The dog has fought to give this power to the worthy man, Manawee. He has fought to keep this power from an aspect of ancient human nature that would misuse it. The giving of power into the right hands is as important as the finding of the names.

The heroic dog gives the names to Manawee, who presents them to the young women's father. The young women are ready to go away with Manawee. They have all along been waiting for Manawee to discover and retain conscious knowing of their intrinsic natures.

So we see that the two things which prevent progress in these matters are the distractions of one's appetites and the dark stranger—this sometimes being the innate oppressor within the psyche and sometimes a person or situation in the outer world. Regardless, each traveler knows innately how to defeat these looters and marauders. Keep hold of the names, the names are all.

The Interior Woman

Sometimes women become tired and cranky while waiting for their mates to understand them. The women say, "Why can't they know what I think, what I want?" Women become fatigued with asking this question. Yet, there is a solution to this dilemma, a solution which is efficient and effective.

If a woman wants a mate who is responsive in this way, she will reveal to him the secret of women's duality. She will tell him about the interior woman, that one who, added to herself, makes two. She does this by teaching her mate to ask her two deceptively simple questions that will cause her to feel seen, heard, and known.

The first question is this: "What do you want?" Almost everyone asks some version of this, just as a matter of course. But there is yet one more essential question, and that is: "What does your deeper self desire?"

If one overlooks a woman's dual nature and takes a woman at face value, one is in for a big surprise, for when the woman's wildish nature rises from her depths and begins to assert itself, she often has interests, feelings, and ideas which are quite different from those she expressed before.

To securely weave a relationship, a woman will also ask the same two questions of her mate. As women, we learn to poll both sides of our nature and that of others as well. From the information we receive reciprocally from both sides, we can very clearly determine what is valued most and how to respond accordingly.

When a woman consults her own dual nature, she is in the process of looking, canvassing, taking soundings of material that is beyond consciousness, and therefore often astonishing in content and process, and most often very valuable.

To love a woman, the mate must also love her untamed nature.

If she takes a mate who cannot or will not love this other side, she shall surely in some way be dismantled and be left to limp about unrepaired.

So men, as much as women, must name their dual natures. The most valued lover, the most valuable parent, the most valued friend, the most valuable "wilderman," is the one who wishes to learn. Those who are not delighted by learning, those who cannot be enticed into new ideas or experiences, cannot develop past the road post they rest at now. If there is but one force which feeds the root of pain, it is the refusal to learn beyond this moment.

We know that the creature Wild Man is seeking his own earthy woman. Afeared or not, it is an act of deepest love to allow oneself to be stirred by the wildish soul of another. In a world where humans are so afraid of "losing," there are far too many protective walls against being dissolved in the numinosity of another human soul.

The mate for the wildish woman is the one who has a soulful tenacity and endurance, one who can send his own instinctual nature to peek under the tent of a woman's soul-life and comprehend what he sees and hears there. The good match is the man who keeps returning to try to understand, who does not let himself be deterred by the sideshows on the road.

So, the wildish task of the man is to find her true names, and not to misuse that knowledge to seize power over her, but rather to apprehend and comprehend the numinous substance from which she is made, to let it wash over him, amaze him, shock him, even spook him. And to stay with it. And to sing out her names over her. It will make her eyes shine. It will make his eyes shine.

But, lest one rest too soon, there is yet another aspect to naming the dualities, a more fearsome one yet, but one essential to all lovers. While one side of a woman's dual nature might be called Life, Life's "twin" sister is a force named Death. The force called Death is one of the two magnetic forks of the wild nature. If one learns to name the dualities, one will eventually bump right up against the bald skull of the Death nature. They say only heroes can stand it. Certainly the wildish man can stand it. Absolutely, the wildish woman can stand it. They are in fact wholly transformed by it.

So now please meet Skeleton Woman.

CHAPTER 5

Hunting:
When the Heart
Is a Lonely Hunter

Skeleton Woman:
Facing the Life/Death/Life Nature of Love

Wolves are good at relationships. Anyone who has observed wolves sees how deeply they bond. Mates are most often for life. Even though they clash, even though there is dissension, their bonds carry them over and through harsh winters, plentiful springs, long walks, new offspring, old predators, tribal dances, and group sings. The relational needs of humans are no different.

While the instinctual lives of wolves include loyalty and life-long bonds of trust and devotion, humans sometimes have trouble with these matters. If we were to use archetypal terms to describe what determines the strong bonds among wolves, we might surmise that the integrity of their relationships is derived from their synchronization with the ancient pattern of all nature—what I call the Life/Death/Life cycle.

The Life/Death/Life nature is a cycle of animation, development, decline, and death that is always followed by re-animation. This cycle affects all physical life and all facets of psychological life. Everything—the sun, novas, and the moon, as well as the affairs of humans and those of the tiniest creatures, cells and atoms alike—have this fluttering, then faltering, then fluttering again.

Unlike humans, wolves do not deem the ups and downs of life, energy, power, food, nor opportunity as startling or punitive. The

137

peaks and valleys just are, and wolves ride them as efficiently, as fluidly, as possible. The instinctual nature has the miraculous ability to live through all positive boon, all negative consequence, and still maintain relationship to self, to others.

Among wolves, the cycles of nature and fate are met with grace and wit and the endurance to stay tight with one's mate and to live long and as well as can be. But in order for humans to live and give loyalty in this most fit manner, in this way which is most wise, most preserving, and most feeling, one has to go up against the very thing one fears most. There is no way around it, as we shall see. One must sleep with Lady Death.

In wise stories, love is seldom a romantic tryst between two lovers. For instance, some stories from the circumpolar regions describe love as a union of two beings whose strength together enables one or both to enter into communication with the soul-world and to participate in fate as a dance with life and death.

The story I am about to relate to you is a hunting story about love. It is set in the frozen north. To understand this story, we have to see that there, in one of the harshest environs and one of the most stressed hunting cultures in the world, love does not mean a flirtation or a pursuit for simple ego-pleasure, but a visible bond composed of the psychic sinew of endurance, a union which prevails through bounty and austerity, through the most complicated and most simple days and nights. The union of two beings is seen as *angakok* magic in itself, as a relationship through which "the powers that be" become known to both individuals.

But there are requirements for this kind of union. In order to create this enduring love, one invites a third partner to the union. The third partner I call Skeleton Woman. She could also be called Lady Death, and as such, she is another Life/Death/Life figure in one of its many guises. In this form, Lady Death is not a disease, but a deity.

In a relationship she has the role of the oracle who knows when it is time for cycles to begin and end.[1] As such, she is the wildish aspect of relationship, the one of whom men are most terrified . . . and sometimes women also, for when faith in the transformative has been lost, the natural cycles of increase and attrition are feared as well.

To create enduring love, Skeleton Woman must be admitted to the relationship and be embraced by both lovers. Here, in an old Inuit setting and amplified into an original literary story from a short five-line spoken-poem given me by Mary Uukalat, is the Skeleton Woman. Here, too, are the psychic stages for mastery of her embrace. Let us peer at the images which rise from the smoke of this tale.

Skeleton Woman

SHE HAD DONE SOMETHING of which her father disapproved, although no one any longer remembered what it was. But her father had dragged her to the cliffs and thrown her over and into the sea. There, the fish ate her flesh away and plucked out her eyes. As she lay under the sea, her skeleton turned over and over in the currents.

One day a fisherman came fishing, well, in truth many came to this bay once. But this fisherman had drifted far from his home place, and did not know that the local fishermen stayed away, saying this inlet was haunted.

The fisherman's hook drifted down through the water, and caught, of all places, in the bones of Skeleton Woman's rib cage. The fisherman thought, "Oh, now I've really got a big one! Now I really have one!" In his mind he was thinking of how many people this great fish would feed, how long it would last, how long he might be free from the chore of hunting. And as he struggled with this great weight on the end of the hook, the sea was stirred to a thrashing froth, and his kayak bucked and shook, for she who was beneath struggled to disentangle herself. And the more she struggled, the more she tangled in the line. No matter what she did, she was inexorably dragged upward, tugged up by the bones of her own ribs.

The hunter had turned to scoop up his net, so he did not see her bald head rise above the waves, he did not see the little coral creatures glinting in the orbs of her skull, he did not see the crustaceans on her old ivory teeth. When he turned back with his net, her entire body, such as it was, had come to the surface and was hanging from the tip of his kayak by her long front teeth.

"Agh!" cried the man, and his heart fell into his knees, his eyes hid in terror on the back of his head, and his ears blazed bright red. "Agh!" he screamed, and knocked her off the prow with his oar and began paddling like a demon toward shoreline. And not realizing she was tangled in his line, he was frightened all the more for she appeared to stand upon her toes while chasing him all the way to shore. No matter which way he zigged his kayak, she stayed right behind, and her breath rolled over the water in clouds of steam, and her arms flailed out as though to snatch him down into the depths.

"Aggggggghhhh!" he wailed as he ran aground. In one leap he was out of his kayak, clutching his fishing stick and running, and the coral-white corpse of Skeleton Woman, still snagged in the fishing line, bumpety-bumped behind right after him. Over the rocks he ran, and she followed. Over the frozen tundra he ran and she kept right up. Over the meat laid out to dry he ran, cracking it to pieces as his mukluks bore down.

Throughout it all she kept right up, in fact grabbed some of the frozen fish as she was dragged behind. This she began to eat, for she had not gorged in a long, long time. Finally, the man reached his snowhouse and dove right into the tunnel and on hands and knees scrabbled his way into the interior. Panting and sobbing he lay there in the dark, his heart a drum, a mighty drum. Safe at last, oh so safe, yes safe, thank the Gods, Raven, yes, thank Raven, yes, and all-bountiful Sedna, safe . . . at . . . last.

Imagine when he lit his whale oil lamp, there she—it—lay in a tumble upon his snow floor, one heel over her shoulder, one knee inside her rib cage, one foot over her elbow. He could not say later what it was, perhaps the firelight softened her features, or the fact that he was a lonely man. But a feeling of some kindness came into his breathing, and slowly he reached out his grimy hands and, using words softly like a mother to a child, began to untangle her from the fishing line.

"Oh, na, na, na." First he untangled the toes, then the ankles. "Oh, na, na, na." On and on he worked into the night, until dressing her in furs to keep her warm, Skeleton Woman's bones were all in the order a human's should be.

He felt into his leather cuffs for his flint, and used some of his hair to light a little more fire. He gazed at her from time to time as he oiled the precious wood of his fishing stick and rewound the gut line. And she in the furs uttered not a word—she did not dare—lest this hunter take her out and throw her down to the rocks and break her bones to pieces utterly.

The man became drowsy, slid under his sleeping skins, and soon was dreaming. And sometimes as humans sleep, you know, a tear escapes from the dreamer's eye; we never know what sort of dream causes this, but we know it is either a dream of sadness or longing. And this is what happened to the man.

The Skeleton Woman saw the tear glisten in the firelight, and she became suddenly soooo thirsty. She tinkled and clanked and crawled over to the sleeping man and put her mouth to his tear. The single tear was like a river and she drank and drank and drank until her many-years-long thirst was slaked.

Then, while lying beside him, she reached inside the sleeping man and took out his heart, the mighty drum. She sat up and banged on both sides of it: *Bom, Bomm! . . . Bom, Bomm!*

As she drummed, she began to sing out "Flesh, flesh, flesh! Flesh, flesh, flesh!" And the more she sang, the more her body filled out with flesh. She sang for hair and good eyes and nice fat hands. She sang the divide between her legs, and breasts long enough to wrap for warmth, and all the things a woman needs.

And when she was done, she also sang the sleeping man's clothes off and crept into his bed with him, skin against skin. She returned the great drum, his heart, to his body, and that is how they awakened, wrapped one around the other, tangled from their night together, in another way now, a good and lasting way.

The people who cannot remember how she came to her first ill-fortune say she and the fisherman went away and were consistently well fed by the creatures she had known in her life underwater. The people say that it is true and that is all they know.

Death in the House of Love

Inability to face and untangle the Skeleton Woman is what causes many love relationships to fail. To love, one must not only be strong, but wise. Strength comes from the spirit. Wisdom comes from experience with Skeleton Woman.

As we see in the tale, if one wishes to be fed for life, one must face and develop a relationship with the Life/Death/Life nature. When we have that, we are no longer bumbling along fishing for fantasies, but are made wise about the necessary deaths and startling births that create true relationship. When we face Skeleton Woman we learn that passion is not something to go "get" but rather something generated in cycles and given out. It is Skeleton Woman who demonstrates that a shared living together through all increase and decrease, through all endings and beginnings, is what creates an unparalleled devotional love.

This story is an apt metaphor for the problem of modern love, the fear of the Life/Death/Life nature, the Death aspect in particular. In much of western culture, the original character of the Death nature has been covered over by various dogmas and doctrines until it is split off from its other half, Life. We have erroneously been trained to accept a broken form of one of the most profound and basic aspects of the wild nature. We have been taught that death is always followed by more death. It is simply not so, death is always in the process of incubating new life, even when one's existence has been cut down to the bones.

Rather than seeing the archetypes of Death and Life as opposites, they must be held together as the left and right side of a single thought. It is true that within a single love relationship there are many endings. Yet, somehow and somewhere in the delicate layers of the being that is created when two people love one another, there is both a heart and breath. While one side of the heart empties, the other fills. When one breath runs out, another begins.

If one believes that the Life/Death/Life force has no stanza beyond death, it is no wonder that some humans are frightened of commitment. They are terrified to go through even one ending. They cannot bear to pass from the veranda into the inner rooms. They are fearful, for they sense that there in the breakfast room of the house of love sits Lady Death, tapping her toe, folding and refolding her gloves. Before her is a work list, on one side what is living, on the other, what is dying. She means to carry through. She means to maintain a balance.

The archetype of the Life/Death/Life force is grossly misunderstood throughout many modern cultures. Some no longer understand that Lady Death represents an essential creation pattern. Through her loving ministrations, life is renewed. In many folklores the female figures of death often receive much sensational press: she carries a scythe and "harvests" the unsuspecting, she kisses her victims and leaves their corpses scattered behind her, or she drowns people and then wails long into the night.

But in other cultures, such as East Indian and Mayan, which have preserved teachings about the wheel of life *and* death, Lady Death enfolds the already dying, easing their pain, giving them comfort. In *curanderisma*, she is said to turn the baby in the womb to the headfirst position so it can be born. She is said to guide the hands of the midwife, to open the pathways of the mother's milk in the breasts, as well as to comfort anyone who weeps alone. Rather than vilifying her, those who know her in full cycle respect her largess and her lessons.

Archetypally, the Life/Death/Life nature is a basic component of the instinctive nature. This is personified through world myth and folklore as *Dama del Muerte*, Lady Death; *Coatlicue*; *Hel*; *Berchta*; *Ku'an Yin*; *Baba Yaga*; Lady in White; Compassionate Nightshade; and as a group of women called by the Greeks *Graeae*, the Gray Ladies. From the *Banshee*, in her carriage made of night-cloud, to *La Llorona*, the weeping woman at the river, from the dark angel who brushes humans with a wing tip, collapsing them into an ecstasy, to swampfire that appears when death is imminent, stories are filled with these remnants of the old creation Goddess personifications.[2]

Much of our knowledge of the Life/Death/Life nature is contaminated by our fear of death. Therefore our abilities to move with the cycles of this nature are quite frail. These forces do not "do something" to us. They are not thieves who rob us of the things we cherish. This nature is not a hit-and-run driver who smashes what we value.

No, no, the Life/Death/Life forces are part of our own nature, part of an inner authority that knows the steps, knows the dance of Life and Death. It is composed of the aspects of ourselves who know when something can, should, and must be born and when it must die. It is a deep teacher if we can only learn its tempo. Rosario Castellanos, the Mexican mystic and ecstatic poet, writes about surrender to the forces that govern life and death:

> . . . dadme la muerte que me falta . . .
> . . . give me the death I need . . .

Poets understand that there is nothing of value without death. Without death there are no lessons, without death there is no dark for the diamond to shine from. While those who are initiated are unafraid of Lady Death, the culture often encourages that we throw Skeleton Woman over the cliffs, for not only is she fearsome, it takes too long to learn her ways. A soul-less world encourages faster, quicker, thrashing about to find the one filament that seems to be *the one* that will burn forever and right now. However, the miracle we are seeking takes time: time to find it, time to bring it to life.

The modern search for a perpetual motion machine rivals the search for a perpetual love machine. It is not surprising that people trying to love become confused and harried, as in the story "The Red Shoes," and dance a mad dance, unable to stop the frantic jig, and whirl right past the things they, in their deepest hearts, cherish most.

Yet, there is another way, a better way, which takes into account human foibles, fears, and quirks. And as so often happens in the cycles of individuation, most of us just stumble over it.

The First Phases of Love

The Accidental Finding of Treasure

In all tales there is material that can be understood as a mirror reflecting the illnesses or the well-being of one's culture or one's own inner life. Also in tales there are mythic themes that can be understood as describing stages of and instruction for maintaining balance in both inner and outer worlds.

While the Skeleton Woman could be interpreted as representing the movements within a single psyche, I find this tale most valuable when understood as a series of seven tasks that teach one soul to love another deeply and well. These are: discovering another person as a kind of spiritual treasure, even though one may not at first realize what one has found. Next in most love relationships comes the chase and the hiding, a time of hopes and fears for both. Then comes the untangling and understanding of the Life/Death/Life aspects of the relationship and the development of compassion for the task. Next come the relaxing into trust, the ability to rest in the presence and goodwill of the other, and after that, a time of sharing both future dreams and past sadness, these being the beginning of healing archaic wounds with regard to love. Then, the use of the heart to sing up new life, and finally, the intermingling of body and soul.

The first task, the finding of treasure, is found in dozens of tales throughout the world that describe the catching of a creature from beneath the sea. When this occurs in the narrative, we always know that a big struggle will soon take place between what lives in the topside world and what lives or has been repressed into the underworld. In this tale, the fisherman snags more than he ever expected. "Oh, it's a big one," he thinks as he turns to gain his net.

He does not realize that he is bringing up the scariest treasure he will ever know, that he is bringing up more than he can yet handle. He does not know that he will have to come to terms with it, that he is about to have all his powers tested. And worse, he does not know that he does not know. That is the state of all lovers at the beginning: they are blind as bats.

Humans who do not know any better have the proclivity to approach love the same way the fisherman in the story approaches the hunt: "Ah, I hope I get a big one, one that will feed me for a long time to come, one that will excite me, make my life easier, one I can brag about to all the other hunters back home."

This is the natural progression of the naive or famished hunter. The very young, the uninitiated, the hungry, and the wounded have values that revolve around the finding and the winning of trophies. The very young truly do not know what they are seeking yet, the hungry seek sustenance, and the wounded seek consolation for previous losses. Yet all will have treasure "happen upon" them.

When one is in the company of the great powers of the psyche, in this case the Life/Death/Life woman, and one is naive, then one is sure to get more than what one is fishing for. So often we entertain the fantasy of being fed from the deep nature, through a love affair, a job, or by money, and we hope these feedings will last for a long time. We would like not to do any further work. In truth, there are even times when we would like to be fed without doing much work at all. In reality, we know nothing of value ever develops this way. But we wish it anyway.

To lay inert and only dreaming of a perfect love is easy. It is an anesthetization from which we might never recover but for ruthlessly snagging something valuable, yet outside our awareness. For the naive and wounded, the miracle of the psyche's ways is that even if you are halfhearted, irreverent, didn't mean to, didn't really hope to, don't want to, feel unworthy to, aren't ready for it, you will accidentally stumble upon treasure anyway. Then it is your soul's work to not overlook what has been brought up, to recognize treasure as treasure no matter how unusual its form, and to consider carefully what to do next.

The fisherman motif shares some archetypal symbolism with that of the hunter, and these two represent, among many things, the psychological elements of humans that seek to know, that strive to nourish self through merging with the instinctual nature. In stories, as in life, the hunter and fisherman begin their quest in one of three ways: in a sacred, or mean-spirited, or bumbling manner. In the Skeleton Woman story, we can see that the fisherman is a little on the bumbling side. He is not mean-spirited but he does not exactly have sacred attitude or intention either.

Sometimes lovers begin this way too. At the beginning of a relationship they are only fishing for a little excitement, or a little "help me make it through the night" antidepressant. Without realizing it, they unwittingly enter a part of their own and the other person's psyches in which Skeleton Woman resides. While their egos may be fishing for fun, this psychical space is sacred ground for Skeleton Woman. If we troll these waters, we are guaranteed to hook her for certain.

The fisherman thinks he is pursuing simple nourishment and nurture, when in fact, he is bringing up the entire elemental feminine nature, the neglected Life/Death/Life nature. It cannot be overlooked, for wherever new life begins, the Death Queen shows up. And when this occurs, at least for the moment, people pay rapt and fearful attention.

In the opening motif—that of a woman lying under the ocean—Skeleton Woman is similar to Sedna,[3] a Life/Death/Life figure from Inuit mythology. Sedna is the great deformed creation Goddess who lives in the Inuit underworld. Sedna's father threw her over the edge of his kayak, for unlike other dutiful daughters of the tribe, she had run off with a dog-man. Like the father in the fairy tale "The Handless Maiden," Sedna's father chopped off her hands. Her fingers and limbs sank to the bottom of the sea, where they became fish and seals and other life forms that sustained the Inuit ever after.

What was left of Sedna sank to the bottom of the sea. There she became all bones and long, long hair. In the Inuit rite, earthbound shamans swim down to her, bringing peace-food to quiet her snarling dog-husband and guardian. The shamans comb her long, long hair while singing to her, begging her to heal the soul or body of a person above, for she is the great *angakok*, magician; she is the great northern gate of Life and Death.

Skeleton Woman, who spent an eon lying under the water, can also be understood as a woman's unused and misused Life/Death/Life force. In her vital and resurrected form, she governs the intuitive and emotive abilities to complete the life cycles of birthings and endings, grievings and celebrations. She is the one who peers at things. She can tell when it is time for a place, a thing, an act, a group, or a relationship to die. This gift, this psychological sensitivity, awaits those who would lift her to consciousness through the act of loving another.

A part of every woman and every man resists knowing that in all love relationships Death must have her share. We pretend we can love without our illusions about love dying, pretend we can go on without our superficial expectations dying, pretend we can progress and that our favorite flushes and rushes will never die. But in love, psychically, everything becomes picked apart, everything. The ego does not want it to be so. Yet it is how it is meant to be, and the person of a deep and wildish nature is undeniably drawn to the task.

What dies? Illusion dies, expectations die, greed for having it all, for.wanting to have all be beautiful only, all this dies. Because love always causes a descent into the Death nature, we can see why it takes abundant self-power and soulfulness to make that commitment. When one commits to love, one also commits to the revivification of the essence of Skeleton Woman and all her teachings.

The fisherman in the story is slow to realize the nature of what he has caught. This is true of everyone at first. It is hard to realize what you are doing when you are fishing in the unconscious. If you are inexperienced, you do not know that down there lives the Death nature. Once you find out what you are dealing with, your impulse is to throw her back. We become like the mythical fathers who throw their wild daughters out of the kayak and into the sea.

We know that relationships sometimes falter when they move from the anticipatory stage to the stage of facing what is really on the end of one's hook. This is as true of the relationship between a mother and her eighteen-month-old child as it is between parents and their teenager, as between friends, as that between lovers of a lifetime or of just a little time. The relationship begun in all goodwill flaps and sways, and sometimes staggers, when the "sweetheart" stage is over. Then, instead of enacting a fantasy, the more challenging relationship begins in earnest and all one's craft and wisdom must be called into action.

The Skeleton Woman who lies under the water represents an inert form of deep instinctual life, which knows by heart the creating of Life, the creating of Death. If lovers insist on a life of forced gaiety, perpetual pleasuramas, and other forms of deadening intensity, if they insist on sexual *Donner und Blitz* thunder and lightning all the time, or a torrent of the delectable and no strife at all, there goes the Life/Death/Life nature right over the cliff, drowned in the sea again.

Refusing to allow all the cycles of life and death in the love relationship causes the Skeleton Woman nature to be ripped from her psychic lodgings and drowned. Then the love relationship takes on a strained ". . . let us never be sad, let us always have fun" face to be maintained at all costs. The soul of the relationship sinks out of sight, set to drift under water, senseless and useless.

Skeleton Woman is always thrown over the cliff when one or both lovers cannot stand her or understand her. She is thrown over the cliff when we misapprehend the use of transformative cycles: when things must die and be replaced by others. If lovers cannot stand these Life/Death/Life processes, they cannot love one another over and beyond hormonal aspirations.

Throwing this mysterious nature over the cliff always causes the woman lover, and the soulful force in men, to become a skeleton, bereft of a genuine love or nourishment. As a woman often takes keen notice of biological and emotional cycles, the life and death cycles are at the center of her concern. Since there can be little new life without a decline in that which has gone previously, lovers who insist on attempting to keep everything at a psyche-scintillating peak will spend their days in an increasingly ossified relationship. The desire to force love to live on in its most positive form only is what causes love ultimately to fall over dead, and for good.

The fisherman's challenge is to face Lady Death, her embrace, and her life and death cycles. Unlike other tales in which an underwater creature is captured but then released, thereby granting the fisherman a wish in gratitude, Lady Death is not letting go, Lady Death is not graciously granting any wishes. She surfaces, like it or not, for without her there can be no real knowledge of life, and without that knowing, there can be no fealty, no real love or devotion. Love costs. It costs bravery. It costs going the distance, as we shall see.

I see a phenomenon time and again in lovers regardless of gender. It goes something like this: two people begin a dance to see if they would care to love one another. Suddenly, Skeleton Woman is accidentally hooked. Something in the relationship begins diminishing and slides into entropy. Often the painful pleasure of sexual excitement is abating, or one sees the other's frail, injured underside, or sees the other as "not quite trophy material," and that's when the bald and yellow-toothed old girl rises to the surface.

It seems so gruesome, yet this is the premier time when there is a real opportunity to show courage and to know love. To love means to stay with. It means to emerge from a fantasy world into a world where sustainable love is possible, face to face, bones to bones, a love of devotion. To love means to stay when every cell says "run!"

When lovers are able to tolerate the Life/Death/Life nature, when they are able to understand it as a continuum—as a night between two days—and as *the* force that creates a love that endures a lifetime, they are able to face the Skeleton Woman in the relationship. Then together they are strengthened, and both are called to deeper understanding of the two worlds they live in, one the mundane world, the other, the world of spirit.

During my twenty-plus years of practice, men and women have burrowed into my sofa saying with happy terror, "I met someone—I didn't mean to, I was just minding my own business, I wasn't looking—and wham! I met this someone with a capital *S. Now* what am I going to do?" As they continue to nurture the new relationship, they begin to cower. They shrink, they worry. Are they having love anxiety over this person? No. They are feeling fearful because they are beginning to glimpse a bald skull rising from beneath the waves of their passion. Ai! What shall they do?

I tell them this is a magic time. It does little to calm them. I tell them we shall now see something wonderful. They have little faith. I tell them to hold on, and this they are able to do, but barely. Before I know it, from the viewpoint of the analysis, the little boat of their love relationship is rowing faster and faster. It careens into shore, and before you can say jackrabbit, they are running for their lives, and as analyst I am running along beside them trying to put a word in, while guess-who bumpety-bumps along behind.

For most, when first confronting Skeleton Woman, the impulse is to run like the wind, and as far away as possible. Even running is part of the process. It is only human to do so, but not for long and not forever.

The Chase and the Hiding

The Death nature has an odd habit of surfacing in love affairs just at the time we feel we have won over a lover, just as we feel we have landed "a big fish." That's when the Life/Death/Life nature surfaces and scares everyone sideways. That is when more contortions go on about why love cannot, will not, should not "work" for either party concerned. That is where all the diving into the burrow is done. It is an effort to become invisible. Invisible to the lover? No. Invisible to the Skeleton Woman. That is what all the running and hiding is about. But, as we see, there is nowhere to hide.

Rational psyche goes fishing for something deep and not only lands it but is so shocked it can barely stand it. Lovers have a sense that something is chasing them. Sometimes they think it is the other who is doing the chasing. In reality, it is Skeleton Woman. At first, when we learn to truly love, we misunderstand many things. We think the other is chasing us, when in fact our intention to relate to another human being in a special way is what hooks Skeleton Woman so she cannot escape from us. Wherever love is nascent, the Life/Death/Life force will always surface. Always.

So here are the fisherman and the Skeleton Woman, all tangled up with each other. As Skeleton Woman bumps along behind the terrified fisherman, she begins a primitive participation in life; she becomes hungry and eats dried fish. Later, as she comes even more to life, she will quench her thirst with the fisherman's tear.

We see this odd phenomenon in all love affairs: the faster he runs, the more she picks up speed. When one or the other lover attempts to run from the relationship, the relationship is paradoxically invested with more life. And the more life that is created, the more frightened the fisherman becomes. And the more he runs, the more life is created. This phenomenon is one of life's central tragi-comedies.

One person in such a situation dreamed of meeting a woman/lover whose soft body opened like a cabinet. Inside her body cavity were embryos shining and throbbing, daggers on shelves dripping with blood, and bags packed with the first green color of spring. The dreamer was given great pause, for this was a dream about the Life/Death/Life nature.

These glimpses into the interiority of Skeleton Woman cause the lovers-in-training to seize their fishing sticks and hie across the land at breakneck speed in an effort to put as much distance as possible between themselves and her. Skeleton Woman is great and mysterious, she is dazzlingly numinous. Psychically, she stretches from horizon to horizon and from heaven to hell. She is much to embrace. Yet, it is no wonder people run to embrace her. What one fears can strengthen, can heal.

The running-and-hiding phase is the time during which lovers try to rationalize their fear of the Life/Death/Life cycles of love. They say, "I can do better with someone else," or "I don't want to give up my (fill in the blank)___," or "I don't want to change my life," or "I don't want to face my wounds or anyone else's," or "I'm not ready yet," or "I don't want to be transformed without first knowing in absolute detail what I will look like/feel like afterward."

It is a time when thoughts are all jumbled together, when one makes a desperate dive for shelter, and the heart beats, not from cherishing and being cherished as much as from abject terror. To be trapped by Lady Death! Ai! The horror of meeting the Life/Death/Life force face-to-face! Double Ai!

Some make the mistake of thinking they are running away from a relationship with the lover. They are not. They are not running away from love, or the pressures of the relationship. They are trying to outrun the mysterious Life/Death/Life force. Psychology diagnoses this as "fear of intimacy, fear of commitment." But those are only symptoms. The deeper issue is one of misbelief and distrust. Those who run away forever fear to truly live according to the cycles of the wild and integral nature.

So here the Death Woman chases the man across water, across the boundary of the unconscious to the conscious land mass of the mind. The conscious psyche becomes aware of what it has caught and tries desperately to outrun it. We do this constantly in our lives. Something fearsome raises its head. We aren't paying attention and keep pulling it up, thinking it is some booty. It is a trove, but not the kind we've imagined. It is a treasure we've unfortunately been taught to fear, So we attempt to run away or throw it back, or prettify it and make it what it is not. But this will not work. Eventually, we all have to kiss the hag.

The same process follows in love. We want only beauty but wind up facing the "baddie" instead. We push Skeleton Woman away, but she proceeds. We run. She follows. She is the great teacher we have been saying we want. "No, not this teacher!" we shriek when she arrives. We want a different one. Too bad. This is the teacher everyone gets.

There is a saying that when the student is ready the teacher appears. This means the interior teacher surfaces when the soul, not the ego, is ready. This teacher comes whenever the soul calls—and thank goodness, for the ego is never fully ready. If it were solely up to the ego's readiness to draw this teacher to us, we would remain essentially teacherless for life. We are blessed, since the soul continues transmitting its desire regardless of the ever-changing opinions of our egos.

People fear that when things become tangled and frightening in love relationships that the end is near, but this is not so. Because this is an archetypal matter and because Skeleton Woman does the work of Fate, the hero *is supposed to* take off across the horizon, the Death Woman *is supposed to* come right along behind, the lover-in-training *is supposed to* dive into his little hut and gasp and choke and hope he is safe. And Skeleton Woman *is supposed to* follow him right into his safe haven. He *is supposed to* untangle her, and so forth.

For modern lovers the idea of "taking space" is like the fisherman's little snowhouse, where he thinks he is safe. Sometimes this fear of confronting the death nature is distorted into "begging off," trying to keep only the pleasurable sides of the relationship going without dealing with Skeleton Woman. That will never work.

It causes lovers who are not "taking space" immense anxiety, for they themselves are willing to meet Skeleton Woman. They have primed themselves, they have reinforced themselves, they are attempting to keep their fears balanced. And now, just as they are ready to untangle this mystery, just as one or the other is about to drum on the heart and sing up a life together, one lover cries "Not yet, not yet" or "No, not ever."

There is a vast difference between the need for solitude and renewal, and the desire to "take space" to avoid the inevitable intercourse with Skeleton Woman. But intercourse, meaning exchange with and acceptance of the Life/Death/Life nature, *is* the next step in order to strengthen one's ability to love. Those who enter into relationship with her will gain an enduring skill for love. Those who won't, won't. There is no way around it.[4]

All the "not readies," all the "I need times," are understandable, but only for a short while. The truth is that there is never a "completely ready," there is never a really "right time." As with any descent to the unconscious, there comes a time when one simply hopes for the best, pinches one's nose, and jumps into the abyss. If this were not so, we would not have needed to create the words *heroine*, *hero*, or *courage*.

The work of learning the Life/Death/Life nature has to be done. Put off, Skeleton Woman sinks beneath the water, but will rise again and again and give chase again and again. It is her work to do this. It is our work to learn. If one wishes to love, there is no getting around it. The work of embracing her is a *task*. Without a task that challenges, there can be no transformation. Without a task there is no real sense of satisfaction. To love pleasure takes little. To love truly takes a hero who can manage his own fear.

Granted, many, many people come to this "escape-and-hide" stage. Some unfortunately arrive here over and over again. The entrance to this burrow is rutted with all the scrambling. But those who care to love emulate the fisherman. They strive to light the fire and face the Life/Death/Life nature. They contemplate what they fear, and paradoxically, respond with both conviction and wonder.

Untangling the Skeleton

The Skeleton Woman tale contains a "suitor test" theme. In a suitor test, lovers must prove their rightful intentions and powers, these usually demonstrating that they have the *cojones* or *ovarios* to face a powerful and fearsome numinosity of some sort . . .

though here we call it the Life/Death/Life nature, others might call it an aspect of the Self, or the spirit of Love, yet others might say God or *Gracia*, a spirit of energy, or any number of appellations.

The fisherman shows his rightful intent, his powers, and his increasing involvement with Skeleton Woman by untangling her. He looks at her all bent this way and that and he sees in her a glimmer of something, he knows not what. He had run from her, panting and sobbing. Now he thinks to touch her. She is touching his heart in some way just by being. When we comprehend the loneliness of the Life/Death/Life nature within the psyche, that one, who through no fault of her own, is constantly thrown away . . . then perhaps we too can be touched by her travail.

If it is love we are making, even though we are apprehensive or frightened, we are willing to untangle the bones of the Death nature. We are willing to see how it all goes together. We are willing to touch the not-beautiful[5] in another, and in ourselves. Behind this challenge is a cunning test from the Self. It is found even more clearly in tales where the beautiful appears ugly in order to test someone's character.

In the tale "Diamonds, Rubies, and Pearls," a good but reviled stepdaughter draws water for a wealthy stranger and is rewarded by having diamonds, rubies, and pearls spill from her mouth when she speaks. The stepmother orders her own lazy daughters to stand at the same well and wait upon the wealthy stranger. But this time a stranger in rags approaches. When she begs for a dipper of water the evil daughters haughtily refuse. The stranger rewards them by causing snakes, toads, and lizards to fall from their mouths ever after.

In fairy-tale justice, as in the deep psyche, kindness to that which seems less, is rewarded by good, and refusal to do good for one who is not beautiful, is reviled and punished. It is the same in the great feeling states such as love. When we enlarge or extend ourselves to touch the not-beautiful, we are rewarded. If we spurn the not-beautiful, we are severed from real life and left out in the cold.

For some, it is easier to think higher, more beautiful thoughts and to touch those things that positively transcend us than to touch, help, and assist the not-so-positive. Even more so, as the story illustrates, it is easy to turn away the not-beautiful and feel falsely righteous about it. This is the love problem of dealing with Skeleton Woman.

What is the not-beautiful? Our own secret hunger to be loved is the not-beautiful. Our disuse and misuse of love is the not-beautiful. Our dereliction in loyalty and devotion is unlovely, our sense of soul-separateness is homely, our psychological warts, inadequacies, misunderstandings, and infantile fantasies are the not-beautiful. Additionally, the Life/Death/Life nature, which births, destroys, incubates, and births again, is considered by our cultures the not-beautiful.

To untangle Skeleton Woman is to understand that conceptual error and to set it aright. To untangle Skeleton Woman is to understand that love does not mean all glimmering candles and increase. To untangle Skeleton Woman means that one finds heartening rather than fear in the darkness of regeneration. It means balm for old wounds. It means changing our ways of seeing and being to reflect the health rather than dearth of soul.

To love, we touch the basic and not-so-lovely bony woman, untangling the sense of this nature for ourselves, bringing her back to order, letting her live again. It is not enough to haul the unconscious to the surface, not even enough to accidentally drag her home. It stops the progression of love to be afeared or disdainful of her for very long.

Untangling the mystery of the Skeleton Woman begins to break the spell—that is, the fear that one will be consumed, made dead forever. Archetypally, to untangle something requires a descent, the following of a labyrinth down into the underworld or to the place where matters are revealed in entirely new ways. One must follow what at first appears to be a convoluted process, but in effect is a profound pattern for renewal. In fairy tales, to loosen the girdle, undo the knot, untie, and untangle means to begin to understand something previously closed to us, to understand its applications and uses, to become mage-like, a knowing soul.

When the fisherman untangles Skeleton Woman, he begins to have "hands-on" knowledge of Life's and Death's articulations. The skeleton is an excellent image for the Life/Death/Life nature. As a psychic image, the skeleton is composed of hundreds of small and large odd-shaped sticks and knobs in continuous harmonious relationship to one another. When one bone turns, the rest turn, even if imperceptibly. The Life/Death/Life cycles are like that exactly. When Life moves, the bones of Death move sympathetically. When Death moves, the bones of Life begin to turn too.

Also, when one tiny bone is out of place, chipped, spurred, subluxed, it hurts the integrity of the whole. When the Life/Death/Life nature in oneself or in a relationship is suppressed, the same occurs. One's life limps along, catches, hobbles, protects movement. When there is hurt to these structures and cycles, there is always interruption of libido. Love is not possible then. We lie under the water; just bones, drifting back and forth.

To untangle this nature means to learn her attenuations, habits, movements. It means to learn the cycles of life and death, to memorize them and so to see how they all go together, how they are all a single organism, just as the skeleton is a single organism.

Fear is a poor excuse for not doing the work. We are all afraid. It is nothing new. If you are alive, you are fearful. Among the Inuit, Raven is the trickster. In his undeveloped side, he is a creature of appetite. He likes pleasure only, attempts to avoid all uncertainty and the fears that uncertainty brings. He is a good deal cautious and a good deal greedy, both. He is fearful if something does not immediately look fulfilling. He pounces when it does.

He likes bright abalone shell, silver beads, endless vittles, gossip, and warm sleeps over the smoke hole. The lover-to-be may be like Raven who wants "a sure thing." Like Raven, the ego is afraid passion will end, and tries to avoid the end of the meal, the end of the fire, the end of the day, and an end to pleasure. Raven, like ego, becomes wily, and always to his detriment, for when he forgets his soul, he loses his power.

The ego fears that if we admit the Life/Death/Life nature into our lives, we will never be happy again. Have we been so very perfectly happy all along, ai? No. But the undeveloped ego is very simple, like an unsocialized child, and not particularly a happy-go-lucky child either; rather more like a child who is watching all the time to see which slice is the biggest, which bed the softest, which lover the most handsome.

Three things differentiate living from the soul versus living from ego only. They are: the ability to sense and learn new ways, the tenacity to ride a rough road, and the patience to learn deep love over time. The ego, however, has a penchant and a proclivity to avoid learning. Patience is not ego's strong suit. Enduring in relationship is not Raven's forte. So it is not from the ever-changing ego that we love another, but rather from the wild soul.

"A wild patience," as poet Adrienne Rich[6] puts it, is required in order to untangle the bones, to learn the meaning of Lady Death, to have the tenacity to stay with her. It would be a mistake to think that it takes a muscle-bound hero to accomplish this. It does not. It takes a heart that is willing to die and be born and die and be born again and again.

The untangling of Skeleton Woman reveals that she is ancient, and old beyond discriminate time. It is she, Lady Death, who measures energy versus distance, she who weighs time versus libido, she who hefts spirit versus survival. She meditates on it, she studies it, she considers, and then she moves to invest it with a spark or two, or a sudden blaze of wildfire, or to tamp it down a bit, bank it down, or put out its life altogether. She knows what is required. She knows when it is time.

In untangling her we acquire the ability to sense what comes next, to better comprehend how all the aspects of nature's psyche interrelate, how we can participate. To untangle her means to gain articulate knowledge of self and other. It means to strengthen our ability to follow the phases, projects, eras of incubation, birthing, and transformations peaceably and with as much grace as we can marshal.

So in this sense, a lover who once was rather artless about love becomes far better at it through having observed this Skeleton Woman, and from having sorted her bones. As one begins to ascertain the patterns of Life/Death/Life, one can anticipate the cycles of the relationship in terms of increase following deficit and attrition following abundance.

A person who has untangled Skeleton Woman knows patience, knows better how to wait. He is not shocked or afraid of spareness. He is not overwhelmed by fruition. His needs to attain, to "have right now," are transformed into a finer craft of finding all facets of relationship, observing how cycles of relationship work together. He is not afraid to relate to the beauty of fierceness, the beauty of the unknown, the beauty of the not-beautiful. And in learning and working at all these, he becomes the quintessential wild lover.

How does a man learn these things? How does anyone learn them? Enter into direct dialogue with the Life/Death/Life nature by listening to the inner voice that is not ego. Learn by asking the Life/Death/Life nature direct questions about love and loving and then listen to her answers. Through all, we learn to not be misled by the nagging voice at the back of the mind that says, "This is silly . . . I'm just making this all up." We learn to ignore that voice and listen to what is heard beyond that. We learn to follow what we hear—all those things that bring us closer to acute awareness, the love of devotion, and a clear view of the soul.

It is good to make a meditative and daily practice of untangling the Life/Death/Life nature over and over again. The fisherman sings a little one-line song over and over to aid the untangling. It is a song to help awareness, to help untangle the Skeleton Woman nature. We do not know what he is singing. We can only guess. When we are untangling this nature, it would be good for us to sing something like this: What must I give more death to today, in order to generate more life? What do I know should die, but am hesitant to allow to do so? What must die in me in order for me to love? What not-beauty do I fear? Of what use is the power of the not-beautiful to me today? What should die today? What should live? What life am I afraid to give birth to? If not now, when?

If we sing the song of consciousness till we feel the burn of truth, we throw a burst of fire into the darkness of psyche so we can see what we're doing . . . what we're truly doing, not what we wish to think we're doing. This is the untangling of one's feelings and the beginning of understanding why love and life are to be lived by the bones.

To face Skeleton Woman, one need not take on the role of the solar hero, nor do armed battle, nor risk one's life in the wilderness. One need only care to untangle her. This power in knowing the Life/Death/Life nature awaits lovers who go beyond running away, who push beyond a desire to find themselves safe.

The ancients who sought this life and death knowledge called it the Pearl of Great Price, the Inimitable Treasure. Holding the threads of these mysteries and untangling them brings a powerful knowing about Fate and Time, time for all things, all things in their own time, rolling with the rough, gliding on the smooth. There is no knowledge more preserving, more nutritive, more strengthening of love than this.

That is what awaits the lover who will sit by the fire with Skeleton Woman, who will contemplate her and allow the feeling for her to rise. It waits for those who will touch her not-beauty and who will untangle her Life/Death/Life nature with tenderness.

The Sleep of Trust

In this stage of relationship, a lover returns to a state of innocence, a state in which he is still awed by the emotional elements, a state in which he is full of wishes, hopes, and dreams. Innocence is different than naïveté. There is an old saying in the backwoods I come from: "Ignorance is not knowing anything and being attracted to the good. Innocence is knowing everything, and still being attracted to the good."

Let us see how far we have come now. The fisherman-hunter has brought the Life/Death/Life nature to the surface. He has, outside his will, been "pursued" by her. But he has also managed to face her; he has felt compassion for her tangled state, and he has touched her. All these are leading him into a full participation with her. All these are leading him into a transformation, into love.

While the metaphor of sleep can denote a psychic unconsciousness, here it symbolizes creation and renewal. Sleep is the symbol of rebirth. In creation myths, souls go to sleep while a transformation of some duration takes place, for in sleep, we are re-created, renewed.

> . . . Sleep that knits up the raveled sleeve of care, [sleep is] sore labor's bath, [the] balm of hurt minds, great Nature's second course, chief nourisher in life's feast.
>
> —Shakespeare, *Macbeth*, II, ii, 36

If you could lay your eyes upon the most fire-hardened, most cruel and unpitying person alive, during sleep and at the moment of waking, you would see in them for a moment the untainted child spirit, the pure innocent. In sleep we are once again brought back to a state of sweetness. In sleep we are remade. We are re-assembled from the inside out, fresh and new as innocents.

This state of wise innocence is entered by shedding cynicism and protectionism, and by reentering the state of wonder one sees in most humans who are very young and many who are very old. It is a practice of looking through the eyes of a knowing and loving spirit, instead of through those of the whipped dog, the hounded creature, the mouth atop a stomach, the angry wounded human. Innocence is a state that is renewed as one sleeps. Unfortunately, many throw it aside with the coverlet as they arise each day. It would be better to take an alert innocence with us and draw it close for warmth.

Though an initial return to this state may require scraping away years of jaded viewpoints, decades of callous and carefully constructed bulwarking, once one has returned one never has to pry for it, dig for it, ever again. To return to an alert innocence is not so much an effort, like moving a pile of bricks from here to there, as it is standing still long enough to let the spirit find you. It is said that all that you are seeking is also seeking you, that if you lie still, sit still, it will find you. It has been waiting for you a long time. Once it is here, don't move away. Rest. See what happens next.

This is the way to approach the Death nature, not as wily and shrewd, but with the trust of spirit. The word *innocent* is often used to mean a person of no knowing, or a simpleton. But the roots of the word mean to be free of injury or hurt. In Spanish, the word *inocente* is understood to mean a person who tries not to harm another, but who *also* is able to heal any injury or harm to herself.

La inocente is the name often given to a *curandera* healer, one who heals others of injury or harm. To be an innocent means to be able to see clearly what is the matter and to mend it. These are the powerful ideas behind innocence. It is considered not only an attitude about avoiding harm to others or self but also an ability to mend and restore oneself (and others). Think of it. What a boon to all the cycles of loving.

By way of this metaphor of innocent sleep, the fisherman trusts the Life/Death/Life nature enough to rest and to revivify in her presence. He is entering into a transition that will take him to a deeper understanding, a higher stage of maturity. When lovers enter this state, they are surrendering to the forces within themselves, those that have trust, faith, and the profound power of innocence. In this spiritual sleep, the lover trusts that the works of his soul will be worked in him, that all will be as it should be. This lover sleeps the sleep of the wise instead of the wary.

There is wariness that is real, when danger is near, and wariness that is unwarranted and that comes from having been wounded previously. The latter causes men and women, both, to act touchy and disinterested even when they feel they would like to display warmth and caring. Persons who are afraid of being "taken for a ride" or of "being trapped"—or who vociferously state their claims over and over again of wanting to "be free"—are those who let the gold slip right through their fingers.

Many times I've heard a man say he has "a good woman" who is enamored of him and he of her, but he just can't "let go" enough to see what he really feels about her. The turning point for such a person is when he allows himself to love "even though" . . . even though he has pangs, even though he is nervous, even though he has been wounded previously, even though he fears the unknown.

Sometimes there are no words to help one's courage. Sometimes you just have to jump. There has to be at some point in a man's life a time when he will trust where love takes him, where he fears more being trapped in some dry cracked riverbed of a psyche than being out in lush but uncharted territory. When a life is too controlled, there becomes less and less life to control.

In this stage of innocence, the fisherman returns to being a young soul, for in his sleep he is unscarred, and there is no memory of what he was yesterday or before. In sleep, he is not striving to gain place or position. In his sleep he is renewed.

Within the masculine psyche, there is a creature, an unwounded man, who believes in the good, who has no doubts about life, who is not only wise but who also is not afraid to die. Some would identify this as a warrior self. But it is not that. It is a spirit self, and a young spirit at that, one who regardless of being tormented, wounded, and exiled continues to love, because it is in its own way self-healing, self-mending.

Women will testify to seeing this creature lurking in a man outside of his awareness. This young spirit's ability to bring the power of healing to bear on his own psyche is so awesome that it is astounding. His trust is not dependent on his lover not to hurt him. His is a trust that any wound that comes to him can be healed, a trust that new life follows old. A trust that there is deeper meaning in all these things, that seemingly petty events are not without meaning, that all things of one's life—the ragged, the jagged, and the lilting and the soaring—all can be used as life's energy.

It must be said too that sometimes as a man becomes more free, and closer to the Skeleton Woman, his lover becomes more fearful and has some work of her own to do regarding untangling, observing, the sleep that returns innocence, learning to trust the Life/Death/Life nature. When both are well initiated, they together then have the power with which to balm any hurt, outlive any pain.

Sometimes a person is afraid to "go to sleep" in the other's presence, afraid to return to a psychic innocence, or afraid the other person will take advantage of him. Such people project all manner of motives onto the other, and simply do not trust themselves. Yet, it is not their lovers they mistrust. It is the Life/Death/Life nature they have not yet reckoned with. It is this Death nature that they need to trust. As in sleep, the Life/Death/Life nature in its most wildish form is as simple as a graceful exhalation (ending) and inhalation (beginning). The only trust required is to know that when there is one ending there will be another beginning.

In order to do this, if we are lucky, we are worn down and slip into trust by giving in to its pull. The steeper way is by forcibly throwing ourselves into a trusting state of mind—forcing ourselves to remove all the conditions, all the ifs and onlys. However, there is usually no sense waiting till we feel strong enough to trust, because that day will never come. So yes, we take the chance that what we have been taught by the culture to believe about the Life/Death/Life nature is wrong, and that our instincts are right.

For love to thrive, the mate must trust that whatever will be, will be transformative. Man or woman, each must let themselves enter that state of sleep that returns one to a wise innocence, one that creates and re-creates, as it should, those deeper coils of Life/Death/Life experience.

Giving the Tear

As the fisherman sleeps, a tear is released from the corner of his eye. Skeleton Woman spies it, is filled with thirst, and awkwardly crawls to him to drink from the cup of his eye. What, we ask, could he be dreaming that would cause such a tear to come forth?

Tears carry creative power. In mythos, the giving of tears causes immense creation and heartfelt reunion. In herbal folklore, tears are used as a binder, to secure elements, unite ideas, join souls. In fairy tales, when tears are thrown, they frighten away robbers or cause rivers to flood. When sprinkled, they call the spirits. When poured onto the body, they heal lacerations and restore sight. When touched, they cause conception.

When one has ventured this far into relationship with the Life/Death/Life nature, the tear that is cried is the tear of passion and compassion mixed together, for oneself, and for the other. It is the hardest tear to cry and especially for men and certain kinds of "street-tough" women.

This tear of passion and compassion is most often wept after the accidental finding of treasure, after the fearful chase, after the untangling—for it is the combination of these that causes the exhaustion, the disassembling of defenses, the facing of oneself, the stripping down to the bones, the desire for both knowledge and relief. These cause a soul to peer into what the soul truly wants, and to weep for loss and love of both.

As surely as Skeleton Woman was brought to the surface, now this tear, this feeling in the man, is also brought to the surface. It is an instruction in loving both self and another. Stripped now of all the bristles and hooks and shivs of the daytime world, the man draws Skeleton Woman to lie beside him, to drink and be nourished by his deepest feeling. In his new form he is able to feed the thirsty other.

Her ghost has been summoned by his weeping—ideas and

powers from far off in the psychic world unite over the warmth of his tear. The history of the symbol of water as creator, as pathway, is long and varied. Spring comes in a rain of tears. Entry to the lower world is upon a waterfall of tears. A tear, heard by anyone of heart, is understood as a cry to come closer. And so does the fisherman cry, and closer she does come. Without his tear, she would remain only bones. Without his tear, he would never awaken to love.

The tear of the dreamer comes when a lover-to-be allows himself to feel and to bind up his own wounds, when he allows himself to see the self-destruction he has wrought by his loss of faith in the goodness of self, when he feels cut away from the nurturing and revivifying cycle of the Life/Death/Life nature. Then, he weeps, for he feels his loneliness, his acute homesickness for that psychic place, for that wild knowing.

This is the man healing, the man growing in understanding. He takes on his own medicine-making, he takes on the task of feeding the "deleted other." Through his tears, he begins to create.

To love another is not enough, to be "not an impediment" in the life of the other is not enough. It is not enough to be "supportive" and "there for them," and all the rest. The goal is to be *knowledgeable* about the ways of life and death, in one's own life and in panorama. And the only way to be a knowing man is to go to school in the bones of Skeleton Woman. She is waiting for the signal of deep feeling, that one tear that says, "I admit the wound."

This admission feeds the Life/Death/Life nature, causes the bond to be made and the deep knowing in a man to begin. We all have made the mistake of thinking someone else can be our healer, our thriller, our filling. It takes a long time to find it is not so, mostly because we project the wound outside ourselves instead of ministering to it within.

There is probably nothing a woman wants more from a man than for him to dissolve his projections and face his own wound. When a man faces his wound, the tear comes naturally, and his loyalties within and without are made clearer and stronger. He becomes his own healer; he is no longer lonely for the deeper Self. He no longer applies to the woman to be his analgesic.

There is a story that describes this well. In Greek myth, there was a man named Philoctetes. It is told he inherited the magic bow and arrow of Heracles. Philoctetes was wounded in the foot during battle. However, this wound would not heal, and instead grew so malodorous, and his cries of pain so horrible, that his companions abandoned him on the island Lemnos and left him there to die.

Philoctetes barely escaped starvation by using Heracles' bow to shoot small game. But his wound festered and the smell grew ever greater, so that any sailor even remotely near the island had to steer clear. However, a group of men conspired to brave the stench of Philoctetes' wound in order to steal the magical bow and arrow from him.

The men drew lots and the task fell to the youngest.[7] The older men encouraged him to be quick and travel under cover of night. And so the young man set sail. But on the wind, and overwhelming the smell of the sea, came another odor so horrible that the man had to wrap his face in a cloth wrung in seawater in order to breathe freely. Nothing, however, could protect his ears from Philoctetes' terrible cries.

The moon was shrouded in cloud. Good, he thought as he moored his boat and crept to the side of the agonized Philoctetes. As he reached for the precious bow and arrow, the moon suddenly shed her light upon the haggard face of the dying old man. And something in the young man—he knew not what—suddenly moved him to tears. The young man was overwhelmed with a compassion and mercy that endured.

Instead of stealing the old man's bow and arrows, the young man purified Philoctetes' wound, bound it, and stayed with him, feeding him, cleaning him, building fires, and caring for the old man till he could carry him to Troy, where he could be healed by the semi-divine physician Aesculapius. And thus the story comes to a close.

The tear of compassion is wept in response to realizing the stinking wound. The stinking wound has different configurations and sources for each person. For some it means spending a lifetime pulling oneself up the mountain hand over hand—belatedly to find we've been working our way up the wrong mountain. For some it is unresolved and unmedicated issues of abuse in childhood.

For others, it is a crushing loss of some sort in life or in love. One young man suffered loss of his first love and had no support from anyone, and no understanding about how to heal from it. For years he had wandered broken, yet protesting that he was not injured. One man was a rookie player for a pro ball team. He accidentally but permanently injured his leg so that his lifelong dream disappeared overnight. The stinking wound was not only the tragedy, not only the injury, but for twenty years' time the only medicine he poured into the wound was bitterness, substance abuse, carousing. When men have wounds like these, you can smell them coming. No woman, no love, no attention heals such a wound, only self-compassion, only attendance to one's own wounded state.

When the man cries the tear, he has come upon his pain, and he knows it when he touches it. He sees how his life has been lived protectively because of the wound. He sees what of life he has missed because of it. He sees how he hamstrings his love for life, for himself, and for another.

In fairy tales, tears change people, remind them of what is important, and save their very souls. Only a hardness of heart inhibits weeping and union. There is a saying I translated from the Sufi long ago, a prayer really, asking God to break one's heart: "Shatter my heart so a new room can be created for a Limitless Love."

The internal feeling of tenderness that moves the fisherman to untangle Skeleton Woman also allows him to feel other forgotten longings, to resurrect his self-compassion. Because he is in a state of innocence, that is, thinking all things are possible, he is unafraid to say his soul desires. He is unafraid to wish, for he believes his need will be met. It is a great relief for him to believe his soul will be fulfilled. When the fisherman cries his true feeling, the reunion with the Life/Death/Life nature is furthered.

The fisherman's tear draws Skeleton Woman to him; causes her to thirst, causes her to desire further participation with him. As in fairy tales, tears call things to us, they correct things, provide the missing part or piece. In the African tale "Golden Falls," a magician shelters a runaway slave girl by crying so many tears he creates a waterfall under which she takes refuge. In the African tale "Bone Rattle," souls of dead healers are summoned by the sprinkling of children's tears upon the earth. We are reminded again and again of the power of this great feeling. There is drawing power in tears, and within the tear itself, powerful images that guide us. Tears not only represent feeling but are also lenses through which we gain an alternative vision, another point of view.

In the story, the fisherman is letting his heart break—not break down, but break open. It is not the love of *la teta*, the breast milk mother, he wants; not the love of lucre, not the love of power or fame or sexuality. It is a love that comes upon him, a love he has always carried within him but has never acknowledged before.

A man's soul is seated more deeply and more clearly as he apprehends this relationship. The tear comes. She drinks. Now something else will develop and be reborn within him, something he can give to her: a vast and oceanic heart.

The Later Phases of Love

Heart as Drum, and Singing Up

It is told that the skin or body of a drum determines who and what will be called into being. Some drums are believed to be journeying drums transporting the drummer and listeners (also called "passengers" in certain traditions) to various and sundry places. Other kinds of drums are powerful in other ways.

It is said that drums made of human bone call the dead. Drums made of the hide of certain animals call those specific animal spirits. Drums that are particularly beautiful call Beauty. Drums with bells attached call child-spirits and weather. Drums that are low in voice call the spirits who can hear that tone. Drums high in voice call spirits who can hear that tone, and so on.

A drum made of heart will call the spirits that are concerned with the human heart. The heart symbolizes essence. The heart is one of the few essential organs humans and animals must have to live. Remove one kidney, the human lives. Additionally, take both legs, the gallbladder, one lung, one arm, and the spleen; the human lives—not well perhaps, but there is life. Take away certain brain functions and the human still lives. Take the heart, the person is gone instantly.

The psychological and physiological center is the heart. In Hindu *Tantras*, which are instructions from the Gods to humans, the heart is the *Anāhata chakra*, the nerve center that encompasses feeling for another human, feeling for oneself, feeling for the earth, and feeling for God. It is the heart that enables us to love as a child loves: fully, without reservation, and with no hull of sarcasm, depreciation, or protectionism.

When Skeleton Woman uses the fisherman's heart, she uses the central motor of the entire psyche, the only thing that really matters now, the only thing capable of creating pure and innocent feeling. They say it is the mind that thinks and creates. This story says otherwise. It suggests that it is the heart that thinks and calls the molecules, atoms, feelings, yearnings, and whatever else need be, into one place to create the matter that fulfills Skeleton Woman's creation.

The story contains this promise: allow Skeleton Woman to become more palpable in your life, and she will make your life larger in return. When you free her from her tangled and misunderstood state and realize her as both teacher and lover, she becomes ally and partner.

Giving one's heart for new creation, for new life, for the forces of Life/Death/Life, is a descent into the feeling realm. It may be difficult for us, especially if we have been wounded by disappointment or by sorrow. But it is meant to be drummed through, to bring to full life the Skeleton Woman, to come close to the one who has always been close to us.

When a man gives his whole heart, he becomes an amazing force—he becomes an inspiratrice, a role that in the past was reserved for women only. When Skeleton Woman sleeps with him, he becomes fertile, he is invested with feminine powers in a masculine milieu. He carries the seeds of new life and of necessary deaths. He inspires new works within himself, but also in those near him.

Over the years I have seen this in others and experienced it myself. It is a profound occasion when you create something of value through your lover's belief in you, through his heartfelt feeling about your work, your project, your subject. It is an amazing phenomenon. And it is not necessarily limited to a lover; it can occur through anyone who gives his or her heart to you in a deep manner.

So, the man's bond with the Life/Death/Life nature will eventually give him ideas by the dozens and life plots and situations and musical scores and colors and images without parallel—for the Life/Death/Life nature as related to the Wild Woman archetype, has at its disposal all that ever was and all that ever will be. When Skeleton Woman creates, sings flesh onto herself, the person whose heart she uses feels it, is filled with creation themselves, bursts with it, brims over from it.

The story illustrates also a power that originates in the psyche and is represented by the symbols of drumming and singing. In mythos, songs heal wounds and are used to bring game closer. Persons are summoned by the singing of their names. Pain is relieved, magic breaths restore the body. The dead are called or resurrected through song.

It is told that all creation was accompanied by a sound or word said aloud, a sound or word whispered or spoken on the breath. In mythos, singing is considered to issue from a mysterious source, one that enwisens the whole of creation, all the animals and the humans and the trees and plants and all who hear it. In storytelling it is said that anything that has "sap" has singing.

The creation hymn produces psychic change. The tradition of such is vast: there are love-producing songs in Iceland, and among the Wichita and the Micmac. In Ireland, magic power is called down by magic song. In one Icelandic story, a person falls on the ice crags and severs a limb, but it is regenerated through the singing of song.

In almost all cultures, at the creation the Gods give the people songs, telling them that to use them will call the Gods back at any time, that song will bring to them the things they need as well as transform or banish those things they do not want. In this manner the giving of song is a compassionate act that enables humans to call the Gods and the great forces into human circles. Song is a special kind of language that accomplishes this in a way the spoken voice cannot.

Since time out of mind, the song, like the drum, has been used to create a non-ordinary consciousness, a trance state, a prayer state. All humans and many animals are susceptible to having their consciousness altered by sound. Certain sounds, like a dripping faucet or an insistent car horn, can make us anxious, even angry. Other sounds, like the ocean's roar or the wind in the trees, can fill us with good feeling. The sound of thudding—as in footsteps—causes a snake to feel a negative tension. But being softly sung to can cause a snake to dance.

The word *pneuma* (breath) shares its origins with the word *psyche*; they are both considered words for soul. So when there is song in a tale or mythos, we know that the gods are being called upon to breathe their wisdom and power into the matter at hand. We know then that the forces are at work in the spirit world, busy crafting soul.

So the singing of song and using the heart as drum are both mystical acts awakening layers of the psyche not much used or seen. The breath or pneuma flowing over us shakes open certain apertures, rouses certain otherwise inaccessible faculties. We cannot say for each person what will be sung up, drummed up, because these open such odd and unusual apertures in the human who participates thusly. However, one can be assured that whatever is enacted will be numinous and arresting.

The Dance of Body and Soul

Through their bodies, women live very close to the Life/Death/Life nature. When women are in their right instinctual minds, their ideas and impulses to love, to create, to believe, to desire are born, have their time, fade and die, and are reborn again. One might say that women consciously or unconsciously practice this knowledge every moon cycle of their lives. For some this moon that tells the cycles is up in the sky. For others it is a Skeleton Woman who lives in their own psyches.

From her very flesh and blood and from the constant cycles of filling and emptying the red vase in her belly, a woman understands physically, emotionally, and spiritually that zeniths fade and expire, and what is left is reborn in unexpected ways and by inspired means, only to fall back to nothing, and yet be reconceived again in full glory. As you can see, the cycles of Skeleton Woman run throughout and under and in the entire woman. It cannot be otherwise.

Sometimes men who are still running away from the Life/Death/Life nature are afraid of such a woman, for they sense she is a natural ally of Skeleton Woman. But it was not always this way. The symbol of death as spiritual transformer is a remnant of a time when Lady Death was welcomed as a close relative, as one's own sister, brother, father, mother, or lover. In feminine imagery, the Death Woman, Death Mother, or Death Maiden always was understood as the carrier of destiny, the maker, the harvest maiden, the mother, the river-walker, and the re-creator; all of these in cycle.

Sometimes the one who is running from the Life/Death/Life nature insists on thinking of love as a boon only. Yet love in its fullest form is a series of deaths and rebirths. We let go of one phase, one aspect of love, and enter another. Passion dies and is brought back. Pain is chased away and surfaces another time. To love means to embrace and at the same time to withstand many many endings, and many many beginnings—all in the same relationship.

The process is complicated by the fact that much of our over-civilized culture has a difficult time tolerating the transformative. But there are better attitudes with which to embrace the Life/Death/Life nature. Throughout the world, though it is called by different names, many see this nature as *un baile con La Muerte*, a dance with death; Death as a dancer, with Life as its dance partner.

Way up in the Great Lakes dune country where I grew up, people lived who still spoke in the biblical dialect of *thee* and *hast* and *thus*. My childhood friend, Mrs. Arle Scheffeler, a silver-haired mother who had lost her only son in World War II, still kept to this archaic prose. One summer night I dared ask her if she still missed her son, and she gently explained her sense of life and death in terms a child could understand. The story she cryptically called, "Dead Bolt,"[8] went, in part, like this: A woman welcomes a traveler named Death to her fire. The old woman is not afraid.

She seems to know Death as a life-giver as well as a death-dealer. She is certain Death is the cause of all tears and all laughter.

She tells Death he is welcome at her hearth, that she has loved him through "all my crops bursting, and all my fields falling, through my children borning, my children dying." She tells him she knows him and that he is her friend: "Thou hast caused me great weeping and dancing, Death. So call out the rounds now! I do know the steps!"

To make love, if we are to love, *bailamos con La Muerte*, we dance with Death. There will be flowing, there will be draining, there will be live birth and still birth and yet born-again birth of something new. To love is to learn the steps. To make love is to dance the dance.

Energy, feeling, closeness, solitude, desire, ennui, all rise and fall in relatively closely packed cycles. One's desire for nearness, and for separations, waxes and wanes. The Life/Death/Life nature not only teaches us to dance these, but teaches that the solution for malaise is always the opposite; so new action is the cure for boredom, closeness is the cure for loneliness, solitude is the cure for feeling cramped.

Without the knowledge of this dance, a person is inclined, during various still-water times, to extrovert the need for new and personal action into spending too much money, doing danger, roping reckless choices, taking a new lover. It is the dummling's or fool's way. It is the way of those who do not know.

At first we all think we can outrun the death aspect of the Life/Death/Life nature. The fact is we cannot. It follows right along behind us, bumpety-bump, thumpety-thump, right into our houses, right into consciousness. If in no other way, we learn of this darker nature when we concede that the world is not a fair place, that chances are lost, that opportunities come to us unbidden, that the Life/Death/Life cycles prevail whether we wish them to or not. Yet if we live as we breathe, take in and let go, we cannot go wrong.

In this story there are two transformations, one of the hunter, one of Skeleton Woman. In modern terms, the hunter's transformation goes something like this. First he is the unconscious hunter. "Hello, it's just me. I'm here fishing and minding my own business." Then he is the scared and fleeing hunter. "What? You want me? Oh, I think I must go now." Now he reconsiders and begins to untangle his feelings and finds a way to relate to her. "I feel my soul drawn to you. Who are you really, how are you put together?"

Then he sleeps. "I will trust you. I allow myself to expose innocence." And his tear of deep feeling is revealed and it nourishes her. "I have waited a long time for you." His heart is lent to create her wholly. "Here, take my heart and bring yourself to life in my life." And so the hunter-fisherman is loved in return. This is a typical transformation of a person learning to truly love.

Skeleton Woman's transformations take a slightly different trajectory. First, as the Life/Death/Life nature, she is used to having her relationships with humans end right after the initial hooking. It is no wonder she heaps so many blessings on those who will go the distance with her, for she is used to having humans cut bait and dash for land.

First she is thrown away and exiled. Then she is accidentally caught by someone who is afraid of her. She begins to return to life from an inert state; she eats, she drinks from him who has raised her up, she transforms herself by the strength of his heart, by his strength to face her. . . and himself. She is transformed from being a skeleton into a living being. She is loved by him, and he by her. She empowers him as he empowers her. She, who is the great wheel of nature, and he, the human being, now live in harmony with one another.

We see in the story what Death requires of love. It requires its tear—its feeling—and its heart. It requires to be made love to. The Life/Death/Life nature requires of lovers that they face this nature straight-on, that they neither faint nor feint from her, that their commitment to one another is far more than "being together," that their love is based on their combined learning and strength to meet this nature, to love this nature, to dance with this nature together.

Skeleton Woman sings up for herself a lush body. This body Skeleton Woman sings up is functional in all ways; it is not the pieces and parts of woman-flesh idolized by some in certain cultures, but rather an entire woman's body, one that can feed babies, make love, dance and sing, give birth, and bleed without dying.

This singing of flesh onto oneself is another common folk motif. In African, Papuan, Jewish, Hispanic, and Inuit stories, bones are transformed into a person. The Mejícaña *Coatlicue* brings mature humans forth from bones of the dead in the underworld. A Tlingit shaman sings off the clothes of the woman he loves. All over the world in stories, magic results from singing. Singing brings increase.

Also all over the world, various fairies, nymphs, and giantesses have breasts so long they can throw them over their shoulders. In Scandinavia, among the Celts, and in the circumpolar region, stories tell of women who can create their bodies at will.

We see from the story that the giving of body is one of the last in the phases of love. This is as it should be. It is good to master the first stages of meeting with the Life/Death/Life nature and let the literal body-to-body experiences come after. I caution women, do not engage a lover who wants to go from accidental catching to giving body. Insist on all the phases. Then the last phase will take care of itself, the time of body union will come in its own right time.

When the union is begun in the body phase, the process of facing the Life/Death/Life nature can still be accomplished later . . . but it takes much more resolve. It is harder work, for the pleasure-ego must be dragged away from its carnal interest so that the foundation work can be done. The little dog in the Manawee story points out just how hard it is to remember what path one is on when one's nerves are being thrummed by delight.

So, to make love is to merge the breath and the flesh, spirit and matter; one fits into the other. In this tale there is a mating of the mortal and immortal, and this too is true in a love relationship that will last. There is an immortal soul-to-soul connection that we have little ability to describe or perhaps even to decide, but that we experience deeply. There is a wonderful tale from India in which a mortal beats a drum so the fairies can dance before the Goddess Indra. For this service the drummer is granted a fairy wife. There is something like this in the love relationship too; something is awarded to the man who will enter into cooperative relationship with the psychic feminine realm, which is mysterious to him.

In the end of the story, the fisherman is breath to breath, skin to skin, with the Life/Death/Life nature. What this means is different for each man. How he experiences this deepening of her relationship with him is also unique. We only know that in order to love we must kiss the hag, and more. We must make love with her.

But the tale also tells how to come into cooperative and rich relationship with what one fears. She is just what he must lend his heart to. When the man merges with the psychological and spiritual as represented by the Skeleton Woman, he becomes close as he can be to her, and this causes him to be close as can be to his female lover. To find this eminent life and love adviser, one only need stop running, do some untangling, face the wound and one's own yearning with compassion, give one's entire heart to the process.

So, in the end, in the fleshing-out of herself, the Skeleton woman enacts the entire creation process, but rather than beginning as a baby, in the way Westerners are taught to think about life and death, she begins as ancient bones and fleshes out her life from there. She teaches the man to make new life. She shows him that the way of the heart is the way of creation. She shows him that creation is a series of births and deaths. She teaches that protectionism creates nothing, selfishness creates nothing, holding on and screaming effects nothing. Only letting go, giving heart, the great drum, the great instrument of the wild nature, only this creates.

That is how love relationship is meant to work, each partner transforming the other. The strength and power of each is untangled, shared. He gives her the heart drum. She gives him knowledge of the most complicated rhythms and emotions imaginable. Who knows what they will hunt together? We only know that they will be nourished to the end of their days.

CHAPTER 6

Finding One's Pack:
Belonging as
Blessing

The Ugly Duckling

Sometimes life goes wrong for the wildish woman from the beginning. Many women had parents who surveyed them as children and puzzled over how this small alien had managed to infiltrate the family. Other parents were always looking heavenward, ignoring or abusing the child or giving her the old icicle eye.

Let women who have had this experience take heart. You have avenged yourself by having been, through no fault of your own, a handful to raise and an eternal thorn in their sides. And perhaps even today you are able to inspire them to abject fear when you come a-knocking. That's not too shabby as innocent retribution goes.

See to it now that you spend less time on what they didn't give you and more time on finding the people you belong to. You may not belong to your original family at all. You may match your family genetically, but temperamentally you may belong to another group of people. Or you may belong to your family perfunctorily while your soul leaps out, runs down the road, and is gluttonously happy munching spiritual cookies somewhere else.

Hans Christian Andersen[1] wrote dozens of literary stories about children who were orphans. He was a premier advocate of the lost and neglected child and he strongly supported searching for and finding one's own kind.

His rendering of "The Ugly Duckling" was first published in

1845. The ancient motif underlying the tale is about the unusual and the dispossessed, a perfect Wild Woman demi-history. For the last two centuries "The Ugly Duckling" has been one of the few stories to encourage successive generations of "outsiders" to hold on till they find their own.

It is what I would call a psychological and spiritual root story. A root story is one that contains a truth so fundamental to human development that without integration of this fact, further progression is shaky, and one cannot entirely prosper psychologically until this point is realized. So, here is "The Ugly Duckling," that I wrote as a literary story based on the eccentric version originally told in the Magyar language by the *falusias mesélök*, rustic tellers from my family.[2]

~~~~~~~~~~~~~~~~~~~~~~~~~~~~~~~

The Ugly Duckling

IT WAS NEAR THE TIME of harvest. The old women were making green dolls from corn sheaves. The old men were mending the blankets. The girls were embroidering their white dresses with blood-red flowers. The boys were singing as they pitched golden hay. The women were knitting scratchy shirts for the coming winter. The men were helping to pick and pull and cut and hoe the fruits the fields had brought forth. The wind was just beginning to loosen the leaves a little more, and then a little more, each day. And down by the river, there was a mother duck brooding on her nest of eggs.

Everything was going as it should for this mother duck, and finally, one by one her eggs began to tremble and shake until the shells cracked, and out staggered all her new ducklings. But there was one egg left, a very big egg. It just sat there like a stone.

An old duck came by and the duck mother showed off her new children. "Aren't they good-looking?" she bragged. But the unhatched egg caught the old duck's attention and she tried to dissuade the duck mother from sitting on that egg any longer.

"It's a turkey egg," exclaimed the old duck, "not a proper kind of egg at all. Can't get a turkey into the water, you know." She knew, for she had tried.

But the duck mother felt that she had been sitting for such a long time, a little longer would not hurt. "I'm not worried about that," she said, "but do you know that scoundrel father of these ducklings hasn't come to visit me once?"

But eventually the big egg began to shudder and roll. It finally broke open, and out tumbled a big, ungainly creature. His skin was etched with curly red-and-blue veins. His feet were pale purple. His eyes, transparent pink.

The duck mother cocked her head and stretched her neck and peered at him. She couldn't help herself: she pronounced him ugly. "Maybe it is a turkey after all," she worried. But when the ugly duckling took to the water with the other offspring, the duck mother saw that he swam straight and true. "Yes, he's one of my own, even though he's very peculiar in appearance. But actually, in the right light . . . he is almost handsome."

So she presented him to the other creatures in the farmyard, but before she knew it, another duck shot across the courtyard and bit the ugly duckling right in the neck. The duck mother cried, "Stop!" But the bully sputtered, "Well, he looks so strange and ugly. He needs to be pushed around."

And the queen duck with the red rag on her leg said, "Oh, another brood! As though we don't have enough mouths to feed. And that one over there, that big ugly one, well, surely he was a mistake."

"He's not a mistake," said the duck mother. "He's going to be very strong. He just laid in the egg too long and is yet a little mis-shapen. He'll straighten out though. You'll see." She groomed the ugly duckling's feathers and licked his cowlicks.

But the others did all they could to harass the ugly duckling. They flew at him, bit him, pecked him, hissed and screeched at him. And their torment of him grew worse as time went on. He hid, he dodged, he zigzagged left and right, but he could not escape. The duckling was as miserable as any creature could be.

At first his mother defended him, but then even she grew tired of it all, and exclaimed in exasperation, "I wish you would just go away." And so the ugly duckling ran away. With most of his feathers pulled out and looking extremely bedraggled, he ran and ran until he reached a marsh. There he lay down at the water's edge with his neck stretched out and sipped as he could from the water now and then.

From the rushes two ganders watched him. They were young and full of themselves. "Say there, you ugly thing," they sniggered. "Want to come with us over to the next county? There's a gaggle of young unmarried geese over there, just right for the choosing."

Suddenly shots rang out and the ganders fell with a thud and the marsh water ran red with their blood. The ugly duckling dived for cover and all around were shots and smoke and dogs barking.

At last the marsh became quiet and the duckling ran and flew as far away as he could. Toward nightfall he came to a poor hovel; the door was hanging by a thread, there were more cracks than walls. Here lived an old raggedy woman with her uncombed cat and her cross-eyed hen. The cat earned her keep with the old woman by catching mice. The hen earned her keep by laying eggs.

The old woman felt lucky to have found a duck. Maybe it will lay eggs, she thought, and if not, we can kill it and eat it. So the duck stayed, but he was tormented by the cat and hen, who asked him, "What good are you if you cannot lay and you cannot catch?"

"What I love best," sighed the duckling, "is to be 'under,' whether it is under the wide blue sky or under the cool blue water." The cat could make no sense of being underwater and criticized the duckling for his stupid dreams. The hen could make no sense of getting her feathers all wet, and she made fun of the duckling too. In the end, it was clear there would be no peace for the duckling there, so he left to see if things would be better down the road.

He came upon a pond and as he swam there it became colder and colder. A flock of creatures flew overhead, the most beautiful he had ever seen. They cried down to him, and hearing their sounds made his heart leap and break at the same time. He cried back in a sound he had never before made. He had never seen creatures more beautiful than they, and he had never felt more bereft.

He turned and turned in the water to watch them till they flew out of sight, then he dove to the bottom of the lake and huddled there, trembling. He was beside himself, for he felt a desperate love for those great white birds, a love he could not understand.

A colder wind began and blew harder and harder through the days, and snow came upon frost. The old men broke the ice in the milk pails, and the old women spun long into the night. The mothers fed three mouths at once by candlelight and the men searched for the sheep under white skies at midnight. The young men went waist-deep in the snow to go to milking and the girls imagined they saw the faces of handsome young men in the flames of the fire while they cooked. And down at the pond nearby, the duckling had to swim faster and faster in circles to keep a place for himself in the ice.

One morning the duckling found himself frozen in the ice and it was then that he felt he would die. Two mallards flew down and skidded onto the ice. They surveyed the duck. "You are ugly," they barked. "Too bad, so sad. Nothing can be done for such as you." And off they flew.

Luckily a farmer came by and freed the duckling by breaking the ice with his staff. He lifted the duckling up and tucked him under his coat and marched home. In the farmer's house the children reached for the duckling, but he was afraid. He flew up to the rafters, making all the dust fall down into the butter. From there he dove right into the milk pitcher, and as he struggled out all wet and woozy, he fell over into the flour barrel. The farmer's wife chased him with her broom, and the children screamed with laughter.

The duckling flapped through the cat's door and, outside at last, lay in the snow half dead. From there he struggled on till he came to another pond, then another house, another pond, another house, and the entire winter was spent this way, alternating between life and death.

And even so, the gentle breath of spring came again, and the old women shook out the feather beds, and the old men put away their long underwear. New babies came in the night, while fathers paced the yard under starry skies. During daylight, the young girls put daffodils in their hair and young men studied girls' ankles. And on a pond nearby, the water became warmer and the ugly duckling who floated there stretched his wings.

How strong and big his wings were. They lifted him high over the land. From the air he saw the orchards in their white gowns, the farmers plowing, the young of all of nature hatching, tumbling, buzzing, and swimming. Also paddling on the pond were three swans, the same beautiful creatures he had seen the autumn before; those that so caused his heart to ache. He felt pulled to join them.

What if they act as though they like me, and then just as I join them, they fly away laughing? thought the duckling. But he glided down and landed on the pond, his heart beating hard.

As soon as they saw him, the swans began to swim toward him. No doubt I am about to meet my end, thought the duckling, but if I am to be killed, then rather by these beautiful creatures than by hunters, farm wives, or long winters. And he bowed his head to await the blows.

But, la! In the reflection in the water he saw a swan in full dress: snowy plumage, sloe eyes, and all. The ugly duckling did not at first recognize himself, for he looked just like the beautiful strangers, just like those he had admired from afar.

And it turned out that he was one of them after all. His egg had accidentally rolled into a family of ducks. He was a swan, a glorious swan. And for the first time, his own kind came near him and touched him gently and lovingly with their wing tips. They groomed him with their beaks and swam round and round him in greeting.

And the children who came to feed the swans bits of bread cried out, "There's a new one." And as children everywhere do, they ran to tell everyone. And the old women came down to the water, unbraiding their long silver hair. And the young men cupped the deep green water in their hands and flicked it at the young girls, who blushed like petals. The men took time away from milking just to breathe the air. The women took time away from mending just to laugh with their mates. And the old men told stories about how war is too long and life too short.

And one by one, because of life and passion and time passing, they all danced away; the young men, the young women, all danced away. And the old ones, the husbands, the wives, they all danced away. The children and the swans all danced away . . .

leaving just us . . . and the springtime . . . and down by the river, another mother duck begins to brood on her nest of eggs.

The problem of the exiled one is primeval. Many fairy tales and myths center around the theme of the outcast. In such tales, the central figure is tortured by events outside her venue, often due to a poignant oversight. In "The Sleeping Beauty" the thirteenth fairy is overlooked and not invited to the christening, which results in a curse being placed upon the child, effectively exiling everyone in one way or another. Sometimes exile is enforced through sheer meanness, as when the stepmother casts her step-daughter out into the dark wood in "Vasalisa the Wise."

Other times exile comes about as the result of a naive error. The Greek God Hephaestus took his mother's, Hera's, side in an argument with Zeus, her husband. Zeus became infuriated and hurled Hephaestus off Mount Olympus, banishing and crippling him.

Sometimes exile comes from striking a bargain one does not understand, such as in the tale of a man who agrees to wander as a beast for a certain number of years in order to win some gold, and later discovers he's given his soul to the devil in disguise.

"The Ugly Duckling" theme is universal. All stories of "the exile" contain the same nucleus of meaning, but each is surrounded by different frills and furbelows reflecting the cultural background of the story as well as the poetry of the individual teller.

The core meanings we are concerned with are these: The duckling of the story is symbolic of the wild nature, which, when pressed into circumstances of little nurture, instinctively strives to continue no matter what. The wild nature instinctively holds on and holds out, sometimes with style, other times with little grace, but holds on nevertheless. And thank goodness for that. For the wildish woman, duration is one of her greatest strengths.

The other important aspect of the story is that when an individual's particular kind of soulfulness, which is both an instinctual and a spiritual identity, is surrounded by psychic acknowledgment and acceptance, that person feels life and power as never before.

Ascertaining one's own psychic family brings a person vitality and belongingness.

Exile of the Unmatched Child

In the story, the various creatures of the village peer at the "ugly" duckling and one way or another pronounce him unacceptable. He is not ugly in reality, but he does not match the others. He is so different that he looks like a black bean in a bushel of green peas. The mother duck at first tries to defend this duckling whom she believes to be her offspring. But finally she is profoundly divided emotionally and withdraws from caring for the alien child.

His siblings and others of his community fly at him, peck at him, torment him. They mean to chase him away. And the ugly duckling is heartbroken really, to be rejected by his own. It is a terrible thing, especially since he really did nothing to warrant it other than look different and act a little different. If truth be told, we have here, before the creature is even half grown, a duckling with a massive psychological complex.

Girl children who display a strong instinctive nature often experience significant suffering in early life. From the time they are babies, they are taken captive, domesticated, told they are wrongheaded and improper. Their wildish natures show up early. They are curious, artful, and have gentle eccentricities of various sorts, ones that, if developed, will constitute the basis for their creativity for the rest of their lives. Considering that the creative life is the soul's food and water, this basic development is excruciatingly critical.

Generally, early exile begins through no fault of one's own and is exacerbated by the misunderstanding, the cruelty of ignorance, or through the intentional meanness of others. Then, the basic self of the psyche is wounded early on. When this happens, a girl begins to believe that the negative images her family and culture reflect back to her about herself are not only totally true but are also totally free of bias, opinion, and personal preference. The girl begins to believe that she is weak, ugly, unacceptable, and that this will continue to be true no matter how hard she tries to reverse it.

A girl is banished for the exact reasons we see in "The Ugly

Duckling." In many cultures, there is an expectation when the female child is born that she is or will become a certain type of person, acting in a certain time-honored way, that she will have a certain set of values, which if not identical to the family's, then at least based on the family's values, and which at any rate will not rock the boat. These expectations are defined very narrowly when one or both parents suffer from a desire for "the angel child," that is, the "perfect" conforming child.

In some parents' fantasy whatever child they have will be perfect, and will reflect only the parents' ways and means. If the child is wildish, she may, unfortunately, be subjected to her parents' attempts at psychic surgery over and over again, for they are trying to re-make the child, and more so trying to change what her soul requires of her. Though her soul requires seeing, the culture around her requires sightlessness. Though her soul wishes to speak its truth, she is pressured to be silent.

Neither the child's soul nor her psyche can accommodate this. Pressure to be "adequate," in whatever manner authority defines it, can chase the child away, or underground, or set her to wander for a long time looking for a place of nourishment and peace.

When culture narrowly defines what constitutes success or desirable perfection in anything—looks, height, strength, form, acquisitive power, economics, manliness, womanliness, good children, good behavior, religious belief—then corresponding mandates to measure oneself against these criteria are introjected into the psyches of all the members of that culture. So the issues of the exiled wildish woman are usually twofold: inner and personal, and outer and cultural.

Let us attend here to the inner issues of the exile, for when one develops adequate strength—not perfect strength, but moderate and serviceable strength—in being oneself and finding what one belongs to, one can then influence the outer community and cultural consciousness in masterful ways. What is moderate strength? It is when the internal mother who mothers you isn't one hundred percent confident about what to do next. Seventy-five percent confident will do nicely. Seventy-five percent is a goodly amount. Remember, we say that a flower is blooming whether it is in half, three-quarters, or full bloom.

Kinds of Mothers

While we can interpret the mother in the story as symbolic of one's external mother, most who are grown up now have as a legacy from their actual mother, an internal mother. This is an aspect of psyche that acts and responds in a manner identical to a woman's experience in childhood with her own mother. Further, this internal mother is made from not only the experience of the personal mother but also other mothering figures in our lives, as well as the images held out as the good mother and the bad mother in the culture at the time of our childhoods.

For most adults, if there was trouble with the mother once but there is no more, there is still a duplicate mother in the psyche who sounds, acts, responds the same as in early childhood. Even though a woman's culture may have evolved into more conscious reasoning about the role of mothers, the internal mother will have the same values and ideas about what a mother should look like, act like, as those in one's childhood culture.[3]

In depth psychology, this entire maze is called *the mother complex*. It is one of the core aspects of a woman's psyche, and it is important to recognize its condition, strengthening certain aspects, arighting some, dismantling others, and beginning over again if necessary.

The duck mother in the story has several qualities, which we'll analyze one by one. She is representative of, all at the same time, an ambivalent mother, a collapsed mother, and an unmothered mother. By examining these mothering structures, we can begin to assess whether our own internal mother complex staunchly sustains our unique qualities, or whether it needs a long overdue adjustment.

THE AMBIVALENT MOTHER

In our story the duck mother is cut away, forced away from her instincts. She is taunted for having a child who is different. She is divided emotionally, and as a result collapses, and withdraws her caring from the alien child. Although initially she tries to stand firm, the duckling's "otherness" begins to jeopardize the mother's safety in her own community, and she tucks her head and dives.

Have you not witnessed a mother forced to such a decision, if not fully, then partially? The mother bends to the desires of her village, rather than aligning herself with her child. Right into the present, mothers still act out the well-founded fears of centuries of women before them; to be shut out of the community is to be ignored and regarded with suspicion at the least, and to be hunted down and destroyed at the worst. A woman in such environs will often try to mold her daughter so that she acts "properly" in the outer world—thereby hoping to save her daughter and herself from attack.

This is a mother and a child who are then both divided. In "The Ugly Duckling," the duck mother is psychically divided and this causes her to be pulled in several different directions, which is what ambivalence is all about. Any mother who has ever been under fire will recognize her. One pull is her own desire to be accepted by her village. Another is for self-preservation. The third pull is to respond to the fear that she and her child will be punished, persecuted, or killed by the village. This fear is a normal response to an abnormal threat of psychic or physical violence. The fourth pull is the mother's instinctual love for her child and the preservation of that child.

It is not uncommon in punitive cultures for women to be torn between being accepted by the ruling class (her village) and loving her child, be it a symbolic child, creative child, or biological child. This is an old, old story. Women have died psychically and spiritually for trying to protect the unsanctioned child, whether it be their art, their lover, their politics, their offspring, or their soul life. At the extreme, women have been hanged, burned, and murdered for defying the village proscriptions and sheltering the unsanctioned child.

A mother with a child who is different must have the endurance of Sisyphus, the fearsomeness of the Cyclops, and the tough hide of Caliban[4] to go against a mean-spirited culture. The most destructive cultural conditions for a woman to be born into and to live under are those that insist on obedience without consultation with one's soul, those with no loving forgiveness rituals, those that force a woman to choose between soul and society, those where compassion for others is walled off by economic tiers or caste systems, where the body is seen as something needing to be "cleaned" or as a shrine to be regulated by fiat, where the new, the unusual, or the different engenders no delight, and where curiosity and creativity are punished and denigrated instead of rewarded, or rewarded only if one is not a woman, where painful acts are perpetrated on the body and called holy, or whenever a woman is punished unjustly, as Alice Miller puts it succinctly, "for her own good,"[5] where the soul is not recognized as a being in its own right.

When a woman has this ambivalent mother construct in her own psyche, she may find herself giving in too easily; she may find herself afraid to take a stand, to demand respect, to assert her right to do it, learn it, live it in her own way.

Whether these issues derive from an internal construct or an external culture, in order for the mothering function to withstand such constraints, she must have some very fierce qualities, qualities that, in many cultures, are considered masculine. For generations, sadly, the mother who wanted to engender esteem in herself and her offspring needed the very qualities that were expressly forbidden to her: vehemence, fearlessness, and fearsomeness.

For a mother to happily raise a child who is slightly or largely different in psyche and soul needs from that of the mainstream culture, she must have a start on some heroic qualities herself. She must be able, like the heroines of myths, to find and obtain these qualities if they are not allowed, to shelter them, unleash them at the right time, and stand for herself and what she believes. There is almost no way to make oneself ready for this, other than to take a deep draft of courage, and then act. Since time out of mind a considered act of heroism has been the cure for stultifying ambivalence.

THE COLLAPSED MOTHER

Finally, the duck mother can no longer stand the harassment of the child she has helped into the world. But what is even more telling is that she can no longer tolerate the torment she herself experiences from her community as she attempts to protect her "alien" child. So she collapses. She cries to the little duckling, "I wish you were far away." And the tortured duckling runs away.

When a mother collapses psychologically, it means she has lost her sense of herself. She may be a malignantly narcissistic mother who feels entitled to be a child herself. More likely she has been severed from the wildish Self and has been frightened into the collapse by some real threat, psychic or physical.

When people collapse, they usually slide into one of three feeling states: a muddle (they are confused), a wallow (they feel no one adequately sympathizes with their travail), or a pit (an emotional replay of an old wounding, often an uncorrected and unaccounted-for injustice done to them when they themselves were children).

The way to cause a mother to collapse is to divide her emotionally. The most common way, time out of mind, has been to force her to choose between loving her child and fearing what harm the village will visit on her and the child if she does not comply with the rules. In *Sophie's Choice* by William Styron, the heroine, Sophie, is a prisoner in a Nazi extermination camp. She stands before the Nazi commandant with her two children in her arms. The commandant forces her to choose which of the two children will live and which will die by telling Sophie that if she refuses to make a choice both children will be killed.

While to be forced to make such a choice is unthinkable, it is a psychic choice that mothers have been forced to make for eons. Obey the rules and kill off your children, or else. It goes on. When a mother is forced to choose between the child and the culture, there is something abhorrently cruel and unconsidered about that culture. A culture that requires harm to one's soul in order to follow the culture's proscriptions is a very sick culture indeed. This "culture" can be the one a woman lives in, but more damning yet, it can be the one she carries around and complies with within her own mind.

There are countless literal examples of this throughout the world,[6] some of the most heinous examples being found in America where it has been traditional to force women away from their loved ones and from the things they love. There was the long and ugly history of breaking families forced into slavery in the eighteenth, nineteenth, and twentieth centuries. There is in the last many centuries the proscription that mothers should surrender their sons to the nation for the sake of war, and be glad of it. There are the forced "repatriations" that continue yet today.[7]

There have been various fashions at various times throughout the world that proscribe that a woman should not be allowed to love and shelter whomever she loves and in whichever way she wishes.

One of the least-spoken-about oppressions of women's soul lives concerns millions of unmarried mothers or never-married mothers throughout the world, including the United States, who, in this century alone, were pressured by cultural mores to hide their condition or their children, or else to kill or surrender their offspring, or to live a half-life under assumed identities and as reviled and disempowered citizens.[8]

For generations women accepted the role of legitimizing humans through marriage to a man. They agreed that a human was not acceptable unless a man said so. Without that "masculine" protection, the mother is vulnerable. It is ironic then that in "The Ugly Duckling" the father is mentioned only once. That is when the duck mother is brooding on the ugly duckling egg. She laments about the father of her offspring: "That scoundrel hasn't come to visit me once." For a long time in our culture, the father—unfortunately, and for whatever reasons[9]—was unable or unwilling to "be there" for anyone, most sorely, even himself. One could easily say that for many, many wildish girl children, the father was a collapsed man, just a shade who hung himself along with his coat in the closet every night.

When a woman has a collapsing mother construct within her psyche and/or her culture, she is wobbly about her worth. She may feel that choices between fulfilling outer demands and the demands of soul are life-and-death issues. She may feel like a tormented outsider who belongs nowhere—which is relatively normal for the exile—but what is not normal is to sit down and cry about it and do nothing. One is supposed to get to one's feet and go off in search of what one belongs to. For the exile, that is always the next step, and for a woman with an internalized collapsing mother, it is the quintessential step. If a woman has a collapsing mother, she must refuse to become one to herself also.

THE CHILD MOTHER OR THE UNMOTHERED MOTHER

The image portrayed by the duck mother in the tale, as we can see, is very unsophisticated and naive. By far the most common kind of fragile mother is the unmothered mother. In the story, she who is so insistent on having babies eventually turns from her child. There are many reasons a human and/or psychic mother might act thusly. She may be an unmothered woman herself. She may be one of the fragile mothers, psychically very young or very naive.

She may be so psychically dislocated that she considers herself unlovable even by a baby. She may have been so tortured by her family and her culture that she cannot imagine herself worthy of touching the hem of the "radiant mother" archetype that accompanies new motherhood. You see, there are no two ways about it: a mother must be mothered in mothering her own offspring. Though a woman has an inalienable spiritual and physical bond with her offspring, in the world of the instinctual Wild Woman, she does not just suddenly become a fully formed temporal mother all by herself.

In olden times, the blessings of the wildish nature normally came through the hands and words of the women who nurtured the younger mothers. Especially first-time mothers have within them, not an experienced old crone, but a child-mother. A child-mother can be any age, eighteen or forty, it doesn't matter. Every new mother begins as a child-mother. A child-mother is old enough to have babies and has good instincts in the right direction, but she needs the mothering of an older woman or women who essentially prompt, encourage, and support her in her mothering of her children.

For eons this role was served by the older women of the tribe or village. These human "Goddess-mothers," who were later relegated by religious institutions to the role of "godmother," constituted an essential female-to-female nutritional system that nourished the young mothers in particular, teaching them how to nourish the psyches and souls of their young in return. When the Goddess-mother role became more intellectualized, "godmother" came to mean someone who made sure the child did not stray from the precepts of the Church. Much was lost in the transmigration.

The older women were the arks of instinctual knowing and behavior who could invest the young mothers with the same. Women give this knowing to each other through words, but also by other means. Complicated messages about what and how to be are sent simply through a look, a touch with the palm of the hand, a murmur, or a special kind of "I cherish you" hug.

The instinctual self always blesses and helps those who come after. It is this way among healthy creatures and among healthy humans. In this way the child-mother is swept across the threshold into the circle of mature mothers, who welcome her with jokes, gifts, and stories.

This woman-to-woman circle was once the domain of Wild Woman, and it had open membership; anyone could belong. But all we have left of this today is the little tatter called a "baby shower," where all the birthing jokes, mother gifts, and genitalia stories are squeezed into two hours' time, no longer available to the woman throughout her entire lifetime as a mother.

In most parts of industrialized countries today, the young mother broods, births, and attempts to benefit her offspring all by herself. It is a tragedy of enormous proportions. Because many women were born to fragile mothers, child-mothers, and unmothered mothers, they may themselves possess a similar internal style of "selfmothering."

The woman who has a child-mother or unmothered mother construct in her psyche, or glorified in the culture and maintained at work and in the family, is likely to suffer from naive presentiments, lack of seasoning, and in particular a weakened instinctual ability to imagine what will happen one hour, one week, one month, one year, five years, ten years from now.

A woman with a child-mother within takes on the aura of a child pretending to be a mother. Women in this state often have an undifferentiated "long live everything" attitude, a "do everything, be everything to everyone" brand of hyper-momism. They are not able to guide and support their children, but like the farmer's children in "The Ugly Duckling" story who are so thrilled to have a creature in the house but do not know how to give it proper care, the child-mother winds up leaving the child battered and bedraggled. Without realizing it, the child-mother tortures her offspring with various forms of destructive attention and in some cases lack of useful attention.

Sometimes the frail mother is herself a swan who has been raised by ducks. She has not been able to find her true identity soon enough to benefit her offspring. Then, as her daughter comes upon the great mystery of the wildish nature of the feminine in adolescence, the mother too finds herself having sympathy pangs and swan urges. The daughter's search for identity may even inaugurate the mother's "maiden" journey for her lost self at last. So in that household, between the mother and the daughter, there will be two wildish spirits down in the basement holding hands and hoping to be called upstairs.

So these are the things that can go awry when the mother is cut away from her own instinctive nature. But do not sigh too hard or too long, for there is help for all of this.

THE STRONG MOTHER, THE STRONG CHILD

The remedy is in gaining mothering for one's young internal mother. This is gained from actual women in the outer world who are older and wiser and preferably who have been tempered like steel; they are fire-hardened for having gone through what they have gone through. Regardless of the cost even now, their eyes *see*, their ears *hear*, their tongues *speak*, and they are kind.

Even if you had the most wonderful mother in the world, you may eventually have more than one. As I have often told my own daughters, "You are born to one mother, but if you are lucky, you will have more than one. And among them all you will find most of what you need." Your relationships with *todas las madres*, the many mothers, will most likely be ongoing ones, for the need for guidance and advisory is never outgrown, nor, from the point of view of women's deep creative life, should it ever be.[10]

Relationships between women, whether the women share the same bloodlines or are psychic soulmates, whether the relationship is between analyst and analysand, between teacher and apprentice, or between kindred spirits, are kinship relationships of the most important kind.

While some who write in psychology today tout the leaving of the entire mother matrix as though it were a coup, that, if not accomplished, taints one forever, and though some say that denigration of one's personal mother is good for an individual's mental health, in truth, the construct and concept of the wild mother can never and should never be abandoned. For if it is, a woman abandons her own deep nature, the one with all the knowing in it, all the bags of seeds, all the thorn needles for mending, all the medicines for work and rest and love and hope.

Rather than disengaging from the mother, we are seeking a wild and wise mother. We are not, cannot be, separate from her. Our relationship to this soulful mother is meant to turn and turn, and to change and change, and it is a paradox. This mother is a school we are born into, a school we are students in, a school we are teachers at, all at the same time, and for the rest of our lives. Whether we have children or not, whether we nourish the garden, the sciences, or the thunderworld of poetics, we always brush against the wild mother on our way to anywhere else. And this is as it should be.

But what shall we say for the woman who truly has had an experience of destructive mothering in her own childhood? Of course that time cannot be erased, but it can be eased. It cannot be sweetened up, but it can be rebuilt, strongly, and properly, now. It is not the rebuilding of the internal mother that is so frightening to so many, but rather the fear that something essential died back then, something that can never be brought back to life, something that received no nourishment, for psychically one's own mother was dead herself. For you, I say, be at peace, you are not dead, you are not lethally injured.

As in nature, the soul and the spirit have resources that are astonishing. Like wolves and other creatures, the soul and spirit are able to thrive on very little, and sometimes for a long time on nothing. To me, it is the miracle of miracles that this is so. Once I was transplanting a hedgerow of lilac. One great bush was dead from a mysterious cause, but the rest were shaggy with purple in springtime. The dead one cracked and crunched like peanut brittle as I dug it out. I found that its root system was attached to all the other living lilacs up and down the fence line.

Even more astounding, the dead one was the "mother." She had the thickest and oldest roots. All her big babies were doing fine even though she herself was *botas arribas*, boots up, so to speak.

Lilacs reproduce with what is called a sucker system, so each tree is a root offshoot of the primal parent. In this system, even if the mother fails, the offspring can survive. This is the psychic pattern and promise for those with little or no, as well as those who have had torturous mothering. Even though the mother somehow falls over, even though she has nothing to offer, the offspring will develop and grow independently and still thrive.

Bad Company

The ugly duckling goes from pillar to post trying to find a place to be at rest. While the instinct about exactly where to go may not be fully developed, the instinct to rove until one finds what one needs is well intact. Yet there is a kind of pathology sometimes in the ugly duckling syndrome. One keeps knocking at the wrong doors even after one knows better. It is hard to imagine how a person is supposed to know which doors are right doors if one has never known a right door to begin with. However, the wrong doors are those that cause you to feel the outcast all over again.

This is the "looking for love in all the wrong places" response to exile. When a woman turns to repetitive compulsive behavior—repeating over and over again a behavior that is not fulfilling, that causes decline instead of sustained vitality—in order to salve her exile, she is actually causing more damage because the original wounded state is not being attended to and she incurs new wounding with each foray.

This is like putting some puny medicine on your nose when you have a gash in your arm. Different women choose different kinds of "wrong medicine." Some choose the obviously wrong, such as bad company, overindulgences that are harmful or soul-stealing, things that first build a woman way up and then tear her down to ground zero minus five.

The solutions to these bad choices are severalfold. If the woman were able to sit herself down and peer into her own heart, she would see there a need to have her talents, her gifts, and her limitations respectfully acknowledged and accepted. So, to begin healing, stop kidding yourself that a little feel-good of the wrong sort will take care of a broken leg. Tell the truth about your wound, and then you will get a truthful picture of the remedy to apply to it. Don't pack whatever is easiest or most available into the emptiness. Hold out for the right medicine. You will recognize it because it makes your life stronger rather than weaker.

Not Looking Right

Like the ugly duckling, an outsider learns to stay away from situations where one may be able to act right but still doesn't look right. The duckling, for instance, can swim well, but still doesn't look right. Conversely, a woman may look right, but may not be able to act right. There are many sayings about persons who cannot hide what they are (and in their hearts don't wish to), all the way from the east Texan "You can dress 'em up, but you can't take 'em out" to the Spanish "She was a woman with a black feather under her skirt."[11]

In the story, the duckling begins to act like a dummling,[12] the one who can't do anything right . . . he flaps dust into the butter and falls into the flour barrel, but not until he has first fallen into the milk pitcher. We all have had times like this. Can't do anything right. Try to make it better. Makes it worse instead. Duckling had no business in that house. But you see what happens when one is desperate. One goes to the wrong place for the wrong thing. As one of my dear late colleagues used to say, "You can't get milk at the ram's house."[13]

While it is useful to make bridges even to those groups one does not belong to, and it is important to try to be kind, it is also imperative to not strive too hard, to not believe too deeply that if one acts just right, if one manages to tie down all the itches and twitches of the wildish *criatura*, that one can actually pass for a nice, restrained, subdued, and demure lady-woman. It is that kind of acting, that kind of ego-wish to belong at all costs, that knocks out the Wild Woman connection in the psyche. Then instead of a vital woman you have a nice woman who is de-clawed. Then you have a well-behaved, well-meaning, nervous woman, panting to be good. No, it is better, more graceful, and far more soulful to just be what and as you are and let the other creatures be what they are too.

Frozen Feeling, Frozen Creativity

Women deal with exile in other ways. Like the duckling who becomes frozen in the ice of the pond, they freeze up. Freezing up is the worst thing a person can do. Coldness is the kiss of death to creativity, relationship, life itself. Some women act as though it is an achievement to be cold. It is not. It is an act of defensive anger.

In archetypal psychology to be cold is to be without feelings. There are stories of the frozen child, the child who could not feel, the corpses frozen in the ice, during which time nothing could move, nothing could become, nothing could be born. For a human to be frozen means to purposely be without feeling, especially toward oneself, but also and sometimes even more so toward others. While it is a self-protective mechanism, it is hard on the soul-psyche, for the soul does not respond to iciness, but rather warmth. An icy attitude will put out a woman's creative fire. It will inhibit the creative function.

This is a serious problem, yet the story gives us an idea. The ice must be broken and the soul taken out of the freeze.

When writers, for example, feel dry, dry, dry, they know that the way to become moist is to write. But if they're locked in ice, they won't write. There are painters who are gasping to paint, but they're telling themselves, "Get out of here. Your work is weirdly strange and ugly." There are many artists who've not yet gotten a good foothold or who are old war-horses at developing their creative lives, and yet and still, every time they reach for the pen, the brush, the ribbons, the script, they hear, "You're nothing but trouble, your work is marginal or completely unacceptable—because you yourself are marginal and unacceptable."

So what is the solution? Do as the duckling does. Go ahead, struggle through it. Pick up the pen already and put it to the page and stop whining. Write. Pick up the brush and be mean to yourself for a change, paint. Dancers, put on the loose chemise, tie the ribbons in your hair, at your waist, or on your ankles and tell the body to take it from there. Dance. Actress, playwright, poet, musician, or any other. Generally, just stop talking. Don't say one more word unless you're a singer. Shut yourself in a room with a ceiling

or in a clearing under the sky. Do your art. Generally, a thing
cannot freeze if it is moving. So move. Keep moving.

The Passing Stranger

Although in the story the farmer taking the duck home seems to be
a literary device to further the story rather than an archetypal leitmotif about exile, there is a thought here that I think is valuable.
The person who might take us out of the ice, who might even psychically free us from our lack of feeling, is not necessarily going
to be the one to whom we belong. It may be, as in the story,
another of those magical but fleeting events that again came
along when we least expected it, an act of kindness from a passing
stranger.

This is another example of nourishment of the psyche that
occurs when one is at the end of one's rope and cannot stand it
anymore. Then a something that is sustaining appears out of
nowhere to assist you, and then disappears into the night, leaving
you wondering, Was that a person or a spirit? It might be a sudden
gust of luck that brings something very needed in through your
door. It might be as simple a thing as a respite, a let-up in pressure,
a small space of rest and repose.

This is not a fairy tale we are talking about now, but real life.
Whatever it might be, it is a time when the spirit, in one way or
another, feeds us, pulls us out, shows us the secret passage, the
hiding place, the escape route. And this coming when we are
down and feeling stormy dark or darkly calm is what pushes us
through the channel to the next step, the next phase in learning the
strength of the exile.

Exile as Boon

If you have attempted to fit whatever mold and failed to do so, you
are probably lucky. You may be an exile of some sort, but you
have sheltered your soul. There is an odd phenomenon that occurs
when one keeps trying to fit and fails. Even though the outcast is
driven away, she is at the same time driven right into the arms of
her psychic and true kin, whether these be a course of study, an art

form, or a group of people. It is worse to stay where one does not belong at all than to wander about lost for a while and looking for the psychic and soulful kinship one requires. It is never a mistake to search for what one requires. Never.

There is something useful in all this torque and tension. Something in the duckling is being tempered, being made strong by this exile. While this situation is not one we would wish on anyone for any reason, its effect is similar to pure natural carbon under pressure producing diamonds—it leads eventually to a profound magnitude and clarity of psyche.

There is an aspect of alchemy, wherein the base substance of lead is pounded about and beaten down. While exile is not a thing to desire for the fun of it, there is an unexpected gain from it; the gifts of exile are many. It takes out weakness by the pounding. It removes whininess, enables acute insight, heightens intuition, grants the power of keen observation and perspective that the "insider" can never achieve.

Even though there are negative aspects to it, the wild psyche can endure exile. It makes us yearn that much more to free our own true nature and causes us to long for a culture to match. Even this yearning, this longing makes a person go on. It makes a woman go on looking, and if she cannot find the culture that encourages her, then she usually decides to construct it herself. And that is good, for if she builds it, others who have been looking for a long time will mysteriously arrive one day enthusiastically proclaiming that they have been looking for this all along.

The Uncombed Cats and Cross-Eyed Hens of the World

The uncombed cat and the cross-eyed hen find the duckling's aspirations stupid and nonsensical. It gives just the right perspective on the touchiness and the values of others who denigrate those who are not like themselves. Who would expect a cat to like the water? Who would expect a hen to go swimming? No one, of course. But too often, from the exile's point of view, when people are not alike, it is the exile who is inferior, and the limitations and/or motives of the other are not properly weighed or evaluated.

Well, in the spirit of not wanting to make one person less and another person more, or any more than we have to for the purposes of discussion, let us just say that here the duckling has the same experience that thousands of exiled women have—that of a basic incompatibility with dissimilar persons, which is no one's fault, even though most women are too obliging and take it on as though it is their fault personally.

When this happens, we see women who are ready to apologize for taking up space. We see women who are afraid to just say "No, thank you," and leave. We see women who listen to someone telling them they are wrongheaded over and over again without understanding that cats don't swim and hens don't dive under water.

I must admit, I sometimes find it useful in my practice to delineate the various typologies of personality as cats and hens and ducks and swans and so forth. If warranted, I might ask my client to assume for a moment that she is a swan who does not realize it. Assume also for a moment that she has been brought up by or is currently surrounded by ducks.

There is nothing wrong with ducks, I assure them, or with swans. But ducks are ducks and swans are swans. Sometimes to make the point I have to move to other animal metaphors. What if you were raised by the mice people? But what if you're, say, a swan. Swans and mice hate each other's food for the most part. They each think the other smells funny. They are not interested in spending time together, and if they did, one would be constantly harassing the other.

But what if you, being a swan, had to pretend you were a mouse? What if you had to pretend to be gray and furry and tiny? What if you had no long snaky tail to carry in the air on tail-carrying day? What if wherever you went you tried to walk like a mouse, but you waddled instead? What if you tried to talk like a mouse, but instead out came a honk every time? Wouldn't you be the most miserable creature in the world?

The answer is an unequivocal yes. So why, if this is all so and too true, do women keep trying to bend and fold themselves into shapes that are not theirs? I must say, from years of clinical observation of this problem, that most of the time it is not because of deep-seated masochism or a malignant dedication to self-destruction or anything of that nature. More often it is because the woman simply doesn't know any better. She is unmothered.

There is a saying, *tu puedes saber muchas cosas*, you can know about things, but it is not the same as *sentido*, possessing sense. The duckling seems to know "things," but he has no sense. He is unmothered, meaning untaught at the most basic level. Remember, it is the mother who teaches by expanding the innate talents of the offspring. Animal mothers who teach their offspring to hunt are not exactly teaching them "how to hunt," for that is in their bones already. But they are teaching them what to watch out for, what to pay attention to; those things are not known to them until the mother shows them, thereby activating new learning and innate wisdom.

It is the same for the woman in exile. If she is an ugly duckling, if she is unmothered, her instincts have not been sharpened. She learns instead by trial and error. Usually many trials; many, many errors. But there is hope, for you see, the exile never gives up. She keeps going till she finds the guide, the scent, till she finds the trail, till she finds home.

Wolves never look more funny than when they have lost the scent and scrabble to find it again: they hop in the air; they run in circles; they plow up the ground with their noses; they scratch the ground, then run ahead, then back, then stand stock-still. They look as if they have lost their wits. But what they are really doing is picking up all the clues they can find. They're biting them down out of the air, they're filling up their lungs with the smells at ground level and at shoulder level, they are tasting the air to see who has passed through it recently, their ears are rotating like satellite dishes, picking up transmissions from afar. Once they have all these clues in one place, they know what to do next.

Though a woman may look scattered when she has lost touch with the life she values most and is running about trying to recapture it, she is most often gathering information, taking a taste of this, grabbing up a paw of that. At the very most one might briefly explain to her what it is that she is doing. Then, let her be. As soon as she processes all the information from the clues she's gathered, she'll be moving in an intentional manner again. Then the desire for membership in the uncombed cat and cross-eyed hen club will diminish to nothing.

Remembrance and Continuance No Matter What

We all have a longing that we feel for our own kind, our wild kind. The duckling, you will recall, ran away after being tortured without mercy. Next he had a run-in with a gaggle of geese and was almost killed by hunters. He was chased from the barnyard and from a farmer's home, and finally exhausted, he shivered at the edge of the lake. There is no woman among us who does not know his feeling. And yet, it is just this longing that leads us to hang on, to go on, to proceed with hope.

Here is the promise from the wild psyche to all of us. Even though we have only heard about, glimpsed, or dreamt a wondrous wild world that we belonged to once, even though we have not yet or only momentarily touched it, even though we do not identify ourselves as part of it, the memory of it is a beacon that guides us toward what we belong to, and for the rest of our lives. In the ugly duckling, a knowing yearning stirs when he sees the swans lift up into the sky, and from that single event his remembrance of that vision sustains him.

I worked with a woman who was near the last straw and thinking suicide. A spider making its web on her porch caught her eye. Precisely what it was in that wee beastie's act that chopped the ice around her soul so she could go free and grow again, we will never know. But I am convinced, both as psychoanalyst and as *cantadora*, that many times it is the things of nature that are the most healing, especially the very accessible and the very simple ones. The medicines of nature are powerful and straightforward: a ladybug on the green rind of a watermelon, a robin with a string of yarn, a weed in perfect flower, a shooting star, even a rainbow in a glass shard in the street can be the right medicine. Continuance is a strange thing: it puts out tremendous energy, it can be fed for a month on five minutes of contemplating quiet water.

It is interesting to note that among wolves, no matter how sick, no matter how cornered, no matter how alone, afraid, or weakened, the wolf will continue. She will lope even with a broken leg.

She will go near others seeking the protection of the pack. She will strenuously outwait, outwit, outrun, and outlast whatever is bedeviling her. She will put her all into taking breath after breath. She will drag herself, if necessary, just like the duckling, from place to place, till she finds a good place, a healing place, a place for thriving.

The hallmark of the wild nature is that it goes on. It perseveres. This is not something we do. It is something we are, naturally and innately. When we cannot thrive, we go on till we can thrive again. Whether it be our creative life that we are cut away from, whether it be a culture or a religion we are cast out of, whether it be a familial exiling, a banishment by a group, or sanctions on our movements, thoughts, and feelings, the inner wild life continues and we go on. The wild nature is not native to any particular ethnic group. It is the core nature of women from Benin, Cameroon, and New Guinea. It is in women from Latvia, The Netherlands, and Sierra Leone. It is the center of Guatemalan women, Haitian women, Polynesian women. Name a country. Name a race. Name a religion. Name a tribe. Name a city, a village, a lone outpost. The women all have this in common—the Wild Woman, the wild soul. They all go on feeling for and following the wild.

So, if women must, they will paint blue sky on jail walls. If the skeins are burnt, they will spin more. If the harvest is destroyed they will sow more immediately. Women will draw doors where there are none, and open them and pass through into new ways and new lives. Because the wild nature persists and prevails, women persist and prevail.

The duckling is led to within an inch of his life. He has felt lonely, cold, frozen, harassed, chased, shot at, given up on, unnourished, out there way out of bounds, at the edge of life and death and not knowing what will come next. And now comes the most important part of the story: spring approaches, new life quickens, a new turn, a new try is possible. The most important thing is to hold on, hold out, for your creative life, for your solitude, for your time to be and do, for your very life; hold on, for the promise from the wild nature is this: after winter, *spring always comes.*

Love for the Soul

Hold out. Hold on. Do your work. You will find your own way. At the end of the tale, the swans recognize the duckling as one of their own before he does. That is rather typical of the exiled women. After all that hard wandering, they manage to wander over the frontier into home territory and often don't realize for a time that people's looks have ceased to be disparaging and are more often neutral, when they are not admiring and approving.

One would think that now that they are on their own psychic ground they would be deliriously happy. But, no. For a time at least, they are terribly distrustful. Do these people really regard me? Am I really safe here? Will I be chased away? Can I really sleep with both eyes closed now? Is it all right to act like . . . a swan? After a time, these suspicions fall away and the next stage of coming back to oneself begins: acceptance of one's own unique beauty; that is, the wild soul from which we are made.

There is probably no better or more reliable measure of whether a woman has spent time in ugly duckling status at some point or all throughout her life than her inability to digest a sincere compliment. Although it could be a matter of modesty, or could be attributed to shyness—although too many serious wounds are carelessly written off as "nothing but shyness"[14]—more often a compliment is stuttered around about because it sets up an automatic and unpleasant dialogue in the woman's mind.

If you say how lovely she is, or how beautiful her art is, or compliment anything else her soul took part in, inspired, or suffused, something in her mind says she is undeserving and you, the complimentor, are an idiot for thinking such a thing to begin with. Rather than understand that the beauty of her soul shines through when she is being herself, the woman changes the subject and effectively snatches nourishment away from the soul-self, which thrives on being acknowledged, on being seen.

So that is the final work of the exile who finds her own: to not only accept one's own individuality, one's specific identity as a certain kind of person, but also to accept one's beauty . . . the shape of one's soul and the fact that living close to that wild creature transforms us and all that it touches.

When we accept our own wild beauty, it is put into perspective, and we are no longer poignantly aware of it anymore, but neither would we forsake it or disclaim it either. Does a wolf know how beautiful she is when she leaps? Does a feline know what beautiful shapes she makes when she sits? Is a bird awed by the sound it hears when it snaps open its wings? Learning from them, we just act in our own true way and do not draw back from or hide our natural beauty. Like the creatures, we just are, and it is right.

For women this searching and finding is based on the mysterious passion that women have for what is wild, what is innately themselves. We have been calling the object of this yearning Wild Woman . . . but even when women do not know her by name, even when they do not know where she resides, they strain toward her: they love her with all their hearts. They long for her, and that longing is both motivation and locomotion. It is this yearning that causes us to search for Wild Woman and find her. It is not as hard as one might first imagine, for Wild Woman is searching for us too. We are her young.

The Mistaken Zygote

OVER THE YEARS of my practice it became clear that this issue of belonging sometimes needs to be hailed from a lighter side, for levity can shake some of the pain out of a woman. I began to tell my clients this story I created called "The Mistaken Zygote," mainly as a way to help them look at their outsider material with a more empowering metaphor. This is how the story goes.

Have you ever wondered how you managed to end up in such an odd family as yours? If you have lived your life as an outsider, as a slightly odd or different person, if you are a loner, one who lives at the edge of the mainstream, you have suffered. Yet there also comes a time to row away from all that, to experience a different vantage point, to emigrate back to the land of one's own kind.

Let there be no more suffering, no more attempting to figure where you went wrong. The mystery of why you were born to whomever you were born to is over, *finis*, *terminado*, finished. Rest for a moment at the bow and refresh yourself in the wind coming from your homeland.

For years women who carry the mythic life of the Wild Woman archetype have silently cried, "Why am I so different? Why was I born into such a strange [or unresponsive] family?" Wherever their lives wanted to burst forth, someone was there to salt the ground so nothing could grow. They felt tortured by all the proscriptions against their natural desires. If they were nature children, they were kept under roofs. If they were scientists, they were told to be mothers. If they wanted to be mothers, they were told they'd better fit the mold entirely. If they wanted to invent something, they were told to be practical. If they wanted to create, they were told a woman's domestic work is never done.

Sometimes they tried to be good according to whichever standards were most popular, and didn't realize till later what they really wanted, how they needed to live. Then, in order to have a life, they experienced the painful amputations of leaving their families, the marriages they had promised under oath would be till death, the jobs that were to be the springboards to something more stultifying but better paying. They left dreams scattered all over the road.

Often the women were artists who were trying to be sensible by spending eighty percent of their time doing labor that aborted their creative lives on a daily basis. Although the scenarios are endless, one thing remains constant: they were pointed out very early on as "different" with a negative connotation. In actual fact, they were passionate, individual, inquiring, and in their right instinctive minds.

So the answer to Why me, Why this family, Why am I so different, is, of course, that there are no answers to these questions. Still, the ego needs something to chew on before it will let go, so I propose three answers regardless. (The analysand may pick whichever one she likes, but she must pick at least one. Most pick the last one, but any are sufficient.) Prepare yourself. Here they are.

We are born the way we are, and into the odd families we came through 1) just because (almost no one will believe this), 2) the

Self has a plan, and our pea-brains are too tiny to parse it (many find this a hopeful idea), or 3) because of the Mistaken Zygote Syndrome (well . . . yes, maybe . . . but what is that?).

Your family thinks you're an alien. You have feathers, they have scales. Your idea of a good time is the forest, the wilds, the inner life, the outer majesty. Their idea of a good time is folding towels. If this is so for you in your family, then you are a victim of the Mistaken Zygote Syndrome.

Your family moves slowly through time, you move like the wind; they are loud, you are soft, or they are silent and you sing. You know because you just know. They want proof and a three-hundred-page dissertation. Sure enough, it's the Mistaken Zygote Syndrome.

You've never heard of that? Well see, the Zygote Fairy was flying over your hometown one night, and all the little zygotes in her basket were hopping and jumping with excitement.

You were indeed destined for parents who would have understood you, but the Zygote Fairy hit turbulence and, oops, you fell out of the basket over the wrong house. You fell head over heels, head over heels, right into a family that was not meant for you. Your "real" family was three miles farther on.

That is why you fell in love with a family that wasn't yours, and that lived three miles over. You always wished Mrs. and Mr. So-and-So were your real parents. Chances are they were meant to be.

This is why you tap-dance down the hallways even though you come from a family of television spores. This is why your parents are alarmed every time you come home or call. They worry, "What will she do next? She embarrassed us last time, God only knows what she will do now. Ai!" They cover their eyes when they see you coming and it is not because your light dazzles them.

All you want is love. All they want is peace.

The members of your family, for their own reasons (because of their preferences, innocence, injury, constitution, mental illness, or cultivated ignorance), are not so good at being spontaneous with the unconscious, and of course your visit home conjures the trickster archetype, the one who stirs things up. So before you've even broken bread together, the trickster madly dances by just dying to drop one of her hairs into the family stew.

Even though you don't mean to upset the family, they will be upset no matter what. When you show up, everyone and everything seems to go quite mad.

It is a sure sign of wild zygotes in the family if the parents are offended all the time and the children feel as though they can never do anything right.

The unwild family wants only one thing, but the Mistaken Zygote is never able to figure out what that is, and if she could, it would make her hair stand up in exclamation points.

Prepare yourself, I will tell you this big secret. This is what they really want from you, that mysterious, momentous thing.

The unwild want consistency.

They want you to be exactly the same today as you were yesterday. They wish you not to change with the days, but to remain as at the beginning of Steaming Time.

Ask the family if they want consistency and they will answer affirmatively. In all things? No, they will say, only in the things that matter. Whatever these things are that count in their value systems, they are too often anathema to the wild nature of women. Unfortunately, "the things that matter" to them are not cohesive with "the things that matter" to the wild child.

~~~~~~~~~~~~~~~~~~~~~~~~~~~~~~~~~~~~~

Consistency in manner is an impossible sentence for Wild Woman, for her strength is her adaptation to change, her innovation, her dancing, her howling, her growling, her deep instinctual life, her creative fire. She does not show consistency through uniformity, but rather through her creative life, through her consistent perceptions, quick-sightedness, flexibility, and deftness.

If we were to name only one thing that makes the Wild Woman what she is, it would be her responsiveness. The word *response* comes from the Latin "to pledge, to promise"—and that is her strong suit. Her perceptive and deft responses are a consistent promise and pledge to the creative forces, be it *Duende*, the goblin-spirit behind passion, or Beauty, Art, or the Dance, or Life. Her promise to us, if we will not thwart it, is that she will cause us to live. She will cause us to live fully alive, responsively and consistently so.

In this way, the Mistaken Zygote gives her fealty, not to her family but to her interior Self. This is why she feels torn. You might say her wolf mother has hold of her tail, her worldly family has hold of her arms. It is not long before she is crying in pain, snarling and biting herself and others, and finally, the deathly quiet. You look in her eyes and you see *ojos del cielo*, sky eyes, the eyes of a person who is no longer here.

While socialization for children is an important thing, to kill the interior *criatura* is to kill the child. The West Africans recognize that to be harsh with a child is to cause its soul to retreat from its body, sometimes just a few feet away, other times many days' walk away.

While the needs of the child's soul must be balanced with her need for safety and physical care and with carefully examined notions about "civilized behavior," I always worry for those who are too well behaved; they often have that "faint soul" look in their eyes. Something is not right. A healthy soul shines through the persona on most days and blazes through on others. Where there is gross injury, the soul flees.

Sometimes it drifts or bolts so far away that it takes masterful propitiation to coax it back. A long time must pass before such a soul will trust enough to return, but it can be accomplished. The retrieval requires several ingredients: naked honesty, stamina, tenderness, sweetness, ventilation of rage, and humor. Combined, these make a song that calls the soul back home.

What are soul needs? They lie in two realms: nature and creativity. In these realms lives *Na'ashjé'ii Asdzáá*, Spider Woman, the great creation spirit of the Dineh. She gifts her people with protection. Her purview, among others, is teaching the love of beauty.

The soul's needs are found in the hovel of those three old (or young, depending on what day it is) sisters—Clotho, Lachesis, and Atropos—who make the red thread, meaning the passion, of a woman's life. They weave the ages of a woman's life, tying them off as each is completed and the next is begun. They are found in the woods of the huntress spirits, Diana and Artemis, both of whom are wolf women who represent the ability to hunt, track, and recover various aspects of the psyche.

The soul's needs are governed by *Coatlicue*, the Aztec Goddess of female self-sufficiency, who gives birth squatting and square on her feet. She teaches about the lone woman's life. She is a maker of babies, meaning new potential for life, but she is also a death mother who wears skulls on her skirt, and when she walks they sound like the rattles on a snake, for they are skull rattles, and because skull rattles sound also like rain, through sympathetic resonance, they draw down rain for the earth. She is the protectoress of all lone women and those so *mágia*, so filled with powerful thoughts and ideas, they must live out at the edge of who-knows-where in order not to daze the village too much. *Coatlicue* is the especial protectoress of the female outsider.

What is the basic nutrition for the soul? Well, it differs from creature to creature, but here are some combinations. Consider them psychic macrobiotics. For some women air, night, sunlight, and trees are necessities. For others, words, paper, and books are the only things that satiate. For others, color, form, shadow, and clay are the absolutes. Some women must leap, bow, and run, for their souls crave dance. Yet others crave only a tree-leaning peace.

There is yet another issue to be dealt with. Mistaken Zygotes learn to be survivors. It is tough to spend years among those who cannot help you to flourish. Being able to say that one is a survivor is an accomplishment. For many, the power is in the name itself. And yet comes a time in the individuation process when the threat or trauma is significantly past. Then is the time to go to the next stage after survivorship, to healing and *thriving*.

If we stay as survivors only without moving to thriving, we limit ourselves and cut our energy to ourselves and our power in the world to less than half. One can take so much pride in being a survivor that it becomes a hazard to further creative development. Sometimes people are afraid to continue beyond survivor status, for it is just that—a status, a distinguishing mark, a "damn-straight, bet your buttons, better believe it" accomplishment.

Instead of making survivorship the centerpiece of one's life, it is better to use it as one of many badges, but not the only one. Humans deserve to be dripping in beautiful remembrances, medals, and decorations for having lived, truly lived and triumphed. Once the threat is past, there is a potential trap in calling ourselves by names taken on during the most terrible time of our lives. It creates a mind-set that is potentially limiting. It is not good to base the soul identity solely on the feats and losses and victories of the bad times. While survivorship can make a woman tough as beef jerky, at some point, allying with it exclusively begins to inhibit new development.

When a woman insists "I am a survivor" over and over again once the time for its usefulness is past, the work ahead is clear. We must loosen the person's clutch on the survivor archetype. Otherwise nothing else can grow. I liken it to a tough little plant that managed—without water, sunlight, nutrients—to send out a brave and ornery little leaf anyway. In spite of it all.

But thriving means, now that the bad times are behind, to put ourselves into occasions of the lush, the nutritive, the light, and there to flourish, to thrive with bushy, shaggy, heavy blossoms and leaves. It is better to name ourselves names that challenge us to grow as free creatures. That is thriving. That is what was meant for us.

Ritual is one of the ways in which humans put their lives in perspective, whether it be Purim, Advent, or drawing down the moon. Ritual calls together the shades and specters in people's lives, sorts them out, puts them to rest. There is a particular image from *El Día de los Muertos*, Day of the Dead, celebrations that can be applied to help women in the transition from surviving to thriving. It is based on the rite of *ofrendas*, which are altars to those who have passed from this life. *Ofrendas* are tributes, memorials, and expressions of deepest regard for the loved ones no longer on this earth. I find it helps many women to make an *ofrenda* to the child they once were, rather like a testament to the heroic child.

Some women choose objects, writings, clothing, toys, mementos from events, and other symbols from childhood that will be portrayed. They arrange the *ofrenda* in their own way, tell the story that goes with it or not, and then leave it up for as long as they wish. It is the evidence of their past hardship, valor, and triumph over adversity.[15]

This way of looking at the past accomplishes several things: it gives perspective, a compassionate rendering of times past, by laying out what one experienced, what one has made of it, what is admirable. It is the admiring of it, rather than the being of it, that releases the person.

To be the child survivor beyond its time is too over-identified with an injured archetype. To realize the injury, and yet memorialize it, allows thriving to come forth. Thriving is what was meant for us on this earth. Thriving, not just surviving, is our birthright as women.

Do not cringe and make yourself small if you are called the black sheep, the maverick, the lone wolf. Those with slow seeing say a nonconformist is a blight on society. But it has been proven over the centuries, that being different means standing at the edge, means one is practically guaranteed to make an original contribution, a useful and stunning contribution to her culture.[16]

When seeking guidance, don't ever listen to the tiny-hearted. Be kind to them, heap them with blessing, cajole them, but do not follow their advice.

If you have ever been called defiant, incorrigible, forward, cunning, insurgent, unruly, rebellious, you're on the right track. Wild Woman is close by.

If you have never been called these things, there is yet time. Practice your Wild Woman. *Ándele!* And again.

✢ CHAPTER 7

Joyous Body:
The Wild Flesh

I have been taken with the way wolves hit their bodies together when they run and play, the old wolves in their way, the young ones in theirs, the skinny ones, the fat ones, the long-legged, the lop-tailed, the floppy-eared, the ones whose broken limbs healed crookedly. They all have their own body configurations and strengths, their own beauty. They live and play according to what and who and how they are. They do not try to be what they are not.

Up in the northlands, I watched one old wolf who had only three legs; she was the only one who could fit through a crevasse where blueberries were branching. I once saw a gray wolf crouch and leap in such a flash it left the image of a silver arc in the air for a second afterward. I remember a delicate one, a new mother, still fulsome in the belly, picking her way through the pool moss with the grace of a dancer.

Yet, despite their beauty and ability to stay strong, wolves are sometimes talked about in this way: "Ah, you are too hungry, your teeth are too sharp, your appetites too interested." Like wolves, women are sometimes discussed as though only a certain temperament, only a certain restrained appetite, is acceptable. And too often added to that is an attribution of moral goodness or badness according to whether a woman's size, height, gait, and shape conform to a singular or exclusionary ideal. When women are relegated to moods, mannerisms, and contours that conform to a single ideal of beauty and behavior, they are captured in both body and soul, and are no longer free.

In the instinctive psyche, the body is considered a sensor, an informational network, a messenger with myriad communication systems—cardiovascular, respiratory, skeletal, autonomic, as well as emotive and intuitive. In the imaginal world, the body is a powerful vehicle, a spirit who lives with us, a prayer of life in its own right. In fairy tales, as personified by magical objects that have superhuman qualities and abilities, the body is considered to have two sets of ears, one for hearing in the mundane world, the other for hearing the soul; two sets of eyes, one set for regular vision, another for far-seeing; two kinds of strength, the strength of the muscles and the invincible strength of soul. The list of twos about the body goes on.

In systems of body work such as Feldenkrais method, Ayurveda, and others, the body is understood variously as having six senses, not five. The body uses its skin and deeper fascia and flesh to record all that goes on around it. Like the Rosetta stone, for those who know how to read it, the body is a living record of life given, life taken, life hoped for, life healed. It is valued for its articulate ability to register immediate reaction, to feel profoundly, to sense ahead.

The body is a multilingual being. It speaks through its color and its temperature, the flush of recognition, the glow of love, the ash of pain, the heat of arousal, the coldness of nonconviction. It speaks through its constant tiny dance, sometimes swaying, sometimes a-jitter, sometimes trembling. It speaks through the leaping of the heart, the falling of the spirit, the pit at the center, and rising hope.

The body remembers, the bones remember, the joints remember, even the little finger remembers. Memory is lodged in pictures and feelings in the cells themselves. Like a sponge filled with water, anywhere the flesh is pressed, wrung, even touched lightly, a memory may flow out in a stream.

To confine the beauty and value of the body to anything less than this magnificence is to force the body to live without its rightful spirit, its rightful form, its right to exultation. To be thought ugly or unacceptable because one's beauty is outside the current fashion is deeply wounding to the natural joy that belongs to the wild nature.

Women have good reason to refute psychological and physical standards that are injurious to spirit and which sever relationship with the wild soul. It is clear that the instinctive nature of women values body and spirit far more for their ability to be vital, responsive, and enduring than by any measure of appearance. This is not to dismiss who or what is considered beautiful by any segment of culture, but to draw a larger circle that embraces all forms of beauty, form, and function.

Body Talk

A friend and I once performed a tandem storytelling called "Body Talk" about discovering the ancestral blessings of our kith and kin. Opalanga is an African American *griot* and she is very tall, like a yew tree, and as slender. I am *una Mexicana*, and am built close to the ground and am of extravagant body. In addition to being mocked for being tall, as a child she was told that the split between her front teeth was the sign of being a liar. I was told that my body shape and size were the signs of being inferior and of having no self-control.

In this concurrent telling about body, we spoke of the slings and arrows we received throughout our lives because, according to the great "they," our bodies were too much of this and not enough of that. In our telling, we sang a mourning song for the bodies we were not allowed to enjoy. We rocked, we danced, we looked at each other. We were each thinking the other is so mysterious-looking in such a beautiful way, how could anyone have thought otherwise?

How amazed I was to hear that as an adult she had journeyed to the Gambia in West Africa and found some of her ancestral people, who, lo! had among their tribe, many people who were very tall like the yew trees and as slender, and who had splits between their front teeth. This split, they explained to her, was called *Sakaya Yallah*, meaning "opening of God" . . . and it was understood as a sign of wisdom.

How surprised she was when I told her, that as an adult, I had journeyed to the Isthmus of Tehuantepec in Mexico and found some of my ancestral people, who lo! were a tribe with giant women who were strong, flirtatious, and commanding in their size. They had patted me[1] and plucked at me, boldly remarking that I was not quite fat enough. Did I eat enough? Had I been ill? I must try harder, they explained, for women are *La Tierra*, made round like the earth herself, for the earth holds so much.[2]

So in the performance, as in our lives, our personal stories, which began as experiences both oppressive and depressive, end with joy and a strong sense of self. Opalanga understands that her height is her beauty, her smile one of wisdom, and that the voice of God is always close to her lips. I understand my body as not separate from the land, that my feet are made to hold my ground, my body a vessel made to carry much. We learned, from powerful people outside our own United States culture, to revalue the body, to refute ideas and language that would revile the mysterious body, or that would ignore the female body as an instrument of knowing.[3]

To take much pleasure in a world filled with many kinds of beauty is a joy in life to which all women are entitled. To support only one kind of beauty is to be somehow unobservant of nature. There cannot be only one kind of songbird, only one kind of pine tree, only one kind of wolf. There cannot be one kind of baby, one kind of man, or one kind of woman. There cannot be one kind of breast, one kind of waist, one kind of skin.

My experiences with women of size in Mexico caused me to question the entire set of analytic premises about women's various sizes and shapes and especially weights. One old psychological premise in particular seemed grotesquely erroneous: the idea that all women of size are hungry for something; that "inside them is a thin person screaming to get out." When I suggested this "screaming thin woman" metaphor to one of the majestic Tehuana tribeswomen, she peered at me somewhat alarmed. Did I mean "possession by an evil spirit?[4] Who would have put such an evil thing inside a woman?" she asked. It was beyond her comprehension that a woman would be considered by "healers" or anyone else to have a screaming woman within because she was naturally big.

While compulsive and destructive eating disorders that distort body size and body image are real and tragic, they are not the norm for most women. Women who are big or small, wide or narrow, short or tall, are most likely to be so simply because they inherited the body configuration of their kin; if not their immediate kin, then those a generation or two back. To malign or judge a woman's inherited physicality is to make generation after generation of anxious and neurotic women. To make destructive and exclusionary judgments about a woman's inherited form, robs her of several critical and precious psychological and spiritual treasures. It robs her of pride in the body type that was given to her by her own ancestral lines. If she is taught to revile this body inheritance, she is immediately slashed away from her female body identity with the rest of the family.

If she is taught to hate her own body, how can she love her mother's body that has the same configuration as hers?[5]—her grandmother's body, the bodies of her daughters as well? How can she love the bodies of other women (and men) close to her who have inherited the body shapes and configurations of their ancestors? To attack a woman thusly destroys her rightful pride of affiliation with her own people and robs her of the natural lilt she feels in her body no matter what height, size, shape she is. In essence, the attack on women's bodies is a far-reaching attack on the ones who have gone before her as well as the ones who will come after her.[6]

Instead, harsh judgments about body acceptability create a nation of hunched-over tall girls, short women on stilts, women of size dressed as though in mourning, very slender women trying to puff themselves out like adders, and various other women in hiding. Destroying a woman's instinctive affiliation with her natural body cheats her of confidence. It causes her to perseverate about whether she is a good person or not, and bases her self-worth on how she looks instead of who she is. It pressures her to use up her energy worrying about how much food she consumes or the readings on the scale and tape measure. It keeps her preoccupied, colors everything she does, plans, and anticipates. It is unthinkable in the instinctive world that a woman should live preoccupied by appearance this way.

It makes utter sense to stay healthy and strong, to be as nourishing to the body as possible.[7] Yet I would have to agree, there is in many women a "hungry" one inside. But rather than hungry to be a certain size, shape, or height, rather than hungry to fit the stereotype; women are hungry for basic regard from the culture surrounding them. The "hungry" one inside is longing to be treated respectfully, to be accepted,[8] and in the very least, to be met without stereotyping. If there really is a woman "screaming to get out" she is screaming for cessation of the disrespectful projections of others onto her body, her face, her age.

The pathologizing of variation in women's bodies is a deep bias endorsed by many psychological theorists, most certainly by Freud. For instance, in his book on his father, Sigmund, Martin Freud relates how the entire family actively disliked and ridiculed stout people.[9] The reasons for Freud's views are beyond the scope of this work; however, it is difficult to understand how such an attitude would assist a balanced viewpoint toward women's bodies.

Yet, suffice it to say that various practitioners of psychology continue to hand down this bias against the natural body, encouraging women to turn their attentions to a constant monitoring of body, thereby robbing them of deeper and finer relationships with their given form. Angst about the body robs a woman in some large share of her creative life and her attention to other things.

This encouragement to begin trying to carve her body is remarkably similar to the carving, burning, peeling off layers, stripping down to the bones the flesh of the earth itself. Where there is a wound on the psyches and bodies of women, there is a corresponding wound at the same site in the culture itself, and finally on Nature herself. In a true holistic psychology all worlds are understood as interdependent, not as separate entities. It is not amazing that in our culture there is an issue about carving up a woman's natural body, that there is a corresponding issue about carving up the landscape, and yet another about carving up the culture into fashionable parts as well. Although a woman may not be able to stop the dissection of culture and lands overnight, she can stop doing so to her own body.

The wild nature would never advocate the torture of the body, culture, or land. The wild nature would never agree to flog the form in order to prove worth, prove "control," prove character, be more visually pleasing, more financially valuable.

A woman cannot make the culture more aware by saying "Change." But she can change her own attitude toward herself, thereby causing devaluing projections to glance off. She does this by taking back her body. By not forsaking the joy of her natural body, by not purchasing the popular illusion that happiness is only bestowed on those of a certain configuration or age, by not waiting or holding back to do anything, and by taking back her real life, and living it full bore, all stops out. This dynamic self-acceptance and self-esteem are what begins to change attitudes in the culture.

The Body in Fairy Tales

There are many mythos and fairy tales that describe the frailties and the wildness of the body. There is Greek Hephaestus, the lame worker of precious metals; the Mexican *Hartar*, the double-bodied one; Venus-born-of-the-sea; the littlest tailor, who was ugly but could create new life; the women of Giant Mountain, who are courted for their strength; Thumbelina, who is able to travel about magically; and many more.

In fairy tales certain magic objects have transportive and sensory abilities that are apt metaphors for body, such as magic leaf, magic carpet, cloud. Sometimes cloaks, shoes, shields, hats, and helmets give the power of invisibility, superior strength, far-vision, and so forth. These are archetypal kith and kin. Each enables the physical body to enjoy deepened insight, hearing, flight, or protection of some sort for both psyche and soul.

Before the invention of carriages, coaches, chariots, before the domestication of animals for hauling and riding, it appears the motif that represented the sacred body was the magical object. Articles of clothing, amulets, talismans, and other objects, when related to in a certain way, transported the person across the river or the world

The magic carpet is an excellent symbol of the sensory and psychic value of the natural body. Fairy tales in which the flying carpet motif appears mimic the not-very-conscious attitude toward body in our own culture. The magic carpet is at first thought to be quite ordinary and without much value. But for those who seat themselves in its dense pile and say "Arise," the carpet instantly trembles, rises a bit, hovers, and then, zoom! away it flies, transporting the rider to a different place, center, viewpoint, knowing.[10] The body, through its states of arousal, awareness, and sensory experiences—such as listening to music, for instance, or hearing a loved one's voice or smelling a certain fragrance—has the ability to transport us elsewhere.

In fairy tales, as in mythos, the carpet signifies a form of loco- motion, but of a certain kind—the kind that enables us to see into the world and into the underlife as well. In the Middle Eastern sto- ries, it is the vehicle for spirit flight of the shamans. The body is no dumb thing from which we struggle to free ourselves. In proper perspective, it is a rocket ship, a series of atomic cloverleafs, a tangle of neurological umbilici to other worlds and experiences.

In addition to the magic carpet, there are other symbols for the body. One story in particular illustrates three. This tale was given to me by Fahtah Kelly. It is called simply, "The Tale of the Magic Carpet."[11] In it, a sultan sends three brothers to search for "the finest object on earth." Whichever brother is deemed to have found the ultimate treasure will win an entire kingdom. One brother searches and brings back an ivory wand through which one can see into whatever one wishes. One brother brings back an apple whose smell can cure any affliction. The third brother brings back a magic carpet that can transport a person anywhere simply by his thinking of the place.

"So, which is the greater?" asks the sultan. "The ability to see far? The ability to heal and recover? Or the ability for spirit flight?"

By turn, each brother glorifies the object he has found. Yet the sultan finally waves his hand and proclaims, "None of these is greater than the other, for without one, the others would be of no use." And the kingdom is given in equal shares to each brother.

Embedded in this tale are potent images that allow us to imagine what a true aliveness of body really is. This tale (and others like it) describe the fabulous powers of intuition, insight, sensory healing, and the rapture hidden in the body.[12] We tend to think of body as this "other" that does its thing somewhat without us, and that if we "treat" it right, it will make us "feel good." Many people treat their bodies as if the body is a slave, or perhaps they even treat it well but demand it follow their wishes and whims as though it were a slave nonetheless.

Some say the soul informs the body. But what if we were to imagine for a moment that the body informs the soul, helps it adapt to mundane life, parses, translates, gives the blank page, the ink, and the pen with which the soul can write upon our lives? Suppose, as in fairy tales of the shapechangers, the body is a God in its own right, a teacher, a mentor, a certified guide? Then what? Is it wise to spend a lifetime chastising this teacher who has so much to give and teach? Do we wish to spend a lifetime allowing others to detract from our bodies, judge them, find them wanting? Are we strong enough to refute the party line and listen deep, listen true to the body as a powerful and holy being?[13]

The idea in our culture of body solely as sculpture is wrong. Body is not marble. That is not its purpose. Its purpose it to protect, contain, support, and fire the spirit and soul within it, to be a repository for memory, to fill us with feeling—that is the supreme psychic nourishment. It is to lift us and propel us, to fill us with feeling to prove that we exist, that we are here, to give us grounding, heft, weight. It is wrong to think of it as a place we leave in order to soar to the spirit. The body is the launcher of those experiences. Without body there would be no sensations of crossing thresholds, there would be no sense of lifting, no sense of height, weightlessness. All that comes from the body. The body is the rocket launcher. In its nose capsule, the soul looks out the window into the mysterious starry night and is dazzled.

The Power of the Haunches

What constitutes a healthy body in the instinctual world? At the most basic level—the breast, the belly, anywhere there is skin, anywhere there are neurons to transmit feeling—the issue is not what shape, what size, what color, what age, but does it feel, does it work as it is meant to, can we respond, do we feel a range, a spectrum of feeling? Is it afraid, paralyzed by pain or fear, anesthetized by old trauma, or does it have its own music, is it listening, like Baubo, through the belly, is it looking with its many ways of seeing?

I had two watershed experiences when I was in my early twenties, experiences that went against everything I had been taught about body up to then. While at a women's weeklong gathering and at night at the fire near the hot springs, I saw a naked woman of about thirty-five; her breasts were emptied out by childbearing, her belly striated from birthing children. I was very young and I remember feeling sorry for the assaults on her fair and thin skin. Someone was playing maracas and drums, and she began to dance, her hair, her breasts, her skin, her limbs all moving in different directions. How beautiful she was, how vital. Her grace was heartbreaking. I had always smiled at that phrase, "fire in her loins." But that night I saw it. I saw the power in her haunches. I saw what I had been taught to ignore, the power of a woman's body when it is animated from the inside. Almost three decades later, I can still see her dancing in the night and I am still struck by the power of body.

The second awakening involved a much older woman. Her hips were, according to common standard, too pear-shaped, her bosom very tiny in comparison, and she had thin purply little veins all over her thighs, a long scar from a serious surgery going around her body from rib cage to spine in the manner in which apples are peeled. Her waist was perhaps four hands wide.

It was a mystery then why the men buzzed about her as though she were honeycomb. They wanted to take a bite out of her pear thighs, they wanted to lick that scar, hold that chest, lay their cheeks upon her spidery veins. Her smile was dazzling, her gait so beautiful, and when her eyes looked, they truly took in what they were looking at. I saw again what I had been taught to ignore, the power *in* the body. The cultural power *of* the body is its beauty, but power *in* the body is rare, for most have chased it away with their torture of or embarrassment by the flesh.

It is in this light that the wildish woman can inquire into the numinosity of her own body and understand it not as a dumbbell that we are sentenced to carry for life, not as a beast of burden, pampered or otherwise, who carries us around for life, but a series of doors and dreams and poems through which we can learn and know all manner of things. In the wild psyche, body is understood as a being in its own right, one who loves us, depends on us, one to whom we are sometimes mother, and who sometimes is mother to us.

~~~~~~~~~~~~~~~~~~~~~

La Mariposa, Butterfly Woman

TO TELL YOU ABOUT THE POWER of the body in another way, I have to tell you a story, a true, rather long story.

For years, tourists have thundered across the great American desert, hurrying through the "spiritual circuit": Monument Valley, Chaco Canyon, Mesa Verde, Kayenta, Keams Canyon, Painted Desert, and Canyon de Chelly. They peer up the pelvis of the Mother Grand Canyon, shake their heads, shrug their shoulders, and hurry home, only to again come charging across the desert the next summer, looking, looking some more, watching, watching some more.

Underneath it all is the same hunger for numinous experience that humans have had since the beginning of time. But sometimes this hunger is exacerbated, for many people have lost their ancestors.[14] They often do not know the names of those beyond their grandparents. They have lost, in particular, the family stories. Spiritually, this situation causes sorrow . . . and hunger. So many are trying to re-create something important for soul sake.

For years tourists have come also to Puyé, a big dusty mesa in the middle of "nowhere," New Mexico. Here the *Anasazi*, the ancient ones, once called to each other across the mesas. A prehistoric sea, it is said, carved the thousands of grinning, leering, and moaning mouths and eyes into the rock walls there.

The Diné (Navajo), Jicarilla Apache, southern Ute, Hopi, Zuni, Santa Clara, Santa Domingo, Laguna, Picuris, Tesuque, all these desert tribes come together here. It is here that they dance themselves back into lodgepole pine trees, back into deer, back into eagles and *Katsinas*, powerful spirits.

And here too come visitors, some of whom are very starved of their geno-myths, detached from the spiritual placenta. They have forgotten their ancient Gods as well. They come to watch the ones who have *not* forgotten.

The road up to Puyé was built for horse hooves and moccasins. But over time automobiles became more powerful and now locals and visitors come in all manner of cars, trucks, convertibles, and vans. The vehicles all whine and smoke up the road in a slow, dusty parade.

Everyone parks *trochimochi*, willy-nilly, on the lumpy hillocks. By noon, the edge of the mesa looks like a thousand-car pileup. Some people park next to six-foot-tall hollyhocks thinking they will just knock over the plants to get out of their cars. But the hundred-year-old hollyhocks are like old iron women. Those who park next to them are trapped in their cars.

The sun turns into a fiery furnace by midday. Everyone trudges in hot shoes, burdened with an umbrella in case it rains (it will), an aluminum folding chair in case they tire (they will), and if they are visitors, perhaps a camera (if they're allowed), and pods of film cans hanging around their necks like garlic wreaths.

Visitors come with all manner of expectations, from the sacred to the profane. They come to see something that not everyone will be able to see, one of the wildest of the wild, a living numen, *La Mariposa*, the Butterfly Woman.

The last event of the day is the Butterfly Dance. Everyone anticipates with great delight this one-person dance. It is danced by a woman, and oh what a woman. As the sun begins to set, here comes an old man resplendent in forty pounds of formal-dress turquoise. With the loudspeakers squawking like a chicken espying a hawk, he whispers into the 1930s chrome microphone, "An' our nex' dance is gonna be th' Butterfly Dance." He limps away on the cuffs of his jeans.

Unlike a ballet recital, where the act is announced, the curtains part, and the dancers wobble out, here at Puyé, as at other tribal dances, the announcement of the dance may precede the dancer's appearance by anywhere from twenty minutes to forever. Where is the dancer? Tidying up the camper, perhaps. Air temperatures over 100 degrees are common, so last-minute repairs to sweat-streaked body paint are needed. If a dance belt, which belonged to the dancer's grandfather, breaks on the way to the arena, the dancer would not appear at all, for the spirit of the belt would need to rest. Dancers delay because a good song is playing on "Tony Lujan's Indian Hour" on radio Taos, KKIT (after Kit Carson).

Sometimes a dancer does not hear the loudspeaker and must be summoned by footrunner. And then always, of course, the dancer must speak to all relatives on the way to the arena, and most certainly stop to allow the little nephews and nieces a good look. How awed the little children are to see a towering *Katsina* spirit who looks suspiciously, a little at least, like Uncle Tomás, or a corn dancer who seems to strongly resemble Aunt Yazie. Lastly, there is the ubiquitous possibility that the dancer is still out on the Tesuque highway, legs dangling out the maw of a pickup truck while the muffler smudges the air black for a mile downwind.

While awaiting the Butterfly Dance in giddy anticipation, everyone chatters about butterfly maidens and the beauty of the Zuni girls who danced in ancient red-and-black garb with one shoulder bared, bright pink circles painted on their cheeks. They laud the young male deer-dancers who danced with pine boughs bound to their arms and legs.

Time passes.

And passes.

And passes.

People jingle coins in their pockets. They suck their teeth. The visitors are impatient to see this marvelous butterfly dancer.

Unexpectedly then, for everyone is bored to scowls, the drummer's arms begin drumming the sacred butterfly rhythm, and the chanters begin to cry to the Gods for all they are worth.

To the visitors, a butterfly is a delicate thing. "O fragile beauty," they dream. So they are necessarily shaken when out hops Maria Lujan.[15] And she is big, really *big*, like the Venus of Willendorf, like the Mother of Days, like Diego Rivera's heroic-size woman who built Mexico City with a single curl of her wrist.

And Maria Lujan, oh, she is old, very, very old, like a woman come back from dust, old like old river, old like old pines at timberline. One of her shoulders is bare. Her red-and-black *manta*, blanket dress, hops up and down with her inside it. Her heavy body and her very skinny legs made her look like a hopping spider wrapped in a tamale.

She hops on one foot and then the other. She waves her feather fan to and fro. She is The Butterfly arrived to strengthen the weak. She is that which most think of as not strong: age, the butterfly, the feminine.

Butterfly Maiden's hair reaches to the ground. It is thick as ten maize sheaves and it is stone gray. And she wears butterfly wings—the kind you see on little children who are being angels in school plays. Her hips are like two bouncing bushel baskets and the fleshy shelf at the top of her buttocks is wide enough to ride two children.

She hops, hops, hops, not like a rabbit, but in footsteps that leave echoes.

"I am here, here, here . . .

"I am here, here, here . . .

"Awaken you, you, you!"

She sways her feather fan up and down, spreading the earth and the people of the earth with the pollinating spirit of the butterfly. Her shell bracelets rattle like snakes, her bell garters tinkle like rain. Her shadow with its big belly and little legs dances from one side of the dance circle to the other. Her feet leave little puffs of dust behind.

The tribes are reverent, involved. But some visitors look at each other and murmur "This is it? *This* is the Butterfly Maiden?" They are puzzled, some even disillusioned. They no longer seem to remember that the spirit world is a place where wolves are women, bears are husbands, and old women of lavish dimensions are butterflies.

Yes, it is fitting that Wild Woman/Butterfly Woman is old and substantial, for she carries the thunderworld in one breast, the underworld in the other. Her back is the curve of the planet Earth with all its crops and foods and animals. The back of her neck carries the sunrise and the sunset. Her left thigh holds all the lodgepoles, her right thigh all the she-wolves of the world. Her belly holds all the babies that will ever be born.

Butterfly Maiden is the female fertilizing force. Carrying the pollen from one place to another, she cross-fertilizes, just as the soul fertilizes mind with nightdreams, just as archetypes fertilize the mundane world. She is the center. She brings the opposites together by taking a little from here and putting it there. Transformation is no more complicated than that. This is what she teaches. This is how the butterfly does it. This is how the soul does it.

Butterfly Woman mends the erroneous idea that transformation is only for the tortured, the saintly, or only for the fabulously strong. The Self need not carry mountains to transform. A little is enough. A little goes a long way. A little changes much. The fertilizing force replaces the moving of mountains.

Butterfly Maiden pollinates the souls of the earth: It is easier than you think, she says. She is shaking her feather fan, and she's hopping, for she is spilling spiritual pollen all over the people who are there, Native Americans, little children, visitors, everyone. She is using her entire body as a blessing, her old, frail, big, short-legged, short-necked, spotted body. This is woman connected to her wild nature, the translator of the instinctual, the fertilizing force, the mender, the rememberer of old ideas. She is *La voz mitológica*. She is Wild Woman personified.

The butterfly dancer must be old because she represents the soul that is old. She is wide of thigh and broad of rump because she carries much. Her gray hair certifies that she need no longer observe taboos about touching others. She is allowed to touch everyone: boys, babies, men, women, girl children, the old, the ill, and the dead. The Butterfly Woman can touch everyone. It is her privilege to touch all, at last. This is her power. Hers is the body of *La Mariposa*, the butterfly.

~~~~~~~~~~~~~~~~~~~~~~~~~~~~~~~~~~

The body is like an earth. It is a land unto itself. It is as vulnerable to overbuilding, being carved into parcels, cut off, overmined, and shorn of its power as any landscape. The wilder woman will not be easily swayed by redevelopment schemes. For her, the questions are not how to form but how to feel. The breast in all its shapes has the function of feeling and feeding. Does it feed? Does it feel? It is a good breast.

The hips, they are wide for a reason, inside them is a satiny ivory cradle for new life. A woman's hips are outriggers for the body above and below; they are portals, they are a lush cushion, the handholds for love, a place for children to hide behind. The legs, they are meant to take us, sometimes to propel us; they are the pulleys that help us lift, they are the *anillo*, the ring for encircling a lover. They cannot be too this or too that. They are what they are.

There is no "supposed to be" in bodies. The question is not size or shape or years of age, or even having two of everything, for some do not. But the wild issue is, does this body feel, does it have right connection to pleasure, to heart, to soul, to the wild? Does it have happiness, joy? Can it in its own way move, dance, jiggle, sway, thrust? Nothing else matters.

When I was a child, I was taken on a field trip to the Museum of Natural History in Chicago. There I saw the sculptures of Malvina Hoffman, dozens of life-size dark bronze sculptures in a great hall. She had sculpted the mostly naked bodies of people of the world and she had wild vision.

She lavished her love on the thin calf of the hunter, the long breasts of the mother with two grown children, the cones of flesh on the chest of the virgin, the old man's nuts hanging to mid thigh, the nose with nostrils bigger than the eyes, the nose hooked like a hawk's, the nose straight like a corner. She had fallen in love with ears like semaphores, and ears low near the chin and small as pecans. She had loved each hair coiled like a snake basket, or each hair wavy as a ribbon unfurling, or each hair straight as fever grass. She had the wild love *of* body. She understood the power *in* the body.

There is a line in Ntozake Shange's *for colored girls who have considered suicide/when the rainbow is enuf*.[16] In the play, the woman in purple speaks after having struggled to deal with all the psychic and physical aspects of herself that the culture ignores or demeans. She sums herself up in these wise and peaceful words:

here is what i have . . .
poems
big thighs
lil tits
&

so much love

This is the power of the body, our power, the power of the wildish woman. In mythos and fairy tales, deities and other great spirits test the hearts of humans by showing up in various forms that disguise their divinity. They show up in robes, rags, silver sashes, or with muddy feet. They show up with skin dark as old wood, or in scales made of rose petal, as a frail child, as a lime-yellow old woman, as a man who cannot speak, or as an animal who can. The great powers are testing to see if humans have yet learned to recognize the greatness of soul in all its varying forms.

Wild Woman shows up in many sizes, shapes, colors, and conditions. Stay awake so you can recognize the wild soul in all its many guises.

CHAPTER 8

Self-preservation:
Identifying Leg Traps,
Cages, and Poisoned Bait

The Feral Woman

In the Oxford English Dictionary the word *feral* derives from Latin *fer* . . . meaning "wild beast." In common usage, a feral creature is one who was once wild, then domesticated, and who has reverted back to a natural or untamed state once again.

I postulate the feral woman as one who was once in a natural psychic state—that is, in her rightful wild mind—then later captured by whatever turn of events, thereby becoming overly domesticated and deadened in proper instincts. When she has opportunity to return to her original wildish nature, she too easily steps into all manner of traps and poisons. Because her cycles and protective systems have been tampered with, she is at risk in what used to be her natural wild state. No longer wary and alert, she easily becomes prey.

There is a specific pattern to the loss of instinct. It is essential to study this pattern, to actually memorize it, so that we can guard the treasures of our basic natures and those of our daughters as well. In the psychic woods there are many leg traps made of rusted iron that lie just below the leafy green of the forest floor. Psychologically, the same is true of the greater world. There are various lures to which we are susceptible: relationships, people, and ventures that are tempting, but inside that good-looking bait is something sharpened to a point, something that kills our spirit as soon as we bite into it.

Feral women of all ages, and especially the young, have a tremendous drive to compensate for long famines and exiles. They are endangered by excessive and mindless striving toward people and goals that are not nurturant, substantive, or enduring. No matter where they live or in what time, there are cages waiting always; too-small lives into which women can be lured or pushed.

If you have ever been captured, if you have ever endured *hambre del alma*, a starvation of the soul, if you have ever been trapped, and especially if you have a drive to create, it is likely that you have been or are a feral woman. The feral woman is usually extremely hungry for something soulful, and often will take any poison disguised on a pointed stick, believing it to be the thing for which her soul hungers.

Though some feral women veer away from traps at the last moment with only minor losses of fur, far more stumble into them unwittingly, knocked temporarily senseless, while others are broken by them, and still others manage to disentangle themselves and drag themselves off to a cave to nurse their injuries alone.

In order to avoid these snares and enticements that are tripped by a woman's time spent in capture and famine, we must be able to see them in advance and sidestep them. We have to redevelop insight and caution. We have to learn to veer. To be able to see the right turns, we have to be able to see the wrong ones.

There is what I believe to be the remnants of an old women's teaching tale that explicates the plight of the starved and feral woman. It is variously known by names such as "The Devil's Dancing Shoes," "The Red-Hot Shoes of the Devil," and "The Red Shoes." Hans Christian Andersen wrote his rendition of this old tale and titled it with the latter name. Like a true raconteur, he surrounded the core of the story with much of his own ethnic wit and sensitivity.

The following is a Magyar-Germanic version of "The Red Shoes" that my aunt Tereza used to tell us when we were children, one that I use here with her blessing. In her artful way, she always began the tale by saying, "Look at your shoes, and be thankful they are plain . . . for one has to live very carefully if one's shoes are too red."

The Red Shoes

ONCE THERE WAS a poor motherless child who had no shoes. But the child saved cloth scraps wherever she found them and over time sewed herself a pair of red shoes. They were crude but she loved them. They made her feel rich even though her days were spent gathering food in the thorny woods until far past dark.

But one day as she trudged down the road in her rags and her red shoes, a gilded carriage pulled up beside her. Inside was an old woman who told her she was going to take her home and treat her as her own little daughter. So to the wealthy old woman's house they went, and the child's hair was cleaned and combed. She was given pure white undergarments and a fine wool dress and white stockings and shiny black shoes. When the child asked after her old clothes, and especially her red shoes, the old woman said the clothes were so filthy, and the shoes so ridiculous, that she had thrown them into the fire, where they were burnt to ashes.

The child was very sad, for even with all the riches surrounding her, the humble red shoes made by her own hands had given her the greatest happiness. Now, she was made to sit still all the time, to walk without skipping, and to not speak unless spoken to, but a secret fire began to burn in her heart and she continued to yearn for her old red shoes more than anything.

As the child was old enough to be confirmed on The Day of The Innocents, the old woman took her to an old crippled shoemaker to have a special pair of shoes made for the occasion. In the shoemaker's case there stood a pair of red shoes made of finest leather that were finer than fine; they practically glowed. So even though red shoes were scandalous for church, the child, who chose only with her hungry heart, picked the red shoes. The old lady's eyesight was so poor she could not see the color of the shoes and so paid for them. The old shoemaker winked at the child and wrapped the shoes up.

The next day, the church members were agog over the shoes on the child's feet. The red shoes shone like burnished apples, like hearts, like red-washed plums. Everyone stared; even the icons on the wall, even the statues stared disapprovingly at her shoes. But she loved the shoes all the more. So when the pontiff intoned, the choir hummed, the organ pumped, the child thought nothing more beautiful than her red shoes.

By the end of the day the old woman had been informed about her ward's red shoes. "Never, never wear those red shoes again!" the old woman threatened. But the next Sunday, the child couldn't help but choose the red shoes over the black ones, and she and the old woman walked to church as usual.

At the door to the church was an old soldier with his arm in a sling. He wore a little jacket and had a red beard. He bowed and asked permission to brush the dust from the child's shoes. The child put out her foot, and he tapped the soles of her shoes with a little wig-a-jig-jig song that made the soles of her feet itch. "Remember to stay for the dance," he smiled, and winked at her.

Again everyone looked askance at the girl's red shoes. But she so loved the shoes that were bright like crimson, bright like raspberries, bright like pomegranates, that she could hardly think of anything else, hardly hear the service at all. So busy was she turning her feet this way and that, admiring her red shoes, that she forgot to sing.

As she and the old woman left the church, the injured soldier called out, "What beautiful dancing shoes!" His words made the girl take a few little twirls right there and then. But once her feet had begun to move, they would not stop, and she danced through the flower beds and around the corner of the church until it seemed as though she had lost complete control of herself. She did a gavotte and then a *csárdás* and then waltzed by herself through the fields across the way.

The old woman's coachman jumped up from his bench and ran after the girl, picked her up, and carried her back to the carriage, but the girl's feet in the red shoes were still dancing in the air as though they were still on the ground. The old woman and the coachman tugged and pulled, trying to pry the red shoes off. It was such a sight, all hats askew and kicking legs, but at last the child's feet were calmed.

Back home, the old woman slammed the red shoes down high

on a shelf and warned the girl never to touch them again. But the girl could not help looking up at them and longing for them. To her they were still the most beauteous things on the face of the earth.

Not long after, as fate would have it, the old woman became bedridden, and as soon as her doctors left, the girl crept into the room where the red shoes were kept. She glanced up at them so high on the shelf. Her glance became a gaze and her gaze became a powerful desire, so much so that the girl took the shoes from the shelf and fastened them on, feeling it would do no harm. But as soon as they touched her heels and toes, she was overcome by the urge to dance.

And so out the door she danced, and then down the steps, first in a gavotte, then a *csárdás*, and then in big daring waltz turns in rapid succession. The girl was in her glory and did not realize she was in trouble until she wanted to dance to the left and the shoes insisted on dancing to the right. When she wanted to dance round, the shoes insisted on dancing straight ahead. And as the shoes danced the girl, rather than the other way around, they danced her right down the road, through the muddy fields, and out into the dark and gloomy forest.

There against a tree was the old soldier with the red beard, his arm in a sling, and dressed in his little jacket. "Oh my," he said, "what beautiful dancing shoes." Terrified, she tried to pull the shoes off, but as much as she tugged, the shoes stayed fast. She hopped on one foot and then the other trying to take off the shoes, but her one foot on the ground kept dancing even so, and her other foot in her hand did its part of the dance also.

And so dance, and dance and dance, she did. Over highest hills and through the valleys, in the rain and in the snow and in the sunlight, she danced. She danced in the darkest night and through sunrise and she was still dancing in twilight as well. But it was not good dancing. It was terrible dancing, and there was no rest for her.

She danced into a churchyard and there a spirit of dread would not allow her to enter. The spirit pronounced these words over her, "You shall dance in your red shoes until you become like a wraith, like a ghost, till your skin hangs from your bones, till there is nothing left of you but entrails dancing. You shall dance door to door through all the villages and you shall strike each door three times and when people peer out they will see you and fear your fate for themselves. Dance red shoes, you shall dance."

The girl begged for mercy, but before she could plead further, her red shoes carried her away. Over the briars she danced, through the streams, over the hedgerows and on and on, dancing, still dancing till she came to her old home and there were mourners. The old woman who had taken her in had died. Yet even so, she danced on by, and dance she did, as dance she must. In abject exhaustion and horror, she danced into a forest where lived the town's executioner. And the ax on his wall began to tremble as soon as it sensed her coming near.

"Please!" she begged the executioner as she danced by his door. "Please cut off my shoes to free me from this horrid fate." And the executioner cut through the straps of the red shoes with his ax. But still the shoes stayed on her feet. And so she cried to him that her life was worth nothing and that he should cut off her feet. So he cut off her feet. And the red shoes with the feet in them kept on dancing through the forest and over the hill and out of sight. And now the girl was a poor cripple, and had to find her own way in the world as a servant to others, and she never, ever again wished for red shoes.

Brutal Loss in Fairy Tales

It is more than reasonable to ask why there are such brutal episodes in fairy tales. It is a phenomenon found worldwide in mythos and folklore. The gruesome conclusion to this tale is typical of fairy-tale endings wherein the spiritual protagonist is unable to complete an attempted transformation.

Psychologically, the brutal episode communicates an imperative psychic truth. This truth is so urgent—and yet so easy to disregard by saying, "Oh, um hmmm, I do understand," and to then go traipsing off to one's doom anyway—that we are unlikely to heed the alarm if it is stated in lesser terms.

In the modern technological world, the brutal episodes of fairy tales have been replaced by images in television commercials, such as those showing a family snapshot with one member blotted out and a trail of blood over the photograph to show what happens when a person drives while drunk, or attempting to dissuade people from using illegal drugs by showing an egg bubbling in a frying pan and pointing out that this is what happens to the brain on drugs. The brutal motif is an ancient way of causing the emotive self to pay attention to a very serious message.

The psychological truth in "The Red Shoes" is that a woman's meaningful life can be pried, threatened, robbed, or seduced away from her unless she holds on to or retrieves her basic joy and wild worth. The tale calls our attention to traps and poisons we too easily take onto ourselves when we are caught in a famine of wild soul. Without a firm participation with the wild nature, a woman starves and falls into an obsession of "feel betters," "leave me alones" and "love me—please."

When she is starved, a woman will take any substitutes offered, including those that, like dead placebos, do absolutely nothing for her, as well as destructive and life-threatening ones that hideously waste her time and talents or expose her life to physical danger. It is a famine of the soul that makes a woman choose things that will cause her to dance madly out of control—then too, too near the executioner's door.

So in order to understand this tale further, we have to see how a woman can so drastically lose her way by losing her instinctual and wild life. The way to hold on to what we have, the way to find our way back to the wild feminine, is to see what mistakes a woman so trapped can make. Then we can backtrack and repair. Then we can have reunion.

As we shall see, the loss of the handmade red shoes represents the loss of a woman's self-designed life and passionate vitality, and the taking on of a too-tame life. This eventually leads to loss of accurate perception, which leads to excess, which leads to loss of the feet, the platform on which we stand, our basis, a deep part of our instinctual nature that supports our freedom.

"The Red Shoes" shows us how a deterioration begins and what state we come to if we make no intervention in our own wildish behalf. Let there be no mistake, when a woman makes efforts to intervene and fight her demon, whatever that demon may be, it is one of the most worthy battles known, both archetypally and in consensual reality. Even though she might, as in the tale, hit ground-zero-minus-five bottom via famine, capture, injured instinct, destructive choices, and all the rest, remember, at bottom is where the living roots of psyche are. It is there that a woman's wild underpinnings are. At bottom is the best soil to sow and grow something new again. In that sense, hitting bottom, while extremely painful, is also the sowing ground.

Though we would never wish the poisonous red shoes and the subsequent decrease of life onto ourselves or others, there is in its fiery and destructive center a something that fuses fierceness to wisdom in the woman who has danced the cursed dance, who has lost herself and her creative life, who has driven herself to hell in a cheap (or expensive) handbasket, and yet who has somehow held on to a word, a thought, an idea until she could escape her demon through a crack in time and live to tell about it.

So the woman who has danced out of control, who has lost her footing and lost her feet and understands that bereft state at the end of the fairy tale, has a special and valuable wisdom. She is like a saguaro, a fine and beautiful cactus that lives in the desert. Saguaros can be shot full of holes, carved upon, knocked over, stepped on, and still they live, still they store life-giving water, still they grow wild and repair themselves over time.

Though fairy tales end after ten pages, our lives do not. We are multi-volume sets. In our lives, even though one episode amounts to a crash and burn, there is always another episode awaiting us and then another. There are always more opportunities to get it right, to fashion our lives in the ways we deserve to have them. Don't waste your time hating a failure. Failure is a greater teacher than success. Listen, learn, go on. That is what we are doing with this tale. We are listening to its ancient message. We are learning about deteriorative patterns so we can go on with the strength of one who can sense the traps and cages and baits before we are upon them or caught in them.

Let us begin to unravel this very important tale by understanding what happens when the vital life we value most, no matter what it might look like to others, the life we love most, is devalued and turned to ashes.

The Handmade Red Shoes

In the tale we see that the child loses the red shoes she has fashioned for herself, those that made her feel rich in her own special way. She was poor, but she was innovative; she was finding her way. She had progressed from having no shoes to having shoes that gave her a sense of soul in spite of the difficulties of her outer life. The handmade shoes are marks of her rising out of a mean psychic existence into a passionate life of her own design. Her shoes represent an enormous and literal step toward integration of her resourceful feminine nature in day-to-day life. It does not matter that her life is imperfect. She has her joy. She will evolve.

In fairy tales, we can understand this typically poor but inventive character as a psychological motif for one who is rich in spirit and who slowly becomes more conscious and more powerful over a long period of time. It could be said that this character exactly portrays all of us, for we all make progress slowly but surely.

Socially, shoes send a signal, a way of recognizing one type of person from another. Artists often wear shoes that are quite different from those worn by, say, engineers. Shoes can tell something about what we are like, sometimes even who we are aspiring to be, the persona we are trying out.

The archetypal symbolism of the shoe goes back to ancient times, when shoes were a mark of authority: rulers had them, slaves didn't. Even today, much of the modern world is taught to make immoderate judgments about a person's intelligence and abilities based on whether he or she wears shoes or not, as well as whether those who wear shoes are "well-heeled" or not.

This version of the tale grows out of our having lived in the cold north countries where shoes are understood as instruments of survival. Keeping the feet dry and warm keeps a person alive in bitter cold and wet. I can remember my aunt telling me that to steal someone's only pair of shoes in winter was a crime equal to murder. A woman's creative and passionate nature is at the same risk if she cannot hold on to her sources of growth and joy. These are her warmth, her protection.

The symbol of shoes can be understood as a psychological metaphor; they protect and defend what we stand on—our feet. In archetypal symbolism, feet represent mobility and freedom. In that sense to have shoes to cover the feet is to have the conviction of our beliefs and the wherewithal to act on them. Without psychic shoes a woman is unable to negotiate inner or outer environs that require acuity, sense, caution, and toughness.

Life and sacrifice go together. Red is the color of life and of sacrifice. To live a vibrant life, we must make sacrifices of various sorts. If you want to go to university, you must sacrifice time and money and give intense concentration to the venture. If you want to create, you have to sacrifice superficiality, some security, and often your desire to be liked, to draw up your most intense insights, your most far-reaching visions.

Problems arise when there is much sacrifice but no life forthcoming from it all. Then red is the color of blood-loss rather than blood-life. This is exactly what occurs in the tale. One sort of vibrant and beloved red is lost when the child's handmade red shoes are burned. This sets up a yearning, an obsession, and finally an addiction to another kind of red: the one of fast-breaking, cheap thrills; sex without soul; the one that leads to a life without meaning.

So, understanding all aspects of the fairy tale as components of a single woman's psyche, we can see that the child's making of the red shoes accomplishes a major feat: she takes life from shoeless/slave status—just going on one's way, nose to the road, looking neither left nor right—to a consciousness that pauses to create, that notices beauty and feels joy, that has passion and registers satiation . . . and all the things that make up the integral nature we call wild.

The fact that the shoes are red indicates that the process is going to be one of vibrant life, which includes sacrifice. This is right and proper. The fact that these shoes are handmade and pieced from scraps points to the child symbolizing the creative spirit, who, being motherless and untaught for whatever reasons, has pieced this all together for herself using native perception. And brava! what a fine and soulful accomplishment.

If well enough could only be left alone, this situation would progress nicely for the creative self. In the tale, the child is delighted by her handiwork; the fact that she could manage it, the fact that she had the patience to search and gather, to design, to piece and fit, to make her ideas manifest. No matter that at first the product is crude; many of the creation Gods through all cultures and through all time did not create perfectly the first time. The first try can always stand improvement, and the second and often the third and fourth as well. That has nothing to do with one's goodness and skill. It is just life, evocative and evolving.

But if the child is left alone, she will make another pair of red shoes, and another, and another, until they are not so crude. She will progress. But even beyond her wondrous display of ingenuity and thriving in difficult circumstances, the shining fact for her is that these shoes she has made cause her enormous joy, and joy is her life's blood, spirit-food and soul-life all in one.

Joy is the kind of feeling a woman has when she lays the words down on the paper just so, or hits the notes *al punto*, right on the head, the first time. Whew. Unbelievable. It is the kind of feeling a woman has when she finds she is pregnant and wants to be. It is the kind of joy a woman feels when she looks at people she loves enjoying themselves. It is the kind of joy a woman feels when she has done something that she feels dogged about, that she feels intense about, something that took risk, something that made her stretch, best herself, and succeed—maybe gracefully, maybe not, but she did it, created the something, the someone, the art, the battle, the moment; her life. That is a woman's natural and instinctive state of being. Wild Woman emanates up through that kind of joy. That sort of soulful situation summons her by name.

But, in the story, as fate would have it, one day, in direct opposition to the simple red shoes pieced from scraps, the simple joy for life, along comes a gilded carriage creaking and rolling into the child's life.

The Traps

Trap #1: The Gilded Carriage, the Devalued Life

In archetypal symbolism, the carriage is a literal image, a conveyance that carries something from one place to another. In modern dream material and contemporary folklore it has been mostly supplanted by the automobile, which has the same archetypal "feel" to it. Classically, this sort of "carrying" conveyance is understood as the central mood of the psyche that transports us from one place in the psyche to another, from one idea to another, from one thought to another, and from one endeavor to another.

Climbing into the old woman's gilded carriage here is very similar to entering the gilded cage; it supposedly offers something more comfortable, less stressful, but in effect it captures instead. It entraps in a way that is not immediately perceivable, since gilt tends to be so dazzling at first. So imagine we are going down the road of our own lives, in our handmade shoes, and a mood comes over us, something like this: "Maybe something else would be better; something that isn't so difficult, something that takes less time, energy, and striving."

It often happens in women's lives. We are in the midst of an endeavor, and feeling anywhere from bad to good about it. We are just making up our lives as we go along and doing the best we can. But soon something washes over us, something that says, This is pretty hard. But look at that beautiful something-or-other over there. That gussied-up thing looks easier, finer, more compelling. All of a sudden the gilded carriage rolls up, the door opens, the little stairs drop down, and we step in. We have been seduced. This temptation occurs on a regular and sometimes daily basis. Sometimes it is hard to say no.

So we marry the wrong person because it makes our economic lives easier. We give up on the new piece we're working on and go back to using the easier but old tired-out one we've been pushing around the floor for the last ten years. We don't take that good poem into the finer-than-fine range but leave it in its third draft instead of raking through it one more time.

The gilded carriage scenario overwhelms the simple joy of red shoes. While we could interpret this as a woman's quest for material goods and comforts, more often it expresses a simple psychological desire to not have to toil so at the basic matters of creative life. The desire to have it easier is not the trap; that is something the ego naturally desires. Ah, but the price. The price is the trap. The trap is sprung when the child goes to live with the rich old woman. There she must remain proper and silent . . . no overt yearning allowed, and more specifically, no fulfillment of that yearning. This is the beginning of soul famine for the creative spirit.

Classical Jungian psychology emphasizes that the loss of soul occurs particularly at mid-life, somewhere at, or after, age thirty-five. But for women in modern culture, soul loss is a danger every single day, whether you are eighteen or eighty, married or not, regardless of your bloodline, education, or economics. Many "educated" people smile indulgently when they hear that "primitive" people have endless lists of experiences and events they feel can steal their souls away from them—from sighting a bear at the wrong time of year to entering a house that has not yet been blessed after a death occurred there.

Though much in modern culture is wondrous and life-giving, it also has more wrong-time bears and unblessed places of the dead in a square block than throughout a thousand square miles of outback. The central psychic fact remains that our connection to meaning, passion, soulfulness, and the deep nature is something we have to keep watch over. There are many things that try to force, sweep, seduce away those handmade shoes, seeming simple things like saying, "Later, I'll do that dance, planting, hugging, finding, planning, learning, peace-making, cleansing . . . later." Traps, all.

Trap #2: The Dry Old Woman, the Senescent Force

In dream and fairy-tale interpretation, whoever owns the "conveyor of attitudes," the gilded carriage, is understood as the main value pressing down upon the psyche, forcing it forward, locomoting it in the direction it pleases. In this case, the values of the old woman who owns the carriage begin to drive the psyche.

In classical Jungian psychology the archetypal figure of the elder is sometimes called a "senex" force. In Latin, *senex* means "old man." More properly, and without the gender attribution, the symbol of the elder can be understood as the *senescent force*: that which acts in a way that is peculiar to the aged.[1]

In fairy tales, this aged force is personified by an old person who is often portrayed as one-sided in some way, indicating that one's psychic process is also developing in a one-sided manner. Ideally, an old woman symbolizes dignity, mentoring, wisdom, self-knowledge, tradition-bearing, well-defined boundaries, and experience . . . with a good dose of crabby, long-toothed, straight-talking, flirtatious sass thrown in for good measure.

But when an old fairy-tale woman uses these attributes negatively, as in "The Red Shoes," we are forewarned that aspects of psyche that should remain warm are about to be frozen in time. Something normally vibrant within the psyche is about to be starched flat, given a drubbing, or distorted beyond recognition. When the child enters the old woman's gilded carriage and subsequently her household, she is captured just as surely as if she purposely stuck her paw into a double DD fang-hanger trap.

As we see in the tale, being taken in by the old woman, rather than dignifying the new, allows the senescent attitude to destroy innovation. Rather than mentoring her ward, the old woman will attempt to calcify her. The old woman in this tale is not a sage, but rather is dedicated to repetition of a single value without experimentation or renewal.

By way of all the scenes at church, we see that the single value is that the opinion of the collective matters more than anything, and should eclipse the needs of the individual wild soul. A collective is often thought of as the culture[2] that surrounds an individual. While this is true, Jung's definition was "the many as compared to the one." We are influenced by many collectives, both groups with which we affiliate and those of which we are not members. Whether the collectives surrounding us are academic, spiritual, financial, work-world, familial, or otherwise, they enact powerful rewards and punishments to their members and non-members alike. They work to influence and control all manner of things— from our thoughts to our choice of lovers to our life's work. They may also demean or discourage efforts that are not concomitant with their preferences.

In this tale, the old woman is a symbol of the rigid keeper of collective tradition, an enforcer of the unquestioned status quo, the "behave yourself; don't make waves; don't think too hard; don't get big ideas; just keep a low profile; be a carbon copy; be nice; say 'yes' even though you don't like it, it doesn't fit, it's not the right size, and it hurts." And so on.

To follow such a lifeless value system causes loss of soul-linkage in the extreme. Regardless of collective affiliations or influences, our challenge in behalf of the wild soul and our creative spirit is to *not* merge with any collective, but to distinguish ourselves from those who surround us, building bridges back to them as we choose. We decide which bridges will become strong and well traveled, and which will remain sketchy and empty. And the collectives we favor with relationship will be those that offer the most support for our soul and creative life.

If a woman works at a university, she is in an academic collective. She is not to merge with whatever this collective environ may put forth, but add her own special flavor to it. As an integral creature, unless she has created other strong things in her life to offset this, she cannot afford to deteriorate into a one-sided, peevish, "I do my job, go home, come back . . ." kind of person. If a woman attempts to be a part of an organization, association, or family that neglects to peer into her to see what she is made of, one that fails to ask "What makes this person run?" and one that does not put forth effort to challenge or encourage her in any positive manner . . . then her ability to thrive and create is diminished. The more harsh the circumstances, the more she is exiled to a salted barrens where nothing is allowed to grow.

The separation of a woman's life and mind from flattened-out collective thinking and the development of her unique talents are among the most important accomplishments a woman can fashion, for these acts prevent both soul and psyche from sliding into enslavement. A culture that authentically promotes individual development will never make a slave class of any group or gender.

However, in the tale, the child acquiesces to the old woman's dry values. The child becomes feral then, moving from a natural state to a captured one. Soon she will be tossed into the wilds of the diabolical red shoes, but without innate sensing and unable to perceive the dangers.

If we remove ourselves from our real and passionate lives and enter the gilded carriage of the dry old woman, in effect we adopt the persona and ambitions of the brittle old perfectionist. Then, like all captured creatures, we fall into a sadness that leads to an obsessive yearning, often characterized in my practice as "the restlessness with no name." Thereafter, we are at risk of seizing the first thing that promises to make us feel alive again.

It is important to keep our eyes open and to carefully weigh offers of an easier existence, a trouble-free path, especially if, in exchange, we are asked to surrender our personal creative joy to a cremating fire rather than enkindling one of our own making.

Trap #3: *Burning the Treasure,* Hambre del Alma, *Soul Famine*

There's burning that goes with joy, and there's burning that goes with annihilation. One is the fire of transformation, the other is the fire of decimation only. It is the fire of transformation we want. But many women give up the red shoes and agree to become too cleaned up, too nice, too compliant with someone else's way of seeing the world. We give our joyful red shoes to the destructive fire when we digest values, propagandas, and philosophies whole-sale, psychological ones included. The red shoes are burned to ashes when we paint, act, write, do, be in any way that causes our lives to be diminished, weakening our vision, breaking our spirit bones.

Then a woman's life is overcome by pallor, for she is *hambre del alma,* a starved soul. All she wants is her deep life back. All she wants are those handmade red shoes. The wild joy that these represent might have been burnt in the fire of disuse, or the fire of devaluing one's own work. They might have been burnt in the flames of self-imposed silence.

Too, too many women made a terrible vow years before they knew any better. As young women, they were starved of basic encouragement and support, and so filled with sorrow and resignation, they put down their pens, closed up their words, turned off their singing, rolled up their artwork, and vowed never to touch them ever again. A woman in such a condition has inadvertently entered into the oven along with her handmade life. Her life becomes ashes.

A woman's life may die away in the fire of self-hatred for complexes can bite hard and, at least for a time, successfully frighten her away from coming too near the work or life that matters to her. Many years are spent in *not* going, *not* moving, *not* learning, *not* finding out, *not* obtaining, *not* taking on, *not* becoming.

The vision a woman has for her own life can also be decimated in the flames of someone else's jealousy or someone's plain-out destructiveness toward her. Family, mentors, teachers, and friends are not supposed to be destructive if and when they feel envy, but some decidedly are, in both subtle and not-so-subtle ways. No woman can afford to let her creative life hang by a thread while she serves an antagonistic love relationship, parent, teacher, or friend.

When the personal soul-life is burnt to ashes, a woman loses the vital treasure and begins to act dry-boned as Death. In her unconscious, the desire for the red shoes, a wild joy, not only continues, it swells and floods, and eventually staggers to its feet and takes over, ferocious and famished.

To be in the state of *hambre del alma*, a starved soul, is to be made relentlessly hungry. Then a woman burns with a hunger for anything that will make her feel alive again. A woman who has been captured knows no better, and will take something, anything, that *seems similar* to the original treasure, good or not. A woman who is starved for her real soul-life may look "cleaned up and combed" on the outside, but on the inside she is filled with dozens of pleading hands and empty mouths.

In this state, she will take any food regardless of its condition or its effect, for she is trying to make up for past losses. Yet even though this is a terrible situation, the wild Self will try over and over again to save us. It whispers, whimpers, calls, drags our fleshless carcasses around in our nightdreams until we become conscious of our condition and take steps to reclaim the treasure.

We can better understand the woman who dives into excesses—

the most common being drugs, alcohol, and bad love—and who is driven by soul-hunger by noting the behavior of the starved and ravening animal. Like the starved soul, the wolf has been portrayed as vicious, ravenous, preying upon the innocent and the unguarded, killing to kill, never knowing when enough is enough. As you can see, the wolf has a very bad and unearned fairy-tale and real-life reputation. In actuality, wolves are dedicated social creatures. The entire pack is instinctively organized so healthy wolves kill only what is needed for survival. Only when there is trauma to an individual wolf or to the pack does this normal pattern loosen or change.

There are two instances in which a wolf kills excessively. In both, the wolf is not well. A wolf may kill indiscriminately when it is ill with rabies or distemper. A wolf may kill excessively after a period of famine. The idea that famine can alter the behavior of creatures is quite a significant metaphor for the soul-starved woman. Nine times out of ten a woman with a spiritual/psychological problem that causes her to fall into traps and be badly hurt is a woman who is currently being starved or who has been critically soul-starved in the past.

Among wolves, famine occurs when snows are high and game is impossible to reach. Deer and caribou act as snowplows; wolves follow their paths through the high snow. When the deer are stranded by high snowfalls, no plowing occurs; then the wolves are stranded too. Famine ensues. For wolves the most dangerous time for famine is winter. For woman, a famine may occur at any time, and can come from anywhere, including her own culture.

For the wolf, famine usually ends in springtime when the snows begin to melt. Following a famine, the pack may throw itself into a killing frenzy. Its members won't eat most of the game they kill, and they won't cache it. They leave it. They kill much more than they could ever eat, much more than they could ever need.[3] A similar process occurs when a woman's been captured and starved. Suddenly free to go, to do, to be, she is in danger of going on a rampage of excesses too . . . and feels justified about it. The girl in the fairy tale, too, feels justified in gaining access to the poisonous red shoes at any cost. There is something about famine that causes judgment to be blighted.

So when the treasure of a woman's most soulful life has been burned to ashes, instead of being driven by anticipation, a woman is possessed by voraciousness. So, for instance, if a woman wasn't permitted to sculpt, she may suddenly begin to sculpt day and night, lose sleep, deprive her innocent body of nutrition, impair her health, and who knows what else. Maybe she cannot stay awake a moment longer; ah, reach for the drugs . . . for who knows how long she will be free.

Hambre del alma is also about starvation of the soul's attributes: creativity, sensory awareness, and other instinctual gifts. If a woman is supposed to be a lady who sits with her knees kissing only each other, if she was raised to keel over in the presence of rough language, if she was never allowed anything to drink but pasteurized milk . . . then when she is freed, look out! Suddenly she may not be able to drink enough of those sloe-gin fizzes, she may sprawl like a drunken sailor, and her language will peel the paint off the walls. After famine, there is a fear one will again be captured someday. So one gets while the getting is good.[4]

Overkill through excesses, or excessive behaviors, is acted out by women who are famished for a life that has meaning and makes sense for them. When a woman has gone without her cycles or creative needs for long periods of time, she begins a rampage of— you name it—alcohol, drugs, anger, spirituality, oppression of others, promiscuity, pregnancy, study, creation, control, education, orderliness, body fitness, junk food, to name a few areas of common excess. When women do this, they are compensating for the loss of regular cycles of self-expression, soul-expression, soul-satiation.

The starving woman endures famine after famine. She may plan her escape, yet believe that the cost of fleeing is too high, that it will cost her too much libido, too much energy. She may be ill-prepared in other ways too, such as educationally, economically, spiritually. Unfortunately, the loss of treasure and the deep memory of famine may cause us to rationalize that excesses are desirable. And it is, of course, such a relief and a pleasure to finally be able to enjoy sensation . . . any sensation.

A woman newly free from famine just wants to enjoy life for a change. Her dulled perceptions about the emotional, rational, physical, spiritual, and financial boundaries required for survival endanger her instead. For her there is a pair of poisonous red shoes glowing out there somewhere. She will take them wherever she finds them. That is the trouble with famine. If something looks like it will fill the yearning, a woman will seize it, no questions asked.

Trap #4: *Injury to Basic Instinct, the Consequence of Capture*

Instinct is a difficult thing to define, for its configurations are invisible, and though we sense they have been part of human nature since the beginning of time, no one knows quite where they might be housed neurologically, or precisely how they act upon us. Psychologically, Jung speculated that the instincts derived from the psychoid unconscious, that layer of psyche where biology and spirit might touch. I am of a considered same mind, and would go further to venture that the creative instinct in particular is as much the lyrical language of the Self as is the symbology of dreams.

Etymologically, the word *instinct* derives from the Latin *instinguere*, meaning "impulse," also *instinctus*, meaning "instigation," to incite or impel via an innate prompting. The idea of instinct can be valued positively as an inner something that when blended with forethought and consciousness guides humans to integral behavior. A woman is born with all instinct intact.

Although we could say that the child in the tale has been swept into a new environment, one in which her roughness is smoothed down and her difficult life is removed, in reality her individuation ceases, her striving to develop stops. And when the old woman, a stultifying presence, sees the works of the creative spirit as refuse rather than riches, and burns the handmade red shoes, the child becomes more than silent. She becomes sad, which is the expected state when creative spirit is locked away from natural soul-life. Worse, the child's instinct to properly flee this plight is dulled to a nothing. Instead of aiming toward new life, she sits down in a psychic pool of glue. Lack of fleeing when it is absolutely warranted causes depression. Another trap.

Call the soul what you like—one's marriage to the wild, one's hope for the future, one's fluming energy, one's creative passion, my way, what I do, the Beloved, the wild groom, the "feather on the breath of God."[5] Whatever words or images you may have for this process in your life, it is that which has become captured. That is why the creative spirit of the psyche becomes so bereft.

Through wildlife studies of various species of captive animals, it was found that no matter how lovingly their zoo plazas are constructed, no matter how much their human keepers love them, as indeed they do, the creatures often become unable to breed, their appetites for food and rest become skewed, their vital behaviors dwindle to lethargy, sullenness, or untoward aggressiveness. Zoologists call this behavior in captives "animal depression." Any time a creature is caged, its natural cycles of sleep, mate selection, estrus, grooming, parenting, and so forth deteriorate. As the natural cycles are lost, emptiness follows. The emptiness is not full, like the Buddhist concept of sacred void, but rather empty like being inside a sealed box with no windows.

So too when a woman enters the household of the dry old woman, she experiences lack of resolve, miasma, ennui, simple depressions, and sudden anxiety states that are similar to the symptoms animals display when they have been stunned by capture and trauma. Too much domestication breeds out strong and basic impulses to play, relate, cope, rove, commune, and so forth. When a woman agrees to become too "well-bred" her instincts for these impulses drop down into her darkest unconscious, outside her automatic reach. She is said then to be instinct-injured. What should come naturally comes not at all, or after too much tugging, pulling, rationalizing, fighting with herself.

When I speak of overdomestication as capture, I do not refer to socialization, the process whereby children are taught to behave in more or less civilized ways. Social development is critical and important. Without it, a woman cannot make her way in the world.

But too much domestication is like forbidding the vital essence to dance. In its proper and healthy state, the wild self is not docile or vacuous. It is alert and responsive to any given movement or moment. It is not locked into an absolute and repetitive pattern for any and all circumstances. It has creative choice. The instinct-injured woman has no choice. She just stays stuck.

There are many ways to be stuck. The instinct-injured woman usually gives herself away because she has a difficult time asking for help or recognizing her own needs. Her natural instincts to fight or flee are drastically slowed or extincted. Recognition of the sensations of satiation, off-taste, suspicion, caution, and the drive to love fully and freely are inhibited or exaggerated.

As in the tale, one of the most insidious attacks on the wild self is to be directed to perform properly, implying a reward will follow (if ever). Though this method may (I emphasize "may") temporarily persuade a two-year-old to clean her room (no playing with toys until the bed is made)[6] it will never, never work in a vital woman's life. While consistency, follow-through, and organization are all essential to implementing creative life, the old woman's injunction to "be proper" kills off any opportunity to expand.

It is play, not properness, that is the central artery, the core, the brain stem of creative life. The impulse to play is an instinct. No play, no creative life. Be good, no creative life. Sit still, no creative life. Speak, think, act only demurely, little creative juice. Any group, society, institution, or organization that encourages women to revile the eccentric; to be suspicious of the new and unusual; to avoid the fervent, the vital, the innovative; to impersonalize the personal, is asking for a culture of dead women.

Janis Joplin, a blues singer during the 1960s, is a good example of a feral woman who was instinct-injured by spirit-crushing forces. Her creative life, innocent curiosity, love of life, somewhat irreverent approach to the world during her growing-up years were mercilessly vilified by her teachers and many of those who surrounded her in the "good-girl" white Southern Baptist community of her time.

Though she was an A student and a talented painter, she was ostracized by other girls for not wearing makeup[7] and by neighbors for liking to climb a rock outcropping outside town and singing up there with her friends and for listening to jazz. When she finally escaped to the world of the blues, she was so starved she could no longer tell when enough was enough. She had shaky boundaries, that is, no limits around sex, liquor, and drugs.[8]

There is something about Bessie Smith, Anne Sexton, Edith

Piaf, Marilyn Monroe, and Judy Garland that follows the same instinct-injured pattern of soul-famine: attempting to "fit," becoming intemperate, not being able to stop.[9] We could make a very long list of instinct-injured talented women who in their vulnerable states made very poor choices. Like the child in the tale, they all lost their handmade shoes somewhere along the way and found their way to the poisoned red shoes. They all were filled with sorrow, for they hungered for spirit-food, soul-story, natural roving, self-decoration in keeping with their own needs, God-learning, and a simple and sane sexuality. But they unwittingly chose the cursed shoes—beliefs, actions, ideas that caused life to deteriorate more and more—that turned them into madly dancing specters.

Injury to instinct cannot be underestimated as the root of the issue when women are acting mad, are possessed by obsession, or when they are stuck in less malignant but nevertheless destructive patterns. The repair of injured instinct begins with acknowledging that a capture has taken place, that a soul-famine has followed, that usual boundaries of insight and protection have been disturbed. The process that caused a woman's capture and the ensuing famine has to be reversed. But first, many women go through the next few stages as described in the story.

Trap #5: Trying to Sneak a Secret Life, Split in Two

In this segment of the tale, the child is to be confirmed and is taken to the shoemaker for new shoes. The confirmation motif is a relatively modern addition to this story. Archetypally, it is likely that "The Red Shoes" is a many times overlaid fragment of a far older story or myth about the onset of menarche and the taking on of a less-mother-protected life, a young woman having been taught awareness and response to the outer world by her own female elders in previous years.[10]

It is said that in the matriarchal cultures of ancient India, Egypt, parts of Asia, and Turkey—which are believed to have influenced our concept of the feminine soul for thousands of miles in all directions—the bequeathing of henna and other red pigments to young girls, so that they could stain their feet with it, was a central feature in threshold rites.[11] One of the most important threshold rites regarded first menstruation. This rite celebrated the crossing from childhood into the profound ability to bring forth life from one's own belly, to carry the attendant sexual power and all peripheral womanly powers. The ceremony was concerned with red blood in all its stages: the uterine blood of menstruation, delivery of a child, miscarriage, all running downward toward the feet. As you can see, the original red shoes had many meanings.

The reference to the Day of The Innocents is also a later overlay. It refers to a Christian feast day that, in Europe, eventually eclipsed winter solstice celebrations from the old Pagan world. During the older Pagan celebrations, women practiced ritual cleansing of the feminine body and the feminine soul/spirit in preparation for figurative and literal new life in the coming spring. These rites might have included group grieving for child-bearing loss,[12] including the death of a child, or miscarriage, still-birth, abortion, and other important events in women's sexual and reproductive lives from the old year.[13]

Now in the tale occurs one of the most revealing episodes of psychic repression. The child's voracious desire for soul ruptures the battens of her dried-out behaviors. At the shoemaker's, she sneaks the strange red shoes past the old woman. A ravening hunger for the soul-life has rushed to the surface of the psyche, taking whatever it can lay its hands on, for it knows it will soon be repressed again.

This explosive psychological "sneaking" occurs when a woman suppresses large parts of self into the shadows of the psyche. In the view of analytical psychology, the repression of both negative and positive instincts, urges, and feelings into the unconscious causes them to inhabit a shadow realm. While the ego and superego attempt to continue to censor the shadow impulses, the very pressure that repression causes is rather like a bubble in the sidewall of a tire. Eventually, as the tire revolves and heats up, the pressure behind the bubble intensifies, causing it to explode outward, releasing all the inner content.

The shadow acts similarly. That is why a Scrooge-like person may amaze everyone and suddenly give millions of dollars to an orphans' home. Or why a normally sweet person is capable of

throwing a fit, temporarily acting like a Roman candle gone
berserk. We find that by opening the door to the shadow realm a
little, and letting out various elements a few at a time, relating to
them, finding use for them, negotiating, we can reduce being surprised by shadow sneak attacks and unexpected explosions.

Though the values may change from culture to culture, thereby
positing different "negatives" and "positives" in the shadow, typical impulses that are considered negative and therefore relegated
to the shadowlands are those that encourage a person to steal,
cheat, murder, act excessively in various ways, and so forth in that
vein. The negative shadow aspects tend to be oddly exciting and
yet entropic in nature, stealing balance and equanimity of mood
and life from individuals, relationships, and larger groups.

The shadow also, however, can contain the divine, the luscious,
beautiful, and powerful aspects of personhood. For women especially, the shadow almost always contains very fine aspects of
being that are forbidden or given little support by her culture. At
the bottom of the well in the psyches of too many women lies the
visionary creator, the astute truth-teller, the far-seer, the one who
can speak well of herself without denigration, who can face herself without cringing, who works to perfect her craft. The positive
impulses in shadow for women in our culture most often revolve
around permission for the creation of a handmade life.

These discarded, devalued, and "unacceptable" aspects of soul
and self do not just lie there in the dark, but rather conspire about
how and when they shall make a break for freedom. They burble
down there in the unconscious, they seethe, they boil, till one day,
no matter how well the lid over them is sealed, they explode
outward and upward in an unchanneled torrent and with a will of
their own.

Then it is, as we say up in the backwoods, like trying to put ten
pounds of mud back into a five-pound sack. What has erupted
from shadow is hard to cap once it has been detonated. Though it
would have been far better to have found an integral way to consciously live out one's joy in the creative spirit than to have buried
it at all, sometimes a woman is pushed to the wall, and this is the
outcome.

The shadow life occurs when writers, painters, dancers, mothers, seekers, mystics, students, or journeywomen stop writing, painting, dancing, mothering, looking, peering, learning, practicing. They might stop because whatever they just spent long with did not come out the way they had hoped, or did not receive the recognition it deserved, or countless other reasons. When the maker stops for whatever reason, the energy that naturally flows to her is diverted underground, where it surfaces whenever and wherever it can. Because a woman feels she cannot in daylight go full-bore at whatever it is she wants, she begins to lead a strange double life, pretending one thing in daylight hours, acting another way when she gets a chance.

When a woman pretends to press her life down into a nice tidy little package, all she accomplishes is spring-loading all her vital energy down into shadow. "Fine, I'm fine," such a woman says. We look at her across the room or in the mirror. We know she is not fine. Then one day, we hear she has taken up with a piccolo player and has run off to Tippicanoe to be a pool hall queen. And we wonder what happened, because we know she hates piccolo players and always wanted to live on Orcas Island, not in Tippicanoe, and she never before mentioned anything about pool halls.

Like Hedda Gabler in Henrik Ibsen's play, the wildish woman can pretend to live "an ordinary life" while gritting her teeth, but there is always a price to pay. Hedda sneaks a passionate and dangerous life, playing games with an ex-lover and with Death. Outwardly, she pretends to be content wearing bonnets and listening to her dry husband cavil about his dusty life. A woman can be outwardly polite and even cynical, but inwardly hemorrhaging.

Or, like Janis Joplin, a woman can try to comply until she can't stand it any longer, and then her creative nature, corroded and sickened by being forced into the shadow, erupts violently to rebel against the tenets of "breeding" in reckless ways that disregard one's gifts and one's very life.

You can call it anything you like, but sneaking a life because the real one is not given room enough to thrive is hard on women's vitality. Captured and starved women sneak all kinds of things: they sneak unsanctioned books and music, they sneak friendships, sexual feeling, religious affiliation. They sneak furtive thinking, dreams of revolution. They sneak time away from their mates and families. They sneak a treasure into the house. They sneak their writing time, their thinking time, their soul-time. They sneak a spirit into the bedroom, a poem before work, they sneak a skip or an embrace when no one's looking.

To detour off this polarized path, a woman has to surrender the pretense. Sneaking a counterfeit soul-life never works. It always blows out the sidewall when you're least expecting it. Then it's misery all around. It's better to get up, stand up, no matter how homemade your platform, and live the most you can, the best you can, and forgo the sneaking of counterfeits. Hold out for what has real meaning and health for you.

In the tale, the child ducks the shoes past the old woman with failing eyesight. Here, it is affirmed that the dry and perfectionistic value system itself is devoid of the ability to see closely, to be alert to what is going on all around. It is typical of the injured inner psyche and culture as well, to not notice the personal distress of the self. So the young girl makes one more rotten choice in a long line of several.

Let us surmise that her first step to entrapment, entering the gilded carriage, was made out of ignorance. Let us say letting go of her own handiwork was thoughtless but typical of those who are inexperienced at life. But now she wants those shoes in the shoemaker's case, and paradoxically, that impulse toward new life is right and proper, but she *has* spent too much time at the old woman's, and her instincts do not cry out in alarm as she chooses this deadly potential. In fact, the shoemaker conspires with the child. He winks and smiles about her poor choice. Together they sneak the red shoes by.

Women trick themselves this way. They've thrown away the treasure, whatever it might be, but they're sneaking bits and pieces any way they can. Are they writing? Yes, but secretly, so they have no support, no feedback. The student, is she going for her edge? Yes, but secretly so that she can have no help and no mentor. Is the performer risking putting out completely original work or is she presenting pale imitations so that she becomes mime instead of exemplar? What about the ambitious woman who is pretending to be not ambitious, but who is heartfelt toward accomplishments for herself, her people, her world? She is the powerful dreamer, yet consigns herself to struggle forward in silence. It is deadly to be without a confidante, without a guide, without even a tiny cheering section.

It is difficult to sneak little shreds of life this way but women do it every day. When a woman feels compelled to sneak life, she is in minimal subsistence mode. She sneaks life away from the hearing of "them," whoever the "them" is in her life. She acts disinterested and calm on the surface, but whenever there is a crack of light, her starved self leaps out, runs for the nearest life form, lights up, kicks back, charges madly, dances herself silly, exhausts herself, then tries to creep back to the black cell before anyone notices she is gone.

Women with poor marriages do this. Women made to feel inferior do this. Women filled with shame, women fearing punishment, ridicule, or humiliation do this. Instinct-injured women do this. Sneaking is good for a captured woman only *if* she sneaks the right thing, only if that thing leads to her liberation. In essence, sneaking good and filling and brave pieces of life causes the soul to be even more determined that the sneaking stop, and that it be free to lead life out in the open as it sees fit.

You see, there is something in the wild soul that will not let us subsist forever on piecemeal intake. Because in actuality, it is impossible for the woman who strives for consciousness to sneak little sniffs of good air and then be content with no more. Remember when you were a child and you found out that you couldn't do yourself in by holding your breath? Though you might try to get by on just a little air or no air at all, some big fist bellows takes over, something fierce and demanding that makes you eventually shovel the air in as fast as you can. You gulp it, bite it down until you are breathing fully again.

Blessedly, there is something like that in the soul/psyche as well. It takes us over and forces us to take full breaths of good air. Truly, we know that we cannot really subsist on sneaking little sips of life. The wild force in a woman's soul demands that she have access to it all. We can stay alert and take in the things that are right for us.

The shoemaker in the tale foreshadows the old soldier who brings the dance-yourself-crazy shoes to life later in the story.

There are too many coincidences between this character and what we know of ancient symbolism to think he is just an innocent bystander. The natural predator within the psyche (and that of the culture as well) is a shapechanger, a force that is able to disguise itself, just as traps, cages, and poisoned bait are disguised in order to lure the unaware. We must take into account that he makes a joke out of tricking the old woman.

No, it is likely that he is in league with the soldier, who of course is a depiction of the devil in disguise.[14] In olden times, the devil, the soldier, the shoemaker, the hunchback, and other images were used to portray the negative forces in both earth nature and human nature.[15]

While we could rightfully be proud of the soul brave enough to try to sneak a something, an anything, under such drought conditions, the fact remains that that alone cannot be the sole issue. A whole psychology has to include not only body, mind, and spirit, but also, equally, culture and environ. And in this light, it must be asked at each level how it came to be that any individual woman feels she has to cringe, flinch, grovel, and plead for a life that is her own to begin with. What is in any culture that demands such? Inquiring into the pressures created by each layer of the inner and outer worlds will preclude a woman from thinking that sneaking the devil shoes is, in any way, a constructive choice at all.

Trap #6: Cringing Before the Collective, Shadow Rebellion

The child sneaks on the red shoes, marches off to church, pays no attention to what swirls around her, is reviled by the community. Members of the village "tell" on her. She is chastised. The red shoes are taken away. But it is too late, she is hooked. The issue is not yet obsession, rather that the collective inspires and strengthens her inner starvation by demanding capitulation to its narrow values.

You can try to have a secret life, but sooner or later the super-ego, a negative complex, and/or the culture itself, will hail down. It is hard to hide an unsanctioned something that you are ravenous about. It is hard to hide stolen pleasures even when they are not nourishing ones.

The nature of negative complexes and cultures is to pounce upon any discrepancy between the consensus about what is acceptable behavior and the individual's differing impulse. Just as some people go mad to see a single leaf upon their walkway, negative judgment draws out its saws to amputate any member that does not conform.

Sometimes the collective pressures a woman to be "a saint," to be enlightened, to be politically correct, to "have it together," in order for each of her endeavors to amount to an opus. If we cringe before the collective and acquiesce to pressures for mindless conformity, we are protected from exile, but at the same time also treacherously endanger our wildish lives.

Some think that the times are past when if a woman was called wild she was being cursed. If she was wild, meaning acting her natural soul-self, she was labeled "wrong" and "bad." It is not so that these times are over. What has changed are the types of behaviors that are considered "out of control" for women. For instance, in various parts of the world today, if a woman takes a stand politically, socially, spiritually, familially, environmentally, if she points out that some particular emperor has no clothes, or if she speaks for those who are hurt or who are without voice, too often her motives are examined to see if she has "gone wild," that is, crazy.

For a wild child born into a rigid community, the usual outcome is to experience the ignominy of being shunned. Shunning treats the victim as if she does not exist. It withdraws spiritual concern, love, and other psychic necessities from that person. The idea is to force her to conform, or else to kill her spiritually and/or to drive her from the village to languish and die in the outback.

If a woman is shunned, it is almost always because she has done or is about to do something in the wildish range, oftentimes something as simple as expressing a slightly different belief or wearing an unapproved color—small, small things as well as large ones. It must be remembered that an oppressed woman not so much refuses to fit as she *cannot fit* without also dying. Her spiritual integrity is at stake, and she will try to be free in whatever ways are available, even if they put her at risk.

Here is a recent example. According to CNN, at the onset of the Gulf War, Moslem women from Saudi Arabia, forbidden to drive by religious stricture, climbed into cars and drove. After the war, the women were brought before tribunals that condemned their behavior and, finally, after much interrogation and condemnation, released the women to the custody of their fathers, brothers, or husbands, who had to promise to keep the women in line in the future.

This is a case of a woman's life-giving and life-thriving mark on a crazy world being defined as scandalous, insane, and out of control. Unlike the child in the tale, who allows the culture surrounding her to press her into even more dryness, sometimes the only alternative to cringing before a parched collective is to commit an act drenched in courage. This act need not necessarily be of the earthshaking variety. Courage means to follow the heart. There are millions of women who commit acts of great heart every day. It is not only the singular act that reshapes a dry collective, but also the continuation of those acts. As a young Buddhist nun once told me, "Water drips through stone."

In addition, there is a very hidden aspect to most collectives that encourages oppression of women's wild, soulful, and creative lives, and that is the encouragement within the culture for women themselves to "tell on" one another and to sacrifice their sisters (or brothers) to strictures that do not reflect the relatedness found in the familial values of the feminine nature. These include not only the encouraging of one woman to inform on another and therefore expose her to punishment for behaving in a feminine and integral manner, for registering appropriate horror or dissension to injustice, but also the encouraging of older women to collude in the physical, mental, and spiritual abuse of women who are younger, less powerful, or helpless, and the encouraging of young women to dismiss and neglect the needs of women who are far older than they.

When a woman refuses to support the dry collective, she refuses to stop her wild thinking, and her actions follow accordingly. "The Red Shoes" in essence teaches us that the wild psyche must be properly protected—by unequivocally valuing it our-selves, by speaking out in its interest, by refusing to submit to psychic unhealth. We also learn that the wild, because of its energy and beauty, is *always* eyed by somebody or other, some-thing or other, some group or other, for trophy purposes or as a thing to be reduced, altered, ruled on, murdered, redesigned, or controlled. The wild always needs a guardian at the gate, or it will be misused.

When the collective is hostile to a woman's natural life, rather than accept the derogatory or disrespectful labels that are placed upon her, she can and must, like the ugly duckling, hold on, hold out, and search for that which she belongs to—and preferably out-live, out-thrive, and out-create those who vilified her.

The problem with the girl in the red shoes is that instead of becoming strong for the fight, she is off in la-la land, captured by the romance of those red shoes. The important thing about rebellion is that the form it takes be effective. The girl's fascina-tion with the red shoes actually keeps her from a meaningful rebel-lion, one that would promote change, give a message, cause an awakening.

I wish we could say that by now all the traps for women no longer exist, or that women are so wise that they can spot the traps from far off. But it is not so. We still have the predator in the culture, and it still tries to undercut and destroy all conscious-ness and all bids for wholeness. There is much truth to the saying that freedoms have to be fought for anew every twenty years. Sometimes it seems that they have to be fought for every five minutes.

But the wild nature teaches that we meet challenges as they occur. When wolves are badgered, they don't say, "Oh, no! Not *again*!" They bound, pounce, run, dive, scramble, play dead, go for the throat, whatever needs to be done. So we cannot be shocked that there is entropy, deterioration, hard times. Let us understand that the issues that entrap women's joy will always shift and shape-change, but in our own essential natures we find the absolute stamina, the necessary libido for all necessary acts of heart.

Trap #7: Faking It, Trying to be Good,
Normalizing the Abnormal

As the tale goes on, the girl is chastised for wearing the red shoes to church. Now, though she gazes up at the red shoes on the shelf, she does not touch them. She has, to this point, tried going without her soul-life; that did not work. Next, she tried sneaking a dual life; that did not work either. Now, in a last-ditch stand, she "tries to be good."

The problem with "being good" to the extreme is that it does not resolve the underlying shadow issue, and again, it will rise like a tsunami, like a giant tidal wave, and rush down, destroying everything in its path. In "being good," a woman closes her eyes to everything obdurate, distorted, or damaging around her, and just "tries to live with it." Her attempts to accept this abnormal state further injure her instincts to react, point out, change, make impact on what is not right, what is not just.

Anne Sexton wrote about the fairy tale "The Red Shoes" in a poem also called *"The Red Shoes"*:

> I stand in the ring
> in the dead city
> and tie on the red shoes . . .
> They are not mine.
> They are my mother's.
> Her mother's before.
> Handed down like an heirloom
> but hidden like shameful letters.
> The house and the street where they belong
> are hidden and all the women, too,
> are hidden . . .

Trying to be good, orderly, and compliant in the face of inner or outer peril or in order to hide a critical psychic or real-life situation de-souls a woman. It cuts her from her knowing; it cuts her from her ability to act. Like the child in the tale, who does not object out loud, who tries to hide her starvation, who tries to make it seem as though nothing is burning in her, modern women have the same disorder, normalizing the abnormal. This disorder is rampant across cultures. Normalizing the abnormal causes the spirit, which would normally leap to correct the situation, to instead sink into ennui, complacency, and eventually, like the old woman, into blindness.

There's an important study that gives insight into women's loss of self-protective instinct. In the early 1960s, scientists[16] conducted animal experiments to determine something about the "flight instinct" in humans. In one experiment they wired half the bottom of a large cage, so that a dog placed in the cage would receive a shock each time it set foot on the right side. The dog quickly learned to stay on the left side of the cage.

Next, the left side of the cage was wired for the same purpose and the right side was safe from shocks. The dog reoriented quickly and learned to stay on the right side of the cage. Then, the entire floor of the cage was wired to give random shocks, so that no matter where the dog lay or stood it would eventually receive a shock. The dog acted confused at first, and then it panicked. Finally the dog "gave up" and lay down, taking the shocks as they came, no longer trying to escape them or outsmart them.

But the experiment was not over. Next, the cage door was opened. The scientists expected the dog to rush out, but it did not flee. Even though it could vacate the cage at will, the dog lay there being randomly shocked. From this, scientists speculated that when a creature is exposed to violence, it will tend to adapt to that disturbance, so that when the violence ceases or the creature is allowed its freedom, the healthy instinct to flee is hugely diminished, and the creature stays put instead.[17]

In terms of the wildish nature of women, it is this normalization of violence, and what scientists subsequently termed "learned helplessness," that influences women to not only stay with drunken mates, abusive employers, and groups that exploit and harass them but causes them to feel unable to rise up to support the things they believe in with all their hearts: their art, their loves, their lifestyles, their politics.

The normalizing of the abnormal even when there is clear evidence that it is to one's own detriment[18] to do so applies to all battering of the physical, emotional, creative, spiritual, and instinctive natures. Women face this issue any time they are stunned into doing anything less than defending their soul-lives from invasive projections, cultural, psychic, or otherwise.

Psychically, we become used to the shocks aimed at our wild natures. We adapt to violence against the psyche's knowing nature. We try to be good while normalizing the abnormal. As a result, we lose our power to flee. We lose our power to lobby for the elements of soul and life we find most valuable. When we are obsessed with the red shoes, all kinds of important personal, cultural, and environmental matters fall by the wayside.

There is such loss of meaning when one gives up the life made by hand that all manner of injuries to psyche, nature, culture, family, and so forth are then allowed to occur. The harm to nature is concomitant with the stunning of the psyches of humans. They are not and cannot be seen as separate from one another. When one group talks about how wrong the wild is, and the other group argues that the wild has been wronged, something *is* drastically wrong. In the instinctive psyche, the Wild Woman looks out on the forest and sees a home for herself and all humans. Yet others may look at the same forest and imagine it barren of trees and their pockets bursting with money. These represent serious splits in the ability to live and let live so that all can live.

When I was a child in the 1950s, in the early days of industrial disgraces against the earth, an oil barge sank in the Chicago Basin of Lake Michigan. After a day at the beach, mothers scrubbed their little children with the same fervor they usually reserved for scrubbing wooden floors, for their children were stained with oil globs.

The oil wreck oozed a goo that traveled in great sheets like floating islands as long and wide as city blocks. When these collided with jetties, they broke into gobbets, and sank into the sand and drifted into shore under the waves. For years swimmers could not swim without being covered with black muck. Children building castles would suddenly scoop up a handful of rubbery oil. Lovers could no longer roll in the sand. Dogs, birds, water life, and people all suffered. I remember feeling that my cathedral had been bombed.

Injury to instinct, normalizing the abnormal, is what allowed mothers to wipe the stains of that oil spill, and later, the further sins of factories, refineries, and smelters, off their little children, their laundry, the insides of their loved ones as best they could, and while confused and worried, the women effectively cut away their rightful rage. Not all but most had become used to not being able to intervene in shocking events. There were formidable punishments for breaking silence, for fleeing the cage, for pointing out wrongs, for demanding change.

We can see from similar events that have occurred over our lifetimes that when women do not speak, when not enough people speak, the voice of the Wild Woman becomes silent, and therefore the world becomes silent of the natural and wild too. Silent, eventually, of wolf and bear and raptors. Silent of singings and dancings and creations. Silent of loving, repairing, and holding. Bereft of clear air and water and the voices of consciousness.

But back in those times, and too often today, even though women were infused with a yearning for a wild freedom, they continued outwardly to rub SOS on porcelain, using caustic cleansers, staying, as Sylvia Plath put it, "tied to their Bendix washing machines." There they washed and rinsed their clothes in water too hot for human touch and dreamt of a different world.[19] When the instincts are injured, humans will "normalize" assault after assault, acts of injustice and destruction toward themselves, their offspring, their loved ones, their land, and even their Gods.

This normalizing of the shocking and abusive is refused by repairing injured instinct. As instinct is repaired, the integral wild nature returns. Instead of dancing into the forest in the red shoes until all life becomes tortured and meaningless, we can return to the handmade life, the wholly mindful life, re-make our own shoes, walk our walk, talk our own talk.

While it is true that there is much to learn by dissolving one's projections (you're mean, you hurt me) and looking at how we are mean to ourselves, how we hurt ourselves, this should definitely not be the end of the inquiry.

The trap within the trap is thinking that everything is solved by dissolving the projection and finding consciousness in ourselves. This is sometimes true and sometimes not. Rather than this either/or paradigm—it's either something amiss out there or something awry with us—it is more useful to use an and/and model. Here' is the internal issue *and* here is the external issue. This paradigm allows a whole inquiry and far more healing in all directions. This paradigm supports women to question the status quo with confidence, and to not only look at themselves but also at the world that is accidentally, unconsciously, or maliciously pressuring them. The and/and paradigm is not meant to be used as a blaming model, a blaming of self or others, but is rather a way of weighing and judging accountability, both inner and outer, and what needs be changed, applied for, adumbrated. It stops fragmentation when a woman seeks to mend all within her reach, neither slighting her own needs nor turning away from the world.

Somehow many women are able to maintain themselves in a captured state, but they live a half life or a quarter life or even an *n*th life. They manage, but may become bitter to the end of their days. They may feel hopeless, and often, like a babe who has cried and cried with no human aid forthcoming, they may become deathly silent, and despairing. Fatigue and resignation follow. The cage is locked.

Trap #8: Dancing Out of Control, Obsession and Addiction

The old woman has made three errors in judgment. Though she is supposed to, in the ideal, be the guardian, the guide of the psyche, she is too blind to see the true nature of the shoes she herself paid for. She is unable to see the child becoming enchanted by them or to see through the character of the man with the red beard waiting near the church.

The old man with the red beard gave the soles of the child's shoes a tippy-tap-tap, and this itchy vibration set the child's feet to dancing. She dances now, oh how she dances, except she cannot stop. Both the old woman, who is supposed to act as guardian of the psyche, and the child, who is meant to express the joy of the psyche, are sundered from all instinct and common sense.

The child has tried it all: adapting to the old woman, not adapting, sneaking, "being good," losing control and dancing off, regaining herself and trying to be good again. Here her acute starvation of soul and meaning forces her to once more grasp for the red shoes, strap them on, and begin her last dance, a dance into the void of unconsciousness.

She has normalized a dry cruel life, thereby setting up more yearning in her shadow for the shoes of madness. The man in the red beard has brought something to life, but it is not the child; it is the torturous shoes. The girl begins to whirl and twirl her life away in a manner that, as with addiction, does not bring bounty, hope, or happiness, but trauma, fear, and exhaustion. There is no rest for her.

As she whirls into a churchyard, there is a spirit of dread there who will not allow her to enter. The spirit pronounces this curse over her: "You shall dance in your red shoes until you become like a wraith, like a ghost, till your skin hangs from your bones, till there is nothing left of you but entrails dancing. You shall dance door to door through all the villages and you shall strike each door three times and when people peer out they will see you and fear your fate for themselves. Dance red shoes, you shall dance." The spirit of dread thereby seals her into an obsession that parallels an addiction.

The lives of many creative women have followed this pattern. As a teenager, Janis Joplin tried to adapt to the mores of her small town. Then she rebelled a little, climbing the hills at night and singing out from them, hanging out with "artistic types." After her parents were called to school to account for their daughter's behaviors, she began a double life, acting outwardly unassuming but sneaking across the state line at night to hear jazz. She went on to college, became quite ill from various substance abuses, "reformed," and tried to act normal. Gradually, she began drinking again, put together a little dirt band, dabbled in drugs, and strapped on the red shoes in earnest. She danced and danced till she died of a drug overdose at age twenty-seven.

It was not Joplin's music, her singing, or her creative life finally sprung loose that killed her. It was lack of instinct to recognize the traps, to know when enough was enough, to create boundaries around her own health and welfare, to understand that excesses break small psychic bones, then larger ones, until finally the entire underpinnings of psyche collapse and a person becomes a puddle instead of a powerful force.

She needed only one wise inner construct that she could hold on to, one shred of instinct that would last until she could begin the time-consuming work of rebuilding inner sense and instinct. There is a wild voice that lives inside all of us, one that whispers, "Stay here long enough . . . stay here long enough to revive your hope, to drop your terminal cool, to give up defensive half-truths, to creep, carve, bash your way through, stay here long enough to see what is right for you, stay here long enough to become strong, to try the try that will make it, stay here long enough to make the finish line, it matters not how long it takes or in what style . . . "

ADDICTION

It is not the joy of life that kills the spirit of the child in "The Red Shoes," it is the lack of it. When a woman is unconscious about her starvation, about the consequences of using death-dealing vehicles and substances, she is dancing, she is dancing. Whether these are such things as chronic negative thinking, poor relationships, abusive situations, drugs, or alcohol—they are like the red shoes, hard to pry a person away from once they've taken hold.

In this compensatory addiction to excess, the old dry woman of the psyche plays a major role. She was blind to begin with. Now she takes ill. She is immobile, leaving a total void in the psyche. There is no one to talk sense to the excessive psyche now. Eventually the old woman dies altogether, leaving no safe ground in the psyche at all. And the child dances. At first her eyes are rolled back in her head in ecstasy, but later, as the shoes dance her to exhaustion, her eyes are rolled back in horror.

Within the wild psyche are a woman's fiercest instincts for survival. But, unless she practices her inner and outer freedoms regularly, submission, passivity, and time spent in captivity dull her innate gifts of vision, perception, confidence, and so forth, the ones she needs for standing on her own.

The instinctual nature tells us when enough is enough. It is prudent and life-preserving. A woman cannot make up for a lifetime of betrayal and wounding through the excesses of pleasure, rage, or denial. The old woman of the psyche is supposed to call time, is supposed to say when. In this tale, the old woman is kaput; she is done for.

Sometimes it is difficult for us to realize when we are losing our instincts, for it is often an insidious process that does not occur all in one day, but rather over a long period of time. Too, the loss or deadening of instinct is often entirely supported by the surrounding culture, and sometimes even by other women who endure the loss of instinct as a way of achieving belonging in a culture that keeps no nourishing habitat for the natural woman.[20]

Addiction begins when a woman loses her handmade and meaningful life and becomes fixated upon retrieving anything that resembles it in any way she can. In the story, the child tries again and again to reunite with the diabolical red shoes, even though they increasingly cause her to lose control. She has lost her power of discrimination, her ability to sense what the nature of a thing really is. Because of the loss of her original vitality, she is willing to accept a deadly substitute. In analytical psychology we would say she has given the Self away.

Addiction and ferality are related. Most women have been captured at least for a brief time, and some for interminably long periods. Some were free only *in utero*. All lose varying amounts of instinct for the duration. For some the instinct which senses who is a good person and who is not is injured, and the woman is often led astray. For others, ability to react to injustice is slowed way down and they often become reluctant martyrs poised to retaliate. For still others the instinct to flee or to fight is weakened and they are victimized. The list goes on. Conversely, a woman in her right wildish mind rejects convention when it is neither nurturing nor sensible.

Substance abuse is a very real trap. Drugs and alcohol are very much like an abusive lover who treats you well at first and then beats you up, apologizes, gives you nice treatment for a while, and then beats you up again. The trap is in trying to hang in there for the good while trying to overlook the bad. Wrong. This can never work.

Joplin began carrying out the wildish wishes of others as well. She began to carry a kind of archetypal presence that others were afraid to carry for themselves. They cheered on her rebelliousness as though she could free them by becoming wild *for them*.

Janis made one more try at conformity before she began a long slide into possession. She joined the ranks of other powerful but hurt women who found themselves acting as flying shamans to the masses. They too became exhausted and fell from the sky. Frances Farmer, Billie Holiday, Anne Sexton, Sylvia Plath, Sara Teasdale, Judy Garland, Bessie Smith, Edith Piaf, and Frida Kahlo—sadly, the lives of some of our favorite role models of wild and artistic women ended prematurely and tragically.

A feral woman is not strong enough to carry a longed-for archetype for everyone else without breaking. A feral woman is supposed to be immersed in a healing process. We don't ask a recovering person to carry the piano upstairs. A woman who is returning has to have time to strengthen.

People who are grabbed and taken away by the red shoes always initially feel that whatever substance it is that they are addicted to is a tremendous savior in one sense or another. Sometimes it gives a sense of fantastic power, or a false sense that they have the energy to stay awake all night, create until dawn, go without eating. Or perhaps it allows them to sleep without fearing demons, or calms their nerves, or helps them not care so deeply about all the things they care so deeply about, or maybe it helps them not want to love and be loved anymore. However, in the end, it only creates, as we see in the tale, a blurred background whirling by so fast that no real life is truly being lived. Addiction[21] is a deranged Baba Yaga who eats up lost children and drops them off at the executioner's door.

At the Executioner's House

Trying to Take Shoes Off, Too Late

When the wildish nature has been nearly exterminated, in the most extreme cases, it is possible that a schizoid deterioration and/or psychosis may overwhelm the woman.[22] She may just suddenly stay in bed, refuse to rise, or wander around in her bathrobe, absently leave cigarettes burning three to an ashtray, or cry and not be able to stop, wander in the streets with her hair disheveled, abruptly leave her family to wander. She may feel suicidal, she may kill herself either accidentally or with purpose. But far more commonly, the woman just goes dead. She doesn't feel good or bad; she just doesn't feel.

So what happens to women when their vibrant psychic colors are mushed all together? What happens when you mix scarlet, sapphire, and topaz all together? Artists know. When you stir vibrant colors together, you get a color called mud. Not mud that is fertile, but mud that is sterile, colorless, strangely dead, that does not emit light. When painters make mud on the canvas they must begin all over again.

This is the hard part; this is where the shoes have to be cut off. It hurts to cut oneself away from an addiction to self-destruction. Nobody knows why. You'd think a captured person would be relieved to have turned this corner. You'd think they would feel saved in the nick of time. You'd think they would rejoice. But no, instead they go into a funk, they hear teeth gnashing, and discover they're the ones making that noise. They feel they are bleeding somehow, even though there is no blood. Yet, it is this pain, this severing, this "not having a foot to stand on," so to speak, this no home to go back to, that is exactly what is needed to start over, to start fresh, to go back to the handmade life, the one careful and mindfully crafted by us every day.

Yes there is pain in being severed from the red shoes. But being cut away from the addiction all at once is our only hope. It is a severing that is filled with absolute blessing. The feet will grow back, we will find our way, we will recover, we will run and jump and skip again some day. By then our handmade life will be ready. We'll slip into it and marvel that we could be so lucky to have another chance.

Returning to A Life Made by Hand, Healing Injured Instincts

When a fairy tale ends as this one does, with a death or dismemberment of the protagonist, we ask, How could it have ended differently?

Psychically, it is good to make a halfway place, a way station, a considered place in which to rest and mend after one escapes a famine. It is not too much to take one year, two years, to assess one's wounds, seek guidance, apply the medicines, consider the future. A year or two is scant time. The feral woman is a woman making her way back. She is learning to wake up, pay attention, stop being naive, uninformed. She takes her life in her own hands. To re-learn the deep feminine instincts, it is vital to see how they were decommissioned to begin with.

Whether the injuries be to your art, words, lifestyles, thoughts, or ideas, and if you have knitted yourself up into a many-sleeved sweater, cut through the tangle now and get on with it. Beyond desire and wishing, beyond the carefully reasoned methods we love to talk and scheme over, there is a simple door waiting for us to walk through. On the other side are new feet. Go there. Crawl there if need be. Stop talking and obsessing. Just do it.

We cannot control who brings us into this world. We cannot influence the fluency with which they raise us; we cannot force the culture to instantly become hospitable. But the good news is that, even after injury, even in a feral state, even, for that matter, in an as yet captured state, we can have our lives back.

The psychological soul-plan for coming back into one's own is as follows: Take extra special caution and care to loose yourself into the wild gradually, setting up ethical and protective structures by which you gain tools to measure when something is too much. (You are usually already very sensitive to when something is too little.)

So the return to the wild and free psyche must be made with boldness, but also with consideration. In psychoanalysis we are fond of saying that to be trained as a healer/helper it is as important to learn what not to do as it is to learn what to do. To return to the wild from captivity carries the same caveats. Let us take a closer look.

The pitfalls, traps, and poisoned baits laid out for the wildish woman are specific to her culture. Here I have listed those that are common to most cultures. Women from differing ethnic and religious backgrounds will have additional specific insights. In a symbolic sense, we are composing a map of the woods in which we live. We are delineating where the predators live and describing their modi operandi. It is said that a single wolf knows every creature in her territory for miles around. It is this knowledge that gives her the edge in living as freely as possible.

Regaining lost instinct and healing injured instinct is truly within one's reach, for it returns when a woman pays close attention through listening, looking, and sensing the world around herself, and then by acting as she sees others act; efficiently, effectively, and soulfully. The opportunity to observe others who have instincts well intact is central to retrieval. Eventually, the listening, looking, and acting in an integral manner becomes a pattern with a rhythm to it, one you practice until it is relearned and becomes automatic again.

If our own wild natures have been wounded by something or someone, we refuse to lie down and die. We refuse to normalize this wound. We call up our instincts and do what we have to do. The wildish woman is, by nature, intense and talented. But because of being cut away from her instincts, she is also naive, accustomed to violence, adaptive to expatriation and exmatriation. Lovers, drugs, drink, money, fame, and power cannot much help the damage done. But a gradual re-entry to the instinctual life can. For this, a woman needs a mother, a "good enough" wildish mother. And guess who is waiting to be that mother? The Wild Woman wonders what is taking you so long to be with her, *really* be with her, not just sometimes, or when it's convenient, but consistently.

If you are striving to do something you value, it is so important to surround yourself with people who unequivocally support your work. It is both a trap and a poison to have so-called friends who have the same injuries but no real desire to heal them. These kinds of friends encourage you to act outrageously, outside of your natural cycles, out of sync with your soul-needs.

A feral woman cannot afford to be naive. As she returns to her innate life, she must consider excesses with a skeptical eye and be aware of their costs to soul, psyche, and instinct. Like the wolf pups, we memorize the traps, how they are made, and how they are laid. That is the way we remain free.

Even so, lost instincts do not recede without leaving echoes and trails of feeling, which we can follow to claim them again. Though a woman may be held in the velvet fist of propriety and stricture, whether she is one breath away from destruction through excesses or has just begun to dive into them, she can still hear whispers of the wild God in her blood. Even in these worst circumstances as portrayed in "The Red Shoes," even the most injured instincts can be healed.

To aright all this, we resurrect the wild nature, over and over again, each time the balance tips too far in one direction or another. We will know when there is reason for concern, for generally balance makes our lives larger and imbalance makes our lives smaller.

One of the most important things we can do is to understand life, all life, as a living body in itself, one that has respiration, new cell turnover, sloughing off, and waste material. It would be silly if we expected our bodies not to have waste material more than once every five years. It would be inane to think that just because we ate a day ago we shouldn't be hungry today.

It is just as fatuous to think that once we solve an issue it stays solved, that once we learn, we always remain conscious ever after. No, life is a great body that grows and diminishes in different areas, at different rates. When we are like the body, doing the work of new growth, wading through *la mierda*, the shit, just breathing or resting, we are very alive, we are within the cycles of the Wild Woman. If we could realize that *the work is to keep doing the work*, we would be much more fierce and much more peaceful.

To hold to joy, we may sometimes have to fight for it, we may have to strengthen ourselves and go full-bore, doing battle in whichever ways we deem most shrewd. To prepare for siege, we may have to go without many comforts for the duration. We can go without most things for long periods of time, anything almost, but not our joy, not those handmade red shoes.

The real miracle of individuation and reclamation of Wild Woman is that we all begin the process before we are ready, before we are strong enough, before we know enough; we begin a dialogue with thoughts and feelings that both tickle and thunder within us. We respond before we know how to speak the language, before we know all the answers, and before we know exactly to whom we are speaking.

But like the wolf mother teaching her pups to hunt and take care, this is the way Wild Woman wells up through us. We begin to speak in her voice, taking on her vision and her values. She teaches us to send out the message of our return to those who are like us.

I know several writers who have this glyph taped above their writing desks. I know one who carries it folded up inside her shoe. It is from a poem by Charles Simic and it is the ultimate instruction to us all: "He who cannot howl, will not find his pack."[23]

If you want to re-summon Wild Woman, refuse to be captured.[24] With instincts sharpened for balance—jump anywhere you like, howl at will, take what there is, find out all about it, let your eyes show your feelings, look into everything, see what you can see. Dance in red shoes, but make sure they're the ones you've made by hand. I can promise that you will become one vital woman.

CHAPTER 9

Homing: Returning
to OneSelf

There is human time and there is wild time. When I was a child in
the north woods, before I learned there were four seasons to a
year, I thought there were dozens: the time of night-time thunder-
storms, heat lightning time, bonfires-in-the-woods time, blood-on-
the-snow time, the times of ice trees, bowing trees, crying trees,
shimmering trees, bearded trees, waving-at-the-tops-only trees,
and trees-drop-their-babies time. I loved the seasons of diamond
snow, steaming snow, squeaking snow, and even dirty snow and
stone snow, for these meant the time of flower blossoms on the
river was coming.

These seasons were like important and holy visitors and each
sent its harbingers: pine cones open, pine cones closed, the smell
of leaf rot, the smell of rain coming, crackling hair, lank hair,
bushy hair, doors loose, doors tight, doors that won't shut at all,
windowpanes covered with ice-hair, windowpanes covered with
wet petals, windowpanes covered with yellow pollen, windowpanes pecked with sap gum. And our own skin had its cycles too:
parched, sweaty, gritty, sunburned, soft.

The psyches and souls of women also have their own cycles
and seasons of doing and solitude, running and staying, being
involved and being removed, questing and resting, creating and
incubating, being of the world and returning to the soul-place.
When we are children and young girls, the instinctive nature
notices all these phases and cycles. It hovers quite near us and we
are aware and active at various intervals as we see fit.

Children *are* the wildish nature, and without being told to, they prepare for the coming of these times, greeting them, living with them, and keeping from those times *recuerdos*, mementos, for remembering: the crimson leaf in the dictionary; the angel-wing necklaces from the seeds of the silver maples; snowballs in the meat locker; the special stone, bone, stick, or pod; the peculiar shell; the ribbon from the bird burial; a diary of smells from that time; the calm heart; the excited blood; and all the pictures in their minds.

Once, we lived by these cycles and seasons year after year, and they lived in us. They calmed us, danced us, shook us, reassured us, made us learn creaturally. They were part of our soul-skins—a pelt that enveloped us and the wild and natural world—at least until we were told that there really were only four seasons to a year, and that women themselves really only had three seasons—girlhood, adulthood, and old womanhood. And that was supposed to be that.

But we cannot allow ourselves to sleepwalk wrapped in this flimsy and unobservant fabrication, for it causes women to deviate from their natural and soulful cycles and therefore to suffer from dryness, tiredness, and homesickness. It is far better for us to return to our own unique and soulful cycles regularly, all of them, any of them. The following story can be understood as a commentary on the most important of women's cycles, the return to home, the wild home, the soul-home.

Tales of creatures with mysterious human kinship are told across the world, for such represent an archetype, a universal knowing about an issue of soul. Sometimes fairy tales and folktales erupt from a sense of place, from soulful places in particular. This story is told in the cold countries to the north, in any country where there is an icy sea or ocean. Versions of this story are told among the Celts, the Scots, the tribes of northwest America, Siberian and Icelandic peoples. The story is commonly called "The Seal Maiden" or "Selkie-o, *Pamrauk*, Little Seal"; "*Eyalirtaq*, Flesh of Seal." This special literary version that I wrote for my analysands, and to use in performance, I call "Sealskin, Soulskin." The story tells about where we truly come from, what we are made of, and how we must all, on a regular basis, use our instincts and find our way back home.[1]

~~~~~~

Sealskin, Soulskin

DURING A TIME that once was, is now gone forever, and will come back again soon, there is day after day of white sky, white snow . . . and all the tiny specks in the distance are people or dogs or bear.

Here, nothing thrives for the asking. The winds blow hard so the people have come to wear their parkas and *mamleks*, boots, sideways on purpose now. Here, words freeze in the open air, and whole sentences must be broken from the speaker's lips and thawed at the fire so people can see what has been said. Here, the people live in the white and abundant hair of old Annuluk, the old grandmother, the old sorceress who is Earth herself. And it was in this land that there lived a man . . . a man so lonely that over the years, tears had carved great chasms into his cheeks.

He tried to smile and be happy. He hunted. He trapped and he slept well. But he wished for human company. Sometimes out in the shallows in his kayak when a seal came near he remembered the old stories about how seals were once human, and the only reminder of that time was their eyes, which were capable of portraying those looks, those wise and wild and loving looks. And sometimes then he felt such a pang of loneliness that tears coursed down the well-used cracks in his face.

One night he hunted past dark but found nothing. As the moon rose in the sky and the ice floes glistened, he came to a great spotted rock in the sea, and it appeared to his keen eye that upon that old rock there was movement of the most graceful kind.

He paddled slow and deep to be closer, and there atop the mighty rock danced a small group of women, naked as the first day they lay upon their mothers' bellies. Well, he was a lonely man, with no human friends but in memory—and he stayed and watched. The women were like beings made of moon milk, and their skin shimmered with little silver dots like those on the salmon in springtime, and the women's feet and hands were long and graceful.

So beautiful were they that the man sat stunned in his boat, the water lapping, taking him closer and closer to the rock. He could hear the magnificent women laughing . . . at least they seemed to laugh, or was it the water laughing at the edge of the rock? The man was confused, for he was so dazzled. But somehow the loneliness that had weighed on his chest like wet hide was lifted away, and almost without thinking, as though he was meant, he jumped up onto the rock and stole one of the sealskins laying there. He hid behind an outcropping and he pushed the sealskin into his *qutnguq*, parka.

Soon, one of the women called in a voice that was the most beautiful he'd ever heard . . . like the whales calling at dawn . . . or no, maybe it was more like the newborn wolves tumbling down in the spring . . . or but, well no, it was something better than that, but it did not matter because . . . what were the women doing now?

Why, they were putting on their sealskins, and one by one the seal women were slipping into the sea, yelping and crying happily. Except for one. The tallest of them searched high and searched low for her sealskin, but it was nowhere to be found. The man felt emboldened—by what, he did not know. He stepped from the rock, appealing to her, "Woman . . . be . . . my . . . wife. I am . . . a lonely . . . man."

"Oh, I cannot be wife," she said, "for I am of the other, the ones who live *temeqvanek*, beneath."

"Be . . . my . . . wife," insisted the man. "In seven summers, I will return your sealskin to you, and you may stay or you may go as you wish."

The young seal woman looked long into his face with eyes that but for her true origins seemed human. Reluctantly she said, "I will go with you. After seven summers, it shall be decided."

So in time they had a child, whom they named Ooruk. And the child was lithe and fat. In winter the mother told Ooruk tales of the creatures that lived beneath the sea while the father whittled a bear or a wolf in whitestone with his long knife. When his mother carried the child Ooruk to bed, she pointed out through the smoke hole to the clouds and all their shapes. Except instead of recounting the shapes of raven and bear and wolf, she recounted the stories of walrus, whale, seal, and salmon . . . for those were the creatures she knew.

But as time went on, her flesh began to dry out. First it flaked, then it cracked. The skin of her eyelids began to peel. The hairs of her head began to drop to the ground. She became *naluaq*, palest white. Her plumpness began to wither. She tried to conceal her limp. Each day her eyes, without her willing it so, became more dull. She began to put out her hand in order to find her way, for her sight was darkening.

And so it went until one night when the child Ooruk was awakened by shouting and sat upright in his sleeping skins. He heard a roar like a bear that was his father berating his mother. He heard a crying like silver rung on stone that was his mother.

"You hid my sealskin seven long years ago, and now the eighth winter comes. I want what I am made of returned to me," cried the seal woman.

"And you, woman, would leave me if I gave it to you," boomed the husband.

"I do not know what I would do. I only know I must have what I belong to."

"And you would leave me wifeless, and the boy motherless. You are bad."

And with that her husband tore the hide flap of the door aside and disappeared into the night.

The boy loved his mother much. He feared losing her and so cried himself to sleep . . . only to be awakened by the wind. A strange wind . . . it seemed to call to him, "Oooruk, Oooruuuuk."

And out of bed he climbed, so hastily that he put his parka on upside down and pulled his mukluks only halfway up. Hearing his name called over and over, he dashed out into the starry, starry night.

"Oooooooruuuuk."

The child ran out to the cliff overlooking the water, and there, far out in the windy sea, was a huge shaggy silver seal . . . its head was enormous, its whiskers drooped to its chest, its eyes were deep yellow.

"Ooooooooruuuuk."

The boy scrambled down the cliff and stumbled at the bottom over a stone—no, a bundle—that had rolled out of a cleft in the rock. The boy's hair lashed at his face like a thousand reins of ice.

"Oooooooruuuuk."

The boy scratched open the bundle and shook it out—it was his mother's sealskin. Oh, and he could smell her all through it. And as he hugged the sealskin to his face and inhaled her scent, her soul slammed through him like a sudden summer wind.

"Ohhh," he cried with pain and joy, and lifted the skin again to his face and again her soul passed through his. "Ohhh," he cried again, for he was being filled with the unending love of his mother.

And the old silver seal way out ... sank slowly beneath the water.

The boy climbed the cliff and ran toward home with the seal-skin flying behind him, and into the house he fell. His mother swept him and the skin up and closed her eyes in gratitude for the safety of both.

She pulled on her sealskin. "Oh, mother, no!" cried the child.

She scooped up the child, tucked him under her arm, and half ran and half stumbled toward the roaring sea.

"Oh, mother! No! Don't leave me!" Ooruk cried.

And at once you could tell she wanted to stay with her child, she *wanted* to, but something called her, something older than she, older than he, older than time.

"Oh, mother, no, no, no," cried the child. She turned to him with a look of dreadful love in her eyes. She took the boy's face in her hands, and breathed her sweet breath into his lungs, once, twice, three times. Then, with him under her arm like a precious bundle, she dove into the sea, down, and down, and down, and still deeper down, and the seal woman and her child breathed easily under water.

And they swam deep and strong till they entered the underwater cove of seals where all manner of creatures were dining and singing, dancing and speaking, and the great silver seal that had called to Ooruk from the night sea embraced the child and called him grandson.

"How fare you up there, daughter?" asked the great silver seal.

The seal woman looked away and said, "I hurt a human . . . a man who gave his all to have me. But I cannot return to him, for I shall be a prisoner if I do."

"And the boy?" asked the old seal. "My grandchild?" He said it so proudly his voice shook.

"He must go back, father. He cannot stay. His time is not yet to be here with us." And she wept. And together they wept.

And so some days and nights passed, seven to be exact, during which time the luster came back to the seal woman's hair and eyes. She turned a beautiful dark color, her sight was restored, her body regained its plumpness, and she swam uncrippled. Yet it came time to return the boy to land. On that night, the old grandfather seal and the boy's beautiful mother swam with the child between them. Back they went, back up and up and up to the topside world. There they gently placed Ooruk on the stony shore in the moonlight.

His mother assured him, "I am always with you. Only touch what I have touched, my firesticks, my *ulu*, knife, my stone carvings of otters and seal, and I will breathe into your lungs a wind for the singing of your songs."

The old silver seal and his daughter kissed the child many times. At last, they tore themselves away and swam out to sea, and with one last look at the boy, they disappeared beneath the waters. And Ooruk, because it was not his time, stayed.

As time went on, he grew to be a mighty drummer and singer and a maker of stories, and it was said this all came to be because as a child he had survived being carried out to sea by the great seal spirits. Now, in the gray mists of morning, sometimes he can still be seen, with his kayak tethered, kneeling upon a certain rock in the sea, seeming to speak to a certain female seal who often comes near the shore. Though many have tried to hunt her, time after time they have failed. She is known as *Tanqigcaq*, the bright one, the holy one, and it is said that though she be a seal, her eyes are capable of portraying those human looks, those wise and wild and loving looks.

Loss of Sense of Soul as Initiation

The seal is one of the most beautiful of all symbols for the wild soul. Like the instinctual nature of women, seals are peculiar creatures who have evolved and adapted over eons. Like the seal woman, actual seals only come onto the land in order to breed and nurse. The mother seal is intensely devoted to her pup for about two months, loving, guarding, and feeding it solely from her own body stores. During this time, the thirty-pound pup quadruples in weight. Then the mother swims out to sea and the now viable and grown pup begins an independent life.

Among ethnic groups throughout the world, including many in the circumpolar region and West Africa, it is said that humans are not truly animated until the soul gives birth to the spirit, tenders and nurses it, filling it up with strength. Eventually the soul is believed to retreat to a farther home while the spirit begins its independent life in the world.[2]

The symbol of seal as a representation of soul is all the more compelling because there is a "docility" about seals, an accessibility well known to those who live near them. Seals have a sort of dogness about them; they are naturally affectionate. A kind of purity radiates from them. But they can also be very quick to react, retreat, or retort if threatened. The soul is like that too. It hovers near. It nurses the spirit. It does not run away when it perceives something new or unusual or difficult.

But sometimes, especially when a seal is not used to humans and just lies about in one of those blissful states that seals seem to enter from time to time, she does not anticipate human ways. Like the seal woman in the story, and like the souls of young and/or inexperienced women, she is unaware of the intentions of others and potential harm. And that is always when the sealskin is stolen.

I have come to the sense over the years of working with "capture" and "theft of treasure" motifs, and from analyzing many men and women, that there is in the individuation processes of almost everyone at least a one-time and significant theft. Some people characterize it as a theft of their "great opportunity" in life. Others define it as a larceny of love, or a robbing of one's spirit, a weakening of the sense of self. Some describe it as a distraction, a break, an interference or interruption of something vital to them: their art, their love, their dream, their hope, their belief in goodness, their development, their honor, their strivings.

Most of the time this major theft creeps up on the person from their blind side. It comes upon women for the same reasons it occurs in this story: because of naïveté, poor insight into the motives of others, inexperience in projecting what might happen in the future, not paying attention to all the clues in the environment, and because fate is always weaving lessons into the weft.

People who have been thusly robbed are not bad. They are not wrong. They are not stupid. But they are, in some significant way, inexperienced, or in a kind of psychic slumber. It would be a mistake to attribute such states only to the young. They can exist in anyone, regardless of age, ethnic affiliation, years of schooling, or even good intentions. It is clear that being stolen from most definitely evolves into a mysterious archetypal initiation[3] opportunity for those who are caught up in it . . . which is almost everyone.

The process of retrieving the treasure and figuring out how to replenish oneself develops four vital constructs in the psyche. When this dilemma is met head-on, and the descent to the *Río Abajo Río*, river beneath the river, is made, it fiercely strengthens our resolve to strive for conscious reclamation. It clarifies, over time, what it is that is most important to us. It fills us up with the need to have a plan for freeing ourselves psychically or otherwise and to enact our newly found wisdom. Finally, and most importantly, it develops our medial nature, that wild and knowing part of psyche that can also traverse the world of soul and the world of humans.

The archetypal core of the "Sealskin, Soulskin" story is extremely valuable, for it gives clear and pithy directions for the exact steps we must take in order to develop and find our way through these tasks. One of the central and most potentially destructive issues women face is that of beginning various psychological initiation processes with initiators who have not completed the process themselves. They have no seasoned persons who know how to proceed. When initiators are incompletely initiated themselves, they omit important aspects of the process without realizing it, and sometimes visit great abuse on the initiate, for they are working with a fragmentary idea of initiation, one that is often tainted in one way or another.[4]

At the other end of the spectrum is the woman who has experienced theft, and who is striving for knowledge and mastery of the situation, but who has run out of directions and does not know there is more to practice in order to complete the learning, and so repeats the first stage, that of being stolen from, over and over again. Through whatever circumstances, she has gotten tangled in the reins. Essentially, she is without instruction. Instead of discovering the requirements of a healthy wildish soul, she becomes a casualty of an uncompleted initiation.

Because matrilineal lines of initiation—older women teaching younger women certain psychic facts and procedures of the wild feminine—have been fragmented and broken for so many women and over so many years, it is a blessing to have the archeology of the fairy tale to learn from. What can be derived from those deep templates echoes the innate patterns of women's most integral psychological processes. In this sense, fairy tales and mythos are initiators; they are the wise ones who teach those who have come after.

So, it is the incompletely initiated or half-initiated women for whom the dynamics in "Sealskin, Soulskin" are most valuable. By knowing all the steps to take to complete the cyclical return to home, even a botched initiation can be untangled, reset, and completed properly. Let us see how this story instructs us to proceed.

Losing One's Pelt

The development of knowing, as in versions of "Bluebeard," "Rapunzel," "Devil's Midwife," and "Briar Rose" and others, begins with suffering. This progresses from first being unaware, then tricked in one way or another, and thence finding one's way to power again, and more so, to depth. The theme of a fateful catching that tests consciousness and ends in a deep knowing is a timeless one in fairy tales with female protagonists. Such tales carry dense instruction to all of us about what our work is if and when we are captured, and how to come back from it with the ability *pasar atravez del basque como una loba*, to slip through the forest like a wolf, *con un ojo agudo*, with a shrewd eye.

"Sealskin, Soulskin" contains a retrograde motif. Sometimes we call such tales "backward stories." In many fairy tales, a human is enchanted and turned into an animal. But here we have the opposite: a creature led into a human life. The story produces an insight into the structure of the female psyche. The seal maiden, like the wildish nature in women's psyches, is a mystical combination that is creatural and at the same time able to live among humans in a resourceful manner.

The pelt in this story is not so much an article as the representation of a feeling state and a state of being—one that is cohesive, soulful, and of the wildish female nature. When a woman is in this state, she feels entirely in and of herself instead of out of herself and wondering if she is doing right, acting right, thinking well. Though this state of being "in one's self" is one she occasionally loses touch with, the time she has previously spent there sustains her while she is about her work in the world. The return to the wildish state periodically is what replenishes her psychic reserves for her projects, family, relationships, and creative life in the topside world.

Eventually every woman who stays away from her soul-home for too long, tires. This is as it should be. Then she seeks her skin again in order to revive her sense of self and soul, in order to restore her deep-eyed and oceanic knowing. This great cycle of going and returning, going and returning, is reflexive within the instinctual nature of women and is innate to all women for all their lives, from throughout girlhood, adolescence, and young adulthood, through being a lover, through motherhood, through being a craftswoman, a wisdom-holder, an elderwoman, and beyond. These phases are not necessarily chronological, for mid-age women are often newborn, old women are intense lovers, and little girls know a good deal about cronish enchantment.

Over and over we lose this sense of feeling we are wholly in our skins by means already named as well as through extended duress. Those who toil too long without respite are also at risk. The soulskin vanishes when we fail to pay attention to what we are really doing, and particularly its cost to us.

We lose the soulskin by becoming too involved with ego, by being too exacting, perfectionistic,[5] or unnecessarily martyred, or driven by a blind ambition, or by being dissatisfied—about self, family, community, culture, world—and not saying or doing anything about it, or by pretending we are an unending source for others, or by not doing all we can to help ourselves. Oh, there are as many ways to lose the soulskin as there are women in the world.

The only way to hold on to this essential soulskin is to retain an exquisitely pristine consciousness about its value and uses. But, since no one can consistently maintain acute consciousness, no one can keep the soulskin absolutely every moment day and night. But we can keep the theft of it to a bare minimum. We can develop that *ojo agudo*, the shrewd eye that watches the conditions all around and guards our psychic territory accordingly. The "Sealskin, Soulskin" story, however, is about an instance of what we might call aggravated theft. This big theft can, with consciousness, be mediated in the future if we will pay attention to our cycles and the call to take leave and return home.

Every creature on earth returns to home. It is ironic that we have made wildlife refuges for ibis, pelican, egret, wolf, crane, deer, mouse, moose, and bear, but not for ourselves in the places where we live day after day. We understand that the loss of habitat is the most disastrous event that can occur to a free creature. We fervently point out how other creatures' natural territories have become surrounded by cities, ranches, highways, noise, and other dissonance, as though we are not surrounded by the same, as though we are not affected also. We know that for creatures to live on, they must at least from time to time have a home place, a place where they feel both protected and free.

We traditionally compensate for loss of a more serene habitat by taking a vacation or a holiday, which is supposed to be the giving of pleasure to oneself, except a vacation is often anything but. We can compensate our workaday dissonance by cutting down on the things we do that cause us to tense our deltoids and trapezii into painful knots. And all this is very good, but for the soul-self-psyche, vacation is not the same as refuge. "Time out" or "time off" is not the same as returning to home. Calmness is not the same as solitude.

We can contain this loss of soul by keeping close to the pelt to begin with. For instance, I see in the talented women in my practice that soulskin theft can come through relationships that are not in their rightful skins themselves, and some relationships are downright poisonous. It takes will and force to overcome these relationships, but it can be done, especially if, as in the story, one will awaken to the voice calling from home, calling one back to the core self where one's immediate wisdom is whole and accessible. From there, a woman can decide with clear-seeing what it is she must have, and what it is she wants to do.

The aggravated theft of the sealskin also occurs far more subtly through the theft of a woman's resources and of her time. The world is lonely for comfort, and for the hips and breasts of women. It calls out in a thousand-handed, million-voiced way, waving to us, plucking and pulling at us, asking for our attention. Sometimes it seems that everywhere we turn there is a someone or a something of the world that needs, wants, wishes. Some of the people, issues, and things of the world are appealing and charming; others may be demanding and angry; and yet others seem so heartrendingly helpless that, against our wills, our empathy overflows, our milk runs down our bellies. But unless it is a life-and-death matter, take the time, make the time, to "put on the brass brassiere."[6] Stop running the milk train. Do the work of turning toward home.

Though we see that the skin can be lost through a devastating and wrong love, it may also be lost in a right and deepest love. It is not exactly the rightness of a person or thing or its wrongness that causes the theft of our soulskins, it is the cost of these things to us. It is what it costs us in time, energy, observation, attention, hovering, prompting, instructing, teaching, training. These motions of psyche are like cash withdrawals from the psychic savings account. The issue is not about these energic cash withdrawals themselves, for these are an important part of life's give and take. But it is being *overdrawn* that causes the loss of the skin, and the paling and dulling of one's most acute instincts. It is lack of further deposits of energy, knowledge, acknowledgment, ideas, and excitement that causes a woman to feel she is psychically dying.

In the story, when the young seal woman loses her pelt, she is involved in a beautiful pursuit, in the business of freedom. She dances and dances, and does not pay attention to what is going on about her. When we are in our rightful wildish nature, we all feel this bright life. It is one of the signs that we are close to Wild Woman. We all enter the world in a dancing condition. We always begin with our own pelts intact.

Yet, at least till we become more conscious, we all go through this stage in individuation. We all swim up to the rock, dance, and don't pay attention. It is then that the more tricksterish aspect of the psyche descends, and somewhere down the road we suddenly look for and can no longer find what belongs to us or to what we belong. Then our sense of soul is mysteriously missing, and more so, it is hidden away. And so we wander about partially dazed. It is not good to make choices when dazed, but we do.

We know poor choice occurs in various ways. One woman marries too early. Another becomes pregnant too young. Another goes with a bad mate. Another gives up her art to "have things." Another is seduced by any number of illusions, another by promises, another by too much "being good" and not enough soul, yet another by too much airiness and not enough earthiness. And in cases where the woman goes with her soulskin half on and half gone, it is not necessarily because her choices are wrong so much as that she stays away from her soul-home too long and dries out and is rather of little use to anyone, least of all herself. There are hundreds of ways to lose one's soulskin.

If we delve into the symbol of animal hide, we find that in all animals, including ourselves, piloerection—hair standing on end—occurs in response to things seen as well as to things sensed. The rising hair of the pelt sends a "chill" through the creature and rouses suspicion, caution, and other protective traits. Among the Inuit it is said that both fur and feathers have the ability to see what goes on far off in the distance, and that is why an *angakok*, shaman, wears many furs, many feathers, so as to have hundreds of eyes to better see into the mysteries. The sealskin is a symbol of soul that not only provides warmth, but also provides an early warning system through its vision as well.

In hunting cultures, the pelt is equal to food as the most important product for survival. It is used to make boots, to line parkas, for waterproofing to keep ice hoar away from the face and wrists.

The pelt keeps little children safe and dry, protects and warms the vulnerable human belly, back, feet, hands, and head. To lose the pelt is to lose one's protections, one's warmth, one's early warning system, one's instinctive sight. Psychologically, to be without the pelt causes a woman to pursue what she thinks she should do, rather than what she truly wishes. It causes her to follow whoever or whatever impresses her as strongest—whether it is good for her or not. Then there is much leaping and little looking. She is jocular instead of incisive, laughs things off, puts things off. She pulls back from taking the next step, from making the necessary descent and holding herself there long enough for something to happen.

So you can see that in a world that values driven women who go, go, go, the stealing of soulskins is very easy, so much so that the first theft occurs somewhere between the ages of seven and eighteen. By then, most young women have begun to dance on the rock in the sea. By then most will have reached for the soulskin but not found it where they left it. And, though this initially seems meant to cause the development of a medial structure in the psyche—that is, an ability to learn to live in the world of spirit and in the outer reality as well—too often this progression is not accomplished, nor is any of the rest of the initiatory experience, and the woman wanders through life skinless.

Though we may have tried to prevent a recurrence of theft by practically sewing ourselves into our soulskins, very few women reach the age of majority with more than a few tufts of the original pelt intact. We lay aside our skins while we dance. We learn the world, but lose our skins. We find that without our skins we begin to slowly dry away. Because most women were raised to bear these things stoically, as their mothers did before them, no one notices there is a dying going on, until one day . . .

When we are young and our soul-lives collide with the desires and requirements of culture and the world, indeed we feel stranded far from home. However, as adults we continue to drive ourselves even farther from home as a result of our own choices about who, what, where, and for how long. If we were never taught to return to the soul-home in childhood, we repeat the "theft and wandering around lost" pattern ad infinitum. But, even when it is our own dismal choices that have blown us off course—too far from what we need—hold faith, for within the soul is the homing device. We all can find our way back.

The Lonely Man

In a story similar to the core of this one, it is actually a human woman who lures a whale-man to copulate with her by stealing his fin. In other stories, the offspring is sometimes a girl, sometimes a fish boy. Sometimes the old one out in the sea is a venerable old female. Because there is so much gender exchange in stories, the maleness and femaleness of the characters in the story are far less important than the proscribed process.

In this spirit, let us consider that the lonely man who steals the sealskin represents the ego of a woman's psyche. The health of the ego is often determined by how well one measures boundaries in the outer world, how strongly one's identity is formed, how well one differentiates past, present, and future, and how closely one's perceptions coincide with consensual reality. It is a timeless motif in human psyche that the ego and the soul vie to control the life force. In early life, the ego, with its appetites, often leads; it is always cooking something up that smells really good. The ego is very muscular during this time. It relegates the soul to back porch kitchen duty.

But at some point, sometimes in our twenties, sometimes our thirties, most often the forties, although some women aren't really ready until they're fifty or sixty or even in their seventies or eighties, we begin at last to let the soul lead. The power shifts away from brickabrack and frick-frack to soulfulness. And though the soul does not assume the lead by killing off the ego, the ego is demoted, one might say, and given a different assignment in the psyche, which is essentially to submit to the concerns of the soul.

From the time we are born, there is a wildish urge within us that desires our souls lead our lives, for the ego can only understand just so much. Imagine the ego on a permanent and relatively short leash; it can only go so far into the mysteries of life and spirit. Usually, it becomes frightened. It has a bad habit of reducing all numinosity to a "nothing but." It demands facts that are observable. Proofs that are of a feeling or mystical nature do not very often sit well with the ego. That is why the ego is lonely. It is very limited in its constructs in this way; it cannot fully participate in the more mysterious processes of soul and psyche. Yet the lonely man yearns for soul, dimly recognizes soulful and wildish things when they are near.

Some people use the words *soul* and *spirit* interchangeably. But in fairy tales the soul is always the pro-*gyn*itor and the pro*gen*itor of spirit. In arcane hermeneutics, the spirit is a being born of the soul. The spirit inherits or incarnates into matter in order to gather news of the ways of the world and carries these back to the soul. When not interfered with, the relationship between soul and spirit is one of perfect symmetry; each enriches the other in turn. Together, the soul and spirit form an ecology, as in a pond where the creatures at the bottom nourish those at the top and those at the top nourish those at the bottom.

In Jungian psychology, the ego is often described as a small island of consciousness that floats in a sea of unconsciousness. However, in folklore the ego is portrayed as a creature of appetite, often symbolized by a not very bright human or animal surrounded by forces very mystifying to it, and over which it attempts to gain control. Sometimes the ego is able to gain control in a most brutish and destructive manner, but in the end, through the heroine's or hero's progress, it most often loses its bid to reign.

In the beginning of one's life, the ego is curious about the soul-world, but more often it is concerned with fulfilling its own hungers. The ego is initially born into us as potential, and is shaped, developed, and filled up with ideas, values, and duties by the world around us: our parents, our teachers, our culture. And this is as it should be, for it becomes our escort, our armor, and our scout in the outer world. However, if the wildish nature is not allowed to emanate upward through the ego, giving it color, juice, and instinctive responsiveness, then although the culture may approve of what has been fashioned in this ego, the soul does not, cannot, will not approve such incompleteness of *its* work.

The lonely man in the tale is attempting to participate in the life of the soul. But like the ego, he is not particularly built for it, and tries to grab at the soul rather than develop a relationship with it. Why does the ego steal the sealskin? Like all other lonely or hungry things, it loves the light. It sees light, and the possibility of being close to the soul, and it creeps up to it and steals one of its essential camouflages. Ego cannot help itself. It is what it is; attracted to the light. Even though it cannot live under the water, it has its own yearning for relationship with the soul. The ego is crude in comparison to the soul. Its way of doing things is usually not evocative or sensitive. But it has a tiny and dimly understood longing for the beautiful light. And this, in some way and for some time, calms the ego.

So, in a hunger for soul, our own ego-self steals the pelt. "Stay with me," whispers the ego. "I will make you happy—by isolating you from your soul-self and your cycles of returning to your soul-home. I will make you very, very happy. Please, please stay." And so, as is right in the beginning of feminine individuation, the soul is pressured into relationship with ego. The mundane function of the soul's subservience to the ego occurs in order for us to learn the world, the ways to gain things, how to work, how to differentiate good from not so good, when to move, when to stay put, how to live with other people, learning the mechanics and machinations of culture, holding a job, holding a baby, taking care of the body, taking care of business . . . all the things of the outer life.

The initial purpose of developing such an important construct within a woman's psyche, the marriage of the seal woman and the lonely man, a marriage in which she is definitely subservient, is to create a temporary arrangement that will ultimately produce a spirit child who can cohabit and translate in and between both the mundane and the wildish worlds. Once this symbolic child is born, developed, initiated, it resurfaces into the outer world and the relationship with soul is healed. Even though the lonely man, the ego, cannot dominate forever—for someday it must submit to the demands of soul for the rest of a woman's life—by living with the seal woman/soul-woman, it has been touched by greatness, and is therefore gratified, enriched, and humbled all at the same time.

The Spirit Child

So we see that the union of opposites between ego and soul produces something of infinite value, the spirit child. And it is true that even when the ego roughly intrudes upon the more subtle aspects of psyche and soul, a cross-fertilization is taking place. Paradoxically, by stealing the soul's protection and its ability to vanish into the water at will, the ego participates in making a child who will claim dual heritage, world and soul, one who will be able to carry messages and gifts back and forth between the two.

In some of the greatest tales, such as the Gaelic "Beauty and the Beast," the Mexican *"Bruja Milagra,"* and the Japanese *"Tsukino Waguma:* The Bear," finding the way back to one's rightful psychic order begins with the feeding of or the caring for a lonely and/or injured woman, man, or beast. That such a child, who will have the ability to traverse two very different worlds, can come from a woman who is in such a skinless state and "married" to something in herself or in the outer world that is so lonely and undeveloped is one of the constant miracles of the psyche. Something occurs within us when we are in such a state, something that produces a feeling state, a tiny new life, a small flame that thrives under imperfect, arduous, or even inhumane conditions.

This spirit child is *la niña milagrosa*, a miracle child, who has the ability to hear the call, hear the far-off voice that says it is time to come back, back to oneself. The child is a part of our medial nature that compels us, for it can hear the call when it comes. It is the child rising out of sleep, out of bed, out of the house, and out into the wind-filled night and down to the wild sea that causes us to assert, "As God is my witness, I shall proceed in this way," or "I *will* endure," or "I shall not be turned away," or "I shall find a way to continue."

It is the child who brings the sealskin, soulskin back to his mother. It is the child who enables her to return to her home. This child is a spiritual power that impels us to continue our important work, to push back, change our lives, better the community, join in helping to balance the world . . . all by returning to home. If one wants to participate in these things, the difficult marriage between soul and ego must be made, the spirit child must be brought to life. Retrieval and return are the goals of mastery.

Regardless of a woman's circumstances, the spirit child, the old seal who rises up from the sea calling his daughter home, and the open sea are always near. Always. Even in places and at times one might least expect them to be present.

Since 1971, I've taught writing as contemplative practice in prisons and penitentiaries across the nation. On a particular trip to a federal women's prison with a group of artist/healers,[7] in order to do performance and teach a group of a hundred women who were intensely involved in a spiritual growth program there, as usual, I saw few "hardened" women. Instead, I saw dozens of women in various stages of seal-womanness. Many, many had been figuratively, but also literally, "captured" through their intensely naive choices. Whatever their reasons for being there, in spite of the most constrained conditions, each woman in her own way was clearly in the process of creating a spirit child, carefully and painfully fashioned from her own flesh, from her own bones. Each woman was searching also for the seal-skin; each was in the process of remembering the way back to the soul-home.

One artist of our troupe, a young black violinist named India Cook, played for the women. We were outdoors in the open yard; it was very cold and the wind was making an *Ooooooo* sound around the backdrop on the open stage. The violinist drew her bow across the strings of her electrified violin and played sternum-piercing music in a minor key. Truly, her violin wept. A big Lakota woman pounded on my arm and hoarsely whispered, "This sound . . . that violin unlocks a place in me. I thought I was locked up good and tight and forever." Her broad face was both puzzled and ethereal. My heart broke on itself, but in a good way, for I saw that no matter what had happened to her—and *much* had happened to her—she could still hear the cry from over the sea, that call from home.

In the "Sealskin, Soulskin" story, the seal maiden tells her child stories about what lives and thrives under the sea. She instructs through her stories, shaping this child who was born of her union with the ego. She is forming the child, teaching it the terrain and the ways of the "other." The soul is preparing this wildish child of the psyche for something very important.

Drying Out and Crippling

Most of a woman's depressions, ennuis, and wandering confusions are caused by a severely restricted soul-life in which innovation, impulse, and creation are restricted or forbidden. Women receive enormous impulse to act from the creative force. We cannot overlook the fact that there is still much thieving and hamstringing of women's talents through cultural restriction and punishment of her natural and wildish instincts.

We can break away from this condition if there is an underground river or even a little freshet pouring from somewhere soulful into our lives. But if a woman "far from home" surrenders all power, she will become first a fog, then a vapor, and finally a wisp of her former wildish self.

All this secreting away of a woman's natural pelt and her subsequent drying out and crippling reminds me of an old story that circulated in our family among the several old country tailors. My late Uncle Vilmos once told it to calm and teach an angry adult in our extended family, one who was being too harsh with a child. Uncle Vilmos had infinite patience and tenderness toward humans and creatures. He was a natural storyteller in the *mesemondók* tradition and skilled in applying stories as gentle medicine.

A MAN CAME TO A SZABÓ, TAILOR, and tried on a suit. As he stood before the mirror, he noticed the vest was a little uneven at the bottom.

"Oh," said the tailor, "don't worry about that. Just hold the shorter end down with your left hand and no one will ever notice."

While the customer proceeded to do this, he noticed that the lapel of the jacket curled up instead of lying flat.

"Oh that?" said the tailor. "That's nothing. Just turn your head a little and hold it down with your chin."

The customer complied, and as he did, he noticed that the inseam of the pants was a little short and he felt that the rise was a bit too tight.

"Oh, don't worry about that," said the tailor. "Just pull the inseam down with your right hand, and everything will be perfect." The customer agreed and purchased the suit.

The next day he wore his new suit with all the accompanying hand and chin "alterations." As he limped through the park with his chin holding down his lapel, one hand tugging at the vest, the other hand grasping his crotch, two old men stopped playing checkers to watch him stagger by.

"*M'Isten*, oh, my God!" said the first man. "Look at that poor crippled man!"

The second man reflected for a moment, then murmured, "*Igen*, yes, the crippling is too bad, but you know I wonder . . . where did he get such a nice suit?"

~~~~~~~~~~~~~~~~~~~~~~~~~~~~~~~~~~~

The reaction of the last old man constitutes a common cultural response toward a woman who has developed an impeccable persona but who is all crippled up with trying to maintain it. Well yes, she is crippled, but look at how nice she looks, look at how good she is, look at how well she's doing. When we become dried out, we try to walk all crippled up in order to make it appear that we are handling everything, that all is well, and just so. Whether it is the soulskin that is missing, or the culture-made skin that doesn't fit, we are crippled by pretending it is otherwise. But, when we do this, life is diminished and the cost to ourselves is very high.

When a woman begins to dry out, it becomes harder and harder for her to function in the hearty wildish nature. Ideas, creativity, life itself thrives on moisture. Women in this condition often have dark man dreams: thugs, prowlers, or rapists threaten them, hold them hostage, steal from them, and far worse. Sometimes these dreams are trauma dreams arising from an actual assault. But most often they are dreams of women who are drying out, who are not giving care to the instinctual side of their lives, who steal from themselves, deprive the creative function, and sometimes make no effort to help themselves, or else work very hard to ignore the call back to the water.

Over the years of my practice, I have seen many women in this dried-out state, some mildly affected, others more so. Concomitantly, I've heard from the same women many injured-animal dreams, these increasing dramatically (in women and men) over the last ten years or so. It is hard not to notice that the increase in injured-animal dreams coincides with the devastations to the wilderness both within as well as outside of people.

In these dreams, the creature—doe, lizard, horse, bear, bull, whale, and so on—is crippled up, much like the man in the tailor story, much like the seal woman. Although dreams of injured animals comment on the condition of a woman's instinctive psyche and her relationship to the wild nature, at the same time these dreams also reflect deep lacerations in the collective unconscious regarding the loss of the instinctual life. If the culture prohibits an integral and sane life for women for whatever reason, she will dream injured-animal dreams. Though the psyche makes every effort to cleanse and strengthen itself regularly, every lash mark "out there" is recorded on the unconscious "in here," so that a dreamer carries the effects of losing her personal ties with Wild Woman, and also the world's loss of relationship with this deep nature.

So sometimes it is not only the woman who is drying out. Sometimes, essential aspects of one's micro-environment—the family or the workplace, for instance—or one's larger culture are caking and cracking to dust also, and these affect and afflict her. In order for her to contribute to helping aright these conditions, a return to her own skin, her own instinctual common sense, and her own return to home are necessary.

As we have seen, it is hard to recognize our condition until we become like seal woman in her distress: peeling, limping, losing juice, going blind. So it is a gift from the immense vitality of the psyche, then, that there is deep in the unconscious a caller, an old one who rises to the surface of our consciousness and begins to incessantly call us back to our true natures.

Hearing the Old One's Call

What is that cry over the sea? This voice on the wind that calls the child from his bed and out into the night is similar to a kind of nightdream that comes into a dreamer's awareness as a disembodied voice and nothing more. This is one of the most powerful dreams a dreamer can dream. In my cultural traditions, whatever is said by this voice in the dream is considered a direct transmission from the soul.

It is said that disembodied voice dreams may occur at any time but particularly when a soul is in distress; then the deep self cuts to the chase, so to speak. Bang! A woman's soul speaks. And it tells her what comes next.

In the story, the old seal rises out of its own element to begin the call. It is a profound feature of the wild psyche that if we do not come on our own, if we aren't paying attention to our own seasons and the time for return, the Old One will come for us, calling and calling until something in us responds.

Thank goodness for this natural homing signal that becomes louder and louder the more we are in need of return. The signal goes off as everything begins to be "too"—in either a negative or positive sense. It can be as much time to go home when there is too much positive stimulation as when there is ceaseless dissonance. Perhaps we have become too intense about something. We can be too worn down by something. We can be overloved, underloved, overworked, underworked . . . each costs much. In the face of "too much" we gradually become dry, our hearts become tired, our energies begin to become spare, and a mysterious longing for—we almost never have a name for it other than "a something"—rises up in us more and more; then the Old One calls.

In this story, it is interesting that the one who hears and responds to the call from the sea is the little spirit child. It is he who ventures out over the ice crags and stones, who dumbly follows the cry, and who accidentally trips over his mother's rolledup sealskin.

The child's restless sleep is an acute and accurate portrayal of the restlessness a woman feels when she is yearning to return to her psychic place of origin. Since the psyche is a complete system, all its elements resonate to the call. A woman's restlessness during this time is often accompanied by irritability and a sense that everything is much too near for comfort, or far too far for peace. She feels anywhere from a little bit to a lot "lost," for she has stayed too long from home. These feelings are just the right feelings to feel. They are a message that says "Come here now." That feeling of being torn comes from hearing, consciously or unconsciously, something calling us, calling us back, something that we cannot say no to without hurting ourselves.

If we don't go when it is time, the soul will come for us, as we see in these lines from a poem called "Woman Who Lives Under the Lake."

> . . . one night
> there's a heartbeat at the door.
> Outside, a woman in the fog,
> with hair of twigs and dress of weed,
> dripping green lake water.
> She says "I am you,
> and I have traveled a long distance.
> Come with me, there is something I must show you . . ."
> She turns to go, her cloak falls open,
> Suddenly, golden light . . . everywhere, golden light . . .[8]

The old seal rises up at night and the child stumbles about at night. In this and many other tales we see the main character discovering an astonishing truth or recovering an invaluable treasure while groping in the dark. This motif is ubiquitous in fairy tales and occurs no matter what, by hook or by crook. Nothing makes the light, the wonder, the treasure stand out so well as darkness. The "dark night of the soul" has almost become a catchphrase in certain parts of the culture. The recovery of the divine is done in the dark of Hel or Hades or "there." The return of the Cristo comes as a glow from the gloaming of hell. The Asian sun Goddess Amaterasu bursts from the darkness beneath the mountain. The Sumerian Goddess Inanna, in her water form, "ignites into a white gold as she lies in a newly plowed trough of black earth."[9] In the mountains in Chiapas, it is said that every day "the yellow sun must burn a hole through the blackest *huipil*, blouse, in order to rise up in the sky."[10]

These images of going about in and through the dark carry an age-old message that says, "Do not fear 'not knowing.' " In various phases and periods of our lives, this is as it should be. This feature of tales and myths encourages us to follow the call, even when we've no idea of where to go, in what direction, or for how long. All we know is that like the child in the tale, we must sit up, get up, and go see. So maybe we stumble around in the dark for a while trying to find what calls us, but because we have managed to not talk ourselves out of being summoned by the wild one, we invariably stumble over the soulskin. When we breathe up that soulstate, we automatically enter the feeling state of "This is right. I know what I need."

For many modern women, it is not the driving about in the dark looking for the soulskin that is most fearsome. Rather it is the diving into the water, the actual return to home, and especially the actual leave-taking, that are far more formidable. Though women come back into themselves, draw on the sealskin, pat it closed, and are all ready to go, it is hard to go; really, really hard to cede, to hand over whatever we've been so busy with, and just leave.

Staying Overlong

In the story, the seal woman dries out as she stays too long. Her afflictions are the same ones we experience by staying overlong. Her skin dries out. Our skin is our greatest sensing organ; it tells us when we are cold, too warm, excited, frightened. When a woman is gone too long from home, her ability to perceive how she's truly feeling and thinking about herself and all other matters begins to dry and crack. She is on "lemming status." Because she is not perceiving what is too much, what is not enough, she runs right over her own edges.

We see in the tale that her hair thins, her weight drops, she becomes an anemic version of what she once was. When we stay too long, we too lose our ideas, our soul-relationship becomes scrawny, our blood runs thin and slowly. Seal woman begins to limp, her eyes lose their moisture, she begins to go blind. When we are overdue for home, our eyes have nothing to sparkle for, our bones are weary, it is as though our nerve sheaths are unwrapped, and we can no longer focus on who or what we are about.

In the wooded hills of Indiana and Michigan, there is a striking group of farm people whose ancestors came up from the hills of Kentucky and Tennessee a long time ago. Though their speech is clotted with grammatical inventions—"I ain't got no . . ." and "We done this the other day . . ."—they are Bible readers and so they also use beautiful and rolling long words such as *iniquities*, *aromatical*, and *canticle*.[11] Also, they have many descriptions that apply to women being worn out and unaware. Backwoods people don't sand their words down fine. They block cut them, string them in chunks they call sentences, and throw them down rough. "Gone too long in harness," "worked her hind legs off," "so tired she can't find her way back to a bright red barn," and the especially brutal descriptor "suckling a dead litter," mean she is draining her life away in a futile or unrewarding marriage, job, or endeavor.

When a woman is too long gone from home, she is less and less able to propel herself forward in life. Instead of pulling in the harness of her choice, she's dangling from one. She's so cross-eyed with tiredness she trudges right on past the place of help and comfort. The dead litter is comprised of ideas, chores, and demands that don't work, have no life, and bring no life to her. Such a woman becomes pale yet contentious, more and more uncompromising, yet scattered. Her fuse burns shorter and shorter. Popular culture calls this "burnout"—but it's more than that, it's *hambre del alma*, the starving soul. Then, there is only one recourse, finally the woman knows she has to—not might, maybe, sort of, but *must*—return to home.

In the story, a promise made becomes a promise broken. The man, who is rather dried out himself with all those long cracks in his face from having been so lonely so long, has gotten the seal woman to enter his house and heart by promising that after a certain period of time he will return her pelt and she can stay with him or return to her own land, as she wishes.

What woman does not know this broken promise by heart? "As soon as I finish this I can go. As soon as I can get away . . . When the springtime comes, I'll go. When the summer's over, I'll go. When the kids are back in school . . . Late in autumn when the trees are so beautiful, I will go. Well, no one can go anywhere in winter. So I'll just wait for spring . . . I really mean it this time."

The return to home is particularly important if one has been bound up in worldly matters and overstayed her time. What is that length of time? It is different for each woman, but suffice to say that women know, absolutely know, when they have stayed overlong in the world. They know when they are overdue for home. Their bodies are in the here and now, but their minds are far, far away.

They are dying for new life. They are panting for the sea. They are living just for next month, just till this semester is past, can't wait till winter is finally over so they can feel alive again, just waiting for a mystically assigned date somewhere in the future when they will be free to do some wondrous thing. They think they will die if they don't . . . you fill in the blank. And there is a quality of mourning to it all. There is angst. There is bereftness. There is wistfulness. There is longing. There is plucking at threads in one's skirt and staring long from windows. And it is not a temporary discomfort. It stays, and grows more and more intense over time.

Yet women continue in their day-to-day routines, looking sheepish, acting guilty and smirky. "Yes, yes, yes, I know," they say. "I should, but, but, but . . ." It is the "buts" in their sentences that are the dead giveaways that they have stayed too long.

An incompletely initiated woman in this depleted state erroneously thinks she is deriving more spiritual credit by staying than she thinks she will gain by going. Others are caught up in, as they say in Mexico, *dar a algo un tirón fuerte*, always tugging at the sleeve of the Virgin, meaning they are working hard and ever harder to prove that they are acceptable, that they are good people.

But there are other reasons for the divided woman. She is not used to letting others take the oars. She may be a practitioner of "kid lit" which is a litany that goes like this: "But my kids need this, my kids need that, et cetera."[12] She does not realize that by sacrificing her need for return, she teaches her children to make the very same sacrifices of their own needs once they are grown.

Some women are afraid that those around them will not understand their need for return. And not all may. But the woman must understand *this* herself: When a woman goes home according to her own cycles, others around her are given their own individuation work, their own vital issues to deal with. Her return to home allows others growth and development too.

Among wolves there are no such divided feelings about going and staying, for they work, whelp, rest, and rove in cycles. They are part of a group that shares in working and caregiving while others take time away. It is a good way to live. It is a way to live that has all the integrity of the wild feminine.

Let us clarify that the going home is many different things to many different women. My Romanian painter friend knew his grandmother was in her going-home state when she took a wooden chair out into the back garden and sat staring at the sun with her eyes wide open. "It is medicine for my eyes, good for you," she said. People knew not to disturb her, or if they didn't know, they soon found out. It is important to understand that going home does not necessarily cost money. It costs time. It costs a strong act of will to say "I am going" and mean it. You can call over your shoulder, as my dear friend Jean recommends, "I'm off for now but I'll be back," but you must keep trekking homeward even so.

There are many ways to go home; many are mundane, some are divine. My clients tell me these mundane endeavors constitute a return to home for them ... although I caution you, the exact placement of the aperture to home changes from time to time, so its location may be different this month than last. Rereading passages of books and single poems that have touched them. Spending even a few minutes near a river, a stream, a creek. Lying on the ground in dappled light. Being with a loved one without kids around. Sitting on the porch shelling something, knitting something, peeling something. Walking or driving for an hour, any direction, then returning. Boarding any bus, destination unknown. Making drums while listening to music. Greeting sunrise. Driving out to where the city lights do not interfere with the night sky. Praying. A special friend. Sitting on a bridge with legs dangling over. Holding an infant. Sitting by a window in a café and writing. Sitting in a circle of trees. Drying hair in the sun. Putting hands in a rain barrel. Potting plants, being sure to get hands very muddy. Beholding beauty, grace, the touching frailty of human beings.

So, it is not necessarily an overland and arduous journey to go home, yet I do not want to make it seem that it is simplistic, for there is much resistance to going home no matter if it be easy or hard.

There is one more way to understand women's delaying the return, one that is far more mysterious, and that is a woman's overidentification with the healer archetype. Now an archetype is an enormous force that is both mysterious and instructive to us. We gain great stores by being near it, by emulating it to some extent, by being in balanced relationship to it. Each archetype carries its own characteristics that support the name we give the archetype: the great mother, the divine child, the sun hero, and so forth.

The great healer archetype carries wisdom, goodness, knowing, caregiving, and all the other things associated with a healer. So, it is good to be generous and kind and helpful like the great healer archetype. But only to a point. Beyond that, it exerts a hindering influence on our lives. Women's "heal everything, fix everything" compulsion is a major entrapment constructed by the requirements placed upon us by our own cultures, mainly pressures to prove that we are not just standing around taking up space and enjoying ourselves, but that we have redeemable value—in some parts of the world, it is fair to say, to prove that we have value and therefore should be allowed to live. These pressures are introduced into our psyches when we are very young and unable to judge or resist them. They become law to us . . . unless or until we challenge them.

But the cries of the suffering world cannot all be answered by a single person all the time. We can truly only choose to respond to those that allow us to go home on a regular basis, otherwise our heart-lights dim to almost nothing. What the heart wishes to help is sometimes different from what the soul's resources be. If a woman values her soulskin, she will decide these matters according to how close she is to and how often she has been "home."

While archetypes may emanate through us for short periods of time, in what we call numinous experience, no woman can emanate an archetype continuously. Only the archetype itself can be ever-able, all giving, eternally energetic. We may try to emulate these, but they are ideals, not achievable by humans, and not meant to be. Yet the trap requires that women exhaust themselves trying to achieve these unrealistic levels. To avoid the trap, one has to learn to say "Halt" and "Stop the music," and of course mean it.

A woman has to go away and be with herself and look into how she came to be trapped in an archetype to begin with.[13] The basic wild instinct that determines "only this far and no farther, only this much and no more" must be retrieved and developed. That is how a woman keeps her bearings. It is preferable to go home for a while, even if it causes others to be irritated, rather than to stay and deteriorate, and then finally crawl away in tatters.

So, women who are tired, temporarily sick of the world, who are afraid to take time off, afraid to stop, wake up already! Lay a blanket over the banging gong that cries for you to infinitely help this, help that, help this other thing. It will be there to uncover again, if you wish it so, when you come back. If we do not go home when it is time, we lose our focus. Finding the skin again, putting it on, patting it tight, going home again, helps us to be more effective when we return. There is a saying, "You can't go home again." It is not true. While you cannot crawl back into the uterus again, you can return to the soul-home. It is not only possible, it is requisite.

Cutting Loose, Diving In

What is homing? It is the instinct to return, to go to the place we remember. It is the ability to find, whether in dark or in daylight, one's home place. We all know how to return home. No matter how long it's been, we find our way. We go through the night, over strange land, through tribes of strangers, without maps and asking of the odd personages we meet along the road, "What is the way?"

The exact answer to "Where is home?" is more complex . . . but in some way it is an internal place, a place somewhere in time rather than space, where a woman feels of one piece. Home is where a thought or feeling can be sustained instead of being interrupted or torn away from us because something else is demanding our time and attention. And through the ages women have found myriad ways to have this, make this for themselves, even when their duties and chores were endless.

I first learned this in the community of my childhood, where many devout women rose before five A.M. and in their long dark dresses wended their way through the gray dawn to kneel in the cold nave of the church, their peripheral vision cut off by babushkas pulled far forward. They buried their faces in their red hands and prayed, told God stories, pulled into themselves peace, strength, and insight. Oftentimes, my Aunt Katerin took me with her. When once I said, "It is so quiet and pretty here," she winked as she shushed me. "Don't tell anyone; it's a very important secret." And so it was, for on the walking path to church at dawn and in the dim interior of the church itself were the only two places of that time where it was forbidden to disturb a woman.

It is right and proper that women eke out, liberate, take, make, connive to get, assert their right to go home. Home is a sustained mood or sense that allows us to experience feelings not necessarily sustained in the mundane world: wonder, vision, peace, freedom from worry, freedom from demands, freedom from constant clacking. All these treasures from home are meant to be cached in the psyche for later use in the topside world.

Although there are many physical places one can go to "feel" her way back to this special home, the physical place itself is not home; it is only the vehicle that rocks the ego to sleep so that we can go the rest of the way by ourselves. The vehicles through and by which women reach home are many: music, art, forest, ocean spume, sunrise, solitude. These take us home to a nutritive inner world that has ideas, order, and sustenance all of its own.

Home is the pristine instinctual life that works as easily as a joint sliding upon its greased bearing, where all is as it should be, where all the noises sound right, and the light is good, and the smells make us feel calm rather than alarmed. How one spends one's time in the return is not important. Whatever revivifies balance is what is essential. That is home.

There is not only time to contemplate, but also to learn, and uncover the forgotten, the disused, and the buried. There we can imagine the future and also pore over the scar maps of the psyche, learning what led to what, and where we will go next. As Adrienne Rich writes about taking back the Self in her evocative poem, "Diving Into the Wreck,"[14]

> There is a ladder.
> The ladder is always there
> hanging innocently
> close to the side of the schooner . . .
> I go down . . .
> I came to explore the wreck . . .
> I came to see the damage that was done
> and the treasures that prevail . . .

The most important thing I can tell you about the timing of this home cycle is this: When it's time, it's time. Even if you're not ready, even if things are undone, even if today your ship is coming in. When it's time, it's time. The seal woman returns to the sea, not because she just feels like it, not because today is a good day to go, not because her life is all nice and tidy—there is no nice and tidy time for anyone. She goes because it is time, and therefore she must.

We all have favorite methods of talking ourselves out of taking the time to go home; yet when we retrieve our instinctive and wildish cycles, we are under a psychic obligation to arrange our lives so that we can live them more and more in accordance. Arguments about the rightness versus the wrongness of leave-taking in order to return home are useless. The simple truth is that when it's time, it's time.[15]

Some women never go home, and instead live their lives *a la zona zombi*, in the zombie zone. The most cruel part of this lifeless state is that the woman functions, walks, speaks, acts, even accomplishes many things, but she no longer feels the effects of what has gone wrong—if she did, her pain would make her immediately turn to the fixing of it.

But, no, a woman in such a state hobbles on, arms out, defended against the painful loss of home, blind and, as they say in the Bahamas, "She gone *sparat*," meaning her soul has gone off without her and left her feeling, no matter what she does, not quite substantial. In this state women have an odd sense that they are accomplishing much but feel little satisfaction. They are doing what they thought they wanted to do, but the treasure in their hands has somehow turned to dust. This is a very good awareness for a woman to have in such a state. Discontent is the secret door to significant and life-giving change.

Women I've worked with who have not been home in twenty or more years always weep upon first setting foot on that psychic ground again. For various reasons, which seemed like good ones at the time, they spent years accepting permanent exile from the homeland; they forgot how immensely good it is for rain to fall on dry earth.

For some, home is the taking up of an endeavor of some sort. Women begin to sing again after years of finding reason not to. They commit themselves to learn something they've been heart-felt about for a long time. They seek out the lost people and things in their lives. They take back their voices and write. They rest. They make some corner of the world their own. They execute immense or intense decisions. They do something that leaves footprints.

For some, home is a forest, a desert, a sea. In truth, home is holographic. It is carried at full power in even a single tree, a solitary cactus in a plant shop window, a pool of still water. It is also at full potency in a yellow leaf lying on the asphalt, a red clay pot waiting for a root bundle, a drop of water on the skin. When you focus with soul-eyes, you will see home in many, many places.

For how long does one go home? As long as one can or until you have yourself back again. How often is it needed? Far more often if you are a "sensitive" and are very active in the outer world. Less so if you have thick skin and are not so "out there." Each woman knows in her heart how often and how long is needed. It is a matter of assessing the condition of the shine in one's eyes, the vibrancy of one's mood, the vitality of one's senses.

How do we balance the need to go home with our daily lives? We pre-plan home into our lives. It is always amazing how easily women can "take time away" if there is illness, if a child needs them, if the car breaks down, if they have a toothache. Going home has to be given the same value, even stated in crisis proportions if necessary. For it is unequivocally true, if a woman doesn't go when it's her time to go, the hairline crack in her soul/psyche becomes a ravine, and the ravine becomes a roaring abyss.

If a woman absolutely values her going-home cycles, those around her will also learn to value them. It is true that significant "home" can be reached by taking time away from the click-clack of daily routine, time that is inviolate and solely for ourselves. "Solely for ourselves" means different things to different women. For some being in a room with the door closed, but still being accessible to others, is a fine return to home. For others though,the place from which to dive to home needs to be without even a tiny interruption. No "Mommy, Mommy, where are my shoes?" No "Honey, do we need anything from the grocery store?"

For this woman, the inlet to her deep home is evoked by silence. *No me molestes.* Utter Silence, with a capital *U* and a capital *S.* For her, the sound of wind through a great loom of trees is silence. For her, the crash of a mountain stream is silence. For her, thunder is silence. For her, the natural order of nature, which asks nothing in return, is her life-giving silence. Each woman chooses both as she can and as she must.

Regardless of your home time, an hour or days, remember, other people can pet your cats even though your cats say only you can do it right. Your dog will try to make you think you are abandoning a child on the highway, but will forgive you. The grass will grow a little brown but it will revive. You and your child will miss each other, but be glad when you return. Your mate may grump. They'll get over it. Your boss may threaten. She or he will get over it too. Staying overlong is madness. Going home is sanity.

When the culture, the society, or the psyche does not support this cycle to return home, many women learn to leap over the gate or dig under the fence anyway. They become chronically ill and purloin reading time in bed. They smile that fangy smile as if all is well and go on a subtle work slowdown for the duration.

When the cycle to return home is disturbed in women, many feel that in order to free themselves to go they must pick a fight with their boss, their children, their parents, or their mate in order to assert their psychic needs. So it occurs that in the midst of some blowup or other, the woman insists, "Well, I'm leaving. Since you're such a ___ [fill in the blank] and you obviously don't care about ___ [fill in the blank], then I'll just be leaving, thank you very much." And rumble, roar, spray of gravel, she's off.

If a woman has to fight for what is rightfully hers, she feels justified, feels absolutely vindicated in her desire to go home. It is interesting to note that if necessary, wolves fight to gain what they want, whether it be food, sleep, sex, or peace. It would appear that to fight for what one wants is a proper instinctual response to being hindered. However, for many women the fight must also or only be fought inside, battled out against the entire internal complex that negates her need to begin with. You can also push an aggressive culture back much better once you've gone home and come back.

If you have to battle each time you go, your relationships with those close to you may need to be weighed carefully. If you can, it is better to teach your people that you will be more and also different when you return, that you are not abandoning them but learning yourself anew and bringing yourself back to your real life. Especially if you are an artist, surround yourself with persons who are understanding about your need for home, for chances are you will need, more often than most, to mine the psychic terrain of home in order to learn the cycles of creation. So be brief, but potent. My friend Normandi, a gifted writer, says she's practiced and gotten it down to this: "I am going." These are the best words ever. Say them. Then go.

Different women have different criteria for what constitutes a useful and/or necessary length of time spent home. Most of us cannot always go for as long as we want, so we go for as long as we can. Now and then we go for as long as we must. Other times, we go until we miss what we left. Sometimes we dip in, dip out, dip in again in bursts. Most women who are coming back into their natural cycles again alternate between these, balancing out circumstances and need. One thing is sure, it's a good idea to keep a little valise by the door. Just in case.

The Medial Woman: Breathing Under Water

In the story, a curious compromise is made. Instead of leaving the child, or taking the child with her forever, seal woman takes the child for a visit to the ones who live "beneath." The child is given recognition as a member of the seal clan through the blood of his mother. There in the underwater home he is educated in the ways of the wild soul.

The child represents a new order in the psyche. His seal mother has breathed some of her own breath, some of her special kind of animation, into this child's lungs, thereby, in psychological terms, transforming him into a medial being,[16] one who is able to bridge both worlds. Yet, even though this child is initiated in the underworld, he cannot stay there, but must come back to earth. Thence forward, he occupies a special role. The child who has dived down and resurfaced is not wholly ego, not wholly soul, but somewhere in between.

There is at the core of all women, what Toni Wolffe, a Jungian analyst who lived in the first half of the twentieth century, called "the medial woman." The medial woman stands between the worlds of consensual reality and the mystical unconscious and mediates between them. The medial woman is the transmitter and receiver between two or more values or ideas. She is the one who brings new ideas to life, exchanges old ideas for innovative ones, translates between the world of the rational and the world of the imaginal. She "hears" things, "knows" things, and "senses" what should come next.

This midway point between the worlds of reason and image, between feeling and thinking, between matter and spirit— between all the opposites and all shades of meaning one can imagine—is the home of the medial woman. The seal woman in the story is an emanation of soul. She is able to live in all worlds, the topside world of matter, and the far world, or underworld, which is her spiritual home, but she cannot stay too long on earth. She and the fisherman, the ego-psyche, create a child who can also live in both worlds, but cannot stay too long in the soul-home.

The seal woman and the child together form a system in a

woman's psyche that is rather like a bucket brigade. The seal woman, soul-self, passes thoughts, ideas, feelings, and impulses up from the water to the medial self, which in turn lifts those things onto land and consciousness in the outer world. The structure also works conversely. The events of our daily lives, our past traumas and joys, our fears and hopes for the future, are all passed hand over hand down to the soul, who makes comments on them in our nightdreams, emanates its feelings upward through our bodies, or pierces us with a moment of inspiration with an idea on the end of it.

The Wild Woman is a combination of common sense and soul-sense. The medial woman is her double and is also capable of both. Like the child in the tale, the medial woman is of this world, but can travel to the deeper reaches of psyche with ease. Some women are born with this as their gift. Other women acquire it as a skill. It matters not which way one arrives at it. But one of the effects of going to home on a regular basis is that the medial woman of the psyche is strengthened each time a woman goes and returns.

Surfacing

The wonder and pain of returning to the wild home place lies in the fact that we can visit, but we cannot stay. No matter how wonderful it is in the deepest home imaginable, we cannot stay under water forever, but must rise back to the surface. Like Ooruk, who is gently placed on the stony shore, we come back to our mundane lives infused with new animation. Even so, it is a sad moment to be placed back on the shore and on our own once again. In ancient mystical rites, initiates returning to the outer world also felt a bittersweet mood pass through them. They were glad and refreshed, but also a little wistful at first.

The remedy for this small mourning is given when seal woman instructs her child, "I am always with you. Only touch what I have touched, my firesticks, my *ulu*, knife, my stone carvings of otters and seal, and I will breathe into your lungs a wind for the singing of your songs."[17] Her words are a special kind of wild promise. They imply that we should not spend much time in immediate yearning to go back. Instead, understand these tools, interact with them, and you will feel her presence as though you are a drum skin that has been tapped by a wild hand.

The Inuit characterize these tools as those belonging to "a real woman." They are what a woman needs to "carve a life for herself." Her knife cuts, dresses, frees, designs, makes materials fit. Her knowledge of the firesticks enables her to create fire under the most austere conditions. Her stone carvings express her mystical knowledge, her healing repertoire, and her personal union with the spirit world.

In psychological terms, these metaphors typify the strengths common to the wild nature. In classical Jungian psychology, some might call this tandem union the ego-self axis. In fairy-tale argot the knife is, among other things, a visionary tool for cutting through obscurity and seeing into hidden things. The tools of fire-making typify the ability to make nourishment for oneself, to transform one's old life into new life, to repel useless negativity. They can be seen as a representation of innate drive that heat-strengthens the base materials of the psyche. Traditionally, the making of fetishes and talismans helps the fairy-tale heroine and hero to remember that the strengths of the world of spirit are close by.

For a modern woman, the *ulu*, her knife, symbolizes insight, her willingness and ability to cut away the superfluous, making clear endings and carving new beginnings. Her fire-making declares her ability to rise from failure, to create passion in her own behalf, to burn something to the ground if necessary. Her stone carvings embody her memory of her own wild consciousness, her union with the natural instinctual life.

Like the seal woman's child, we learn that to come close to the soul-mother's creations is to be filled with her. Even though she has gone to her own people, her full force can be felt through the feminine powers of insight, passion, and connection to the wild nature. Her promise is that if we make contact with the tools of psychic strength we will feel her pneuma; her breath will enter our breath, and we will be filled with a sacred wind for singing. The old Inuit say that the breath of a god and the breath of a human, when commingled, cause a person to create an intense and holy poetry.[18]

It is that holy poetry and singing we are after. We want powerful words and songs that can be heard underwater and over land. It is the wild singing we are after, our chance to use the wild language we are learning by heart under the sea. When a woman speaks her truth, fires up her intention and feeling, stays tight with the instinctive nature, she is singing, she is living in the wild breath-stream of the soul. To live this way is a cycle in itself, one meant to go on, go on, go on.

This is why Ooruk does not try to dive back under the water or beg to go with his mother as she swims out to sea and disappears from sight. This is why he stays on land. He has the promise. As we return to the clacking world, especially if we have been isolated in some way during our trip home, people, machines, and other objects have a slightly unfamiliar cast to them, and even the chatter of those around us sounds a little strange to our ears. This phase of return is called re-entry and it is natural. The feeling of being from an alien world passes after a few hours or a few days. Thereafter, we will spend a good space of time at our mundane life, fueled by the energy we gathered on our journey to home and practicing interim union with soul through the practice of solitude.

In the tale, the seal woman's child begins to enact the medial nature. He becomes a drummer, a singer, a storyteller. In fairy-tale interpretation, the drummer by drumming becomes the heart at the center of whatever new life and new feeling need to arise and reverberate. The drummer is able to frighten things away, as well as to evoke them. The singer carries messages back and forth between the great soul and the mundane self. By nature and tone of voice the singer can dismantle, destroy, build up, and create. The storyteller is said to have crept close and listened to the Gods talking in their sleep.[19]

So through all these creative acts, the child lives what seal woman has breathed into him. The child lives what he has learned under water, the relational life with the wild soul. We find ourselves then, filled with drum beats, filled with singing, filled with listening and saying our own words; new poems, new ways of seeing, new ways of acting and thinking. Instead of trying to "make the magic last," we just live. Instead of resisting or dreading our chosen work, we move into it fluidly; alive, filled with new notions, and curious to see what happens next. After all, the person who has returned to home has survived being carried out to sea by the great seal spirits.

The Practice of Intentional Solitude

In the gray mists of morning, the now-grown child kneels on a rock in the sea and converses with none other than the seal woman. This intentional and daily practice of solitude and communing allows him to be near home in a critical way, not only by diving down to the soul-place for more sustained periods of time, but just as important, by being able to call the soul back up to the topside world for brief periods.

In order to converse with the wild feminine, a woman must temporarily leave the world and inhabit a state of aloneness in the oldest sense of the word. Long ago the word *alone* was treated as two words, *all one*.[20] To be *all one* meant to be wholly one, to be in oneness, either essentially or temporarily. That is precisely the goal of solitude, to be all one. It is the cure for the frazzled state so common to modern women, the one that makes her, as the old saying goes, "leap onto her horse and ride off in all directions."

Solitude is not an absence of energy or action, as some believe, but is rather a boon of wild provisions transmitted to us from the soul. In ancient times, as recorded by physician-healers, religious and mystics, purposeful solitude was both palliative and preventative. It was used to heal fatigue and to prevent weariness. It was also used as an oracle, as a way of listening to the inner self to solicit advice and guidance otherwise impossible to hear in the din of daily life.

Women from ancient times as well as modern aboriginal women often set a sacred place aside for this communion and inquiry. Traditionally it is said to have been set aside during women's menses, for during that time a woman lives much closer to self-knowing than usual; the membrane between the unconscious and the conscious minds thins considerably. Feelings, memories, sensations that are normally blocked from consciousness pass over into cognizance without resistance. When a woman takes solitude during this time, she has more material to sift through.

However, in my exchanges with tribal women from North, Central, and South America, as well as female progeny of some of the Slavic tribes, I find that the "women's places" were used *anytime*, not just during menses, and more so, that each woman often had her own "woman's place," consisting of a certain tree, place at the water's edge, or some natural forest or desert room or ocean cave.

My experience in analyzing women leads me to believe that much of modern women's premenstrual crankiness is not just a physical syndrome but is equally attributable to her being thwarted in her need to take enough time away to revivify and renew herself.[21] I always laugh when I hear someone quoting early anthropologists who claimed that menstruating women of various tribes were considered "unclean" and forced to leave the village until they were "over it." All women know that even if there were such a forced ritual exile, every single woman, to a woman, would, when her time came, leave the village hanging her head mournfully, at least till she was out of sight, and then suddenly break into a jig down the path, cackling all the way.

As in the tale, if we establish a regular practice of intentional solitude, we invite a conversation between ourselves and the wild soul that comes near to our shore. We do this not only just to "be near" the wild and soulful nature, but as in the mystical tradition since time out of mind, the purpose of this union is for us to ask questions, and for the soul to advise.

How does one call up the soul? There are many ways: through meditation, or in the rhythms of running, drumming, singing, writing, painting, music making, visions of great beauty, prayer, contemplation, rite and ritual, standing still, even entrancing moods and ideas. All are psychic summonses that call the soul up from its dwelling place.

However, I advocate using those methods that require no props, no special location, and that can be accomplished as easily in a minute as in a day. This means using one's mind to summon the soul-self. Everyone has at least one familiar state of mind in which to effect this kind of solitude. For myself, solitude is rather like a folded-up forest that I carry with me everywhere and unfurl around myself when I have need. I sit at the feet of the great old trees of my childhood. From that vantage point, I ask my questions, receive my answers, then coalesce my woodland back down to the size of a love note till next time. The experience is immediate, brief, informative.

Truly the only thing one needs for intentional solitude is the ability to tune out distractions. A woman can learn to detach from other people, noise, and chatter, no matter if she is in the midst of a contentious board meeting, no matter if she is being stalked by a house that needs to be cleaned by bulldozer, no matter if she is surrounded by eighty loquacious relatives, fighting, singing, and dancing their way through a three-day wake. If you have ever been a teenager, you definitely know how to tune out. If you have ever been the mother of an insomniac two-year-old, you know how to take intentional solitude. It is not hard to do, just hard to remember to do.

Though we all might prefer to have the kind of sojourn to home that is much more sustained, wherein we depart and no one knows where we are and we return much later, it is also very good to practice taking solitude in a room full of a thousand persons. It may sound odd at first, but frankly, people converse with the soul all the time. But rather than entering the state consciously, many fall into it suddenly, through a reverie, or all at once "snap to" and "find" themselves in it.

Because it is considered such an untoward thing, we have learned to camouflage this interval of soulful communication by naming it in very mundane terms. So, it has been named thusly: "talking to oneself," being "lost in thought," "staring off into space," or "daydreaming." This euphemistic language is inculcated by many segments of our culture, for unfortunately, we are taught from childhood onward to feel embarrassment if found communing with soul, and especially in pedestrian environments such as work or school.

Somehow, the educational and business world has felt that such time spent at being "all one," is unproductive, when in fact it is the most fecund. It is the wild soul who channels ideas into our imagination, whereupon we sort through these to find which we will implement, which are most applicable and productive. It is commingling with soul that causes us to glow bright with spirit, willing to assert our talents, whatever they might be. It is that brief, even momentary, but intentional union that supports us to live out our inner lives so that instead of burying them in the self-inversion of shame, fear of reprisal or attack, lethargy, complacency, or other limiting reasonings and excuses, we let our inner lives wave, flare, blaze on the outside for all to see.

So, in addition to gaining information about whatever we wish to see into, the taking of solitude can be used to assess how we ourselves are doing in any sphere we choose. Earlier in the tale, we saw the child stay under the sea for seven days and nights, this being a learning of one of the oldest cycles of nature. Seven is oft considered a woman's number, a mystical number synonymous with the division of the moon cycle into four parts and equal to menses: waxing, half, full, and waning. It has been usual in the old ethnic women's traditions that at the full moon cycle an inquiry should be made into the state of one's being; the state of one's friendships, one's home life, one's mate, one's children.

In such a state of solitude we can do this, for it is during that time that we bring all aspects of self to bear at one point in time, and we poll them, inquire of them, finding out what they/we/soul wishes right now, and then gaining it if possible. In this way we take vital soundings of our current conditions. There are many aspects of our lives for us to assess on a continuing basis: habitat, work, creative life, family, mate, children, mother/father, sexuality, spiritual life, and so on.

The measurement used in assessment is simple: What needs less? And: What needs more? We are asking from the instinctive self, not in stilted logic, not ego-wise, but Wild Woman–wise, what work, adjustments, loosenings, or emphasizing needs to take place. Are we still on proper course in spirit and soul? Is one's inner life showing on the outside? What needs battening, protection, ballast, or weights? What needs be disposed of, moved, or changed?

After a period of practice, the cumulative effect of intentional solitude begins to act like a vital respiratory system, a natural rhythm of adding knowledge, making minute adjustments, and deleting the unusable over and over again. It is not only potent but pragmatic, for solitude lives low on the food chain; though it costs something in intention and follow-through, it can be done at any time, in any place. Over time, as you practice, you will find yourself designing your own queries to soul. Sometimes you may have only one question. Other times you may have none whatsoever and just wish to rest on the rock near the soul, breathing together.

Women's Innate Ecology

In the tale it is said that many try to hunt the soul to capture and kill her, but no hunter is able. It is one more fairy-tale reference to the indestructibility of the wild soul. Even if we have been working, sexing, resting, or playing out of cycle, it does not kill the Wild Woman, it only tires *us* out. The good news is that we can make the necessary corrections and return to our own natural cycles again. It is through the love for and the caring for our natural seasons that we protect our lives from being dragged into someone else's rhythm, someone else's dance, someone else's hunger. It is through validation of our distinct cycles for sex, creation, rest, play, and work that we relearn to define and discriminate between all our wild senses and seasons.

We know that we cannot live the confiscated life. We know there is a time when the things of men and the people and things of the world must be left for a while. We have learned that we are like amphibians: We can live on land, but not forever, not without trips to the water and to home. Overly civilized and overly oppressive cultures try to keep women from returning home. Too often, she is warned away from the water until she is thin as a dime and dimmed in light.

But when the call for extended leave to home comes, a part of her always hears, has been waiting to hear. When the call to home comes, she will follow, has been secretly or not so secretly preparing to follow. She and all the allies of her inner psyche will restore her ability to return. This empowering process does not apply to just a woman here and a woman there, it applies to all of us. Everyone becomes snagged by land commitments. Yet, the old one out in the sea calls everyone. Everyone must return.

None of these ways to return home are dependent on economics, social status, education, or physical mobility. Even if we can see only one blade of grass, even if we have only a quarter foot of sky to scry, even if we have only a rangy weed coming up through a crack in the sidewalk, we can see our cycles in and with nature. We can all swim out to sea. We can all commune with the seal from the rock. All women must have this union: mothers with children, women with lovers, single women, women with jobs, women in the doldrums, women riding high on the world, introverted women, extroverted women, women with industrial-strength responsibilities.

Jung said, "It would be far better simply to admit our spiritual poverty. . . . When spirit becomes heavy, it turns to water. . . . Therefore the way of the soul . . . leads to the water."[22] The return to home and the intervals of conversing with the seal from the rock in the sea are our acts of innate and integral ecology, for they all are a return to the water, a meeting with the wild friend, the one who above all others, loves us unremittingly, unguardedly, and with profound endurance. We need only look into and learn from those soulful eyes that are "wild and wise and loving."

🔥 CHAPTER 10

Clear Water:
Nourishing the Creative Life

Creativity is a shapechanger. One moment it takes this form, the next that. It is like a dazzling spirit who appears to us all, yet is hard to describe for no one agrees on what they saw in that brilliant flash. Are the wielding of pigments and canvas, or paint chips and wallpaper, evidence of its existence? How about pen and paper, flower borders on the garden path, building a university? Yes, yes. Ironing a collar well, cooking up a revolution? Yes. Touching with love the leaves of a plant, pulling down "the big deal," tying off the loom, finding one's voice, loving someone well? Yes. Catching the hot body of the newborn, raising a child to adulthood, helping raise a nation from its knees? Yes. Tending to a marriage like the orchard it is, digging for psychic gold, finding the shapely word, sewing a blue curtain? All are of the creative life. All these things are from the Wild Woman, the *Río Abajo Río*, the river beneath the river, which flows and flows into our lives.

Some say the creative life is in ideas, some say it is in doing. It seems in most instances to be in a simple being. It is not virtuosity, although that is very fine in itself. It is the love of something, having so much love for something—whether a person, a word, an image, an idea, the land, or humanity—that all that can be done with the overflow is to create. It is not a matter of wanting to, not a singular act of will; one solely must.

The creative force flows over the terrain of our psyches looking for the natural hollows, the *arroyos*, the channels that exist in us.

We become its tributaries, its basins; we are its pools, ponds, streams, and sanctuaries. The wild creative force flows into whatever beds we have for it, those we are born with as well as those we dig with our own hands. We don't have to fill them, we only have to build them.

In archetypal lore there is the idea that if one prepares a special psychic place, then the being, the creative force, the soul source, will hear of it, sense its way to it, and inhabit that place. Whether this force is summoned by the biblical "go forward and prepare a place for the soul" or, as in the film *Field of Dreams*,[1] in which a farmer hears a voice urging him to build a baseball diamond for the spirits of players past, "If you build it, they will come," preparing a fitting place induces the great creative force to advance.

Once that great underground river finds its estuaries and branches in our psyches, our creative lives fill and empty, rise and fall in seasons just like a wild river. These cycles cause things to be made, fed, fall back, and die away, all in their own right time, and over and over again.

Creating one thing at a certain point in the river feeds those who come to the river, feeds creatures far downstream, yet others in the deep. Creativity is not a solitary movement. That is its power. Whatever is touched by it, whoever hears it, sees it, senses it, knows it, is fed. That is why beholding someone else's creative word, image, idea, fills us up, inspires us to our own creative work. A single creative act has the potential to feed a continent. One creative act can cause a torrent to break through stone.

For this reason, a woman's creative ability is her most valuable asset, for it gives outwardly and it feeds her inwardly at every level: psychic, spiritual, mental, emotive, and economic. The wild nature pours out endless possibilities, acts as birth channel, invigorates, slakes thirst, satiates our hunger for the deep and wild life. Ideally, this creative river has no dams on it, no diversions, and especially no misuse.[2]

Wild Woman's river nurtures and grows us into beings that are like her: life givers. As we create, this wild and mysterious being is creating us in return, filling us with love. We are evoked in the way creatures are evoked by sun and water. We are made so alive that we in turn give life out; we burst, we bloom, we divide and multiply, we impregnate, incubate, impart, give forth.

Clearly creativity emanates from something that rises, rolls, surges, and spills into us rather than from something that just stands there hoping that we might, however circuitously, find our way to it. In that sense we can never "lose" our creativity. It is always there, filling us or else colliding with whatever obstacles are placed in its path. If it finds no inlet to us, it backs up, gathers energy, and rams forward again till it breaks through. The only ways we can avoid its insistent energy are to continuously mount barriers against it, or to allow it to be poisoned by destructive negativity and negligence.

If we are gasping for creative energy; if we have trouble pulling down the fertile, the imaginative, the ideational; if we have difficulty focusing on our personal vision, acting on it, or following through with it, then something has gone wrong at the waterspill juncture between the headwaters and the tributary. Perhaps one's creative waters are flowing through a polluting environment wherein the life forms of imagination are killed off before they can grow to maturity. More often than not, when a woman is bereft of her creative life, all these circumstances are at the root of the issue.

There are other more insidious possibilities as well. Perhaps one so admires the gifts of another, and/or the seeming benefits earned or received by another, that one becomes expert in mimicry, sadly content to be a mediocre "them," rather than developing one's own unique gifts to their absolute and startling depths. Perhaps one has become caught in a hyper-fascination or a hero-worship and has no idea how to mine their own inimitable gifts. Perhaps one is afraid, for the waters are deep, the night is dark, and the way is very long; just the right conditions needed for development of one's original and precious gifts.

Since Wild Woman is *Río Abajo Río*, the river beneath the river, when she flows into us, we flow. If the aperture from her to us is blocked, we are blocked. If her currents are toxified by our own negative inner complexes or by the environ of persons around us, the delicate processes that craft our ideas are polluted also. Then we are like a dying river. This is not a slight thing to be ignored. The loss of clear creative flow constitutes a psychological and spiritual crisis.

When a river is tainted, everything begins to die off because, as we know from environmental biology, every life form is dependent on every other life form. If, in an actual river, the sedge at water's edge turns brown starving for oxygen, then the pollens can find nothing vibrant enough to fertilize, water plantain falls over leaving no cribs among its roots for water lilies, willows will not grow catkins, newts find no mates, and mayflies will not hatch. Therefore the fish will not jump, birds will not dive down, and the wolves and other creatures that come to refresh themselves move on or else die from drinking bad water or from eating prey that has eaten the dying plants near the water.

When creativity stagnates in one way or another, there is the same outcome: a starving for freshness, a fragility of fertility, no place for smaller life forms to live in the interstices of larger life forms, no breeding of this idea to that one, no hatch, no new life. Then we feel ill and want to move on. We wander aimlessly, pretending we can get along without the lush creative life or else by faking one; but we cannot, we must not. To bring back creative life, the waters have to be made clean and clear again. We have to wade into the sludge, purify the contaminants, reopen the apertures, protect the flow from future harm.

Among Spanish-speaking people, there is an old old tale called *"La Llorona,"*[3] "The Weeping Woman." Some say it originated in the early 1500s when the conquistadors invaded the Aztec peoples of Mexico, but it is far older than that. It is a tale about the river of life that became a river of death. The *protagonista* is a haunting river woman who is fertile and generous, creating out of her own body. She is poor, breathtakingly beautiful, but rich in soul and spirit.

"La Llorona" is an odd tale, for it continues to evolve throughout time as though it has a big inner life of its own. Like a great marching sand dune that pushes across the land, taking up what is before it, building with and upon it till the land becomes part of its own body, this story builds on the psychic issues of each generation. Sometimes the *La Llorona* tale is told as a story about

Ce. Malinalli or *Malinche*, the native woman said to have been translator and lover to the Spanish conqueror Hernán Cortés.

But the first version of *"La Llorona"* I ever heard described her as the female protagonist in a union-busting war up in the north woods, where I was raised. The next time I heard the tale, *La Llorona* was dealing with an antagonist involved in the forced repatriation of Mexicans from the United States in the 1950s. I heard the story in numerous versions in the Southwest, one being from the old Spanish Land Grant farmers, who said she was involved in the land grant wars in New Mexico; a rich developer took advantage of a poor but beautiful Spanish daughter.

Then there is the spook story; *La Llorona* wanders and wails through a trailer park at night. There is "a prostitute with AIDS" tale; *La Llorona* plies her trade down at the Town River in Austin. The most startling one, I was given by a young child. First I will tell you the general story line of the great *La Llorona* tales, and then a most astonishing twist on the story.

La Llorona

A RICH *HIDALGO*, nobleman, courts a beautiful but poor woman and wins her affections. She bears him two sons, but he deigns not to marry her. One day he announces that he is returning to Spain, where he will marry a rich woman chosen by his family, and that he will take his sons with him.

The young woman is crazed and acts in the manner of the great shrieking madwomen throughout time. She claws his face, she claws her own face, she tears at him, she tears at herself. She picks up the two small sons and runs to the river with them and there throws them into the torrent. The children drown, and *La Llorona* falls to the riverbank in grief and dies.

The *hidalgo* returns to Spain and marries the rich woman. The soul of *La Llorona* ascends to heaven. There the master of the gate tells her she may come to heaven, for she has suffered, but that she may not enter *until* she recovers the souls of her children from the river.

And that is why it is said today that *La Llorona*, the weeping woman, sweeps the riverbanks with her long hair, puts her long stick-fingers into the water to drag the bottom for her children. It is also why living children must not go near the river after dark, for *La Llorona* may mistake them for her own children and take them away forever.[4]

~~~~~~

Now, to a modern *La Llorona*. As the culture is affected by various influences, our thinking, our attitudes, and our issues shift. The *La Llorona* story shifts too. While in Colorado last year collecting ghost stories, Danny Salazar, a ten-year-old child with no front teeth and surrealistically big feet on his skinny (but someday to be tall) body, gave me this tale. He told me that *La Llorona* did not kill her children for the reasons described in the old tale.

"No, no," asserted Danny. *La Llorona* went with a rich *hidalgo* who had factories on the river. But something went wrong. During her pregnancy *La Llorona* drank from the river. Her babies, twin boys, were born blind and with webbed fingers, for the *hidalgo* had poisoned the river with the waste from his factories.

The *hidalgo* told *La Llorona* he didn't want her or her babies. He married a rich woman who wanted the things the factory manufactured. *La Llorona* threw the babies into the river because they would have such a hard life. Then she fell down dead from grief. She went to heaven but Saint Peter told her she could not come into heaven until she found the souls of her sons. Now *La Llorona* looks and looks through the polluted river for her children, but she can hardly see, for the water is so dirty and dark. Now her ghost drags the river bottom with her long fingers. Now she wanders the riverbanks calling for her children all the time.

The Pollution of the Wild Soul

La Llorona belongs to the category of tales that the *cantadoras y cuentistas* in our family call *temblón*, shiver stories. These overtly entertain, but are meant to cause listeners to experience a shiver of awareness that leads to thoughtfulness, contemplation, and action.

Regardless of the shifting motifs within this story over time, the theme remains the same: the destruction of the fertile feminine. Whether the contamination of wild beauty takes place in the inner world or in the outer world, it is painful to witness. In modern culture we sometimes count one as far more devastating than the other, but both are equally critical.

Although I sometimes tell this two-version tale in other contexts,[5] when understood as a metaphor for the deterioration of the creative flow, it causes everyone—women and men alike—to shiver with knowing aplenty. If we view this tale as the condition of a single woman's psyche, we can understand a good deal about the weakening and wasting of a woman's creative process. As in other stories that have harsh endings, the tale is instrumental in teaching a woman what *not* to do, and how to back out of poor choices in order to lessen negative impact. Generally, by taking the opposite psychological tack to that chosen by the protagonist in the tale, we can learn to ride the swell instead of drown in it.

This tale uses the metaphors of the beautiful woman and the pure river of life to describe a woman's creative process in its normative state. But here, when interactive with a destructive animus, both the woman and the river decline. Then a woman whose creative life is dwindling experiences, like *La Llorona*, a sensation of poisoning, deformation, a desire to kill off everything. Subsequently she is driven to seemingly endless searching through the wreckage for her former creative potential.

In order for her psychic ecology to be arighted, the river has to be made clear once again. It is not the quality of our creative products that we are concerned with through this story, but the individual's recognition of the value of one's unique gifts and the methods for caring for the creative life that surrounds those gifts. Always behind the actions of writing, painting, thinking, healing, doing, cooking, talking, smiling, making, is the river, the *Río Abajo Río*; the river under the river nourishes everything we make.

In symbology, the great bodies of water express the place where life itself is thought to have originated. In the Hispanic Southwest, the river symbolizes the ability to live, truly live. It is greeted as the mother, *La Madre Grande*, *La Mujer Grande*, the Great Woman, whose waters not only run in the ditches and riverbeds but spill out of the very bodies of women themselves as their babies are born. The river is seen as the *Gran Dama* who walks the land with a full swirling skirt of blue or silver and sometimes gold, who lays with the soil to make it good for growing.

Some of my old women friends in South Texas say *El Río Grande* could never be a man river, but is a woman river. They laugh and say, How can a river be anything but the *La Dulce Acequia*, the sweet slot, between the thighs of the earth? In northern New Mexico, the river in storm, in wind, in flash flood, is spoken of as the one who is aroused, the one who in her heat rushes to touch everything she can to make it grow.

So we see that the river here symbolizes a form of feminine largess that arouses, excites, makes passionate. Women's eyes flash as they create, their words lilt, their faces flush with life, their very hair seems to shine all the more. They are excited by the idea, aroused by the possibilities, impassioned by the very thought, and at that point, like the great river, they are meant to flow outward and continuously on their own unparalleled creative path. That is the way women feel fulfilled. And this is the condition of the river that *La Llorona* once lived by before destruction occurred.

But sometimes, as in the tale, a woman's creative life is taken over by something that wants to manufacture things of and for ego only, things which have no lasting soul-worth. Sometimes there are pressures from her culture that say her creative ideas are useless, that no one will want them, that it is futile for her to continue. That is pollution. That is pouring lead into the river. That is what poisons the psyche.

Ego satisfaction is allowable and important in its own regard. The problem is that the spewing out of negative complexes attacks all freshness, newness, potential, newborness, things in the pupae stage, the lacuna, as well as the half-grown and the old and revered. When there is too much soulless or mock manufacturing, toxic waste pours into the pure river, killing off both creative impulse and energy.

Poison in the River

There are many myths about the pollution of and the sealing off of the creative and the wild, whether they be about the contamination of purity as personified by the noxious fog that once spread over the island Lecia, where the skeins of life with which the Fates wove were stored,[6] or tales about evildoers stopping up village wells, thereby causing suffering and death. Two of the most profound stories are the latter-day "Jean de Florette" and "Manon of the Spring."[7] In those tales, two men, hoping to deprive a poor hunchbacked man, his wife, and little daughter of the land they are attempting to bring to life with flowers and trees, seal off the spring that feeds that land, causing the destruction of the soulful and hardworking family.

The most common effect of pollution in women's creative life is loss of vitality. This disables a woman's ability to create or act "out there" in the world. Though there are times in a woman's cycles of healthy creative life when the river of creativity disappears underground for a time, something is being developed all the same. We are incubating then. It is a very different sensation than that of spiritual crisis.

In a natural cycle, there is restlessness and impatience, perhaps, but there is never a sense the wild soul is dying. We can tell the difference by assessing our anticipation: even when our creative energy is involved in a long incubation, we still look forward to the outcome, we feel the pops and surges of that new life turning and humming within us. We do not feel desperate. There is no lunging and grasping.

But when the creative life dies because we are not tending to the health of the river, that is another matter entirely. Then, we feel exactly like the dying river; we feel loss of energy, we feel tired; there is nothing creeping, roiling, lifting leaves, cooling off, warming up. We become thick, slow in a negative way, poisoned by pollution, or by a backup and stagnation of all our riches. Everything feels tainted, unclear, and toxic.

How might a woman's creative life become polluted? This sludging of creative life invades all five phases of creation: inspiration, concentration, organization, implementation, and sustenance. Women who have lost one or more of these report that they "can't think" of anything new, useful, or empathic for themselves. They are easily "distracted" by love affairs, too much work, too much play, by tiredness, or by fear of failure.[8]

Sometimes they cannot coalesce the mechanics of organization, and their project lays scattered about in a hundred places and pieces. Sometimes the problems issue from a woman's naïveté about her own extroversion: She thinks that by making a few motions in the outer world, she has really done something. This is like making the arms but not the legs or the head of a thing and calling it done. She feels necessarily incomplete.

Sometimes a woman trips over her own introversion and wants to simply wish things into being; she may think that just thinking the idea is good enough, and there need be no outer manifestation. Except she feels bereft and unfinished anyway. These are all manifestations of pollution in the river. What is being manufactured is not life but something that inhibits life.

Other times she is under attack by those around her, or by the voices yammering in her head: "Your work is not right enough, not good enough, not this enough, not that enough. It is too grandiose, too infinitesimal, too insignificant, takes too long, is too easy, too hard." This is pouring cadmium into the river.

There is another story that describes the same process, but uses different symbolism. In Greek mythos there is an episode wherein the Gods decree that a group of birds called the Harpies[9] shall punish a soul named Phineus. Each time Phineus's food is magically laid out, the flock flies in, steals some of the food, scatters some, and defecates on the rest, leaving the poor man ravenously hungry.[10]

This literal pollution can also be understood figuratively as a string of complexes within the psyche whose sole raison d'être is to foul things up. This tale is most definitely a *temblón*, shiver story; it makes us shiver in recognition, for we have all experienced this. The "Harpy Syndrome" destroys via denigration of one's talents and efforts, and through a most disparaging internal dialogue. A woman brings up an idea and the Harpy shits upon it. The woman says, "Well, I thought I would do this and this." The Harpy says, "That's a stupid idea, no one cares about that, it's ridiculously simplistic. Well, mark my words, your ideas are all dumb, people will laugh, you really have nothing to say." This is Harpy-talk.

Excuses are another form of pollution. From women writers,

painters, dancers, and other artists, I have heard every excuse con-
cocted since the earth cooled. "Oh, I'll get around to it one of these
days." In the meantime, she has the grinning depression. "I keep
busy, yes I squeeze in my writing here and there, why I wrote two
poems last year, yes, and finished one painting and part of another
over the last eighteen months, yes, the house, the kids, the husband, the boyfriend, the cat, the toddler, need my consummate
attention. I am going to get around to it, I don't have the money, I
don't have the time, I can't find the time, I can't make the time, I
can't start until I have the finest most expensive instruments or
experiences, I just don't feel like it right now, the mood is not right
yet. I just need at least a day's worth of time to get it done, I just
need to have a few days' time to get it done. I just need to have a
few weeks of time to myself to get it done, I just, just, just . . ."

Fire on the River

Back in the 1970s the Cuyahoga River at Cleveland became so
polluted it began to burn. Polluted creative flow can suddenly
erupt in a toxic fire that burns not only on the fuel of garbage in the
river but incinerates all the life forms as well. Too many psychic
complexes all working at the same time can cause immense
damage to the river. Negative psychological complexes rear up
and question your worth, your intention, your sincerity, and your
talent. They also send exhortations that assert unequivocally that
you must labor to "earn a living" doing things that exhaust you,
leave you no time to create, destroying your will to imagine.

Some of the malevolent complexes' favorite thieveries and
punishments of women's creativity revolve around promising the
soul-self "time to create" somewhere off in the foggy future. Or
promising that when one has several days in a row free, then the
rumpus will begin at last. It's hogwash. The complex has no such
intention. It is another way of suffocating the creative impulse.

Alternatively the voices may whisper, "Only if you have a doctorate degree will your work be decent, only if you are lauded by
the Queen, only if you receive such and such award, only if you
are published in such and such magazine, only if, if, if."

This only-iffing is like stuffing the soul with junk food. It is one thing to be fed with any old thing; it is quite another to be truly nourished. Most often the logic of the complex is extremely faulty, even though it will try to convince you otherwise.

One of the greatest problems of the creative complex is the accusation that whatever you're doing won't work because you're not thinking logically, you're not being logical, what you have done so far isn't logical and is therefore doomed to failure. First of all, the primary stages of creating are not logical—nor should they be. If the complex succeeds in stopping you with this, it has you. Tell it to sit down and be quiet or go away till you're done. Remember, if logic were all there really was to the world, then surely all men would ride sidesaddle.

I've seen women work long, long hours at jobs they despise in order to buy very expensive items for their houses, mates, or children. They put their considerable talents on the back burner. I've seen women insist on cleaning everything in the house before they could sit down to write . . . and you know it's a funny thing about house cleaning . . . it never comes to an end. Perfect way to stop a woman.

A woman must be careful to not allow over-responsibility (or over-respectability) to steal her necessary creative rests, riffs, and raptures. She simply must put her foot down and say no to half of what she believes she "should" be doing. Art is not meant to be created in stolen moments only.

The scattering of plans and projects, as if by a wind, occurs when a woman attempts to organize a creative idea and it just somehow keeps being blown away, becoming more and more confused and disordered. She is not tracking it in any concrete way because, again, she doesn't have time to write it all down and organize it, or she is called by so many other things, that she loses her place and cannot pick it up again.

It may also be that a woman's creative process is misunderstood or disrespected by those around her. It is up to her to inform them that when she has "that look" in her eyes, it does not mean she is a vacant lot waiting to be filled. It means she is balancing a big cardhouse of ideas on a single fingertip, and she is carefully connecting all the cards using tiny crystalline bones and a little spit, and if she can just get it all to the table without it falling down or flying apart, she can bring an image from the unseen world into being. To speak to her in that moment is to create a Harpy wind that blows the entire structure to tatters. To speak to her in that moment is to break her heart.

And yet, a woman may do this to herself by talking away her ideas until all the arousal is gone from them, or by not putting her foot down about people creeping off with her creative tools and materials, or by the simple oversight of not buying the right equipment to execute the creative work properly, or by stopping and starting so many times, by allowing everyone and their cat to interrupt her at will, that the project falls into a shambles.

If the culture in which a woman lives attacks the creative function of its members, if it splits or shatters any archetype or perverts its design or meaning, these will be incorporated in their broken state into the psyches of its members in the same way; as a broken-winged force rather than a hale one filled with vitality and possibility.

When these injured elements about how to allow the creative life and how to nourish it are activated within a woman's psyche, it is hard to have a dit of insight into what is wrong. Being in a complex is like being inside a black bag. It is dark, you cannot see what has hold of you, you only know you're captured by a something. Then we are temporarily unable to organize our thoughts or priorities, and like bagged creatures, we begin to act without contemplation. Although acting without contemplation can be very useful at times, such as in the premise of "first thought, right thought," in this instance it is not so.

During a poisoned or stalled creation, a woman gives the beautiful soul-self "pretend eating." She tries to disregard the condition of the animus. So she throws a little workshop to it here and drops a little reading time for it there. But in the end, this has no substance. The woman is kidding no one but herself.

So when this river dies, it is without its flow, without its life force. The Hindus say that without Shakti, the personified feminine life force, Shiva, who encompasses the ability to act, becomes a corpse. She is the life energy that animates the male principle, and the male principle in turn animates action in the world.[11]

So we see that the river must be reasonably balanced between its pollutions and its cleansings, or else all comes to nothing. But in order to carry on in this manner, the immediate environ must be nutritive and accessible. In matters of survival it is an incontrovertible fact that the less available the essentials—food and water, safety and shelter—the fewer the options. And the fewer the options, the less creative life, for creativity thrives on the many, on the endless combinations of all things.

The destructive *hidalgo* in the tale is a deep but immediately recognizable part of a wounded woman. He is her animus, who causes her to struggle, not with creating—often she cannot even get to that point—but rather with her gaining a clear permission, a solid inner support system to create at will. A healthy animus is meant to involve himself with the work of the river, and this is as it should be. Well integrated, he is the helper, watching to see if anything need be done. But in the *La Llorona* story, the animus is one-sided; he takes over, prevents vital new life, and insists on dominating the life of the psyche. When a malignant animus gains such power, a woman may denigrate her own work, or else, at the other extreme, attempt to fake real work. When any of these take place, a woman has fewer and fewer creative options. The animus gains power to push the woman around, denigrates her work, thereby inauthenticating it in one way or another. He does this by ruining the river.

Let us look first at the parameters of the animus in general, then we can proceed to understanding how a woman's creative life deteriorates when there is negative animus influence, and what she can and must do about it. Creativity is meant to be an act of clear consciousness. Its actions reflect the clarity of the river. The animus, that which funds outer action, is the man on the river. He is the steward. He is caregiver and protector of the water.

The Man on the River

Before we can understand what the man in the *La Llorona* story has done by polluting the river, we have to see how what he represents is meant to be a positive construct in a woman's psyche. By classical Jungian definition, *animus* is the soul-force in women, and is considered masculine. However, many women psychoanalysts, including myself, have, through personal observation, come to refute the classical view and to assert instead that the revivifying source in women is not masculine and alien to her, but feminine and familiar.[12]

Nevertheless, I believe the masculine concept of animus has great relevance. There is tremendous correlation between women who are afraid to create—afraid to manifest their ideas in the world, or else are doing so in some manner that is disrespectful or haphazard—and their dreams may present many images of injured or injuring men. Conversely, the dreams of women strong in outer manifesting ability often feature a strong male figure who consistently appears in various guises.

Animus can best be understood as a force that assists women in acting in their own behalf in the outer world. Animus helps a woman put forth her specific and feminine inner thoughts and feelings in concrete ways—emotionally, sexually, financially, creatively, and otherwise—rather than in a construct that patterns itself after a culturally imposed standard of masculine development in any given culture.

The male figures in women's dreams seem to indicate that animus is not the soul of a woman, but "of, from, and for" the soul of a woman.[13] In its balanced and nonperverted form, animus is an essential "bridging man." This figure often has wondrous capabilities that cause him to rise to the work as bringer and bridger. He is like a merchant of soul. He imports and exports knowledge and products. He chooses the best of what is offered, arranges the best price, supervises the integrity of the exchanges, follows up, follows through.

Another way to understand this is to think of Wild Woman, the soul-Self, as the artist and the animus as the arm of the artist.[14] Wild Woman is the driver, the animus hustles up the vehicle. She makes the song, he scores it. She imagines, he offers advice. Without him the play is created in one's imagination, but never written down and never performed. Without him the stage may be filled to bursting, but the curtains never part and the marquee remains dark.

If we were to translate the healthy animus into Spanish metaphor, he would be *el agrimensor*, the surveyor, who knows the lay of the land and with his compass and his thread measures the distance between two points. He defines the edges and establishes boundaries. Also call him *el jugador*, the gamesman, the one who studies and knows how to and where to place the marker to gain or to win. These are some of the most important aspects of a robust animus.

So the animus travels the road between two territories and sometimes three: underworld, inner world, and outer world. All a woman's feelings and ideas are bundled up and carted across those spans—in every direction—by the animus, who has a feeling for all worlds. He brings ideas from "out there" back into her, and he carries ideas from her soul-Self across the bridge to fruition and "to market." Without the builder and maintainer of this land bridge, a woman's inner life cannot be manifested with intent in the outer world.

You needn't call him animus, call him by what words or images you like. But also understand that there is currently within women's culture a suspicion of the masculine, for some a fear of "needing the masculine," for others, a painful recovery from being crushed by it in some way. Generally this wariness comes from the barely-beginning-to-be-healed traumas from family and culture during times previous, times when women were treated as serfs, not selfs. It is still fresh in Wild Woman's memory that there was a time when gifted women were tossed away as refuse, when a woman could not have an idea unless she secretly embedded and fertilized it in a man who then carried it out into the world under his own name.

But ultimately I think we cannot throw away any metaphor that helps us see and be. I wouldn't trust a palette that had red missing from it, or blue, or yellow, or black, or white. Neither would you. The animus is a primary color in the palette of the female psyche.

So, rather than being *the* soul-nature of women, animus, or the contra-sexual nature of women, is a profound psychic intelligence with ability to act. It travels back and forth between worlds, between the various nodes of the psyche. This force has the ability to extrovert and to act out the desires of the ego, to carry out the impulses and ideas of the soul, to elicit a woman's creativity, in manifest and concrete ways.

The key aspect to a positive animus development is actual *manifestation* of cohesive inner thoughts, impulses, and ideas. Though we speak here of positive animus development, there is also a caveat: An integral animus is developed in full consciousness and with much work of self-examination. If one does not carefully peer into one's motives and appetites each step of the way, a poorly developed animus results. This deleterious animus can and will senselessly carry out unexamined ego impulses, pumping out various blind ambitions and fulfilling myriad unexamined appetites. Further, animus is an element of women's psyches that must be exercised, given regular workouts, in order for her and it to be able to act in whole ways. If the useful animus is neglected in a woman's psychic life, it atrophies, exactly like a muscle that has lain inert too long.

While some women theorize that a warrior-woman nature, the Amazonian nature, the huntress nature, can supplant this "masculine-within-the-feminine element," there are to my sights many shades and layers of masculine nature, such as a certain kind of intellectual rule making, law giving, boundary setting, that are extremely valuable to women who live in the modern world. These masculine attributes do not arise from women's instinctual psychic temperament in the same form or tone as those from her feminine nature.[15]

So, living as we do in a world that requires both meditative and outward action, I find it very useful to utilize the concept of a masculine nature or animus in woman. In proper balance animus acts as helper, helpmate, lover, brother, father, king. This does *not* mean animus is king of the woman's psyche, as an injured patriarchal point of view might have it. It means there is a kingly aspect existent in the woman's psyche, a kingly element that when developed attitudinally, acts and mediates in loving service to the wild nature. Archetypally, the king symbolizes a force that is meant to work in a woman's behalf and for her well-being, governing what she and soul assign to him, ruling over whatever psychic lands are granted to him.

So that is how it is supposed to be, but in the tale the animus has sought other goals at the expense of the wild nature, and as the river fills up with waste, the flow itself begins to poison other aspects of the creative psyche, and especially the unborn children of the woman.

What does it mean when the psyche has given the animus the power of the river and it is misused? Someone told me when I was a child that it was as easy to create for good as it was to create for bad. I have not found this to be so. It is far harder to keep the river clear. It is far easier to let it molder. Let us say then that keeping the flow clear is a natural challenge we all face. We hope to remedy clouding as quickly and as extensively as we are able.

But what if something takes over the creative flow, making it muddier and muddier? What if we become trapped by that, what if we somehow perversely begin to somehow derive issue from it, to not only like it but rely on it, make a living by it, feel alive through it? What if we use it to get us out of bed in the morning, to take us somewhere, to make us a somebody in our own minds? Those are the traps that wait for all of us.

The *hidalgo* in this story represents an aspect of women's psyche that, to put it colloquially, has "gone bad." It has become corrupt, it derives benefit from its manufacturing of poison, it is somehow tied to unhealthy life. He is like a king who rules through a misguided hunger. He is neither wise nor can he ever be loved by the woman he purports to serve.

It is very good for a woman to have in her psyche a devoted animus figure, strong, able to see far, hearing both in the outer world and the underworld, able to predict what is likely to occur next, deciding laws and justice by the sum of what he senses and sees in all worlds. But the one in this story is an infidel. The role of the animus as portrayed by the well-realized *hidalgo*, king or mentor, in a woman's psyche is supposed to be able to help her realize her possibilities and goals, make manifest the ideas and ideals she holds dear, weigh the justice and integrity of things, take care of the armaments, strategize when she is threatened, help her unite all her psychic territories.

When the animus has become a menace the way we see in this tale, a woman loses confidence in her decisions. As her animus becomes more weakened by its one-sidedness—its falsehoods, thefts, posturings to and about her—the water of the river turns from something that is essential to life to something to be approached with the same caution as a hired killer. Then there is a famine in the land and pollution on the river.

To create is *creare* in Latin,[16] meaning to produce, to make (life), to produce where there was nothing before. It is the drinking from the polluted river that causes cessation of inner and therefore outer life. In the tale, this pollution causes deformation of the children, and these children represent young ideas and ideals. The children represent our ability to produce a something where there was once a nothing. We can recognize that this deformation of new potential is taking place when we begin to question our ability, and especially our legitimacy, to think, or act, or be.

Gifted women, even as they reclaim their creative lives, even as beautiful things flow from their hands, from their pens, from their bodies, still question whether they are writers, painters, artists, people, *real* ones. And of course they are real ones even though they might like to bedevil themselves with what constitutes "real." A farmer is a real farmer when she looks out over the land and plans the spring crops. A runner is real when she takes the first step, a flower is real when it is yet in its mother stem, a tree is real when it is still a seed in the pine cone. An old tree is a real living being. Real is what has life.

Animus development varies from woman to woman. It is not a perfectly formed creature that springs forth from the thighs of the Gods. It appears to have an innate or inborn quality to it, but also has to "grow up," be taught and trained. It is meant to be a strong and direct force. But when there is damage to the animus through all the myriad forces of culture and self, something weary, or mean-spirited, or a deadness some call "being neutral" interposes itself between the inner world of psyche and the outer world of the blank page, clear canvas, waiting dance floor, boardroom, gathering. This "something"—usually somehow slitty-eyed, misunderstood, or misappropriated—clots the river, clogs thinking, jams the pen and the brush, locks the joints for an interminable period of time, crusts over fresh ideas, and thusly we suffer.

There is an odd phenomenon in the psyche: When a woman is afflicted with a negative animus, any effort at a creative act touches it off so that it attacks her. She picks up a pen, the factory on the river spews its poison. She thinks about applying to school, or takes a class, but stops in the middle, choking on the lack of inward nourishment and support. A woman revs up but continuously falls back. There are more unfinished needlework projects, more never-realized flower beds, more hikes never taken, more notes never written just to say "I care," more foreign languages never learned, more music lessons abandoned, more weft hanging on the loom waiting and waiting . . .

These are the deformed life forms. These are *La Llorona*'s poisoned children. And they are all tossed into the river, they are all tossed back into the polluted waters that so afflicted them to begin with. In the best archetypal circumstances what is supposed to happen is that they burble around and like a phoenix rise from the ashes in a new form. But here something is wrong with the animus and therefore weights are awry in one's ability to differentiate one impulse from the other, let alone to manifest and implement one's ideas in the world. And the river is so filled with the excrement of complexes, nothing can rise from it for new life.

And so here is the hard part: We have to go into the sludge and look for the precious gifts that lie under it all. Like *La Llorona*, we have to drag the river for our soul-life, for our creative lives. And one more thing, also difficult: We must clean up the river so *La Llorona* can see, so she and we can find the souls of the children and be at peace to create again.

The culture makes the "factories" and pollution worse through its immense power to devalue the feminine—and its misunderstanding of the bridging nature of the masculine.[17] Culture too often holds a woman's animus in exile by pressing one of those insoluble and nonsensical questions that complexes pretend are valid, and before which many women are cowed: "But are you a *real* writer [artist, mother, daughter, sister, wife, lover, worker, dancer, person]?" "Are you *really* talented [gifted, worthy]?" "Do you *really* have anything to say that is worthwhile [enlightening, will help humankind, find a cure for anthrax]?"

Not surprisingly, when a woman's animus is taken up with psychic manufacturing of a negative sort, a woman's output dwindles as her confidence and creative muscle wane. Women in this predicament tell me they "cannot see a way out" of their so-called writer's block, or for that matter the cause of it. Their animus is sucking all the oxygen out of the river, and they feel "extremely tired" and suffer "tremendous loss of energy," can't seem to "get going," feel "held back by something."

Taking Back the River

The Life/Death/Life nature causes Fate, relationship, love, creativity, and all else to move in large and wild patterns, one following the other in this order: creation, increase, power, dissolution, death, incubation, creation, and so on. Theft or absence of ideas, thoughts, feelings is the outcome of a disturbed flow. Here is how to take back the river.

Receive nurturance to begin the cleanup of the river. Troublesome contaminants in the river are obvious when a woman turns away sincere compliments about her creative life. There may be only a little pollution, as in the offhanded "Oh, how nice you are to give such a compliment," or there may be massive trouble on the river: "Oh, this old thing" or "You must be out of your mind." And also the defensive "Of course I'm wonderful, how could you fail to notice?" These are all signs of injured animus. Good things flow into the woman but are immediately poisoned.

To reverse the phenomenon, a woman practices taking in the compliment (even if initially it looks as though she is lunging at the compliment in order to keep it for herself this time), savors it, fights off the malignant animus that wants to tell the giver of the compliment "That's what you think, you don't really know all the mistakes she's made, you don't really see what a drip she is . . . etcetera."

Negative complexes are particularly attracted to the juiciest ideas, the most revolutionary and wonderful ideas, and the most rampant forms of creativity. So, there are no two ways about it, we must summon up a clearer-acting animus and the older one must be laid to rest, that is, sent down to the archival layer of the psyche where we file away deflated and folded impulses and catalysts. There they become artifacts rather than actors or affects.

Respond; that is how to clear the river. Wolves lead immensely creative lives. They make dozens of choices every day, decide this way or that, estimate how far, concentrate on their prey, calculate the chances, seize opportunity, react powerfully to accomplish their goals. Their abilities to find the hidden, to coalesce intention, to focus on the desired outcome, and to act in their own behalf to gain it, are the exact characteristics required for creative follow-through in humans.

To create one must be able to respond. Creativity is the ability to respond to all that goes on around us, to choose from the hundreds of possibilities of thought, feeling, action, and reaction that arise within us, and to put these together in a unique response, expression, or message that carries moment, passion, and meaning. In this sense, loss of our creative milieu means finding ourselves limited to only one choice, divested of, suppressing, or censoring feelings and thoughts, not acting, not saying, doing, or being.

Be wild; that is how to clear the river. In its original form, the river does not flow in polluted, we manage that. The river does not dry up, we block it. If we want to allow it its freedom, we have to allow our ideational lives to be let loose, to stream, letting anything come, initially censoring nothing. That is creative life. It is made up of divine paradox. It is an entirely interior process. To create one must be willing to be stone stupid, to sit upon a throne on top of a jackass and spill rubies from one's mouth. Then the river will flow, then we can stand in the stream of it raining down. We can put out our skirts and shirts to catch as much as we can carry.

Begin; this is how to clear the polluted river. If you're scared, scared to fail, I say begin already, fail if you must, pick yourself up, start again. If you fail again, you fail. So what? Begin again. It is not the failure that holds us back but the reluctance to begin over again that causes us to stagnate. If you're scared, so what? If you're afraid something's going to leap out and bite you, then for heaven's sake, get it over with already. Let your fear leap out and bite you so you can get it over with and go on. You will get over it. The fear will pass. In this case, it is better if you meet it head-on, feel it, and get it over with, than to keep using it to avoid cleaning up the river.

Protect your time; this is how to banish pollutants. I know a fierce painter here in the Rockies who hangs this sign on the chain that closes off the road to her house when she is in a painting or thinking mode: "I am working today and am not receiving visitors. I know you think this doesn't mean you because you are my banker, agent, or best friend. But it does."

Another sculptor I know hangs this sign on her gate: "Do not disturb unless I've won the lottery or Jesus has been sighted on the Old Taos Highway." As you can see, the well-developed animus has excellent boundaries.

Stay with it. How to further banish this pollution? By insisting nothing will stop us from exercising the well-integrated animus, by continuing our soul-spinning, our wing-making ventures, our art, our psychic mending and sewing, whether we feel strong or not, whether we feel ready or not. If necessary by tying ourselves to the mast, the chair, the desk, the tree, the cactus—wherever we create. It is essential, even though often painful, to put in the necessary time, to not skirt the difficult tasks inherent in striving for mastery. A true creative life burns in more ways than one.

Negative complexes that arise along the way are banished or transformed—your dreams will guide you the last part of the way—by putting your foot down, once and for all, and by saying, "I love my creative life more than I love cooperating with my own oppression." If we were to abuse our children, Social Services would show up at our doors. If we were to abuse our pets, the Humane Society would come to take us away. But there is no Creativity Patrol or Soul Police to intervene if we insist on starving our own souls. There is just us. We are the only ones to watch over the soul-Self and the heroic animus. It is bitterly harsh to water them once a week, or once a month, or even once a year. They each have their own circadian rhythms. They need us and need the water of our craft every day.

Protect your creative life. If you would avoid *hambre del alma*, the starved soul, name the problem for what it is—and fix it. Practice your work every day. Then, let no thought, no man, no woman, no mate, no friend, no religion, no job, and no crabbed voice force you into a famine. If necessary, show your incisors.

Craft your real work. Build that hut of warmth and knowing.

Pull your energy from over there to over here. Insist on a balance between pedestrian responsibility and personal rapture. Protect the soul. Insist on quality creative life. Let neither your own complexes, your culture, intellectual detritus, nor any high-sounding, aristocratic, pedagogical, or political la-la steal it away from you.

Lay out nourishment for the creative life. Although many things are good and nutritious for the soul, most fall into Wild Woman's four basic food groups: time, belonging, passion, and sovereignty. Stock up. These keep the river clean.

When the river is cleansed again it is free to flow; a woman's creative output increases and thereafter continues in natural cycles of increase and decrease and increase again. Nothing will be carried off or fouled for long. Whatever contaminants occur naturally are neutralized efficiently. The river returns as our system of nourishment, one we can enter without fear, one we can drink from without worry, one beside which we can calm the tormented soul of *La Llorona*, healing her children and restoring them to her. We can dismantle the polluting process of the factory, seat a new animus. We can live our lives as we wish and as we see fit, there beside the river, holding our many babies in our arms, showing them their reflections in the clear, clear water.

Focus and the Fantasy Mill

In North America, the tale of "The Little Match Girl" is best known in the Hans Christian Andersen version. At its core, it describes what lack of nurture, lack of focus look like, and what they lead to. It is a very old tale told the world over in various ways; sometimes it is a charcoal burner who uses his last coals to warm himself while he dreams of times past. In some versions the symbol of matches is exchanged for something else, as in "The Little Flowerseller," about a broken-hearted man who gazes into the centers of his last flowers and is spirited away from this life.

Though some might look at the superficial story rendering and say these are maudlin stories, meaning they have excessive emotional "sweetness," it would be a mistake to dismiss them lightly. The stories actually are, at their base, profound expressions of psyche being negatively mesmerized to the point that real and vibrant life begins to "die" in spirit.[18]

The following "Little Match Girl" was given to me by my Aunt Katerina, who had come to America after World War II. During the war, her simple Hungarian farming village had been overrun and occupied three times by three different hostile armies. She always began the tale by saying that soft dreams under hard conditions are no good, that in tough times we must have tough dreams, real dreams, those that, if we will work diligently and drink our milk to the health of the Virgin, will come true.

The Little Match Girl

THERE WAS A LITTLE GIRLCHILD who had neither a mother nor a father, and she lived in the dark forest. There was a village at the edge of the forest and she had learned she could buy matches for a half-penny there, and that she could sell them on the street for a full penny. If she sold enough matches, she could buy a crust of bread, return to her lean-to in the forest, and sleep there dressed in all the clothes she owned.

The winter came and it was very cold. She had no shoes, and her coat was so thin she could see through it. Her feet were past the point of being blue, her toes were white; so were her fingers and the end of her nose. She wandered the streets and begged strangers, would they please buy matches from her? But no one stopped and no one paid her any attention.

So she sat down one evening saying, "I have matches. I can light a fire and I can warm myself." But she had no kindling and no wood. She decided to light the matches anyway.

As she sat there with her legs straight out in front of her, she struck the first match. As she did, it seemed that the cold and the snow disappeared altogether. What she saw instead of swirling snow was a room, a beautiful room with a great dark green ceramic stove with a door with iron scrollwork. The stove emanated so much heat it made the air wavy. She snuggled up close to the stove and it felt heavenly.

But all of a sudden the stove went out, and she was again sitting in the snow, shivering so bitterly the bones in her face chimed. And so she struck the second match, and the light fell upon the wall of the building next to where she sat and she could suddenly see through it. In the room behind the wall was a snowy cloth covering a table, and there on the table were china plates of the purest white, and on a platter was a goose that had just been cooked, and just as she was reaching for this repast, the vision disappeared.

She was again in the snow. But now her knees and her hips no longer hurt. Now the cold was stinging and burning its way up her arms and torso, and so she lit the third match.

And in the light of the third match was a beautiful Christmas tree, beautifully decorated with white candles with lacy ruffs, and beautiful glass ornaments, and thousands and thousands of little dots of light that she couldn't quite make out.

And she looked up the trunk of this enormous tree, that went higher and higher, and stretched farther and farther toward the ceiling until it became the stars in the heavens over her head, and suddenly a star blazed across the sky, and she remembered her mother had told her that when a soul dies, a star falls.

And out of nowhere her grandmother appeared, so warm and so kind, and the child felt so happy to see her. The grandmother picked up her apron and put it around the child, held her close with both arms, and the child was content.

But the grandmother began to fade. And the child struck more and more matches to keep the grandmother with her . . . and more and more matches to keep the grandmother with her . . . and more and more . . . and together she and the grandmother began to rise together up into the sky where there was no cold and no hunger and no pain. And in the morning, between the houses, the child was found still, and gone.

Staving Off Creative Fantasy

This child lives in an environ where people do not care. If you are in one of these, get out. This child is in a milieu where what she has, little fires on sticks—the beginnings of all creative possibility—is not valued. If you are in this predicament, turn your back and walk away. This child is in a psychic situation in which there are few options. She has resigned herself to her "place" in life. If this has happened to you, unresign yourself and come out kicking ass. When Wild Woman is cornered, she does not surrender, she comes ahead, claws out and fighting.

What is the Match Girl to do? If her instincts were intact, her choices would be many. Walk to another town, sneak into a wagon, stow away in a coal cellar. Wild Woman would know what to do next. But the Match Girl doesn't know Wild Woman anymore. The little wild child is freezing, all that is left of her is a person who goes about in a trance.

Being with real people who warm us, who endorse and exalt our creativity, is essential to the flow of creative life. Otherwise we freeze. Nurture is a chorus of voices both from within and without that notices the state of a woman's being, takes care to encourage it, and if necessary, gives comfort as well. I'm not certain how many friends one needs, but definitely one or two who think your gift, whatever it may be, is *pan de cielo*, the bread of heaven. Every woman is entitled to an Allelujia Chorus.

When women are out in the cold, they tend to live on fantasies instead of action. Fantasy of this sort is the great anesthetizer of women. I know women who have been gifted with beautiful voices. I know women who are natural storytellers; almost everything out of their mouths is freshly formed and finely wrought. But they are isolated, or feel disenfranchised in some way. They are shy, which is often a cover for a starving animus. They have difficulty gaining a sense that they are supported from within, or by friends, family, community.

To avoid being the Little Match Girl, there is one major action you must take. Anyone who does not support your art, your life, is not worth your time. Harsh but true. Otherwise one walks right in and dresses in the rags of the Match Girl and is compelled to live a quarterlife that freezes all thought, hope, gifts, writings, playings, designing, and dancing.

Warmth should be the major pursuit of the Little Match Girl. But in the story it is not. Instead she tries to sell off the matches, her sources of warmth. Doing so leaves the feminine no warmer, no richer, no wiser, and with no further development.

Warmth is a mystery. It somehow heals and engenders us. It is the loosener of too-tight things, it enhances flow, the mysterious urge to *be*, the maiden flight of fresh ideas. Whatever warmth is, it draws us closer, and closer yet.

The Match Girl is not in an environment where she can thrive. There is no warmth, no kindling, no firewood. If we were in her place what could we do? We could first of all not entertain the fantasyland the Match Girl builds by lighting matches. There are three kinds of fantasies. The first is the pleasure fantasy; it is a form of mind ice-cream, strictly for enjoyment, such as daydreams. The second kind of fantasy is intentional imaging. This kind of fantasy is like a planning session. It is used as a vehicle to take us forward into action. All successes—psychological, spiritual, financial, and creative—begin with fantasies of this nature. Then there is the third kind of fantasy, the kind that brings everything to a halt. This is the kind of fantasy that hinders right action during critical times.

Unfortunately, this is the kind the Match Girl spins. It is a fantasy that has nothing to do with reality. It has to do with feeling nothing can be done, or that a thing is too hard to do, so one might as well sink into idle fantasy. Sometimes the fantasy is in a woman's mind. Sometimes it comes to her through a liquor bottle, a needle—or lack of one. Sometimes the smoke of a weed is the transporter, or many forgettable rooms, complete with bed and stranger. Women in these situations are playing out the Little Match Girl in every night of fantasies and more fantasies, and waking up dead and frozen at every daybreak. There are many ways to lose one's intent, to lose one's focus.

So what will reverse this and restore soul-esteem and self-esteem? We have to find something very different than what the Match Girl had. We have to take our ideas to a place where there is support for them. This is an enormous step concomitant with focus: to find nurture. Very few of us can create solely under our own steam. We need all the pats from angel wings that we can find.

Most of the time people have wonderful ideas: I'm gonna paint that wall a color I like; I'm going to create a project the entire town can be involved with; I'm going to make some tiles for my bathroom, and if I really like them, I'm going to sell some of them; I'm going to go back to school, sell my house and travel, have a child, leave this and begin that, go my way, clean up my act, help aright this injustice or that, protect the unprotected.

Those kinds of projects need nurture. They need vital support—from *warm* people. Little Match Girl is tattered. Like the old folk song, she's been down so long it looks like up to her. No one can thrive at her level. We want to put ourselves in a situation where, like the plants and trees, we can turn toward the sun. But there has to be a sun. To do this we have to *move*, not just sit there. We have to do something that makes our situation different. Without a move, we are back out on the streets selling matches again.

Friends who love you and have warmth for your creative life are the very best suns in the world. When a woman, like the Little Match Girl, has no friends she also becomes frozen by anguish, and sometimes by anger as well. Even if one has friends, those friends may not be suns. They may give comfort instead of informing the woman about her increasingly frozen circumstances. They comfort her—but that is far different from nurture. Nurture moves you from one place to another. Nurture is like psychic Wheaties.

The difference between comfort and nurture is this: if you have a plant that is sick because you keep it in a dark closet, and you say soothing words to it, that is comfort. If you take the plant out of the closet and put it in the sun, give it something to drink, and then talk to it, that is nurture.

A frozen woman without nurture is inclined to turn to incessant "what if" daydreams. But even if she is in this frozen condition, *especially* if she is in such a frozen condition, she must refuse the comforting fantasy. The comforting fantasy will kill us dead for certain. You know how lethal fantasies go: "Some day . . ." and "If I only had . . ." and "He will change . . ." and "If I just learn to control myself . . . when I get really ready, when I have enough xyz, when the kids are grown, when I am more secure, when I find someone else, and as soon as I . . ." and so on.

The Little Match Girl has an internal grandmother who instead of barking "Wake up! Get up! No matter what it takes, find warmth!" takes her away into a fantasy life, takes her to "heaven." But heaven will not help the Wild Woman, the trapped wild child, or the Little Match Girl in this situation. These comforting fantasies must not be ignited. They are seductive and lethal distractions from the real work.

We see the Match Girl making some kind of trade-off, some kind of ill-conceived commerce in the story when the child sells her matches, the only thing she has that might keep her warm. When women are disconnected from the nurturing love of the wild mother, they are on the equivalent of a subsistence diet in the outer world. The ego is just eking out a life, just taking the barest of nourishment from without and returning each night from whence she began, over and over. There she sleeps, exhausted.

She cannot awaken to a life with a future because her wretched life is like a hook upon which she hangs daily. In initiations, spending a significant period of time under difficult conditions is part of a dismemberment that severs one from ease and complacency. As an initiatory passage, it will come to a conclusion, and the newly "sanded down" woman will commence a refreshed and enwisened spiritual and creative life. However, women in the Match Girl condition could be said to be involved in an initiation that has gone awry. The hostile conditions do not serve to deepen, only to decimate. Another venue, another environ, with different supports and guides, must be chosen.

Historically, and particularly in men's psychology, illness, exile, and suffering are often understood as an initiatory dismemberment, sometimes carrying great meaning. But, for women, there are additional archetypes of initiation that rise out of women's innate psychology and physicality; giving birth is one, the power of blood is another, as are being in love or receiving nurturant love. Being given the blessing by someone she looks up to, being taught in a deep and supportive way by one older than she, all these are initiations that are intense, and that have their own tensions and resurrections.

The Match Girl could be said to have come so close, yet remained so far from the transitional stage of movement and action that would have completed the initiation. While she has the materials for an initiatory experience in her wretched life, there is no one within or without to guide the psychic process.

Psychically, in the most negative sense, winter brings the kiss of death—that is, a coldness—to anything it touches. Coldness spells the end of any relationship. If you want to kill something, just be cold to it. As soon as one becomes frozen in feeling, thinking, or action, relationship is not possible. When humans want to abandon something in themselves or leave someone else out in the cold, they ignore them, disinvite them, leave them out, go out of their way to have to even hear their voice or lay eyes upon them. This is the situation in the psyche of the Match Girl.

The Match Girl wanders the streets and she begs strangers to buy matches from her. This scene shows one of the most disconcerting things about injured instinct in women, the giving of light for little price. The little lights on sticks here are like the bigger lights, the skulls on the sticks, in the Vasalisa story. They represent wisdom, but more importantly, they ignite consciousness, replacing dark with light, relighting that which has burned out. Fire is the major symbol of the revivificator in the psyche.

Here we have the Match Girl in great need, begging to be given to, offering in fact a thing of far greater value—a light—than value received in return—a penny. Whether this "great value given for less value received" is within our psyches or experienced by us in the outer world, the outcome is the same: more loss of energy. Then a woman cannot respond to her own needs. Something that wants to live begs for it, but is not answered. Here we have someone who, like Sophia, the Greek spirit of wisdom, takes light from the abyss, but sells it off in fits and starts of useless fantasy. Bad lovers, rotten bosses, exploitative situations, wily complexes of all sorts tempt a woman to these choices.

When the Match Girl decides to burn the matches, she uses her resources to fantasize instead of act. She uses her energy in a momentary kind of way. This shows up in obvious ways in a woman's life. She's determined to go to college, but takes three years to make up her mind which one. She is going to do that series of paintings but since she has no place to hang such a show, she doesn't make painting a priority. She wants to do this or that but she doesn't take the time to learn, to develop the sensitivity or skill to do it well. She has ten notebooks full of dreams, but is caught in her fascination with interpretation and cannot put their meanings into action. She knows she must leave, begin, stop, go, but she doesn't.

And so we see why. When a woman is frozen of feeling, when she can no longer feel herself, when her blood, her passion, no longer reach the extremities of her psyche, when she is desperate; then a fantasy life is far more pleasurable than anything else she can set her sights upon. Her little match lights, because they have no wood to burn, instead burn up the psyche as though it were a big dry log. The psyche begins to play tricks on itself; it lives now in the fantasy fire of all yearning fulfilled. This kind of fantasizing is like a lie: If you tell it often enough, you begin to believe it.

This sort of conversion angst, wherein problems or issues are diminished by enthusiastically fantasizing unrealizable solutions or nicer times, does not only assail women, it is the major stumbling block of humankind. The stove in the Match Girl fantasy represents warm thoughts. It is also a symbol of the center, the heart, the hearth. It tells us her fantasy is for the true self, the heart of the psyche, the warmth of a home within.

But all of a sudden the stove goes out. The Match Girl, like all women in this psychic predicament, finds herself back sitting in the snow again. Here we see that this kind of fantasy is brief but intensely destructive. It has nothing to burn but our energy. Even though a woman might use her fantasies to keep herself warm, she still winds up in the deep freeze.

The Match Girl lights more matches. Each fantasy burns out, and again the child is in the snow and freezing. When the psyche freezes, a woman is turned toward herself and no one else. She lights a third match. This is the fairy-tale three, the magic number, the point at which something new should happen. But in this case, because fantasy overwhelms action, nothing new occurs.

It is ironic that the story contains a Christmas tree. The Christmas tree evolved from a pre-Christian symbol of life everlasting—the evergreen. One could say it is this that might save her, the idea of the ever-green, ever-growing, ever-moving soul-psyche. But the room has no ceiling. The idea of life cannot be contained in the psyche. The mesmerizing has taken hold.

The grandmother is so warm, so kind, yet she is the final morphia, the final dram of hemlock. She draws the child into the sleep of death. In its most negative sense this is the sleep of complacency, the sleep of numbness—"It's all right, I can stand it"; the sleep of denial—"I just look the other way." This is the sleep of malignant fantasy, wherein we hope all travail will magically disappear.

It is a psychic fact that when libido or energy wanes to the point where its breath no longer shows on the mirror, some representation of the Life/Death/Life nature shows up, here portrayed by the grandmother. It is her work to arrive at the death of something, to incubate the soul that has left its husk behind, and to care for the soul till it can be born anew.

And that is the blessedness of everyone's psyche. Even in the event of such a painful ending as the Match Girl's, there is a ray of light. When enough time, discontent, and pressure have been brought to bear, the Wild Woman of the psyche will hurl new life into a woman's mind, giving her opportunity to act in her own behalf once more. As we can see from the suffering involved, it is far better to heal one's addiction to fantasy than wait around wishing and hoping to be raised from the dead.

Renewing the Creative Fire

So now let us imagine that we have everything all together, we are clear about our intention, we are not drowning in escapist fantasy, we are integrated and our creative life flourishes. We need one more attribute; we need to know what to do not *if*, but *when* we lose focus; that is, when we wear down for a time. What? After all this work, we might lose our focus? Yes, it will only be lost temporarily, but it is the natural order. Here is a fine tale about it, that in our family is called "The Three Gold Hairs."

There is a saying in our family that story has wings. Via transocean migrations by my Magyar foster family, a number of the stories I carry flew over the Carpathian Mountains with them when they fled their villages during the wars. There they lodged for a time in the Urals, thence sailing over an ocean to North America. The little ragged band, and their stories shaped by their experiences, then traveled overland down through the great forests to the Great Lakes basin.

The little core of "The Three Gold Hairs" was given to me by my "Tante" Kata, a gifted healer and powerful prayer-maker who grew up in Eastern Europe, and I have amplified that kernel here. In my research, I have spotted quite different Teutonic and Celtic stories that revolve around the leitmotif of "golden hair." The leitmotif or kernel of a story represents an archetypal juncture in the psyche. That is the nature of archetypes ... they deposit some nuance of themselves at the point of contact with psyche. As symbolic representations, they sometimes leave behind an evidence—wending their ways into the life stories, dreams, and ideas of every mortal. Dwelling who knows where, the archetypes constitute, one might say, a set of psyche instructions that traverse time and space and enwisen each new generation.

The theme of this story is about how one regains focus once one has lost it. Focus is composed of sensing, hearing, and following the directions of the soul-voice. Many women are quite good at focusing, but when they lose touch with it, they become scattered like a feather bed burst all over the countryside.

It is important to have a container for all that we sense and hear from the wild nature. For some women it is their journals, where they keep track of every feather that flies by, for others it is the creative art, they dance it, paint it, make it into a script. Remember Baba Yaga? She has a big pot; she moves through the sky in a cauldron that is actually a pestle and a mortar. In other words, she has a container in which to put things. She has a way of thinking, a way of moving from one place to another that is contained. Yes, containment is the solution to the problem of all loss of energy, that and one more thing. Let us see ...

The Three Gold Hairs

ONCE, WHEN IT WAS DEEPEST, darkest night, the sort of night when the land is black and the trees seem like gnarled hands against the dark blue sky, it was on exactly this kind of night that a lone old man staggered through the forest. Though boughs scratched his face, half-blinding his eyes, he held out a tiny lantern before him. Therein the candle burned lower and lower.

The old man was a sight to behold with his long yellow hair, cracked yellow teeth, and curved amber fingernails. His back was rounded like a bag of flour, and so ancient was he that his skin hung in furbelows from chin, arms, and hips.

The old one progressed through the forest by grasping a sapling and pulling his body forward, grasping another sapling, and pulling himself forward, and with this rowing motion and by the small breath left in him, he made his way through the forest.

Every bone in his feet pained like fire. The owls in the trees screeched right along with his joints as he propelled himself forward in the dark. Way off in the distance, there was a tiny flickering light, a cottage, a fire, a home, a place of rest, and he labored toward that little light. Just as he reached the door, he was so tired, so exhausted, the tiny light in his little lantern died, and the old man fell through the door and collapsed.

Inside was an old woman sitting before a beautiful roaring fire, and now she hurried to his side, gathered him into her arms, and carried him to the fire. She held him in her arms as a mother holds her child. She sat and rocked him in her rocking chair. There they were, the poor frail old man, just a sack of bones, and the strong old woman rocking him back and forth saying, "There, there. There, there. There, there."

And she rocked him all through the night, and by the time it was not yet morning but almost, he had grown much younger, he was now a beautiful young man with golden hair and long strong limbs. And still she rocked him. "There, there. There, there. There, there."

And as morning approached even more closely, the young man had turned into a very small and very beautiful child with golden hair plaited like wheat.

Just at the moment of dawn, the old woman plucked three hairs very quickly from the child's beautiful head and threw them to the tiles. They sounded like this: *Tiiiiiiiing! Tiiiiiiiiing! Tiiiiiiiiing!*

And the little child in her arms crawled down from her lap and ran to the door. Looking back at the old woman for a moment, he gave her a dazzling smile, then turned and flew up into the sky to become the brilliant morning sun.[19]

~~~~~~

Things are different at night, so to understand this story we must descend to a night-consciousness, a state in which we are more quickly aware of every creak and snap. Night is when we are closer to ourselves, closer to essential ideas and feelings that do not register so much during the daylight hours.

In mythos, night is the world of Mother Nyx, the woman who made the world. She is the Old Mother of Days, one of the Life and Death crones. When it is night in a fairy tale, for interpretation's sake, we know we are in the unconscious. *San Juan de la Cruz*, Saint John of the Cross, called such "the dark night of the soul." In this tale, night typifies a time when energy in the form of an old, old man becomes weaker and weaker. It is a time when we are on our last foot in some important way.

To lose focus means to lose energy. The absolutely wrong thing to attempt when we've lost focus is to rush about struggling to pack it all back together again. Rushing is not the thing to do. As we see in the tale, sitting and rocking is the thing to do. Patience, peace, and rocking renew ideas. Just holding the idea and the patience to rock it are what some women might call a luxury. Wild Woman says it is a necessity.

This is something the wolves know all about. When an intruder appears, wolves may growl, bark, or even bite the interloper, but also they may, from a good distance, draw back into their group and sit together as a family would. They just sort of sit there and breathe together. Rib cages go in and out, up and down. They're focusing themselves, regrounding themselves, returning to the center of themselves and deciding what is critical, what to do next. They're deciding they're "not going to do anything right now, just going to sit here and breathe, just gonna rock together."

Now many times when ideas aren't unfolding or operating smoothly, or we aren't working them well, we lose focus. It is part of a natural cycle and it occurs because the idea has gotten stale or we have lost our ability to see it in a fresh way. We have ourselves grown old and creaky like the old man in "Three Gold Hairs." Although there are many theories on creative "blocks," the truth is that mild ones come and go like weather patterns and like seasons—with the exceptions of the psychological blocks we talked about earlier, such as not getting down to one's truth, fear of being rejected, being afraid to say what one knows, worrying about one's adequacy, pollution of the basic flow, settling for mediocrity or pale imitations, and so on.

This story is so excellent because it delineates the entire cycle of an idea, the little tiny light accorded it, which of course is the idea itself, and that it becomes fatigued and is near extinguished, all as part of its natural cycle. In fairy tales, when something bad happens it means that something new has to be tried, a new energy has to be introduced, a helper, healer, magic force has to be consulted.

Here again we see old *La Que Sabe*, the two-million-year-old woman. She is "the one who knows." To be held in her arms before her fire is restorative, reparative.[20] It is to this fire and to her arms that the old man drags himself, for without these he will die.

The old man is tired out from a long time at the work we give to him. Have you ever seen a woman work like the devil had hold of her big toe, only to suddenly collapse and go no further? Have you ever seen a woman hell's-a-popping about some social issue only to one day turn her back and say "Hell with it." Her animus has worn out and is in need of being rocked by *La Que Sabe*. The woman whose idea or energy has waned, withered, or ceased altogether needs to know the way to this old woman *curandera*, healer, and must carry the tired animus there for renewal.

I work with many women who are deeply involved in social activism. There is no doubt about it, at the far turn of this cycle they become tired out, dragging themselves through the forest on creaking legs, the lantern flickering, ready to go out. This is the time when they say, "I've had it. I quit, I'm turning in my press pass, my badge, my union suit, my . . ." whatever it is. They're going to immigrate to Auckland. They're going to watch TV and eat bean curd cookies and never look out the window onto the world again. They're going to buy bad shoes, move to a neighborhood where nothing ever happens, they're going to watch the shopping channel for the rest of their lives. From now on they're going to mind their own business, look the other way . . . on and on.

Whatever their idea of respite, even though they're speaking from abject tiredness and frustration, I say that respite is a good idea, it is time to rest. To which they usually screech, "Rest! How can I rest when the whole world is going to hell right before my very eyes?"

But in the end, a woman must rest now, rock now, regain her focus. She must become younger, recover her energy. She thinks she cannot, but she can, for the circle of women, be they mothers, students, artists, or activists, always closes to fill in for those who go on rest leave. A creative woman has to rest now and return to her intense work later. She has to go see the old woman in the forest, the revivifier, the Wild Woman in one of her many leitmotifs. Wild Woman *expects* that the animus will wear out on a regular basis. She is not shocked that he falls through her door. She is not shocked when we fall through the door. She is ready. She will not rush to us in a panic. She will just pick us up and hold us till we regain our power again.

And neither should we panic when we lose our momentum or focus. But like her, we must calmly hold the idea and be with it a while. Whether our focus is on self-development, world issues, or relationship doesn't matter, the animus will wear down. It is not a matter of if, it is a matter of when. Completing long endeavors, such as finishing school, concluding a manuscript, fulfilling one's opus, caregiving an ill person, all these have their times when the once-young energy turns old, falls down, and can go on no longer.

For women, it is best if they understand this at the onset of an endeavor, for women tend to be surprised by fatigue. Then they wail, they mutter, they whisper about failure, inadequacy, and such. No, no. This losing of energy is as it is. It is Nature.

The assumption of eternal strength in the masculine is in error. It is a cultural introject that must be routed from the psyche. This misconception causes both the masculine energies in the inner landscape and males in the culture to feel an unwarranted sense of failure if they tire or need rest. All naturally need a break to restore strength. The modus operandi of the Life/Death/Life nature is cyclical and applies to everyone and all things.

In the story, three hairs are thrown to the floor. In my family there is a saying: "Throw some gold on the floor." This is derived from *desprender las palabras*, which in the tradition of *cuentistas*, storytellers, and healers in my family, means to throw away some of the words of the story in order to make it stronger.

The hair is symbolic of thought, that which issues from the head. To throw some away or down makes the boychild somehow lighter, causing him to shine even more brightly. Likewise your worn-out idea or endeavor can shine more brightly if you will take some of it and throw it away. It is the same idea as the sculptor removing more marble in order to reveal more of the hidden form beneath. A powerful way to renew or strengthen one's intention or action that has become fatigued is to throw some ideas away, and focus.

Take three hairs out of your endeavor and throw them to the ground. There they become like a wake-up call. Throwing them down makes a psychic noise, a chime, a resonance in the woman's spirit that causes activity to occur again. The sound of some of one's many ideas falling away becomes like an announcement of a new era or a new opportunity.

In reality, old *La Que Sabe* is giving the masculine a light pruning. We know that cutting away the deadwood helps a tree to grow stronger. We also know that pinching off the heads of blossoms of certain plants helps them grow far more bushy, far more lush. For the wildish woman, the animus's cycle of increase and decrease is natural. It is an archaic process, an ancient process. Time out of mind, it is how women approached the world of ideas and the outer manifestation of them. This is how women do it. The old woman in the fairy tale "Three Gold Hairs" teaches us, re-teaches us really, how it is done.

So what is the point of this reclamation and focus, this calling back of what has been lost, this running with the wolves? It is to go for the jugular, to get right down to the seed and to the bones of everything and anything in your life, because that's where your pleasure is, that's where your joy is, that's where a woman's Eden lies, that place where there is time and freedom to be, wander, wonder, write, sing, create, and not be afraid. When wolves perceive pleasure or danger, they at first become utterly still. They become like statues, utterly focused so they can see, so they can hear, so they can sense what is *there*, sense what is there in its most elemental form.

This is what the wildish nature offers us: the ability to see what is before us through focusing, through stopping and looking and smelling and listening and feeling and tasting. Focusing is the use of all of our senses, including intuition. It is into this world that women come in order to claim their own voices, their own values, their imaginations, their clairvoyance, their clear-seeing, their stories, and the ancient memories of women. And these are the work of focus and creation. If you've lost focus, just sit down and be still. Take the idea and rock it to and fro. Keep some of it and throw some away, and it will renew itself. You need do no more.

CHAPTER 11

Heat: Retrieving a Sacred Sexuality

The Dirty Goddesses

There is a being who lives in the wild underground of women's natures. This creature is our sensory nature, and like any integral creature it has its own natural and nutritive cycles. This being is inquiring, relational, bounding with energy sometimes, quiescent at other times. It is responsive to stimulus involving the senses: music, movement, food, drink, peace, quiet, beauty, darkness.[1]

It is this aspect of a woman that has heat. Not a heat as in "Let's have sex, baby, baby." But like a fire underground that burns high, then low, in cycles. From the energy released there, a woman acts as she sees fit. A woman's heat is not a state of sexual arousal but a state of intense sensory awareness that includes, but is not limited to, her sexuality.

Much could be written about uses and abuses of women's sensory nature and how she and others either stoke the fire against its natural rhythms or try to douse it in its entirety. But let us instead focus on an aspect that is fervent, definitely wild, and giving off a heat that keeps us warmed with good feeling. In modern women this sensory expression has been given short shrift and, in many places and times, has been banned altogether.

There is an aspect of women's sexuality that in ancient times was called the sacred obscene, not in the way we use the word obscene today, but meaning sexually wise in a witty sort of way. There were once Goddess cults that were in some part devoted to irreverent female sexuality. The rites were not derogatory, but were concerned with portraying parts of the unconscious that remain, yet today, mysterious and largely uncharted.

The very idea of sexuality as sacred, and more specifically, obscenity as an aspect of sacred sexuality, is vital to the wildish nature. There were Goddesses of obscenity in the ancient women's cultures—so-called for their innocent yet wily lewdness. However, language, in English at least, makes it very difficult to understand the "obscene Goddesses" in any way other than a vulgar one. Here is what the word *obscene* and other related words mean. From these meanings, I think you can see why this aspect of old Goddess worship was pushed underground.

I would like you to consider these three dictionary definitions and develop your own conclusions:

• *Dirt*: Middle English, *drit*, probably from Icelandic—excrement. It has been extended to include filth; generally, soil, dust, etc. and *obscenity* of any kind, especially language.

• *Dirty word*: an *obscene* word, also currently used for something that has become socially or politically unpopular or suspect, often through unmerited criticism and denigration or from being out of line with current trends.

• *Obscene*: from old Hebrew, *Ob*, meaning a wizard, sorceress.

All this denigration, yet there are remnants of stories throughout world culture that have survived various purges. These inform us that the obscene is not vulgar at all, but rather seems more like some fantastic nature creature that you dearly wish would visit you and be one of your best friends.

Some years back, when I began telling "dirty Goddess stories," women smiled and then laughed to hear about the exploits of women, both real and mythological, who had used sexuality, sensuality, in order to make a point, to lighten sadness, to cause laughter, and in that way to set something aright that had gone awry in the psyche. I was also taken by how women approached the threshold of laughter with regard to these matters. First they had to set aside all their training that said it wasn't ladylike to laugh such a laugh.

I saw how ladylikeness in the wrong situation actually throttled a woman rather than allowing her to breathe. To laugh you have to be able to exhale and take another breath in quick succession. We know from kinesiology, and various other body therapies such as Hakomi, that to take a breath causes one to feel one's emotions, that when we wish not to feel, we hold our breath instead.

In laughter, a woman breathes fully, and when she does, she may begin to feel unsanctioned feelings. And what could these feelings be? Well, they turn out not to be feelings so much as relief and remedies for feelings, often causing the release of stopped-up tears or the reclamation of forgotten memories, or the bursting of chains on the sensual personality.

It became clear to me that the importance of these old Goddesses of obscenity was demonstrated by their ability to loosen what was too tight, to lift gloom, to bring the body into a kind of humor that belongs not to the intellect but to the body itself, to keep these passages clear. It is the body that laughs at coyote stories, Uncle Trungpa[2] stories, Mae West lines, and so forth. The mischief and humor of the obscene Goddesses can cause a vital form of medicine to spread throughout the endocrine and neurological systems of the body.

The following three stories embody the obscene in the way we are using the word here, to mean a kind of sexual/sensual enchantment that causes good emotional feeling. Two are ancient, and one is modern. They are about the dirty Goddesses. I call them so for they have wandered underground for a long time. In the positive sense, they belong to the fertile earth, the mud, the muck of the psyche—the creative substance from which all art originates. In fact, the dirty Goddesses represent that aspect of Wild Woman that is both sexual and sacred.

Baubo: The Belly Goddess

There is a powerful saying: *Ella habla por en medio en las piernas*, "She speaks from between her legs." Little "between-the-legs" stories are found all over the world. One is the story of Baubo, a Goddess from ancient Greece, the so-called "Goddess of obscenity." She has older names, such as *Iambe*, and it appears the

Greeks borrowed her from far older cultures. There have been archetypal wild Goddesses of sacred sexuality and Life/Death/Life fertility since the beginning of memory.

There is only one popular reference to Baubo in writings existent from ancient times, giving the direct impression that her cult was destroyed, and buried under the stampede of various conquests. I have a strong sense that somewhere, perhaps under all those sylvan hills and forest lakes in Europe and the East, there are temples to her, complete with artifacts, and bone icons.[3]

So, it is not by accident that few have heard of Baubo, but remember, one shard of archetype can carry the image of the whole. And we have the shard, for we have a story in which Baubo appears. She is one of the most lovely and picaresque of all the highnesses who lived on Olympus. This is my *cantadora*, storytelling version based on the old wildish remnant of Baubo still glinting in post-matriarchal Greek mythos and the Homeric hymns.[4]

THE EARTH MOTHER, Demeter, had a beautiful daughter called Persephone who was playing out in the meadow one day. Persephone came upon one particularly lovely bloom, and reached out her fingertips to cup its lovely face. Suddenly the ground began to shake and a giant zigzag ripped across the land. Up from deep within the earth charged Hades, the God of the Underworld. He stood tall and mighty in a black chariot driven by four horses the color of ghost.

Hades seized Persephone into his chariot, her veils and sandals flying. Down, down, down into the earth he reined his horses. Persephone's screams grew more and more faint as the rift in the earth healed over as though nothing had ever happened.

The voice of the maiden crying out echoed through the stones of the mountains, bubbled up in a watery cry from underneath the sea. Demeter heard the stones cry out. She heard the watery crying. And then, over all the land came an eerie silence, and the smell of crushed flowers.

And tearing her wreath from her immortal hair, and unfurling down from each shoulder her dark veils, Demeter flew out over the land like a great bird, searching for, calling for her daughter.

That night an old crone at the edge of a cave remarked to her sisters that she had heard three cries that day; one, a youthful voice crying out in terror; and another calling plaintively; and a third, that of a mother weeping.

Persephone was nowhere to be found, and so began Demeter's crazed and months-long search for her beloved child. Demeter raged, she wept, she screamed, she asked after, searched every land formation underneath, inside, and atop, begged mercy, begged death, but no matter what, she could not find her heart-child.

So, she who had made everything grow in perpetuity, cursed all the fertile fields of the world, screaming in her grief, "Die! Die! Die!" Because of Demeter's curse, no child could be born, no wheat could rise for bread, no flowers for feasts, no boughs for the dead. Everything lay withered and sucked at parched earth or dry breasts.

Demeter herself no longer bathed. Her robes were mud drenched, her hair hung in dreadlocks. Even though the pain in her heart was staggering, she would not surrender. After many ask-ings, pleadings, and episodes, all leading to nothing, she finally slumped down at the side of a well in a village where she was unknown. And as she leaned her aching body against the cool stone of the well, along came a woman, or rather a sort of woman. And this woman danced up to Demeter wiggling her hips in a way suggesting sexual intercourse, and shaking her breasts in her little dance. And when Demeter saw her, she could not help but smile just a little.

The dancing female was very magical indeed, for she had no head whatsoever, and her nipples were her eyes and her vulva was her mouth. It was through this lovely mouth that she began to regale Demeter with some nice juicy jokes. Demeter began to smile, and then chuckled, and then gave a full belly laugh. And together the two women laughed, the little belly Goddess Baubo and the powerful Mother Earth Goddess, Demeter.

And it was just this laughing that drew Demeter out of her depression and gave her the energy to continue her search for her daughter, which, with the help of Baubo, and the crone Hekate, and the sun Helios, was ultimately successful. Persephone was restored to her mother. The world, the land, and the bellies of women thrived again.

~~~~~~

I have always loved this little Baubo more than any other Goddess in Greek mythology, perhaps better than any figure, period. She is no doubt drawn from the Neolithic belly Goddesses who are mysterious figures with no heads, and sometimes no feet and no arms. It is paltry to say they are "fertility figures," for they are far more than that. They are the talismans of women-talk—you know, the kind women would never, never, ever say in front of a man unless it was an unusual circumstance. That kind of talk.

These little figures represent sensibilities and expressions unique in all the world; the breasts, and what is felt within those sensitive creatures, the lips of the vulva, wherein a woman feels sensations that others might imagine but only she knows. And the belly laugh being one of the best medicines a woman can possess.

I have always thought the kaffeeklatsch was a remnant of ancient women's ritual of being together, a ritual, like the old one, of belly talk, women talking from the guts, telling the truth, laughing themselves silly, feeling enlivened, going home again, everything better.

Sometimes it is hard to get men to go away so women can be alone with each other. I just know that in ancient times women encouraged men to go away on "the fishing trip." This is a ruse used by women since time immemorial to make men leave for a while so a woman can either be by herself or be with other women. Women desire to live in a solely female atmosphere from time to time, whether in solitude by themselves or with others. This is a natural feminine cycle.

Male energy is nice. It is more than nice; it is sumptuous, it is grand. But sometimes it is like too much Godiva chocolates. We yearn for some clean cold rice for a few days and a clear hot broth to clear the palate. We must do this from time to time.

Additionally, the little belly Goddess Baubo raises the

interesting idea that a little obscenity can help to break a depression. And it is true that certain kinds of laughter, which come from all those stories women tell each other, those women stories that are off-color to the point of being completely tasteless . . . those stories stir libido. They rekindle the fire of a woman's interest in life again. The belly Goddess and the belly laugh are what we are after.

So in your self-healing trove, put small "dirt stories," Baubo kinds of stories. This diminutive form of story is powerful medicine. The funny, "dirty" story can not only lift depression but can cut the black heart right out of rage, leaving a happier woman than before. Try it, you'll see.

Now I cannot say a great deal about the next two aspects of the Baubo story, for they are meant to be discussed in small groups and among women only, but I can say this much: Baubo has another aspect; she sees through her nipples. It is a mystery to men, but when I suggest such to women, they nod their heads enthusiastically and say, "I know just what you mean!"

To see through the nipples is certainly a sensory attribute. The nipples are psychic organs, responsive to temperature, fear, anger, noise. They are a sensing organ as much as the eyes in the head.

And as for "speaking from the vulva," it is, symbolically, speaking from the *primae materia*, the most basic, most honest level of truth—the vital *os*. What else is there to say but that Baubo speaks from the mother lode, the deep mine, literally the depths. In the story of Demeter searching for her daughter, no one knows what words Baubo actually spoke to Demeter. But we can have some ideas.

Coyote Dick

I think the jokes that Baubo told to Demeter were women's jokes about those beautifully shaped transmitters and receivers: genitalia. If so, perhaps Baubo told Demeter a story like this one, which I heard some years back from an old trailer park manager down in Nogales. His name was Old Red and he claimed Native blood.

He was not wearing his teeth, and hadn't shaved in a couple of days. His nice old wife, Willowdean, had a pretty, but battered, face. Her nose, she told me, had once been broken in a bar fight. They owned three Cadillacs, none of which ran. She had a Chihuahua dog that she kept in a playpen in the kitchen. He was the kind of man who wore his hat while sitting on the toilet.

I was researching stories and had pulled my little Napanee trailer onto their grounds. "So do you know any stories about these parts?" I began, meaning the land and environs.

Old Red looked at his wife real sly with a rubbery smile and provoked her by sneering. "I'm gonna tell her about Coyote Dick."[5]

"Red, don't tell her that story. Red, don't you tell her."

"I'm gonna tell her about Coyote Dick anyway," asserted Old Red.

Willowdean put her head in her hands and spoke to the table, "Don't tell her that story Red, I mean it."

"I'm telling her right now, Willowdean."

Willowdean sat sideways in her chair, her hand across her eyes like she had just gone blind.

This is what Old Red told me. He said he heard this story "from a Navajo who heard it from a Mexican who heard it from a Hopi."

ONCE UPON A TIME there was Coyote Dick, and he was both the smartest and the dumbest creature you could ever hope to meet. He was always hungry for something, and always playing tricks on people to get what he wanted, and any other time he was always sleeping.

Well, one day while Coyote Dick was sleeping, his penis got really bored and decided to leave Coyote and have an adventure on its own. So the penis disattached itself from Coyote Dick and ran down the road. Actually, it hopped down the road, having just one leg and all.

So it hopped and it hopped, and it was having a good time and it hopped off the road and out into the woods, where—Oh no!—it hopped right into a grove of stinging nettles. "Ouch!" it cried. "Ow, ow, ow!" it screeched. "Help! Help!"

The sound of all this crying woke Coyote Dick, and when he reached down to start his heart with the accustomed crank, it was gone! Coyote Dick ran down the road holding himself between the legs, and finally came upon his penis in the worst trouble you can imagine. Gently, Coyote Dick lifted his adventurous penis out of the nettles, patted him and soothed him down, and put him back where he belonged.

Old Red laughed like a maniac, coughing fit, eyes bulging and all. "And that is the story of ol' Coyote Dick."

Willowdean admonished him, "You forgot to tell her the ending."

"What ending? I already told her the ending," grumped Old Red.

"You forgot to tell her the real ending of the story, you old tank of gas."

"Well, if you remember it so well, you tell her." The doorbell rang and he rose up from his creaky chair.

Willowdean looked at me straight and her eyes sparkled. "The end of the story is the moral." At that moment, Baubo took hold of Willowdean, for she began to giggle, then guffaw, and finally belly laugh so long, and with tears even, that it took her two minutes to say these last two sentences, what with repeating each word two or three times between gasps.

"The moral is that those nettles, even once Coyote Dick got out of them, made his cock itch like crazy forever after. And that's why men are always sliding up to women, and wanting to rub up against them with that 'I'm so itchy' look in their eyes. You know, that universal cock has been itching ever since that first time it ever ran away."

I don't know what it was about it that struck me, but we sat there in her kitchen, shrieking and pounding the table till we had practically lost all muscle control. Afterward, the sensation reminded me of just having eaten a big bite of good horseradish.

This truly is the kind of story I think Baubo told. Her repertoire includes anything that makes women laugh like that, unrestrained, not caring about showing your tonsils, letting your belly hang out, letting your breasts shake. There is something about a sexual laugh that is different from a laugh about more tame things. A "sexual" laugh seems to reach both far and deep into the psyche, shaking all manner of things loose, playing upon our bones, and making a delightful feeling course through the body. It is a form of wildish pleasure that belongs in every woman's psychic repertoire.

The sacred and the sensual/sexual live very near one another in the psyche, for they all are brought to attention through a sense of wonder, not from intellectualizing but through experiencing something through the physical pathways of the body, something that for the moment or forever, whether it is a kiss, a vision, a belly laugh, or whatever, changes us, shakes us out, takes us to a pinnacle, smooths out our lines, gives us a dance step, a whistle, a true burst of life.

In the sacred, the obscene, the sexual, there is always a wild laugh waiting, a short passage of silent laughter, or crone-nasty laughter, or the wheeze that is a laugh, or the laugh that is wild and animal, or the trill that is like a run on the musical scale. Laughter is a hidden side of women's sexuality; it is physical, elemental, passionate, vitalizing, and therefore arousing. It is a kind of sexuality that does not have a goal, as does genital arousal. It is a sexuality of joy, just for the moment, a true sensual love that flies free and lives and dies and lives again on its own energy. It is sacred because it is so healing. It is sensual for it awakens the body and the emotions. It is sexual because it is exciting and causes waves of pleasure. It is not one-dimensional, for laughter is something one shares with oneself as well as with many others. It is a woman's wildest sexuality.

Here is another peek at women's stories and the dirty Goddesses. This is a story I found as a child. It is amazing what children hear that adults think they do not hear.

A Trip to Rwanda

I was about twelve years old, and we were at Big Bass Lake up in Michigan. After cooking breakfast and lunch for forty people, all my nice and round female relatives, my mother and my aunts, were lying out in the sun on chaise lounges, sunning themselves, talking and joking. The men were "fishing"—which meant they were off having a good time cussing and telling their own kinds of jokes and stories. I was playing somewhere near the women.

Suddenly I heard piercing shrieks. Filled with alarm I raced to where the women were. But they were not crying out in pain. The women were laughing, and my one auntie kept saying over and over again when she could get her breath between shrieks, ". . . covered their faces . . . covered their faces!" And this mysterious sentence would send all of them off into fits of laughter once again.

They shrieked, screamed, gulped, and shrieked some more for a long, long time. On one of my aunts' laps lay a magazine. Much later, as all the women dozed in the sun, I slipped the magazine out from under her sleeping hand and lay under the chaise reading with big eyes. On the page was an anecdote from World War II. It went something like this:

~~~~~~~~~~~~~~~~~~~

GENERAL EISENHOWER WAS going to visit his troops in Rwanda. [It might have been Borneo. It might have been General Mac-Arthur. The names meant little to me then.] The governor wanted all the native women to stand by the side of the dirt road and cheer and wave to welcome Eisenhower as he drove by in his jeep. The only problem was that the native women never wore any clothes other than a necklace of beads and sometimes a little thong belt.

No, no, that would never do. So the governor called the headman of the tribe and told him the predicament. "No worry," said the head man. If the governor could provide several dozen skirts and blouses, he would see to it that the women dressed in them for this one-time special event. And these the governor and local missionaries managed to provide.

However, on the day of the great parade, and just minutes before Eisenhower was to drive down the long road in his jeep, it was discovered that while all the native women dutifully wore the skirts, they did not like the blouses, and had left them at home. So now all the women were lined up and down both sides of the road, skirted but bare-breasted, and with not another stitch on and no underwear at all.

Well the governor had apoplexy when he heard and he angrily summoned the headman, who assured him that the headwoman had conferred with him, and assured him that the women had agreed on a plan to cover their breasts when the general drove by. "Are you sure?" bellowed the governor.

"I am sure. Very, very sure," said the headman.

Well, there was no time left to argue and we can only guess at General Eisenhower's reaction as his jeep came chugging by and woman after bare-breasted woman gracefully lifted up the front of her full skirt and covered her face with it.

I lay under the chaise stifling my laughter. It was the silliest story I had ever heard. It was a wonderful story, a thrilling story. But intuitively, I also knew it was contraband, so I kept it to myself for years and years. And sometimes in the midst of hard times, during tense times, and even before taking tests in college, I would think of the women from Rwanda covering their faces with their skirts, and no doubt laughing into them. And I would laugh and feel centered, strong, and down-to-earth.

This no doubt is the other gift of women's jokings and shared laughter. It all becomes a medicine for the tough times, a strengthener for later. It is good, clean, dirty fun. Can we imagine the sexual and the irreverent as sacred? Yes, especially when they are medicinal, leading to a wholeness and mending of heart. Jung noted that if someone came to his office complaining of a sexual issue, the real issue was more often a problem of spirit and soul. When a person told of a spiritual problem, often it was really a problem about the sexual nature.

In that sense, sexuality can be fashioned as a medicine for the spirit and is therefore sacred. When sexual laughter is *un remedio*, medicine, it is sacred laughter. And whatever causes healing laughter is sacred as well. When laughter helps without doing harm, when laughter lightens, realigns, reorders, reasserts power and strength, this is the laughter that causes health. When the laughter makes people glad they are alive, happy to be here, more conscious of love, heightened with eros, when it lifts their sadness and severs them from anger, that is sacred. When they are made bigger, made better, more generous, more sensitive, that is sacred.

In the Wild Woman archetype, there is much room for the nature of the dirty Goddesses. In the wild nature, the sacred and the irreverent, the sacred and the sexual, are not separate from one another, but live together like, I suspect, a group of old, old women just waiting down the road for us to drop by. They are there in your psyche, waiting for you to show up, trying out their stories on one another, and laughing like dogs.

CHAPTER 12

Marking Territory:
The Boundaries of Rage
and Forgiveness

The Crescent Moon Bear

Under the tutelage of Wild Woman we reclaim the ancient, the intuitive, and the passionate. When our lives reflect hers, we act cohesively. We carry through, or learn to if we don't already know how. We take the steps to make our ideas manifest in the world. We regain focus when we lose it, attend to personal rhythms, draw closer to friends and mates who are in accord with wildish and integral rhythms. We choose relationships that nurture our creative and instinctive lives. We reach out to nurture others. And we are willing to teach receptive mates about wildish rhythms if need be.

But there is another aspect to mastery, and that is dealing with what can only be called women's rage. The release of that rage is required. Once women remember the origins of their rage, they feel they may never stop grinding their teeth. Ironically, we also feel very anxious to disperse our rage, for it feels distressing and noxious. We wish to hurry up and do away with it.

But repressing it will not work. It is like trying to put fire into a burlap bag. Neither is it good to scald ourselves or someone else with it. So there we are holding a powerful emotion that we feel came upon us unbidden. It is a little like toxic waste; there it is, no one wants it, but there are few disposal areas for it. One has to travel far in order to find a burial ground. Here is a literary version of a brief Japanese tale that I've detailed over the years. I call it

375

"*Tsukina Waguma*, The Crescent Moon Bear." I believe it can help us see our way through this matter. The core of the story was given to me as "The Bear," by Sgt. I. Sagara, WWII veteran and patient at Hines Veteran's Assistance Hospital in Illinois many years ago.

~~~~~~

THERE ONCE WAS a young woman who lived in a fragrant pine forest. Her husband was away fighting a war for many years. When finally he was released from duty, he trudged home in a most foul mood. He refused to enter the house, for he had become used to sleeping on stones. He kept to himself and stayed in the forest day and night.

His young wife was so excited when she learned her husband was coming home at last. She cooked and shopped and shopped and cooked and made dishes and dishes and bowls and bowls of tasty white soybean curd and three kinds of fish, and three kinds of seaweed, and rice sprinkled with red pepper, and nice cold prawns, big and orange.

Smiling shyly, she carried the food to the woods and knelt beside her war-weary husband and offered to him the beautiful food she had prepared. But he sprang to his feet and kicked the trays over so that the bean curd spilled, the fish jumped into the air, the seaweed and rice spilled into the dirt, and the big orange prawns went rolling down the path.

"Leave me alone!" he roared, and turned his back on her. He became so enraged she was frightened of him. Time after time this occurred until finally, in desperation, the young wife found her way to the cave of the healer who lived outside the village.

"My husband has been badly injured in the war," the wife said. "He rages continuously and eats nothing. He wishes to stay outside and will not live with me as before. Can you give me a potion that will make him loving and gentle once again?"

The healer assured her, "This I can do for you, but I need a special ingredient. Unfortunately, I am all out of hair from the crescent moon bear. So, you must climb the mountain, find the black bear, and bring me back a single hair from the crescent moon at its throat. Then I can give you what you need, and life will be good again."

Some women would have felt daunted by this task. Some women would have thought the entire effort impossible. But not she, for she was a woman who loved. "Oh! I am so grateful," she said. "It is so good to know that something can be done."

So she readied for her journey, and the next morning she went out to the mountain. And she sang out *"Arigato zaishö,"* which is a way of greeting the mountain and saying, "Thank you for letting me climb upon your body."

She climbed into the foothills where there were boulders like big loaves of bread. She ascended up to a plateau covered with forest. The trees had long draping boughs and leaves that looked like stars.

"Arigato zaishö," she sang out. This was a way of thanking the trees for lifting their hair so she could pass underneath. And so she found her way through the forest and began to climb again.

It was harder now. The mountain had thorny flowers that seized the hem of her kimono, and rocks that scraped her tiny hands. Strange dark birds flew out at her in the dusk and frightened her. She knew they were *muen-botoke*, spirits of the dead who had no relatives, and she sang out prayers for them: "I will be your relative. I will lay you to rest."

Still she climbed, for she was a woman who loved. She climbed till she saw snow on the mountain peak. Soon her feet were wet and cold, and still she climbed higher, for she was a woman who loved. A storm began, and the snow blew straight into her eyes and deep into her ears. Blinded, still she climbed higher. And when the snow stopped, the woman sang out *"Arigato zaishö,"* to thank the winds for ceasing to blind her.

She took shelter in a shallow cave and could barely pull all of herself into it. Though she had a full pack of food, she did not eat, but covered herself in leaves and slept. In the morning, the air was calm and little green plants even showed through the snow here and there. "Ah," she thought, "now, for the crescent moon bear."

She searched all day and near twilight found thick cords of scat and needed look no farther, for a gigantic black bear lumbered across the snowfall, leaving behind deep pad and claw marks. The crescent moon bear roared fiercely and entered its den. She reached into her bundle and placed the food she had brought in a bowl. She set the bowl outside the den and ran back to her shelter to hide. The bear smelled the food and came lurching from its den, roaring so loudly it shook loose little stones. The bear circled around the food from a distance, sampled the wind many times, then ate the food up in one gulp. The great bear reared up, snuffled the air again, and then disappeared into its den.

The next evening the woman did the same, setting out the food, but this time instead of returning to her shelter she retreated only halfway. The bear smelled the food, heaved itself out of its den, roared to shake the stars from the skies, circled, tested the air very cautiously, but finally gobbled up the food and crawled back into its den. This continued for many nights until one dark blue night the woman felt brave enough to wait even closer to the bear's den.

She put the food in the bowl outside the den and stood right by the opening. When the bear smelled the food and lumbered out, it saw not only the usual food but also a pair of small human feet as well. The bear turned its head sideways and roared so loudly it made the bones in the woman's body hum.

The woman trembled, but stood her ground. The bear hauled itself onto its back legs, smacked its jaws, and roared so that the woman could see right up into the red-and-brown roof of its mouth. But she did not run away. The bear roared even more and put out its arms as though to seize her, its ten claws hanging like ten long knives over her scalp. The woman shook like a leaf in high wind, but stayed right where she was.

"Oh, please, dear bear," she pleaded, "please, dear bear, I've come all this way because I need a cure for my husband." The bear brought its front paws to earth in a spray of snow and peered into the woman's frightened face. For a moment, the woman felt she could see entire mountain ranges, valleys, rivers, and villages reflected in the bear's old, old eyes. A deep peace settled over her, and her trembling ceased.

"Please, dear bear, I've been feeding you all these past nights. Could I please have one of the hairs from the crescent moon on your throat?" The bear paused, This little woman would be easy food. Yet suddenly he was filled with pity for her. "It is true," said the crescent moon bear, "you've been good to me. You may have one of my hairs. But take it quickly, then leave here and go back to your own."

The bear raised its great snout so that the white crescent on its throat showed, and the woman could see the strong pulse of the bear's heart there. The woman put one hand on the bear's neck, and with her other took hold of a single glossy white hair. Quickly, she pulled it. The bear reared back and cried out as though wounded. And this pain then settled into annoyed huffs.

"Oh, thank you, crescent moon bear, thank you so much." The woman bowed and bowed. But the bear growled and lumbered forward a step. It roared at the woman in words she could not understand and yet words she had somehow known all her life. She turned and fled down the mountain as fast as she could. She ran under the trees with leaves shaped like stars. And all the way through she cried *"Arigato zaishö,"* to thank the trees for lifting their boughs so she could pass. She stumbled over the boulders that looked like big loaves of bread, crying *"Arigato zaishö,"* to thank the mountain for letting her climb upon its body.

Though her clothes were ragged, her hair askew, her face soiled, she ran down the stone stairs that led to the village, down the dirt road and right through the town to its other side, and into the hovel where the old healer sat tending the fire.

"Look, look! I have it, I found it, I claimed it, a hair of the crescent moon bear!" cried the young woman.

"Ah good," said the healer with a smile. She peered closely at the woman and took the pure white hair and held it out toward the light. She weighed the long hair in one old hand, measured it with one finger, and exclaimed, "Ah. Yes! This is an authentic hair from the crescent moon bear." Then suddenly she turned and threw the hair deep into the fire, where it popped and crackled and was consumed in a bright orange flame.

"No!" cried the young wife. "What have you done!?"

"Be calm. It is good. All is well," said the healer. "Remember each step you took to climb the mountain? Remember each step you took to capture the trust of the crescent moon bear? Remember what you saw, what you heard, and what you felt?"

"Yes," said the woman, "I remember very well."

The old healer smiled at her gently and said, "Please now, my daughter, go home with your new understandings and proceed in the same ways with your husband."

~~~~~~~~~~~~~~~~~~~~~~~~~~~~~~

Rage as Teacher

The central motif of this story, the quest for a magical item, is found throughout the world. In some cases it is a woman who makes the journey, in others a man. The magical thing being sought is an eyelash, a nose hair, a tooth, a ring, a feather, or some other physical element. Variations on the motif of an animal part or pelt as treasure are found in Korea, Germany, and the Urals. In China, the donor is often a tiger. In Japan, the animal in the story is sometimes a bear, sometimes a fox. In Russia, the object sought is the beard of a bear. In one tale from my family, the hair sought is a whisker from the chin of the Baba Yaga herself.

"The Crescent Moon Bear" story belongs to a category of tales I call aperture stories. Aperture stories allow us to glimpse their hidden healing structures and deeper meanings, rather than just their overt contents. The content of this story shows us that patience will help anger, but the larger transmission is about what a woman must do in order to restore order in the psyche, thereby healing the angry self.

In aperture stories, things are implied rather than stated. In this tale, the understructure reveals an entire model for dealing with, and healing from rage: by seeking a wise and calm healing force (going to the healer), accepting the challenge of going into psychic territory one has never approached before (climbing the mountain), recognizing the illusions (dealing with climbing the boulders, running under the trees), putting one's old and obsessive thoughts and feelings to rest (meeting the *muen-botoke*, restless spirits without relatives to bury them), soliciting the great compassionate Self (patiently feeding the bear and the bear returning her kindness), understanding the roaring side of the compassionate psyche (recognizing that the bear, the compassionate Self, is not tame).

The story demonstrates the importance of bringing this psychological knowledge down to earth in our real lives (coming down off the mountain and back into the village), learning that healing is in the process of questing and practice, not in a single idea (destruction of the hair). The heart of the story is, "Apply all these things to one's rage, and all will be well" (advice from the healer to go home and apply these principles).

This story is one of a group of stories that begin with the protagonist appealing to or soliciting an injured, lonely creature of one sort or another. If we look at the story as if all components were part of a single woman's psyche, we can see that the psyche has a very angry and tortured sector as represented by the image of the husband home from the war. The loving spirit of the psyche, the wife, takes it upon herself to find a cure for this anger and rage so she and her love can live in peace and with love once again. This is a worthy endeavor for all women, for it treats rage and often allows us to find our way to forgiveness.

The tale shows us that patience is a good thing to apply to fresh or old rage, as is embarking on a quest for its healing. Though each person's healing and insight will be different, the story proposes some interesting ideas about how to go about the process.

A great philosopher-prince named Shotoku Taishi lived in Japan at the turn of the sixth century. He taught, among other things, that one must do psychic work in both the inner and outer worlds. But even more so, he taught tolerance for every human, every creature, *and every emotion.* The balanced valuing of emotion is certainly an act of self-respect.

Even raw and messy emotions can be understood as a form of light, crackling and bursting with energy. We can use the light of rage in a positive way, in order to see into places we cannot usually see. A negative use of rage concentrates destructively in one tiny spot until, like acid creating an ulcer, it burns a black hole right through all the delicate layers of the psyche.

But there is another way. All emotion, even rage, carries knowledge, insight, what some call enlightenment. Our rage can, for a time, become teacher . . . a thing not to be rid of so fast, but rather something to climb the mountain for, something to personify via various images in order to learn from, deal with internally, then shape into something useful in the world as a result, or else let it go back down to dust. In a cohesive life, rage is not a stand-alone item. It is a substance waiting for our transformative efforts. The cycle of rage is like any other cycle; it rises, falls, dies, and is released as new energy. Attention to the matter of rage begins the process of transformation.

Allowing oneself to be taught by one's rage, thereby transforming it, disperses it. One's energy returns to use in other areas, especially the area of creativity. Although some people claim they can create out of their chronic rage, the problem is that rage confines access to the collective unconscious—that infinite reservoir of imaginal images and thoughts—so that a person creating out of rage tends to create the same thing over and over again, with nothing new coming through. Untransformed rage can become a constant mantra about how oppressed, hurt, and tortured we were.

One of my friends and fellow performance artists, who claims to have been enraged forever, refuses all help in dealing with it. When she writes scripts about war, she writes about how bad people are; when she writes scripts about the culture, similar bad characters arise. When she writes scripts about love, the same bad people with the identical bad intentions show up. Rage corrodes our trust that anything good can occur. Something has happened to hope. And behind the loss of hope is usually anger; behind anger, pain; behind pain, usually torture of one sort or another, sometimes recent, but more often from long ago.

In physical post-trauma work, we know that the sooner injury is dealt with, the less its effects spread or worsen. Also the more quickly a trauma is contained and dealt with, the faster the recovery time. This is true for psychological trauma as well. What condition would we be in if we'd broken a leg as a child, and thirty years later it still had not been properly set?

The original trauma would cause tremendous disruption of other systems and rhythms in the body, such as the immune and skeletal systems, locomotion patterns, and so on. That is precisely the situation with old psychological trauma. For many it was not attended to at the time, whether out of ignorance or neglect. Now, one is home from the war, so to speak, but it feels as though one is still at war in the mind and body. Yet by harboring rage—that is, the fallout of trauma—instead of questing for solutions to it, what caused it, what we can do with it, we seal ourselves into a room full of it for the rest of our lives. That is no way to live, intermittently or otherwise. There is a life beyond thoughtless rage. As we see in the tale, it takes a conscious practice to contain and heal such. But we can do it. It truly takes only climbing through one step at a time.

Bringing in the Healer: Climbing the Mountain

So rather than trying to "behave" and not feel our rage or rather than using it to burn down every living thing in a hundred-mile radius, it is better to first ask rage to take a seat with us, have some tea, talk a while so we can find out what summoned this visitor. At first rage acts like the angry husband in the story. It doesn't want to talk, it doesn't want to eat, just wants to sit there and stare, or rail, or be left alone. It is at this critical point that we call the healer, our wisest self, our best resources for seeing beyond ego irritation and aggravation. The healer is always the "far-seer." She is the one who can tell us what good can come from exploring this emotive surge.

Healers in fairy tales generally represent a calm and unperturbed aspect of the psyche. Even though the world may be falling to pieces outwardly, the inner healer is unswayed by it all and maintains the calm to figure out the best way to proceed. Every woman's psyche contains this "fixer." It is part of the wild and natural psyche and we are born with it. If we have lost track of its whereabouts, we can call it again by looking calmly at the situation causing us rage, projecting ourselves into the future, and from that vantage point deciding what would make us feel proud of our past behavior, and then acting that way.

The outrage or irritation we naturally feel about various aspects of life and culture is exacerbated when there were repeated incidents of disrespect, harrowing, neglect, or high ambiguity[1] in childhood. A person thusly injured is sensitized to further injury and utilizes all defenses to avoid them.[2] Gross losses of power, meaning loss of certainty that we are worthy of care, respect, and concern, cause extreme sorrow and angry childhood vows to, once grown, never allow oneself to be harmed like that ever again.

Additionally, if a woman was raised to have fewer positive expectations than others in the family, with harsh restraints on her freedoms, deportment, language, and so forth, her normal anger is likely to escalate over issues, tones of voice, gestures, words, and other sensory triggers that remind her of the original events.[3] Sometimes educated guesses can be made about the wounds of childhood by closely inspecting what matters adults irrationally lose their tempers over.[4]

We want to use anger as a creative force. We want to use it to change, develop, and protect. So, whether a woman is dealing with the aggravation of the moment with an offspring, or some sort of a searing lengthy burn, the perspective of the healer is the same: When there is calm, there can be learning, there can be creative solutions, but where there is firestorm, inside or out, it burns hot and leaves nothing but ash. We want to be able to look back on our actions with honor. We want something useful to show for feeling angry.

While it is true that we sometimes need to vent our rage before we can progress to a learning calm, this needs be done in containment of some sort. Otherwise it is like throwing a lighted match onto gasoline. The healer says yes, this rage can be changed, but I need something from another world, something from the instinctual world, the world where animals still talk and the spirits live—something from the human imagination.

In Buddhism there is a questing action called *nyübu*, which means to go into the mountains in order to understand oneself and to remake one's connections to the Great. It is a very old ritual related to the cycles of preparing the earth, sowing, and harvesting. While it might be good to go into the real mountains if possible, there are also mountains in the underworld, in one's own unconscious, and luckily, we all carry the entrance to the underworld right in our own psyches, so we can go into the mountains for renewal with dispatch.

In mythos, a mountain is sometimes understood as a symbol describing the levels of mastery one must attain before one can ascend to the next level. The lowest part of the mountain, the foothills, often represents the urge toward consciousness. All that occurs in the foothills is thought of in terms of maturing consciousness. The middle part of the mountain is often thought of as the steeping part of the process, the part that tests the knowledge learned at lower levels. The higher mountain represents intensified learning; the air is thin there, it takes endurance and determination to stay at the tasks. The peak of the mountain represents confrontation with the ultimate wisdom, such as that in mythos wherein the old woman lives atop the mountain, or as in this story, the wise old bruin.

So, it is good to take to the mountain when we don't know what else to do. When we are drawn to quests we know little about, this makes life and develops soul. In climbing the unknown mountain we gain true knowledge of the instinctive psyche and the creative acts of which it is capable—that is our goal. Learning occurs differently for each person. But the instinctual viewpoint that emanates from the wild unconscious, and that is cyclical, begins to be the only one that makes sense of and gives meaning to life, our lives. It unerringly informs us about what to do next. Where can we find this process that will free us? On the mountain.

On the mountain we find additional clues about how to transform the hurt, negativism, and grudge-holding aspects of rage, all usually felt and often warranted initially. One is the phrase *"Arigato zaishö,"* which the woman sings to thank the trees and the mountains for allowing her to pass. Figuratively translated, the phrase means "Thank you, Illusion." In Japanese, *zaishö* means a clear way of looking at matters that interfere with deeper understandings of ourselves and the world.

An illusion occurs when something creates an image that is not real, such as heat waves on a road that make the road seem wavy. That there are heat waves is accurate, but the road is not really wavy. That is the illusion. The first piece of information is accurate, but the second piece, the conclusion, is not.

In the story the mountain allows the woman passage and the trees lift their limbs to let her pass. This symbolizes a lifting of illusions that allows the woman to proceed on her quest. In Buddhism there are said to be seven veils of illusion. As each is discarded a person is said to understand another aspect of the true nature of life and the self. To lift the veils makes one strong enough to tolerate what life is about; and to see into the patterns of events, people, and things; and eventually to learn not to take the first impression so deadly seriously, but to look behind and beyond.

In Buddhism, the lifting of the veils is necessary for enlightenment. The woman in this tale is on a journey to bring light into the darkness of rage. To do this she must understand the many layers of reality there on the mountain. We have so many illusions about life. "She is beautiful, therefore she is desirable" can be an illusion. "I am good, therefore I will be accepted" may also be an illusion. When we look for our truth, we are also looking to dispel our illusions. When we are able to see through these illusions, which in Buddhism would be called "barriers to enlightenment," we are able to discover the hidden side of rage.

These are some common illusions about rage. "If I lose my rage, I will be changed; I will become weaker." (The first premise is correct, but the conclusion is inaccurate.) "I learned my rage from my father [mother, grandmother, etc.] and I am doomed to feel this way all my life." (First statement, accurate; conclusion, inaccurate.) These illusions are challenged by questing, by asking, studying, peering under the trees, and by climbing the body of the mountain. We lose our illusions when we take the risk to meet the aspect of our nature that is truly wild; a mentor of life, rage, patience, suspicion, wariness, secretiveness, remoteness, and resourcefulness . . . the crescent moon bear.

While the woman is on the mountain, birds fly out at her. They are *muen-botoke*, spirits of dead people who have no family to feed them, comfort them, lay them to rest. When she prays for them, she becomes their family, she cares for them and comforts them. This is a useful way to understand the orphaned dead of the psyche. These are the creative thoughts and words and ideas in a woman's life that have suffered premature death, and that deeply contribute to her rage. In a way, one could say rage is the result of ghosts not laid properly to rest. There are suggestions for how to deal with the *muen-botoke* of a woman's psyche at the end of this chapter under *Descansos*.

As in the story, it is a worthy task to propitiate the wise bear, the instinctive psyche, and to keep offering it spiritual food, whether that be church, prayer, archetypal psychology, dreamlife, art, rock climbing, canoeing, travel, or whatever else. To come close to the mystery of the bear, one gives it food. It is quite a journey, this fixing of rage: stripping down illusions, taking rage as teacher, asking the help of the instinctual psyche, laying the dead past to rest.

The Spirit Bear

What does the symbol of bear, as opposed to fox, or badger, or quetzal, teach us about dealing with the angry self? To the ancients, bear symbolized resurrection. The creature goes to sleep for a long time, its heartbeat decreases to almost nothing. The male often impregnates the female right before hibernation, but miraculously, the egg and sperm do not unite right away. They float separately in her uterine broth until much later. Near the end of hibernation, the egg and sperm unite and cell division begins, so that the cubs will be born in the spring when the mother is awakening, just in time to care for and teach her new offspring. Not only by reason of awakening from hibernation as though from death, but much more so because the she-bear awakens with new young, this creature is a profound metaphor for our lives, for return and increase coming from something that seemed deadened.

The bear is associated with many huntress Goddesses: Artemis and Diana in Greece and Rome, and *Muerte* and *Hecoteptl*, mud women deities handed down through the Latina cultures. These Goddesses bestowed upon women the power of tracking, knowing, "digging out" the psychic aspects of all things. To the Japanese the bear is a symbol of loyalty, wisdom, and strength. In northern Japan where the Ainu tribe lives, the bear is one who can talk to God directly and bring messages back for humans. The crescent moon bear is considered a sacred being, one who was given the white mark on his throat by the Buddhist Goddess Kwan-Yin, whose emblem is a crescent moon. Kwan-Yin is the Goddess of Deep Compassion and the bear is her emissary.[5]

In the psyche, the bear can be understood as the ability to regulate one's life, especially one's feeling life. Bearish power is the ability to move in cycles, be fully alert, or quiet down into a hibernative sleep that renews one's energy for the next cycle. The bear image teaches that it is possible to maintain a kind of pressure gauge for one's emotional life, and most especially that one can be fierce and generous at the same time. One can be reticent and valuable. One can protect one's territory, make one's boundaries clear, shake the sky if need be, yet be available, accessible, engendering all at the same time.

The hair from the throat of the bear is a talisman, a way to remember what one has learned. As we see, it is invaluable.

The Transformative Fire and Right Action

The bear shows great compassion toward the woman, allowing her to pluck one of his hairs. She hurries back down the mountain, practicing all the gestures, songs, and praises that spontaneously rose out of her as she climbed the mountain. She comes running to the healer, so anxious. She might have said, "Look, I did it, I did what you told me. I endured. I triumphed." The old healer, who is also kind, takes a moment, lets the woman savor her accomplishment, and then throws the hard-won hair into the fire.

The woman is stunned. What has this crazy healer done? "Go home," says the healer. "Practice what you have learned." In Zen, the moment the hair is thrown into the fire and the healer speaks her simple words, *that* is the moment of true enlightenment. Notice that enlightenment does not occur on the mountain. It occurs when, by burning the hair of the crescent moon bear, the projection of magical cure is dissolved. We all face this issue, for we all hope that if we work hard and have a high holy quest, we will come up with a something, a substance, a material something or other that will—flash!—make everything orderly forever.

But that is not the way it works. It works exactly the way it is rendered in the story. We can have all the knowledge in the universe, and it comes down to one thing: practice. It comes down to going home and step-by-step implementing what we know. As often as necessary, and for as long as possible, or forever, whichever comes first. It is very reassuring to know that when one is in a burgeoning rage one knows precisely and with the skill of a craftswoman what to do about it: wait it out, release illusions, take it for a climb on the mountain, speak with it, respect it as a teacher.

We are given many markers in this story, many ideas about coming to balance: making patience, giving the enraged one kindness and time to get over his rage through introspection and questing. There is an old saying:

Before Zen, mountains were mountains and trees were trees.
During Zen, mountains were thrones of the spirits
    and trees were the voices of wisdom.
After Zen, mountains were mountains and trees were trees.

While the woman was on the mountain, learning, everything was magic. Now that she is off the mountain, the so-called magical hair has been burned in the fire that destroys illusion, and now it is time for "after Zen." Life is supposed to become mundane again. Yet she has the bounty of her experience on the mountain. She has knowing. The energy that was bound up in rage can be used for other things.

Now a woman who has come to terms with rage returns to mundane life with new knowing, a new sense that she can more artfully live her life. Yet one day in the future, a something—a look, a word, a tone of voice, a feeling of being patronized, unappreciated, or manipulated against one's will, one of these—will crop up again. Then her residue of pain will catch fire.[6]

Rage left over from old injuries can be compared to the trauma of a shrapnel wound. One can pick out almost all the pieces of shattered metal from the missile, but the tiniest shards remain. One would think that if most are out, that would be that. Not so. On some occasions, those tiniest shards twist and turn within and cause an ache that feels like the original wounding (rage rising up) all over again.

But it is not the original and vast rage that causes this welling up, it is the very small particles of it, the irritants still left in the psyche that can never be fully excised. These cause a pain that is almost as intense as that of the original injury. Then a person tightens up, fearing the full blow of the pain, in effect causing more pain. They are involved in drastic maneuvers on three fronts: one in trying to contain the outside event, one in attempting to contain the pain broadcasting from the old injury inside, and one trying to secure safety of position by running, head down in a psychological crouch.

It is too much to ask a single individual to take on the equivalent of a gang of three and try to KO all of them at one time. That is why it is imperative to stop in the midst of it all, withdraw, and take solitude. It is too much to try to fight and handle feeling gutshot at the same time. A woman who has climbed the mountain withdraws, deals with the older event first, then the more recent event, decides her position, shakes out her ruff, puts up her ears, and goes back out to act with dignity.

None of us can entirely escape our history. We can certainly put it in the background, but it is there nevertheless. However, if you will do these things for yourself, you will bridge the rage and eventually everything will calm down and be fine. Not perfect, but fine. You'll be able to move ahead. The time of the shrapnel rage will be over. You'll handle it better and better each time because you'll know when it is time to call in the healer again, to climb the mountain, to release yourself from the illusions that the present is an exact and calculated replay of the past. A woman remembers that she can be both fierce and generous at the same time. Rage is not like a kidney stone—if you wait long enough, it will pass. No, no. You must take right action. Then it will pass, and more creation will come to your life.

Righteous Rage

To turn the other cheek, that is, to remain silent in the face of injustice or mistreatment, has to be weighed very carefully. It is one thing to use passive resistance as a political tool as Gandhi taught masses of people to do, but it is quite another matter when women are encouraged or forced to be silent in order to survive an impossible situation of corrupt or unjust power in the family, community, or world. Then women are amputated from the wild nature and their silence is not serenity but an enormous defense against being harmed. It is a mistake for others to think that just because a woman is silent, it always means she approves of life as is.

There are times when it becomes imperative to release a rage that shakes the skies. There is a time—even though these times are very rare, there is definitely a time—to let loose all the fire-power one has. It has to be in response to a serious offense; the offense has to be big and against the soul or spirit. All other reasonable avenues for change have to be attempted first. If these fail, then we have to choose the right time. There is definitely a right time for full-bore rage. When women pay attention to the instinctual self, like the man in the following tale, they know when it is time. Intuitively, they know and they act. And it is right. Right as rain.

This story is from the Mideast. In Asia, versions of it are told by Sufis, Buddhists, and Hindus.[7] It belongs to the category of story that treats of performing the forbidden or unsanctioned act in order to redeem life.

~~~~~~~~~~~~~~~~~~~~

The Withered Trees

THERE WAS A SOUL whose very bad temper had cost him more wasted time and loss of good friends than any other element in his life. He approached an old wise man in rags and asked, "How can I ever bring this demon of rage under control?" The old man instructed the younger man to post himself at a parched oasis far off in the desert and to sit there among all the withered trees and to draw up the brackish water for any traveler who might venture there.

And the man, trying to overcome his rage, rode out to the desert to the place of the withered trees. For months, garbed in robes and burnoose against the flying sand, he drew the sour water and gave it to all who approached. Years passed and he suffered no more fits of temper.

One day a dark rider came to the dead oasis, and gave a haughty glance down at the man who offered him water from a bowl. The rider scoffed at the clouded water, refused it, and began to ride on.

The man offering water was immediately enraged, so much so he was blinded by it, and seizing the rider down from his camel, killed him on the spot. Oh la! He was immediately aggrieved that he had been consumed by such rage. And look what it had come to.

Suddenly, up rode another rider at great speed. The rider looked down upon the visage of the dead man and exclaimed, "Thank Allah, you have killed the man who was on his way to murder the king!" And at that moment, the cloudy water of the oasis turned clear and sweet and the withered trees of the oasis blushed green and burst into joyous bloom.

We understand this tale symbolically. It is not a tale about killing people. It is a teaching about not unleashing anger indiscriminately, but at the right time. The tale begins when the man learns to give out water, life, even under drought conditions. To give out life is an innate impulse in most women. They are very good at it most of the time. However, there is also a time for the gust from the gut, a time for righteous anger, rightful rage.[8]

Many women are sensitive the way sand is sensitive to the wave, the way trees are sensitive to the quality of the air, the way a wolf can hear another creature step into her territory from over a mile away. The splendid gift of women so attuned is to see, hear, sense, receive, and transmit images and ideas and feelings with lightning speed. Most women can feel the slightest change in someone else's temperament, can read faces and bodies—this being called intuition—and often from a plethora of tiny clues that coalesce to give her information, she knows what is on their minds. In order to use these wild gifts, women remain open to all things. But it is this very openness that leaves their boundaries vulnerable, thereby exposing them to injuries of spirit.

Like the man in the "Withered Trees" story, a woman may face the same issue to greater or lesser degrees. She may carry a form of scattershot rage that compels her to pick, pick, pick, or use coldness like an anesthesia, or give out sweet words while meaning to punish or demean. She may force her own will on those who are dependent on her or she may threaten them with severance of relationship or affection. She may withhold praise, or even the giving of credit where credit is due, and in general act quite instinct-injured. It is a given that a person who treats others in this manner is under intensive attack in her own psyche by a demon who does exactly the same to her.

Many a woman so afflicted decides to embark on a clean-up campaign, and resolves not to be petty anymore, to be "nicer," to be more giving. This is worthy, and often a relief to those around her, as long as she does not become over-identified with being a giving person like the man in the story. He is out in the oasis, and by serving others, he begins to feel better and better. He becomes identified with the evenness yet flatness of his life.

So too, a woman who avoids all confrontation begins to feel better. But it is temporary. This is not the learning we are after. The learning we are after is to know when to allow right anger and when not. The tale is not about striving for gentle sainthood. It is about knowing when to act in an integral and wild manner. Most of the time wolves avoid confrontation, but when they must enforce territory, when something or someone constantly hounds them, or corners them, they explode in their own powerful way. This happens rarely, but the ability to express this anger is within their repertoire and it should be within ours too.

There has been much speculation that an angry woman is awesome in her power to cause fear and trembling in those around her. But that is far too much projection of the viewer's personal angst for any woman to justly carry. In her instinctual psyche, a woman has the power, when provoked, to be angry in a mindful way—and that *is* powerful. Anger is one of her innate ways to begin to reach out to create and preserve the balances that she holds dear, all that she truly loves. It is both her right, and at certain times and in certain circumstances, a moral duty.

For women, this means there is a time to reveal your incisors, your powerful ability to defend territory, to say "This far and no farther, the buck stops here, and hold on to your hat, I've got something to say, this is definitely going to change."

Like the man in the beginning of "The Withered Trees," and like the warrior in "The Crescent Moon Bear," many women often have within them a tired-out, battle-fatigued soldier who just doesn't want to hear it anymore, doesn't want to talk about it, doesn't want to deal with it. A parched oasis in the psyche rises up because of this. This is, without or within, always an area of great silence, just waiting for, just begging for a roaring to take place, a breaking, shattering, shaking something that will create life again.

The man in the story is initially taken aback by his deed of killing the rider. Yet, when he understands that, in that instance, "first thought, right thought" applied, he is released from the too-simple rule of "never be angry." As in "The Crescent Moon Bear," enlightenment does not occur during the deed itself, it occurs once illusion is destroyed, and one gains insight into the underlying meaning.

Descansos

So, we have seen that we wish to make rage into a fire that cooks things rather than into a fire of conflagration. We have seen that the work on rage cannot be completed without the ritual of forgiveness. We have spoken about women's rage often deriving from the situation in her family of origin, from the surrounding culture, and sometimes from adult trauma. But regardless of the source of the rage, something has to happen to recognize it, bless it, contain it, and release it.

Women who are tortured often develop a dazzling kind of perception that has uncanny depth and breadth. Although I would never wish anyone tortured in order to learn the secret ins and outs of the unconscious, the fact is, having lived through a gross repression causes gifts to arise that compensate and protect.

In that respect a woman who has lived a torturous life and delved deeply into it definitely has inestimable depth. Though she came to it through pain, if she has done the hard work of clinging to consciousness, she will have a deep and thriving soul-life and a fierce belief in herself regardless of occasional ego-waverings.

There is a time in our lives, usually in mid-life, when a woman has to make a decision—possibly the most important psychic decision of her future life—and that is, whether to be bitter or not. Women often come to this in their late thirties or early forties. They are at the point where they are full up to their ears with everything and they've "had it" and "the last straw has broken the camel's back" and they're "pissed off and pooped out." Their dreams of their twenties may be lying in a crumple. There may be broken hearts, broken marriages, broken promises.

A body who has lived a long time accumulates debris. It cannot be avoided. But if a woman will return to the instinctual nature instead of sinking into bitterness, she will be revivified, reborn. Wolf pups are born each year. Usually they are these little mewling, sleepy-eyed, dark-furred creatures covered in dirt and straw, but they are immediately awake, playful, and loving, wanting to be close and comforted. They want to play, want to grow. The woman who returns to the instinctual and creative nature will come back to life. She will want to play. She will still want to grow, both wide and deep. But first, there has to be a cleansing.

I would like to introduce you to the concept of *Descansos* as I've developed it in my work. If you ever traveled in Old Mexico, New Mexico, southern Colorado, Arizona, or parts of the South, you've seen little white crosses by the roadway. These are *descansos*, resting places.[9] You'll also find them on the edges of cliffs along particularly scenic but dangerous roads in Greece, Italy, and other Mediterranean countries. Sometimes crosses are clustered in twos or threes or fives. People's names are inscribed upon them— Jesús Mendéz, Arturo Buenofuentes, Jeannie Abeyta. Sometimes the names are spelled out in nails, sometimes they are painted on the wood or carved into it.

Often they are profusely decorated with artificial or real flowers or they glisten with chopped-up new straw glued to wood slats, making them shine like gold in the sun. Sometimes the *descanso* is just two sticks or two pieces of pipe tied across one another with twine and stuck in the ground. In the rockiest passes, the cross is just painted onto a large rock at the roadside.

Descansos are symbols that mark a death. Right there, right on that spot, someone's journey in life halted unexpectedly. There has been a car accident, or someone was walking along the road and died of heat exhaustion, or a fight took place there. Something happened there that altered that person's life and the lives of other persons forever.

Women have died a thousand deaths before they are twenty years old. They've gone in this direction or that, and have been cut off. They have hopes and dreams that have been cut off also. Anyone who says otherwise is still asleep. All that is grist for the mill of *descansos*.

While all these things deepen individuation, differentiation, growing up and growing out, blossoming, becoming awake and aware and conscious, they are also profound tragedies and have to be grieved as such.

To make *descansos* means taking a look at your life and marking where the small deaths, *las muertes chiquitas*, and the big deaths, *las muertes grandotas*, have taken place. I like to make a time-line of a woman's life on a big long sheet of white butcher paper, and to mark with a cross the places along the graph, starting with her infancy all the way to the present where parts and pieces of her self and her life have died.

We mark where there were roads not taken, paths that were cut off, ambushes, betrayals, and deaths. I put a little cross along the time-line at the places that should have been mourned, or still need to be mourned. And then I write in the background "forgotten" for those things that the woman senses but which have not yet surfaced. I also write "forgiven" over those things the woman has for the most part released.

I encourage you to make *descansos*, to sit down with a time-line of your life and say "Where are the crosses? Where are the places that must be remembered, must be blessed?" In all are meanings that you've brought forward into your life today. They must be remembered, but they must be forgotten at the same time. It takes time. And patience.

Remember in "The Crescent Moon Bear" the woman said a prayer and laid the wandering orphaned dead to rest. That is what one does in *descansos*. *Descansos* is a conscious practice that takes pity on and gives honor to the orphaned dead of your psyche, laying them to rest at last.

Be gentle with yourself and make the *descansos*, the resting places for the aspects of yourself that were on their way to somewhere, but never arrived. *Descansos* mark the death sites, the dark times, but they are also love notes to your suffering. They are transformative. There is a lot to be said for pinning things to the earth so they don't follow us around. There is a lot to be said for laying them to rest.

Injured Instinct and Rage

Women (and men) tend to try to draw an end to old episodes by saying "I/he/she/they did the best they could." But to say "they did the best they could" is not forgiveness. Even if true, that peremptory statement cuts off the possibility of healing. It is like applying a tourniquet above a deep wound. To leave that tourniquet on after a time causes gangrene for lack of circulation. Denying anger and pain does not work.

If a woman is instinct-injured, she is typically faced with several challenges regarding rage. First, she often has a problem with intrusion recognition; she is slow to notice territory violations and does not register her own anger until it is upon her. Like the man at the beginning of "The Withered Trees" her temper comes upon her in a kind of ambush.

This lag is the result of instincts injured by exhortations to little girls to not notice dissension, to try to be peacemakers at all costs, to not interfere, and to stand the pain until everything calms down or temporarily goes away. Typically such women do not act upon the rage they feel but jump the gun, or have a delayed reaction weeks, months, or even years later, realize what they should have, could have, would have said or done.

This is usually *not* caused by shyness or introversion but by too much "fifth and sixth guess" thinking, too much trying to be nice to one's own detriment, and not enough acting from soul. The wild soul knows when and how to act if a woman will only listen. Right response carries insight and right amounts of compassion and strength mixed together. Injured instinct must be arighted by practicing and enforcing strong boundaries and by practicing firm and, when possible, generous responses, but solid ones nevertheless.

A woman may have difficulty releasing anger even when it impedes her own life, even when it causes her to obsessively dwell upon events years old as though they happened yesterday. Dwelling on trauma and doing so intensely for a period of time is very important to healing. But eventually all injury has to be given sutures and be allowed to heal over into scar tissue.

Collective Rage

Collective anger or rage is also a natural function. There is such a phenomenon as group hurt, group grief. Women who become socially, politically, or culturally conscious often find that they have to deal with a collective rage that seeps upward through them again and again.

It is psychically sound for women to feel this anger. It is psychically sound for them to use this anger about injustice to invent ways to elicit useful change. It is *not* psychologically sound for them to neutralize their anger so they will not feel, so they will therefore not press for evolution and change. As with personal rage, collective anger is also a teacher. Women can consult with it, question it in solitude and with others, and act upon their conclusions. There is a difference between carrying around old ingrown rage and stirring it with a new stick to see what constructive uses can come of it.

Collective rage is well utilized as motivation to seek out or offer support, to conceive of ways to impel groups or individuals into dialogue, or to demand accountability, progress, improvements. These are proper processes in the patterns of women coming to consciousness. These are appropriate to their caring about what is essential and important to them. It is part of the healthy instinctual psyche to have deep reactions to disrespect, threat, injury. Devout reaction is a natural and expected part of learning about the collective worlds of soul and psyche.

Stuck in Old Rage

If and when rage again becomes a dam to creative thought and action, then it must be softened or changed. For those who have spent considerable time working through a trauma, whether it was caused by someone's cruelty, neglect, lack of respect, recklessness, arrogance, ignorance, or even fate, there comes a time to forgive in order to release the psyche to return to a normal state of calm and peace.[10]

When a woman has trouble letting go of anger or rage, it's often because she's using rage to empower herself. While that may have been wisdom at the beginning, now she must be careful, for ongoing rage is a fire that burns her own primary energy. To be in this state is like speeding through life "pedal to the metal"; trying to live a balanced life with the accelerator pressed all the way to the floor.

Neither is the fieriness of rage to be mistaken as a substitute for a passionate life. It is not life at its best; it is a defense that, once the time of needing it for protection is past, costs plenty to keep. After a time it burns interminably hot, pollutes our ideas with its black smoke, and occludes other ways of seeing and apprehending.

Now I'm not going to tell you a big, fat lie and say you can cleanse all your rage today or next week and it will be gone forever. The angst and torment of times past rise up in the psyche on a cyclical basis. Although a deep purging discharges most of the archaic hurt and rage, the residue can never completely be swept clear. But it should leave a very light ash, not a hungry fire. So the clearing of residual rage must become a periodic hygienic ritual, one that releases us, for to carry old rage beyond the point of its usefulness is to carry a constant, if unconscious, anxiety.

Sometimes people become confused and think that to be stuck in an outdated rage means to fuss and fume and to act out and toss and throw things. It does not mean that in most cases. It means to be tired all the time, to carry a thick layer of cynicism, to dash the hopeful, the tender, the promising. It means to be afraid you will lose before you open your mouth. It means to reach flashpoint inside whether you show it on the outside or not. It means bilious entrenched silences. It means feeling helpless. But there is a way out, and it is through forgiveness.

"Oh, argh, forgiveness?" you say. Anything but that? But you know in your heart that someday, sometime, it will come to that. It may not come until the deathbed time, but it will come. Consider this: Many people have trouble with forgiveness because they have been taught that it is a singular act to be completed in one sitting. That is not so. Forgiveness has many layers, many seasons. In our culture there is a notion that forgiveness is a 100 percent proposition. All or nothing. It is also taught that forgiveness means to overlook, to act as though a thing has not occurred. This is not true either.

A woman who can work up a good 95 percent forgiveness of someone or something tragic and damaging almost qualifies for beatification, if not sainthood. If she is 75 percent forgiving and 25 percent "I don't know if I ever can forgive fully, and I don't even know if I want to," that is more the norm. But 60 percent forgiveness accompanied by 40 percent "I don't know, and I'm not sure, and I'm still working on it," is definitely fine. A level of 50 percent or less forgiveness qualifies for work-in-progress status. Less than 10 percent? You've either just begun or you're not really trying yet.

But, in any case, once you've reached a bit more than halfway, the rest will come in time, usually in small increments. The important part of forgiveness is *to begin and to continue*. The finishing of it all is a life work. You have the rest of your life to work at the lesser percentage. Truly, if we could understand all, all could be forgiven. But for most people it takes a long time in the alchemical bath to come to this. It is all right. We have the healer, so we have the patience to see it through.

Some people, by innate temperament, are more easily able to forgive than others. For some it is a gift, for most it has to be learned as a skill. Essential vitality and sensitivity seem to affect the ability to pass things off. High vitality and high sensitivity do not always allow wrongs to be passed off easily. You are not bad if you do not forgive easily. You are not a saint if you do. Each to her own, and all in due time.

To truly heal, however, we must say our truth, and not only our regret and pain but also what harm was caused, what anger, what disgust, and also what desire for self-punishment or vengeance was evoked in us. The old healer of the psyche understands human nature with all its foibles and gives pardon based on the telling of the naked truth. She not only gives second chances, she most often gives many chances.

Let us look at four levels of forgiveness. These stages I've developed and used in my work with traumatized people over the years. Each level has several layers. These can be dealt with in whatever order and for however long one desires, but I've listed them in the order I encourage my own clients to begin working.

Four Stages of Forgiveness

1. to forego—to leave it alone
2. to forebear—to abstain from punishing
3. to forget—to aver from memory, to refuse to dwell
4. to forgive—to abandon the debt

FOREGO[11]

To begin to forgive, it is good to forego for a while. That is, to take a break from thinking about the person or event for a while. It is not leaving something undone, but rather more like taking a vacation from it. This prevents us from being exhausted, allows us to strengthen in other ways, to have other happiness in our lives.

This is good practice for the final letting go that comes with forgiveness later on. Leave the situation, memory, issue as many times as you need to. The idea is not to overlook but to become agile and strong at detaching from the issue. To forego means to take up that weaving, that writing, to go to that ocean, to do some learning and loving that strengthens you, and to allow the issue to drop away for a time. This is right, good, and healing. The issues of past injury will bedevil a woman far less if she assures the wounded psyche that she will give it healing balms now and deal with the entire issue of who caused what injury later.

FOREBEAR[12]

The second phase is to forebear, particularly in the sense of abstaining from punishing; neither thinking about it nor acting on it in small or large ways. It is extremely useful to practice this kind of containment, for it coalesces the issue into one place instead of allowing it to flow everywhere. This builds focus toward the time when one proceeds to the next steps. This does not mean to go blind or dead and lose self-protective vigilance. It means to give a bit of grace to the situation and see how that assists.

To forebear means to have patience, to bear up against, to channel emotion. These are powerful medicines. Do as much as you can. This is a cleansing regime. You need not do all; you can choose one, such as patience, and practice that. You can refrain from punitive uttering, muttering, from acting resentful, hostile. To refrain from unnecessary punishing strengthens integrity of action and soul. To forebear is to practice generosity, thereby allowing the great compassionate nature to participate in matters that have previously caused emotion ranging all the way from minor irritation to rage.

FORGET[13]

To forget means to aver from memory, to refuse to dwell—in other words, to let go, to loosen one's hold, particularly on memory. To forget does not mean to make yourself brain-dead. Conscious forgetting means letting go of the event, not insisting it stay in the foreground, but rather moving it off a stage, allowing it to be relegated to the background.

We practice conscious forgetting by refusing to summon up the fiery material, we refuse to recollect. To forget is an active, not a passive, endeavor. It means to not haul up certain materials or turn them over and over, to not work oneself up by repetitive thoughts, pictures, or emotions. Conscious forgetting means willfully dropping the practice of obsessing, intentionally outdistancing and losing sight of it, not looking back, thereby living in a new landscape, creating new life and new experiences to think about instead of the old ones. This kind of forgetting does not erase memory, it lays the emotion surrounding the memory to rest.

FORGIVE[14]

There are many ways and portions to forgiving a person, a community, a nation for an offense. It is important to remember that a "final" forgiveness is not surrender. It is a conscious decision to cease to harbor resentment, which includes forgiving a debt and giving up one's resolve to retaliate. You are the one who decides when to forgive and what ritual to use to mark the event. You decide what debt you will now say needs not be paid further.

Some choose blanket pardon: releasing a person from any restitution now or ever. Others choose to call a halt to redress in process, abandoning the debt, saying whatever has been done is done, and the payback is now enough. Another kind of pardon is to release a person without his having made any emotional or other sort of restitution.

To some, a finalizing of forgiving means to regard the other indulgently, and this is easiest with regard to relatively benign offenses. One of the most profound forms of forgiveness is to give compassionate aid to the offending person in one form or another.[15] This does not mean you should stick your head in the snake's basket, but instead respond from a stance of mercy, security, and preparedness.[16]

Forgiveness is the culmination of all foregoing, forebearing, and forgetting. It does not mean giving up one's protection, but one's coldness. One deep form of forgiveness is to cease excluding the other, which includes ceasing to stiff-arm, ignore, or act coldly toward, insisting on being neither patronizing nor phony. It is better for the soul-psyche to closely limit time and repartee with people who are difficult for you than to act like an unfeeling mannequin.

Forgiveness is an act of creation. You can choose from many time-honored ways to do it. You can forgive for now, forgive till then, forgive till the next time, forgive but give no more chances— it's a whole new game if there's another incident. You can give one more chance, give several more chances, give many chances, give chances only if. You can forgive part, all, or half of an offense. You can devise a blanket forgiveness. You decide.[17]

How does one you know if she has forgiven? You tend to feel sorrow over the circumstance instead of rage, you tend to feel sorry for the person rather than angry with him. You tend to have nothing left to remember to say about it all. You understand the suffering that drove the offense to begin with. You prefer to remain outside the milieu. You are not waiting for anything. You are not wanting anything. There is no lariat snare around your ankle stretching from way back there to here. You are free to go. It may not have turned out to be a *happily ever after*, but most certainly there is now a fresh *Once upon a time* waiting for you from this day forward.

✍ CHAPTER 13

Battle Scars:
Membership in the
Scar Clan

Tears are a river that take you somewhere. Weeping creates a river around the boat that carries your soul-life. Tears lift your boat off the rocks, off dry ground, carrying it downriver to someplace new, someplace better.

There are oceans of tears women have never cried, for they have been trained to carry mother's and father's secrets, men's secrets, society's secrets, and their own secrets, to the grave. A woman's crying has been considered quite dangerous, for it loosens the locks and bolts on the secrets she bears. But in truth, for the sake of a woman's wild soul, it is better to cry. For women, tears are the beginning of initiation into the Scar Clan, that timeless tribe of women of all colors, all nations, all languages, who down through the ages have lived through a great something, and yet who stood proud, still stand proud.

All women have personal stories as vast in scope and as powerful as the numen in fairy tales. But there is one kind of story in particular, which has to do with a woman's secrets, especially those associated with shame; these contain some of the most important stories a woman can give her time to unraveling. For most women, these secret stories are her own personal ones, embedded, not like jewels in a crown, but like black gravel under the skin of the soul.

Secrets as Slayers

Over my twenty-year practice, I've listened to thousands of "secret stories," stories that, in the main, were kept hidden for many years, sometimes for almost a lifetime. Whether a woman's secret is shrouded in self-imposed silence, or whether she has been threatened by someone more powerful than she, she deeply fears disenfranchisement, being considered an undesirable person, disruption of relationships that are important to her, and sometimes even physical harm if she reveals her secret.

Some women's secret stories are about having told a bald-faced lie or having done a purposeful meanness that caused someone else trouble or pain. However, in my experience, these are rare. More women's secrets revolve around having violated some social or moral code of their culture, religion, or personal value system. Some of these acts, events, and choices, particularly those related to women's freedom in any and all arenas of life, were often held out by the culture as being shamefully wrong for women, but not for men.

The problem of secret stories surrounded by shame is that they cut a woman off from her instinctive nature, which is in the main, joyous and free. When there is a black secret in the psyche, a woman can go nowhere near it, and in fact protects herself from coming into contact with anything that will remind her of it or cause her already chronic pain to crest to an even more intense level.

This defensive maneuver is common, and, as in the aftereffects of trauma, secretly influences women's choices in what she will or will not undertake in the outer world: which books, films, or events she will or will not involve herself with; what she will or won't laugh about; and what interests she gives herself to. In this sense, there is an entrapment of the wild nature which ought to be free to do, be, look into whatever it likes.

Generally, secrets follow the same themes found in high drama. These are some of the themes of secrets: betrayal; forbidden love; unsanctioned curiosity; desperate acts; forced acts; unrequited love; jealousy and rejection; retribution and rage; cruelty to self or others; disapproved desires, wishes, and dreams; disapproved sexual interests and lifestyles; unplanned pregnancies; hatred and aggression; accidental death or injury; broken promises; loss of courage; loss of temper; incompletion of something; inability to do something; behind-the-scenes intervention and manipulation; neglect; abuse; and the list goes on, most of the themes falling under the category of the sorrowful error.[1]

Secrets, like fairy tales and dreams, also follow the same energy patterns and structures as those found in drama. But secrets, instead of following the heroic structure, follow the tragic structure. The heroic drama begins with a heroine on a journey. Sometimes she is not psychologically awake. Sometimes she is too sweet and doesn't perceive danger. Sometimes she has already been mistreated and makes the desperate moves of a captured creature. However she begins, the heroine eventually falls into the clutches of whatever or whoever, and is sorely tested. Then, through her wit and because she has people who care for her, she is freed and stands taller as a result.[2]

In a tragedy the heroine is snatched, forced, or drives straight into hell and is subsequently overwhelmed. No one hears her cries, or else her pleas are ignored. She loses hope, loses touch with the preciousness of her life, and collapses. Instead of being able to savor her triumph over adversity, or her wisdom of choices and her endurance, she is degraded and deadened. The secrets a woman keeps are almost always heroic dramas that have been perverted into tragedies that go nowhere.

But there is good news. The way to change a tragic drama back into a heroic one is to open the secret, speak of it to someone, write another ending, examine one's part in it and one's attributes in enduring it. These learnings are equal parts pain and wisdom. The having lived through it is a triumph of the deep and wild spirit.

The shame-filled secrets women carry are old, old tales. Any person who has kept a secret to her own detriment has been buried by shame. In this universal plight, the pattern itself is archetypal: the heroine has either been forced to do something or, through the loss of instinct, has been trapped into something. Typically, she is powerless to aright the sad condition. She is in some way sworn or shamed into secrecy. She complies for fear of loss of love, loss of regard, loss of basic subsistence. To seal the secret further, a curse is placed upon the person or persons who would reveal it. A terrible something or other is threatened if the secret is ever revealed.

Women have been advised that certain events, choices, and circumstances in their lives, usually having to do with sex, love, money, violence, and/or other difficulties rampant in the human condition, are of the most shameful nature and are therefore completely without absolution. This is untrue.

Everyone makes poor choices in words or deeds before they know any better and before they realize what the consequences will be. There is nothing on this planet or in this universe that is outside the bounds of forgiveness. Nothing. "Oh no!" you're saying, "this *one* thing I did is totally without pardon." I said *nothing* that a human may have done, is doing, or might do, is outside the bounds of forgiveness. Nothing.

The Self is not a punitive force that rushes about punishing women, men, and children. The Self is a wildish God who understands the nature of creatures. It is often hard for us to "act right," especially when the basic instincts, including intuition, are cut away. Then it is difficult to speculate on outcome before, rather than after the fact. The wildish soul has a deeply compassionate side that takes this into account.

In the archetype of the secret, an enchantment of sorts is cast like a black net across part of a woman's psyche, and she is encouraged to believe that the secret must never be revealed, and further, she must believe that if she does reveal it all decent persons who come across her shall revile her in perpetuity. This additional threat, as well as the secret shame itself, causes a woman to carry not one burden but two.

This sort of enchantment threat is a pastime only among persons inhabiting a small and black space in their hearts. Among persons of warmth and love for the human condition, quite the opposite is true. They would help to draw out the secret, for they know it makes a wound that will not heal until the matter is given words and witness.

The Dead Zone

The keeping of secrets cuts a woman off from those who would give her love, succor, and protection. It causes her to carry the burden of grief and fear all by herself, and sometimes for an entire group, whether family or culture. Further, as Jung said, keeping secrets cuts us off from the unconscious. Where there is a shaming secret, there is always a dead zone in the woman's psyche, a place that does not feel or respond properly to her own continuing emotional life events or to the emotional life events of others.

The dead zone is greatly protected. It is a place of endless doors and walls, each locked with twenty locks, and the *homunculi*, the little creatures in women's dreams, are always busy building more doors, more dams, more security, lest the secret escape.

There is no way to fool the Wild Woman, however. She is aware of the dark bundles in a woman's mind that are tied round and round with ropes and bands. These spaces in a woman's mind do not respond to light or grace, so covered over are they. And, of course, since the psyche is greatly compensatory, the secret will find its way out anyway, if not in actual words, then in the form of sudden melancholias, intermittent and mysterious rages, all sorts of physical tics, torques, and pains, dangling conversations that end suddenly and without explanation, and sudden odd reactions to movies, films, and even television commercials.

The secret always finds its way out, if not in direct words, then somatically, and most often not in a way that it can be dealt with and helped in a straightforward manner. So what does the woman do when she finds the secret leaking out? She runs after it with great expenditure of energy. She beats, bundles, and burrows it back down into the dead zone again, and builds larger defenses. She calls her *homunculi*—the inner guardians and ego defenders—to build more doors, more walls. The woman leans against her latest psychic tomb, sweating blood and breathing like a locomotive. A woman who carries a secret is an exhausted woman.

My *nagynénik*, aunts, used to tell a little story about this matter of secrets. They called it "*Arányos Haj*, Golden Hair, The Woman with Hair of Gold."

The Woman With Hair of Gold

THERE WAS A VERY STRANGE but beautiful woman with long golden hair as fine as spun gold. She was poor and without mother or father, and lived in the woods alone and wove upon a loom made of black walnut boughs. A brute who was the son of the coal burner tried to force her into marriage, and in an effort to buy him off, she gave him some of her golden hair.

But he did not know or care that it was spiritual, not monetary, gold that she gave him, so when he sought to trade her hair for merchandise in the marketplace, people jeered at him and thought him mad.

Enraged, he returned by night to the woman's cottage and with his own hands murdered her and buried her body by the river. For a long time no one noticed that she was missing. No one inquired of her hearth or health. But in her grave, the woman's golden hair grew and grew. The beautiful hair curled and spiraled upward through the black soil, and it grew looping and twirling more and more, and up and up, until her grave was covered by a field of swaying golden reeds.

Shepherds cut the curly reeds to make flutes, and when they played them, the tiny flutes sang and would not stop singing,

Here lies the woman with golden hair
murdered and in her grave,
killed by the son of the coal burner
because she wished to live.

And that is how the man who took the life of the woman with golden hair was discovered and brought to justice so that those who live in the wild woods of the world, like we ourselves do, were safe again once more.

While this tale overtly gives the usual instruction to be careful in lonely places out in the woods, the inner message is profound, and that is that the life force of the beautiful wilderwoman personified by her hair continues to grow and to live and to emanate conscious knowing even though overtly silenced and buried. The leitmotifs of this tale are probably fragments of a much larger and more ancient death-and-resurrection story centering around a female Godhead.

This segment is beautiful and valuable, and additionally it tells us something about the nature of secrets and even, perhaps, what it is that is killed off in the psyche when a woman's life is not properly valued. In this tale, the murder of the woman who lives out in the woods is the secret. She represents a *kore*, the woman-who-will-not-marry. This aspect of the female psyche represents that which wishes to keep to herself alone. This is mystical and solitary in a good way, for the *kore* is taken up with the sorting and weaving of ideas, thoughts, and endeavors.

It is this self-contained wilderwoman that is most injured by trauma or by the keeping of a secret . . . this integral sense of self that needs not have much around itself in order to be happy; this heart of the female psyche who weaves in the forest on the black walnut loom and is at peace there.

No one in the fairy tale asks about the absence of this vital woman. This is not unusual in fairy tales or in real life. The families of the dead women in "Bluebeard" do not come seeking their daughters either. Culturally, this needs no interpretation. Sadly, we all know what it means, and many women, too many, understand that lack of inquiry firsthand. Often the woman who carries secrets meets with the same response. Though people may perceive that at center her heart is pierced, they may accidentally or purposefully go blind to the evidence of her injury.

But part of the miracle of the wild psyche is that no matter how badly a woman is "killed," no matter how injured, her psychic life continues, and it rises above ground where in soulful circumstances it will sing its way up and out again. Then wrongful harm done is consciously apprehended and the psyche begins restoration.

It is an interesting idea, is it not, that a woman's life force can continue to grow even though she is seemingly without life? It is a promise that under even the most anemic conditions the wildish life force will keep our ideas alive and developing, albeit only for a while, underground. Life will pry and scrabble its way above ground in time. This living force will not let the matter rest until the buried woman's whereabouts and circumstances are revealed.

As with the shepherds in the story, this involves drawing a breath and putting the soul-breath or *pneuma* through the reeds, in order to know the true state of affairs in the psyche and what must be done next. This is the work of crying out. Then the digging work follows.

While some secrets are strengthening—for instance, those used as part of a strategy in order to gain a competitive goal, or those happy ones kept just for the pleasure of savoring them—the secrets of shame are very different, as different as a beribboned medal versus a bloody knife. The latter must be brought up, witnessed by compassionate humans under generous conditions. When a woman keeps a shameful secret it is horrifying to see the enormous amounts of self-blame and self-torture she endures. All the blame and torture that were promised to descend upon the woman if she tells the secret does so anyway, even though she has told no one; it all attacks her from within.

The wildish woman cannot live with this. Shameful secrets cause a person to become haunted. She cannot sleep, for a shaming secret is like a cruel barbed wire that catches her across the gut as she tries to run free. The secrets of shame are destructive not only to a woman's mental health but to her relationships with the instinctive nature. Wild Woman digs things up, throws them into the air, chases them around. She does not bury and forget. If she buries at all, she remembers what, and where, and it will not be long before she has disinterred it again.

Keeping shame a secret is profoundly disturbing to the psyche. Secrets erupt in dream material. An analyst must often go beyond the manifest, and sometimes even the archetypal content of a dream in order to see that it is in fact broadcasting the very secret the dreamer cannot, dare not, tell aloud.

There are many dreams that, when analyzed, are understood to be about immense and extensive feelings that the dreamer, in real life, is unable to cry out. Some of these dreams pertain to secrets. Some of the most common dream images I've seen are lights, electric and otherwise, flickering and/or going out, dreams in which the dreamer becomes ill from eating something, those in which the dreamer cannot move out of danger, and those wherein the dreamer tries to call out, but no voice issues forth.

Remember *canto hondo*, the deep song, and *hambre del alma*, the starved soul? In time, these two forces, through dreams and the woman's own wild life force, rise to the surface of the psyche and break out the necessary cry, the cry that frees. A woman finds her voice then. She sings out, cries out the secret, and is heard. Her psychic footing will be restored.

In the tradition of my families' ethnic and religious practices, the core meaning of this fairy tale and others similar to it are medicines to be applied to wounds which are kept secret. In prayerful *curanderisma* they are considered encouragement, advice, and resolution. What stands behind the formation of fairy-tale wisdom is the fact that for both women and men, woundings to the self, soul, and psyche through secrets and otherwise, are part of most persons' lives. Neither can the subsequent scarring be avoided. But there is help for these injuries, and absolutely there is healing.

There are general wounds, and there are wounds that are specific to males, and there are wounds that are specific to females. Abortion leaves a scar. Miscarriage makes a scar. Losing a child of any age makes a scar. Sometimes being close to another person lays down scar tissue. There may be extensive scarring as the result of naive choices, from being entrapped, as well as from right but difficult choices. There are as many shapes of scars as there are types of psychic woundings.

Repressing secret material surrounded by shame, fear, anger, guilt, or humiliation effectively shuts down all other parts of the unconscious that are near the site of the secret.[3] It is like shooting an anesthetic into, say, a person's ankle in order to do a surgery. Much of the leg above and below the ankle is also affected by the anesthesia and no longer has feeling. This is how secret keeping works in the psyche. It is a constant IV drip of anesthetic that numbs far more than the area at issue.

No matter what kind of secret, no matter how much pain is

involved in keeping the secret, the psyche is affected in the same way. Here is one example. One woman, whose husband forty years earlier had committed suicide three months after they were married, was urged by his family to not only hide the evidence of his major depressive illness but also her deep emotional grief and anger from that time. As a result, she developed a "dead zone" regarding his anguish, her anguish, as well as her rage at the cultural stigma attached to the entire event.

She allowed the husband's family to betray her by agreeing to their requirement that she never reveal the fact of their cruel treatment of her husband over the years. And each year on the anniversary of her husband's suicide, there was dead silence from the family. No one called to say "How are you feeling? Would you like some company? Do you miss him? I know you must. Shall we go out and do something together?" The woman dug her husband's grave once more and buried her grief alone, year after year.

Eventually she began to avoid other days of commemoration: anniversaries and birthdays, including her own. The dead zone spread from the center of the secret outward, not only overtly covering commemorative events, but then stretching to celebratory events, and even beyond. All of these familial and friendship events were disparaged by the woman, who overtly considered them a waste of time.

To her unconscious, however, they were empty gestures, for no one had come close to her in her times of despair. Her chronic grief, that shameful secret keeping, had eaten into the area of her psyche that governed relatedness. Most often we wound others where, or very close to where, we have been wounded ourselves.

If a woman desires, however, to retain all her instincts and abilities to move freely within her psyche, she can reveal her secret or secrets to one trustworthy human being, and recount them as many times as necessary. A wound is usually not disinfected once and then forgotten, but is tended to and washed several times while it heals.

When a secret is finally told, the soul needs more response than "Hmmmmm, oh really, that's too bad," or "Oh well, life is tough," from both the teller and the listener. The teller has to try not to depreciate the matter. And it is a blessing if the listener is a person who can listen with a full heart and can wince, shiver, and feel a ray of pain cross his or her own heart and not collapse. Part of healing from a secret is to tell it so that others are moved by it. In this way a woman begins to recover from shame by receiving the succor and tending she missed during the original trauma.

In small and confidential groups of women, I bring about this exchange by asking the women to gather together and to bring photographs of their mothers, aunts, sisters, mates, grandmothers, and other women who are significant to them. We line up all the pictures. Some are cracked, some peeling, some damaged by water or coffee cup rings; some have been torn in two and taped back together; some are wrapped in glassine tissue. Many have beautiful archaic writing on the back saying "Oh, you kid!" or "Love forever" or "This is me with Joe at Atlantic City" or "Here I am with my groovy roommate" or "These are the girls from the factory."

I suggest each woman begin by saying, "These are the women of my bloodline" or "These are the women from whom I inherited." Women look at these pictures of their female family and friends, and with a deep compassion, begin to tell the stories and secrets of each as they know them: the big joy, the big hurt, the big travail, the big triumph in each woman's life. Throughout the time we spend together there are many moments when we can go no further, for many, many tears lift many, many boats out of dry dock and off we all sail away together for a while.[4]

What is valuable here is a true cleaning of the feminine laundry once and for all. The common proscription against washing the family laundry in public is ironic because usually the "dirty laundry" does not ever get washed within the family either. Down in the darkest corner of the cellar, the family "dirty laundry" just lies there stiff with its secret forever. The insistence on keeping a thing private is poison. In reality, it means that a woman has no support around her to deal with the issues that cause her pain.

Many of the personal secret stories of women are the kind that family and friends are inadequate to discuss; they disbelieve or attempt to make light of or bypass them, and they truly have understandable reason to do so. If they do discuss them, candle them, work with them, they would have to share the grief with the woman. No standing about composed. No "Ohhh, wellll . . ." and then silence. No "We must try to keep busy and not dwell on such things." Instead, were a woman's mate, family, community to share the grief over the death of the golden-haired woman, they would all have to take their place in the cortege. They would all have to weep at the grave. No one could wriggle out of it, and it would be very hard on them.

When women give more thought to the matter of their own secret shame than other members of their family or community, they alone consciously suffer.[5] The psychological purpose of family—to pull together—never occurs. Yet the wild nature demands that one's environ be cleansed of irritants and threats, that matters which oppress be reduced as much as possible. So, it is usually a matter of time before a woman calls up her courage from the soul bones, cuts herself a golden reed, and plays the secret in her own strong voice.

But here is what to do about shame-filled secrets, based on study of archetypal advice extrapolated from dozens of fairy tales such as "Bluebeard," "Mr. Fox," "Robber Bridegroom," "Mary Culhane,"[6] and others, where the heroine refuses to keep the secret in one way or another, and so is finally freed to live fully alive.

See what you see. Say it to someone. It is never too late. If you feel you cannot say it aloud, write it down for them. Choose a person whom you instinctively believe to be trustworthy. The can of worms you are worried about opening is far better off being out there than festering inside yourself. If you prefer, seek a therapist who knows how to deal with secrets. This will be a person of mercy, with no particular drum to bang about right and wrong, who knows the difference between guilt and remorse and about the nature of grieving and resurrection of spirit.

Whatever the secret is, we understand that it is now part of our work for life. Redemption heals a once-open wound. But there will be a scar nevertheless. With changes of weather the scar can and will ache again. That is the nature of a true grief.

For years, classical psychology of all types erroneously thought that grief was a process that you did once, preferably over a year's period of time, and then it was done with, and anyone who was unable or unwilling to complete this over the prescribed time period had something rather wrong with them. But we know now what humans have known instinctively for centuries: that certain hurts and harms and shames can never be done being grieved; the loss of a child through death or relinquishment being one of the most, if not *the* most, enduring.

In a study[7] of diaries written over many years' time, Paul C. Rosenblatt, Ph.D., found that people may recover from the worst of their soul-grief in the first year or two after a tragedy, depending on a person's support systems and so forth. But afterward, the person continues to experience periods of active grieving. Although the episodes become farther and farther apart in time and shorter in duration, each recurrence carries close to the same intensity of gut-staggering grief as the first occasion.

This data helps us to understand the normalcy of long-term grief. When a secret is not told, grieving goes on anyway, and for life. The keeping of secrets interferes with the natural self-healing hygiene of psyche and spirit. This is one more reason to say our secrets. Telling and grieving resurrect us from the dead zone. They allow us to leave the death cult of secrets behind. We can grieve and grieve hard, and come out of it tear-stained, rather than shame-stained. We can come out deepened, fully acknowledged, and filled with new life.

Wild Woman will hold us while we grieve. She is the instinctual Self. She can bear our screaming, our wailing, our wishing to die without dying. She will put the best medicine in the worst places. She will whisper and murmur in our ears. She will feel pain for our pain. She will bear it. She will not run away. Although there will be scars and plenty of them, it is good to remember that in tensile strength and ability to absorb pressure, a scar is stronger than skin.

The Scapecoat

Sometimes in my work with women I show them how to make a full-length scape*coat* from cloth or some other material. A scapecoat is a coat that details in painting, writing, and with all manner of things pinned and stitched to it all the name-calling a woman has endured in her life, all the insults, all the slurs, all the traumas, all the wounds, all the scars. It is her statement of her experience of being scape*goat*ed. Sometimes it takes only a day or two to make such a coat, other times it takes months. It is exceedingly helpful in detailing all the hurts and slams and slashes of a woman's life.

At first, I made a scapecoat for myself. It soon became so heavy it needed a chorus of Muses to carry the train. I had in mind that I would make this scapecoat and then, having put all this psychic refuse together in one psychic object, I would disperse some of my old woundedness by burning the scapecoat. But you know, I kept the coat hung from the ceiling in the hallway and every time I walked near it, instead of feeling bad, I felt good. I found myself admiring the *ovarios* of the woman who could wear such a coat and still be walking foursquare, singing, creating, and wagging her tail.

I found this also to be true of the women I worked with. They never want to destroy their scapecoats once they have made them. They want to keep them forever, the nastier and the gorier, the better. Sometimes we also call them battlecoats, for they are proof of the endurance, the failures, and the victories of individual women and their kinswomen.

It is also a good idea for women to count their ages, not by years, but by battle scars. "How old are you?" people sometimes ask me. "I am seventeen battle scars old," I say. Usually people don't flinch, and rather happily begin to count up their own battle scar ages accordingly.

As the Lakota painted glyphs on animal hides to record the events of winter, and the Nahuatl, the Maya, and the Egyptians had their codices recording the great events of the tribe, the wars, the triumphs, women have their scapecoats, their battlecoats. I wonder what our granddaughters and great-granddaughters will think of our lives recorded thusly. I hope it will all have to be explained to them.

Let there be no mistake about it, for you have earned it by the hard choices of your life. If you are asked your nationality, ethnic origin, or blood line, smile enigmatically. Say, "Scar Clan."

✍ CHAPTER 14

La Selva Subterránea:
Initiation in the
Underground Forest

The Handless Maiden

If a story is seed, then we are its soil. Just hearing the story allows us to experience it as though we ourselves were the heroine who either falters or wins out in the end. If we hear a story about a wolf, then afterward we rove about and know like a wolf for a time. If we hear a story about a dove finding her young at last, then for a time after, something moves behind our own feathered breasts. If it be a story of wresting the sacred pearl from beneath the claw of the ninth dragon, we feel exhausted afterward, and satisfied. In a very real way, we are imprinted with knowing just by listening to the tale.

Among Jungians this is called "participation mystique"—a term borrowed from anthropologist Levy-Bruhl—and it is used to mean a relationship wherein "a person cannot distinguish themselves as separate from the object or thing they behold." Among Freudians, it is called "projective identification." Among anthropologists, it is sometimes called "sympathetic magic." All these terms mean the ability of the mind to step away from its ego for a time and merge with another reality, that is, another way of comprehending, a different way of understanding. Among healers from my heritage, this means experiencing and learning ideas via a prayerful or non-ordinary state of mind and bringing the insights and knowledge one has gained in the circumstance back into consensual reality.[1]

418

"The Handless Maiden" is a remarkable story, one in which we find the toes of the old night religions peeking out from under the layers of the tale. The story is formed in such a way that listeners participate in the heroine's test of endurance, for the tale has such amplitude that it takes long to tell it, and even longer to absorb. Customarily, I teach this tale over seven nights' time, and sometimes, depending on the listeners, over seven weeks' and occasionally seven months' time—spending one night, week, or month for each labor in the story—and there is a reason for this.

The story pulls us into a world that lies far below the roots of trees. From that perspective we see that "The Handless Maiden" offers material for a woman's entire life process. It deals with most of the key journeys of a woman's psyche. Unlike other tales we have looked at in this work that speak to a specific task or a specific learning taking place over a few days' or weeks' time, "The Handless Maiden" covers a many-years-long journey—the journey of a woman's entire lifetime. So this story is something special, and a good rhythm for assimilating it, is to read it and sit with your Muse, turning it part by part, over a generous period of time.

"The Handless Maiden" is about women's initiation into the underground forest through the rite of endurance. The word *endurance* sounds as though it means "to continue without cessation," and while this is an occasional part of the tasks underlying the tale, the word *endurance* also means "to harden, to make sturdy, to make robust, to strengthen," and this is the principal thrust of the tale, and the generative feature of a woman's long psychic life. We do not just go on to go on. Endurance means we are making something substantial.

The teaching of endurance occurs all throughout nature. The pads of wolf pups' paws are soft as clay when the pups are born. It is only the ranging, the roaming, the treks on which their parents take them that toughen them up. Then they can climb and bound over sharp gravel, over stinging nettle, even over broken glass, without being hurt.

I have seen wolf mothers plunge their pups into the coldest streams imaginable, run until a pup is splay-legged and can hardly keep up and then run some more. They are toughening up the sweet little spirit, investing it with strength and resilience. In mythos, the teaching of endurance is one of the rites of the Great Wild Mother, the Wild Woman archetype. It is her timeless ritual to make her offspring strong. It is she who toughens us up, makes us potent and enduring.

And where does this learning take place, where are these attributes acquired? *La selva subterránea*, the underground forest, the underworld of female knowing. It is a wild world that lives under this one, under the world perceived by ego. While there, we are infused with instinctive language and knowledge. From that vantage point we understand what cannot be so easily understood from the point of view of the topside world.

The maiden in this tale masters several descents. As she completes one round of descent and transformation, she plunges into yet another. These alchemical rounds are complete, each with a *nigredo*, loss, *rubedo*, sacrifice, and *albedo*, coming of light, following one upon the other. The king and the king's mother each have a round themselves. All this descending and loss and finding and strengthening portrays women's lifelong initiation into the renewal of the wild.

"The Handless Maiden" story is called, in different parts of the world, "Silver Hands," "The Handless Bride," and "The Orchard." Folklorists number more than a hundred versions of the tale. The core of the literary version I've written here was given to me by my Aunt Magdalena, one of the great women farmer/field workers of my young life. Other variations are found throughout Eastern and Middle Europe. But truth be told, the deep womanly experience underlying the tale is found anywhere there is a yearning for the Wild Mother.

My Aunt Magdalena had a sly storytelling habit. She caught her listeners off guard by beginning a fairy tale with "This happened ten years ago," and then proceeded to tell a tale from the medieval era, complete with knights, moats, and all. Or she'd say "Once upon a time, just last week . . ." and then she'd tell a tale about a time before humans wore clothing.

So, here is the modern-ancient "Handless Maiden."

ONCE UPON A TIME a few days ago, the man down the road still owned a large stone that ground the villagers' grain to flour. The miller had fallen on hard times and had nothing left but the great rough millstone in a shed, and the large flowering apple tree behind it.

One day, as he carried his silver-lipped ax into the forest to cut deadwood, a strange old man stepped from behind a tree. "There's no need for you to torture yourself by cleaving wood," wheedled the old man. "I shall dress you in riches if you will but give me what stands behind your mill."

"What is there behind my mill but the flowering apple tree?" thought the miller, and agreed to the old man's bargain.

"In three years' time, I'll come take what is mine," chortled the stranger, and he limped away, disappearing between the staves of the trees.

The miller met his wife on the path. She had run from their house, apron flying, hair askew. "Husband, husband, at the stroke of the hour, into our house came a finer clock upon the wall, our rustic chairs were replaced by those hung in velvet, and the paltry cupboard abounds now with game, our trunks and boxes are over-flowing. Pray tell, how has this happened?" And even at that moment, golden rings appeared on her fingers and her hair was drawn up into a golden circlet.

"Ah," said the miller, looking in awe as his own doublet turned to satin. Before his eyes his wooden shoes with the heels worn to nothing so he walked tilted backward, they too turned into fine shoes. "Well, it is from a stranger," he gasped. "I came upon an odd man in a dark frock coat in the forest and he promised great wealth if I gave him what is behind our mill. Surely, wife, we can plant another apple tree."

"Oh, my husband!" wailed the woman, and she looked as though she had been struck dead. "The man in the black coat was the Devil, and what stands behind the mill is the tree, yes, but our daughter is also there sweeping the yard with a willow broom."

And so the parents stumbled home, weeping tears on all their finery. Their daughter stayed without husband for three years and had a temperament like the first sweet apples of spring. The day the Devil came to fetch her she bathed and put on a white gown and stood in a circle of chalk she'd drawn around herself. When the Devil reached out to grab her, an unseen force threw him across the yard.

The Devil screamed, "She must not bathe any more else I cannot come near her." The parents and the girl were terrified. And so some weeks went by and the daughter did not bathe until her hair was matted, her fingernails like black crescents, her skin gray, her clothes darkened and stiff with dirt.

Then, with the maiden every day more and more resembling a beast, the Devil came again. But the girl wept and wept. Her tears ran through her fingers and down her arms—so much so that her dirty hands and arms became purest white and clean. The Devil was enraged. "Chop off her hands, otherwise I cannot come near her." The father was horrified. "You want me to sever the hands of my own child?" The Devil bellowed, "Everything here will die, including you, your wife, and all the fields for as far as you can see."

The father was so frightened he obeyed, and begging his daughter's forgiveness he began to sharpen his silver-lipped ax. The daughter submitted, saying, "I am your child, do as you must."

And this he did, and in the end no one could say who cried out in anguish the louder, the daughter or the father. Thus ended the girl's life as she had known it.

When the Devil came again, the girl had cried so much the stumps that were left of her limbs were again clean, and the Devil was again thrown across the yard when he attempted to seize her. Cursing in words that set small fires in the forest, he disappeared forever, for he had lost all claim to her.

The father had aged one hundred years, and his wife also. Like true people of the forest, they continued as best they could. The old father offered to keep his daughter in a castle of great beauty and with riches for life, but the daughter said she felt it more fitting she become a beggar girl and depend on the goodness of others for sustenance. And so she had her arms bound in clean gauze, and at daybreak she walked away from her life as she had known it.

She walked and walked. High noon caused her sweat to streak the dirt on her face. The wind disheveled her hair until it was like a stork's nest of twigs all tangled this way and that. In the midst of the night she came to a royal orchard where the moon had put a gleam on all the fruits that hung from the trees.

She could not enter because the orchard was surrounded by a moat. But, she fell to her knees, for she was starved. A ghostly spirit in white appeared and shut one of the sluice gates so that the moat was emptied.

The maiden walked among the pear trees and somehow she knew that each perfect pear had been counted and numbered, and that they were guarded as well. Nevertheless, a bough bent itself low, its limb creaking, so she could reach the lovely fruit at its tip. She put her lips to the golden skin of the pear and ate while standing there in the moonlight, her arms bound in gauze, her hair afright, appearing like a mud woman, the handless maiden.

The gardener saw it all, but recognized the magic of the spirit who guarded the maiden, and did not interfere. After the girl finished eating the single pear, she withdrew across the moat and slept in the shelter of the wood.

The next morning the king came to count his pears. He found one missing, and looking high and looking low, he could not find the vanished fruit. The gardener explained: "Last night two spirits drained the moat, entered the garden at high moon, and one without hands ate the pear that offered itself to her."

The king said he would keep watch that night. At dark he came with his gardener and his magician, who knew how to speak with spirits. The three sat beneath a tree and watched. At midnight, the maiden came floating through the forest, her clothes dirty rags, her hair awry, her face streaked, her arms without hands, and the spirit in white beside her.

They entered the orchard the same way as before. Again, a tree gracefully bent one of its boughs to within her reach and she supped on the pear at its tip.

The magician came close, but not too close, to them and asked, "Are you of this world or not of this world?" And the girl answered, "I was once of *the* world, and yet I am not of *this* world."

The king questioned the magician. "Is she human or spirit?" The magician answered that she was both. The king's heart leapt and he rushed to her and cried, "I shall not forsake you. From this day forward, I shall care for you." At his castle he had made for her a pair of silver hands, which were fastened to her arms. And so it was that the king married the handless maiden.

In time, the king had to wage war in a far-off kingdom, and he asked his mother to care for his young queen, for he loved her with all his heart. "If she gives birth to a child, send me a message right away."

The young queen gave birth to a happy babe and the king's mother sent a messenger to the king telling him the good news. But on the way to the king the messenger tired, and coming to a river, felt sleepier and sleepier and finally fell entirely asleep by the river's edge. The Devil came out from behind a tree and switched the message to say the queen had given birth to a child that was half dog.

The king was horrified at the message, yet sent back a message saying to love the queen and care for her in this terrible time. The lad who ran with the message again came to the river, and feeling heavy as though he had eaten a feast, soon fell asleep by the side of the water. Whereupon the Devil again stepped out and changed the message to say "Kill the queen and her child."

The old mother was shaken by her son's command and sent a messenger to confirm. Back and forth the messengers ran, each one falling asleep at the river and the Devil changing messages that became increasingly terrible, the last being "Keep the tongue and eyes of the queen to prove she has been killed."

The old mother could not stand to kill the sweet young queen. Instead she sacrificed a doe, took its tongue and eyes, and hid them away. Then she helped the young queen bind her infant to her breast, and veiling her, said she must flee for her life. The women wept and kissed one another good-bye.

The young queen wandered till she came to the largest, wildest forest she had ever seen. She picked her way over and through and around trying to find a path. Near dark, the spirit in white, the same one as before, appeared and guided her to a poor inn run by kindly woodspeople. Another maiden in a white gown took the queen inside and knew her by name. The child was laid down.

"How do you know I am a queen?" asked the maiden.

"We who are of the forest follow these matters, my queen. Rest now."

So the queen stayed seven years at the inn and was happy with her child and her life. Her hands gradually grew back, first as little baby hands, pink as pearl, and then as little girl hands, and then finally as woman's hands.

During this time the king returned from the war, and his old mother wept to him, "Why would you have me kill two innocents?" and displayed to him the eyes and the tongue.

Hearing the terrible story, the king staggered and wept inconsolably. His mother saw his grief and told him these were the eyes and tongue of a doe and that she had sent the queen and her child off into the forest.

The king vowed to go without eating or drinking and to travel as far as the sky is blue in order to find them. He searched for seven years. His hands became black, his beard moldy brown like moss, his eyes red-rimmed and parched. During this time he neither ate nor drank, but a force greater than he helped him live.

At last he came to the inn kept by the woodspeople. The woman in white bade him enter, and he laid down, so tired. The woman placed a veil over his face and he slept. As he breathed the breath of deepest sleep, the veil billowed and gradually slipped from his face. He awakened to find a lovely woman and a beautiful child gazing down at him.

"I am your wife and this is your child." The king was willing to believe but saw that the maiden had hands. "Through my travails and yet my good care, my hands have grown back," said the maiden. And the woman in white brought the silver hands from a trunk where they'd been treasured. The king rose and embraced his queen and his child and there was great joy in the forest that day.

All the spirits and the dwellers of the inn had a fine repast. Afterward, the king and queen and baby returned to the old mother, held a second wedding, and had many more children, all of whom told this story to a hundred others, who told this story to a hundred others, just as you are one of the hundred others I am telling it to.

The First Stage—The Bargain Without Knowing

In the first stage of the story, the susceptible and acquisitive miller makes a poor bargain with the Devil. He thought to enrich himself, but too late realizes the price is going to be very, very high. He thought he was trading his apple tree for wealth, but instead he finds he has given his daughter to the Devil.

In archetypal psychology, we take all the elements of a fairy tale to be descriptions of the aspects in a single woman's psyche. So, regarding this tale, as women, we must ask ourselves here at the beginning, "What poor bargain does every woman make?"

Though we might respond with different answers on different days, there is one answer that is constant to all women's lives. Though we hate to admit it, over and over again the poorest bargain of our lives is the one we make when we forfeit our deep knowing life for one that is far more frail; when we give up our teeth, our claws, our sense, our scent; when we surrender our wilder natures for a promise of something that seems rich but turns out to be hollow instead. Like the father in the tale, we make this bargain without realizing the sorrow, the pain, and the dislocation it will cause us.

We can be smart in the ways of the world, and yet almost every mother's daughter, if given half a chance, chooses the poor bargain at first. The making of this awful bargain is a matter of enormous and meaningful paradox. Even though choosing poorly could be seen as a pathologically self-destructive act, it far more often turns into a watershed event that brings vast opportunity to redevelop the power of the instinctive nature. In this respect, though there is loss and sadness, the poor bargain, like birth and death, constitutes a rather utilitarian step off the cliff planned by the Self in order to bring a woman deep into her wildness.

A woman's initiation begins with the poor bargain she made long ago while still slumbering. By choosing whatever appealed to her as riches, she surrendered, in return, dominion over some and often every part of her passionate, creative, and instinctive life. That female psychic slumber is a state approximating somnambulism. During it, we walk, we talk, yet we are asleep. We love, we work, but our choices tell the truth about our condition; the voluptuous, the inquiring, the good and incendiary sides of our natures are not fully sentient.

This is the state of the daughter in the tale. She is a lovely creature to behold, an innocent. Yet, she could forever sweep the yard behind the mill—back and forth, and back and forth—and never develop knowing. Her metamorphosis has no metabolism.

So, the tale begins with the unintended but acute betrayal of the young feminine, of the innocent.[2] It can be said that the father, who symbolizes the function of the psyche that is supposed to guide us in the outer world, is, in fact, very ignorant about how the outer world and the inner world work in tandem. When the fathering function of the psyche fails to have knowing about issues of soul, we are easily betrayed. The father does not realize one of the most basic things that mediates between the world of soul and the world of matter—that is, that many things that present themselves to us are not as they seem upon first contact.

The initiation into this kind of knowing is the initiation that none of us wants, even though it is the one all of us, sooner or later, receive. So many tales—"Beauty and the Beast," "Bluebeard," "Reynard the Fox"—begin with the father endangering the daughter.[3] But, in a woman's psyche, even though the father bumbles into a lethal deal because he knows nothing of the dark side of the world or the unconscious, the horrible moment marks a dramatic beginning for her; a forthcoming consciousness and shrewdness.

No sentient being in this world is allowed to remain innocent forever. In order for us to thrive, our own instinctive nature drives us to face the fact that things are not as they first seem. The wild creative function pushes us to learn about the many states of being, perception, and knowing. These are the many conduits through which the Wild Woman speaks to us. Loss and betrayal are the first slippery steps of a long initiatory process that pitches us into *la selva subterránea*, the underground forest. There, sometimes for the first time in our lives, we have a chance to cease walking into walls of our own making and learn to pass through them instead.

While in modern society a women's loss of innocence is often ignored, in the underground forest a woman who has lived through the demise of her innocence is seen as someone special, in part because she has been hurt, but much more so because she has gone on, because she is working hard to understand, to peel back the layers of her perceptions and her defenses to see what lies underneath. In that world, her loss of innocence is treated as a rite of passage.[4] That she can now see more clearly is applauded. That she has endured and continues to learn gives her both status and honor.

Making a poor bargain is not only representative of the psychology of young women, it holds true for women of any age who are without initiation or who are dangling in an incomplete initiation in these matters. How does any woman involve herself in such a bargain? The story opens with the symbol of the mill and the miller. Like them, the psyche is a grinder of ideas; it masticates concepts and breaks them down into usable nourishment. It takes in raw material, in the form of ideas, feelings, thoughts, and perceptions, and breaks them open in a way that makes them usable for our nourishment.

This psychic ability is often called processing. When we process, we sort through all the raw material in the psyche, all the things we've learned, heard, longed for, and felt during a period of time. We break these down into parts, asking, "How shall I use this best?" We use these processed ideas and energies to implement our most soulful tasks and to fund our various creative endeavors. In this way a woman remains both sturdy and lively.

But in the story, the mill is not milling. The psyche's miller is unemployed. This means nothing is being done with all the raw material that comes into our lives on a daily basis, and that no sense is being made of all the grains of knowing that blow into our faces from the world and from the underworld. If the miller[5] has no work, the psyche has stopped nourishing itself in critically important ways.

The milling of grain has to do with the creative urge. For whatever reason, the creative life of a woman's psyche is at a standstill. A woman who feels thusly senses that she is no longer fragrant with ideas, that she is not fired with invention, that she is not grinding finely to find the pith of things. Her mill is silenced.

There appears to be a natural slumber that comes upon humans at certain times in their lives. From raising my own, and from my work with the same group of gifted children over a period of years, I saw that this sleep seems to descend upon children at age eleven or thereabouts. That is when they begin to take acute measurements about how they compare with others. During this time their eyes go from clear to hooded, and though they are always in motion like Mexican jumping beans, they are often dying of terminal cool. Whether they are being too cool or too well-behaved, in neither state are they responsive to what goes on deep inside, and a sleep gradually covers over their bright-eyed, responsive natures.

Let us further imagine that during this time we are offered something for nothing. That somehow we have twisted ourselves around to believe that if we will remain asleep something will accrue to us. Women know what this means.

When a woman surrenders her instincts that tell her the right time to say yes and when to say no, when she gives up her insight, intuition, and other wildish traits, then she finds herself in situations that promised gold but ultimately give grief. Some women relinquish their art for a grotesque financial marriage, or give up their life's dream in order to be a "too-good" wife, daughter, or girl, or surrender their true calling in order to lead what they hope will be a more acceptable, fulfilling, and especially, more sanitary life.

In these ways, and others, we lose our instincts. Instead of our lives being filled with the possibility of enlightenment, we are covered over with a kind of "endarkenment" instead. Our outer ability to see into the nature of things and our inner seeing are both snoring away so that when the Devil comes a-knocking, we sleepwalk over to the door and let him in.

The Devil symbolizes the dark force of the psyche, the predator, who in this tale is not recognized for what he is. This Devil is an archetypal bandit who needs, wants, sucks up light. Theoretically, if he were given light—that is, a life with the possibility of love and creativity—then the Devil would no longer be the Devil.

In this tale, the Devil is present because the young girl's sweet light has attracted him. Her light is not just any light but the light of a maiden soul trapped in a somnambulistic state. Oh, what a tasty morsel. Her light glows with heartbreaking beauty, but she is unaware of her value. Such a light, whether it be the glow of a woman's creative life, her wild soul, her physical beauty, her intelligence, or her generosity, always attracts the predator. Such a light that is also unaware and unprotected is always a target.

I worked with a woman who was quite taken advantage of by others, be they spouse, children, mother, father, or stranger. She was forty years old, and still at this bargain/betrayal stage of inner development. By her sweetness, her warm and welcoming voice, her lovely manner, she not only attracted those who took away an ember from her, but so large a crowd gathered before her soulful fire that they blocked her from receiving any of its warmth herself.

The poor bargain she had made was to never say no in order to be consistently loved. The predator of her own psyche offered her the gold of being loved if she would give up her instincts that said "Enough is enough." She realized fully what she was doing to herself when she had a dream that she was on her hands and knees in a crowd, trying to reach through the forest of legs for a precious crown someone had thrown into a corner.

The instinctual layer of her psyche was pointing out that she had lost her sovereignty over her own life, and that it was going to be hands-and-knees work to get it back. To retrieve her crown, this woman had to reevaluate her time, her giving, her attentions to others.

The flowering apple tree in the tale symbolizes a beauteous aspect of women, the side of our nature that has its roots sunk into the world of the Wild Mother, where it is nurtured from below. The tree is the archetypal symbol of individuation; it is considered immortal, for its seeds will live on, its root system shelters and revivifies, it is home to an entire food chain of life. Like a woman, a tree also has its seasons and its stages of growth; it has its winter, it has its spring.

In the Northwoods apple orchards, farmers call their mares and their dogs "Girl," and their flowering fruit trees "Lady." The orchard trees are the young naked women of spring—the "first nose," as we used to say. Of all the things that most meant spring, the fragrance of clustered fruit blossoms outranked the crazed robins jumping around doing triple-gainers in the side yard, and outscored the new crops coming in like tiny flames of green fire in black dirt.

Also, there was a saying about apple trees: "Young in spring, bitter fruit: other side, sweet as ice." This meant the apple had a dual nature. In the late spring it looked lovely and round and as though drizzled with sunrise. Yet it was too tart to eat; it would make all your nerves stand up and go awk! But, later in the season, to bite into the apple was like breaking open sweet candy running with juice.

The apple tree and the maiden are interchangeable symbols of the feminine Self, and the fruit is a symbol of nourishment and maturation of our knowledge of that Self. If our knowledge about the ways of our own soul is immature, we cannot be nourished from it, for the knowing is not yet ripe. As with apples, it takes time for maturation, and the roots must find their ground and at least a season must pass, sometimes several. If the maiden soul sense remains untested, nothing more can occur in our lives. But if we can gain underworld roots, we can become mature, nourishing to soul, Self, and psyche.

The flowering apple tree is a metaphor for fecundity, yes. But more so it signifies the densely sensual creative urge and the ripening of ideas. All these are the work of *las curanderas*, the root women, who live deep in the crags and *montañas*, mountains, of the unconscious. They mine the deep unconscious there, and deliver up the work to us. We work the work they give to us, and as a result a potent fire, shrewd instincts, and deep knowing springs to life, and we develop and grow in depth in both inner and outer worlds.

Here we have a tree symbolizing the abundance of wild and free nature in a woman's psyche and yet the value of this is not understood by the psyche. One could say the entire psyche is asleep to the vast possibilities in the feminine nature. When we speak of a woman's life in relationship to the symbol of the tree, we mean the feminine blossoming energy that belongs to us and that comes to us in cycles, ebbing and returning to us on a regular basis as psychic spring follows psychic winter. Without the renewal of this flowering impulse in our lives, hope is covered over, and the earth of our minds and hearts remains in an unmoving state. The flowering apple tree is our deep life.

We see the psyche's devastating underestimation of the value of the young elemental feminine—when the father says of the apple tree, "Surely we can plant another." The psyche does not recognize its own creator-Goddess in her flowering tree embodiment. The young self is traded off without realizing her dearness or her role as root messenger for the Wild Mother. Yet, it is this breach of knowing that causes the initiation of endurance to begin.

The unemployed miller, down on his luck, had begun to chop wood. It is hard work to chop wood, is it not? There is much heaving and hauling. Yet this chopping of wood symbolizes vast psychic resources, the ability to provide energy for one's tasks, to develop one's ideas, to bring the dream, whatever it be, within reach. So when the miller begins to chop away, we could say the psyche has begun to do the very hard work of bringing light and warmth to itself.

But, the poor ego is always looking for an easy way out. When the Devil suggests he will relieve the miller of hard work in exchange for the light of the deep feminine, the ignorant miller agrees. We seal our own fates in this way. Deep in the wintry parts of our minds, we are hardy stock and know there is no such thing as a work-free transformation. We know that we will have to burn to the ground in one way or another, and then sit right in the ashes of who we once thought we were and go on from there.

But, another side of our natures, a part more desirous of languor, hopes it won't be so, hopes the hard work can cease so slumber can resume. When the predator comes along, we are already set up for him; we are relieved to imagine that maybe there is an easier way.

When we shun the chopping of wood, the hands of the psyche will be chopped off instead . . . for without the psychic work, the psychic hands wither. But this desire for a bargain over hard work is so human and so common that it is amazing to find a person alive who has not made the compact. The choice is so usual that if we were to give example after example of women (or men) wanting to quit the chopping of wood and have a more easy life, thus losing their hands—that is, their grasp on their own lives—well, we would be here a long time.

For instance, a woman marries for wrong reasons and cuts off her creative life. A woman has one sexual preference, and forces herself to another. A woman wants to be, go, do a big something, and stays home and counts paper clips instead. A woman wants to live life, but saves little shreds of life as though they are string. A woman is her own person, yet gives an arm, a leg, or an eyeball away to every lover who comes down the pike. A woman flows with radiant creativity, and invites her vampirish friends to a group siphon. A woman needs to go on with her life and something in her says, "No, being snared is being safe." This is the Devil's "I'll give you this, if you'll give me that," the bargain without knowing.

So what was meant to be the nutritive and flowering tree of the psyche loses power, loses its blossoms, loses energy, is sold out, is forced into forfeiting its potential, not understanding the bargain it has made. The entire drama almost always begins and establishes its strong hold outside a woman's consciousness.

Yet, it must be emphasized that this is where everyone begins. In this tale the father represents the outer world point of view, the collective ideal that pressures women to be wilted rather than wildish. Even so, there is no shame and no blame if you have given away the flowering boughs. Yes, you have suffered for it, no doubt. And you may have given it away for years, even for decades. But there is hope.

The mother in the fairy tale announces to the entire psyche what has occurred. She says, "Wake up! See what you have done!" And everybody wakes up so fast, it hurts.[6] But still it is good news, for the wishy-washy mother of the psyche, the one that once helped to dilute and dull feeling function, has just awakened to the horrible meaning of the bargain. Now a woman's pain becomes conscious. When it is conscious, she can do something with it. She can use it to learn with, to grow strong with, to become a knowing woman.

Over the long term, there will be even better news yet. That which has been given away can be reclaimed. It can be restored to its proper place in the psyche. You will see.

The Second Stage—The Dismemberment

In the second stage of the story, the parents stumble home, weeping tears on all their finery. Three years to the day the Devil comes to fetch the daughter. She has bathed and put on a white gown. She stands inside a chalk circle she's drawn around herself. When the Devil reaches out to seize her, an unseen force throws him across the yard. He orders her not to bathe. She devolves to an animal-like condition. But she weeps on her hands, and again the Devil cannot touch her. He orders the father to cut off her hands so she cannot weep on them. This is done, and thus her life as she has known it is ended. But she cries on the stumps of her arms and the Devil again cannot overwhelm her, and he gives up.

The daughter has done remarkably well considering the circumstances. Yet we are numb once we have passed through this stage and realize what has been done to us, how we surrendered to the will of the predator and the frightened father so that we wound up being made handless.

After this, spirit reacts by moving when we move, by reaching when we reach, by walking when we walk, but it has no feeling to it. We are numb when we realize what has come to pass. We are horrified to fulfill our barter. We think our internal parental constructs are supposed to always be alert, responsive, and protective of the flowering psyche. Now we see what happens when they are not.

Three years pass between the making of the bargain and the Devil's return. These three years represent a time when a woman does not have clear consciousness about the fact that she herself is the sacrifice. She is the burnt offering that has been made for some poor bargain. In mythology the three-year period is the time of mounting momentum, as in the three years of winter that precede *Ragnarok*, the Twilight of the Gods, in Scandinavian mythology. In myths like these, three years of something occurs, then comes a destruction, then from that ruin is born a new world of peace.[7]

This number of years is symbolic of the time when a woman wonders what will happen to her now, wonders if what she fears most—being totally carried off by a destructive force—is really going to occur. The fairy-tale symbol of three follows this pattern: The first try is no good. The second try, still no good. The third turn, ah, now something will happen.

Soon enough energy will be stirred at last, enough soul-wind has been raised to cause the psychic vessel to sail far and away. Lao-tzu[8] says, "Of the one comes two, and of the two, three. And from the three come ten thousand." By the time we come to the "three" power of anything, that is, to the transformative moment, the atoms leap, and where there was once lassitude there is now locomotion.

Remaining without husband for three years can be understood as the psyche in an incubation, one in which it would be too difficult and distracting to have another relationship. The work of these three years is to strengthen oneself as much as one can, to use all one's psychic resource for oneself, to become as conscious as possible. That means stepping outside our suffering and seeing what it means, how it goes, what pattern it is following, studying others with the same pattern who have come through it all, and imitating what makes sense to us.

It is this kind of observation of predicaments and solutions that bids a woman to stay to herself, and this is right, for as we find further in the story, the maiden's task is to find the bridegroom in the underworld, not in the topside world. In hindsight, women see the preparation for their initiatory descent mounting over a long period of time, sometimes years, till finally and suddenly over the edge and into the rapids they go, most often pushed over, but occasionally entering by a graceful dive from the cliffs . . . but rarely.

This period of time is sometimes characterized by an ennui. Women will often say their mood is such that they cannot quite put their finger on what it is they want, whether it be work, lover, time, creative work. It is hard to concentrate. It is hard to be productive. This nerve-restlessness is typical of this spiritual developmental stage. Time alone, and not very far down the road, will take us to the edge we need fall, step, or dive over.

At this point in the tale, we see a fragment of the old night religions. The young woman bathes, dresses in white, draws a chalk circle around herself. It is an old Goddess ritual to bathe—purify—to don the white gown—the garb of descent to the land of the dead—and to draw a circle of magic protection—sacred thought—around oneself. All these the maiden does in a rather trancelike state, as though she is drawing instruction from far away in time.

There is a crisis point for us when we are waiting for what we are sure will be our destruction, our ending. This causes us, like the maiden, to cock our ears toward a faraway voice coming from ancestral time, a voice that tells us how to stay strong, how to keep spirit simple and pure. Once in my own despair I dreamt a voice that said, "Touch sun." After the dream, every day, wherever I went, I put my back, or the sole of my foot, or my palm on the sun-cats—the rectangles of sunlight—on walls, floors, and doors. I leaned and rested on those golden shapes. They acted as a turbine to my spirit. I cannot say how, only that it was so.

If we listen to dream voices, to images, to stories—especially those from our own lives, and to our art, to those who have gone before, and to each other, something will be handed out to us, even several somethings that are ritual, personal psychological rites, these serving to steady this stage of the process.[9]

The bones of this tale are from the time when it is said that Goddesses combed the hair of mortal women and loved them so. In this sense then, we understand that the descents in this tale are those that draw a woman to the ancient past, to her ancestral motherlines in the underworld. This is the task, to return through the mists of time to the place of *La Que Sabe*, who is expecting us. She has extensive underworld teachings for us that will be of great value to our spirits and to us in the outer world.

In the old religions, dressing oneself in purity and preparing for one's death makes one immune, inaccessible to evil. Placing the old protection of the Wild Mother about oneself—the chalk circle of prayer, highest thought, or concern for an outcome beneficial for the soul's sake—these enable our psychological descent to continue without swerving off course, without our vitality being extinguished by the devilish opposing force of the psyche.

Here we are, all dressed up and as protected as we can be,

awaiting our fate. But the maiden weeps, cries on her hands. At first when the psyche cries unconsciously, we are unable to hear it except for a feeling of helplessness that comes over us. The maiden continues to weep. Her tears are a germination of that which preserves her, that which purifies the wound she has received.

C. S. Lewis wrote about the bottle of child's tears that heals any wound with just one drop. Tears, in mythos, melt the icy heart. In "The Stone Child,"[10] a story I've amplified from a song-poem given to me years ago by my beloved Inuit *madrina*, Mary Uukalat, a boy's hot tears cause a cold stone to break open, releasing a protective spirit. In the tale "Mary Culhane," the demon who has seized Mary cannot enter any house where tears have been cried by a true heart; these the demon considers "holy water." All through history, tears have done three works: called the spirits to one's side, repelled those who would muffle and bind the simple soul, and healed the injuries of poor bargains made by humans.

There are times in a woman's life when she cries and cries and cries, and even though she has the succor and support of her loved ones, still and yet she cries. Something in this crying keeps the predator away, keeps away unhealthy desire or gain that will ruin her. Tears are part of the mending of rips in the psyche where energy has leaked and leaked away. The matter is serious, but the worst does not occur—our light is not stolen—for tears make us conscious. There is no chance to go back to sleep when one is weeping. Whatever sleep comes then is only rest for the physical body.

Sometimes a woman says, "I am sick of crying, I am tired of it, I want it to stop." But it is her soul that is making tears, and they are her protection. So she must keep on till the time of need is over. Some women marvel at all the water their bodies can produce when they weep. This will not last forever, only till the soul is done with its wise expression.

The Devil tries to approach the daughter and cannot, for she has both bathed and cried. He admits his power is weakened by such holy water and demands she no longer bathe. But rather than this debasing her, it has the opposite effect.[11] She begins to resemble an animal then, infused with the powers of the underlying wildish nature, and this, too, is protection. It may be at this stage that a woman takes less or a different sort of interest in her appearance. She may go about dressed more like a tangle of twigs than a person. As she contemplates her plight, many former preoccupations recede.

"Well," says the Devil, "if I peel away your civilized layer maybe I can steal your life forever." The predator wishes to degrade her, weaken her by his proscriptions. The Devil thinks that if the maiden became unbathed and dirty, then he would be able to rob her of herself. But just the opposite occurs, for the sooty woman, the mud woman, is beloved by the Wild Woman and protected by her unequivocally.[12] It would appear that the predator does not understand that his proscriptions only put her closer to her powerful wild nature.

The Devil cannot come close to the wildish self. Being thus has a purity that eventually repels thoughtless or destructive energy. The combination of this and her pure tears prevents access to the vile thing that wishes her doom so it can live more fully.

Next, the Devil instructs the father to mutilate his daughter by chopping off her hands. If the father does not comply, the demon threatens to kill off the entire psyche: "Everything here will die, including you, your wife, and all the fields for as far as you can see." The Devil's goal is to cause the daughter to lose her hands—that is, her psychic ability to grasp, to hold, to help herself or others.

The fathering element of the psyche is not mature, cannot hold its power against this intense predator, and so chops off his daughter's hands. He attempts to plead for his daughter, but the price—destruction of the entire creative force of the psyche—is too high. The daughter submits to the desecration, and the blood sacrifice is completed, that which in ancient times denoted a full descent to the underworld.

In the act of losing her hands, the woman makes her way into *la selva subterránea*, the underworld initiation ground. If this were a Greek play, the tragic chorus would now cry out and weep, for even though the act causes her to learn immense power, at this time a woman's innocence has been slain and will never return in the same way again.

The silver-lipped ax comes from another archeological layer of the old wild feminine in which silver is the special color of the spirit world and of the moon. The silver-lipped ax is so called for in olden times it was made of forge-blackened steel, and its blade was sharpened by whetstone till it turned a bright silverish color. In the old Minoan religion, the ax of the Goddess was used to mark the ritual path of the initiate and to mark the places designated as holy. I have heard from two old Croatian "talers" that in the old women's religions, a small ritual ax was used to sever the umbilical cord of the newborn, freeing the child from the underworld so it could live in this world.[13]

The silver of the ax is related to the silver hands that will eventually belong to the maiden. Here is a tricky passage, for it presents the idea that the removal of psychic hands may be ritual. In old women's healing rites in Eastern and Northern Europe, there was the concept of the young sapling being pruned with an ax in order to grow more full.[14] Long ago there was a deep devotion to living trees. They were valued, for they symbolized the ability to die and return back to life. They were esteemed for all the life-giving things they provided people, such as firewood for warmth and cooking, wands for cradles, staffs for walking, walls for shelter, medicine for fever, and also as places to climb to see far and, if necessary, to hide from the enemy. The tree was truly a great wild mother.

In ancient women's religion, this sort of ax innately belongs to the Goddess, not to the father. This sequence in the fairy tale strongly suggests that the father's ownership of the ax comes about in the story as a result of the scrambling together of the old and the newer religions, the older one itself having been dismembered, certainly dis-remembered. Yet, regardless of the mists of time and/or the overlays covering these old ideas about women's initiation, by following a tale such as this one we can extract what we need from the tangle; we can re-piece the map that shows the path of descent and the way back up again.

We can understand the removal of psychic hands in much the same way the symbol was understood by the ancients. In Asia, the celestial ax was used to cut one away from the unillumined self. This motif of cutting as initiation is central to our story. If, in our modern societies, the hands of the ego must be sundered in order to regain our wild office, our feminine senses, then go they must in order to take us away from all seductions of meaningless things within our reach, whatever it is that we can hold on to in order not to grow. If it is so that the hands must go for a while, then so be it. Let them go.

The father wields the silver cutting tool, and though he has a sense of terrible regret, he holds more dear his own life and that of the psyche all around, although some storytellers in our family clearly emphasize that the life he most fears losing is his own. If we understand the father as an organizing principle, a sort of ruler of the external or worldly psyche, then we can see that a woman's overt self, her mundane, ruling ego-self, does not want to die.

This is completely understandable. Such is always the case in a descent. Some of what we are is drawn to the descent as though it is something lovely, dark, and bittersweet. At the same time we are repelled by it, crossing psychic streets, highways, and even continents to avoid it. Yet here we are shown that the flowering tree must suffer the amputation. The only way we can stand the thought of this is by the promise that someone, somewhere in the underside of the psyche, waits for us, waits to help us, heal us. And this is so. A great Someone waits to restore us, to transform what has deteriorated, and to bind up the limbs that have been hurt.

In the farmlands out where I grew up, lightning and hail storms were called "cutting storms," sometimes also "reaper storms," as in Grim Reaper, for they cut down the living beings all around: livestock and sometimes also humans, but mostly bearing-plants and trees. After a great storm, entire families crept from their root cellars and bent over the land, seeing what help the crops, the flowers, the trees might need. The littlest children picked up the strewn boughs full of leaves and fruit. The older children propped up plants still living but slashed. They bound them up with wooden dowels, kindling splints, and white rag bandages. The adults dismantled and buried that which had been struck down irrevocably.

There is a loving family like this waiting for the maiden in the underworld, as we shall see. In this metaphor of cutting off the hands, we see that something will come of it. In the underworld, whenever a thing is not able to live, it is taken down and cut apart to be used in another way. This woman of the story is not old, not sick, yet she must be dismantled for she cannot be the way she has been anymore. Yet forces are waiting for her to help her heal.

By cutting off her hands, the father deepens the descent, hastens the *disolutio*, the difficult loss of all one's dearest values, which mean everything, the loss of vantage point, the loss of horizon lines, the loss of one's bearings about what one believes and for what reasons. In aboriginal rites worldwide, the idea is definitely to confuse the ordinary mind so that the mystical can be easily introduced to the initiates.[15]

With the cutting off of the hands, the importance of the rest of the psychic body and its attributes is emphasized and we know that the foolish ruling father of the psyche has not long to live, for the deep and dismembered woman is going to do her work, with or without his assistance and protection. And as gruesome as it may seem at first, this new version of her body is going to help.

So it is in this descent that we lose our psychic hands, those parts of our bodies that are like two small human beings in and of themselves. In olden times, the fingers were likened to legs and arms, and the wrist joint was likened to the head. Those beings can dance, they can sing. I once clapped cadence with Reneé Heredia, a great flamenco guitarist. In flamenco, the palms of the hands speak, they make sounds that are words, like "Faster, oh beautiful one, soar now, be deeper, ah, feel me, feel this music, feel this and this and this." The hands are beings in their own right.

If you study crèche scenes from the Mediterranean, more often than not you see that the hands of the shepherds and the Wise Men, or of Mary and Joseph, are all extended with palms facing the Divine Child, as though the child were a light that could be received up through the skin of the palms. In Mexico, you see this also in statues of the great Goddess Guadalupe showering her healing light down upon us by showing us the palms of her hands. The power of the hands is recorded throughout history. At Kayenta on the Diné (Navajo) reservation there is a certain hogan with an ancient red handprint beside the door. It means, "We are safe here."

As women, we touch many people. We know our palm is a kind of sensor. Whether in a hug or a pat or just a touch on the shoulder, we take a reading of the persons we touch. If we are connected in any way to *La Que Sabe*, we know what another human feels by sensing them with our palms. For some, information in the form of images and sometimes even words comes to them, informing them of the feeling state of others. One might say there is a form of radar in the hands.

Hands are not only receivers but transmitters. When one shakes a person's hand, one can send a message, and often unconsciously does so by pressure, intensity, duration, and skin temperature. Persons who consciously or unconsciously intend meanness have touches that feel as though they are poking holes in the psychic soul-body of the other. At the other psychological pole, hands laid upon a person can soothe, comfort, remove pain, and heal. This is woman's knowledge through the centuries, handed down mother to daughter.[16]

The predator of the psyche knows all about the deep mystery associated with hands. In too many parts of the world, an egregiously pathological way of demonstrating inhumanity is to kidnap an innocent person and cut off their hands; to dismember the human feeling, seeing, and healing function. The killer does not feel, so he does not wish for his victim to feel either. This is exactly the intention of the Devil, for the unredeemed aspect of the psyche does not feel, and in its insane envy of those who do, it is driven to a cutting hatred. To murder a woman by cutting is a theme of many tales. But this Devil is more than a murderer, he is a mutilator. He requires mutilation, not decorative or simple initiatory scarification, but the kind that intends to disable a woman forever.

When we say a woman's hands are cut off, we mean she is bound away from self-comfort, from immediate self-healing, so very helpless to do anything except follow the age-old path. So it is proper that we continue to weep during this time. It is our simple and powerful protection against a demon so hurtful that none of us can fully comprehend its motive or raison d'être.

In fairy tales there is the leitmotif called the "thrown object." The heroine who is being pursued takes a magical comb from her hair and throws it down behind her, where it grows into a forest of trees so thick you couldn't poke a pitchfork between them. Or the heroine has a little vial of water, which she uncorks, sprinkling its contents behind her as she runs. The droplets turn into a flood, effectively slowing down her pursuer.

In the story, the young woman cries and cries all over her stumps and the Devil is repelled by some sort of force field around her. He cannot seize her as he had intended. Here, tears are the "thrown object," the watery wall that keeps out the Devil, not because the Devil is moved or made soft by them—he is not— but because there is something about the purity of true tears that causes the Devil's power to be broken. And we find this to be true when we cry for the love of God that nothing, nothing, is on the horizon but the most bleak, the most dark and unredeemed possibilities, and yet the tears save us from being burnt to the ground for no useful end.[17]

The daughter must grieve. I am amazed how little women cry nowadays, and then apologetically. I worry when shame or disuse begins to steal away such a natural function. To be a flowering tree and to be moist is essential, otherwise you will break. Crying is good, it is right. It does not cure the dilemma, but it enables the process to continue instead of collapsing. And now, the maiden's life as she has known it, her understanding of life to this point, is over, and she goes down to another level of the underworld. And we continue in her footsteps. We go onward, even though we are vulnerable and so peeled of ego-protection, like a tree skinned of its bark. Yet we are powerful, for we have learned to sling the Devil across the yard.

At this time, we see in our lives that no matter what we do, our ego-plans slip from our grasp. There will be a change in our lives, a big one, no matter what nice plans the little temperamental conductor-ego has for the next movement. Our own powerful destiny begins to rule our lives—not the mill, not the sweeping, not the sleeping. Our lives as we once knew them are over. We are desirous of being alone, perhaps being left alone. We can no longer rely on the fatherly dominant culture; we are in the midst of learning our real lives for the first time. We go on.

It is a time when all that we value loses its lilt. Jung reminds us of the term used by Heraclitus, *enantiodromia*—meaning to flow backward. But this flowing backward can be more than a regression into the personal unconscious, it can be a heartfelt return to workable ancient values, more deeply held ideas.[18] If we understand this stage of the initiation of endurance as a step backward, it must also be considered a step ten leagues down and back into the realm of Wild Woman.

All this causes the Devil to throw his rump over his shoulder and stomp off. In this sense, when a woman feels she has lost her touch, lost her usual way with the world, she is powerful still in her pureness of soul, she is strong in her insistence on her sorrow, and this causes the thing that wishes to destroy her to withdraw.

The psychic body has lost its precious hands, it is true. But the rest of the psyche will compensate for the loss. We still have feet that know the way, a soul-mind with which to see far, breasts and belly to sense with, just like the exotic and enigmatic belly Goddess, Baubo, who represents the deep instinctual nature of women . . . and who also has no hands.

With this incorporeal and uncanny body we go forward. We are about to make the next descent.

The Third Stage—The Wandering

In the third stage of the story, the father offers to keep his daughter in riches for life, but the daughter says she will go forth and depend upon fate. At daybreak, with her arms bound in clean gauze, she walks away from her life as she has known it.

She becomes disheveled and animal-like again. Late at night, starving, she comes to an orchard in which all the pears are numbered.[19] A spirit drains the moat around the orchard, and while the mystified gardener watches, the young woman eats the pear that offers itself to her.

Initiation is the process by which we turn from our natural inclination to remain unconscious and decide that, whatever it takes— suffering, striving, enduring—we will pursue conscious union with the deeper mind, the wild Self. In the tale, the mother and father attempt to draw the maiden back into an unconscious state: "Ah, stay here with us, you are injured, but we can make you forget." Will she, now that she has defeated the Devil, rest on her laurels so to speak? Will she retire, handless, injured, to the recesses of the psyche where she can be taken care of for the rest of her life by just drifting along and doing what she is told?

No, she will not withdraw like an acid-scarred beauty into a dim room forever. She will dress, psychically medicate herself as best she can, and descend another stone staircase to an even deeper realm of the psyche. The old dominant part of the psyche offers to keep her safe and hidden forever, but her instinctual nature says no to that, for it feels it must strive to live fully awake no matter what.

The maiden's wounds are wrapped in white gauze. White is the color of the deathland, and also the color of the alchemical *albedo*, the resurrection of the soul from the underworld. The color is a harbinger of the cycle of descent and return. Here at the beginning, the maiden becomes a wanderer, and this in and of itself is a resurrection into a new life, and a death in the old. To wander is a very good choice.

Women in this stage often begin to feel both desperate and adamant to go on this inward journey, no matter what. And so they do, as they leave one life for another, or one stage of life for another, or sometimes even one lover for no other lover than themselves. Progressing from adolescence to young womanhood, or from married woman to spinster, or from mid-age to older, crossing over the crone line, setting out wounded but with one's own new value system—that is death and resurgence. Leaving a relationship or the home of one's parents, leaving behind outmoded values, becoming one's own person, and sometimes, driving deep into the wildlands because one just *must*, all these are the fortune of the descent.

So off we go, down into a different world, under a different sky, with unfamiliar ground beneath our boots. And yet we go vulnerably, for we have no grasping, no holding on to, no clinging to, no knowing—for we have no hands.

The mother and father—the collective and egoistic aspects of the psyche—no longer have the power they once had. They have been chastened by blood that has been spilt through their reckless disregard. Even though they make the offer to keep the maiden in comfort, they are helpless now to direct her life, for destiny draws her to live as a wanderer. In this sense, her mother and father die. Her new parents are the wind and the road.

The archetype of the wanderer constellates, that is, causes another to emerge: that of the lone wolf or the outsider. She is outside the seeming happy families of the villages, outside the warm room and out in the cold; that is her life now.[20] This becomes the living metaphor for women on the journey. We begin somehow not to feel a part of the life that carnivals about us. The calliope seems far away, the barkers, the hucksters, the whole magnificent circus of outer life wobbles and then falls to dust as we descend farther into the underworld.

Here, the old night religion again comes up from the road to meet us. While the old tale of Hades grabbing off Persephone to the underworld is a fine drama, far older stories from the matria-centered religions, such as those about Ishtar and Inanna, point toward a definite "yearning to love" bond between the maiden and the king in the underworld.

In these old religious versions, the maiden need not be seized and dragged into the underworld by some dark God. The maiden knows she must go, knows it is part of divine rite. Although she may be fearful, she *wants* to go meet her king, her bridegroom in the underworld, from the beginning. Making her descent in her own way, she is transformed there, learns deep knowing there, and ascends again to the outer world.

Both the classical Persephone myth and the core of the fairy tale "The Handless Maiden" are fragmentary dramas which derive from the more cohesive ones portrayed in the older religions. What was once a longing to find the underworld Beloved became, somewhere in time, a lust and seizure in later myths.

In the time of the great matriarchies, it was understood that a woman would naturally be led to the underworld, guided there and therein by the powers of the deep feminine. It was considered part of her instruction, and an achievement of the highest order for her to gain this knowledge through firsthand experience. The nature of this descent is the archetypal core of both "The Handless Maiden" fairy tale and the Demeter/Persephone myth.

So now in the tale, the maiden wanders about for the second time in her unwashed animal state. This is the proper mode of descent—the "I don't care so much for things of the world" mode. And as we see, her beauty shines regardless. The idea of being unwashed also is from ritual of olden times, the culmination of which is the bathing and putting on of new clothes to represent having crossed into new or renewed relationship with the Self.

We see that the handless maiden has gone through one entire descent and transformation—the one of awakening. In certain alchemical tracts there are three stages described as being necessary to transformation: the *nigredo*, the black or the dark dissolving stage, the *rubedo*, the red or the sacrificial stage, and the *albedo*, the white or the resurgent stage. The bargain with the Devil was the *nigredo*, the darkening; the chopping off of her hands was the *rubedo*, the sacrifice; and the leaving of home wrapped in white, the *albedo*, is the new life. And now, as the wanderer, she is plunged back into the *nigredo* again. But now the old self is gone, and the deep self, the naked self, is the powerful wanderer.[21]

Now the maiden is not only haggard but hungry. She kneels before an orchard as though it is an altar—and it is—the altar of the wild underground Gods. As we descend to the primary nature, the old, automatic ways of nourishing ourselves are eliminated. Things of the world that used to be food for us lose their taste. Our goals no longer excite us. Our achievements no longer hold interest. Everywhere we look in the topside world, there is no food for us. So, it is one of the purest miracles of the psyche that when we are so defenseless help comes, and right on time.

The vulnerable maiden is visited by an emissary from the soul, the spirit in white. This spirit in white removes the barriers to her being nourished. It empties the moat by adjusting the sluice gate. The moat has hidden meaning. According to the ancient Greeks, in the underworld the river called Styx separates the land of the living from the land of the dead. Its waters are filled with the memories of all past deeds of the dead since the beginning of time. The dead can decipher these memories and keep them in order, for they have heightened vision that comes from being without material body.

But for the living, the river is poison. Unless the living are accompanied across by a spirit guide, they will drown and sink to another level of the underworld, one that is like a mist, and there they will wander forever. Dante had his Virgil, *Coatlicue* had a living snake who accompanied her to the fire world, and the handless maiden has the spirit in white. So, you see, first a woman escapes from the not-awake mother and the greedy, bumbling father, and then gives herself over to be guided by the wild soul.

In the tale, the spirit guide escorts the handless maiden across to the underworld realm of the trees, the king's orchard. This, too, is a remnant of the old religion. Spirit guides are always assigned to the young initiates in the old religions. Greek mythos is filled with reports of young women being accompanied by wolf women or lion women or other figures who served as initiators. Even in current religious rites that are concomitant with nature, such as among the Diné (Navajo), the mysterious *yeibecheis* are animal elementals who accompany initiation as well as healing rites.

The psychic idea embodied here is that the underworld, like the unconscious of humans, swirls with many unusual and compelling features, images, archetypes, seductions, threats, treasures, tortures, and tests. It is important for a woman's individuation journey that she have spiritual good sense, or be assisted by a guide who does, so that she does not fall into the phantasmagoria of the unconscious, so that she does not lose herself in this tantalizing material. As we see in the tale, it is more important to stay with one's hunger and go forward from there.

Like Persephone before her, and the Life/Death/Life Goddesses before her, the maiden finds her way into a land where there are magical orchards and a king awaits her. The old religion now begins to glow in this tale with more and more intensity. In Greek myths[22] there were two trees twined over the door to the underworld, and Elysium, the place where the dead who had been found virtuous were sent, was composed of what?—yes, orchards.

Elysium is described as a place of perpetual day, where souls may elect to be reborn on earth whenever they please. It is the doppelgänger, the double of the topside world. Difficult things may occur here, but their meaning and the learning they provide are different from those in the topside world. In the topside world, all is interpreted in the light of simple gains and losses. In the underworld or other world, all is interpreted in light of the mysteries of true sight, right action, and the development of becoming a person of intense inner strength and knowing.

In the tale the action now centers on the fruit tree, which in ancient times was called the Tree of Life, Tree of Knowing, Tree of Life and Death, or Tree of Knowledge. Unlike trees with needles or leaves, the fruit tree is a tree of bountiful food—and not just food, for a tree stores water in its fruit. Water, the primal fluid of growth and continuance, is soaked up by the roots, which feed the tree by capillary action—a network of billions of cell plexuses too small to see—and water arrives in the fruit and plumps it out into a beauteous thing.

Because of this, the fruit is considered to be invested with soul, with a life force that develops from *and* contains some measure of water, air, earth, food, and seed, which on top of it all also tastes divine. Women who are fed by the fruit and water and seed of the work in the underground forests are plumped out psychologically accordingly; their psyches become gravid and carry on a continual ripening.

Like a mother offering the babe her breast, the pear tree in the orchard bends down to give the maiden its fruit. This mother's juice is that of regeneration. Eating the pear nourishes the maiden, but a more poignant action is this: the unconscious, the fruit of it, bends to feed her. In this sense, the unconscious bestows a kiss of itself upon her lips. It gives her a taste of the Self, the breath and the substance of her own wild God, a wild communion.

The hailing of Mary by her kinswoman Elizabeth[23] in the New Testament is probably a remnant of this ancient understanding among women: "Blessed be the fruit of thy womb," she says. In the prior night religions, the woman, just having been initiated and pregnant with knowing, would be welcomed back into the world of the living with a lovely blessing from her kinswomen.

The remarkable idiom of the story is that during the darkest times the feminine unconscious, the uterine unconscious, Nature, feeds a woman's soul. Women describe that in the midst of their descent they are in the darkest dark and are touched by the brush of a wing tip and feel lightened. They feel an inner nourishing taking place, a spring of blessed water bursting forth over parched ground . . . from where they do not know. This spring does not solve suffering, but rather nourishes when nothing else is forthcoming. It is manna in the desert. It is water from stones. It is food out of thin air. It quells the hunger so we can go on. And that is the whole point . . . to go on. To go on toward our knowing destiny.

The tale resurrects the memory of a very old promise; the promise is that the descent will nourish even though it is dark, even though one feels one has lost one's way. Even in the midst of not knowing, not seeing, "wandering blind," there is a "Something," an inordinately present "Someone" who keeps pace. We go left, it goes left. We go right, it follows close behind, bearing us up, making a way for us.

Now we are in another *nigredo* of wandering and not knowing what will become of us, and yet in this very raggedy condition we are brought to sup on the Tree of Life. To eat of the Tree of Life in the land of the dead is an ancient impregnation metaphor. In the land of the dead, it was believed a soul could invest itself in a fruit, or any edible thing, so that its future mother would eat it, and the soul hidden within the fruit would begin its regeneration in her flesh. So here, at the almost midway point, through the substance of the pear, we are being given the body of the Wild Mother, we are eating that which we will ourselves become.[24]

The Fourth Stage—Finding Love in the Underworld

The next morning the king comes to count his pears. One is missing and the gardener reveals what he's seen. "Last night two spirits drained the moat, entered the garden at high moon, and one without hands ate the pear that offered itself to her."

That night, the king keeps watch with his gardener and with his magician, who knows how to speak with the spirits. At midnight, the maiden comes floating through the forest, her clothes dirty rags, her hair awry, her face streaked, her arms without hands, and with the spirit in white beside her.

Again, another tree gracefully bends itself to her reach and she sups on the pear at its bough's end. The magician comes close, but not too close, and asks, "Are you of this world or not of this world?" The maiden answers, "I was once of *the* world, and yet I am not of *this* world."

The king questions the magician, "Is she human or spirit?" The magician answers that she is both. The king rushes to her, pledging his loyalty and love: "I shall not forsake you. From this day forward, I shall care for you." They marry, and he has made for her a pair of silver hands.

The king is a wisening creature in the underworld psyche. He is not just any old king, but one of the chief watchers of a woman's unconscious. He watches over the botany of the growing soul—his (and his mother's) orchard is rich with the trees of life and death. He is of the family of the wild Gods. Like the maiden, he is able to endure much. And like the maiden, he has another descent ahead of him. But more of that later.

In a sense, one could say he is trailing the maiden. The psyche always shadows its own process. This is a most sacred premise. It means that if you are wandering, there is another—at least one, and often more—who is seasoned and experienced and who waits for you to knock at the door, rap on stone, eat a pear, or just show up, in order to announce your arrival in the underworld. This loving presence waits and watches for the wandering seeker. Women are well aware of this. They call it a little flicker of light or insight, a presentiment, or a presence.

The gardener, the king, and the magician are three mature personifications of the archetypal masculine. They correspond to the sacred trinity of the feminine personified by the maiden, mother, and crone. In this story, the ancient triple Goddesses or the Three-Goddesses-in-One are represented this way: the maiden is portrayed by the handless woman, the mother and crone are both portrayed by the king's mother, who enters the tale later. The twist in the tale that makes it "modern" is that the devil image portrays a figure that in ancient women's initiation rites was normally portrayed by the crone in her dual nature as life-bringer and life-taker. In this tale the Devil is portrayed as the life-taker only.

However, back in misty time, it is a good bet that this sort of story originally presented the crone playing the part of the

initiator/trouble-causer, making things difficult for the sweet
young heroine so embarkation from the land of the living to the
land of the dead could occur. Psychically, this is cohesive with
concepts in Jungian psychology, theology, and the old night religions that the Self, or in our parlance, the Wild Woman, seeds the
psyche with perils and challenges in order that the human in
despair drives herself back down into her original nature looking
for answers and strength, thereby reuniting with the great wild
Self and, as much as possible thereafter, moving as one.

In one way this distortion in the tale distorts our information
about the ancient processes of a woman's return to the underworld. But actually, this replacement of devil for crone is strikingly relevant to us today, for in order to discover the ancient ways
of the unconscious, we often find ourselves fighting off the Devil
in the form of cultural, familial, or intra-psychic injunctions that
devalue the soul-life of the wild feminine. In this sense, the tale
works either way, both by leaving enough bones of the old ritual
so we can reconstruct it, and by showing us how the natural
predator tries to cut us away from our rightful powers, how it tries
to take our soulful work from us.

The major agents of transformation present in the orchard at
this time are, in the approximate order of their appearance: the
maiden, spirit in white, gardener, king, magician, mother/crone,
and devil. Traditionally they represent the following intra-psychic
forces.

THE MAIDEN

As we have seen, the maiden represents the heartfelt and formerly
sleepy psyche. But a warrior-heroine lies beneath her soft exterior.
She has the endurance of the lone wolf. She is able to bear the dirt,
grime, betrayal, hurt, loneliness, and exile of the initiate. She is
able to wander the underworld and return, enriched, to the topside
world. Although she may not be able to articulate them when she
first descends, she is following the instructions and directions of
the old Wild Mother, Wild Woman.

THE SPIRIT IN WHITE

Throughout legend and fairy tales the spirit in white is the guide, the one who has an innate and gentle knowing, who is rather like a trailblazer for the woman's journey. Among some of the *mese-mondók*, this spirit was thought to be a piece of an old and precious shattered God that still invested itself in each human. By way of dress the spirit in white is closely related to myriad Life/Death/Life Goddesses from various cultures who all dress in radiant white—*La Llorona*, Berchta, Hel, and so on. This implies that the spirit in white is a helper of the mother/crone who, in archetypal psychology, is also a Life/Death/Life Goddess.

THE GARDENER

The gardener is a cultivator of soul, a regenerative keeper of seed, soil, and root. He is similar to the Hopi *Kokopelli*, who is a hump-backed Spirit who comes to the villages each spring and fertilizes the crops as well as the women. The gardener's function is regeneration. The psyche of a woman must constantly sow, train, and harvest new energy in order to replace what is old and worn out. There is a natural entropy, or wearing down and using up, of psychic parts. This is good, this is how the psyche is supposed to work, but one must have energies-in-training ready to backfill. This is the role of the gardener in the psychic work. He keeps track of the need for change and replenishing. Intra-psychically, there is constant living, constant death-dealing, constant replacement of ideas, images, energies.

THE KING

The king[25] represents a trove of knowledge in the underworld. He carries the ability to take inner knowing out into the world and put it into practice, without mincing, muttering, or apologizing. The king is the son of the mother queen/crone. Like her, and probably following her lead, he is involved in the mechanisms of vital process of the psyche: the failing, dying, and return of consciousness. Later in the story, when he wanders looking for his lost queen, he will undergo a kind of death that will transform him from a civilized king to a wild one. He will find his queen and so be reborn. In psychic terms this means that the old central attitudes of the psyche will die as the psyche learns more. The old attitudes will be replaced by either new or renewed viewpoints concerning just about everything in a woman's life. In this sense the king represents renewal of the ruling attitudes and laws in a woman's psyche.

THE MAGE

The mage, or magician,[26] whom the king brings with him to interpret what he sees, represents the direct magic of a woman's power. Such things as the split-second recall, the thousand-league vision, the hearing over miles, the empathic ability to see from behind anyone's eyes—human or animal—all these belong to the instinctual feminine. It is the magician who shares in these and also, traditionally, helps to maintain them and enact them in the outer world. Though the mage can be of either gender, here it is a powerful male figure similar to the stalwart brother in fairy tales who so loves his sister that he will do all to help her. The mage always has crossover potential. In dreams and in tales, he appears as a man as often as he shows up as a woman. He can be male, female, animal, or mineral, just as the crone, his female counterpart, can also effect her guises with ease. In conscious life, the mage assists a woman's ability to become whatever she wishes and to portray herself as she wishes at any given moment.

THE QUEEN MOTHER/CRONE

The queen mother/crone in this tale is the king's mother. This figure represents many things, among them fecundity, the vast authority to see into the tricks of the predator, and the ability to soften curses. The word *fecundity*, which sounds like drum talk when said aloud, means more than fertile, it means pregnable, the way soil is pregnable. She is that black soil glittering with mica, black hairy roots, and all life that has gone before, broken down into a fragrant sludge of humus. The word *fertility* has behind it the sense of seeds, eggs, beings, ideas. Fecundity is the basal matter in which seeds are laid, prepared, warmed, incubated, saved. This is why the old mother is often called by her oldest names—Mother Dust, Mother Earth, Mam, and Ma—for she is the muck that makes ideas happen.

THE DEVIL

In this story the dual nature of the woman's soul, which both badgers and heals her, has been replaced by a single figure, the Devil. As we have noted before, this devil figure represents the natural predator of a woman's psyche, a *contra naturam*, an "against nature" aspect that opposes the development of psyche and attempts to kill off all soul. It is a force that is split off from its life-giving aspect. It is a force that must be overcome and contained. The devil figure is not the same as another natural source of badgering and baiting that also goes on in the female psyche, the force that I call the alter-soul. The alter-soul is oppositional and positive. It often shows up in women's dreams and in fairy tales and mythos as a cronish shape-changing figure that magnetizes and harasses the woman into a descent that ideally ends in a reunion with her deepest resources.

So, here in this underworld orchard awaits the gathering together of those powerful parts of the psyche, both male and female. They form a *conjunctio*. This word is from alchemy and means a higher transformative union of unlike substances. When these opposites are rubbed together they result in the activation of certain intra-psychic processes. They act like flint struck against rock in order to make fire. It is through the conjunction and pressure of dissimilar elements inhabiting the same psychic space that soulful energy, insight, and knowing are made.

The presence of the sort of *conjunctio* we have in this story signals an activation of a verdant Life/Death/Life cycle. When we see this rare and precious gathering, we know that a spiritual death will take place, that a spiritual marriage is imminent, also that a new life will be born. These factors predict what is to come. *Conjunctio* is not something one goes out and gets. It is something that occurs because hard, hard work is being done.

So, here we are, in our mud clothes, walking down a road we've never seen, and with the mark of the wild nature glowing through us more and more. It is fair to say that this *conjunctio* is insisting on a striking revision of the old you. If you are here in the orchard, and there are these identifiable psychic aspects with you, there is no turning back—we are going forward.

Now what more about these pears? They are there for those who hunger on their long underworld journey. Several fruits are used traditionally to represent the female womb, most often pears, apples, figs, and peaches, although generally any objects that have outer and inner forms, and at their center a seed that can grow into a living thing—eggs, for instance—can connote this "life within life" quality of the feminine. Here pears, archetypally, represent a burst of new life, a seed of new selfhood.

In much of myth and fairy tale, the fruit trees are under the dominion of the Great Mother, the old Wild Mother, and the king and his men are her stewards. The pears in the orchard are numbered, for in this transformative process all things are attended to. It is not a haphazard design. All is recorded and tallied. The old Wild Mother knows how much she has of these transformative substances. The king comes to count the pears, not in jealous ownership, but to discover if anyone new has arrived in the underworld to begin a deep initiation. The soul world always awaits the novice and the wanderer.

The pear bending to feed the maiden is like a bell pealing throughout the underworld orchard, calling forth the sources and forces—the king, the mage, the gardener, and presently the old mother; all of these rush forward to greet, sustain, and assist the novitiate.

Holy figures throughout the ages assure and reassure us that on the transformative open road there is already "a place set for us." And to this place, by scent, by intuition, we are dragged or spirited by destiny. We all arrive in the king's orchard eventually. It is only right and proper.

In this episode, the three masculine attributes of a woman's psyche—the gardener, king, and magician—are the watchers, questioners, and helpers in the underworld journey, where nothing is as it first seems. As the kingly aspect of a woman's underground psyche learns that there has been a change in the order of the orchard, he comes with the mage of the psyche, who can understand matters of the human *and* spirit worlds, who delves into the distinctions between the psychic this and that in the unconscious.

And so they watch as the spirit again drains the moat. As we mentioned before, this moat carries a symbolic meaning similar to that of the Styx, which was a poisonous river on which the souls of the dead were ferried from the land of the living to the land of the dead. It was not poisonous to the dead, but only to the living. Beware then the sensation of repose and accomplishment that can seduce humans into feeling that a spiritual deed or completion of a spiritual cycle is a point where one may stop and rest on her laurels forevermore. The moat is a resting place for the dead, a completion at the end of life, but the living woman cannot stay too long near it, else she becomes lethargic in the cycles of soul-making.[27]

Through this circular river symbol, the moat, the tale warns us that this water is not just any water but a certain kind. It is a boundary water, much like the circle the maiden drew around herself to keep the Devil away. When one crosses into or through a circle, one is entering into or passing through to another state of being, another state of awareness, or lack of one.

Here, the maiden is passing through the state of unconsciousness reserved for the dead. She is not to drink of this water or wade through it, but rather pass through its dry bed. Because a woman must pass through the land of the dead in a descent, sometimes she becomes confused and thinks she must die forever. But this is not so. The task is to pass through the land of the dead as a living creature, for that is how consciousness is made.

So this moat is a very important symbol, and the fact that the spirit in the tale drains it helps us to understand what we must do on our own journey. We must not lie down and go to happy sleep over what has been thus far attained in our work. Neither should we jump into the river in a crazy attempt to hasten the process. There is death with a lowercase *d* and there is Death with a capital *D.* The one the psyche seeks in this process of Life/Death/Life cycles is *la muerte por un instante,* death for now, not *La Muerte Eterna,* Death For a Long Time.

The magician comes close, but not too close, to the spirit and the young woman. He asks, "Are you of this world or not of this world?" And the maiden, dressed in the unkempt and wild attire of a *criatura* stripped of ego and accompanied by the glowing white body of a spirit, tells the mage she is in the land of the dead even though she is one of the living. "I was once of *the* world, and yet I am not of *this* world." When the king asks the magician, "Is she human or spirit?" the magician answers that she is both human and spirit.

The maiden's cryptic reply acknowledges that she belongs to the land of the living and yet is stepping to the Life/Death/Life cadence, and that because of this she is a human being in descent as well as a shade of her former self. She may live in the topside world days, but the work of transformation occurs in the underworld, and she is able to live in both, like *La Que Sabe*, "she who knows." All this is in order to learn her way, in order to clear her way, to the true and wild self.

To delve the meaning of the Handless Maiden material, here are a few questions to help women begin to clarify their journeys in the underworld. The questions are phrased so they can be answered both individually and collectively. The asking of questions creates a luminous net that is woven as women talk among themselves, and they drop this net into their collective mind and raise it filled with the glimmering, the streaming, the inert, the strangled, and the breathing forms of the inner lives of women for all to see and work with.

In answering one question, other questions come, and to learn more we answer those too. Here are some of the questions: How does one live in the topside world and the underworld at the same time and on a day-to-day basis? What does one have to do to come down into the underworld on one's own? What circumstances in life help women with the descent? Do we have a choice about going or staying? What spontaneous help have you received from the instinctive nature during such a time?

When women (or men) are in this state of dual citizenship, they sometimes make the mistake of thinking that to go away from the world, to leave the mundane life, with its chores, its duties that not only beckon but irritate beyond reason, that this is a sterling idea. But this is not the best way, for the outer world at these times is the only rope left around the ankle of the woman who is wandering, working, hanging upside down in the underworld. It is an excruciatingly important time, when the mundane must play its proper role in exerting an "otherworldly" tension and balance that helps lead to a good end.

And so we wander on our way asking ourselves—if truth be

known, muttering to ourselves really—"Am I of this world or the other?" and answering "I am of both." And we remind ourselves of this as we go along. A woman in such a process must be of both worlds. It is the wandering in such a manner that helps to wring out every last bit of resistance, every last possibility of hubris, to flatten every last objection we might think up, for wandering this way is tiring. But this special kind of fatigue causes us to finally surrender ego fears and ambitions and just follow what comes. As a result, our understanding of our time in the underground forests will be deep and complete.

In the tale, the second pear bends to feed the maiden, and since this king is the son of the old Wild Mother, and since this orchard belongs to her, the young maiden in fact tastes the fruit of the secrets of life and death. As the fruit is a primal image of cycles of flowering, growing, ripening, and receding, eating it internalizes in the initiate a psychic clock or timepiece that knows the Life/Death/Life patterns and that forever after chimes when it is time to let one thing die and then turn to the birthing of another.

In what manner do we find this pear? We immerse ourselves in the mysteries of the feminine, the cycles of the earth, of insects, animals, birds, trees, flowers, the seasons, the flow of rivers and their water levels, the shagging and thinning coats of animals as they live through the seasons, the cycles of opacity and sheerness in our own individuation processes, our cycles of need and waning in sexuality, religiosity, ascent, and descent.

To eat the pear means to feed our deep creative hunger to write, paint, sculpt, weave, to say our piece, to stand up for, put forward hopes and ideas and creations the likes of which the world has never seen before. It is immensely nourishing to reintegrate into our modern lives whichever ancient feminine patterns and principles of innate sensibility and cycles that enrich our lives now.

This is the true nature of the psychic tree: it grows, it gives, it is used up, it leaves its seed for new; it loves us. Such is the Life/Death/Life mystery. It is a pattern, an ancient one from before water, before light, an unwavering one. Once we learn these cycles and their symbolic representations, be they of pear, of tree, of orchard, of stages and ages of a woman's life, we can count on them to repeat themselves over and over again, in the same cycle and in the same manner. The pattern is this: In all dying there is uselessness that becomes useful as we pick our way through it all. What knowing we will come to reveals itself as we go along. In all livingkind, loss brings a full gain. Our work is to interpret this Life/Death/Life cycle, to live it as gracefully as we know how, to howl like a mad dog when we cannot—and to go on, for ahead lies the loving underworld family of the psyche that will embrace and assist us.

The king helps the maiden live more ably in the underworld of her work. And this is good, for sometimes in the descent a woman feels less like an acolyte and more like a poor monster who has accidentally strayed from the mad doctor's laboratory. From their vantage point, however, the underworld figures see us as a blessed life in struggle. By underworld sights, we are a strong flame beating against a dark glass in order to break it and be freed. And all the helping forces there in the lower home rush to support us.

In olden times, stories of woman's descent to the underworld revealed that such was embarked upon in order to marry the king (in some rites there seemed to be no king, and the acolyte probably married whatever imago of the Wild Woman of the underworld existed), and here in the tale we see a remnant of this when the king takes one look at the maiden and immediately, without faint heart or doubt, loves her as his own. He recognizes her as his own, *not* in spite of her handless, wildish, wandering state, but because of it. The theme of being so without, and yet so sustained, continues. Even though we wander about in an unwashed, forlorn, semi-blinded, and handless state, a great force from the Self can love us, and holds us to its heart.

Women in this state often feel a great excitement, the kind a woman feels when she has met a mate who is so much of what she has dreamt of. It is an odd time, a paradoxical time, for we are aboveground, and yet below ground. We are wandering, yet we are loved. We are not rich, yet we are fed. In Jungian terms this state is called the "tension of the opposites," wherein something from each pole of the psyche is constellated at one time, creating new ground. In Freudian psychology it is called a "bifurcation," wherein the essential disposition or attitude of the psyche is divided into two polarities: black and white, good and bad. Among storytellers from my culture, this state is called *nacio dos vesas*, being "twice-born." It is the time where a second birth occurs through a magical source, and whereafter the soul now lays claim to two bloodlines, one from the physical world, one from the world unseen.

The king says he will protect her and love her. Now the psyche is more conscious; there will be a marriage, a very interesting one, between the living king of the land of the dead and the handless woman from the land of the living. A marriage between two such disparate parties would test the most magnificent love between two people, would it not? Yet this marriage is related to all those picaresque marriages in fairy tales where two energetic but dissimilar lives are joined. The cinder girl and the prince, the woman and the bear, the young girl and the moon, the seal maiden and the fisherman, the desert maiden and the coyote. The soul takes on the knowing of each entity. This is what is meant by being twice born.

In fairy-tale marriages, as in those in the topside world, the great love and union between dissimilar entities may last forever, or only until the lesson has been completed. In alchemy, the marriage of opposites means that a death and a birth will soon take place, and we shall see these next in this tale.

The king orders for the maiden a pair of spirit-hands, which will act in her behalf in the underworld. It is in this phase that a woman becomes adroit in the journey; her submission to it is complete, she has gotten her footing, as they say, and also her "handing." To have one's "handing" in the underworld proceeds from learning to summon, direct, comfort, and appeal to the powers of that world, but also to ward off its unwelcome aspects such as sleepiness, and so forth. If the symbol of the hand in the topside world carries a sensory radar with regard to others, the symbolic hand of the underworld can see in the dark and across time.

The idea of replacing lost parts with limbs of silver, gold, or wood has a long, long history through the ages. In fairy tales from Europe and the circumpolar regions, silverwork is the art of the *homunculi*, the hobs, *dvergar*, kobold, gremlins, and elves, which translated into psychological terms are those elemental aspects of spirit that live deep in the psyche and mine it for precious ideas.

These creatures are little psychopomps, that is, messengers who travel between the soul-force and human beings. Since time out of mind, the things fashioned of precious metals are associated with these industrious, often rather grumpy ferreters. It is another example of the psyche at work in our behalf even though we are not present in all workplaces at all times.

As in all things of the spirit, the silver hands carry both history and mystery. There are many myths and tales delineating where magical prostheses originated, who formed them, who cast them, carried them, poured them, cooled them, polished and fit them. Among the classical Greeks, silver is one of the precious metals of Hephaestus's forge. Like the maiden, the God Hephaestus was maimed in a drama concerning his parents. It is likely that Hephaestus and the king in the tale are interchangeable figures.

Hephaestus and the maiden with silver hands are archetypally brother and sister; they both have parents who are unaware of their value. When Hephaestus was born, his father, Zeus, demanded he be given away, and his mother, Hera, complied—at least till the child was grown. Then she restored Hephaestus to Olympus. He had become a goldsmith and silversmith of astonishing abilities. An argument ensued between Zeus and Hera, as Zeus was a jealous God. Hephaestus took his mother's side in the disagreement, and Zeus threw the young man down to the foothills, shattering his legs.

Hephaestus, now crippled, refused to give up and die. He fired his forge with the hottest fire he'd ever built and there formed for himself a pair of legs, made of silver and gold from the knees down. He went on to make all manner of magical things and became a God of love and mystical restoration. He can be said to be the patron of those things and humans that are dismembered, split, sundered, cracked, chipped, and distorted. He has a special love for those who are born crippled and for those whose hearts or dreams are broken.

To all of these he applies remedies that he fashions at his wondrous metal forge, piecing a heart back together with veins of finest goldwork, making a crippled limb strong via gold and silver overlay and investing it with magical function that compensates for the injury.

It is not by accident that the one-eyed, the lame, those with withered limbs or other physical differences have, through time, been sought out as possessing a special knowing. Their injury or difference forces them early on into parts of the psyche normally reserved for the very, very old. And they are watched over by this loving artisan of the psyche, Hephaestus. At one point he made twelve maidens whose limbs were of silver and gold, and who walked and talked and spoke. Legend says he fell in love with one and petitioned the Gods to make her human, but that is another story in and of itself.

To be given silver hands is to be invested with the skills of spirit hands—the healing touch, the ability to see in the dark, the ability to have powerful knowing through physical sensing. They carry an entire psychic *médica* with which to nurture, remedy, and support. At this stage the maiden is invested with the touch of the wounded healer. These psychic hands will cause her to better grasp the mysteries of the underworld, but they will also be retained as gifts once she completes her work and ascends again.

It is typical of this portion of the descent that uncanny, odd, and healing acts occur that come from outside the will of the ego and that are the result of being given spirit hands—that is, a mystical healing vigor. In olden times, these mystical abilities belonged to the old women of the villages. But they did not gain them at the first gray hair; they were accumulated over the hard and long years of this work, this work of endurance. And that is what we too are about.

The hands of silver, you might say, represent the maiden's coronation into yet another role. She is thus crowned, not with a crown upon her head but with silver hands at the ends of her arms. This is her coronation as queen of the underworld. To apply just a little more paleo-mythology at this point, let us consider that in Greek mythology, Persephone was not only a mother's daughter, but also the queen of the land of the dead.

In lesser-known stories about her, she endures various torments such as hanging for three days upon the World Tree in order to redeem the souls who have not enough suffering of their own to deepen their spirits. This female *Cristo/Crista* is echoed in "The Handless Maiden." The parallel is further amplified by the fact that Elysium, where Persephone lived in the underworld, means "apple-land"—*alisier* being a pre-Gallic word for *sorb*, apple—and the Arthurian *Avalon* also meaning the same. The handless maiden is directly associated with the blossoming apple tree.

This is an ancient cryptology. When we learn to read it, we see that Persephone of the apple-land, the handless maiden, and the flowering apple tree are the same sojourner to the wildlands. In all these, we see that fairy tales and mythos have left us a clear map to the knowings and the practices of the past and the way for us to proceed in the present.

Now, here at the end of the fourth labor of the handless maiden, we *could* say the maiden's work in the descent is complete, for she is made the queen of life and death. She is the lunar woman who knows what passes in the night, even the sun itself must roll past her underground in order to renew itself for day. But this is still not the *lysis*, the resolution. We are only at the midpoint of transformation, a place of being held in love, yet poised to make a slow dive into another abyss. And so, we continue.

The Fifth Stage—The Harrowing of the Soul

The king goes off to war in a faraway kingdom, asking his mother to care for his young queen and requesting that a message be sent to him if his wife has a child. The young queen gives birth to a happy babe and the joyous message is sent. But the messenger falls asleep at the river, and the Devil steps out and changes the message to say "The queen has given birth to a child who is half dog."

The king is horrified, yet sends back a message saying to love the queen and care for her in this terrible time. The messenger again falls asleep at the river, and the Devil again steps out and changes the message to "Kill the queen and her child." The old mother, shaken by this request, sends a messenger to confirm, and back and forth the messengers run, falling asleep at the river each time. The Devil's changed messages become increasingly vicious, the last being "Keep the tongue and eyes of the queen to prove she has been killed."

The king's mother refuses to kill the sweet young queen. Instead she sacrifices a doe, keeping its tongue and eyes and hiding them away. She helps the young queen bind her infant to her breast, and veiling her, says she must run for her life. The women weep and kiss each other good-bye.

Like Bluebeard, Jason of golden fleece fame, the *hidalgo* in "La Llorona," and other fairy-tale and mythological husbands/lovers, the king marries and is then called away. Why are these mytho-husbands always trotting off so soon after the wedding night? The reason is different in each tale, but the essential psychic fact is the same: The kingly energy of the psyche falls back and recedes so that the next step in the woman's process can occur; the testing of her newly found psychic stance. In the king's case, he has not abandoned her, for his mother watches over her in his absence.

The next step is the formation of the maiden's relationship to the old Wild Mother and to birthing. There is testing of the love bond between the maiden and the king, and the maiden and the old mother. One has to do with love between opposites, the other has to do with love of the deep female Self.

The departure of the king is a universal leitmotif in fairy tales. When we feel, not a withdrawal of support but a lessening of the nearness of that support, we can be sure that a testing period is about to begin; we will be required to nourish ourselves on soul memory alone till the loved one returns. Then our nightdreams, particularly the most striking, penetrating ones, are the only love we shall have for a time.

Here are some of the dreams women have said sustained them mightily during this next phase.

One gentle and spirited mid-aged woman dreamt she saw in the loam of the earth a pair of lips, and that she lay upon the ground and those lips whispered to her, and then, unexpectedly, they kissed her on the cheek.

Another very hardworking woman dreamt a deceptively simple dream: that she slept one entire night in perfect sleep. When she awoke from the dream, she said she felt rested to perfection, that not a muscle bundle, not a nerve, not a cell was out of place anywhere within her entire system.

Yet another woman dreamt that she had open-heart surgery and that the operating room had no roof so that the overhead operating light was the sun itself. She could feel the light from the sun touch her exposed heart. She heard the surgeon say no further surgery was necessary.

Dreams like these are experiences of the wild feminine nature and of the One who illumines all. Emotionally and often physically profound, they are feeling states that are like a food cache. We can draw from them when spiritual sustenance is spare.

As the king trots off on some adventure, his psychic contribution to the descent is held in place by love and memory. The maiden understands that the kingly principle of the underworld is committed to her and will not forsake her, as he promised before they married. Often at this time a woman is "full of herSelf." She is pregnant, meaning filled with a nascent idea about what her life can become if she will only pursue her work. It is a magical and frustrating time, as we shall see, for this is a cycle of descents, so there is yet another around the bend.

It is because of the burst of new life that a woman's life seems again to stumble too near the edge, and jumps right into the abyss again. But this time, the love of the inner masculine and the old Wild Self will sustain her as never before.

The union of the king and queen of the underworld produces a child. A child made in the underworld is a magic child who has all the potential associated with the underworld, such as acute hearing and innate sensing, but here it is in its *anlage*, or "that which shall become," stage. It is at this time that women on the journey have startling ideas, some might call them grandiose, that are the result of having new and youthful eyes and expectations. Among the very young, this may be as straightforward as finding new interests and new friends. For older women, it can mean an entire tragicomedic epiphany of divorce, reconstitution, and a customized happily-ever-after.

The spirit-baby sets sedentary women off climbing the Alps at age forty-five. The spirit-baby causes a woman to throw over her life of floor wax fixation and sign up for university instead. It is the spirit-babe that causes women who are diddling around doing the safe thing to take to the open road bent under their tinker's pack.

To give birth is the psychic equivalent of becoming oneself, one self, meaning an undivided psyche. Before this birth of new life in the underworld, a woman is likely to think all parts and personalities within her are rather like a hodgepodge of vagrants who wander in and out of her life. In the underworld birth, a woman learns that anything that brushes by her *is* a part of her. Sometimes this differentiation of all the aspects of psyche is hard to do, especially with the tendencies and urges we find repulsive. The challenge of loving unappealing aspects of ourselves is as much of an endeavor as any heroine has ever undertaken.

Sometimes we are afraid that to identify more than one self within the psyche might mean that we are psychotic. While it is true that people with a psychotic disorder also experience many selves, identifying with or against them quite vividly, a person with no psychotic disorder holds all the inner selves in an orderly and rational manner. They are put to good use; the person grows and thrives. For the majority of women, mothering and raising the internal selves is a creative work, a way of knowledge, not a reason for becoming unnerved.

So, the handless maiden is waiting to have a child, a new little wild self. The body in pregnancy does what it wants and knows to do. The new life latches on, divides, swells. A woman at this stage of the psychic process may enter another *enantiodromia*, the psychic state in which all that was once held valuable is now not so valuable anymore, and further, may be replaced by new and extreme cravings for odd and unusual sights, experiences, endeavors.

For instance, for some women, to be married was once the end-all and be-all. But in an *enantiodromia*, they want to be cut loose: marriage is bad, marriage is blah, marriage is unecstatic *scheisse*, shit. Exchange the word *marriage* for the words *lover*, *job*, *body*, *art*, *life*, and *choices* and you see the exact mind-set of this time.

And then there are the cravings. Oh, la! A woman may crave to be near water, or be belly down, her face in the earth, smelling that wild smell. She may have to drive into the wind. She may have to plant something, weed something, pull things out of the ground, or put them into the ground. She may have to knead and bake, rapt in dough up to her elbows.

She may have to trek into the hills, leaping from rock to rock trying out her voice against the mountain. She may need hours of starry nights where the stars are like face powder spilt on a black marble floor. She may feel she will die if she does not dance naked in a thunderstorm, sit in perfect silence, return home ink-stained, paint-stained, tear-stained, moon-stained.

A new self is on the way. Our inner lives, as we have known them, are about to change. While this does not mean we should throw away the decent and especially the supportive aspects of our lives in some kind of demented housecleaning, it does mean that in the descent the topside world and ideals pale, and for a time we shall be restless and unsatisfied, for the satisfaction, the fulfillment, is in the process of being born in the inner reality.

What it is we are hungering for can never be fulfilled by a mate, a job, money, a new this or that. What we hunger for is of the other world, the world that sustains our lives as women. And this child-Self we are awaiting is brought forth by just this means—by waiting. As time passes in our lives and our work in the underworld, the child develops and will be born. In most cases, a woman's nightdreams will presage the birth; women literally dream of a new baby, a new home, a new life.

Now the king's mother and the young queen stay with each other. The king's mother is—guess who?—old *La Que Sabe*. She knows the ways of it all. The queen mother represents both a Demeter-like mothering and a Hekate-like[28] cronation in the unconscious of women.[29]

This womanly alchemy of maiden, mother, and *la curandera*, healer crone, is echoed in the relationship between the handless maiden and the king's mother. They are a similar psychic equation. Though in this tale the king's mother is a little sketchy, like the maiden at the beginning of the tale with her rite of the white gown and the chalk circle, the old mother knows her ancient rites also, as we shall see.

Once the childSelf is born, the old queen mother sends a message about the young queen's infant to the king. The messenger seems normal enough, but as he nears a stream of water, he becomes more and more sleepy, falls asleep, and the Devil jumps out. This is a clue that tells us there will again be a challenge to the psyche during its next labor in the underworld.

In Greek mythos, in the underworld there is a river called Lethe, and to drink of its waters causes one to forget all things said and done. Psychologically this means to fall asleep to one's actual life. The runner who is supposed to enable communication between these two main components of the new psyche cannot yet hold its own against the destructive/seductive force in the psyche. The communicating function of the psyche becomes sleepy, lies down, falls asleep, and forgets.

So, guess who is always out and about? Why, the old tracker of maidens, the hungry Devil. By the word *Devil* in the story, we see how this story was overlaid by more recent religious material. In the story, the messenger, stream, and the sleep that causes forgetfulness reveal that the old religion is right underneath the story line, just the next layer down.

This has been the archetypal pattern of descent since the beginning of time, and we too follow this timeless system. Likewise, we have a history of terrible chores behind us. We have seen Death's steamy breath. We have braved the clutching forests, the marching trees, the roots that trip, the fog that blinds. We are psychic heroines with a valise full of medals. And who can blame us now? We want to rest. We deserve to rest for we have been through a lot. And so we lie down. Next to a lovely stream. The sacred process is not forgotten, just ... just ... well, we would like to take a break, just for a while you know, just going to close our eyes for a minute ...

And before we know it, the Devil hops in on all four feet and changes the message meant to convey love and celebration into one meant to disgust. The Devil represents the psychic aggravation that bedevils us as it sneers, "Have you gone back to your old ways of innocence and naïveté now that you are loved? Now that you gave birth? Do you think being tested is all over, you foolish woman?"

And because we are near Lethe, we snore on. This is the error all women make—not once, but many times. We forget to remember the Devil. The message is changed from a triumph, "The queen has given birth to a beautiful child," to a slur, "The queen has given birth to a half dog." In a similar version of the story, the changed message is even more explicit: "The queen has given birth to a half dog for she has copulated with the beasts in the forest."

This half-dog image in the story is not an accident, but in fact a glorious fragment of the old Goddess-centered religions of Europe across to Asia. During those times people worshipped a triple-headed Goddess. The triple-headed Goddesses are represented in various systems by Hekate, the Baba Yaga, Mother Holle, Berchta, Artemis, and others. Each appeared as or had close association with these animals.

In the older religions, these and other powerful and wild female deities carried the female initiation traditions and taught women all the stages of a woman's life, from maiden through mother through crone. Giving birth to a half dog is a skewed degradation of the ancient wild Goddesses whose instinctual natures were considered holy. The newer religion attempted to pollute the sacred meanings of the triple Goddesses by insisting that the holy ones bred with animals and encouraged their followers to do likewise.

It was at this point that the archetype of the Wild Woman was pushed down and entombed far, far underground, and the wildish in women began to not only dwindle but had to be spoken about in whispers and in secret places. In many cases, women who loved the old Wild Mother had to guard their lives carefully. Finally, the knowing came through only in fairy tales, folklore, trance states, and nightdreams. And thank The Goodness for that.

While in "Bluebeard" we learned about the natural predator as one who cut off women's ideas, feelings, and actions, here in "The Handless Maiden," we study a far more subtle but immensely powerful aspect of the predator, one we must face in our psyches, and more and more on a daily basis in our own outer society.

"The Handless Maiden" reveals how the predator has the ability to twist human perceptions and the vital comprehensions we need to develop moral dignity, visionary scope, and responsive action in our lives and in the world. In "Bluebeard," the predator lets no one live. In "The Handless Maiden," the Devil allows life, but attempts to prevent a woman's reconnection with the deep knowledge of the instinctual nature that contains an automatic rightness of perception and action.

So when the Devil changes the message in the tale, it can be considered in one sense a true record of an actual historical event, one that is particularly relevant to modern women in their psychic work of descent and awareness. Remarkably, many aspects of culture (meaning the collective and dominant belief system of a group of persons living close enough to influence one another) still act as the Devil regarding women's inner work, personal lives, and psychic processes. By carving away this, and blotting out that, and severing a root here, and sealing up an opening there, the "devil" in the culture, and the intra-psychic predator, cause generations of women to feel fearful yet wander about with not the simplest clues about the causes, or about their own loss of the wild nature, which could reveal all to them.

While it is true that the predator has a taste for prey that is in some way soul-hungry, soul-lonely, or in some other way disempowered, fairy tales show us that the predator is drawn also to consciousness, reform, release, and new freedom. As soon as it becomes aware of such, it is on the spot.

Myriad story lines point out the predator, those in this work as well as fairy tales such as "Cap of Rushes" and "All Fur," and continuing with the mythos about the Greek Andromeda and the Azteca Malinche. The devices used are denigration of the protagonist's purpose, disparaging language used to describe the prey, blind judgments, proscriptions, and unwarranted punishments. These are the means by which the predator changes the life-giving messages between soul and spirit into death-dealing messages that cut our hearts, cause shame, and even more importantly inhibit us from taking rightful action.

At the cultural level, we can give many examples of how the predator shapes ideas and feelings in order to steal women's light. One of the most striking examples of loss of natural perception is in the generations of women[30] whose mothers broke the tradition of teaching, preparing, and welcoming their daughters into the most basic and physical aspect of being women, menstruation. In our culture, but also in many others, the Devil changed the message so that first blood and all subsequent cycles of blood became surrounded with humiliation rather than wonder. This caused millions of young women to lose their inheritance of the miraculous body and instead to fear that they were dying, diseased, or being punished by God. The culture and the individuals within the culture picked up the Devil's twisted message without examining it, and passed it on with much affect, thus turning a woman's time of heightened sensation, emotionally and sexually, into a time of shame and punishment.

As we can see from the story, when the predator invades a culture, be it a psyche or a society, the various aspects or individuals of that culture have to use cunning insight, read between the lines, hold their own place, so as not to be swept away by the outrageous but exciting claims of the predator.

When there is too much predator and not enough wild soul, the economic, social, emotional, and religious structures of culture gradually begin to distort the most soulful resources, both in spirit and in the outer world. Natural cycles are starved into unnatural shapes, lacerated with unwise uses, or else put to death. The value of what is wild and visionary is denigrated, and dark speculations are made about how dangerous the instinctual nature really is. Thus stripped of authentic sanctity and meaning, destructive and painful means and methods are rationalized as superior.

However, no matter how much the Devil lies and tries to change the beautiful messages about a woman's real life to mean-spirited, jealous, and life-draining ones, the king's mother truly sees what is occurring and refuses to sacrifice her daughter. In modern terms, she would not muffle her daughter, would not warn her against speaking her truth, would not encourage her to pretend to be less in order to manipulate more. This wild mother figure from the underworld risks retribution to follow what she knows to be the wisest course. She outsmarts the predator instead of colluding. She does not give in. She knows what is integral, knows what will help a woman thrive, knows a predator when she sees one, knows what to do about it. Even when pressured by the most distorted cultural or psychic messages, even with a predator loose in the culture or in the personal psyche, we can all still hear her original wild instructions, and follow them.

This is what women learn when they dig down to the wild and instinctive nature, when they do the work of deep initiation and development of consciousness. They take on a massive enabling through the development of uninterrupted sight, hearing, being, and doing. Women learn to look for the predator instead of trying to shoo it away, ignore it, or be nice to it. They learn the tricks, disguises, and the ways the predator thinks. They learn to "read between the lines" in messages, injunctions, expectations, or customs that have been perverted from the truthful into the manipulative. Then, whether the predator is emanating from within one's own psychic milieu or from the culture outside oneself, or both, we are shrewd and able to meet it head-on and do what needs be done.

The Devil in the tale symbolizes anything that corrupts understanding of the deep feminine processes. You know, it does not take a Torquemada[31] to hound the souls of women. They can be also hounded simply by the goodwill of new but unnatural ways, which when taken too far rob a woman of her nourishing wildish nature and her ability to make soul. A woman need not live as though she were born in 1000 B.C. Nevertheless, the old knowing is universal knowing, eternal and immortal learning, which will be as relevant five thousand years from now as it is today, and as it was five thousand years ago. It is archetypal knowing, and that kind of knowledge is timeless. It is a good idea to remember that the predator is timeless also.

In another sense entirely, the switcher of messages, being an innate and contrary force that exists in the psyche and in the world, naturally opposes the new childSelf. Yet, paradoxically, because we must respond to fight it or balance it, the battle itself strengthens us immeasurably. In our personal psychic work, we receive switched messages from the Devil constantly—"I am good; I am not so good. My work is deep work; my work is silly. I am making a difference; I am not getting anywhere. I am brave; I am a coward. I am knowing; I ought to be ashamed of myself." These are confusing to say the least.

So, the king's mother sacrifices a doe instead of the young queen. In the psyche, as in the culture at large, there is an odd psychic quirk. Not only when people are hungry and deprived does the Devil show up but also sometimes where there has been an event of great beauty, in this case the birth of the beautiful new baby. Again, the predator is always attracted to light, and what is more light than new life?

However, there are other dissemblers within the psyche that also attempt to demean or tarnish the new. In women's process of learning the underworld, it is a psychic fact that when one has given birth to a beautiful thing something mean will also arise, even if only momentarily, something that is jealous, lacks understanding, or shows disdain. The new child will be called down, called ugly, and condemned by one or more persistent antagonists. The birth of the new causes complexes, both negative mother and negative father, and other negating creatures to rise from the psychic landfill and attempt, at the very least, to sharply criticize the new order, and at the very most to attempt to dispirit the woman and her new offspring, idea, life, or dream.

This is the same scenario of the ancient fathers, Kronos and Uranos and Zeus as well, who always attempted to eat or banish their offspring out of some dark fear that the children would gain succession over them. In Jungian terms, this destructive force would be called a complex, an organized set of feelings and ideas in the psyche that is unconscious to the ego and therefore more or less can have its way with us. In the psychoanalytic milieu the antidote is consciousness of one's foibles and gifts, so that the complex is unable to act on its own.

In Freudian terms, this destructive force would be said to emanate from the id, a dark, indefinite, but infinite psychic land where, scattered like wreckage and made blind from lack of light, live all forgotten, repressed, and revulsive ideas, urges, wishes, and actions. In this psychoanalytic milieu, resolution is brought about by remembering base thoughts and urges, bringing them to consciousness, describing, naming, and cataloging them, in order to leach their potency.

According to some stories from Iceland, this magical destructive force in the psyche is sometimes *Brak*, the ice man. There is an ancient story in which the perfect murder is committed. *Brak* the ice man kills a human woman who will not return his affections. He kills her with an icicle shaped like a dagger. The icicle, as well as the man, melts away in the next day's sun, and there is no weapon left to indict the killer. And there is nothing left of the killer either.

The dark ice man figure from the world of mythos has the same uncanny appearance/disappearance mystique as complexes in the human psyche, as well as the same modus operandi as the Devil in this tale of the handless maiden. That is why the Devil's appearance is so disorienting to the initiate. Like the ice man, he comes out of nowhere, does his killing work, then disappears, dissolves into nowhere, leaving no trail.

This story, however, leaves us an excellent clue: if you feel you have lost your mission, your oomph, if you feel confused, slightly off, then look for the Devil, the ambusher of the soul within your own psyche. If you cannot see, hear, catch it in the act, assume it is at work, and above all stay awake—no matter how tired you become, no matter how sleepy, no matter how much you want to shut your eyes to your true work.

In reality when a woman has a devil complex, it occurs exactly like this. She is walking along, doing well, minding her own business, and all of a sudden—boom! the Devil jumps out, and all her good work loses energy, begins to limp, coughs, coughs some more, and finally falls over. What we might call the demon complex, uses the voice of the ego, attacks one's creativity, one's ideas and dreams. In the tale, it appears as a ridicule or cheapening of a woman's experience of the world and the underworld, trying to split apart the natural *conjunctio* of the rational and the mysterious. The Devil lies, and says a woman's time in the underworld has produced a brute, when in fact it has produced a beautiful child.

When various saints wrote that they wrestled to keep faith with their chosen God, that they were all night assailed by the Devil, who burnt their ears with words meant to weaken their resolve, shook their eyeballs loose with horrible apparitions, and in general dragged their souls over broken glass, they were speaking of this very phenomenon, the Devil jumping out. This psychic ambush is meant to loosen your faith not only in yourself but in the very careful and delicate work you are doing in the unconscious.

It takes goodly amounts of faith to continue at this time, but we must and we do. The king, the queen, and the king's mother, all elements of the psyche are pulling in one direction, in our direction, and so must we persevere with them. At this point it is a work moving into the homestretch. It would be so wasteful and even more painful to abandon it now.

The king of our psyches has a stalwartness. He will not keel over at the first blow. He will not shrivel up with hatred and retribution as the·Devil hopes. The king, who loves his wife so, is shocked at the skewed message but sends a message back saying to care for the queen and their child in his absence. This is the test of our inner certainty . . . can two forces remain connected even if one or the other is held out as abominable and despicable? Can one stand by the other no matter what? Can union continue even when seeds of doubt are strenuously being planted? Thus far the answer is yes. The test of whether there can be a marriage of enduring love between the wild underworld and the earthly psyche is being met, and impressively.

On the way back to the castle, the messenger again falls asleep at the river and the Devil changes the message to "Kill the queen." Here the predator is hoping the psyche will become polarized and kill itself off, rejecting one entire aspect of itself, that crucial one, the newly awakened one, the knowing woman.

The king's mother is horrified at this message, and she and the king correspond back and forth many times, each trying to clarify the other's messages, until finally the Devil changes the king's message to read, "Kill the queen and cut out her eyes and tongue for proof."

Here we already have a maiden without worldly grasp, without hands, for the Devil ordered these cut off. Now he demands further amputations. He wants her now also without true speaking and without true sight as well. This is quite a devil, and yet what he requires gives us tremendous pause. For what he wants to see take place are the very behaviors that have burdened women since time immemorial. He wants the maiden to obey these tenets: "Don't see life as it is. Don't understand the life and death cycles. Don't pursue your yearnings. Don't speak of all these wildish things."

The old Wild Mother, personified by the king's mother, is angry about the Devil's command, and says, This is too much to ask. She just simply refuses. In women's work the psyche says, "This is too much. This I cannot, will not, tolerate." And the psyche begins, as a result of its spiritual experience in this initiation of endurance, to act more shrewdly.

The old Wild Mother could have gathered up her skirts, saddled a brace of horses, and charged far afield to find her son and determine what possession had overtaken him that he would wish to murder his lovely queen and his firstborn child, but she does not. Instead, in time-honored fashion, she sends the young initiate off to yet another symbolic initiation site, the woods. In some rites, the initiatory site was in a cave, or under a mountain, but in the underworld, where tree symbolism abounds, it is most often a forest.

Understand what this signifies: Sending the maiden off to another initiatory site would have been the natural course of events anyway, even had not the Devil jumped out and changed the messages. In the descent there are several sites for initiation, one following upon the other, all having their own lessons and comforts. The Devil, you might say, practically insures that we will feel an urgency to get up and hie on to the next one.

Remember, there is a natural time after childbearing when a woman is considered to be of the underworld. She is dusted with its dust, watered by its water, having seen into the mystery of life and death, pain and joy during her labor.[32] So, for a time she is "not here" but rather still "there." It takes time to re-emerge.

The maiden is like a postpartum woman. She rises from the underworld birthing chair where she has given birth to new ideas, a new life view. Now she is veiled, her babe is given to breast, and she goes on. In the Grimm brothers' version of "The Handless Maiden," the newborn child is male and is called Sorrowful. But in the Goddess religions, the spiritual child born from the woman's venture with the king of the underworld is called Joy.

Here, another sash from the old religion trails across the ground. Following the birth of the maiden's new self, the king's mother sends the young queen off to a long initiation that, as we shall see, will teach her the definitive cycles of a woman's life.

The old Wild Mother gives the maiden a dual blessing: she binds the infant to the maiden's milk-full breast so the childSelf can be nourished no matter what happens next. Then, in the tradition of the old Goddess cults, she wraps the maiden in veils, this being the main apparel a Goddess wears when traveling on sacred pilgrimage, when she wishes not to be recognized or diverted from her intention. In Greece, numerous sculptures and bas-reliefs show the initiate of the Eleusinian rite being veiled and awaiting the next step in initiation.

What is this symbol of veiling? It marks the difference between hiding and disguising. This symbol is about keeping private, keeping to oneself, not giving one's mysterious nature away. It is about preserving the eros and *mysterium* of the wild nature.

Sometimes we have difficulty keeping our new life energy in the transformative pot long enough for something to accrue to us. We must keep it to ourselves without giving it all away to whomever asks, or to whichever stealthy inspiration suddenly happens upon us, telling us it would be good to tip the pot and empty our finest soulfulness out into the mouths of others or onto the ground.

Putting a veil over something increases its action or feeling. This is known among women far and wide. There was a phrase my grandmother used, "veiling the bowl." It meant to put a white cloth over a bowl of kneaded dough to cause the bread to rise. The veil for the bread and the veil for the psyche serve the same purpose. There is a potent leavening in the souls of women in descent. There is a powerful fermenting going on. To be behind the veil increases one's mystical insight. From behind the veil, all humans look like mist beings, all events, all objects, are colored as though in a dawn, or in a dream.

In the 1960s women veiled themselves with their hair. They grew it very long, ironed it, and wore it as a curtain, as a way to veil their faces—as though the world was too split open, too naked—as though their hair could seclude and protect their tender selves. There is a Mideastern dance with veils, and of course modern Moslem women wear the veil. The babushka from Eastern Europe, and the *trajes* worn on women's heads in Central and South America are also mementos of the veil. East Indian women wear veils as a matter of course, and African women do also.

As I looked about the world, I began to feel a little sorry for modern women who did not have veils to wear. For to be a free woman and use a veil at will is to hold the power of the Mysterious Woman. To behold such a woman veiled is a powerful experience.

I once saw a sight that has held me in the thrall of the veil for life: my cousin Éva, preparing for her night wedding. I, about eight years old, sat on her traveling suitcase with my flower girl headdress askew already, one of my anklets up and the other swallowed by my shoe. First she put on her long white satin gown with forty small satin-covered buttons down the back, and then the long white satin gloves with ten satin-covered buttons each. She drew the floor-length veil down over her lovely face and shoulders. My Aunt Teréz fluffed the veil all out, muttering to God to make it perfect. My Uncle Sebestyén stopped in the doorway aghast, for Éva was no longer a mortal. She was a Goddess. Behind the veil her eyes seemed silvery, her hair starry somehow; her mouth looked like a red flower. She was of only herself, contained and powerful, and just out of reach in a right kind of way.

Some say the hymen is the veil. Others, that illusion is the veil. And none are wrong. But there is more. Ironically, though the veil has been used to hide one's beauty from the concupiscence of others, it is also *femme fatale* equipment. To wear a veil of a certain kind, at a certain time, with a certain lover, and with certain looks, is to exude an intense and smoky erotimine that causes true abated breath. In feminine psychology, the veil is a symbol for women's ability to take on whatever presence or essence they wish.

There is a striking numinosity to the veiled one. She inspires such awe that all those she encounters stop in their tracks, so struck with reverence for her apparition that they must leave her alone. The maiden in the tale is veiled to set out on her journey, therefore she is untouchable. No one would dare to raise her veil without her permission. After all the invasiveness of the Devil, once again she is protected. Women undergo this transformation also. When they are in this veiled state, sensible persons know better than to invade their psychic space.

So too, after all the false messages in the psyche, and even in exile, we are protected by some superior wisening, some sumptuous and nourishing solitude that originated in our relationship with the old Wild Mother. We are on the road again, but safe-guarded. By wearing the veil, we are designated as one who belongs to Wild Woman. We are hers, and though not unreach-able, in some ways we are held away from total immersion in mundane life.

The amusements of the upper world do not dazzle us. We are wandering in order to find the place, the homeland in the uncon-scious. As fruit trees in blossom are referred to as wearing beau-tiful veils, we and the maiden are now flowering apple trees on the move, looking for the forest to which we belong.

The slaying of the deer once was a revivification rite, one that would have been led by an old woman like the king's mother, for she would be the designated "knower" of the life and death cycles. In the sacrifice of the doe we see more of the hem of the old reli-gion. The sacrifice of a deer was an ancient rite meant to release the deer's gentle yet bounding energy.

Like women in descent, this sacred animal was known as a hardy survivor of cold and most despairing winters. Deer were considered wholly efficient at foraging, birthing, and living with the inherent cycles of nature. It is likely that the participants of such a ritual belonged to a clan, and that the idea of the sacrifice was to teach initiates about death, as well as to infuse them with the qualities of the wild creature itself.

Here and again is the sacrifice—a double *rubedo*, blood sacri-fice, in fact. First there is the sacrifice of the deer, the animal sacred to the ancient Wild Woman bloodline. In ancient rite, to kill a deer out of cycle was to violate the old Wild Mother. The killing of creatures is dangerous work, for various kind and helpful enti-ties travel in the guise of animals. Killing one out of cycle was thought to endanger the delicate balances of nature and to cause retribution of mythic proportions.

But the larger point is that the sacrifice was one of a mother-creature, a doe, which represented the female body of knowing. Then, by consuming the flesh of that creature and by the wearing of its pelt for warmth and in order to show clan membership, one *became* that creature. This was a sacred ritual since time and beyond. To keep the eyes, ears, snout, horns, and various viscera was to have the power symbolized by their various functions; far seeing, sensing from afar, swift motion, hardy body, the timbre to summon one's own kind, and so forth.

The second *rubedo* transpires when the maiden is separated from both the good old mother and the king. This is a period when we are charged to remember, to persist in spiritual nourishment even though we are separated from those forces that have sustained us in the past. We cannot stay in the ecstasy of perfect union forever. For most of us, it is not our path to do so. Our work is rather to be weaned at some point from these most exciting forces, yet to remain in conscious connection to them and to proceed to the next task.

It is a fact that we can become fixated on a particularly lovely aspect of psychic union and attempt to stay there forever, sucking at the sacred tit. This does not mean nurture is destructive. Quite the contrary, nurture is absolutely essential to the journey, and in substantial amounts. In fact, if it is not present in adequate amounts, the seeker will lose energy, fall into depression, and fade to a whisper. But if we stay at a favorite place in the psyche, such as only in beauty, only in rapture, individuation slows to a slog. The naked truth is that those sacred forces we find within our own psyches someday must be left, at least temporarily, so that the next stage of the process can occur.

As in the tale where the two women tearfully bid each other good-bye, we must say good-bye to precious internal forces that have helped immeasurably. Then, with our new childSelf held to our heart and breast, we step onto the road. The maiden is on her way again, wandering toward a great woods in all great faith that something will come from that great hall of trees, something soul-making.

The Sixth Stage—The Realm of the Wild Woman

The young queen comes to the largest, wildest forest she's ever seen. No paths are discernible. She picks her way over and through and around. Near dark, the same white spirit who helped her at the moat earlier guides her to a poor inn run by kindly woodspeople. A woman in white bids her enter and calls her by name. When the young queen asks how she knows her name, the woman in white says, "We who are of the forest follow these matters, my queen."

So the queen stays seven years at the forest inn, and is happy with her child and her life. Her hands gradually grow back, first as little baby hands, then as little girl hands, and finally as woman's hands.

Though this episode is briefly attended to in the tale, it is truly the longest both in time passed and in terms of bringing the task to fruition. The maiden has wandered again, and comes home, so to speak, for seven years—separated from her husband, it is true, but otherwise experiencing enrichment and restoration.

Her state has again aroused the compassion of a spirit in white—now her guiding spirit—and it leads her to this home in the forest. Such is the infinitely merciful nature of the deep psyche during a woman's journey. There is always the next helper and the next. This spirit who leads and shelters her is of the old Wild Mother, and as such is the instinctual psyche that always knows what comes next and what comes next after that.

This large wild forest that the maiden finds is the archetypal sacred initiatory ground. It is like *Leuce*, the wild forest the ancient Greeks said grew in the underworld, filled with the sacred and ancestral trees and full of beasts, both wild and tame. It is here that the handless maiden finds peace for seven years. Because it is a treeland, and because she is symbolized by the flowering apple tree, this is her homeland at last, the place where her fiery and flowering soul regains its roots.

And who is the woman in the deep wood who runs the inn? Like the spirit dressed in glowing white, she is an aspect of the old triple Goddess, and if absolutely every phase of the original fairy tale were here, there would also be a kindly/fierce old woman at the inn in some capacity or other. But that passage of this story has been lost, somewhat like a manuscript in which some of the pages have been ripped out. The missing element was probably originally suppressed during one of those storms that raged between proponents of the old nature religion and those of the newer religion around which religious belief was to be the dominant. But what remains is potent. The water of the story is not only deep but clear.

What we see are two women who over seven years' time come to know one another. The spirit in white is like the telepathic Baba

Yaga in "Vasalisa," who is a representation of the old Wild Mother. As the Yaga says to Vasalisa, even though she's never seen her before, "Oh, yes, I know your people," this female spirit who is an innkeeper in the underworld already knows the young queen, for she is also of the sacred One who knows all.

Again the story breaks significantly. The exact tasks and learnings of those seven years are not alluded to, other than to say that they were restful and revivifying. Although we might say the story breaks because the learnings of the old nature religion that underlie this story were traditionally kept secret and therefore would not be in such a tale, it is much more likely that there are another seven aspects, tasks, or episodes to this story, one for each year the maiden was in the forest of learning. But, hold fast, nothing is lost in the psyche, remember?

We can remember and resurrect all that occurred during those seven years from little shards we have from other sources on women's initiation. Woman's initiation is an archetype, and although an archetype has many variations, its core remains constant. So, here is what we know about initiation from candling other fairy tales and myths, both oral and written.

The maiden stays for seven years, for that is the time of a season of a woman's life. Seven is the number accorded to the moon's cycles, and it is the number of other terms of sacred time: seven days of creation, seven days to a week, and so forth. But beyond these mystical understandings is one far greater and it is this:

A woman's life is divided into phases of seven years each. Every seven-year period stands for a certain set of experiences and learnings. These phases can be understood concretely as terms of adult development, but they may more so be understood as spiritual stages of development that do not necessarily correspond to a woman's chronological age, although sometimes that is so.

Since the beginning of time, women's lives have been divided into phases, most having to do with the changing powers of her body. Sequentializing a woman's physical, spiritual, emotional, and creative life is useful so that she is able to anticipate and prepare for "what comes next." What comes next is the province of the instinctual Wild Woman. She always knows. Yet, across time, as the old wild initiation rites fell away, the instruction of the younger women by the older women about these inherent womanly stages was also hidden away.

Empirical observation of women's restlessness, yearning, changing, and growing brings the old patterns or phases of women's deep life back to light. Though we can put specific titles to the stages, they are all cycles of completion, aging, dying, and new life. The seven years the maiden spends in the forest teach her the details and dramas connected to these phases. Here are cycles of seven years each, stretching across a woman's entire lifetime. Each has its rites and its tasks. It is up to us to fill them in.

I offer the following to you only as metaphors for psychic depth. The ages and stages of a woman's life provide both tasks to accomplish and attitudes in which to root herself. For instance, if according to the following schema we live to be old enough to enter the psychic place and phase of the mist beings, the place where all thought is new as tomorrow and old as the beginning of time, we will find ourselves entering yet another attitude, another manner of seeing, as well as discovering and accomplishing the tasks of consciousness from that vantage point.

The following metaphors are fragments. But given expansive enough metaphors we can construct, from what is known and from what we sense about the ancient knowing, new insights for ourselves that are both numinous and make sense right now and today. These metaphors are loosely based on empirical experience and observation, developmental psychology, and phenomena found in creation myths, all of which contain many old traces of human psychology.

These phases are not meant to be tied inexorably to chronological age, for some women at eighty are still in developmental young maidenhood, and some women at age forty are in the psychic world of the mist beings, and some twenty year olds are as battle scarred as long-lived crones. The ages are not meant to be hierarchical, but simply belong to women's consciousness and to the increase of their soul-lives. Each age represents a change in attitude, a change in tasking, and a change in values.

0–7   age of the body and dreaming/socialization, yet
            retaining imagination

7–14	age of separating yet weaving together reason and the imaginal
14–21	age of new body/young maidenhood/unfurling yet protecting sensuality
21–28	age of new world/new life/exploring the worlds
28–35	age of the mother/learning to mother others and self
35–42	age of the seeker/learning to mother self/seeking the self
42–49	age of early crone/finding the far encampment/giving courage to others
49–56	age of the underworld/learning the words and rites
56–63	age of choice/choosing one's world and the work yet to be done
63–70	age of becoming watchwoman/recasting all one has learned
70–77	age of re-youthanization/more cronedom
77–84	age of the mist beings/finding more big in the small
84–91	age of weaving with the scarlet thread/understanding the weaving of life
91–98	age of the ethereal/less to saying, more to being
98–105	age of pneuma, the breath
105 +	age of timelessness

For many women, the first half of these phases of a woman's knowing, say to about age forty or so, clearly moves from the substantive body of instinctual infant realizations to the bodily knowing of the deep mother. But in the second round of phases, the body becomes an internal sensing device almost exclusively, and women become more and more subtle.

As a woman transits through these cycles, her layers of defense, protection, density become more and more sheer until her very soul begins to shine through. We can sense and see the movement of the soul within the body-psyche in an astonishing way as we grow older and older.

So, seven is the number of initiation. In archetypal psychology there are literally dozens of references to the symbol of seven. One reference I find most valuable in helping women to differentiate the tasks ahead of them, and in stating their current whereabouts in the underground forest, is from the ancient attributions given to the seven senses. These symbolic attributes were believed to belong to all humans and seem to have constituted an initiation into the soul through the metaphors and actual systems of the body.

For instance, according to ancient teaching in Nahua healing, the senses represent aspects of soul or the "inward holy body," and they are to be worked and developed. While the work is too long to lay out here, there are said to be seven senses, therefore seven task areas: animation, feeling, speech, taste, sight, hearing, and smelling.[33]

Each sense was said to be under the influence of an energy from the heavens. To bring this artfully down to earth now, when women who are working in a group speak of these things, they can describe them, explore them, comb them out by using the following metaphors, from the same ritual, in order to peer into the mysteries of the senses: fire animates, earth gives a sense of feeling, water gives speech, air gives taste, mist gives sight, flowers give hearing, the south wind gives smelling.

My feeling is strong from the little rag left of the old initiatory rite in this part of the tale, mainly the phrase "seven years," that the stages of a woman's entire life, and matters such as those of the seven senses and other cycles and events that are traditionally numbered in sevens, were brought to the attention and mixed into the work of the initiate of olden times. One old storytelling fragment that intrigues me greatly came from Cratynana, an old and beloved Swabian teller in our extended family. She said that long ago women used to go away for several years to a place in the mountains, just like men went away for a long time with the army in the king's service.

So, in this time of the maiden's learning in the deep woods, there is another miracle. Her hands begin to grow back in phases, first those of a baby. We can take this to mean that her understanding of all that has occurred is at first imitative, like the behavior of a baby. As her hands grow into those of a child, she develops a concrete but not absolute understanding of all things. When finally they become women's hands, she has a practiced and deeper grasp of the non-concrete, the metaphoric, the sacred path she has been on.

As we practice the deep instinctive knowing about all manner of things we are learning over a lifetime, our hands return to us, the hands of womanhood. It is amusing sometimes to watch ourselves as we first enter a psychic stage of our own individuation by clumsily imitating the behavior we would like to master. Later as we go along, we grow into our own spiritual phrasing, into our own rightful and one-of-a-kind shapes.

Sometimes I use my other literary version of this tale in performance and analysis. The young queen goes to the well. As she bends over to draw water, her child falls into the well. The young queen begins to shriek, and a spirit appears and asks why she does not rescue her child. "Because I have no hands!" she cries. "Try," calls the spirit, and as the maiden puts her arms in the water, reaching toward her child, her hands regenerate then and there, and the child is saved.

This too is a powerful metaphor for the idea of saving the child-Self, the soul-Self, from being lost again in the unconscious, from forgetting who we are and what our work is. It is at this point in our lives that even very charming people, very enchanting ideas, very alluring calliope music can be turned away with ease, and especially if they do not nurture a woman's union with the wild.

For many women the transformation from feeling oneself swept away or enslaved by every idea or person who raps at her door to being a woman shining with *La Destina*, possessed of a deep sense of her own destiny, is a miraculous one. With eyes on straight, palms outward, with the hearing of the instinctual self intact, the woman goes into life in this new and powerful manner.

In this version the maiden has done the work so that when she needs the help of her hands to sense and guard her progression, they are there. They are regenerated through the fear of losing the childSelf. The regeneration of a woman's grasp on her life and work sometimes causes a momentary hiatus in the work, for she may not be totally confident about her newfound strengths. She may have to try them out for a time to realize how great their reach is.

We often have to re-form our ideas of "once without power (hands), always without power." After all our losses and sufferings we find that if we will reach we will be rewarded by grasping the child that is most precious to us. This is how a woman feels, that at long last, she has grasped her life again. She has palms "to see with," and to fashion life with once more. All through she has been helped by intra-psychic forces, and she has matured greatly. She is truly "within herSelf" now.

So we are almost to the end of walking the vast land of this long story. There is but one more stretch of crescendo and completion ahead. Since this is an induction into the mystery/mastery of endurance, let us press forward on this last leg of the underworld journey.

The Seventh Stage—The Wild Bride and Bridegroom

Now the king returns and he and his mother comprehend that the Devil has sabotaged their messages. The king vows a purification—to go without eating or drinking and to travel as far as the sky is blue in order to find the maiden and their child. He searches for seven years. His hands become black, his beard moldy brown like moss, his eyes red-rimmed and parched. During this time he neither eats nor drinks, but a force greater than himself helps him live.

At last he comes to the inn kept by the woodspeople. There he is covered by a veil, sleeps, and wakens to find a lovely woman and a beautiful child gazing down at him. "I am your wife and this is your child," says the young queen. The king is willing to believe but sees that the maiden has hands. "Through my travails and yet my good care, my hands have grown back," she says. And the spirit-woman in white brings the silver hands from a trunk where they'd been treasured. There is a spiritual feast. The king, queen, and child return to the king's mother, and hold a second wedding.

Here at the end, the woman who has made this sustained descent has melded together a sturdy quaternity of spiritual powers: the kingly animus, the childSelf, the old Wild Mother, and the initiated maiden. She has been washed and purified many times. Her ego's desire for the safe life is no longer lead dog. Now this quaternity leads the psyche.

It is the suffering and wandering of the king that brought about the final reunion and remarriage. Why does he, who is king of the underworld, have to wander? Is he not the king? Well, the truth of the matter is that kings too have to do psychic work, even archetypal kings. Within this tale is the old and extremely cryptic idea that when one force of the psyche changes, the others must shift as well. Here the maiden is no longer the woman he married, no longer the frail wandering soul. Now she is initiated, now she knows her woman's ways in all matters. Now she is wizened with the stories and counsel of the old Wild Mother. She has hands.

So the king must suffer to develop himself. In some ways this king remains in the underworld, but as an animus figure, he represents a woman's adaptation to collective life—he carries the dominant ideas she has learned in her journey to the topside, or outer society. Except he has not yet walked in her shoes, and this he must do in order to carry what she is and what she knows out into the world.

After the old Wild Mother informs him that he has been duped by the Devil, he himself is plunged into his own transformation through wandering and finding, just as the maiden had done before him. He has not lost his hands, but he has lost his queen and his offspring. So the animus follows a path quite similar to that of the maiden.

This empathic replay reorganizes a woman's way of being in the world. To reorient the animus in this manner is to initiate and integrate it into a woman's personal work. This may be how there came to be male initiates at the essentially feminine initiation at Eleusis; these men took on the tasks and travails of female learning in order to find their psychic queens and psychic offspring. The animus enters its own seven-year initiation. In this manner that which a woman has learned will be reflected not only in her inner soul but will also be written upon her and acted upon outwardly as well.

The king wanders also in the forest of initiation, and here again we have the sense that there are seven more episodes missing—the seven stages of animus initiation. But again, we have fragments to extrapolate from, we have our ways and means. One of the clues is that the king does not eat for seven years and yet is sustained. To not be nourished has to do with reaching under our urges and appetites to some deeper meaning that stands behind and down. The king's initiation has to do with learning a kind of deepening with regard to understanding appetites, sexual[34] and otherwise. It has to do with learning the value and balance of cycles that sustain human hope and happiness.

Additionally, since he is animus, his seeking has also to do with finding the fully initiated feminine in the psyche and keeping that as his main goal, regardless of whatever else crosses his path. Thirdly, his initiation into the wild self, as he becomes animal in nature for seven years, and does not bathe for seven years, in order to peel away whatever layers of over-civilizing chitin he has learned. This animus is doing the real work in preparation for showing and acting true to the soul-Self of the newly initiated woman in day-to-day life.

The story line that refers to the veil being placed over the king's face while he sleeps is most likely another fragment from the old mystery rites. There is a beautiful sculpture in Greece of just this: a male initiate veiled with his head bowed as though resting or waiting or asleep.[35] Now we see that the animus cannot be acting beneath *her* level of knowing, or she will become split again between what she feels and knows inwardly and how she, through her animus, behaves outwardly. So the animus must wander about in nature, in its own masculine nature, in the forest also.

It is no wonder that both the maiden and king are caused to walk psychic lands where such processes take place. They can be learned only in the wildish nature, only next to the skin of Wild Woman. It is usual that a woman so initiated should find her underworld love of the wild nature surfacing in her topside-world life. Psychically she has the fragrance of wood fire about her. It is usual that she begins to act *here* what she has learned *there*.

One of the most amazing things about this long initiation is that the woman undergoing this process continues to do all the regular living of topside life: loving lovers; birthing babies; chasing children; chasing art; chasing words; carrying food, paints, skeins; fighting for this and the other; burying the dead; doing all the workaday tasks as well as this deep, faraway journey.

A woman, at this time, is often torn in two directions, for there comes over her an urge to wade into the forest as though it is a river and to swim in the green, to climb to the top of a crag and sit face into the wind. It is a time when an inner clock strikes an hour that forces a woman to have sudden need of a sky to call her own, a tree to throw her arms about, a rock to press her cheek against. Yet she must live her topside life as well.

It is to her extreme credit that even though she many times wishes to, she does not drive her car into the sunset. At least not permanently. For it is this outer life that exerts the right amount of pressure to take on the underworld tasking. It is better to stay in the world during this time rather than leave it, for the tension is better and tension makes a precious and deeply turned life that can be made no other way.

So we see the animus in its own transformation, readying to be an equal partner to the maiden and childSelf. At last they are reunited and there is a return to the old mother, the wise mother, the mother who can bear it all, who helps with her wit and wisdom . . . and they are all united and have love of one another.

The attempt of the demonic to overtake the soul has failed irrevocably. The endurance of soul has been tested and met. A woman goes through this cycle once every seven years, the first time very faintly, and usually, one time at least, very hard, and thereafter in a rather memorial or renewing sort of manner. Here at the last, let us rest now and look over this lush panorama of women's initiation and its tasks. Once we have been through the cycle, we can choose any or all tasks to renew our lives at any time and for any reason. Here are some:

• to leave the old parents of the psyche, descend to the psychic land unknown, while depending on the goodwill of whomever we meet along the way
• to bind the wounds inflicted by the poor bargain we made somewhere in our lives
• to wander psychically hungry and trust nature to feed us
• to find the Wild Mother and her succor
• to make contact with the sheltering animus of the underworld
• to converse with the psychopomp (the magician)
• to behold the ancient orchards (energic forms) of the feminine
• to incubate and give birth to the spiritual childSelf

• to bear being misunderstood, to be severed again and again from love

• to be made sooty, muddy, dirty

• to stay in the realm of the woodspeople for seven years till the child is the age of reason

• to wait

• to regenerate the inner sight, inner knowing, inner healing of the hands

• to continue onward even though one has lost all, save the spiritual child

• to re-trace and grasp her childhood, girlhood, and womanhood

• to re-form her animus as a wild and native force; to love him; and he, her

• to consummate the wild marriage in the presences of the old Wild Mother and the new childSelf

The fact that both the handless maiden and the king suffer through the same seven-years-long initiation is the common ground between feminine and masculine. It gives us a strong idea that instead of antagonism between these two forces, there can be profound love, especially if it is rooted in the seeking of one's own self.

"The Handless Maiden" is a real-life story about us as real women. It is not about one part of our lives, but about the phases of an entire lifetime. It teaches, in essence, that for women the work is to wander into the forest over and over again. Our psyches and souls are specifically suited to this so that we can traverse the psychic underland, stopping here and here and here, listening to the voice of the old Wild Mother, being fed by the fruits of spirit, and being reunited with everything and everyone beloved by us.

The time with Wild Woman is hard at first. To repair injured instinct, banish naïveté, and over time to learn the deepest aspects of psyche and soul, to hold on to what we have learned, to not turn away, to speak out for what we stand for . . . all this takes a boundless and mystical endurance. When we come up out of the underworld after one of our undertakings there, we may appear unchanged outwardly, but inwardly we have reclaimed a vast and womanly wildness. On the surface we are still friendly, but beneath the skin, we are most definitely no longer tame.

✻ CHAPTER 15

Shadowing:
Canto Hondo,
The Deep Song

Shadowing means to have such a light touch, such a light tread, that one can move freely through the forest, observing without being observed. A wolf shadows anyone or anything that passes through her territory. It is her way of gathering information. It is the equivalent of manifesting and then becoming like smoke, and then manifesting again.

Wolves can move ever so softly. The sound they make is in the manner of *los ángeles tímidos*, the shyest angels. First they fall back and shadow the creature they're curious about. Then, all of a sudden, they appear ahead of the creature, peeking half-face with one golden eye from behind a tree. Abruptly, the wolf turns and vanishes in a blur of white ruff and plumed tail, only to backtrack and pop up behind the stranger again. That is shadowing.

The Wild Woman has been shadowing human women for years. Now we see a glimpse of her. Now she is invisible again. Yet she makes so many appearances in our lives, and in so many different forms, we feel surrounded by her images and urges. She comes to us in dreams or in stories—especially stories from our own personal lives—for she wants to see who we are, and if we are ready to join her yet. If we but look at the shadows we cast, we see that they are not two-legged human shadows but the lovely shapes of a something free and wild.

We are meant to be permanent residents, not just tourists in her territory, for we are derived from that land: it is our motherland and our inheritance at the same time. The wild force of our soul-psyches is shadowing us for a reason. There is a saying from medieval times that if you are in a descent, and pursued by a great power—and if this great power is able to snag your shadow, then you too shall become a power in your own right.

The great and good wild force of our own psyches means to place its paw on our shadows, and in that manner she claims us as her own. Once the Wild Woman snags our shadows, we belong to ourselves again, we are in our own right environ and in our rightful home.

Most women are not afraid of this, in fact, they crave the reunion. If they could this very moment find the lair of the Wild Woman, they would dive right in and jump happily into her lap. They only need to be set in the right direction, which is always down, down into one's own work, down into one's own inner life, down through that tunnel to the lair.

We began our search for the wild, whether as girlchildren or as adult women, because in the midst of some ardent endeavor we felt that a wild and supportive presence was near. Perhaps we found her tracks across fresh snow in a dream. Or psychically, we noticed a bent twig here and there, pebbles overturned so their wet sides faced upward . . . and we knew that something blessed had passed our way. We sensed within our own psyches the sound of a familiar breath from afar, we felt tremors in the ground, and we innately knew that something powerful, someone important, some wild freedom within us was on the move.

We could not turn from it, but rather followed, learning more and more how to leap, how to run, how to shadow all things that came across our psychic ground. We began to shadow the Wild Woman and she lovingly shadowed us in return. She howled and we tried to answer her, even before we remembered how to speak her language, and even before we exactly knew to whom we were speaking. And she waited for us, and encouraged us. This is the miracle of the wild and instinctual nature. Without full knowing, we knew. Without full sight, we understood that a miraculous and loving force existed beyond the boundaries of ego alone.

As a child, Opal Whitely wrote these words about reconciliation with the power of the wild.

Today near eventime I did lead
the girl who has no seeing
a little way into the forest
where it was darkness and shadows were.
I led her toward a shadow
that was coming our way.
It did touch her cheeks
with its velvety fingers.
And now she too
does have likings for shadows.
And her fear that was is gone.

The things that have been lost to women for centuries can be found again by following the shadows they cast. And make a candle to Guadalupe, for these lost and stolen treasures still cast shadows across our nightdreams and in our imaginal daydreams and in old, old stories, in poetry, and in any inspired moment. Women across the world—your mother, my mother, you and I, your sister, your friend, our daughters, all the tribes of women not yet met—we all dream what is lost, what next must rise from the unconscious. We all dream the same dreams worldwide. We are never without the map. We are never without each other. We unite through our dreams.

Dreams are compensatory, they provide a mirror into the deep unconscious most often reflecting what is lost, and, what is yet needed for correction and balance. Through dreams, the unconscious constantly produces teaching images. So, like a fabled lost continent, the wild dreamland rises out of our sleeping bodies, rises steaming and streaming to create a sheltering motherland over all of us. This is the continent of our knowing. It is the land of our Self.

And this is what we dream: We dream the archetype of Wild Woman, we dream of reunion. And we are born and reborn from this dream every day and create from its energy all during the daytime. We are born and reborn night after night from this same wild dream, and we return to daylight grasping a coarse hair, the soles of our feet black with damp earth, our hair smelling like ocean, or forest or cook fire.

It is from that land that we step into our day clothes, our day lives. We travel from that wildish place in order to sit before the computer, in front of the cook pot, before the window, in front of the teacher, the book, the customer. We breathe the wild into our corporate work, our business creations, our decisions, our art, the work of our hands and hearts, our politics, spirituality, plans, home-life, education, industry, foreign affairs, freedoms, rights, and duties. The wild feminine is not only sustainable in all worlds; it *sustains* all worlds.

Let us admit it. We women are building a motherland; each with her own plot of soil eked from a night of dreams, a day of work. We are spreading this soil in larger and larger circles, slowly, slowly. One day it will be a continuous land, a resurrected land come back from the dead. *Munda de la Madre*, psychic motherworld, coexisting and coequal with all other worlds. This world is being made from our lives, our cries, our laughter, our bones. It is a world worth making, a world worth living in, a world in which there is a prevailing and decent wild sanity.

When we think of reclamation it may bring to mind bulldozers or carpenters, the restoration of an old structure, and that is the modern usage of the word. However, the older meaning is this: The word *reclamation* is derived from the old French *reclaimer*, meaning "to call back the hawk which has been let fly." Yes, to cause something of the wild to return when it is called. It is there-fore by its meaning an excellent word for us. We are using the voices of our minds, our lives, and our souls to call back intuition, imagination; to call back the Wild Woman. And she comes.

Women cannot get away from this. If there is to be change, we are it. We carry *La Que Sabe*, the One Who Knows. If there is to be inner change, individual woman must do it. If there is to be world change, we women have our own way of helping to achieve it. Wild Woman whispers the words and the ways to us, and we follow. She has been running and stopping and waiting to see if we are catching up. She has something, many things, to show us.

So, if you are on the verge of breaking away, taking a risk—daring to act in proscribed ways, then dig up the deepest bones possible, fructifying the wild and natural aspects of women, of life, of men, of children, of earth. Use your love *and* good instincts to know when to growl, to pounce, to take a swipe, when to kill, when to retreat, when to bay till dawn. To live as closely as possible to the numinous wild a woman must do more head tossing, more brimming, have more sniffing intuition, more creative life, more "get-down-dirty," more solitude, more women's company, more natural life, more fire, more spirit, more cooking of words and ideas. She must do more recognition of sorority, more seeding, more root stock–keeping, more kindness to men, more neighborhood revolution, more poetry, more painting of fables and facts, longer reaches into the wild feminine. More terrorist sewing circles, and more howling. And, especially, much more *canto hondo*, much more deep song.

She must shake out her pelt, strut the old pathways, assert her instinctual knowledge. We can all assert membership in the ancient scar clan, proudly bear the battle scars of our time, write our secrets on walls, refuse to be ashamed, lead the way through and out. Let us not overspend on anger. Instead let us be empowered by it. Most of all let us be cunning and use our feminine wits.

Let us keep in mind that the best cannot and must not hide. Meditation, education, all the dream analysis, all the knowledge of God's green acre is of no value if one keeps it all to oneself or one's chosen few. So come out, come out wherever you are. Leave deep footprints because you can. Be the old woman in the rocking chair who rocks the idea until it becomes young again. Be the courageous and patient woman in "The Crescent Moon Bear" who learns to see through illusion. Don't be distracted by burning matches and fantasies like the Little Match Girl.

Hold out till you find the ones you belong to like the Ugly Duckling. Clear the creative river so *La Llorona* can find what belongs to her. Like the Handless Maiden, let the enduring heart lead you through the forest. Like *La Loba*, collect the bones of lost valuables and sing them back to life. Forgive as much as you can, forget a little, and create a lot. What you do today influences your matri-lineal lines in the future. The daughters of your daughters of your daughters are likely to remember you, and most importantly, follow in your tracks.

The ways and means of living with the instinctive nature are many, and the answers to your deepest questions change as you change and as the world changes, so it cannot be said: "Do this, and this, in this particular order, and all will be well." But, over my lifetime as I've met wolves, I have tried to puzzle out how they live, for the most part, in such harmony. So, for peaceable purposes, I would suggest you begin right now with any point on this list. For those who are struggling, it may help greatly to begin with number ten.

GENERAL WOLF RULES FOR LIFE
 1. Eat
 2. Rest
 3. Rove in between
 4. Render loyalty
 5. Love the children
 6. Cavil in moonlight
 7. Tune your ears
 8. Attend to the bones
 9. Make love
 10. Howl often

✻ CHAPTER 16

The Wolf's Eyelash

If you don't go out in the woods, nothing will ever happen and your life will never begin.

"Don't go out in the woods, don't go out," they said.

"Why not? Why should I not go out in the woods tonight?" she asked.

"A big wolf lives there who eats humans such as you. Don't go out in the woods, don't go out. We mean it."

Naturally, she went out. She went out in the woods anyway, and of course she met the wolf, just as they had warned her.

"See, we told you," they crowed.

"This is my life, not a fairy tale, you dolts," she said. "I have to go to the woods, and I have to meet the wolf, or else my life will never begin."

But the wolf she encountered was in a trap, in a trap this wolf's leg was in.

"Help me, oh help me! Aieeeee, aieeee, aieeee!" cried the wolf. "Help me, oh help me!" he cried, "and I shall reward you justly." For this is the way of wolves in tales of this kind.

"How do I know you won't harm me?" she asked—it was her job to ask questions. "How do I know you will not kill me and leave me lying in my bones?"

"Wrong question," said this wolf. "You'll just have to take my word for it." And the wolf began to cry and wail once again and more.

"Oh, aieee! Aieeee! Aieeee!
There's only one question
worth asking fair maiden,
woooooooooor
aieeeee th'
soooooooooool?"

"Oh you wolf, I will take a chance. Alright, here!" And she
sprang the trap and the wolf drew out its paw and this she bound
with herbs and grasses.

"Ah, thank you kind maiden, thank you," sighed the wolf.
And because she had read too many of the wrong kind of tales,
she cried, "Go ahead and kill me now, and let us get this over
with."

But no, this did not come to pass. Instead this wolf put his paw
upon her arm.

"I'm a wolf from another time and place," said he. And plucking a lash from his eye, gave it to her and said, "Use this, and be
wise. From now on you will know who is good and not so good;
just look through my eyes and you will see clearly.

For letting me live,
I bid you live
in a manner as never before.
Remember, there's only one question
worth asking fair maiden,
woooooooooor
aieeeee th'
soooooooooool?"

And so she went back to her village,
happy to still have her life.
And this time as they said,
"Just stay here and be my bride,"
or "Do as I tell you,"
or "Say as I want you to say,
and remain as unwritten upon
as the day you came,"
she held up the wolf's eyelash

and peered through
and saw their motives
as she had not see them before.
And the next time
the butcher weighed the meat
she looked through her wolf's eyelash
and saw that he weighed his thumb too.
And she looked at her suitor
who said "I am so good for you,"
and she saw that her suitor
was so good for exactly nothing.
And in this way and more,
she was saved,
from not all,
but from many,
misfortunes.

But more so, in this new seeing, not only did she see the sly and cruel, she began to grow immense in heart, for she looked at each person and weighed them anew through this gift from the wolf she had rescued.

And she saw those who were truly kind
and went near to them,
she found her mate
and stayed all the days of her life,
she discerned the brave
and came close to them,
she apprehended the faithful
and joined with them,
she saw bewilderment under anger
and hastened to soothe it,
she saw love in the eyes of the shy
and reached out to them,
she saw suffering in the stiff-lipped
and courted their laughter,
she saw need in the man with no words
and spoke for him,
she saw faith deep in the woman

who said she had none,
and rekindled hers from her own.
She saw all things
with her lash of wolf,
all things true,
and all things false,
all things turning against life
and all things turning toward life,
all things seen only
through the eyes of that
which weighs the heart with heart,
and not with mind alone.

This is how she learned that it is true what they say, that the wolf is the wisest of all. If you listen closely, the wolf in its howling is always asking the most important question—not where is the next food, not where is the next fight, not where is the next dance?—

but the most important question
in order to see into and behind,
to weigh the value of all that lives,
woooooooooor
aieeeee th'
soooooooooool?
woooooooooor
aieeeee th'
soooooooooool?
Where is the soul?
Where is the soul?

Go out in the woods, go out. If you don't go out in the woods, nothing will ever happen and your life will never begin.

> *Go out in the woods,*
> *go out.*
> *Go out in the woods,*
> *go out,*
> *Go out in the woods,*
> *go out.*

𝕀𝕤 AFTERWORD
STORY AS MEDICINE

Here I will lay out for you the *ethos* of story in my family's ethnic traditions, those that my storymaking and poetry are rooted in, and a bit about my use of *las palabras*, words, and *los cuentos*, stories, for assisting the life of the soul.

To my eyes, *Historias que son medicina*: Stories are medicine.

"... Whenever a fairy tale is told, it becomes night. No matter where the dwelling, no matter the time, no matter the season, the telling of tales causes a starry sky and a white moon to creep from the eaves and hover over the heads of the listeners. Sometimes, by the end of the tale, the chamber is filled with daybreak, other times a star shard is left behind, sometimes a ragged thread of storm sky. And whatever is left behind is the bounty to work with, to use toward the soul-making ..."[1]

My work in the humus of stories does not come from my training as a psychoanalyst alone, but equally from my long life as the child of a deeply ethnic and non-literate family heritage. Although my people could not read or write or did so haltingly, they were wise in ways that are often lost to modern culture.

There were times in my growing-up years that stories and jokes and songs and dances were demonstrated at the table during a meal or at a wedding or wake, but most of what I carry, tell raw, or write into literary stories, was received not while sitting in a formal circle but during hard work, tasks requiring intensity and concentration.

To my mind, story, in every way possible, thrives only on hard work—intellectual, spiritual, familial, physical, and integral. It never comes easy. It is never "just picked up," or studied in one's "off times." Its essence cannot be born nor maintained in air-conditioned comfort, it cannot grow to any depth in an enthusiastic but non-committed mind, neither can it live in gregarious but shallow environs. Story cannot be "studied." It is learned through assimilation, through living in its proximity with those who know it, live it, and teach it—more so through all the day-to-day mundane tasks of life, much more than the clearly ceremonial times.

The healing medicine of story does not exist in a vacuum.[2] It cannot exist divorced from its spiritual source. It cannot be taken on as a mix-and-match project. There is an integrity to story that comes from a real life lived in it. A story is clearly illumined from being raised up in it.

In my family's oldest traditions, which stretch far back, as my *abuelitas* say, "for as many generations as there are generations," the times for story, the tales chosen, the exact words employed to convey them, the tones of voice used for each, the endings and beginnings, the unfolding of the text, and especially *the intention* behind each are most often dictated by an acute inner sensibility, more so than any outer pull or "opportunity."

Some traditions set aside specific times for telling stories. Among my friends from several pueblo tribes, stories of Coyote are reserved for winter telling. My *comadres* and relatives in the south of Mexico tell about "the great wind from the east" in the springtime only. In my foster family certain tales cooked in their Eastern European heritage are told only in autumn after harvest. In my blood family, my *El dia de los muertos* stories are traditionally begun in early winter and carried on through the dark of winter until the return of spring.

In the old and integral healing rites germane to *curanderisma*, and the *mesemondók*, every detail is weighed very carefully against the tradition: when to tell a story, which story, and to whom, how long and in what form, what words, and under which conditions. We carefully consider the time, the place, the health or lack of health of the person, the mandates in the person's inner and outer lives, and several other critical factors as well, in order to arrive at the medicine needed. In the most basic ways there is a spirit, both holy and whole, behind our ages-old rituals; and we tell stories when we are summoned by their covenant with us, not vice versa.[3]

In using story as medicine, as in a vigorous psychoanalytic training as well as in other rigorously taught and supervised healing arts, we are trained carefully to know what to do and when, but most especially we are trained in *what not to do*. This, perhaps more than anything, separates stories as entertainment—a worthy form in and of itself—from stories as medicine.

In my "farthest-back" culture, although we bridge the modern world, there is at the root a timeless storyteller legacy, wherein one teller hands down his or her stories and the knowledge of the medicine in them to one or more *las semillas* "seed" persons. "Seeds" are people "who have the gift from birth onward." They are the future story-keeps whom the elder has hopes for. Those who have shown a talent are recognizable. Several old ones will agree and squire them, help and protect them while they learn.

The lucky ones will, with much difficulty, discomfort, and inconvenience, enter a rigorous and many-years-long course of work that will teach them to carry on the tradition as they learned it, with all the proper preparations, blessings, percussions, essential insights, ethics, and attitudes that constitute the body of healing knowledge, according to its requirements—not theirs—according to its initiations, according to its prescribed forms.

These forms and lengths of time "in training" cannot be shunted aside or modernized. They cannot be learned in a few weekends or a few years' time. They demand long periods of time for a reason, and that is so that the work does not become trivialized, changed, or misused, as it often does when in the wrong hands, or when used for the wrong reasons, or when appropriated with all good intention coupled with ignorance.[4] No good can come from that.

How "seeds" are chosen is a mysterious process that defies exact definition except for those who know it well, for it is not based on a set of rules, nor imagination, but rather on time-honored relationship, face-to-face, one person to another. The elder chooses the younger, one chooses another, sometimes they find their way to us, but more often we stumble over each other, and both recognize the other as though over eons. Desire to be like this is not the same as being this.

Typically those in family who carry this talent are called out in childhood. The elders who carry the gift have their eyes peeled, often looking for the one who is *"sin piel,"* the skinless one, the one who feels so much and so deeply and who observes the larger patterns of life and the smaller details as well. They are looking as I, now in my fifth decade, look for those who have come to certain acuities from having, for decades, and for a lifetime, lived in careful listening.

The training of *curanderas, cantadoras y cuentistas* is very similar because in my heritage, stories are considered to be written like *un tatuaje del destino*, a light tattoo on the skin of the one who has lived them.

It is believed that talent in healing derives from the reading of this faint writing upon the soul and the development of what is found there. Story, as one part of a five-part healing discipline, is considered the destiny of one who carries such inscribing. Not all carry such, but those who do have their own futures written upon them. They are called *"Las unicas,"* those who are one of a kind.[5]

So, one of the first questions we ask when we meet a teller/healer is, *"Quienes son tus familiares? Quienes son tus padres?"* "Who are your people?" In other words, from what family line of healers do you come? This does not mean what school did you go to? This does not mean what classes did you take, what workshops have you been to? It means literally, from whose spiritual lines do you descend? As always, we look for authenticity in age, knowing rather than intellectual smartness, a religious devotion that is unshakable and imbedded in daily life, the gentle courtesies and attitudes that are clearly inherent in a person who has knowledge of that Source from which all healing derives.[6]

In the *cantadora/cuentista* tradition, there are parents and grand-parents and sometimes *madrinas y padrinos*, Godparents of a story, and these being the person who taught the story and its meanings and momentum to you, who gifted you with it (the mother or father of the story), and the person who taught it to the person who taught it to you (*abuelo o abuela*, grandfather or grandmother of the story). This is as it should be.

Gaining explicit permission to tell another's tale and the proper crediting of that tale, if permission to it is given, is absolutely essential, for it maintains the genealogical umbilicus; we are on one end, the life-giving placenta on the other. It is a sign of respect, and one might say, of befitting manners in one properly raised in stories to ask and receive permission,[7] to not take work that has not been given freely, to respect the work of others, for their work and their lives together make the work they give out. A story is not just a story. In its most innate and proper sense, it is someone's life. It is the numen of their life and their first-hand familiarity with the stories they carry that makes the story "medicine."

The Godparents of the tale are those who gave a blessing along with the gifting of the story. Sometimes it takes a long, long time to tell the ancestry of a story before we can begin the story proper. This listing of the mother of the story, and the grandmother of the story, and so on, is not a long, boring preamble, but spiced with small stories in and of itself. The longer story that follows is then like a second course, like that at a feast.

In every authentic story and healing tradition that I know, the relating of a story begins with the bringing up, hauling up of psychic contents, both collective and personal. The process is a long exertion in time and energy, both intellectual and spiritual; it is in no way an idle practice. It costs much and takes long. Though there are *intercambiamos cuentos*, story trades, wherein two people who have come to know each other well exchange stories as a gift to one another, this occurs because they have developed, if they are not born to it, a kinship relationship. And this is as it should be.

Although some use stories as entertainment alone, and although television in particular too often uses storylines that depict the necrosis of life, tales are, in one of their oldest senses, a healing art. Some are called to this healing art, and the best, by my lights, are those who have genuinely lain with the story, and found all its matching parts inside themselves and at depth . . . they have had a long mentorship, a long spiritual "discipleship," and a long time perfecting their disciplines. Persons such as these are immediately recognizable by their presence alone.

In dealing with stories, we are handling archetypal energy, which we could metaphorically describe as being like electricity. This electrical power can animate and enlighten, but in the wrong place, wrong time, wrong amount, wrong teller, wrong story, unprepared teller, person who may know some of what to do, but does not know what *not* to do,[8] like any medicine, it will not have the desired effect, or else a deleterious one. Sometimes people who are "story collectors" do not realize what they are asking when they ask for a story of this dimension, or attempt to use it without blessing.

Archetype changes us. Archetype infuses a recognizable integrity, a recognizable endurance—if there is no change in the teller, there has been no fidelity, there has been no real contact with the archetype, no transmission—only rhetorical translation or self-interested aggrandizement. The handing down of story is a large and far-reaching responsibility. To detail the parameters of such would fill several volumes were I to attempt to describe the healing processes in their completeness using story as a single component among many. But in the limited space here, let the most important part be conveyed—that we are charged to make certain that people are completely and fully wired for the stories they carry and tell.

Among the best of the teller-healers I know, and I have been blessed to know many, *their stories grow out of their lives* as roots grow a tree. The stories have grown *them*, grown them into who they are. We can tell the difference. We know when someone has "grown" a story facetiously and when the story has genuinely grown them. It is the latter that underlies the integral traditions.

Sometimes a stranger asks me for one of the stories I've mined, shaped, and carried over the years. As the keeper of these stories, given to me on the basis of promises asked for and promises kept, I do not separate them from the other words and rites that surround them, especially those developed and nurtured in the roots of *familia*. This choice depends on no five-point plan, but on a science of soul. Relationship and relatedness are everything.

The master-apprentice model provides the kind of careful atmosphere in which I have been able to help my learners seek and develop the stories that will accept them, that will shine through them, not just lay on the surface of their being like dime-store jewelry. There are ways and there are ways. There are few easy ways but no easy ways that I know of that also have integrity. There are much more and far more tortuous and difficult ways that have integrity and are worth it.

Absolutely, one is enabled in the healing art, in the medicine of story, by the amount of self that one is willing to sacrifice and put into it, and I mean the word *sacrifice* in every nuance of the word. Sacrifice is not a suffering that one chooses oneself, nor is it a "convenient suffering" in which the terminus is controlled by the "sacrificee." Sacrifice is not a great striving or even a substantial discomfort. It is in somewise "entering a hell not of one's own making," and returning from it, fully chastened, fully focused, fully devoted. No more, no less.

There is a saying in my family: the gatekeeper of stories will exact their due from you, that is, force you to live a certain kind of life, a daily discipline, bend you to many years of study—not idle study as ego finds it convenient, but one built upon exacting patterns and requirements. I cannot emphasize this enough.

In the family traditions of dealing with story, in the *mesemondók* as well as the *cuentista* traditions I learned and have used since I was a child, there is what is called *La invitada*, "the guest" that is, the empty chair; this being present at every telling in one way or another. Sometimes during a tell, the soul of one or more of the listeners comes and sits there, for it has a need. Although I may have an entire evening of material I had carefully considered, I may change the progression to accommodate, to mend, or play with the sense of spirit that comes to the empty chair. "The guest" speaks for the needs of all.

* * *

I tell people to do their own mining of stories from their own lives, and insist upon it with those I teach, *especially* the stories from their own heritages, for if at the least, one turns always to the tales directly from the translators of Grimms, for instance, then the tales of their personal heritage—as soon as their old ones die off— shall be lost to them forever. I am a strong supporter of those who bring back the stories of their heritages, preserving them, saving them from death by neglect. Of course, it is the old people who are the bones of the entire healing and spiritual structures everywhere on the face of the earth.

Look to your people, your life. It is not by accident that this advice is the same among great healers and great writers as well. Look to the *real* that you yourself live. The kinds of tales found there can never come from books. They come from eyewitness accounts.

The authentic mining of stories from one's own life and the lives of one's own people, and the modern world as it relates to one's own life as well, means that there will be discomfort and trials. You know you are on the right path if you have experienced these: the scraped knuckles, the sleeping on cold ground—not once, but over and over again—the groping in the dark, the walking in circles in the night, the bone-chilling revelations, and the hair-raising adventures on the way—these are worth every- thing. There must be a little, and in many cases, a good deal of blood spilled on every story, on every aspect of your own life, if it is to carry the numen, if a person is to carry a true medicine.

I hope you will go out and let stories, that is life, happen to you, and that you will work with these stories from your life—your life—not someone else's life—water them with your blood and tears and your laughter till they bloom, till you yourself burst into bloom. That is the work. The only work.[9]

✺ ADDENDUM

In response . . .

In response to readers asking about various aspects of my work
and life, we have expanded some sections of this work in small
ways, adding several anecdotes, clarifications, and various additional notes, expanding the afterword, and publishing here a
prose-poem for the first time that was part of the original manuscript. All of these ministrations were done carefully and without
disturbing the cadence of the work.

Three years later . . .

Many readers have written to express appreciation, to share news
of their reading groups who have been studying *Women Who Run
With the Wolves*, and to send blessings and inquiries about future
works. They have read this book carefully and closely, and often
more than once.[1]

In all, I have been gently astonished to find that the spiritual
roots of my work, even though quietly stated in the subtext of the
book, were so evident to so many readers. My warmest gratitude
for readers' blessings sent our way, their kind words, thoughtful
insights, great generosities of heart, beautiful gifts made by hand,
and their abundant gestures for strengthening and sheltering—
such as including my work, the welfare of my family and loved
ones, and myself—in their everyday devotions. All these gestures
are preciously held in my heart.

512

Long ago, but not so far away . . .

Here I will try to comment on some of the interests that readers have conveyed to us.

Many have asked about how the writing of *Women Who Run With the Wolves* began. "The writing began long before the writing began."[2] It began by being born into the unusual and quixotic family structures that *El destino* had prepared for me. It began with decades of being filled up by heartbreaking beauty and seeing much hope-lost in cultural, societal, and other kinds of storms. It began as the result of loves and lives both harsh and dear. "The writing began long before the writing began"—this I can say with confidence.

The actual physical writing by hand began in 1971, after a pilgrimage from the desert to my homeplace where I asked for and received blessings from my elders to write a special body of work rooted in the song-language of our spiritual roots. Promises were given by all in many directions then, and have been kept all these years and to the letter . . . the most important being, "Do not forget us and what we have suffered for."[3]

Women Who Run With the Wolves is the first part of a five-part series encompassing one hundred tales on the inner life. The entire twenty-two hundred pages of work took just over twenty years to write. In its essence, the work strives to de-pathologize the integral instinctual nature, and to demonstrate its soulful and essential psychic ties to the natural world. The basic premise that runs through all my work asserts that all human beings are born gifted.

On voice . . .

The work was purposefully written in a blend of the scholarly voice via my training as a psychoanalyst, and equally so, in the voice of the traditions of healing and hard work that reflect my ethnic origins—immigrant, lower working class, and *Católicos* all. The heritage of my growing up is the rhythm of labor, and this shapes me first and foremost as *una poeta*, as poet.

As it represents both a psychological and spiritual document, various bookshops have placed *Women Who Run With the Wolves* in several sections at the same time: Psychology, Poetry, Women's Studies, and Religious Studies. Some have said it defies category, or has begun a new one of its own. I do not know if this is so, but, at its root, I hoped it would be as much an artwork as a psychological work on spirit.

A reader's note . . .
Women Who Run With the Wolves strives to assist the conscious work of individuation. The book is best approached as a contemplative work that is written in twenty-some sections. Each section stands on its own.

Ninety-nine percent of the letters we receive relate how the reader is reading the work not only to themselves, but also to and with a loved one: mother to daughter, granddaughter to grandmother, lover to lover, and in weekly or monthly reading groups. Because the work cannot be read in a week or a month's time, it lends itself to being studied. The work itself invites the personal lives of each reader to be weighed against what is proposed there, decided for or against, passed close to, deepened, returned to, and seen through an ongoing maturation process.

Take your time reading. The work was written slowly over a long period of time. I wrote, went away, and thought about it,[4] came back and wrote some more, went away, thought some more, and came back and wrote some more. Most people read this work the way it was written. A little at a time, then go away, think about it, then come back again.[5]

Remember . . .
Psychology, in its oldest sense, means the study of the soul. Although essential and valuable insights have been contributed in the last century and more will be contributed yet, the mapping of human nature, in all its precious variety, is far from complete. Psychology is not one hundred or so years old. Psychology is thousands of years old. The names of many noble men and women who contributed to psychological knowledge are properly honored. But psychology did not begin there. It began with anyone and everyone who heard a voice greater than their own, and who felt compelled to seek its source.

Some have said that my work constitutes "a newly emerging field." I must say, with all due respect, that the essence of the work

I've been given to do is from very old tradition. This kind of work does not fit restfully under the category of "emerging" anything. Thousands of people in every generation worldwide, mostly old ones who are often "uneducated" but wise in many ways, have watched over and protected its exact and intricate parameters. It has always been alive and thriving because they have been alive and thriving, and held the work to certain shapes and means.[6]

A caveat . . .
The matter of individual maturation is a custom endeavor. There can be no rote, "do this, then this." The process of each individual is *unique* and cannot be codified into a "do these ten easy steps and all will be well." This kind of work is not easy and it is not for everyone. If you seek a healer, analyst, therapist, or counselor, make certain they derive from a discipline that has solid predecessors, that they truly know how to do what they hold themselves out as able to do. Ask friends, relatives, and co-workers whom you trust for their recommendations. Make certain whichever teacher you choose is trained, and adequately, in both methods and ethics.[7]

Life now . . .
I am underground writing and working much of the time, but . . . "there are occasional sightings." I continue to live as I have lived for many years now . . . ardently introverted, yet fiercely dedicated to striving to be in the world. I continue to work as analyst, poet, and writer, as well as caring for my large extended family. I continue to speak on social issues, persevere to record audio, paint, compose, translate, teach, and help to train young psychoanalysts. I teach literature, writing, psychology, mythopoetics, contemplative life, and other subjects at various universities as visiting scholar.[8]

Sometimes people ask what has been the most memorable event over the past few years. Certainly there have been many, but the one that pierced my heart completely was the happiness of the elders in our family when this work was first published—for them, the first book from one of their own in print ever. A particular image: When my eighty-four-year-old father saw this book for the first time, he cried out in his broken English, "A book, a book, a real book!" And right there in his garden, he began to dance an old *Csíbraki* dance from the old country.

The work . . .

As *cantadora* (keeper of the old stories), and as an ethnic woman from two cultures, it would be hard *not* to recognize that humans are very diverse culturally, psychologically, and otherwise. Such being so, it seems to me that it would be an error to think that any one way is *the* way. This particular work is offered as a contribution to what is known and what is needed in a true psychology of women—one that includes *all* the kinds of women that exist, and *all* the kinds of lives they lead.

My observations and experiences over these twenty-some years of practice with both women and men have led me to the idea that regardless of one's state, stage, or station in life, one must have psychological and spiritual strength in order to go forward—in small ways, as well as against the considerable winds that are, from time to time, in effect in every person's life.

Strength does not come *after* one climbs the ladder or the mountain, nor *after* one "makes it"—whatever that "it" represents. Strengthening oneself is *essential* to the process of striving— *especially before and during*—as well as after. It is my belief that attention to and devotion to the nature of soul represents the quintessential strength.

There is much afoot at any given time that can make a shambles of spirit and soul by attempting to destroy intent, or by pressuring one to forget the important questions: Questions such as, not only what are the pragmatics of a situation, but also "where is the soul in this matter?" One proceeds in life, gains ground, reverses injustice, and stands against the winds, through strength of spirit.

This strengthening, whether with words, prayer, contemplations of various kinds, or by other means, comes from a numen, a greatness that rests at the center of the psyche and yet is greater than the whole of the psyche. This numen is entirely accessible, must be attended to and nourished. Its existence, regardless of its many appellations, is an incontrovertible psychic fact.

Difficult and rich—this is what a person in an authentic maturation finds at the essence of it all—and it shows, both inside and outside, on the person who strives toward it. This we know, there is a noticeable difference between a considered life of depth and one based on phantasmagoric beliefs. On this journey toward "true home," though we may, from time to time, turn back to record or measure from whence we came, we do not turn back in order to turn back.

✺ NOTES

Sometimes I call endnotes such as these *los cuentitos*, little stories. They are the offspring of the larger text and are meant to be a separate work of art in and of themselves. They are meant to be read straight through, if one wishes, without referring back to the larger text. I invite you to read them both ways.

INTRODUCTION
Singing Over the Bones

1. The language of storytelling and poetry is the powerful sister of the dream language. From the analysis of many dreams (both contemporary and ancient ones taken from written accounts) over the years, as well as sacred texts and the works of mystics such as Catherine of Siena, Francis of Assisi, Rumi, and Eckhart and the work of many poets such as Dickinson, Millay, Whitman, and so on, there appears to be within the psyche a poetry-making and art-making function that arises when a person spontaneously or purposely ventures near the instinctive core of the psyche.

This place in the psyche, where the dreams, stories, poetry, and art meet, constitutes the mysterious habitat of the instinctual or wild nature. In contemporary dreams and poetry and in the older folktales and writings of mystics, the entire milieu of the core is understood as a being with a life of its own. It is most often symbolized in poetry, painting, dance, and dreams as either one of the vast elements such as ocean, vault of sky, loam of earth, or as a power with personhood, such as *Queen of Heaven, The White Doe, The Friend, The Beloved, The Lover,* or *The Mate.*

From the core, numinous matters and ideas rise up through the person who experiences "being filled by something not-I." Also, many artists carry their own ideas and matters born of ego to the edge of the core and drop them in, sensing rightfully that they will be returned newly infused or washed with the core's remarkable psychic sense of life. Either way, this causes a sudden and profound awakening, changing, or informing of the senses, mood, or heart of the human. When one is freshly informed, one's mood is changed. When one's mood is changed, one's heart is changed. That is why the images and language that arise from that core are so important. In combination, they have the power to change one thing into another in a way that is difficult and tortuous to accomplish by will alone. In this sense, the core Self, the instinctual Self, is both healer and life-bringer.

2. *Ego/Self axis* is a phrase used by Edward Ferdinand Edinger (*Ego and Archetype* [New York: Penguin, 1971]) to describe Jung's view of the ego and Self as being a complementary relationship, each—the mover and the moved—needing one another to function. (C. G. Jung, *Collected Works*, vol. 11, 2nd ed. [Princeton: Princeton University Press, 1972], para. 39).

3. "*Para La Mujer Grande*, the Great Woman," © 1971, C. P. Estés, from *Rowing Songs for the Night Sea Journey: Contemporary Chants* (Privately published, 1989).

4. See Afterword, *Story as Medicine*, about the ethnic traditions I follow regarding the boundaries of story.

5. *El duende* is literally the goblin wind or force behind a person's actions and creative life, including the way they walk, the sound of their voice, even the way they lift their little finger. It is a term used in *flamenco* dance, and is also used to describe the ability to "think" in poetic images. Among Latina *curanderas* who recollect story, it is understood as the ability to be filled with spirit that is more than one's own spirit. Whether one is the artist or whether one is the watcher, listener, or reader, when *el duende* is present, one sees it, hears it, reads it, feels it underneath the dance, the music, the words, the art; one knows it is there. When *el duende* is not present, one knows that too.

6. Vasalisa is an Anglicized version of the Russian name Wassilissa. In Europe, the w is pronounced as v.

7. One of the most critical cornerstones in developing a body of study about the psychology of women is that women themselves observe and describe what takes place in their own lives. A woman's ethnic affiliations, her race, her religious practices, her values are all of a piece, and must all be taken into account for together they constitute her soul sense.

CHAPTER ONE
The Howl: Resurrection of the Wild Woman

1. *E. coli*. Partial abbreviation for *Escherichia coli*, a bacillus that causes gastroenteritis and comes from drinking contaminated water.

2. Romulus and Remus, and the twins of Navajo mythos—these are just some of the many famous twins in mythos.

3. Old Mexico.

4. Poem "Luminous Animal" by blues poet Tony Moffeit from his book *Luminous Animal* (Cherry Valley, New York: Cherry Valley Editions, 1989).

5. This story was given to me by my aunt, Tirezianany. In a Talmudic version of this story called "The Four Who Entered Paradise," the four rabbis enter *Pardes*, Paradise, to study the heavenly mysteries and three of the four go mad in one way or another when they gaze upon the *Shekhinah*—the ancient female Deity.

6. *The Transcendent Function* from C. G. Jung, *Collected Works*, vol. 8, 2nd ed. (Princeton: Princeton University Press, 1972), pp. 67–91.

7. This ancient being is also called by some, "woman outside time."

CHAPTER TWO

Stalking the Intruder: The Beginning Initiation

1. The natural predator appears in fairy tales personified as robber, animal groom, rapist, thug, and sometimes as evil woman of various stripe. Women's dream images closely follow the distribution pattern of natural predator in female protagonist fairy tales. Deleterious relationships, abusive authority figures, and negative cultural prescriptions influence dream and folkloric images as much as or more so than one's own innate archetypal patterning, the latter referred to by Jung as archetypal nodes inherent in each person's psyche. The image properly belongs to the "meeting the Life and Death force" motif rather than the "meeting the witch" category.

2. There are quite different published versions of Bluebeard in the collections of Jakob and Wilhelm Grimm, Charles Perrault, Henri Pourrat, and others. There are oral versions existent throughout Asia and Mezo-America as well. The literary Bluebeard I wrote has the peculiarity of the key that will not stop bleeding. This element is a characteristic peculiar to our family story of Bluebeard that was handed down to me from my aunt. The time she and other Magyar, French, and Belgian women were forced into a slave labor camp during World War II shapes the story I carry.

3. In folklore, mythos, and dreams, the natural predator almost always has a predator or stalker of itself as well. It is the battle between these two that finally brings about a change or a balance. When it does not, or when no other goodly antagonist arises, the story is most often called a horror story. The lack of a positive force that is successfully antithetical to the negative predator strikes the deepest fear into the hearts of humans.

Too, in day to day life, there are plenty of light-stealers and consciousness-killers afoot. In the main, a predatory person misappropriates a woman's creative juice, taking it for their own pleasure or use, leaving her whitened and wondering what happened, while they themselves somehow grow more rosy and hearty. The predatory person desires that a woman not heed her instincts lest she perceive that a siphon has been attached to her mind, her imagination, her heart, her sexuality, or whatever else.

The pattern of surrendering one's core life may have begun in childhood, fostered by caretakers who wanted the child's gifts and loveliness to augment the caretaker's own emptiness and hunger. To be trained thusly gives enormous power to the innate predator and sets one out to be prey for others. Until one's instincts are put back in proper order, a woman so raised is exceedingly vulnerable to being overwhelmed by the unspoken and devastating psychic needs of others. Generally, a woman with good instincts knows the predator is insinuated nearby when she finds herself involved in a relationship or situation that causes her life to become smaller rather than larger.

4. Bruno Bettelheim, *Uses of Enchantment: Meaning and Importance of Fairytales* (New York: Knopf, 1976).

5. von Franz, for instance, says Bluebeard "is a murderer, and nothing more . . ." M. L. von Franz, *Interpretation of Fairytales* (Dallas: Spring Publications, 1970), p. 125.

6. To my mind Jung was speculating that the creator and the created were both in evolution, with one's consciousness influencing the other. It is a remarkable idea that a human might influence the force behind archetype.

7. The malfunctioning telephone call is one of the top twenty most common

dream scenarios that humans dream. In the typical dream, the phone will not work, or the dreamer cannot figure out how it works. The phone wires have been cut, the numbers on the keypad are out of order, the line is busy, the emergency number has been forgotten or is not functioning properly. These sorts of telephone situations in dreams are very close in timbre to the misstated or deviously switched message in letters, such as in the folktale "The Handless Maiden" when the devil changes a celebratory message to a malicious one.

8. To protect the identities of those involved, the name and location of the group has been changed.

9. To protect the identities of those involved, the name and location of the group has been changed.

10. To protect the identities of those involved, the name and location of the group has been changed.

11. To protect the identities of those involved, the name and location of the group has been changed.

CHAPTER THREE
Nosing Out the Facts:
The Retrieval of Intuition as Initiation

1. The Vasalisa and Persephone stories have many equivalencies.

2. The various beginnings and endings of tales constitute a lifelong study. Steve Sanfield, a superb Jewish teller, author, poet, and the first storyteller-in-residence in the United States in the seventies, kindly handed down to me the craft of collecting endings and beginnings as an art form in and of itself.

3. The term "good-enough mother," I first noted in Donald Winnicott's work. It is an elegant metaphor, one of those phrases that says pages in but three simple words.

4. In Jungian psychology the mother structure in the psyche could be said to be built in layers, the archetypal, personal, and cultural. It is the sum of these that constitutes the adequacy or lack of it in the internalized mother structure. As noted in developmental psychology, the building of an adequate internal mother appears to be accomplished in stages, each subsequent stage being built upon the mastery of the previous one. Abusing a child can dismantle or unseat the mother imago in the psyche, splitting the subsequent layers into polarities that are antagonistic rather than cooperative with one another. This can not only decommission previous stages of development, but also destabilize further ones, causing them to be constructed in fragmentary or idiosyncratic ways.

It is possible to remedy these developmental lags that destabilize the formation of trust, strength, and self-nurturance, for this matrix appears to be built less like a brick wall (that would fall down if too many of the bricks below were removed) and to be woven more like a net. This is why so many women (and men) function quite well even with many holes or lags in their nurturant systems. They tend to favor the aspects of the mothering complex where there is least damage to the psychic net. Seeking wise and nourishing guidance can help to mend this net no matter how many years a person has lived with injury.

5. Fairy tales utilize the symbols of *stepfamily, stepmother, stepfather,* and *stepsiblings* both negatively and positively. Because of the high remarriage rate in the United States, there is some sensitivity about the use of this symbol in its negative light, but there are many stories about positive and kindly stepfamilies and foster

families in fairy tales as well, some of the most well known motifs being that of the kindly old couple in the forest who happen upon an abandoned child, and the step-parent who welcomes a child crippled in some way and nurses the child back to health or helps the child to find extraordinary power.

6. This is not to mean one should turn from being warm when warranted and of one's own free choice. The kind of niceness we are speaking of here is a kind that is slavish and borders on fawning. It is born of desperately wanting something and feeling disempowered. It is similar to the child who is afraid of dogs, saying "nice doggy, nice doggy," hoping this will appease the dog.

There is an even more malignant kind of "niceness" in which a woman uses her wiles to propitiate others. She feels she must pleasurably tweak others in order to gain what she believes would not be forthcoming otherwise. It is a malignant form of being nice. It puts a woman in the position of grinning and bowing, trying to make the other feel good so that they will be nice to her, support her, pass her, give her favors, not betray her, and so forth. She is agreeing not to be herself. She loses her shape and takes on the facade the other most seems to desire. While this may be a powerful camouflage tactic in a dire situation in which a woman has little or no control, if a woman voluntarily finds reason to be in this position most of the time, she is kidding herself about something very serious and has relinquished her main source of power: speaking candidly in her own behalf.

7. *Mana* is a Melanesian word which Jung derived from anthropological studies near the beginning of the twentieth century. He understood *mana* as describing the magical quality surrounding and emanating through certain people, talismans, natural elements like sea and mountain, trees, plants, rocks, places, and events. However, the anthropological characterization of that time does not take into account tribal people's personal testimonies that put forth that mana experience is pragmatic and mystical at the same time; it both informs and moves. Additionally, from the report of mystics throughout time who have documented their ups and downs with so-called *mana*, we know that affiliation with the core nature that produces this effect is much like being in love; one feels bereft without it. Though initially it may take up much time and incubation, later one comes to a rich and deep relationship with it.

8. The homunculi are the little creatures, such as the wee people, elves, and other "little people." Although some say the homunculus is a sub-human, those in whose heritage they figure feel they are supra-human; wisely trickerish and engendering in their own ways.

9. Some denigrate the concept of the animal psyche, or separate themselves away from the idea that humans are both soulful and animal. Part of the problem lies in the perception that animals are not soulful or soul-filled. But the word itself, *animal*, is from the Latin, meaning a living creature, even more properly "anything living," and especially, *animalis*: having the breath of life, from *anima*, meaning air, breath, and life. At some point in time, perhaps not too far down the road, we may be amazed that this anthropocentrism ever took root, in the same way many are now amazed that discrimination against humans based on skin color was once an acceptable value for many.

10. Without attention it will continue to be damned in various ways, in those who come after her. She can ease this by giving time to its repair now. We are not speaking of perfection but of building a certain sturdiness.

11. In workshops with women in prison, we sometimes make twig dolls together. We make dolls out of beans, apples, wheat, corn, cloth, and rice paper. Some women draw on these materials with paints, some stitch, some glue them together. In the end, there are dozens and dozens of dolls laid out in rows, many

times made from the same materials, but all as different and unique as the women who crafted them.

12. One of the most central problems of older theories about women's psychology is that the views of women's lives were quite limited. It was not imagined that she could be as much as she is. Classical psychology was more the study of women all folded up, rather than women trying to break free, or women stretching and reaching. The instinctual nature demands a psychology that observes women striving as well as women who are uncrinking from years of living hunched over.

13. This intuition we are speaking of is not the same as the typological functions Jung delineates: feeling, thinking, intuition, and sensation. In the female (and male) psyche, intuition is more than typology. It is of the instinctive psyche, of the soul, and it appears to be innate, having a maturation process, having perceiving, conceptualizing, and symbolizing abilities. It is a function belonging to all women (and men) regardless of typology.

14. In most cases it appears that it is best to go when you are called (or pushed), when you have some semblance of being able to be nimble and resilient, than to hold back, resist, hold off, until the psychic circumstances erupt and drag you bloody and bruised through it all anyway. Sometimes there is no possibility of being poised. But when there is, it is less energy-consuming to proceed than to resist.

15. Mother Night, one of the Life/Death/Life Goddesses from the Slavic tribes.

16. Throughout Mezo-America, *la máscara*, the mask, connotes that a person has mastered union with the spirit portrayed by both the mask and the spirit-clothing one wears. This identification with spirit through clothing and face adornment has almost faded away completely in Western society. However, spinning of thread and weaving of cloth are ways to invite or be informed by spirit all in itself. There is serious evidence that the making of thread and cloth were once religious practices used to teach the cycles of life and death and beyond.

17. It is good to have many personae, to make collections, sew up several, collect them as we go along in life. As we become older, with such a collection at our behest, we find we can portray any aspect of self most anytime we wish. However, at some point, most particularly as one grows into and past mid-life and on into old age, one's personas shift and meld in mysterious ways. Eventually, there is a kind of "meltdown," a loss of personae complete, thereby revealing what would, in its greatest light, be called "the true self."

18. To work in an organic manner, one simplifies, stays more toward sensing and feeling, rather than toward over-intellectualization. Sometimes it is helpful, as one of my late colleagues, J. Vanderburgh, used to say, to think in terms that would be understood by a bright ten-year-old.

19. These coincidentally are also the same qualities of successful soul life, but also of successful business and economic life.

20. Jung felt one might be able to contact the oldest source through night dreams. (*C. G. Jung Speaking*, edited by William McGuire and R.F.C. Hull [Princeton: Princeton University Press, 1977].)

21. It is actually a phenomenon of hypnogogic and hypnopompic states that are somewhere between sleep and waking. It is well documented in sleep laboratories that a question asked in the beginning "twilight" stage of sleep seems to sort through the brain's "facts on file" during later stages of sleep, increasing the capability of bringing a direct answer to mind upon awakening.

22. There was an old woman who lived in a shack in the woods near where I grew up. She ate a teaspoon of dirt a day. Said it kept the sorrows away.

23. Throughout the oral and written fairy-tale tradition, there are many contradictions regarding this. Some tales say that being wise when one is young will cause

one to live a long time. Others caution that being old while young is not so good. In comparison, some of these are proverbs that can be understood many different ways depending on the culture and time period from which they derive. Others however, to my mind, seem to be a kind of koan rather than an instruction. In other words, the phrases are meant to be contemplated rather than understood literally, a contemplation that might eventually bring a satori or sudden realization.

24. This alchemy may have derived from observations far older than metaphysical writings. Several old woman storytellers from both Eastern Europe and Mexico have told me that the black, red, white symbolism derives from the menstrual and reproductive cycle of women. As all women who have menstruated know, black is representative of the sloughed lining of the uterus that is not pregnant. Red symbolizes both the retention of blood in the uterus during pregnancy as well as the "bloody show," that spot of blood that announces the commencement of labor and hence the arrival of new life. White is the mother's milk that flows to feed the new charge. This is considered a complete cycle of intense transformation. It causes me to muse over whether alchemy was a later effort to create a vessel similar to the uterus and an entire set of symbols and actions that would give some proximity to the cycles of menses, gravida, delivery, and nursing. It seems likely that there is an archetype of pregnancy that is not to be taken literally and that it affects or rouses both genders who then must find a way to meaningfully symbolize it for themselves.

25. I've studied the color red in mythos and fairy tales for many years; the red thread, the red shoes, the red cape, and so forth. I believe many fragments from mythos and fairy tales are derived from the old "red Goddesses" who are deities governing the full spectrum of female transformation—all "red" events—sexuality, birth, and the erotic, and originally part of the three sisters archetype of birth, death, and rebirth, as well as part of the rising and dying sun mythos throughout the world.

26. Nineteenth century anthropology erroneously characterized that tribal reverence to deceased elders and grandparents, and the ritual preservation of elders' life stories, were a form of "worship." This unfortunate projection still permeates various "modern" literatures. By my lights, however, having decades of leading the family ritual of *Dia de los muertos,* "ancestral worship," the term coined long ago in classical anthropology, ought to more accurately be called ancestor *kinship,* that is, ongoing relationship with one's venerated elders. The kinship ritual respects the family, blesses the idea that we are not separate from one another, that a single human life is not meaningless, and especially that the good and remarkable deeds of those who have gone before us are of immense value to teach us and guide us.

27. Many female bones have been found at Çatal Hüyük, a Neolithic town under excavation in Anatolia.

28. There are other variations of this story as well as other episodes and in some cases, epilogues or anticlimaxes tacked onto the end of the central story.

29. We see the highly symbolized pelvis shape in bowls and icons from East Balkan and Yugoslavian sites which Gimbutas dates to 5–6000 B.C. Marija Gimbutas, *The Goddesses and Gods of Old Europe: Myths and Cult Images* (Berkeley: University of California Press, 1974. Updated edition, 1982).

30. The image of the dit also appears in dreams, often as a something that is transformed into a useful thing. Some of my colleagues who are physicians speculate that this may symbolize the embryo or egg in its earliest stage. The story givers in our family often refer to the dit as the ova.

31. It is possible that the spirit and consciousness of an individual has a genderlike "feel" to it, and that this masculinity or femininity of spirit and so forth, regardless of physical gender, is innate.

CHAPTER FOUR
The Mate: Union With the Other

1. This rhyme at the end of the story is traditional in west Africa. It was taught to me by Opalanga, a *griot.*

2. There is a child's song in Jamaica that may be a remnant of this tale: *"Just to make sure the yes/ is a yes to the end/ I ask her again/ and again and again and again."* This song was given into my care by V. B. Washington, who has been across all my living, a mother to me.

3. The dog acts somewhat differently in a community of dogs than as a pet in a family of humans.

4. Robert Bly, personal communication, 1990.

CHAPTER FIVE
Hunting: When the Heart Is a Lonely Hunter

1. This does not mean that the relationship comes to an end, but that certain aspects of relationship shed their skins, lose their shells, disappear without a trace, leave no forwarding address, and then suddenly show up again in a different form, color, and texture.

2. During one of my visits to the verdantland of Mexico, I developed a toothache, and a *boticario* sent me to a woman who was known for easing the pain from teeth. While she applied her medicines, she told me about *Txati,* the great spiritwoman. It is clear from her rendering that *Txati* is a Life/Death/Life Goddess, but as yet I find no references to her in academic literature. Among other things *mi abuelita, la curandera* told me was that *Txati* is a great healer who is both the breast and the grave. *Txati* carries with her a copper bowl; turned one way, it contains and spills forth nourishment, turned the other way it becomes the container for the soul of the newly dead. *Txati* is the watcher over childbearing, lovemaking, and death.

3. There are many versions of the Sedna story. She is a powerful deity who lives beneath the water and who is propitiated by healers who ask her to restore health and life to those who are ill or dying.

4. Certainly the "taking of space" can be a valid need for solitude, but it is perhaps the most popular "white lie" of relationships of our time. Rather than talking about what is troubling, one "takes space" instead. This is an adult version of "the dog ate my homework," or "my grandmother died . . ." for the fifth time.

5. And also the not-yet beautiful.

6. From the haunting poem "Integrity." Adrienne Rich, *The Fact of a Door-frame, Poems Selected and New, 1950–1984.* New York: W. W. Norton, 1984.

7. The inclusion of the younger binding the wound of the elder is an inclusion from our familial story "The Wound That Stank."

8. This is a condensation of a very long story that usually takes "three evenings during lightning-bug season" to tell properly.

CHAPTER SIX
Finding One's Pack: Belonging as Blessing

1. Though some Jungian analysts feel that Andersen was "neurotic," and therefore his work not useful to study, I find his work, particularly *the story themes* he chose to embellish, aside from *his way* of embellishing them, very important, for

they portray the suffering of little children, the suffering of the soul Self. This cutting, slicing, and dicing of youthful soul is *not only* an issue common to the time and place where Andersen lived. It continues to be a worldwide and critical issue of soul. Though the issue of abuse of the souls and spirits of children, adults, or the elderly is one that would be diminished by romantic intellectualizations, I find that Andersen faces it squarely. Classical psychology in general predates society's understanding of the breadth and depth of child abuse across class and culture. And fairy tales pre-date psychology in uncovering the facts of humans' purposeful harm to one another.

2. The rustic teller is one who tends not to have been too much overlaid by cynicism, and one who retains good common sense and a sense of the night world as well. By this definition, an educated person raised in an asphalt metropolis could be a rustic. The word more pertains to state of mind rather than to the physical habitat of the person. As a child, I heard "The Ugly Duckling" I drew on from "the three Katies," my elderly paternal aunts, rustics all.

3. This is one of the major reasons an adult undertakes an analysis or a self-analysis: to sort and arrange the parental, cultural, historical, and archetypal factors and complexes so that as in the La Llorona stories, the river is kept clear as possible.

4. Sisyphus, Cyclops, and Kaliban; these three male figures from Greek mythos are known for their endurance, ability to be fierce, and their thick skin. In cultures where women are not allowed to develop in all directions, they are most often inhibited in the development of these so called masculine powers. When there is a psychic and cultural demeaning of masculine development in women, women are constrained from holding the chalice, the stethoscope, the paint brush, the purse strings, political office, and so forth.

5. See Alice Miller's works: *Drama of the Gifted Child, For Your Own Good, Thou Shalt Not Be Aware* (in bibliography).

6. Examples of cutting a woman away from her own way of working and living do not have to be dramatic to make the point. Among the most recent are laws that make it difficult or impossible for a woman (or man) to earn income at home and thereby stay close to the business world, the hearth, and one's children all at the same time. Laws that prevent one from maintaining the cohesiveness of work, family, and personal life are long overdue for being changed.

7. There is still much slavery in the world. Sometimes it is not called that, but when a person is not free "to leave," and will be punished if they "flee," that is slavery. If people are "forced out" whenever someone has the mind to, that also represents a slave state. If a person is forced into painful work or demeaning choices not in their best interest but in order to gain basic subsistence or basic protection, this too constitutes a slavery. Under slaveries of all kinds, families and spirits are broken and lost for years, if not forever.

There still exists literal slavery as well. A person recently returned from a Caribbean island related to me that in one of the luxury hotels there, a Middle Eastern prince had arrived with his retinue that included several female slaves. The entire hotel staff was scurrying about trying to keep them from crossing the path of a well-known black official in the Civil Rights movement from the United States who was also a guest at the hotel.

8. These included child-mothers as young as twelve, teenagers, and women who were older, those pregnant from a night of love, or a night of pleasure, or a night of love and pleasure, also those who were victims of incest-rape as well; all went unmothered and were viciously attacked because their culture was poised to harm both the infant and the mother with aspersions and ostracism.

9. There are any number of writers who have published on this subject. See the

works of Robert Bly, Guy Corneau, Douglas Gillette, Sam Keen, John Lee, Robert L. Moore, and so on.

10. It is one of the silliest myths about growing older, that a woman becomes so complete that she needs nothing and is a fountain of everything for everyone else. No, she continues as a tree that needs water and air no matter how old it becomes. The old woman is the same as a tree; there is no finality, no sudden completion, rather a grandeur of roots and branches, and with proper care, much flowering.

11. Given to me by my friend Faldiz, an Iberian woman, and a kindred spirit.

12. Jung used this word to connote the innocent fool in fairy tales who almost always wills out in the end.

13. From Jan Vanderburgh, personal communication.

14. There has been a bias in Jungian psychology that can obscure the diagnosis of a serious disturbance, and that is that introversion is a normal state regardless of the degree of a person's deathly quietude. In fact a deadly silence that sometimes passes for introversion more often hides deep trauma. When a woman is "shy" or deeply "introverted" or painfully "modest," it is important to look beneath and see if it is innate or if it is injury.

15. Carolina Delgado, a Jungian social worker and artist from Houston, uses *ofrendas* like sand tray, as a projective tool to delineate the psychic state of the individual.

16. The list of "different" women is very long. Think of any role model of the last few centuries, and she is most likely to have begun at the edge or to have come out of a sub-group, or from outside the mainstream.

CHAPTER SEVEN
Joyous Body: The Wild Flesh

1. Tehuana women are always patting and touching not only their babies and not only their men, not only the grandmas and grandpas, not only the food, the clothes, the family pets, but each other as well. It is a very touching culture that seems to make people blossom.

Likewise, watching wolves play, one sees they hit against each other in a kind of rolling dance. It is that connection through the skin that communicates something like, "You belong, we belong."

2. It appears from informal observations among various isolated native groups that although there are tribal loners—perhaps living with the tribe only part-time and not necessarily following the values of the core tribe all the time—the central groups approach males and females respectfully regardless of shape, size, and age. Sometimes they tease each other about one thing or another, but it is not mean or exclusionary. This approach to body, gender, and age is part of a larger view and love of diverse nature.

3. Some have argued that a regard for living in some of the old ways or with certain "aboriginal, old, or ancient" values is sentimental: a maudlin wishing for times past, an illogical fairy fantasy. This reasoning says that women in times past had it hard, disease was rampant, and so on. It is true that women in the past and present worlds had to/have to work hard, often under abusive conditions, were/are mistreated, disease was/is rampant. These are true and are so for men as well.

However, in the native groups and from my own people, both Latina and Hungarian, who are most definitely tribal, clan-making, totem-creating, spinning, weaving, planting, sewing, engendering people, I find that no matter how hard life is or how difficult it becomes, the old values—even if one has to dig for them or relearn them—support soul and psyche throughout. Many of our so called "old ways" are a form of nutrition that never spoils and actually increases the more one uses them.

While there is a sacred and a profane approach to everything, I think there is little sentimentality but rather clear sensibility in the admiring or emulating of certain "ancient values." In many cases to attack the legacy of old and soulful values is to, once again, attempt to sever a woman from the legacies of her matrilineal lines. It is peaceable to the soul to take from the past knowledge, present power, and the future of ideas all at once.

4. If there were an "evil spirit" in women's bodies, it would be mostly introjected by a culture that is very confused about the natural body. While it is true that a woman can be her own worst enemy, a child is not born hating her own body, but rather, as we see from observing a baby, taking an absolute joy in the finding and the using of her body.

5. Or her father's for that matter.

6. For years there has been an enormous amount of material written and circulated without question with regard to human body size and configuration, women's in particular. With few exceptions the majority of the work comes from writers who seem distressed or repelled by various configurations. It is important to hear equally from women who are mentally healthy regardless of configuration but, especially, those who are healthy and of size. Though not within the scope of this book, "the screaming woman within" appears to be in the main a profound projection and introjection by culture. This needs to be examined very closely and understood in terms of deeper cultural prejudices and pathologies involving many ideas other than size, such as hypertrophic sexuality in the culture, soul-hunger, hierarchical structure and caste in body configuration, and so on. It would be good to put the culture on the analyst's couch so to speak.

7. From an archetypal perspective, it is possible that some of the obsession with carving the physical body erupts when one's world or *the* world seems so out of control that people attempt to control the tiny real estate of their own bodies instead.

8. Accepted in the sense of parity, as well as cessation of derision.

9. Martin Freud, *Glory Reflected: Sigmund Freud, Man and Father* (New York: Vanguard Press, 1958).

10. In the magic carpet stories, there are many different descriptions of the condition of the carpet: It was red, blue, old, new, Persian, East Indian, came from Istanbul, was owned by a little old lady who only took it out on . . . and so on.

11. The magic carpet is a central archetypal motif in mideastern wonder tales. One is called "Prince Housain's Carpet," similar to "The Story of Prince Ahmed," and is found in the *Arabian Nights* collection.

12. There are natural substances in the body, some well documented such as serotonin, that seem to cause a sense of well-being, some say even a joyous feeling. Traditionally, these states are accessed by prayer, meditation, contemplation, insight, the use of intuition, trance, dance, certain physical activity, song, and other deep states of soul locus.

13. In intercultural inquiries, I have been impressed with groups that are pushed out of the mainstream, and who yet retain and strengthen their integrity even so. It is fascinating to see that time after time, the disenfranchised group that maintains its dignity is often eventually admired and sought out by the very mainstream that once ousted it.

14. One of many ways of losing touch is to no longer know where one's kith and kin are buried.

15. Pseudonym to protect her privacy.

16. Ntozake Shange, *for colored girls who have considered suicide when the rainbow is enuf* (New York: Macmillan, 1976).

CHAPTER EIGHT
Self-preservation:
Identifying Leg Traps, Cages, and Poisoned Bait

1. From the Latin root *sen*, meaning old, come these related words: Señora, Señor, senate, and senile.

2. There are inner cultures as well as outer cultures. They behave remarkably alike.

3. Barry Holston Lopez defines this in his work *Of Wolves and Men* as "meat drunk" (New York: Scribner, 1978).

4. One can as easily "go excessive" whether brought up in the streets or in silk stockings. False friends, affectations, deadening of pain, protectionist behavior, opacity of one's own light, all these can come upon people regardless of background.

5. From Abbess Hildegard of Bingham, also known as St. Hildegard. Ref: MS2 Weisbaden, Hessische Lantesbibliother.

6. The technique of "No cookie until you do your homework" is called the Primack principle or "grandma's rule" in Psychology 101. Even classical psychology seems to acknowledge that such a rule is the province of the elder.

7. Joplin was not making a political statement by not wearing makeup. Like many adolescents, her skin was broken-out, and, it seems while in high school, she saw herself as a buddy to males rather than as a potential sweetheart.

In the 1960s in the United States, many newly militant women avoided makeup in order to make a political statement, essentially saying they did not wish to present themselves as delectables to be consumed by men. In comparison, both genders in many native cultures don face and body paint to both repel and attract. In essence, for women, self-decoration is a creative province of the feminine, and how or whether one chooses to decorate oneself is a personal language either way, conveying whatever a woman wishes.

8. For a very fine biography of Janis Joplin, who lived a modern version of "The Red Shoes", see Myra Friedman, *Buried Alive: The Biography of Janis Joplin* (New York: Morrow, 1973). There is an updated version published by Harmony Books, NY, 1992.

9. This is not to overlook organic etiology and in some cases iatrogenic deteriorations in some.

10. The most modern versions we have of "The Red Shoes" story probably show more clearly how the original matter of these rites were distorted and corrupted than a thousand pages of historical research. Nevertheless, the remaining versions, though remnants, are invaluable for sometimes the more recent and brutal overlays of a fairy tale tell us exactly what we need to know in order to survive and thrive in a culture and/or psychic environ that mimics the destructive process shown in the tale itself. In that sense we are lucky in an odd way, to have a fragmentary tale that clearly marks the psychic traps waiting for us in the here and now.

11. The rites of ancient and contemporary aboriginal women are often called "puberty" and "fertility" rites. However, those phrases have been envisioned from a mostly male viewpoint in anthropology, archeology, and ethnology since at least the

middle of the nineteenth century. They are phrases that unfortunately distort and fragment the process of women's lives rather than representing the actual reality.

Metaphorically, a woman passes both upward and downward through the bone holes of her own pelvis many times and in different ways and each time there is potential to gain new knowing. This process goes on throughout a woman's entire life. The so-called "fertility" phase does not begin at menstruation and end at menopause.

More properly all "fertility" rites ought to be called threshold rites; each one named according to its specific transformative power, not only what might be accomplished overtly but what is accomplished internally. The Diné (Navajo) blessing ritual called "The Beauty Way" is a good example of language and naming that define the heart of the matter.

12. *Mourning Unlived Lives—A Psychological Study of Childbearing Loss* by Jungian analyst Judith A. Savage is an excellent book and one of the few of its kind on this issue of enormous significance to women (Wilmette, Illinois: Chiron, 1989).

13. Rites, such as hatha and tantric yogas, and dance, and other enactments that order one's relationship with one's body are immensely re-empowering.

14. In some folklores, it is said that the Devil is not comfortable in human form, that the fit isn't quite right, thereby causing the Devil to limp about. In fairy-tale sense the girl in "The Red Shoes" comes to be severed from her feet and therefore has to limp about too for she has "danced with the Devil" so to speak, having taken on his "limping," i.e., his subhuman excessive and deadening life.

15. In Christian times, the ancient shoemaker's tools became synonymous with the devil's torture tools: rasp, pincers, pliers, nippers, hammer, awl, and so forth. In Pagan times shoemakers shared the spiritual responsibility of propitiating the animals from which shoe leather, soles, linings, and wrappings came. By the 1500s, it was asserted throughout non-Pagan Europe that "fals prophetes are maid of Tinklaris and schoeclouters . . . false prophets are made [up] of tinkers and shoemakers."

16. Studies on normalization of violence and learned helplessness have been conducted by experimental psychologist Martin Seligman, Ph.D., and others.

17. In the 1970s in her landmark book on battered women (*The Battered Woman* [New York: Harper & Row, 1980 edition]), Lenore E. Walker applied this principle to the mystery of why women stayed with partners who grossly mistreated them.

18. Or to those around us who are young or helpless.

19. The women's movement, N.O.W., and other organizations, some ecologically oriented, others educational and rights oriented were/are headed up by, developed, and expanded by, and the memberships composed of many, many women who took great risks to step forward and speak out, and perhaps most importantly, to continue, in full voice. In the area of rights there are many voices and directives from both men and women.

20. This keeping a woman in line by her female peers and older women lessens controversy and enhances safety for women who must live under hostile conditions. Under other circumstances however, this psychologically pitches women into full scale betrayals of one another, thereby cutting off another matrilineal inheritance—that of having elders who will speak for younger women, who will intervene, adjudicate, go to council with whomever in order to maintain a balanced society and rights for all.

In other cultures where each gender is understood as either sister or brother, the hierarchical parameters imposed by age and power are softened by caretaking relationships and responsibility for and to each person.

For women who have been betrayed as children, there is a continuing expectation that one will also be betrayed by lover, employer, and culture. Her first experiences with betrayal often came from an incident, one or many, from within her own female or familial lines. It is another miracle of the psyche that such a woman can still trust so very much even though she has been betrayed so very much.

Betrayals occur when those who have power see the trouble and look away. Betrayal occurs when people break promises, hedge on vows of help, protection, speaking for, standing with, withdrawing from acts of courage and acting preoccupied, indifferent, unaware, and so forth instead.

21. Addiction is anything that depletes life while making it "appear" better.

22. The starvation, ferality, or addiction is not the cause of psychosis per se, but rather a primary and on-going attack on the strength of the psyche. An opportunistic complex could theoretically inundate the weakened psyche. This is why it is important to repair injured instinct so that insofar as possible the person does not continue in a deteriorative or vulnerable condition.

23. Charles Simic, *Selected Poems* (New York: Braziller, 1985).

24. *"The Elements of Capture,"* © 1982, C. P. Estés, Ph.D., from post-doctoral thesis.

Take an original.

Domesticate her early, preferably before speech or locomotion.

Over-socialize her in the extreme.

Cause a famine for her wild nature.

Isolate her from the sufferings and freedoms of others so she has nothing to compare her life with.

Teach her only one point of view.

Let her be needy (or dry or cold) and let all see it, yet none tell her.

Let her be split off from her natural body, thereby removing her from relationship with this being.

Cut her loose in an environ where she can over-kill on things previously denied her, things both exciting and dangerous.

Give her friends who are also famished and who encourage her to be intemperate.

Let her injured instincts for prudence and protection continue without repair.

Because of her excesses, (not enough food, too much food, drugs, not enough sleep, too much sleep, etc.) let Death insinuate itself close by.

Let her struggle with "good-girl" persona restoration and succeed at it, but only from time to time.

Then, and finally, let her have a frantic reinvolvement in psychologically or physiologically addictive excesses that are deadening in and of themselves or through misuse (alcohol, sex, rage, compliance, power, etc.).

Now she is captured. Reverse the process, and she will learn to be free. Repair her instincts and she will become strong again.

CHAPTER NINE
Homing: Returning to OneSelf

1. The core theme of this story, the finding of love and home, and the facing of the death nature is one of many found throughout the world. (Also the device of "having to break off frozen words from the lips of the speaker and thaw them by the fire to see what was said," is found worldwide throughout the cold countries.)

2. It is also said among various ethnic groups that the soul does not incarnate into the flesh or give birth to the spirit until it is assured that the body which it is to inhabit is truly prospering. In our oldest traditions, that is why a child is often not

named until seven days after birth, or else two lunar cycles after, or after even a longer time has passed, thereby proving the flesh is strong enough to be invested with soul that in turn gives birth to spirit. Further, many hold to the sensible idea that therefore a child should never be beaten, for it drives the spirit out of its body, and it is a very long and arduous process to retrieve it and return it to its rightful home again.

3. The initiatory process—the word *initiation* comes from the Latin *initiare*, meaning to begin, to introduce, to instruct. An *initiate* is one who is beginning a new way, who has come forward to be introduced and instructed. An *initiator* is one who commits to the deep work of recounting what they know about the path, who shows the "how-to" and guides the initiate so that she will master the challenges and thereby grow in power.

4. In botched initiations, the initiator sometimes looks only for the foibles of the initiate and forgets or overlooks the other seventy percent of initiation: the strengthening of a woman's talents and gifts. Often an initiator creates difficulty without support, contrives perils and then sits back. This is a carryover from a fragmented male style of initiation; one that believes that shame and humiliation strengthen a person. They deliver the difficulty, but not the support. Or there is great attention to procedure, but the critical needs of feeling and soul life are tacked on as afterthought. From the soul's and spirit's points of view, a cruel or inhumane initiation never strengthens sorority or affiliation. It is beyond comprehension.

Lacking competent initiators or in a milieu of initiators who suggest and support abusive procedures, a woman will attempt self-initiation. Hers is a very admirable undertaking and a dazzling accomplishment if she even three-quarters attains it. It is extremely commendable for she must listen closely to the wild psyche as to what comes next, and then after that, and next after that, and follow it without the assurances that it has been done this way and produced the proper effect a thousand times before.

5. There is negative perfectionism and positive perfectionism. The negative sort often revolves around the fear of being found inadequate. A positive perfectionism gives best effort, stays with something productive for mastery's sake. Positive perfectionism urges the psyche to learn to do things *better*; how to write better, speak, paint, eat, relax, worship better, and so on. Positive perfectionism makes certain actions consistently in order to recognize a dream.

6. "Putting on the brass brassiere" is a stock phrase from Yancey Ellis Stockwell, a vibrant therapist and a fine storyteller in her own right.

7. Sponsored by Women's Alliance and many gifted healers, one being the very gentle physician at the prison, Dr. Tracy Thompson, and the energetic healer-teller Kathy Park.

8. From the poem, "Woman Who Lives Under the Lake," © 1980, C. P. Estés, *Rowing Songs For the Night Sea Journey; Contemporary Chants* (Privately published, 1989).

9. From the poem, "Come Cover Me With Your Wildness," © 1980, C. P. Estés. Ibid.

10. Translated into English from the poem *La bolsita negra*, © 1970, C. P. Estés. Ibid.

11. Their word-pictures and say-it-like-it-is phrases found their way into both the Hispanic and Eastern European ethnic groups in that part of the country.

12. It need not be the kidlets. It can be anything. "My houseplants. My dog. My schoolwork. My mate. My petunias." It's all just a ruse. At heart the woman is trembling to go, but trembling to stay as well.

13. The "be all things to all people" complex attacks a woman's adequacy,

urging her to act as though she *is* the "great healer." But for a human to attempt to enact an archetype is rather like attempting to be God. This is not possible to achieve in actuality, and the effort put forth to attempt such is completely draining and very destructive to the psyche.

While an archetype can withstand the projections of human men and women, humans cannot withstand being treated as though they are themselves an archetype and therefore invulnerable and inexhaustible. When a woman is asked/expected to enact the untiring archetype of the great healer, we see her going down for the count in burdensome and negatively perfectionistic roles. When asked to step into the luxurious confines of the archetypal robes of any ideal, it is best to look off into the distance, shake your head, and keep walking toward home.

14. Adrienne Rich, from *The Fact of a Doorframe* (New York: W. W. Norton, 1984), p. 162.

15. In other tales, such as "The Sleeping Beauty," the young sleeping woman awakens, not because she is kissed by the prince, but because it's time . . . the hundred years' curse is up and it is time for her to wake up. The thorn forest surrounding the tower falls away, not because the hero is superior, but because the curse is up and it is time. Fairy tales instruct us over and over: when it's time, it's time.

16. In classical Jungian psychology this child would be called a psychopomp, that is, an aspect of anima or animus, so named after Hermes, who led souls to the underworld. In other cultures, the psychopomp is called *juju, bruja, anqagok, tzaddik*. These words are used both as proper names and sometimes as adjectives to describe the magical quality of an object or person.

17. In the story, the scent of the sealskin causes the child to feel the full impact of his mother's soulful love. Something of the shape of her soul blows through him, not hurting him, but making him aware. Still among some contemporary Inuit families, when a loved one dies, the deceased person's furs, head coverings, leggings, and other personal articles are donned by those who still live. The family and friends so dressed consider this transmission soul to soul and necessary to life itself. It is believed that a powerful remnant of soul is held in the cloth, pelt, and tools of the deceased.

18. Mary Uukulat is my source and gave me the old idea of the breath being made of poem.

19. Ibid.

20. Oxford English Dictionary.

21. Women tend to take adequate time away to respond to crises of physical health—particularly the health of others, but neglect to make maintenance time for their own relationship to their own souls. They tend to not understand soul as the magneto or central generator of their animation and energy. Many women drive their relationship to soul as if it were a not very important instrument. Like any instrument of value, it needs shelter, cleansing, oiling, and repair. Otherwise, like a car, the relationship sludges up, causes deceleration in a woman's daily life, causes her to use up enormous energy for the most simple tasks, and finally busts down out on heartbreak ridge far away from town or telephone. Then, it is a long, long walk back to home.

22. Reference from Robert Bly in an interview published in *The Bloomsbury Review* (January 1990), "The Wild Man In the Black Coat Turns: A Conversation" by Clarissa Pinkola Estés, Ph.D. © 1989, C. P. Estés.

CHAPTER TEN

Clear Water: Nourishing the Creative Life

1. *Field of Dreams*, film based on the novel *Shoeless Joe* by W. P. Kinsella.

2. The problem of stalled creative life usually has several causes: inner negative complexes, lack of support from the outer world, and sometimes also direct sabotage as well.

As regards external destruction of new endeavors and ideas, more creative inquiries are brought to a halt and called inconclusive by manipulating the "either/or" model than almost anything else I can think of. Which came first? The chicken or the egg? This question more often puts an end to peering at a thing and determining its many values. It puts a close to seeing how a thing is constructed and what its uses might be. It is often more useful to use the cooperative and comparative "and/and" model. A thing is this *and* this *and* this. It can be used/not used this way, *and* this way *and* this way.

3. *La Llorona*: Lah Yoh-row-nah, with the accent on the *row* syllable, and roll the *r* a little.

4. The *La Llorona* story has been told since God's Wife sat by the fire. The same story over and over with some small variation, mainly in how she is dressed. "She was dressed like a prostitute and one of the guys picked her up near the river in El Paso. Boy, was he surprised!" "She was dressed in a long white nightgown." "She was dressed in a bridal gown with a long white veil over her face."

Also many Latina parents use *La Llorona* as a sort of mystical baby-sitter. Most children are so awed by the stories of her snatching away children in order to replace her own drowned ones, that youngsters from river towns know to stay away from the water after dark and to come home right on time.

Some who study these tales say they are moral tales meaning to scare people into behaving themselves. Knowing the passion in the blood of those who originate these tales, they strike me as revolutionary tales, stories that are meant to raise consciousness about creating new order. Some tellers call stories like *Llorona*, *Cuentos de la Revolución*, Stories of Revolution.

Stories of struggle, psychic and otherwise, are a very old tradition predating the conquest in Mexico. Some of the old *cuentistas*, storytellers from Mexico in my family, say the so-called Aztec codices are *not* records of war as many scholars have speculated, but picto-stories of the great moral battles faced by all men and women. Many scholars of the old school felt this was impossible for they were certain that the native civilizations did not have the possibility of abstract and symbolic thinking. They felt the members of the old cultures were like children to whom everything was literal. However, we can see by studying the Nahuatl and Mayan poetry from those times, that metaphor was rampant, and there was brilliant ability to think and speak in the abstract.

5. Such as at the Green National Convention at the Continental Divide in the Rocky Mountains in 1991.

6. Given to me by Marik Pappandreas Androupolous, a storyteller from Corinth, and handed down to her by Andrea Zarkokolis, also of Corinth.

7. Marcel Pagnol, *Jean de Florette* and *Manon of the Spring* translated by W. E. van Heyningen (San Francisco: North Point Press, 1988). Both were made into films by Claude Berri (Orion Classic Releases, 1987).

The first work is about evildoers who stop up a spring in order to prevent a young husband and wife from realizing their dream of living free in the wilds, raising their own food, surrounded by wildlife and trees and flowers. Subsequently, the young family is starving, for no water flows onto their lands. The evildoers hope to buy this property for pennies once its reputation as a barren land ensues. The young husband dies, the wife becomes old too soon, and their child grows up with no legacy.

In the second book, the child, a girl, grows up and discovers the plot and avenges her family. Standing in mud to her knees, hands bleeding, she pulls the concrete free. The spring gushes forth again, spilling over and onto the land, pushing rolls of dust before it and bringing the old evil deed of the evildoers to light.

8. "Fear of failure" is one of those catch-phrases that does not really describe what a woman truly fears. Usually a single fear has three parts; one part being a residue from the past (this often being a source of shame), one part being a lack of certainty in the present, and one part being a fear of poor outcome or negative consequences in the future.

Regarding the creative life, one of the most common fears is not precisely a fear of failure, but rather a fear to test the mettle. The thinking goes something like this . . . if you fail, you can pick yourself back up and begin anew; you have infinite chances ahead of you. But, what if you succeed, but in the mediocre range? What if no matter how hard you try, you achieve, yes, but not at the level you wanted to? That is the far more bedeviling issue for those who create. And there are many, many others. That is why the creative life is a deep and complicated path all its own. Yet, even all this complexity should not keep us from it, for the creative life lies right over the heart of the wild nature. Despite our worst fears, there is profound nurturance from the instinctive nature.

9. Once The Harpai were Goddesses of the storm. They were Life and Death deities. Unfortunately, they were split away from being progenitors of both functions and were made into one-sided creatures. As we have seen in the interpretations of the Life/Death/Life nature, any force that governs birth also governs death. In Greece however, the culture which came to be dominated by the thoughts and ideals of a few had so heavily emphasized the death aspect of the Harpai as demon death-bird women that the Harpai's incubating, birthing, and nourishing natures were sliced away. By the time Orestes wrote his play in which the Harpies are killed off or chased to a cave at the ends of the earth, the revivifying nature of these creatures had been thoroughly buried.

10. This is a post-Orestian version. Incidentally, not all negative overlays are patriarchal, and certainly not all patriarchal matters are negative. There is even some value in the old negative patriarchal overlays to myths that once portrayed a strong and healthy feminine, for they not only show us how a conquest culture undercuts the previously held wisdom, but may also show how a subjugated or instinct-injured woman was caused to view herself then, and even today, as well as how she might be healed.

A set of destructive injunctions to and against women (and/or men), leaves behind a sort of archetypal X-ray of what is therefore molded out of shape in a woman's development when she is raised in a culture that does not find the feminine acceptable. So we need not guess. It is all recorded in the overlays of fairy tale and mythos.

11. Many symbols have both masculine and feminine attributions. In the main, it is important for people to decide for themselves which they will use as a magnifying glass to peer into matters of soul and psyche. It makes little sense to argue, as some may be wont to do, over whether the symbol of anything is masculine or feminine, for in the end it appears that these signifiers are only creative ways of looking at a matter, and that the symbol itself actually includes other forces that, because of the Archimedean viewpoint, we cannot fathom. The use of masculine or feminine attribution remains important however, for each is a different lens through which much

can be learned. That is why, in my understanding, I seek out symbols at all, to see what can be learned, how they can be applied, and especially for what wound they may be balm.

12. "Is The Animus Obsolete?" Jennette Jones and Mary Ann Mattoon, in anthology *The Goddess Reawakening*, ed. Shirley Nichols (Wheaton, Illinois: Quest Books, 1989). The chapter details current thinking on animus up through 1987.

13. In mythos, it is routine among the great Goddesses to have a son from their own bodies. Later the son becomes their lover/consort/husband. Though some would take this literally and understand it as describing incest, it is not to be understood that way but rather as a way of describing how the soul gives birth to a masculine potential, which, as it develops, becomes a kind of wisdom and strength and combines with her other powers in many ways.

14. And sometimes the impulse to that arm as well.

15. Essentially, if we cut ourselves away from the idea of masculine nature, we lose one of the strongest polarities for thinking and understanding the mystery of human beings' dual natures at all levels. However, I would rather, if a woman chokes at the very idea of the masculine being a part of the feminine, that she name this bridging nature whatever she likes, so that she is not cut off from imagining and understanding how the polarities work together.

16. Oxford English Dictionary.

17. I would describe this as the masculine's powerful and negotiative nature, one that in many cultures is flattened out in actual men by day labors that are senseless and without soul merit, or by a culture that tricks men into harness and keeps them there until there is little left of them.

18. From my inquiries, there is some indication also that some semblance of this story may be a variant of ancient old year/new year solstice tales, wherein the used-up dies and is reborn again in a vibrant form.

19. Received with love from Kata who endured a Russian labor camp for four years in the 1940s.

20. Transformation by, over, or in the fire is a universal motif. One related to "Three Gold Hairs" is found in Greek mythos, where Demeter, the Great Mother Goddess, holds a mortal infant *in* the fire nightly in order to make him immortal. His mother Metaneira screams bloody murder when she happens upon them, thereby interrupting the practice. Demeter is circumspect as she abandons the fiery process . . . "Too bad," she says to Metaneira, "now the child will only be mortal."

CHAPTER ELEVEN
Heat: Retrieving a Sacred Sexuality

1. Things that stimulate happiness and pleasure are also always "back doors" through which one can be exploited or manipulated.

2. Uncle Tuong-Pa or Trungpa stories are "blue" trickster stories reportedly originating in Tibet. There are trickster stories among all peoples.

3. Çatal Hüyük has a "between the legs" icon high on a wall. The figure is a woman with her legs wide apart, with her "nether mouth" revealed, possibly as oracle. Just the thought of such a figure makes many women chuckle with knowing.

4. Charles Boer, *The Homeric Hymns* (Dallas: Spring Publications, 1987). This is a truly gifted translation.

5. Coyote stories are traditionally told *only* during winter.

CHAPTER TWELVE
Marking Territory:
The Boundaries of Rage and Forgiveness

1. In the family and the proximate cultural milieu.

2. Childhood injuries to instinct, ego, and spirit derive from the child being harshly dismissed, not hearing or seeing the child, not beholding the child, if not with insight, then at least with a decent share of equanimity. In many women there is much injury to having a reasonable expectation that promises will be fulfilled, that one will be treated with dignity, have food when hungry, enjoy freedom to speak, think, feel, and create.

3. In some ways, old emotion is like a mental set of piano strings in the psyche. A rumble from topside can cause a tremendous vibration of those strings in the mind. They can be made to sing out without ever being directly plucked. Events that carry similar overtones, words, visual features of the original events cause a person to "fight" to keep the old material from "singing out."

In Jungian psychology, this eruption of great feeling tone is called constellation of a complex. Unlike Freud, who branded such behavior neurotic, Jung considered it actually a cohesive response, similar to that made by animals who have been previously harassed, tortured, frightened, or injured. The animal tends to react to smells, motions, instruments, sounds which are similar to the original injuring ones. Humans have the same recognition and response pattern.

Many people control old complex material by staying away from persons or events that stir them. Sometimes this is rational and useful and sometimes not. So a man may avoid all women who have red hair similiar to that of his battering father. A woman may steer clear of all contentious argument for it brings up so much in her. However, we try to strengthen our ability to stay in all sorts of situations regardless of complexes because this staying power gives us a voice in the world. It is what gives us ability to change things around us. If we are solely reactive to our complexes we will hide in a hole for the rest of our lives. If we can gain some tolerance of them, utilize them as our allies, for instance use old anger to put teeth into our proclamations, then, we can form and reform many things.

4. There are indeed organic brain syndrome disorders in which raging out of control is a salient feature, and these are treated with medication, not psychotherapy. But here we are speaking of rage induced by memory of previous psychological tortures of one sort or another. I might add that in families where there is a "sensitive," other children in the family with different psychological configurations may not feel as tortured, even though treated similarly.

Children have different needs, different "thicknesses of skin, different capacities for perceiving pain." The one with the least "receivers," so to speak, will consciously feel the least effect of abuse. The child with the most sensors will consciously feel it all, and perhaps strongly sense the wounds of others as well. It is not a matter of truth or not truth, it is a matter of having the ability to receive the transmissions going on around one.

In this matter of childrearing, the old maxim that each child should be raised, not "by the book," but according to what one learns by observing each child's sensitivities, personality, and talents is very fine advice. In the world of nature, even though both are beautiful, a lanky philodendron can go without water seemingly endlessly, but a willow that is far bigger and heavier cannot. There is this natural variation in humans also.

Additionally, it should not be misconstrued that when an adult feels or expresses anger that this is a sure sign of unfinished business in childhood. There is much need and place for rightful and clear anger, especially when previous calls to consciousness have been made in anywhere from dulcet to moderate tones of voice and have gone unheard. Anger is the next step in the hierarchy of calling attention.

However, negative complexes can fuel normal anger into a seething and destructive rage; the catalyst is almost always very tiny, but responded to as though it is of enormous import. In many ways, the dissonances of childhood, the batterings felt there, can positively influence what causes we take on as adults. Many leaders who guide large political, academic, or other kinds of tribes or "families" are doing so in a manner that is far more nourishing and better than the one they themselves were raised in.

5. From old tellers of Japanese heritage, I have heard a variation on "the bear as precious figure" theme in which the bear is strangled by an evil force so that no new life can prevail among the people who worshipped the bruin. The bear's body is buried amidst much grief and mourning. But a woman's tears falling upon the grave bring the bear back to life.

6. The release of old calcified rage, piece by piece or layer by layer, is an essential undertaking for women. It is better to try to take this bomb out into the field in order to detonate it and not to set it off near innocent people. It is worthy to try to discharge it in a way that helps and does not harm. Many times, the continuing sound or sight of a person or project aggravates us even more. It is good to get away from the stimulus, whatever or whoever it might be. There are many ways to do this, change rooms, change venue, change the issue, change the scenery. It helps immensely.

The old saw about slowly counting to ten has powerful reason behind it. If we can even temporarily interrupt the flow of adrenaline and other "fight" chemicals that pour into our systems during initial anger, we can stop the process of being driven back into the feelings and reactions around previously experienced trauma. If we do not make a hiatus for ourselves, the chemicals continue to spill for an extended length of time literally pushing us into increasingly hostile behavior whether we feel sincerely motivated or not.

7. There is a version of this old tale told by the great Sufi teller-healer Indries Shah in *Wisdom of the Idiots* (London: Octagon Press, 1970).

8. To decide to do so depends on several factors, among them: the consciousness of the person or aspect who has done the harm, their ability to yet do more harm and their future intentions, as well as the power equation—whether they are on equal footing or whether there is an unequal power ratio—all these need be assessed.

9. *Descanso* is also used to mean *resting place* as in a burial ground or cemetery.

10. When there has been incest, molestation, or other profound abuses, it may take many years to complete the cycle through forgiveness. In some cases, there may be, for a time, more strength derived by not forgiving, and this too is acceptable. What is not acceptable is a constant "mad-on" about events for the rest of one's life. That excessive boiling is very hard on soul and psyche, as well as the physical body. That must be re-balanced. There are many different approaches for doing this. A therapist who is a strong person and who specializes in these matters ought to be consulted. The question to ask when finding such a professional is, "What is your experience in rage-reduction work and strengthening of spirit?"

11. *Forego*, from Oxford English Dictionary: from O.E. *for gán* or *forgáen*, to go past, to go away.

12. *Forebear*, from Oxford English Dictionary: from M.H.G. *verbern*, to bear with, have patience.

13. *Forget,* from Oxford English Dictionary: from O. Teutonic *getan,* to hold or grasp; with prefix of *for,* means not to hold or not to grasp.

14. *Forgive,* Oxford English Dictionary: from Old English *forziefan,* to give or grant, to give up, cease to harbor resentment.

15. A somewhat different definition of this sort of forgiveness is found in the Oxford English Dictionary: 1865 J. Grote, *Moral Ideas,* viii (1876), 114 "Active forgiveness—the returning of good for evil." This to my mind is the ultimate form of reconciliation.

16. Not only do people have different pacing in forgiving others, the offense also influences the amount of time it takes to forgive. To forgive a misunderstanding is different than forgiving murder, incest, abuse, unjust treatment, betrayal, theft. Depending on what it is, a one-time abuse is sometimes more easily forgivable than repetitive ones.

17. Because the body also has memory, the body must be given attention also. The idea is not to outrun one's rage, but to exhaust it, dismantle it, and reconfigure the libido that is thus freed in a totally different manner than before. This physical release must be accompanied by psychic understanding.

CHAPTER THIRTEEN
Battle Scars: Membership in the Scar Clan

1. I concur with Jung; when one has committed an injustice, one cannot heal from it unless one can tell the absolute truth about it, facing it squarely.

2. I first read of this sort of hamartic and banal scripting in Eric Berne's and Claude Steiner's work.

3. WAE; that is, Jung's Word Association Experiment also found this to be true. In the test, disturbing material resonates, not only upon hearing a word that catalyzes negative associations, but throughout the mention of several more "neutral" words as well.

4. Sometimes photographs and stories of fathers, brothers, husbands, uncles, grandfathers follow (and sometimes the sons and the daughters also) but the main work is with one's preceding female lines.

5. They alone suffer as scapegoat, sin eater, without having the power and benefits of either, i.e. gratitude, honor, and refurbishing from the community.

6. *Mary Culhane and The Dead Man:* this is one of the signature stories of The Folktellers®, two immensely talented and picaresque women from North Carolina named Barbara Freeman and Connie Regan-Blake.

7. Paul C. Rosenblatt, Ph.D., *Bitter, Bitter Tears: Nineteenth-Century Diarists and Twentieth-Century Grief Theories* (Minneapolis: University of Minnesota Press, 1983). Referenced to me by Judith Savage.

CHAPTER FOURTEEN
La Selva Subterránea:
Initiation in the Underground Forest

1. Jung's understanding of participation mystique was based on anthropological views of the late nineteenth century and early twentieth century when many of those who studied tribes felt, and often were, quite separate from them, rather than understanding behaviors in tribes as those on a human continuum that could occur anywhere and in any human culture regardless of race or national origin.

2. This discussion in no way espouses that harm done to an individual is acceptable because it eventually strengthens them.

3. Regarding literal incest by the father and subsequent trauma to the child, see E. Bass and L. Thornton with J. Brister, eds., *I Never Told Anyone: Writings by Women Survivors of Child Abuse* (New York: Harper & Row, 1983). Also B. Cohen; E. Giller; W. Lynn, eds., *Multiple Personality Disorder from the Inside Out* (Baltimore: Sidran Press, 1991).

4. The majority of harsh loss of innocence is supposed to come from the world outside the family. It is a gradual process that almost everyone experiences and that culminates in a painful awakening to the idea that all is not safe or beautiful in the world.

In developmental psychology, this is envisioned as recognizing that one is not "the center of the universe." However, with regard to spirit, it is much more so an awakening and realization of the differences between divine and human natures. Innocence is not meant to be erratically harvested by father or mother. It will come in its own time. The parents are supposed to be there to guide and help if they can, but mostly, to pick up the pieces and set their child back on her feet again.

5. The symbol of the miller is seen in tales in both negative and positive light. Sometimes he or she is stingy, other times generous, as in the stories of the miller who sets out grain for the elves.

6. Waking up gradually—that is, taking down one's defenses slowly and over a period of time—is less painful than having one's defenses penetrated all at once. However in a therapeutic or reparative mode, though faster is more painful initially, the work can sometimes commence and be brought to fruition sooner. However, each to their own, and in their own way.

7. In other tales the three represents a culmination of intense striving and the three can be understood as the sacrifice itself that culminates in a new life.

8. Lao Tzu, ancient philosopher poet. See *Tao Te Ching* (London: The Buddhist Society, 1948). The work is published in many translations by many publishers.

9. There are different methods for different people. Some are very active outwardly, such as dance, some are very active in a different way, the dance of prayer for instance, the dance of the intellect, the dance of the poem.

10. © 1989, C. P. Estés, *Warming the Stone Child: Myths and Stories of the Abandoned and Unmothered Child*, audiotape (Boulder, Colorado: Sounds True, 1989).

11. It is notable that women and men in serious psychic transition often find less interest in things of the outer world for they are thinking, dreaming, and sorting at such deep levels that the appurtenances of the outer world simply fall away. It appears the soul is not very interested in mundane matters unless they have a certain numen to them.

However, this is to be differentiated from a pro-dromal syndrome wherein one's grooming and other day-to-day ministrations deteriorate to nothing and there is an obvious and serious disturbance in mental and social functioning.

12. It is very odd to me that the Ku Klux Klan, in an effort to disparage, calls non-white people "mud people." The old usage of the word mud is intensely positive, in fact probably just the right phrase to empower the deeply wise and powerful instinctive nature. It is from mud (and other earthy substances) that humans and the world were made by the lights of most creation stories.

13. The labrys, the axe, and the open labia of the vulva all share similar shape.

14. Regarding the double axe of the Goddess, it is an ancient symbol, also currently rendered by various women's groups as a symbol of return to the power of womanliness. Additionally, among the members of my *cuentos* research and training

group, *Las Mujeres*, there is much speculation from all sources that the butterfly wings of the labia and the double headed axe are similar symbols from ancient times wherein the shape of the open butterfly was considered to be the shape of the soul.

15. What is mystical is knowing about mundane and spiritual matters from both sides; that is, intellect and first-hand experience of spirit and psyche. Pragmatic mysticism looks for all truth, not just one facet of truth, and then weighs where to stand, how to act.

16. There is a sense in old tales that this is also a feeling and knowing state handed down from all parents to children regardless of gender.

17. As we have seen, tears are multipurpose, they are for both protection and creation.

18. Much of women's culture has been veritably buried for centuries, and we have only inklings of what lies under. Women must have the right to investigate without being cut off before they even set out the archeological grid. The idea is to live a full life, according to one's own instinctive mythos.

19. There is great power in numbers. Many scholars from Pythagoras to the Kabbalists have attempted to understand mathematical mystery. The numbered pears probably carry significance from mysticism and perhaps also from a tonal scale as well.

20. In many ways the handless maiden, the girl with golden hair, and the match girl all face identical issues of being in some way the outsider. The handless maiden story by far encompasses the more complete psychological cycle.

21. You may wonder how many "selfs," that is, centers for consciousness, there are in the psyche. There are many, with one usually the most dominant. Like the pueblos and casitas in New Mexico, the psyche is always in at least three stages—the old fallen down part, the part you live in, and the part under construction. It is like that.

Also, in Jungian theory, the Self with a capital S means the vast soul force. The self with a lower case s signifies the more personal, more limitable person that we are.

22. One of the most extensive "written" records of old rites are those of the ancient Greeks. Though most ancient cultures once had extensive records of rites, ritual laws, and history—and several mediums—sculpture, writing, painting, bardship, architecture, and so forth, conquest after conquest carrying all manner of motives and intentions destroyed most if not all of these. (Subverting a culture requires killing off the holy class: the artists, writers and all their works, the priests and priestesses and healers, the orators, the historians and the keepers of story, all the singers, dancers, and poets . . . all those who have the ability to move the souls and spirits of the people.) However, the bones of many destroyed cultures are still carried in the ark of story across the centuries and delivered right down into our own time.

23. Elizabeth is old and pregnant too with John. This is an intensely mystical passage wherein her husband is struck mute and all.

24. These stages are reached sometimes not so much according to chronological age as according to the needs and timing of psyche and spirit.

25. The archetypal symbol of the king is examined by Robert L. Moore and Douglas Gillette in *King, Warrior, Magician, Lover* (San Francisco: Harper, 1990).

26. The symbols of gardener, king, magician, etc. belong to and find resonance for both men and women. They are not gender specific, but are sometimes understood differently and applied differently by each gender.

27. The first person I heard use the phrase "soul-making" was James Hillman who is himself rather like an idea-spewing incendiary device.

28. The crone of the triple Goddesses of the Greeks.

29. In Hesiod's Theogony (411–52), Persephone and the crone Hekate are said to prefer one another's company above all else.

30. Jean Shinoda Bolen in her clear work on menopause, notes that older women hold the energy of menstrual blood within their bodies and make internal wisdom instead of external children. *The Wise Woman Archetype: Menopause As Initiation* (Boulder, Colorado: Sounds True, 1991).

31. He was the leader of the Inquisition in Spain, a pathologically cruel man, the sanctioned serial killer of his day.

32. This being a consecration rite administered to new mothers by the old healers in my family's *Católico* traditions.

33. From: Ecclus xvii, 5 (scrb/clas lit).

34. For instance, some modern men have lost their sense of sexual cycles ebbing and flowing as they are meant. Some feel nothing, some are stuck in overdrive.

35. In some versions of the tale, the veil is called handkerchief, and it is not the *pneuma*, breath, that causes the veil to be shed, but the little boy plays by taking it on and off his father's face.

AFTERWORD
Story as Medicine

1. Excerpted from the poem entitled, "At the Gates of the City of the Storyteller God," © 1971, C. P. Estés, from *Rowing Songs for the Night Sea Journey: Contemporary Chants* (Privately published, 1989).

2. Here is a rare piece of eyewitness writing that clearly defines the heart of the storytelling art: that ethos, culture, and craft are inseparable. The following words are by the masterful poet and storyteller Steve Sanfield, one who has for decades striven to do the hard work required in psyche's outback.

On the Master Storyteller

"It takes a lifetime, not a few years or even a decade, to become a master of anything. It requires complete immersion in the art. After only twenty years, or thirty at the most, it is a pomposity for us as individual tellers, or for the field as a whole, to lay claim to 'mastery.'

"Should a master storyteller appear, there would be no question about it. He or she would have a 'quality,' intangible probably, that would be instantly recognizable. Having lived a particular story for years or a lifetime, that story would become part of that teller's psyche, and the teller would tell from 'inside' the story. This quality is not often seen . . .

"Proficiency is not enough. Mastery is *not* glibness, gimmicks, audience participation stunts. It is *not* telling to be loved, or for money or fame. Mastery is *not* telling other people's stories. It is *not* trying to please one particular person in the audience or a portion of the audience; it is *not* trying to please anybody. It is listening to your own inner voice, and then putting your heart and soul into every story even if it's just an anecdote or a joke.

"A master teller would be adept at the crafts of performance: movement, grace, voice, and diction. Poetically, the master would strive to 'stretch the language.' Magically, the master would weave a spell from the first word to the final lingering image. Through understanding *earned* by working in the world and living life to the fullest, the teller would have an uncanny sense of who the audience is, and what they need. A true master would select stories, exactly right, for that audience, and that moment. To be able to make those choices requires a vast and significant repertoire. It is the range and quality of repertoire that most distinguishes a master teller.

"A great repertoire builds slowly. The superb teller not only knows the story from the inside out, but knows everything about the story. Stories do not exist in a vacuum . . ."

Excerpted from "Notes from a Conversation at Doc Willy's Bar," recorded by Bob Jenkins. © 1984, Steve Sanfield.

3. Archetype, that is, the irrepressentable force of life, is evocative. That it is powerful is a great understatement. I cannot emphasize enough that the healing disciplines require training with one who knows the way and the ways, one who has unequivocally lived it and for life.

4. My grandmother Katerín said that the most ignorant one is not she who does not know, but "the one who does not know that she does not know." And the person in even worse condition and more of a danger to others is "the one who knows she does not know and docs not care."

5. *La unica que vivio las historias,* the one who has lived the stories.

6. As a lifelong Católica formally consecrated to Her through La Sociedad de Guadalupe as a young child, my taproot and all my most closely heard work derives from devotion to The Son of *La Diosa,* and likewise to His Mother, *Nuestra Señora, Guadalupe,* The Blessed Mother in all Her holy names and faces—in my knowledge and danger, the wildest of the wild, the strongest of the strong.

7. There are oftimes legal ramifications as well.

8. This is the primary tenet of the healing professions. If you cannot help, do no harm. In order to do no harm, one has to *know what not to do.*

9. "Perfect work is cut to fit/ not the shape of the worker/ but the shape of God." Excerpted from the poem, "La Diosa *de la Clarista, un manifiesto pequeño,"* © 1971, C. P. Estés, from *Rowing Songs for the Night Sea Journey: Contemporary Chants* (Privately published, 1989).

ADDENDUM

1. For myself, as for many others, the understanding of many books begins in the re-reading.

2. Excerpted from "Commenting Before the Poems," © 1967, C. P. Estés, from *La Pasionara, Collected Poems,* to be published by Knopf.

3. In *familia,* to suffer does not mean to be a victim, but to be brave in the face of adversity, to be courageous. Even if one may not be able to completely mediate a situation or fate, one must give it their all regardless. I use the word "suffering" in this sense.

4. Writers who are also parents of children often ask, "Where? When did you write?" Late at night, before sunrise, during naptime, on the bus, walking to church, at *missa,* after hours, before hours, in-between hours; whenever, wherever, and on whatever I could.

5. A gentle caution: Because attention to individuation matters can cause heightened thought and feeling, one must take care to not simply become an accumulator of ideas and experiences, but also give goodly amounts of time to the work of bringing their understandings into use in everyday life. My daily practice and that which I teach to others is mainly that of a contemplative in the world, and all the intricacies that such encompasses. Regardless of where or how one begins, a regular practice must be enjoined. It need not be extremely long, but rather concentrated in the time given to it, and focused on as purely as possible, and, of course, enacted daily.

6. See reference in "Afterword, Story As Medicine."

7. There are certain depressions, manias, and other distresses that are organic in nature, meaning they originate from a malfunction of one of the physical systems of the body. Issues of organic origin need to be evaluated by a doctor.

8. The young people I have met at universities, seminaries, and colleges are so yearning to love this world, to learn, to teach, to create, to help. Since they are the future, it is clear that the future holds incredible treasures.

𝖇 EDUCATION OF A YOUNG WOLF: A BIBLIOGRAPHY

This bibliography[1] contains some of the most accessible works on women and psyche. I often recommend them to my students and analysands.[2] Many of these now classic titles, including works by Angelou, de Beauvoir, Brooks, de Castillejo, Cather, Chesler, Friedan, Harding, Jong, Jung, Hong Kingston, Morgan, Neruda, Neumann, and Qoyawayma, as well as anthologies, were ones I read to my students as "soul nutrition" in Psychology of Women courses back in the early 1970s. It was a time when "women's studies" was not a common phrase and many people wondered why there was a need for such a thing.

Since that time many works about women have been published by various presses. Twenty-five years ago these same works would have been relegated to mimeograph circulation or what we used to call "may fly presses," brave publishing ventures, usually under-funded and understaffed, coming to life only long enough to give birth to a handful of important works, before dying away as quickly as they began. Yet even with the publishing ground gained in these past decades, the study of women's lives, psychic or otherwise, is still very young, and far, far from complete. Although there is much more observant and honest work on women's lives being published worldwide and on quite a few subjects that were formerly taboo, there is yet much more to come, both in terms of right and duty to speak as an authority on oneself and one's culture, and in terms of access to the press and distribution channels.

A bibliography is not meant to be a tiresome list. It is not intended to teach a person what to think, but strives to give a body rich things to think about, to expose a person to as many ideas, therefore choices and chances, as possible. A good bibliography aspires to offer overviews of past and present that suggest clear visions for the future. This particular bibliography emphasizes women writers but is inclusive of both genders. These works are, on the whole, excellent, passionate, and original; many are intercultural, all are multi-dimensional. They are filled with data, opinion, and fire. A few reflect a time that is no longer, or a place that is not North America, and they ought to be read in that context. I have added for comparison two or three works which, in my opinion, are abysmal. You will know them when you read them, although your nominations might not be the same as mine.

The writers specified here are varied. Most are specialists, forerunners, some are iconoclasts, outsiders, mainstream, academics, independent, or gypsy scholars. There are many poets represented here, for they are the visionaries and historians of psychic life. In many cases their observations and insights cut so close to the bone that they supersede the suppositions of academic psychology in both accuracy and depth. In any case, most of the authors are *las compañeras o los compañeros*, fellow travelers and contemplatives who arrived at their conclusions through the living of a deep life, and thence carefully describing it.[3] Though there are many, many others as scintillating, here is a lyceum of two hundred plus.

Alegria, Claribel. *Woman of the River*. Pittsburgh: University of Pittsburgh Press, 1989.

———. *Louisa In Realityland*. New York: Curbstone Press, 1989.

———. *Guerrilla Poems of El Salvador*. New York: Curbstone Press, 1989.

Allen, Paula Gunn. *The Sacred Hoop: Recovering the Feminine in American Indian Traditions*. Boston: Beacon Press, 1986.

———. *Grandmothers of the Light: A Medicine Woman's Sourcebook*. Boston: Beacon Press, 1991.

———. *Shadow Country*. Los Angeles: University of California Press, 1982.

Allison, Dorothy. *Bastard Out of Carolina*. New York: Dutton, 1992.

Andelin, Helen B. *Fascinating Womanhood*. Santa Barbara, Calif.: Pacific Press, 1974.

Angelou, Maya. *I Shall Not Be Moved*. New York: Random House, 1990.

———. *All God's Children Need Traveling Shoes*. New York: Random House, 1986.

———. *I Know Why the Caged Bird Sings*. New York: Bantam, 1971.

Education of A Young Wolf: A Bibliography 547

Anzaldúa, Gloria, and Moraga, Cherríe, eds. *This Bridge Called My Back*. New York: Kitchen Table/Women of Color Press, 1983.

Atiya, Nayra. *Khul-Khaal: Five Egyptian Women Tell Their Stories*. Syracuse: Syracuse University Press, 1982.

Atwood, Margaret, *The Robber Bride*. New York: Nan A. Talese/Doubleday, 1993.

Avalon, Arthur. *Shakti and Shakta*. New York: Dover, 1978.

Barker, Rodney. *The Hiroshima Maidens: A Story of Courage, Compassion and Survival*. New York: Viking, 1985.

Bass, Ellen, and Thornton, Louise, eds. *I Never Told Anyone: Writings by Women Survivors of Child Sexual Abuse*. New York: Harper & Row, 1983.

de Beauvoir, Simone. *Memoirs of a Dutiful Daughter*. Translated by James Kirkup. Cleveland: World Publishing Co., 1959.

———. *The Second Sex*. New York: Knopf, 1974.

Bertherat, Thérèse. *The Body Has Its Reasons*. Translated by Thérèse Bertherat and Carol Bernstein. New York: Pantheon Books, 1977.

Bly, Robert. *Iron John: A Book About Men*. Reading, Mass.: Addison-Wesley, 1990.

Boer, Charles. *The Homeric Hymns*. Dallas: Spring Publications, 1987.

Bolen, Jean Shinoda. *Ring of Power: The Abandoned Child, the Authoritarian Father, and the Disempowered Feminine*. San Francisco: HarperCollins, 1992.

———. *Goddesses In Everywoman: A New Psychology of Women*. San Francisco: Harper & Row, 1984.

———. *The Tao of Psychology: Synchronicity and the Self*. San Francisco: Harper & Row, 1979.

Boston Women's Health Book Collective. *The New Our Bodies, Ourselves*. New York: Simon & Schuster, 1984. (look for update)

Brooks, Gwendolyn. *Selected Poems*. New York: Harper & Row, 1984.

Brown, Rita Mae. *Rubyfruit Jungle*. Plainfield, Vt.: Daughters, Inc., 1973.

Browne, E. Susan; Connors, Debra; Stern, Nanci. *With the Power of Each Breath: A Disabled Woman's Anthology*. San Francisco: Cleis Press, 1985.

Budapest, Zsuzsanna E. *The Grandmother of Time*. San Francisco: Harper & Row, 1989.

Castellanos, Rosario. *The Selected Poems of Rosario Castellanos*. Translated by Magda Bogin. St. Paul, Minn.: Graywolf Press, 1988.

de Castillejo, Irene Claremont. *Knowing Woman: A Feminine Psychology*. Boston: Shambhala, 1973.

Castillo, Ana. *My Father Was a Toltec*. Novato, Calif.: West End Press, 1988.

———. *So Far From God*. New York: W.W. Norton, 1993.

Cather, Willa. *My Ántonia*. Boston: Houghton Mifflin, 1988.

———. *Death Comes for the Archbishop*. New York: Vintage, 1971.

Chernin, Kim. *Obsession*. New York: Harper & Row, 1981.

Chesler, Phyllis. *Women and Madness*. Garden City, N.Y.: Doubleday, 1972.

Chicago, Judy. *The Dinner Party: A Symbol of Our Heritage*. Garden City, N.Y.: Anchor, 1979.

———. *Embroidering Our Heritage: The Dinner Party Needlework*. Garden City, N.Y.: Anchor, 1980.

———. *Through the Flower: My Struggle as a Woman Artist*. Garden City, N.Y.: Doubleday, 1975.

———. *The Birth Project*. Garden City, N. Y.: Doubleday, 1982.

Christ, Carol P. *Diving Deep and Surfacing: Women Writers on Spiritual Quest*. Boston: Beacon Press, 1980.

Coles, Robert. *The Spiritual Life of Children*. Boston: Houghton Mifflin, 1990.

Colette. *Collected Stories of Colette*. New York: Farrar, Straus, Giroux, 1983.

Cowan, Lyn. *Masochism: A Jungian View*. Dallas: Spring Publications, 1982.

Craig, Mary. *Spark from Heaven: The Mystery of the Madonna of Medjugorje*. Notre Dame, Ind.: Ave Maria Press, 1988.

Craighead, Meinrad. *The Mother's Songs: Images of God the Mother*. New York: Paulist Press, 1986.

Crow, Mary. *Woman Who Has Sprouted Wings*. Pittsburgh: Latin American Literary Review Press, 1988.

Curb, Rosemary, and Manahan, Nancy, eds. *Lesbian Nuns*. Tallahassee, Fla.: Naiad Press, 1985.

Daly, Mary. *Gyn/ecology*. Boston: Beacon Press, 1978.

———. "in cahoots with Caputi, Jane." *Websters' First New Intergalactic Wickedary of the English Language*. Boston: Beacon Press, 1987.

Derricotte, Toi. *Natural Birth: Poems*. Freedon, Calif.: Crossing Press, 1983.

Dickinson, Emily. *The Complete Poems of Emily Dickinson*. Boston: Little, Brown, 1890.

Doniger, Wendy. *Women, Androgynes, and Other Mythical Beasts*. Chicago: University of Chicago Press, 1980.

Drake, William. *The First Wave: Women Poets in America*. New York: Macmillan, 1987.

Easaran, Eknath, tr. *The Bhagavad Gita*. Berkeley: Nilgiri Press, 1985.

Eisler, Riane. *The Chalice and the Blade*. San Francisco: Harper & Row, 1987.

Ellis, Normandi. *Osiris Awakening: A New Translation of the Egyptian Book of the Dead*. Grand Rapids, Mich.: Phanes Press, 1988.

Erdrich, Louise. *Love Medicine*. New York: Bantam, 1984.

Fenelon, Fania. *Playing for Time*. Translated by Judith Landry. New York: Atheneum, 1977.

Fisher, M.F.K. *Sister Age*. New York: Knopf, 1983.

Forche, Carolyn. *The Country Between Us*. New York: Harper & Row, 1982.

———. *Angel of History*. New York: HarperCollins, 1994.

Foucault, Michel. *Madness and Civilization*. Translated by R. Howard. New York: Pantheon, 1955.

———. *History of Sexuality*. Translated by Robert Hurley. New York: Pantheon, 1978.

Fox, Matthew. *Original Blessing*. Santa Fe: Bear and Company, 1983.

Friedan, Betty. *The Feminine Mystique*. New York: W. W. Norton, 1963.

Friedman, Lenore. *Meetings with Remarkable Women: Buddhist Teachers in America*. Boston: Shambhala, 1987.

Friedman, Myra. *Buried Alive: Biography of Janis Joplin*. New York: Morrow, 1973.

Galland, China. *Longing for Darkness: Tara and the Black Madonna: A Ten Year Journey*. New York: Viking, 1990.

Gaspar De Alba, Alicia; Herrera-Sobek, Maria; Martinez, Demetria. *Three Times a Woman*. Tempe, Ariz.: Bilingual Review Press, 1989.

Gilbert, Sandra, and Gubar, Susan. *The Madwoman in the Attic*. New Haven: Yale University Press, 1979.

Gilligan, Carol. *In a Different Voice*. Cambridge: Harvard University Press, 1982.

Gimbutas, Marija. *The Goddesses and Gods of Old Europe: Myths and Cult Images*. Berkeley and Los Angeles: University of California Press, 1982.

Goldberg, Natalie. *Writing Down the Bones: Freeing the Writer Within*. Boston: Shambhala, 1986.

———. *Long Quiet Highway*. New York: Bantam Books, 1993.

Golden, Renny, and McConnell, Michael. *Sanctuary: The New Underground Railroad.* New York: Orbis Books, 1986.

Goldenburg, Naomi R. *Changing of the Gods: Feminism and the End of Traditional Religions.* Boston: Beacon Press, 1979.

Grahn, Judy. *Another Mother Tongue.* Boston: Beacon Press, 1984.

Guggenbühl-Craig, Adolph. *Power in the Helping Professions.* Dallas: Spring Publications, 1971.

Hall, Nor. *The Moon and the Virgin: Reflections on the Archetypal Feminine.* New York: Harper & Row, 1980.

Harding, M. Esther. *Woman's Mysteries, Ancient and Modern.* New York: Putnam, 1971.

Harris, Jean, and Alexander, Shana. *Marking Time: Letters from Jean Harris to Shana Alexander.* New York: Scribner, 1991.

Heilbrun, Carolyn G. *Writing a Woman's Life.* New York: Ballantine, 1989.

Herrera, Hayden. *Frida: A Biography of Frida Kahlo.* New York: Harper & Row, 1983.

Hillman, James. *Inter-Views: Conversation with Laura Pozzo.* New York: Harper & Row, 1983.

Hoff, Benjamin. *The Singing Creek Where the Willows Grow: The Rediscovered Diary of Opal Whitely.* New York: Ticknor & Fields, 1986.

Hollander, Nicole. *Tales From the Planet Sylvia.* New York: St. Martin's, 1990.

Hull, Gloria T.; Scott, Patricia Bell; Smith, Barbara, eds. *All the Women Are White, All the Blacks Are Men, But Some of Us Are Brave.* New York: Feminist Press, 1982.

Ibarruri, Dolores. *They Shall Not Pass: The Autobiography of La Passionaria.* New York: International Publishers, 1976.

Iglehart, Hallie. *Womanspirit: A Guide to Women's Wisdom.* New York: Harper & Row, 1983.

Jong, Erica. *Fear of Flying.* New York: New American Library, 1974.

———. *Becoming Light: Poems, New and Selected.* New York: HarperCollins, 1991.

Jung, C. G. *Collected Works of C. G. Jung.* Translated by R.F.C. Hull. Princeton: Princeton University Press, 1972.

———, ed. *Man and His Symbols.* Garden City, N.Y.: Doubleday, 1964.

Kalff, Dora. *Sandplay: A Psychotherapeutic Approach to the Psyche.* Santa Monica: Sigo, 1980.

Keen, Sam. *The Faces of the Enemy: Reflections of the Hostile Imagination.* Photography by Ann Page. San Francisco: Harper & Row, 1986.

Kerényi, C. *Zeus and Hera.* Translated by C. Holme. Princeton: Princeton University Press, 1975.

———. *Eleusis: Archetypal Image of Mother and Daughter.* New York: Schocken Books, 1977.

King, Florence. *Southern Ladies and Gentlemen.* New York: Stein & Day, 1975.

Kingston, Maxine Hong. *The Woman Warrior: Memoirs of a Girlhood Among Ghosts.* New York: Knopf, 1976.

Kinkaid, Jamaica. *At the Bottom of the River.* New York: Plume, 1978.

Kinnell, Galway. *The Book of Nightmares.* London: Omphalos and J-Jay Press, 1978.

Klepfisz, Irena. *Dreams of an Insomniac: Jewish Feminist Essays, Speeches and Diatribes.* Portland, Ore.: The Eighth Mountain Press, 1990.

Kolbenschlag, Madonna. *Kiss Sleeping Beauty Goodbye: Breaking the Spell of Feminine Myths and Models.* New York: Doubleday, 1979.

Krysl, Marilyn. *Midwife and Other Poems on Caring.* New York: National League for Nursing, 1989.

Kumin, Maxine. *Our Ground Time Here Will Be Brief.* New York: Penguin, 1982.

Laing, R. D. *Knots.* New York: Vintage, 1970.

Le Sueur, Meridel. *Ripening: Selected Work. 1927–1980.* Old Westbury, N.Y.: Feminist Press, 1982.

Leonard, Linda S. *The Wounded Woman,* Boulder, Colo.: Shambhala, 1983.

Lindbergh, Anne Morrow. *The Gift from the Sea.* New York: Pantheon, 1955.

Lippard, Lucy. *From the Center: Feminist Essays in Women's Art.* New York: E.P. Dutton, 1976.

Lisle, Laurie. *Portrait of an Artist: A Biography of Georgia O'Keeffe.* New York: Seaview, 1980.

López-Pedraza, Rafael. *Cultural Anxiety.* Switzerland: Daimon Verlag, 1990.

Lorde, Audre. *Sister Outsider: Essays and Speeches.* Freedon, California: Crossing Press, 1984.

Luke, Helen M. *The Way of Women, Ancient and Modern.* Three Rivers, Mich.: Apple Farm, 1975.

Machado, Antonio. *Times Alone.* Translated by Robert Bly. Middletown, Conn.: Wesleyan University Press, 1983.

Matsui, Yayori. *Women's Asia.* London: Zed Books, 1987.

Matthews, Ferguson Gwyneth. *Voices from the Shadows: Women with Disabilities Speak Out.* Toronto: Women's Educational Press, 1983.

McNeely, Deldon Anne. *Animus Aeternus: Exploring the Inner Masculine.* Toronto: Inner City, 1991.

Mead, Margaret. *Blackberry Winter.* New York: Morrow, 1972.

Metzger, Deena. *Tree.* Berkeley: Wingbow Press, 1983.

————. *The Woman Who Slept with Men to Take the War Out of Them.* Berkeley: Wingbow Press, 1983.

Millay, Edna St. Vincent. *Collected Poems.* Edited by Norma Millay. New York: Harper & Row, 1917.

Masson, Jeffrey. *The Assault on Truth: Freud's Suppression of the Seduction Theory.* New York: Farrar, Straus, Giroux, 1983.

Miller, Alice. *Thou Shalt Not Be Aware.* Translated by Hildegard Hannum and Hunter Hannum. New York: Farrar, Straus, Giroux, 1984.

————. *For Your Own Good: Hidden Cruelty in Childrearing and the Roots of Violence.* Translated by Hildegard Hannum and Hunter Hannum. New York: Farrar, Straus, Giroux, 1983.

————. *Drama of the Gifted Child.* Translated by Ruth Ward. New York: Basic Books, 1981.

Morgan, Robin. *Sisterhood Is Powerful.* New York: Vintage, 1970.

Mulford, Wendy, ed. *Love Poems by Women.* New York: Fawcett/Columbine, 1990.

Neruda, Pablo. *Residence on Earth.* New York: New Directions, 1973.

Neumann, Erich. *The Great Mother.* Princeton: Princeton University Press, 1963.

Nin, Anais. *Delta of Venus: Erotica.* New York: Harcourt, Brace, Jovanovich, 1977.

Olds, Sharon. *The Gold Cell.* New York: Knopf, 1989.

Olsen, Tillie. *Silences.* New York: Delacorte, 1979.

Orbach, Susie. *Fat Is a Feminist Issue.* New York: Paddington Press, 1978.

Pagels, Elaine. *The Gnostic Gospels.* New York: Random House, 1979.

Partnoy, Alicia, ed. *You Can't Drown the Fire: Latin American Women Writing In Exile.* San Francisco: Cleis Press, 1988.

Perera, Sylvia Brinton. *Descent to the Goddess.* Toronto: Inner City, 1988.

Piaf, Edith. *My Life.* London: Owen, 1990.

Piercy, Marge. *Circles on the Water.* New York: Knopf, 1982.

————, ed. *Early Ripening: American Women's Poetry Now.* London: Pandora, 1987.

————. *The Moon Is Always Female.* New York: Random House, 1980.

————. *Woman on the Edge of Time.* New York: Knopf, 1976.

Pogrebin, Letty Cottin. *Among Friends.* New York: McGraw-Hill, 1987.

Prager, Emily. *A Visit from the Footbinder and Other Stories.* New York: Simon & Schuster, 1982.

Qoyawayma, Polingaysi (White, Elizabeth Q.) *No Turning Back: A Hopi Indian Woman's Struggle to Live In Two Worlds.* As told to Vada F. Carlson. Albuquerque: University of New Mexico Press, 1964.

Raine, Kathleen. *Selected Poems.* Great Barrington, Mass.: Lindisfarne, 1988.

Rich, Adrienne. *The Fact of a Doorframe.* New York: W. W. Norton, 1984.

————. *Diving Into the Wreck.* New York: W. W. Norton, 1973.

————. *Of Woman Born: Motherhood as Experience and Institution.* New York: W. W. Norton, 1976.

Robinson, James M., ed. *The Nag Hammadi Library in English.* San Francisco: Harper & Row, 1977.

Rosen, Marjorie. *Popcorn Venus: Women, Movies and the American Dream.* New York: Coward, McCann, Geoghegan, 1973.

Samuels, A.; Shorter, B.; Plaut, F. *A Critical Dictionary of Jungian Analysis.* London/New York: Routledege & Kegan Paul, 1986.

Sanday, Peggy Reeves. *Female Power and Male Dominance: On the Origins of Sexual Inequalities.* Cambridge: Cambridge University Press, 1981.

Savage, Judith. *Mourning Unlived Lives.* Wilamette, Ill.: Chiron, 1989.

Sexton, Anne. *The Complete Poems.* Boston: Houghton Mifflin, 1981.

————. *No Evil Star.* Ann Arbor: University of Michigan Press, 1985.

Shange, Ntozake. *Nappy Edges.* New York: St. Martin's, 1972.

————. *A Daughter's Geography.* New York: St. Martin's, 1972.

————. *for colored girls who have considered suicide when the rainbow is enuf: a choreopoem.* New York: Macmillan, 1977.

Sheehy, Gail. *Passages.* New York: E. P. Dutton, 1974.

Shikibu, Izumi and Komachi, Onono. *The Ink Dark Moon, Love Poems, Women of the Ancient Court of Japan.* Translated by Jane Hirschfield with Mariko Aratani. New York: Şcribner, 1988.

Silko, Leslie Marmon. *Storyteller.* New York: Seaver Press, 1981.

————. *Ceremony.* New York: Penguin, 1977.

Simon, Jean-Marie. *Guatemala: Eternal Spring, Eternal Tyranny.* London: W. W. Norton, 1987.

Singer, June. *The Boundaries of the Soul: The Practice of Jung's Psychology.* Garden City, N.Y.: Doubleday, 1972.

Spretnak, Charlene. *Lost Goddesses of Early Greece.* Boston: Beacon Press, 1981.

————, ed. *The Politics of Women's Spirituality.* Garden City, N.Y.: Doubleday, 1982.

Starhawk. *Truth or Dare.* New York: Harper & Row, 1979.

Stein, Leon. *The Triangle Fire.* Philadelphia: Lippincott, 1962.

Steinem, Gloria. *The Revolution from Within.* Boston: Little, Brown, 1992.

————. *Outrageous Acts and Everyday Rebellions.* New York: Holt, Rinehart, Winston, 1983.

Stone, Merlin. *When God Was a Woman.* New York: Dial Press, 1976.

————. *Ancient Mirrors of Womanhood*. Boston: Beacon Press, 1984.

Swenson, May. *Cage of Spines*. New York: Rhinehart, 1958.

Tannen, Deborah. *You Just Don't Understand: Women and Men in Conversation*. New York: Morrow, 1990.

Teish, Louisa. *Jambalaya*. San Francisco: Harper & Row, 1985.

Tuchman, Barbara. *A Distant Mirror*. New York: Knopf, 1978.

Tzu, Lao. *Tao Te Ching*. Translated by Stephen Mitchell. San Francisco: Harper & Row, 1988.

von Franz, M. L. *The Feminine In Fairytales*. Dallas: Spring Publications, 1972.

Waldman, Anne. *Fast-Speaking Woman and Other Chants*. San Francisco: City Lights, 1975.

Walker, Alice. *The Color Purple*. New York: Washington Square Press, 1982.

————. *Good Night Willie Lee: I'll See You In the Morning*. New York: Dial Press, 1979.

————. *Her Blue Body: Everything We Know. Earthling Poems*. San Diego: Harcourt, Brace, Jovanovich, 1991.

————. *In Search of Our Mothers' Gardens*. New York: Harcourt, Brace, Jovanovich, 1983.

Walker, Barbara G. *The Woman's Encyclopedia of Myths and Secrets*. San Francisco: Harper & Row, 1983.

————. *The Woman's Dictionary of Symbols and Sacred Objects*. San Francisco: Harper & Row, 1988.

————. *The Crone*. San Francisco: Harper & Row, 1985.

Walker, Lenore, *The Battered Woman*. New York: Harper & Row, 1980.

Warner, Marina. *Alone of All Her Sex: The Myth and Cult of the Virgin Mary*. New York: Knopf, 1976.

Watson, Celia. *Night Feet*. New York: The Smith, 1981.

White, Steve F. *Poets of Nicaragua*. Greensboro: Unicorn Press, 1982.

Whitman, Walt. *Leaves of Grass*. New York: W. W. Norton, 1968.

Wickes, Frances. *The Inner World of Childhood*. New York: Farrar, Straus, Giroux, 1927.

Williams, Terry Tempest. *Refuge*. New York: Pantheon, 1991.

Willmer, Harry. *Practical Jung: Nuts and Bolts of Jungian Psychotherapy*. Wilamette, Ill.: Chiron, 1987.

Wilson, Colin. *The Outsider*. Boston: Houghton Mifflin, 1956.

Wolkstein, Diane, and Kramer, Samuel Noah. *Inanna: Queen of Heaven and Earth*. San Francisco: Harper & Row, 1983.

Wollstonecraft, Mary. *A Vindication of the Rights of Women*. 1792 Reprint. New York: W. W. Norton, 1967.

Woodman, Marion. *Addiction to Perfection*. Toronto: Inner City, 1988.

Woolf, Virginia. *A Room of One's Own*. New York: Harcourt, Brace, 1929.

Yolen, Jane. *Sleeping Ugly*. New York: Coward, McCann & Geoghegan, 1981.

Wynne, Patrice. *The Womanspirit Sourcebook*. San Francisco: Harper & Row, 1988.

Zipes, Jack. *The Brothers Grimm*. New York: Routledge, Chapman and Hall, 1988.

1. This bibliography was developed as an overview of the development of the instinctual nature. I use variations on this core bibliography for other women's issues. Some of the materials in this bibliography show up over and over again in bibliographies attached to other books, usually those written by women on women's issues. These copiously cited works have become a sort of biblio-mantra, and in the main are selections by women who no longer are living, but whose works live on anyway.

2. While I'm not adverse to considering the observations or theories of either gender, or any school, much material is not worth too much time reading, for it is predigested. This means that the pith has been taken out, leaving only the shell—rather like a carousel without the horses, without the music, without the ring, without the riders. The thing still goes round and round, but it is without life.

Re-digested work is another matter altogether. It means repeating something one heard or read or was told, but without asking, is this true? Is this useful? Is this still relevant? Is this the only viewpoint? There is much much work like this in existence. It reminds me of the passing down of the family silver mine. Some mines are played out and are not worth holding on to. Some are dead-end mines; they never produced enough ore worth keeping to begin with.

There is a third detritus and that is diluted work. Diluted work is a pallid copy of an original and strong work. In diluted work, the ability of the primary work to infuse and communicate its original intent, meaning, and medicine to the reader is diminished, fragmented, and distorted. Whenever you can, read first-order work by the person who has lived it, gathered it into one place, analyzed it, and not only loved it, but sacrificed for it as well. Part of reclaiming the wildish nature as we have seen is reconstituting one's discrimination. This is to be applied not only to what is already in our minds, but also to what we put into our minds.

3. Usually I proceed something like this: asking my students to chose three books at a time from this list and to consider them as a puzzle or riddle. Then, to whichever they choose, I add discourses by Kant, Kierkegaard, Mencken, and others. How do they go together? What can one lend the other? Compare, see what happens. Some combinations are bomb materials. Some create seed stock.

✿ ACKNOWLEDGMENTS

This work on the instinctive nature of women has been ongoing now for the better part of twenty-five years. During that time, many people have entered my life, many encouraging and able witnesses. In my traditions, when it comes time to acknowledge people, it usually takes many days to do so; that is why most of our celebrations, from wakes to weddings, must be at least three days long, for the first day must be spent laughing and crying, the second day must be spent fighting and yelling, and the third day must be spent making up, followed by much singing and dancing. So, to all the people in my life who are still singing and dancing:

Bogie, my husband and lover, who helped edit and who learned the transcribing machine so he could help me retype the manuscript . . . over and over. *Tiaja*, who came unbidden and handled administrative matters, did my grocery shopping, made me laugh, further convincing me that a grown daughter is also a sister. *Most especially, my kith and kin, my families, my tribe, my elders*, both living and in spirit—for leaving footprints.

Ned Leavitt, ser humano, my agent, gifted at handing things back and forth between the worlds. *Ginny Faber*, my editor at Ballantine, who during the birth of this book, gave birth to a perfect work, a little wild baby, *Susannah*.

Tami Simon, audio producer, artist, and inspiratrice who burns very bright, for asking what I knew. *Devon Christensen*, the master of detail and the watchkeep on the tiller. *To them and all the fine crew at Sounds True*, including everyone's alter-ego, *The*

Duck, for taking care of business and for their tremendous support so that I could give my time to this written work.

Lucy and Virginia, who arrived out of the mists, and just in time. My gratitude to *Spence*, a gift in and of herself, for sharing these two blessings with me. *The n.o.n.a. girl*, who heard the call, and made her way across rough terrain in order to arrive at just the right moment. *Juan Manuel*, m'hijo, for being a fine *traductor especial*.

My three grown daughters whose lives as women give me inspiration and insight. *My analysands* who, over the years, displayed such breadth and depth, as well as revealing to me the many hues of the shadow, and the many qualities of the light. *Yancey Stockwell* and *Mary Kouri*, who cared for my writing from the beginning. *Craig M.*, for his lifelong and sustaining love. *Jean Carlson*, my fellow crabby old woman, who reminded me to get up and turn three times in a circle. The late *Jan Vanderburgh*, who left one last gift. *Betsy Wolcott*, so generous with her psychic support of other people's joy. *Nancy Pilzner Dougherty*, for saying what could be possible in the future. *Kate Furler*, of Oregon, and *Mona Angniq McElderry*, of Kotzebue, Alaska, for the story-making late into the night twenty-five years ago. *Arwind Vasavada*, Hindu Jungian analyst and elder in my psychic family. *Steve Sanfield*, for also loving the opera woman from the South whose feet didn't go pretty in ice skates.

Lee Lawson, gifted artist and ghost friend, who cut through the soul-stealing la-la and called it like it was. *Normandi Ellis*, poet and author, for reminding me of the *ef* in the ineffable. *Jean Yancey*, just for being alive in my lifetime. *Fran Lees*, *Staci Wertz Hobbit*, and *Joan Jacobs*, for being my gifted and sighted inksisters. *Joann Hildebrand*, *Connie Brown*, *Bob Brown*, *Tom Manning* of Critter Control, *Eleanor Alden*, president of Jung Society at Denver, and *Anne Cole*, horsewoman of the Rockies, for their love and support over these years. *The original wildish women of La Foret*—you were there from the beginning.

My brother and sister griots, cantadoras, y cuentistas y mesemondók, storytellers, folklore researchers, translators, for their friendship and immense generosity: *Nagyhovi Maier*, Magyar gypsy scholar. *Roberta Macha*, Mayan interpreter. *La Pat: Patricia*

Dubrava Kuening, poet and translation specialist. *The men and women of the Native American, Science Fiction, Jewish, Christian, Moslem, and Pagan forums on CIS* for offering obscure and interesting facts. *María de los Angeles Zenaida González de Salazar,* loving expert on the Nahuatl y Aztecas. *Opalanga,* griot and specialist in African-American folklore. *Nagynéni Liz Hornyak, Mary Pinkola, Joseph Pinkola,* and *Roelf Sluman,* Hungarian specialists. *Makoto Nomura,* specialist in Japanese culture. *Cherie Karo Schwartz,* international storyteller, folklore researcher, especially Jewish culture. *J.J. Jerome,* for being a daring teller. *Leif Smith* and *Patricia J. Wagner* of Pattern Research, for being there and being solid. *Arminta Neal,* retired exhibit designer from Denver Museum of Natural History for generously digging into her files. *La Chupatinta: Pedra Abacadaba,* Uvallama village letterwriter. *Tiaja Karenina,* intercultural go-between. *Reina Pennington,* sister Alaskan-traveler, for her blessings. *All the storytellers throughout my life* who gifted me with stories, swapped stories, seeded stories, left stories to me as their spiritual or familial legacy, and who have received my gifts of stories to them in return, taking care of them as they would their own children, and I, the same.

Nancy Mirabella for translating Latina mystics and for telling me about Rocky Mountain Women's Institute. *Rocky Mountain Women's Institute,* for granting me a 1990–91 Associateship to do some work on the *Las Brujas* project, and the support of *Cheryl Bezio-Gorham* and my artist-peers there: *Patti Leota Genack,* painter; *Vicky Finch,* photographer; *Karen Zidwick,* writer; *Hannah Kahn,* choreographer; *Carole McKelvey,* writer; *Dee Farnsworth,* painter. *Women's Alliance* and master weaver *Charlotte Kelly,* for bringing me to teach in the Sierra Madres during the week *Women Who Run With the Wolves* found its publisher. It was a bounty to meet such powerful women activist-healer-artists; they surrounded me during that week like motherships escorting a maiden vessel out to the open sea. *Ruth Zaporah,* performance artist; *Vivienne Verdon-Roe,* filmmaker; *Fran Peavey,* comedienne; *Ying Lee Kelley,* co-chair of Rainbow Coalition; *Naomi Newman,* Jewish storyteller; *Rhiannon,* jazz singer and teller; *Colleen Kelley,* Buddhist artist; *Adele Getty,* author and drummer; *Kyos Featherdancing,* Native American ritualist; *Rachel Bagby,* African-

American singer; *Jalaja Bonheim*, dancer and grace; *Norma Cordell*, Native American teller and teacher; *Tynowyn*, drummaker and musician; *Deena Metzger*, author and bravewoman; *Barbara Borden*, drumwoman; *Kay Tift*, sorter of the strands; *Margaret Pavel*, stringer of the loom; *Gail Benevenuta*, "the voice"; *Rosemary Le Page*, one of the back-strap weavers; *Pat Enochs*, artist of nourishment; *y M'hijas, mis lobitas*, you pups know who you are. And lastly, *the screaming woman*, whom we won't mention.

Jean Shinoda Bolen for being a clear and stalwart *madre del alma*, for setting many examples, and for giving me Valerie. *Valerie Andrews*, author and nomad, for giving me time and for giving me Ned. *Manisha Roy* who held me rapturous about Bengali women. *Bill Harless, Glen Carlson, Jeff Raff, Don Williams, Lyn Cowan, José Arguelles*, for their early support. Those of my talented *Jungian colleagues from IRSJA and IAAP*, who care for and protect both poets and poetry. My *C.G. Jung Center of Colorado colleagues, and analysts-in-training*, past and present, and the psychoanalytic *candidates of IRSJA*, for being excited about learning and continuing with passion toward their true goals.

Molly Moyer, divine roustabout at Tattered Cover who kept whispering encouragement in my ear, and the three great bookstore mothers of Denver who stock their stores with all the intercultural books I had ever hoped for: *Kasha Songer*, The Book Garden; *Clara Villarosa*, The Hue-Man Experience Bookstore; *Joyce Meskis*, The Tattered Cover. Authors *Mark Graham* and *Stephen White, Hannah Green*, the *folks at The Open Door Bookstore, members of Poets of the Open Range, and poets at Naropa Institute*, for support and for caring about words that have meaning. *Sister and brother poets* who let me create through their hearts.

Mike Wesley master Macintosh expert at CW Electronics, for retrieving the entire "lost" manuscript from the hard drive, and *Lonnie Wright*, master service tech who brought my SE30 back from the dead on more than one occasion. *Litforum authors and computer masters across the world*, Japan, Mexico, France, United States, U.K., for computing up at midnight to talk to me about women and wolves.

My most essential teachers: *All librarians*, the keepers of the treasure rooms filled with all of humanity's sighs, sorrows, hopes, and happinesses, my profound gratitude; you have always helped, always been wise, no matter how obscure the request.

Georgia O'Keeffe who, when I was nineteen and told her I was a poet, didn't laugh. *Dorothy Day*, who said that grass roots mattered. As one writer phrased it, for "the madwomen in black," the nuns who were visionaries: *Sisters of the Holy Cross*, especially *Sr. John Michela, Sr. Mary Edith, Sr. Francis Loyola, Sr. John Joseph, Sr. Mary Madeleva*, and *Sr. Maria Isobela y Sr. Maria Concéption*. *Bettina Steinke* who taught me to see the white line that lies on the topmost crease of velvet. *The editor of "The Sixties,"* who wrote back ten words that sustained me for twenty years. To my Jungian and other psychological teachers of whom there are many, but these by their example as artists, *Toni Wolff, Harry Wilmer, James Hillman*, but especially *Carl Gustav Jung*, whose work I use as a springboard, both into his work and also away from it as well. I was immensely attracted to Jung's work for he lived and espoused the life of an artist; he sculpted, wrote, read the tomes, entered the tombs, rowed the rivers; that is an artist's life.

Colorado Council on the Arts and Humanities, Artist in Residence Program, and *Young Audiences*, especially artist-administrators *Daniel Salazar, Patty Ortiz*, and *Maryo Ewell* for their aliveness and enthusiasm. *Marilyn Auer*, editor and associate publisher, *and Tom Auer*, publisher and editor-in-chief of *The Bloomsbury Review*, for the two w's, warmth and wackiness, and the two k's, kindness and kulchur. To those who first published my work, giving spirit-transfusions to continue on with this one: *Tom DeMers, Joe Richey, Anne Richey, Joan Silva, David Chorlton, Antonia Martinez, Ivan Suvanjieff, Allison St. Claire, Andrei Codrescu, José Armijo, Saltillo Armillo, James Taylor III*, and *Patricia Calhoun*, the wild woman of Gilpin County. To those poets who witnessed; *Dana Pattillo, charlie mehrhoff, Ed Ward*, and *the three Marias, Maria Estevez, Maria Ignacio, Maria Reyes Marquez.*

All the hobbits, goblins, toadstools, and *munchkins at Reivers*, one of my favorite writing cafés. Especially *the boys of the treehouse* without whose constant help and opinionation this book could not have been written. The little Colorado and Wyoming villages I live in, *my neighbors, friends, and the servicemen and servicewomen* who brought back stories from all the corners of the earth. *Lois and Charlie*, the mother and father of my husband who gave him so good and deep a love that he is filled with it, and pours it out to me and to our family.

Lastly, to *that one very old oak "message tree"* in the woods where, as a child, I used to write. To *the smell of good dirt, the sound of unencumbered water*, to *the spirits of nature* who all rush out to the road to see who is passing by. To *all women who have gone before me* and made the path a little clearer and a little easier. And with infinite tenderness, to *La Loba*.

⚡ ABOUT THE AUTHOR

Clarissa Pinkola Estés, Ph.D., is an internationally recognized and award-winning poet, a Diplomate senior Jungian psychoanalyst certified via the International Association of Analytical Psychology, Zurich, Switzerland, and a *cantadora*, keeper of the old stories in the Latina tradition. She is past executive director of the C. G. Jung Center for Education and Research in the United States. Her doctorate is in intercultural studies and clinical psychology, and she has taught and practiced privately for twenty-five years.

Women Who Run With the Wolves was begun by Dr. Estés in 1971 and completed over twenty years' time. Her work has been translated into eighteen foreign languages worldwide and has been hailed as a classic and seminal work on the inner lives of women.

Dr. Estés' other published works include *The Gift of Story, A Wise Tale About What Is Enough*. She is the author of a nine-volume bestselling audio series, and *Theatre of the Imagination*, a thirteen-part series that is broadcast on many NPR, Pacifica, and community public radio stations across America.

Dr. Estés, a longtime activist, heads the nascent C. P. Estés Guadalupe Foundation, which has, as one of its goals, to broadcast strengthening stories, via shortwave radio, to trouble spots throughout the world. For her lifetime social activism and writing, she is the recipient of the *Las Primeras* Award from MANA, the National Latina Foundation in Washington, D.C. She was awarded the 1994 President's Medal for social justice from The Union Institute and has received a 1990–91 fellowship from the Rocky Mountain Women's Institute. Dr. Estés is a former Artist-in-Residence for the State of Colorado through the Arts and Humanities Council. Additionally, she is the first recipient of the annual Joseph Campbell festival "Keeper of the Lore" Award.

Women Who Run With the Wolves has received the ABBY Honor Award from the ABA, the Top Hand Award from the Colorado Author's League, and the Gradiva Award from the National Association for the Advancement of Psychoanalysis.

Dr. Estés is married and has three grown children. She is a lifetime member of *La Sociedad de Guadalupe*.

✶ RESOURCES

Clarissa Pinkola Estés, Ph.D., is the creator of a collection of original audio works combining myths and stories with archetypal analysis and psychological commentary. Titles include:

- **Women Who Run With the Wolves:**
  Myths and Stories on the Instinctual Nature of Women (180 minutes)

- **The Creative Fire:**
  Myths and Stories on the Cycles of Creativity (180 minutes)

- **The Boy Who Married an Eagle:**
  Myths and Stories on Male Individuation (90 minutes)

- **The Radiant Coat:**
  Myths and Stories on the Crossing between Life and Death (90 minutes)

- **Warming the Stone Child:**
  Myths and Stories About Abandonment and the Unmothered Child (90 minutes)

- **In the House of the Riddle Mother:**
  Archetypal Motifs in Women's Dreams (180 minutes)

- *The Red Shoes:*
  On Torment and the Recovery of Soul Life (80 minutes)

- *How to Love a Woman:*
  On Intimacy and the Erotic Life of Women (180 minutes)

- *The Gift of Story:*
  A Wise Tale About What Is Enough (60 minutes)

For more information about these and new audio releases by
Dr. Estés, write or call Sounds True Audio, 413 S. Arthur
Avenue, Louisville, CO 80027. Phone 1-800-333-9185.